# Being and Nothingness

"*Being and Nothingness* is a fascinating and intriguing work providing . . . a full-blown metaphysics backed by, and at the same time providing the basis for, a complete theory of man."
*The Times Literary Supplement*

"*Being and Nothingness* is a magnificently imaginative redescription of the human situation. Sartre follows up on leads provided by Hegel and Heidegger in order to replace the Platonic/Aristotelian account of human beings as primarily knowers with a neo-Nietzschean conception of humans as self-creators."
*Richard Rorty*

"Rooted in the tragic circumstance of war and occupation, profoundly marked by Heidegger yet also written against him, Sartre's treatise remains a classic. What accounted for the impact of the work on successive generations was the tension between philosophic argument, social insight and the genius for narrative, for the concrete particular, distinctive of Sartre."
*George Steiner*

"It is full of fascinating and profound analyses of human devices and desires. It is an extremely interesting book . . . It seems to me to have been very well translated by Hazel Barnes."
*Iris Murdoch, New Statesman*

# Jean-Paul
# Sartre

## Being and Nothingness

An essay on phenomenological ontology

Translated by Hazel E. Barnes

Introduction by Mary Warnock
With a new preface by Richard Eyre

 London and New York

*L'Être et le néant* first published 1943
by Éditions Gallimard, Paris

English edition first published in USA 1957
by Methuen & Co. Ltd, New York

First published in United Kingdom 1958
by Methuen & Co. Ltd, London

First published in Routledge Classics 2003
by Routledge
2 Park Square, Milton Park, Abingdon, Oxon, OX14 4RN

*Routledge is an imprint of the Taylor & Francis Group, an informa business*

© 1943 Gallimard, Paris
English translation © 1958 Philosophical Library
Preface to the Routledge Classics edition © 2003 Richard Eyre
© Routledge Classics edition revised by Ms Arlette Elkaïm-Sartre

Typeset in Joanna and Scala Sans by RefineCatch Limited, Bungay, Suffolk
Printed and bound in Great Britain by
TJ International Ltd, Padstow, Cornwall

*British Library Cataloguing in Publication Data*
A catalogue record for this book is available from the British Library

ISBN10: 0–415–27848–1
ISBN13: 978-0–415–27848–5

# CONTENTS

# PREFACE TO THE ROUTLEDGE CLASSICS EDITION

In this country Sartre is as unfashionable as loon pants, so it's hard for us to imagine a world in which, as the novelist Iris Murdoch said when she briefly met Sartre in 1945 in Brussels, "His presence in the city was like that of a pop star. Chico Marx, who was there at about the same time, was less rapturously received."

When I was a student in the 1960s, Sartre didn't quite have poster status – his pipe, glasses and air of bad-temper kept him off walls that celebrated Che, Brigitte Bardot and James Dean – but few student bookshelves lacked a (largely) unread copy of Being and Nothingness, his 632-page exegesis of existentialism. From the little I read, I understood only what suited me but, as I was growing up in a world still scarred by the Holocaust, Hitler, Stalin and nuclear warfare, it wasn't hard to grasp a philosophy which was predicated on the absolute absence of God. And if I understood Sartre superficially, I understood him sufficiently to corroborate my feelings of confusion about my sexual and political identity: "First of all, man exists," he said, "turns up, appears on the scene, and, only afterwards, defines himself." That seemed to describe my condition pretty accurately, and his argument for the reality of "nothingness" hit the mark as far as student life was concerned.

If Sartre's philosophy remained more talked about than read, his novels were popular (Roads to Freedom was serialized by the BBC) and his plays were much performed. In fact, it was practically a legal obligation in the 1960s for student drama groups to perform Huis Clos. Sartre was attracted to the theatre because theatre thrives on metaphor – a room becomes a world, a group of characters becomes a whole society – so plays tend to be about how we live and why we live. In the theatre Sartre was obliged to characterize and animate his philosophical and political propositions, test theory against flesh and

blood. And he was obliged to condense and distil his ideas. "The metaphysician who could not say anything unless he said everything was compelled in
the theatre to give his message briefly," said Iris Murdoch, "and as Sartre
unfortunately could not do everything, as opposed to thinking everything, he
found the theatre, where he had undoubted talent, a sympathetic place to
drop into."

His play, Les Mains sales (Dirty Hands), was first performed in 1948. It's a
noir-ish political thriller, set in a fictional East European country ("Illyria") in
the dying days of the Second World War. A young man is commissioned by a
revolutionary Socialist Party to assassinate the leader of a rival faction, who is
held to be diluting the Party's principles by joining a coalition with Liberal
and Right Wing parties in order to form a government. Not long after the
Labour landslide of 1997, I decided to adapt the play for the Almeida Theatre
in North London. What attracted me to it was partly the topicality of the
debate between means and ends and purity and opportunism, but as much its
exploration of class, of sex, and of growing up. Like Hamlet, Hugo, the play's
protagonist, grows up to grow dead.

My version of Les Mains sales (which I christened The Novice) coincided with
the peace negotiations in Northern Ireland and with rancorous bickering
between Old and New Labour. "Principle," "pragmatism" and "power-
sharing" were words that rained down from all directions, while the metaphor of "dirty hands" was invoked on a daily basis. Sartre's play seemed once
again a play for today just as, it seems to me, Being and Nothingness is a philosophy for today.

The universe which Sartre's philosophy describes is a familiar one to any
contemporary reader in the West: a meaningless, godless and de-personalized
world in which the words "ennui," "angst" and "alienation" are much more
current than "hope" and "compassion." But nevertheless, says Sartre, it's a
world in which we have free will: we are responsible for our actions and are
the sole judges of how they affect others. But that free will is curbed by the
fact that our awareness of ourselves prevents us from ever truly being "ourselves," so we play at being ourselves and become "inauthentic."

To behave "authentically" is to understand that we can make and remake
ourselves by our actions and thus become what our acts define us as being. To
talk rather than act is moral self-deception – "mauvaise foi" (bad faith) –
which involves our behaving as insensate things rather than "authentic"
human beings. In bad faith, we evade responsibility by not exploiting the
possibilities of choice; in short, by not being fully human.

In Being and Nothingness Sartre doesn't present a total system of belief or a
user's manual to life but for me, in spite of being barely literate in philosophy
and in spite of his sometimes impenetrable technical vocabulary, he provides
a topographical account – a moral template – that helps me navigate some of

the more shadowy paths of my existence. And for all his pessimism, in asserting the absolute nature of the individual Sartre defies the inhuman determinism of the contemporary world, where every day we are told that we are "wired" to do this or that by our genetic makeup, or by the pressures of society, or by the structures of economic systems. Sartre presupposes that our lives require a basis in reason but declares that the attempt to uncover that basis is a "futile passion." Oddly I find some comfort in being told this: that we can never hope to understand why we are here and that we have to choose a goal and follow it with passionate conviction, aware of the meaninglessness of our lives and the certainty of our deaths.

For me Sartre's concern with our disposition to evade responsibility and to lie to ourselves – our "bad faith" – is as active a notion as when I first came across it. And in an age where we appear to believe nothing except celebrity, I can't think that a writer who says that we define man only in relation to his commitments is entirely redundant.

I hope the publication of Being and Nothingness in this edition does something to revive interest in a writer whose philosophy in Britain has become as unfashionable as his fiction. What's more he's frequently reviled as a misogynist: the writer Angela Carter once asked, "There is one question that every thinking woman in the Western world must have asked herself at one time or another. Why is a nice girl like Simone de Beauvoir sucking up to a boring old fart like Jean-Paul Sartre?" But just before Christmas a few years ago, I arrived in Paris on the Eurostar. To my astonishment, the magazine kiosks were plastered with photographs of the boring old fart: Sartre had been resurrected as man and philosopher by the popular savant, Bernard-Henri Lévy. Later I heard that there was to be a Place Sartre–De Beauvoir near his favourite café, Les Deux Magots, and that Richard Attenborough was said to be making a film about Simone de Beauvoir's affair with Nelson Algren, with Sartre as the third corner of the amorous triangle. Fame indeed. People might even start to read his books.

Richard Eyre
December 2002

# INTRODUCTION

## by Mary Warnock

Being and Nothingness may well be thought of as Sartre's greatest work; it has also come to be regarded as a text-book of existentialism itself, and this is for many reasons a proper way to read it. There is to be found in these pages, set out with relative perspicuity, almost all the salient ideas of existentialism; and, in addition, the method according to which the book is composed is itself highly characteristic of existentialist philosophers.

There are two aspects of Being and Nothingness which especially mark it as a model of existentialist thought. The first is its treatment of the concrete and the particular. This may be thought of as primarily a matter of method. But the method in question can be seen to arise directly out of the subject-matter, and out of the special interests of Sartre and contemporary existentialist writers. The second characteristic feature of the book is its treatment of the key concept of human freedom. There is a clear connexion between these two features of the book. For the arguments, if such they can be called, for the existence of an extreme of human freedom are arguments which ultimately stem from the verité vécue of the particular human being in the world. One cannot understand the extent of human freedom unless one can understand what it is like to be a human being. It is the nature of human life, in this sense (what it is like), which Being and Nothingness sets out to expound.

But the book has also frequently been thought of as a work which is concerned with ethics; and indeed existentialism in general has frequently been treated as though it were a branch of moral philosophy. This seems to me to be a mistake. Yet the historical fact that it has been so treated leads to the question what, if anything, is the ethical content of Being and Nothingness and what, in the years after its publication, came of the promise which Sartre made at the end of the book, that he would write at greater length on ethics.

Our final question, therefore, must be what has happened to Sartre since the publication of this great existentialist text? Has he fulfilled his promise to write on ethics, and, if so, has this produced anything which could be described as a continuation of *Being and Nothingness*? To this it seems to me that the answer is that he has fulfilled the promise only in a most round-about and paradoxical way, if at all, and that we should therefore regard the present work not only as an important statement of existentialist philosophy, but as the last such statement, since at least Sartre himself has travelled a long way from views contained in it.

There are certain absolutely basic ontological facts which lie behind all the arguments and expositions in *Being and Nothingness*. It has been said that Sartre does not indulge in metaphysics, but only in ontology, and this may be right. But, by whatever name one refers to these basic facts, it is essential to realize that they are supposed by Sartre to function both as the foundation of his arguments, and also as that which is finally confirmed by his descriptions of the world, and they are supposed to be facts of the maximum generality. These are facts, then, about what is in the world. There are two kinds of entity in existence; Beings-in-themselves, and Beings-for-themselves. Beings-in-themselves are non-conscious things, which can be said to have essences, which exist independently of any observer and which constitute all the things in the world. Beings-for-themselves are conscious beings whose consciousness renders them entirely different from other things, in their relation both to themselves and to one another, and to those other things. Given that there are these two kinds of beings in the world, Sartre's whole concern may be seen as an attempt to describe what exactly the relation between them is. And here we come upon an absolutely general concern of existentialist thought, namely to explain and describe being in the world. The world is not treated by any existentialist philosopher primarily as an object of knowledge, nor as an object of perception. There is no tendency to raise the question how we know or prove that there is a world, distinct from those who know or perceive it. Existentialism is, to an extreme degree, anti-Cartesian in this matter: on the one hand, existentialists do not start from "pure consciousness" looking out upon a world about which the question arises "How do I know it exists?" On the other hand they have no hope of and no interest in a description of a "marvellous new science" of the kind envisaged by Descartes. On the contrary, they start all their reflection from the stand-point of a consciousness already engaged in an external world, of "impure" consciousness, modified in all kinds of different ways by its presence in a world of things; and an impersonal or wholly scientific account of the world in terms of regularities and causal connexions seems to them inadequate to the richness of the world as it is actually experienced.

Sartre, then, is attempting, in *Being and Nothingness*, to analyse the connexions between these two radically different kinds of entities. And he proceeds with the analysis by reference to particular features of the world which he describes in the greatest possible concrete detail, so that we are obliged to recognize them and accept them as descriptions of a world we know. From here he can go on to argue that if the description is true, the basic structure of the world must be as he says it is. Alternatively he may start by stating the general features of the world, the distinction between Beings-in-themselves and Beings-for-themselves, and argue that, given this distinction, particular facts must be thus and so. He then produces a story or a description to convince us that they are. There are therefore two overlapping and inter-changeable patterns of analysis in *Being and Nothingness*, but both are character-ized by the use, not merely for illustrative purposes, but as an essential element in the argument of extremely detailed description or anecdote.

It would be easy to multiply examples of this technique. It will perhaps be sufficient to mention two. First, in Sartre's well-known treatment of Bad Faith, he argues from the fact that people are capable of Bad Faith to the most important general characteristic of consciousness itself, namely its being sep-arated from the world of things by a gap or Nothingness. It is the experience of this gap which reveals itself to us first and foremost by our ability to negate propositions, to deny the truth, and to describe things not only truly but also falsely, which makes us conscious of ourselves as different and distinguish-able from the world which surrounds us. In being thus conscious of ourselves we are thereby rendered conscious of the world. Consciousness therefore, as well as imagination and freedom, are all brought into being by the emptiness or Nothingness which "lies at the heart" of Beings-for-themselves.

Sartre starts from the description of Bad Faith, and raises the Kantian-sounding question "How is Bad Faith possible?" He answers this question in terms of the features of consciousness which I have just mentioned, without which no kind of deception, because no kind of false representation could occur. If no false representation could occur, Bad Faith could not occur. But Bad Faith does occur, therefore consciousness must be of this kind. Now it is not enough, in this argument, merely to *state* that Bad Faith occurs, nor even to list in a general way the kind of situation in which we might be satsisfied by the description "Bad Faith." It is an essential part of Sartre's method that we should, as nearly as possible, be presented with the living fact of Bad Faith, and this is the function of the elaborate descriptions contained in chapter 2 of Part I of *Being and Nothingness* . . . the description of the young woman (page 55) and the café waiter (page 59). The point of these descrip-tions is not merely to illustrate a concept, acceptable on other grounds, nor merely to make a general point clear by the citing of a particular example which falls under the general heading. It is rather that we should understand the nature of the phenomenon by accepting the truthfulness of the story, in the way that we may be completely convinced by the truth of the representation of life in a film or a novel; and having thus been induced to believe that this is a way in which people behave, we are then led to accept the rest of the transcendental argument: "Unless consciousness was as I say it is, Bad Faith would not be possible; but you *now realize* that Bad Faith is not only possible, but actual, in your world; therefore consciousness must be as I say."

Another instance of what we may call the anecdotal mode of argument is to be found in Sartre's marvellous treatment of the connexion, not now between Beings-for-themselves and Beings-in-themselves, but between one conscious Being-for-itself and another. In every way this is one of the best parts of *Being and Nothingness*, both in its exposition of the arguments of other philosophers and in its presentation of Sartre's own views. Here, in the first chapter of Part 3, Sartre introduces the idea of Beings-for-others, as a mode of existence fundamental to our experience of the world by, among other things, a brief description (page 259) of someone who is eavesdropping, entirely absorbed in the problem of getting his ear to the keyhole, conscious of himself only in the minimal "non-thetic" way, in which he barely distinguishes himself from his surroundings. But suddenly, while he is thus engaged, he hears a footstep in the hall, and becomes aware that there is someone behind him and he is under observation. Immediately he begins to exist in a different way; he begins to see himself as an eavesdropper; he experiences himself and the other person together in a feeling of shame.

Here, once again, we are made to feel and, as it were, experience in our own persons, the shock which the eavesdropper experiences, the change that his internal feelings undergo at the moment when he is aware of being watched. It would have been possible to present an argument which would have led in the same direction, in a far more external, Aristotelian way; we might, that is, simply have been asked to agree to the fact that the emotion of shame entails the idea of another person, and therefore to agree that, if anyone experiences shame, then that person at least must believe that other people exist. This would have been possible; but it would not have been an existentialist form of argument. As it is, we are asked not to *agree to a proposition* but to *experience, in imagination, a familiar emotion*. And while we are under the impact of it, we are asked whether we do not therefore necessarily believe that other people exist, and that they determine our own mode of existence. To understand the anecdote and reject the general conclusion would be to assert a contradiction.

Here, then, we have just two examples of a genuinely existentialist method of argument, which turns essentially on the presentation of the particular, and above all of the concrete fact. There is another way, too, in which the concrete enters into Sartre's philosophy, which is harder to characterize. For none of the existentialist philosophers, nor for the phenomenologists from whom they took so much, was there a sharp distinction between perceiving one's world, reacting emotionally towards it, and acting upon it. In Sartre's early works, emotions and imagination were both presented as particular modes of perception of the world, and emotion as an incipient way of acting upon it. Thus, in any complete account of the relation between conscious beings and the world there was necessarily bound to enter an account not only of what they knew or perceived of the world, but of what they wanted, what they aspired to do, and how they reacted to the things which surrounded them. Emotional reactions are not a kind of extra, for existentialist thinkers, which may enter briefly into a discussion of ethics (under the headings of Pleasure and Pain, or Love and Hatred) but which are to be excluded entirely from the subject-matter of scientific philosophy, that is, from epistemology and logic. Existentialism does not recognize the boundary between ethics and epistemology, nor between either and ontology (as for logic, it has no interest in it). Just as there is no sharp distinction between knowing and acting on one's knowledge, so there is none between perceiving and feeling. Man's place in nature is that of a uniquely dynamic creature among the inanimate and his dynamism springs from the fact that he is able to see everything around him as relative to his needs, his desires, his aversions and his fears.

With these general remarks in mind it may be worth turning to Sartre's remarks in *Being and Nothingness* about the desirability of a psycho-analysis of things (Part 4, chapter 2, section III, pages 620 following). The aim of such an analysis, Sartre says, would be to explain the meanings which really belong to things. A human being, according to existentialist thought (and here once again there is an obvious link with Husserl), comes into the world surrounded by significant or meaningful objects. The qualities which he perceives in things do not present themselves as "bare" qualities, but as qualities which point beyond themselves, to the most general features of the world as a whole. Now it is of course allowed by such existential psycho-analysis that people differ from each other in their reactions to things. But it would also be argued that there is a number of qualities which things have to which we are bound to react in a standard way, simply because they reveal a truth about the nature of the world and our place in it. Such a quality is viscosity, the significance of which is to reveal to us the threat, the possibility which we must necessarily hate above all others, that we might be in some sense taken over by the mindless In-Itself and that we might totally lose control over our environment.

The exact and detailed description which begins on page 624 has the purpose of spelling out this significance. The nature of viscosity is laid bare here, as it is in *La Nausée*, with a kind of disgusted fascination, not as a metaphor, nor even as, in the ordinary sense, a symbol of the anti-value, but as itself constituting the thing we most hate, and at the same time pointing beyond itself. There is scarcely any parallel in the work of other philosophers with this careful and obsessive obsorption in the actual physical properties of the world, not as a source of scientific laws, but as a source of revelation of the nature of existence itself. Coleridge perhaps more than any other writer in English demonstrated in his detailed description of, for example, the movements of water, the same belief that from the sensible properties of things one could deduce not only their true nature, but the true nature of the universe at large.

*Being and Nothingness*, then, shows itself to be central to the existentialist tradition by its insistence upon the presentation of the concrete fact, not merely by way of example, but as an integral part of its arguments. In addition, Sartre's insistence upon the vast and indeed almost limitless extent of human freedom is equally central to existentialism; but about this I shall be very brief. Whatever criterion may be adopted for marking off existentialist from other philosophers, it would probably be agreed that anyone who is an existentialist must adopt the view that men are free, and that their freedom extends further than they will have thought, before their eyes were opened by the study of philosophy. Essentially, they are free to choose their morality, their attitudes towards God and the world, their approach to death and love. There are notorious difficulties, perhaps particularly for Sartre, in the reconciliation of this extended sphere of human freedom, to belief in which he wishes to convert his readers, with the deterministic account which he gives in *Being and Nothingness* of the inevitable frustrations of love; and it is not possible to discuss these problems here. But there is no doubt that Sartre presents us with an area of human freedom which, most importantly, includes freedom to choose what to do, in the sense of freedom to choose what it is *right* to do.

This freedom, Sartre thinks, can be proved to exist by deduction from the nature of man, as a conscious being, who therefore has a vacancy or lack in himself which, in the nature of the case, he must be free to fill in any way that he can imagine. We cannot, according to this theory, deduce any particular system of ethics from the existential analysis of what there is, but we can discover from the analysis what ethics is and what it is not. "Ontology itself cannot formulate ethical precepts. It is concerned solely with what is, and we cannot possibly formulate imperatives from ontology's indicatives. It does however allow us to catch a glimpse of what sort of ethics will assume its responsibilities when confronted with *a human reality in situation.*" We can understand, moreover, how it is that human beings *inevitably* ascribe values to things. Without any contrivance, just by perceiving the world, they perceive values. Values "spring up round them like partridges." But the chief lesson which we should learn is to avoid the "spirit of seriousness." This is defined on page 646, as that which makes us pretend that values are absolute, given somehow independently of any human subjective judgment. This spirit makes us pretend that the quality of being desirable or undesirable is somehow a quality of the things themselves, like redness or roundness. Once this spirit has been dismissed, then it necessarily follows that a man will recognize himself as the source of all values, and when he has done this it will follow that he realizes that he can choose to value whatever he likes, and is free from the restraint of the conventional, the established or the apparently inescapable bonds of duty or taboo.

But even when all this has been recognized, as Sartre himself clearly sees, the question of what people will actually do still obtrudes itself. To take responsibility for the world is hardly a course of action, and moral philosophy has frequently been required to do more than state that morality is possible; it has been required precisely to explain what sorts of justification would be valid for choices of different kinds. Sartre, at the end of Being and Nothingness (page 645 following) seems both to be saying that no justification of any kind could be given, and also that there might be something more for a moral philosopher to say.

Our final question, therefore, is this: did Sartre go on, after Being and Nothingness, to a genuine ethical theory, as he suggested that he might? (We should notice the famous footnote to page 434 of Being and Nothingness: "These considerations do not exclude the possibility of an ethics of deliverance and salvation. But this can be achieved only after a radical conversion which we cannot discuss here.") It has sometimes been suggested that Sartre's positive approach to moral philosophy was outlined in the essay "Extentialism is a Humanism," first published in 1946. This essay has been translated several times into English, and it became, for a time, a popular starting-point in discussions of existentialist thought. It contained the doctrine that existentialism was a basically hopeful and constructive system of thought, contrary to popular belief, since it encouraged man to action by teaching him that his destiny was in his own hands. Sartre went on to argue that if one believes that each man is responsible for choosing freedom for himself, one is committed to believing also that he is responsible for choosing freedom for others, and that therefore not only was existentialism active rather than passive in tendency, but it was also liberal, other-regarding and hostile to all forms of tyranny. However, I mention this essay here only to dismiss it, as Sartre himself has dismissed it. He not only regretted its publication, but also actually denied some of its doctrines in later works.

For the fulfilment of the promise then, and for the radical conversion, we must look elsewhere. Since the publication of Being and Nothingness, apart from his autobiography, Sartre has published a large number of reviews and articles, and, in 1960, the first volume of The Critique of Dialectical Reason, to which the Question of Method was prefixed as an introduction.

The Question of Method first appeared in 1957, under the title "The present situation of Existentialism." It is of the greatest importance, since it sets out to analyse the connexion, at the time, between existentialism and Marxism, to which in some sense Sartre had become converted. He maintains that every age has a single dominant philosophy, but in addition to this there may be lesser systems which do not merit the title "philosophies," but are "ideologies." These are all of them conceived within the framework of the dominant philosophy, whether their authors realize this or not. Marxism, he argues, is the dominant philosophy of the twentieth century, and existentialism is an ideology which may contribute to, but can neither contradict nor supersede Marxism itself. In fact Sartre here says that the very most that existentialism can do is to refertilize Marxism, and to give life to those parts of it which have become dead or fossilized. The Marxist method, he says, is unduly a priori. Everything which has ever happened is forced by it into the mould of dialectical materialism, with the result that Marxist thinkers tend to overlook the actual facts, or at least to glance at them only cursorily. We are led to believe therefore that existentialism, marked as we have seen by an almost obsessive interest in the concrete and the actual, will breathe new life into Marxism by "interiorizing" it, by rendering it concrete and by presenting the dialectic from within. Sartre claims that existentialism, by still concentrating its attention on the individual, can show how the concept of the class, with which Marxism is concerned, arose. There is an empty space, a mere abstraction, at the very centre of Marxism, Sartre says, and it is this space which he plans to fill with a concrete anthropology.

However, when we turn to the Critique of Dialectical Reason itself, this undertaking seems to have been abandoned. The concept of praxis is the link between the two works. Praxis is deliberate human action; it is the action of the conscious human being upon his non-conscious environment. It was supposed, in the Question of Method, that concentration upon the intentional element in praxis would necessarily entail concentration on the concrete detail of the agent's environment, that is, upon the actual facts which helped him frame his plans. Existentialism would explain what it was like for an individual freely to choose from among the various possibilities open to him. But besides this, the concept of praxis is said to be that which carries within itself a proof that human thought about the world is dialectical in form. New facts are supposed to emerge from the marrying together, in action, of the incompatible elements of thought, or plan, and physical environment, against which the plan has to be measured. By examining the nature of human praxis, Sartre thinks that a foundation can be laid for a general history and anthropology of the world. And by the time we come to the Critique of

*Dialectical Reason* itself, the concrete and the particular have altogether been given up in favour of considerations of the nature of action in general, and of the advance of history in general. Yet in another way, the theme of the *Critique* does bear some relation to the problems posed and left unsolved in *Being and Nothingness*. For the difficulty there was to establish some kind of system to account for or regulate the relation of one person to another. Any two individuals were perpetually striving to dominate, master and possess one another, just as they strove to dominate the rest of their environment; and if one were to systematize the way in which they did in practice solve their problems, or suggest how one might justify one solution rather than another, then one would at once be guilty of the spirit of seriousness, to avoid which was the only *positive* ethical teaching which emerged from the book. Human beings, therefore, seemed condemned to live in total isolation from one another, in the lonely grandeur of choosing freely for themselves, if they did not want to lapse into sentimentality or Bad Faith. But in the *Critique* it is specifically shown how human beings can by their own choice break down this isolation and form themselves into groups. In this way, it looks as if the problems of Being and Nothingness could be solved. If people merely live side by side, without any community of interest, each striving against the other in the context of material scarcity, then this is a *collective*, but not yet a group. The condition of "seriality," the inhuman impotent condition of the collective which is not a group, forms the subject-matter of the first book of the *Critique*. The second book is concerned with the formation of the group. The members of the series come to realize their impotence, and, at that historical moment the impetus towards revolution begins. From the realiz- ation that they can do nothing alone, a kind of "general will" emerges, a dynamic group of individual revolutionaries is formed, and each member "finds himself" in each other member, and their interests become genuinely identical. The formation of this group is, Sartre says, "the beginning of humanity." Thereafter the problem of society and of its individual member is how to keep the group in being, and prevent the lapse back into seriality. The aim of the dialectical movement of history is said to be "totalization," in which the identity of each person with the others in the group shall be finally established.

Even though the *Critique* is never now likely to be finished, we have surely enough of it to entitle us to say that it contains a radical conversion, indeed, but also the end of existentialism, at least for Sartre. The solution of the earlier problems is not a real solution. The undertaking to interiorize Marxism and revivify it with existentialism was not fulfilled. And it seems fairly clear that it could not have been fulfilled. In *Being and Nothingness* a Being-for-itself was free to choose whatever way of life he pleased; but he was doomed in any case to frustration in his relations with others by the nature of his hopeless longing to control and to possess the freedom of the other. These gloomy facts were there presented, as we have seen, in the most direct and concrete way, by the device of getting us to accept that people were of this kind, and could not, given the nature of what there is in the world, be otherwise. In the *Critique*, the conflicts into which people fall are, on the other hand, caused by a contingent scarcity of raw materials, which can in principle be overcome, and if this scarcity is not overcome then people may merge their identity and their freedom into a group. There is very little in the way of concrete or anecdotal argument in the *Critique*; but even if there were, it would no longer constitute a method, a philosophical way of showing that this was the only way to present the facts. In *Being and Nothingness* we are shown people in concrete terms, *because this is how we experience them*, and existentialism aims to analyse how things are and to explain what it is like to be in the world. If Sartre had written anecdotes to illustrate the emergence of the group from the series, these would have been like novels or films commissioned by the government for presentation to party members; they would have been mere decoration, a cultural icing on the solid cake of *a priori* theory. There is nothing which is more crucial to existentialism than the belief that we can know only what we *live*: we know we are free because we experience our own freedom in anguish. We know that we fear the "sticky death of the For-itself in the In-itself" because we know, or are open to persuasion, that viscious things horrify and fascinate us. There is no doubt that the methods of argument used in *Being and Nothingness* can appear grotesque and absurd. But they arise out of the existentialist conviction that to understand a man must find out and experience for himself. For Kierkegaard and for Sartre alike, it was of no use to *tell* people that something was true; they had to *feel* that it was so, and accept it for themselves. Religion which was institutionalized was no religion at all, according to Kierkegaard. For Sartre (the existentialist Sartre) morality according to rules was no morality but only Bad Faith. This was, in fact, the dilemma from which Sartre could not free himself. He was probably right if he thought that as a matter of fact there could not be an existentialist moral philosophy. If the true course of morality lay necessarily in political action, as he came to think, then it would be absurd to suppose that this morality could be presented in terms of the existentialist hero. Such a hero is essentially *not* a political man; for he cares only for his own integrity.

Perhaps it is right, therefore, to regard *Being and Nothingness* as the culmination of a mood—anti-rational, anti-scientific and anti-political. The book itself seems to me to be of tremendous power and interest; and the history of existentialism in general to have a certain fascination, particularly in its manner of converting the scientific aims of Husserl, in psychology and perception, into something so different yet so recognizable. But the time has come to consider existentialism as a part of the history of philosophy, not as a means of salvation nor as a doctrine of commitment. And, as for Sartre himself, we must realize that he is no longer an existentialist at all.

# TRANSLATOR'S PREFACE

This is a translation of all of Jean-Paul Sartre's *L'Etre et le Néant*. It includes those selections which in 1953 were published in a volume entitled *Existential Psychoanalysis*, but I have revised my earlier translation of these and made a number of small changes in technical terminology.

I should like to thank Mr. Forrest Williams, my colleague at the University of Colorado, who has helped me greatly in preparing this translation. Mr. Williams' excellent understanding of both Sartre's philosophy and the French language, and his generous willingness to give his time and effort have been invaluable to me.

I want also to express my appreciation to my friend, Mr. Robert O. Lehnert, who has read large sections of the book and offered many helpful suggestions and who has rendered the task more pleasant by means of stimulating discussions which we have enjoyed together.

Finally I am indebted to the University of Colorado, which through the Council on Research and Creative Work has provided funds for use in the preparation of the typescript.

In a work as long as this there are certain to be mistakes. Since I am the only one who has checked the translation in its entirety, I alone am responsible for whatever errors there may be. I hope that these may be few enough so that the work may be of benefit to those readers who prefer the ease of their own language to the accuracy of the original.

HAZEL E. BARNES
University of Colorado

# INTRODUCTION

## The pursuit of being

### I. THE PHENOMENON

Modern thought has realized considerable progress by reducing the existent to the series of appearances which manifest it. Its aim was to overcome a certain number of dualisms which have embarrassed philosophy and to replace them by the monism of the phenomenon. Has the attempt been successful?

In the first place we certainly thus get rid of that dualism which in the existent opposes interior to exterior. There is no longer an exterior for the existent if one means by that a superficial covering which hides from sight the true nature of the object. And this true nature in turn, if it is to be the secret reality of the thing, which one can have a presentiment of or which one can suppose but can never reach because it is the "interior" of the object under consideration—this nature no longer exists. The appearances which manifest the existent are neither interior nor exterior; they are all equal, they all refer to other appearances, and none of them is privileged. Force, for example, is not a metaphysical conatus of an unknown kind which hides behind its effects (accelerations, deviations, etc.); it is the totality of these effects. Similarly an electric current does not have a secret reverse side; it is nothing but the totality of the physical-chemical actions which manifest it (electrolysis, the incandescence of a carbon filament, the displacement of the needle of a galvanometer, *etc.*). No one of these actions alone is sufficient to reveal it. But no action indicates anything which is behind itself; it indicates only itself and the total series.

The obvious conclusion is that the dualism of being and appearance is no longer entitled to any legal status within philosophy. The appearance refers to the total series of appearances and not to a hidden reality which would drain to itself all the being of the existent. And the appearance for its part is not an inconsistent manifestation of this being. To the extent that men had believed in noumenal realities, they have presented appearance as a pure negative. It was "that which is not being"; it had no other being than that of illusion and error. But even this being was borrowed, it was itself a pretence, and philosophers met with the greatest difficulty in maintaining cohesion and existence in the appearance so that it should not itself be reabsorbed in the depth of non-phenomenal being. But if we once get away from what Nietzsche called "the illusion of worlds-behind-the-scene," and if we no longer believe in the being-behind-the-appearance, then the appearance becomes full positivity; its essence is an "appearing" which is no longer opposed to being but on the contrary is the measure of it. For the being of an existent is exactly what it *appears*. Thus we arrive at the idea of the *phenomenon* such as we can find, for example in the "phenomenology" of Husserl or of Heidegger—the phenomenon or the relative-absolute. Relative the phenomenon remains, for "to appear" supposes in essence somebody to whom to appear. But it does not have the double relativity of Kant's *Erscheinung*. It does not point over its shoulder to a true being which would be, for it, absolute. What it is, it is absolutely, for it reveals itself *as it is*. The phenomenon can be studied and described as such, for it is *absolutely indicative of itself*.

The duality of potency and act falls by the same stroke. The act is everything. Behind the act there is neither potency nor "hexis"[1] nor virtue. We shall refuse, for example, to understand by "genius"—in the sense in which we say that Proust "had genius" or that he "was" a genius—a particular capacity to produce certain works, which was not exhausted exactly in producing them. The genius of Proust is neither the work considered in isolation nor the subjective ability to produce it; it is the work considered as the totality of the manifestations of the person.

That is why we can equally well reject the dualism of appearance and essence. The appearance does not hide the essence, it reveals it; it *is* the essence. The essence of an existent is no longer a property sunk in the cavity of this existent; it is the manifest law which presides over the succession of its appearances, it is the principle of the series. To the nominalism of Poincaré, defining a physical reality (an electric current, for example) as the sum of its various manifestations, Duhem rightly opposed his own theory, which makes of the concept the *synthetic unity* of these manifestations. To be sure phenomenology is anything but a nominalism. But essence, as the principle of the series, is definitely only the concatenation of appearances; that is, itself an appearance. This explains how it is possible to have an intuition of *essences* (the *Wesenchau* of Husserl, for example). The phenomenal being manifests

---

[1] From Greek ἕξις. Sartre seems to have ignored the rough breathing and writes "exis." Tr.

itself; it manifests its *essence* as well as its existence, and it is nothing but the well connected series of its manifestations.

Does this mean that by reducing the existent to its manifestations we have succeeded in overcoming *all* dualisms? It seems rather that we have converted them all into a new dualism: that of finite and infinite. Yet the existent in fact can not be reduced to a *finite* series of manifestations since each one of them is a relation to a subject constantly changing. Although an *object* may disclose itself only through a single *Abschattung*, the sole fact of there being a subject implies the possibility of multiplying the points of view on that *Abschattung*. This suffices to multiply to infinity the *Abschattung* under consideration. Furthermore if the series of appearances were finite, that would mean that the first appearances do not have the possibility of *reappearing*, which is absurd, or that they can be all given at once, which is still more absurd. Let us understand indeed that our theory of the phenomenon has replaced the *reality* of the thing by the *objectivity* of the phenomenon and that it has based this on an appeal to infinity. The reality of that cup is that it is there and that it *is not me*. We shall interpret this by saying that the series of its appearances is bound by a principle which does not depend on my whim. But the appearance, reduced to itself and without reference to the series of which it is a part, could be only an intuitive and subjective plenitude, the manner in which the subject is affected. If the phenomenon is to reveal itself as *transcendent*, it is necessary that the subject himself transcend the appearance toward the total series of which it is a member. He must seize *Red* through his impression of red. By *Red* is meant the principle of the series—the electric current through the electrolysis, *etc*. But if the transcendence of the object is based on the necessity of causing the appearance to be always transcended, the result is that on principle an object posits the series of its appearances as infinite. Thus the appearance, which is *finite*, indicates itself in its finitude, but at the same time in order to be grasped as an appearance-of-that-which-appears, it requires that it be surpassed toward infinity.

This new opposition, the "finite and the infinite," or better, "the infinite in the finite," replaces the dualism of being and appearance. What appears in fact is only an *aspect* of the object, and the object is altogether *in* that aspect and altogether outside of it. It is altogether *within*, in that it manifests itself in that aspect; it shows itself as the structure of the appearance, which is at the same time the principle of the series. It is altogether *outside*, for the series itself will never appear nor can it appear. Thus the outside is opposed in a new way to the inside, and the being-which-does-not-appear, to the appearance. Similarly a certain "potency" returns to inhabit the phenomenon and confer on it its very transcendence—a potency to be developed in a series of real or possible appearances. The genius of Proust, even when reduced to the works produced, is no less equivalent to the infinity of possible points of view which one can take on that work and which we will call the "inexhaust-ibility" of Proust's work. But is not this inexhaustibility which implies a transcendence and a reference to the infinite—is this not an "hexis" at the exact moment when one apprehends it on the object? The essence finally is radically severed from the individual appearance which manifests it, since on principle it is that which must be able to be manifested by an infinite series of individual manifestations.

In thus replacing a variety of oppositions by a single dualism on which they all are based, have we gained or lost? This we shall soon see. For the moment, the first consequence of the "theory of the phenomenon" is that the appearance does not refer to being as Kant's phenomenon refers to the noumenon. Since there is nothing behind the appearance, and since it indicates only itself (and the total series of appearances), it can not be supported by any being other than its own. The appearance can not be the thin film of nothingness which separates the being-of-the-subject from absolute-being. If the essence of the appearance is an "appearing" which is no longer opposed to any being, there arises a legitimate problem concerning the being of this appearing. It is this problem which will be our first concern and which will be the point of departure for our inquiry into being and nothingness.

## II. THE PHENOMENON OF BEING AND THE BEING OF THE PHENOMENON

The appearance is not supported by any existent different from itself; it has its own being. The first being which we meet in our ontological inquiry is the being of the appearance. Is it itself an appearance? It seems so at first. The phenomenon is what manifests itself, and being manifests itself to all in some way, since we can speak of it and since we have a certain comprehension of it. Thus there must be for it a phenomenon of being, an appearance of being, which one can describe as such. Being will be disclosed to us by some kind of immediate access—boredom, nausea, etc., and ontology will be the descrip-tion of the phenomenon of being as it manifests itself; that is, without inter-mediary. However for any ontology we should raise a preliminary question: is the phenomenon of being thus achieved identical with the being of phenom-ena? In other words, is the being which discloses itself to me, which appears to me, of the same nature as the being of existents which appear to me? It seems that there is no difficulty. Husserl has shown how an eidetic reduction is always possible; that is, how one can always pass beyond the concrete phenomenon toward its essence. For Heidegger also "human reality" is ontic-ontological; that is, it can always pass beyond the phemomenon toward its being. But the passage from the particular object to the essence is a passage from homogeneous to homogeneous. Is it the same for the passage from the existent to the phenomenon of being? Is passing beyond the existent toward the phenomenon of being actually to pass beyond it toward its being, as one passes beyond the particular red toward its essence? Let us consider further.

In a particular object one can always distinguish qualities like color, odor, etc. And proceeding from these, one can always determine an essence which they imply, as a sign implies its meaning. The totality "object-essence" makes an organized whole. The essence is not in the object; it is the meaning of the object, the principle of the series of appearances which disclose it. But being is neither one of the object's qualities, distinguishable among others, nor a meaning of the object. The object does not refer to being as to a signification; it would be impossible, for example, to define being as a *presence* since *absence* too discloses being, since not to be *there* means still to be. The object does not *possess* being, and its existence is not a participation in being, nor any other kind of relation. It *is.* That is the only way to define its manner of being; the object does not hide being, but neither does it reveal being. The object does not hide it, for it would be futile to try to push aside certain qualities of the existent in order to find the being behind them; being is being of them all equally. The object does not reveal being, for it would be futile to address oneself to the object in order to apprehend its being. The existent is a phenomenon; this means that it designates itself as an organized totality of qualities. It designates itself and not its being. Being is simply the condition of all revelation. It is being-for-revealing (être-pour-dévoiler) and not revealed being (être dévoilé). What then is the meaning of the surpassing toward the ontological, of which Heidegger speaks? Certainly I can pass beyond this table or this chair toward its being and raise the question of the being-of-the-table or the being-of-the-chair.[2] But at that moment I turn my eyes away from the phenomenon of the table in order to concentrate on the phenomenon of being, which is no longer the condition of all revelation, but which is itself something revealed—an appearance which as such, needs in turn a being on the basis of which it can reveal itself.

If the being of phenomena is not resolved in a phenomenon of being and if nevertheless we can not say anything about being without considering this phenomenon of being, then the exact relation which unites the phenomenon of being to the being of the phenomenon must be established first of all. We can do this more easily if we will consider that the whole of the preceding remarks has been directly inspired by the revealing intuition of the phenomenon of being. By not considering being as the condition of revelation but rather being as an appearance which can be determined in concepts, we have understood first of all that knowledge can not by itself give an account of

[2] Perhaps a more intelligible paraphrase would be, "the question of what it means to be a table or a chair." Tr.

being; that is, the being of the phenomenon can not be reduced to the phenomenon of being. In a word, the phenomenon of being is "ontological" in the sense that we speak of the *ontological* proof of St. Anselm and Descartes. It is an appeal to being; it requires as phenomenon, a foundation which is transphenomenal. The phenomenon of being requires the transphenomenality of being. That does not mean that being is found hidden *behind* phenomena (we have seen that the phenomenon can not hide being), nor that the phenomenon is an appearance which refers to a distinct being (the phenomenon exists only *qua appearance*; that is, it indicates itself on the foundation of being). What is implied by the preceding considerations is that the being of the phenomenon although coextensive with the phenomenon, can not be subject to the phenomenal condition—which is to exist only in so far as it reveals itself—and that consequently it surpasses the knowledge which we have of it and provides the basis for such knowledge.

## III. THE PRE-REFLECTIVE *COGITO* AND THE BEING OF THE *PERCIPERE*

One will perhaps be tempted to reply that the difficulties mentioned above all pertain to a certain conception of being, to a kind of ontological realism entirely incompatible with the very notion of appearance. What determines the being of the appearance is the fact that it appears. And since we have restricted reality to the phenomenon, we can say of the phenomenon that it *is* as it *appears*. Why not push the idea to its limit and say that the being of the appearance is its appearing? This is simply a way of choosing new words to clothe the old "*Esse est percipi*" of Berkeley. And it is in fact just what Husserl and his followers are doing when after having effected the phenomenological reduction, they treat the noema as *unreal* and declare that its *esse* is *percipi*.

It seems that the famous formula of Berkeley can not satisfy us—for two essential reasons, one concerning the nature of the *percipi*, the other that of the *percipere*.

### The nature of the *percipere*

If every metaphysics in fact presupposes a theory of knowledge, every theory of knowledge in turn presupposes a metaphysics. This means among other things that an idealism intent on reducing being to the knowledge which we have of it, ought first to give some kind of guarantee for the being of knowledge. If one begins, on the other hand, by taking the knowledge as a given, without being concerned to establish a basis for its being, and if one then affirms that *esse est percipi*, the totality "perceived-perception," lacks the support of a solid being and so falls away in nothingness. Thus the being of knowledge can not be measured by knowledge; it is not subject to the percipi.[3] Therefore the foundation-of-being (l'être-fondement) for the percipere and the percipi can not itself be subject to the percipi; it must be transphenomenal. Let us return now to our point of departure. We can always agree that the percipi refers to a being not subject to the laws of the appearance, but we still maintain that this transphenomenal being is the being of the subject. Thus the percipi would refer to the percipiens—the known to knowledge and knowledge to the being who knows (in his capacity as being, not as being known); that is, knowledge refers to consciousness. This is what Husserl understood; for if the noema is for him an unreal correlate of noesis, and if its ontological law is the percipi, the noesis, on the contrary, appears to him as reality, of which the principle characteristic is to give itself to the reflection which knows it as "having already been there before." For the law of being in the knowing subject is to-be-conscious. Consciousness is not a mode of particular knowledge which may be called an inner meaning or self-knowledge; it is the transphenomenal dimension of being in the subject. •

Let us look more closely at this dimension of being. We said that consciousness is the knowing being in so far as he is, not in so far as he is known. This means that we must abandon the primacy of knowledge if we wish to establish that knowledge. Of course consciousness can know and know itself. But it is in itself something other than a knowledge turned back upon itself.

All consciousness, as Husserl has shown, is consciousness of something. This means that there is no consciousness which is not a positing of a transcendent object, or if you prefer, that consciousness has no "content." We must renounce those neutral "givens" which, according to the system of reference chosen, find their place either "in the world" or "in the psyche." A table is not in consciousness—not even in the capacity of a representation. A table is in space, beside the window, etc. The existence of the table in fact is a center of opacity for consciousness; it would require an infinite process to inventory the total contents of a thing. To introduce this opacity into consciousness would be to refer to infinity the inventory which it can make of itself, to make consciousness a thing, and to deny the cogito. The first procedure of a philosophy ought to be to expel things from consciousness and to reestablish its true connection with the world, to know that consciousness is a positional consciousness of the world. All consciousness is positional in that it transcends itself in order to reach an object, and it exhausts itself in this same

---

[3] It goes without saying that any attempt to replace the percipere by another attitude from human reality would be equally fruitless. If we granted that being is revealed to man in "acting," it would still be necessary to guarantee the being of acting apart from the action.

positing. All that there is of intention in my actual consciousness is directed toward the outside, toward the table; all my judgments or practical activities, all my present inclinations transcend themselves; they aim at the table and are absorbed in it. Not all consciousness is knowledge (there are states of affective consciousness, for example), but all knowing consciousness can be knowledge only of its object.

However, the necessary and sufficient condition for a knowing consciousness to be knowledge *of* its object, is that it be consciousness of itself as being that knowledge. This is a necessary condition, for if my consciousness were not consciousness of being consciousness of the table, it would then be consciousness of that table without consciousness of being so. In other words, it would be a consciousness ignorant of itself, an unconscious— which is absurd. This is a sufficient condition, for my being conscious of being conscious of that table suffices in fact for me to be conscious of it. That is of course not sufficient to permit me to affirm that this table exists *in itself*— but rather that it exists *for me*.

What is this *consciousness* of consciousness? We suffer to such an extent from the illusion of the primacy of knowledge that we are immediately ready to make of the consciousness of consciousness an *idea ideae* in the manner of Spinoza; that *is*, a knowledge of knowledge. Alain, wanting to express the obvious "To know is to be conscious of knowing," interprets it in these terms: "To know is to know that one knows." In this way we should have defined *reflection* or positional consciousness of consciousness, or better yet *knowledge of consciousness*. This would be a complete consciousness directed toward something which is not it; that is, toward consciousness as object of reflection. It would then transcend itself and like the positional consciousness of the world would be exhausted in aiming at its object. But that object would be itself a consciousness.

It does not seem possible for us to accept this interpretation of the consciousness of consciousness. The reduction of consciousness to knowledge in fact involves our introducing into consciousness the subject-object dualism which is typical of knowledge. But if we accept the law of the knower-known dyad, then a third term will be necessary in order for the knower to become known in turn, and we will be faced with this dilemma: either we stop at any one term of the series—the known, the knower known, the knower known by the knower, *etc.* In this case the totality of the phenomenon falls into the unknown; that is, we always bump up against a non-self-conscious reflection and a final term. Or else we affirm the necessity of an infinite regress (*idea ideae ideae, etc.*), which is absurd. Thus to the necessity of ontologically establishing consciousness we would add a new necessity: that of establishing it epistemologically. Are we obliged after all to introduce the law of this dyad into consciousness? Consciousness of self is not dual. If we wish to avoid an infinite regress, there must be an immediate, non-cognitive relation of the self to itself.

Furthermore the reflecting consciousness posits the consciousness reflected-on, as its object. In the act of reflecting I pass judgment on the consciousness reflected-on; I am ashamed of it, I am proud of it, I will it, I deny it, *etc.* The immediate consciousness which I have of perceiving does not permit me either to judge or to will or to be ashamed. It does not know my perception, does not *posit* it; all that there is of intention in my present con-sciousness is directed toward the outside, toward the world. In turn, this spontaneous consciousness of my perception is *constitutive* of my perceptive consciousness. In other words, every positional consciousness of an object is at the same time a non-positional consciousness of itself. If I count the cigarettes which are in that case, I have the impression of disclosing an objective property of this collection of cigarettes: *they are a dozen.* This property appears to my consciousness as a property existing in the world. It is very possible that I have no positional consciousness of counting them. Then I do not know myself as counting. Proof of this is that children who are capable of making an addition spontaneously can not explain subsequently how they set about it. Piaget's tests, which show this, constitute an excellent refutation of the formula of Alain—To know is to know that one knows. Yet at the moment when these cigarettes are revealed to me as a dozen, I have a non-thetic consciousness of my adding activity. If anyone questioned me, indeed, if anyone should ask, "What are you doing there?" I should reply at once, "I am counting." This reply aims not only at the instantaneous consciousness which I can achieve by reflection but at those fleeting consciousnesses which have passed without being reflected-on, those which are forever not-reflected-on in my immediate past. Thus reflection has no kind of primacy over the consciousness reflected-on. It is not reflection which reveals the conscious-ness reflected-on to itself. Quite the contrary, it is the non-reflective con-sciousness which renders the reflection possible; there is a pre-reflective cogito which is the condition of the Cartesian cogito. At the same time it is the non-thetic consciousness of counting which is the very condition of my act of adding. If it were otherwise, how would the addition be the unifying theme of my consciousnesses? In order that this theme should preside over a whole series of syntheses of unifications and recognitions, it must be present to itself, not as a thing but as an operative intention which can exist only as the revealing-revealed (*révélante-révélée*), to use an expression of Heidegger's. Thus in order to count, it is necessary to be conscious of counting.

Of course, someone may say, but this makes a circle. For is it not necessary that I count in *fact* in order to *be conscious* of counting? That is true. However there is no circle, or if you like, it is the very nature of consciousness to exist "in a circle." The idea can be expressed in these terms: Every conscious existence exists as consciousness of existing. We understand now why the first consciousness of consciousness is not positional; it is because it is one with the consciousness of which it is consciousness. At one stroke it determines itself as consciousness of perception and as perception. The necessity of syntax has compelled us hitherto to speak of the "non-positional consciousness of self." But we can no longer use this expression in which the "of self" still evokes the idea of knowledge. (Henceforth we shall put the "of" inside parentheses to show that it merely satisfies a grammatical requirement.)[4]

This self-consciousness we ought to consider not as a new consciousness, but as *the only mode of existence which is possible for a consciousness of something*. Just as an extended object is compelled to exist according to three dimensions, so an intention, a pleasure, a grief can exist only as immediate self-consciousness. If the intention is not a thing in consciousness, then the being of the intention can be only consciousness. It is not necessary to understand by this that on the one hand, some external cause (an organic trouble, an unconscious impulse, another *Erlebnis*) could determine that a psychic event—a pleasure, for example,—produce itself, and that on the other hand, this event so determined in its material structure should be compelled to produce itself as self-consciousness. This would be to make the non-thetic consciousness a *quality* of the positional consciousness (in the sense that the perception, positional consciousness of that table, would have as addition the quality of self-consciousness) and would thus fall back into the illusion of the theoretical primacy of knowledge. This would be moreover to make the psychic event a thing and to *qualify* it with "conscious" just as I can qualify this blotter with "red." Pleasure can not be distinguished—even logically—from consciousness of pleasure. Consciousness (of) pleasure is constitutive of the pleasure as the very mode of its own existence, as the material of which it is made, and not as a form which would be imposed afterwards upon a hedonistic material. Pleasure can not exist "before" consciousness of pleasure—not even in the form of potentiality or potency. A potential pleasure can exist only as consciousness (of) being potential. Potencies of consciousness exist only as consciousness of potencies.

Conversely, as I showed earlier, we must avoid defining pleasure by the consciousness which I have of it. This would be to fall into an idealism of consciousness which would bring us by indirect means to the primacy of knowledge. Pleasure must not disappear behind its own self-consciousness; it is not a representation, it is a concrete event, full and absolute. It is no more a quality of self-consciousness than self-consciousness is a quality of pleasure. There is no more first a consciousness which receives *subsequently* the affect

---

[4] Since English syntax does not require the "of," I shall henceforth freely translate *conscience (de) soi* as "self-consciousness." Tr.

"pleasure" like water which one stains, than there is first a pleasure (unconscious or psychological) which receives subsequently the quality of "conscious" like a pencil of light rays. There is an indivisible, indissoluble being—definitely not a substance supporting its qualities like particles of being, but a being which is existence through and through. Pleasure is the being of self-consciousness and this self-consciousness is the law of being of pleasure. This is what Heidegger expressed very well when he wrote (though speaking of *Dasein*, not of consciousness): "The 'how' (*essentia*) of this being, so far as it is possible to speak of it generally, must be conceived in terms of its existence (*existentia*)." This means that consciousness is not produced as a particular instance of an abstract possibility but that in rising to the center of being, it creates and supports its essence—that is, the synthetic order of its possibilities.

This means also that the type of being of consciousness is the opposite of that which the ontological proof reveals to us. Since consciousness is not *possible* before being, but since its being is the source and condition of all possibility, its existence implies its essence. Husserl expresses this aptly in speaking of the "necessity of fact." In order for there to be an essence of pleasure, there must be first the *fact* of a consciousness (of) this pleasure. It is futile to try to invoke pretended *laws* of consciousness of which the articulated whole would constitute the essence. A law is a transcendent object of knowledge; there can be consciousness of a law, not a law of consciousness. For the same reasons it is impossible to assign to a consciousness a motivation other than itself. Otherwise it would be necessary to conceive that consciousness in so far as it is an effect, is not conscious (of) itself. It would be necessary in some manner that it should be without being conscious (of) being. We should fall into that too common illusion which makes consciousness semi-unconscious or a passivity. But consciousness is consciousness through and through. It can be limited only by itself.

This self-determination of consciousness must not be conceived as a genesis, as a becoming, for that would force us to suppose that consciousness is prior to its own existence. Neither is it necessary to conceive of this self-creation as an act, for in that case consciousness would be conscious (of) itself as an act, which it is not. Consciousness is a plenum of existence, and this determination of itself by itself is an essential characteristic. It would even be wise not to misuse the expression "cause of self," which allows us to suppose a progression, a relation of self-cause to self-effect. It would be more exact to say very simply: The existence of consciousness comes from consciousness itself. By that we need not understand that consciousness "derives from nothingness." There can not be "nothingness of consciousness" *before* consciousness. "Before" consciousness one can conceive only of a plenum of being of which no element can refer to an absent consciousness. If there is to be nothingness of consciousness, there must be a consciousness which has been and which is no more and a witnessing consciousness which poses the nothingness of the first consciousness for a synthesis of recognitions. Consciousness is prior to nothingness and "is derived" from being.[5]

One will perhaps have some difficulty in accepting these conclusions. But considered more carefully, they will appear perfectly clear. The paradox is not that there are "self-activated" existences but that there is no other kind. What is truly unthinkable is passive existence; that is, existence which perpetuates itself without having the force either to produce itself or to preserve itself. From this point of view there is nothing more incomprehensible than the principle of inertia. Indeed where would consciousness "come" from if it did "come" from something? From the limbo of the unconscious or of the physiological. But if we ask ourselves how this limbo in its turn can exist and where it derives its existence, we find ourselves faced with the concept of passive existence; that is, we can no more absolutely understand how this non-conscious given (unconscious or physiological) which does not derive its existence from itself, can nevertheless perpetuate this existence and find in addition the ability to produce a consciousness. This demonstrates the great favor which the proof a *contingentia mundi* has enjoyed.

Thus by abandoning the primacy of knowledge, we have discovered the *being* of the *knower* and encountered the absolute, that same absolute which the rationalists of the seventeenth century had defined and logically constituted as an object of knowledge. But precisely because the question concerns an absolute of existence and not of knowledge, it is not subject to that famous objection according to which a known absolute is no longer an absolute because it becomes relative to the knowledge which one has of it. In fact the absolute here is not the result of a logical construction on the ground of knowledge but the subject of the most concrete of experiences. And it is not at all *relative* to this experience because it *is* this experience. Likewise it is a non-substantial absolute. The ontological error of Cartesian rationalism is not to have seen that if the absolute is defined by the primacy of existence over essence, it can not be conceived as a substance. Consciousness has nothing substantial, it is pure "appearance" in the sense that it exists only to the degree to which it appears. But it is precisely because consciousness is pure appearance, because it is total emptiness (since the entire world is outside it)—it is because of this identity of appearance and existence within it that it can be considered as the absolute.

---

[5] That certainly does not mean that consciousness is the foundation of its being. On the contrary, as we shall see later, there is a full contingency of the being of consciousness. We wish only to show (1) That *nothing* is the cause of consciousness. (2) That consciousness is the cause of its own way of being.

## IV. THE BEING OF THE *PERCIPI*

It seems that we have arrived at the goal of our inquiry. We have reduced things to the united totality of their appearances, and we have established that these appearances lay claim to a being which is no longer itself appearance. The "*percipi*" referred us to a *percipiens*, the being of which has been revealed to us as consciousness. Thus we have attained the ontological foundation of knowledge, the first being to whom all other appearances appear, the absolute in relation to which every phenomenon is relative. This is no longer the subject in Kant's meaning of the term, but it is subjectivity itself, the immanence of self in self. Henceforth we have escaped idealism. For the latter, being is measured by knowledge, which subjects it to the law of duality; there is only known being including thought itself: thought appears only through its own products; that is, we always apprehend it only as the signification of thoughts produced, and the philosopher in quest of thought must question the established sciences in order to derive it from them as the condition of their possibility. We, on the other hand, have apprehended a being which is not subject to knowledge and which founds knowledge, a thought which is definitely not given as a representation or a signification of expressed thoughts, but which is directly apprehended such as it is—and this mode of apprehension is not a phenomenon of knowledge but is the structure of being. We find ourselves at present on the ground of the phenomenology of Husserl although Husserl himself has not always been faithful to his first intuition. Are we satisfied? We have encountered a transphenomenal being, but is it actually the being to which the phenomenon of being refers? Is it indeed the being of the phenomenon? In other words is consciousness sufficient to provide the foundation for the appearance qua appearance? We have extracted its being from the phenomenon in order to give it to consciousness, and we anticipated that consciousness would subsequently restore it to the phenomenon. Is this possible? We shall find our answer in the examination of the ontological exigencies of the *percipi*.

Let us note first that there is a being of the thing perceived—*as perceived*. Even if I wished to reduce this table to a synthesis of subjective impressions, I must at least remark that it reveals itself *qua table* through this synthesis, that it *is* the transcendent limit of the synthesis, the reason for it and its end. The table is before knowledge and can not be identified with the knowledge which we have of it; otherwise it would be consciousness—i.e., pure immanence—and it would disappear *as* table. For the same cause even if a pure distinction of reason is to separate the table from the synthesis of subjective impressions through which I apprehend it, at least it can not *be* this synthesis; that would be to reduce it to a synthetic activity of connection. In so far then as the known can not be reabsorbed into knowledge, we must discover for it a *being*. This being, we are told, is the *percipi*. Let us recognize first of all that the being of the *percipi* can not be reduced to that of the *percipiens*—i.e., to consciousness—any more than the table is reduced to the bond of representations. At most we can say that it is *relative* to this being. But this *relativity* does not render unnecessary an examination of the being of the *percipi*.

Now the mode of the *percipi* is the *passive*. If then the being of the phenomenon resides in its *percipi*, this being is passivity. Relativity and passivity—such are the characteristic structures of the *esse* in so far as this is reduced to the *percipi*. What is passivity? I am passive when I under-go a modification of which I am not the origin; that is, neither the source nor the creator. Thus my being supports a mode of being of which it is not the source. Yet in order for me to support, it is still necessary that I exist, and due to this fact my existence is always situated on the other side of passivity. "To support passively," for example, is a conduct which I assume and which engages my liberty as much as to "reject resolutely." If I am to be for always "the-one-who-has-been-offended," I must persevere in my being; that is, I myself assume my existence. But all the same I respond on my own account in some way and I assume my offense; I cease to be passive in relation to it. Hence we have this choice of alternatives: either, indeed, I am not passive in my being, in which case I become the foundation of my affections even if at first I have not been the origin of them—or I am affected with passivity in my very existence, my being is a received being, and hence all falls into nothingness. Thus passivity is a doubly relative phenomenon, relative to the activity of the one who acts and to the existence of the one who suffers. This implies that *passivity* can not affect the actual being of the passive existent; it is a relation of one being to another being and not of one being to a nothingness. It is impossible that *the percipere affects the perceptum of* being, for in order for the *perceptum* to be affected it would of necessity have to be already given in some way and exist before having received being. One can conceive of a *creation* on condition that the created being recover itself, tear itself away from the creator in order to close in on itself immediately and assume its being; it is in this sense that a book exists *against* its author. But if the act of creation is to be continued indefinitely, if the created being is to be supported even in its inmost parts, if it does not have its own independence, if it is in *itself* only nothingness—then the creature *is* in no way distinguished from its creator; it is absorbed in him; we are dealing with a false transcendence, and the creator can not have even an illusion of getting out of his subjectivity.[6]

Furthermore the passivity of the recipient demands an equal passivity on the part of the agent. This is expressed in the principle of action and reaction;

---

[6] It is for this reason that the Cartesian doctrine of substance finds its logical culmination in the work of Spinoza.

it is because my hand can be crushed, grasped, cut, that my hand can crush, cut, grasp. What element of passivity can we assign to perception, to knowledge? They are all activity, all spontaneity. It is precisely because it is pure spontaneity, because nothing can get a grip on it that consciousness can not act upon anything. Thus the *esse est percipi* would require that consciousness, pure spontaneity which can not *act* upon anything, give being to a transcendent nothingness, at the same time keeping it in its state of nothingness. So much nonsense! Husserl has attempted to overcome these objections by introducing passivity into the *noesis*; this is the *hyle* or pure flux of experience and the matter of the passive syntheses. But he has only added an additional difficulty to those which we have mentioned. He has introduced in fact those neutral givens, the impossibility of which we have shown earlier. To be sure, these are not "contents" of consciousness, but they remain only so much the more unintelligible. The *hyle* in fact could not be consciousness, for it would disappear in translucency and could not offer that resisting basis of impressions which must be surpassed toward the object. But if it does not belong to consciousness, where does it derive its being and its opacity? How can it preserve at once the opaque resistance of things and the subjectivity of thought? Its *esse* can not come to it from a *percipi* since it is not even perceived, for consciousness transcends it toward the objects. But if the *hyle* derives its being from itself alone, we meet once again the insoluble problem of the connection of consciousness with existents independent of it. Even if we grant to Husserl that there is hyletic stratum for the noesis, we can not conceive how consciousness can transcend this subjective toward objectivity. In giving to the *hyle* both the characteristics of a thing and the characteristics of consciousness, Husserl believed that he facilitated the passage from the one to the other, but he succeeded only in creating a hybrid being which consciousness rejects and which can not be a part of the world.

Furthermore, as we have seen, the *percipi* implies that the law of being of the *perceptum* is relativity. Can we conceive that the being of the thing known is relative to the knowledge? What can the relativity of being mean for an existent if not that the existent has its own being in something other than in itself; that is, *in an existent which it is not*. Certainly it would not be inconceivable that a being should be external to itself if one means that this being is *its own* externality. But such is not the case here. The perceived being is in front of consciousness; consciousness can not reach it, and it can not enter into consciousness; and as the perceived being is cut off from consciousness, it exists cut off from its own existence. It would be no use to make of it an unreal in the manner of Husserl; even as unreal it must exist.

Thus the two determinations of *relativity* and of *passivity*, which can concern modes of being, can on no account apply to being. The *esse* of the phenomenon can not be its *percipi*. The transphenomenal being of consciousness can not provide a basis for the transphenomenal being of the phenomenon. Here we see the error of the phenomenalists: having justifiably reduced the object to the connected series of its appearances, they believed they had reduced its being to the succession of its modes of being. That is why they have explained it by concepts which can be applied only to the modes of being, for they are pointing out the relations between a plurality of already existing beings.

## V. THE ONTOLOGICAL PROOF

Being has not been given its due. We believed we had dispensed with granting transphenomenality to the being of the phenomenon because we had discovered the transphenomenality of the being of consciousness. We are going to see, on the contrary, that this very transphenomenality requires that of the being of the phenomenon. There is an "ontological proof" to be derived not from the reflective *cogito* but from the *pre-reflective* being of the *percipiens*. This we shall now try to demonstrate.

All consciousness is consciousness of something. This definition of consciousness can be taken in two very distinct senses: either we understand by this that consciousness is constitutive of the being of its object, or it means that consciousness in its inmost nature is a relation to a transcendent being. But the first interpretation of the formula destroys itself: to be conscious *of* something is to be confronted with a concrete and full presence which *is not* consciousness. Of course one can be conscious of an absence. But this absence appears necessarily as a pre-condition of presence. As we have seen, consciousness is a real subjectivity and the impression is a subjective plenitude. But this subjectivity can not go out of itself to posit a transcendent object in such a way as to endow it with a plenitude of impressions.[7] If then we wish at any price to make the being of the phenomenon depend on consciousness, the object must be distinguished from consciousness not by its *presence* but by its *absence*, not by its plenitude, but by its nothingness. If being belongs to consciousness, the object is not consciousness, not to the extent that it is another being, but that it is non-being. This is the appeal to the infinite of which we spoke in the first section of this work. For Husserl, for example, the animation of the hyletic nucleus by the only intentions which can find their fulfilment (Erfüllung) in this *hyle* is not enough to bring us outside of subjectivity. The truly objectifying intentions are empty intentions, those which aim beyond the present subjective appearance at the infinite totality of the series of appearances.

We must further understand that the intentions aim at appearances which are never to be given at one time. It is an impossibility on principle for the

---

[7] I.e., in such a way that the impressions are objectified into qualities of the thing. Tr.

terms of an infinite series to exist all at the same time before consciousness, along with the real absence of all these terms except for the one which is the foundation of objectivity. If present these impressions—even in infinite number—would dissolve in the subjective; it is their absence which gives them objective being. Thus the being of the object is pure non-being. It is defined as a *lack*. It is that which escapes, that which by definition will never be given, that which offers itself only in fleeting and successive profiles.

But how can non-being be the foundation of being? How can the absent, *expected* subjective become thereby the objective? A great joy which I hope for, a grief which I dread, acquire from that fact a certain transcendence. This I admit. But that transcendence in immanence does not bring us out of the subjective. It is true that things give themselves in profile; that is, simply by appearances. And it is true that each appearance refers to other appearances. But each of them is already in itself alone a *transcendent being*, not a subjective material of impressions—a *plenitude of being*, not a lack—a *presence*, not an absence. It is futile by a sleight of hand to attempt to found the *reality* of the object on the subjective plenitude of impressions and its *objectivity* on non-being; the objective will never come out of the subjective nor the transcendent from immanence, nor being from non-being. But, we are told, Husserl defines consciousness precisely as a transcendence. In truth he does. This is what he posits. This is his essential discovery. But from the moment that he makes of the *noema* an *unreal*, a *correlate of the noesis*, a noema whose *esse* is *percipi*, he is totally unfaithful to his principle.

Consciousness is consciousness *of* something. This means that transcendence is the constitutive structure of consciousness; that is, that consciousness arises oriented towards a being which is not itself. This is what we call the ontological proof. No doubt someone will reply that the existence of the demand of consciousness does not prove that this demand ought to be satisfied. But this objection can not hold up against an analysis of what Husserl calls intentionality, though, to be sure, he misunderstood its essential character. To say that consciousness is consciousness of something means that for consciousness there is no being outside of that precise obligation to be a revealing intuition of something—i.e., of a transcendent being. Not only does pure subjectivity, if initially given, fail to transcend itself to posit the objective; a "pure" subjectivity disappears. What can properly be called subjectivity is consciousness (of) consciousness. But this consciousness (of being) consciousness must be qualified in some way, and it can be qualified only as revealing intuition or it is nothing. Now a revealing intuition implies something revealed. Absolute subjectivity can be established only in the face of something revealed; immanence can be defined only within the apprehension of a transcendent. It might appear that there is an echo here of Kant's refutation of problematical idealism. But we ought rather to think of

Descartes. We are here on the ground of being, not of knowledge. It is not a question of showing that the phenomena of inner sense imply the existence of objective spatial phenomena, but that consciousness implies in its being a non-conscious and transphenomenal being. In particular there is no point in replying that in fact subjectivity implies objectivity and that it constitutes itself in constituting the objective; we have seen that subjectivity is powerless to constitute the objective. To say that consciousness is consciousness of something is to say that it must produce itself as a revealed-revelation of a being which is not it and which gives itself as already existing when consciousness reveals it.

Thus we have left pure appearance and have arrived at full being. Consciousness is a being whose existence posits its essence, and inversely it is consciousness of a being, whose essence implies its existence; that is, in which appearance lays claim to being. Being is everywhere. Certainly we could apply to consciousness the definition which Heidegger reserves for *Dasein* and say that it is a being such that in its being, its being is in question. But it would be necessary to complete the definition and formulate it more like this: *consciousness is a being such that in its being, its being is in question in so far as this being implies a being other than itself.*

We must understand that this being is no other than the transphenomenal being of phenomena and not a noumenal being which is hidden behind them. It is the being of this table, of this package of tobacco, of the lamp, more generally the being of the world which is implied by consciousness. It requires simply that the being of that which *appears* does not exist *only* in so far as it appears. The transphenomenal being of what exists for *consciousness* is itself in itself (lui-même en soi).

## VI. BEING-IN-ITSELF

We can now form a few definite conclusions about the *phenomenon of being*, which we have considered in order to make the preceding observations. Consciousness is the revealed-revelation of existents, and existents appear before consciousness on the foundation of their being. Nevertheless the primary characteristic of the being of an existent is never to reveal itself completely to consciousness. An existent can not be stripped of its being; being is the ever present foundation of the existent; it is everywhere in it and nowhere. There is no being which is not the being of a certain mode of being, none which can not be apprehended through the mode of being which manifests being and veils it at the same time. Consciousness can always pass beyond the existent, not toward its being, but toward the *meaning of this being*. That is why we call it ontic-ontological, since a fundamental characteristic of its transcendence is to transcend the ontic toward the ontological. The

meaning of the being of the existent in so far as it reveals itself to consciousness is the phenomenon of being. This meaning has itself a being, based on
which it manifests itself.

It is from this point of view that we can understand the famous Scholastic
argument according to which there is a vicious circle in every proposition
which concerns being, since any judgment about being already implies
being. But in actuality there is no vicious circle, for it is not necessary again to
pass beyond the being of this meaning toward its meaning; the meaning of
being is valid for the being of every phenomenon, including its own being.
The phenomenon of being is not being, as we have already noted. But it
indicates being and requires it—although, in truth, the ontological proof
which we mentioned above is not valid *especially* or *uniquely* for it; there is *one*
ontological proof valid for the whole domain of consciousness. But this proof
is sufficient to justify all the information which we can derive from the
phenomenon of being. The phenomenon of being, like every primary phenomenon, is immediately disclosed to consciousness. We have at each instant
what Heidegger calls a pre-ontological comprehension of it; that is, one
which is not accompanied by a fixing in concepts and elucidation. For us at
present, then, there is no question of considering this phenomenon for the
sake of trying to fix the meaning of being. We must observe always:

(1) That this elucidation of the meaning of being is valid only for the
being of the phenomenon. Since the being of consciousness is radically different, its meaning will necessitate a particular elucidation, in terms of the
revealed-revelation of another type of being, being-for-itself (l'être-pour-soi),
which we shall define later and which is opposed to the being-in-itself
(l'être-en-soi) of the phenomenon.

(2) That the elucidation of the meaning of being-in-itself which we are
going to attempt here can be only provisional. The aspects which will be
revealed imply other significations which ultimately we must apprehend and
determine. In particular the preceding reflections have permitted us to distinguish two absolutely separated regions of being: the being of the pre-
reflective cogito and the being of the phenomenon. But although the concept of
being has this peculiarity of being divided into two regions without communication, we must nevertheless explain how these two regions can be
placed under the same heading. That will necessitate the investigation of these
two types of being, and it is evident that we can not truly grasp the meaning
of either one until we can establish their true connection with the notion of
being in general and the relations which unite them. We have indeed established by the examination of non-positional self-consciousness that the being
of the phenomenon can on no account act upon consciousness. In this way
we have ruled out a *realistic* conception of the relations of the phenomenon
with consciousness.

We have shown also by the examination of the spontaneity of the non-reflective cogito that consciousness can not get out of its subjectivity if the latter has been initially given, and that consciousness can not act upon transcendent being nor without contradiction admit of the passive elements necessary in order to constitute a transcendent being arising from them. Thus we have ruled out the *idealist* solution of the problem. It appears that we have barred all doors and that we are now condemned to regard transcendent being and consciousness as two closed totalities without possible communication. It will be necessary to show that the problem allows a solution other than realism or idealism.

A certain number of characteristics can be fixed on immediately because for the most part they follow naturally from what we have just said.

A clear view of the phenomenon of being has often been obscured by a very common prejudice which we shall call "creationism." Since people supposed that God had given being to the world, being always appeared tainted with a certain passivity. But a creation *ex nihilo* can not explain the coming to pass of being; for if being is conceived in a subjectivity, even a divine subjectivity, it remains a mode of intra-subjective being. Such subjectivity can not have even the *representation* of an objectivity, and consequently it can not even be affected with the will to create the objective. Furthermore being, if it is suddenly placed outside the subjective by the fulguration of which Leibniz speaks, can only affirm itself as distinct from and opposed to its creator; otherwise it dissolves in him. The theory of perpetual creation, by removing from being what the Germans call *Selbständigkeit*, makes it disappear in the divine subjectivity. If being exists as over against God, it is its own support; it does not preserve the least trace of divine creation. In a word, even if it had been created, being-in-itself would be *inexplicable* in terms of creation; for it assumes its being beyond the creation.

This is equivalent to saying that being is uncreated. But we need not conclude that being creates itself, which would suppose that it is prior to itself. Being can not be *causa sui* in the manner of consciousness. Being *is* itself. This means that it is neither passivity nor activity. Both of these notions are *human* and designate human conduct or the instruments of human conduct. There is activity when a conscious being uses means with an end in view. And we call those objects passive on which our activity is exercised, in as much as they do not spontaneously aim at the end which we make them serve. In a word, man is active and the means which he employs are called passive. These concepts, put absolutely, lose all meaning. In particular, being is not active; in order for there to be an end and means, there must be being. For an even stronger reason it can not be passive, for in order to be passive, it must be. The self-consistency of being is beyond the active as it is beyond the passive.

Being is equally beyond negation as beyond affirmation. Affirmation is always affirmation of something; that is, the act of affirming is distinguished from the thing affirmed. But if we suppose an affirmation in which the affirmed comes to fulfill the affirming and is confused with it, this affirmation can not be affirmed—owing to too much of plenitude and the immediate inherence of the noema in the noesis. It is there that we find being—if we are to define it more clearly—in connection with consciousness. It is the noema in the noesis; that is, the inherence in itself without the least distance. From this point of view, we should not call it "immanence," for immanence in spite of all connection with self is still that very slight withdrawal which can be realized—away from the self. But being is not a connection with itself. It is itself. It is an immanence which can not realize itself, an affirmation which can not affirm itself, an activity which can not act, because it is glued to itself. Everything happens as if, in order to free the affirmation of self from the heart of being, there is necessary a decompression of being. Let us not, however, think that being is merely one undifferentiated self-affirmation; the undifferentiation of the in-itself is beyond an infinity of self-affirmations, inasmuch as there is an infinity of modes of self-affirming. We may summarize these first conclusions by saying that being is in itself.

But if being is in itself, this means that it does not refer to itself as self-consciousness does. It is this self. It is itself so completely that the perpetual reflection which constitutes the self is dissolved in an identity. That is why being is at bottom beyond the self, and our first formula can be only an approximation due to the requirements of language. In fact being is opaque to itself precisely because it is filled with itself. This can be better expressed by saying that being is what it is. This statement is in appearance strictly analytical. Actually it is far from being reduced to that principle of identity which is the unconditioned principle of all analytical judgments. First the formula designates a particular region of being, that of being in-itself. We shall see that the being of for-itself is defined, on the contrary, as being what it is not and not being what it is. The question here then is of a regional principle and is as such synthetical. Furthermore it is necessary to oppose this formula—being in-itself is what it is—to that which designates the being of consciousness. The latter in fact, as we shall see, has to be what it is.

This instructs us as to the special meaning which must be given to the "is" in the phrase, being is what it is. From the moment that beings exist who have to be what they are, the fact of being what they are is no longer a purely axiomatic characteristic; it is a contingent principle of being in-itself. In this sense, the principle of identity, the principle of analytical judgments, is also a regional synthetical principle of being. It designates the opacity of being-in-itself. This opacity has nothing to do with our position in relation to the in-itself; it is not that we are obliged to apprehend it and to observe it because we are "without." Being-in-itself has no *within* which is opposed to a *without* and which is analogous to a judgment, a law, a consciousness of itself. The in-itself has nothing secret; it is *solid* (*massif*). In a sense we can designate it as a synthesis. But it is the most indissoluble of all: the synthesis of itself with itself.

The result is evidently that being is isolated in its being and that it does not enter into any connection with what is not itself. Transition, becoming, anything which permits us to say that being is not yet what it will be and that it is already what it is not—all that is forbidden on principle. For being *is* the being of becoming and due to this fact it is beyond becoming. It is what it is. This means that by itself it can not even be what it is not; we have seen indeed that it can encompass no negation. It is full positivity. It knows no otherness; it never posits itself as *other-than-another-being*. It can support no connection with the other. It is itself indefinitely and it exhausts itself in being. From this point of view we shall see later that it is not subject to temporality. It is, and when it gives way, one can not even say that it no longer is. Or, at least, a consciousness can be conscious of it as no longer being, precisely because consciousness is temporal. But being itself does not exist as a lack there where it was; the full positivity of being is re-formed on its giving way. It was and at present other beings are: that is all.

Finally—this will be our third characteristic—being-in-itself *is*. This means that being can neither be derived from the possible nor reduced to the necessary. Necessity concerns the connection between ideal propositions but not that of existents. An existing phenomenon can never be derived from another existent qua existent. This is what we shall call the *contingency* of being-in-itself. But neither can being-in-itself be derived from a *possibility*. The possible is a structure of the *for-itself*; that is, it belongs to the other region of being. Being-in-itself is never either possible or impossible. It *is*. This is what consciousness expresses in anthropomorphic terms by saying that being is superfluous (*de trop*)—that is, that consciousness absolutely can not derive being from anything, either from another being, or from a possibility, or from a necessary law. Uncreated, without reason for being, without any connection with another being, being-in-itself is *de trop* for eternity.

Being is. Being is in-itself. Being is what it is. These are the three characteristics which the preliminary examination of the phenomenon of being allows us to assign to the being of phenomena. For the moment it is impossible to push our investigation further. This is not yet the examination of the in-itself—which is never anything but what it is—which will allow us to establish and to explain its relations with the for-itself. Thus we have left "appearances" and have been led progressively to posit two types of being, the in-itself and the for-itself, concerning which we have as yet only superficial and incomplete information. A multitude of questions remain unanswered: What is the ultimate meaning of these two types of being? For what reasons do they both belong to *being* in general? What is the meaning of that being which includes within itself these two radically separated regions of being? If idealism and realism both fail to explain the relations which *in fact* unite these regions which *in theory* are without communication, what other solution can we find for this problem? And how can the being of the phenomenon be transphenomenal?

I have written the present work in order to try answering these questions.

# Part I

The Problem of Nothingness

# 1

# THE ORIGIN OF NEGATION

## I. THE QUESTION

Our inquiry has led us to the heart of being. But we have been brought to an impasse since we have not been able to establish the connection between the two regions of being which we have discovered. No doubt this is because we have chosen an unfortunate approach. Descartes found himself faced with an analogous problem when he had to deal with the relation between soul and body. He planned then to look for the solution on that level where the union of thinking substance and extended substance was actually effected—that is, in the imagination. His advice is valuable. To be sure, our concern is not that of Descartes and we do not conceive of imagination as he did. But what we can retain is the reminder that it is not profitable first to separate the two terms of a relation in order to try to join them together again later. The relation is a synthesis. Consequently the *results* of analysis can not be covered over again by the *moments* of this synthesis.

M. Laporte says that an abstraction is made when something not capable of existing in isolation is thought of as in an isolated state. The concrete by contrast is a totality which can exist by itself alone. Husserl is of the same opinion; for him *red* is an abstraction because color can not exist without form. On the other hand, a spatial-temporal *thing*, with all its determinations, is an example of the concrete. From this point of view, consciousness is an abstraction since it conceals within itself an ontological source in the region of the in-itself, and conversely the phenomenon is likewise an abstraction since it must "appear" to consciousness. The concrete can be only the synthetic totality of which consciousness, like the phenomenon, constitutes only moments. The concrete is man within the world in that specific union of man with the world which Heidegger, for example, calls "being-in-the-world."

We deliberately begin with the abstract if we question "experience" as Kant does, inquiring into the conditions of its possibility—or if we effect a phenomenological reduction like Husserl, who would reduce the world to the state of the noema-correlate of consciousness. But we will no more succeed in restoring the concrete by the summation or organization of the elements which we have abstracted from it than Spinoza can reach substance by the infinite summation of its modes.

The relation of the regions of being is an original emergence and is a part of the very structure of these beings. But we discovered this in our first observations. It is enough now to open our eyes and question ingenuously this totality which is man-in-the-world. It is by the description of this totality that we shall be able to reply to these two questions: (1) What is the synthetic relation which we call being-in-the-world? (2) What must man and the world be in order for a relation between them to be possible? In truth, the two questions are interdependent, and we can not hope to reply to them separately. But each type of human conduct, being the conduct of man in the world, can release for us simultaneously man, the world, and the relation which unites them, only on condition that we envisage these forms of conduct as realities objectively apprehensible and not as subjective affects which disclose themselves only in the face of reflection.

We shall not limit ourselves to the study of a single pattern of conduct. We shall try on the contrary to describe several and proceeding from one kind of conduct to another, attempt to penetrate into the profound meaning of the relation "man-world." But first of all we should choose a basic pattern which can serve us as a guiding thread in our inquiry.

Now this very inquiry furnishes us with the desired conduct; this man that I *am*—if I apprehend him such as he is at this moment in the world, I establish that he stands before being in an attitude of interrogation. At the very moment when I ask, "Is there any conduct which can reveal to me the relation of man with the world?" I pose a question. This question I can consider objectively, for it matters little whether the questioner is myself or the reader who reads my work and who is questioning along with me. But on the other hand, the question is not simply the objective totality of the words printed on this page; it is indifferent to the symbols which express it. In a word, it is a human attitude filled with meaning. What does this attitude reveal to us?

In every question we stand before a being which we are questioning. Every question presupposes a being who questions and a being which is questioned. This is not the original relation of man to being-in-itself, but rather it stands within the limitations of this relation and takes it for granted. On the other hand, this being which we question, we question *about* something. That *about which* I question the being participates in the transcendence of being. I question being about its ways of being or about its being. From this point of view the question is a kind of expectation; I expect a reply from the being questioned. That is, on the basis of a pre-interrogative familiarity with being, I expect from this being a revelation of its being or of its way of being. The reply will be a "yes" or a "no." It is the existence of these two equally objective and contradictory possibilities which on principle distinguishes the question from affirmation or negation. There are questions which on the surface do not permit a negative reply—like, for example, the one which we put earlier, "What does this attitude reveal to us?" But actually we see that it is always possible with questions of this type to reply, "Nothing" or "Nobody" or "Never." Thus at the moment when I ask, "Is there any conduct which can reveal to me the relation of man with the world?" I admit on principle the possibility of a negative reply such as, "No, such a conduct does not exist." This means that we admit to being faced with the transcendent fact of the non-existence of such conduct.

One will perhaps be tempted not to believe in the objective existence of a non-being; one will say that in this case the fact simply refers me to my subjectivity; I would learn from the transcendent being that the conduct sought is a pure fiction. But in the first place, to call this conduct a pure fiction is to disguise the negation without removing it. "To be pure fiction" is equivalent here to "to be only a fiction." Consequently to destroy the reality of the negation is to cause the reality of the reply to disappear. This reply, in fact, is the very being which gives it to me; that is, reveals the negation to me. There exists then for the questioner the permanent objective possibility of a negative reply. In relation to this possibility the questioner by the very fact that he is questioning, posits himself as in a state of indetermination; he *does not know* whether the reply will be affirmative or negative. Thus the question is a bridge set up between two non-beings: the non-being of knowing in man, the possibility of non-being of being in transcendent being. Finally the question implies the existence of a truth. By the very question the questioner affirms that he expects an objective reply, such that we can say of it, "It is thus and not otherwise." In a word the truth, as differentiated from being, introduces a third non-being as determining the question—the non-being of limitation. This triple non-being conditions every question and in particular the metaphysical question, which is our question.

We set out upon our pursuit of being, and it seemed to us that the series of our questions had led us to the heart of being. But behold, at the moment when we thought we were arriving at the goal, a glance cast on the question itself has revealed to us suddenly that we are encompassed with nothingness. The permanent possibility of non-being, outside us and within, conditions our questions about being. Furthermore it is non-being which is going to limit the reply. What being *will be* must of necessity arise on the basis of what it is not. Whatever being is, it will allow this formulation: "Being is that and outside of that, nothing."

Thus a new component of the real has just appeared to us—non-being. Our problem is thereby complicated, for we may no longer limit our inquiry to the relations of the human being to being in-itself, but must include also the relations of being with non-being and the relations of human non-being with transcendent-non-being. But let us consider further.

## II. NEGATIONS

Someone will object that being-in-itself can not furnish negative replies. Did not we ourselves say that it was beyond affirmation as beyond negation? Furthermore ordinary experience reduced to itself does not seem to disclose any non-being to us. I think that there are fifteen hundred francs in my wallet, and I find only thirteen hundred; that does not mean, someone will tell us, that experience had discovered for me the non-being of fifteen hundred francs but simply that I have counted thirteen hundred-franc notes. Negation proper (we are told) is unthinkable; it could appear only on the level of an act of judgment by which I should establish a comparison between the result anticipated and the result obtained. Thus negation would be simply a quality of judgment and the expectation of the questioner would be an expectation of the judgment-response. As for Nothingness, this would derive its origin from negative judgments; it would be a concept establishing the transcendent unity of all these judgments, a propositional function of the type, "X is not."

We see where this theory is leading; its proponents would make us conclude that being-in-itself is full positivity and does not contain in itself any negation. This negative judgment, on the other hand, by virtue of being a subjective act, is strictly identified with the affirmative judgment. They can not see that Kant, for example, has distinguished in its internal texture the negative act of judgment from the affirmative act. In each case a synthesis of concepts is operative; that synthesis, which is a concrete and full event of psychic life, is operative here merely by means of the copula "is" and there by means of the copula "is not." In the same way the manual operation of sorting out (separation) and the manual operation of assembling (union) are two objective conducts which possess the same reality of fact. Thus negation would be "at the end" of the act of judgment without, however, being "in" being. It is like an unreal encompassed by two full realities neither of which claims it; being-in-itself, if questioned about negation, refers to judgment, since being is only what it is—and judgment, a wholly psychic positivity, refers to being since judgment formulates a negation which concerns being and which consequently is transcendent. Negation, the result of concrete psychic operations, is supported in existence by these very operations and is incapable of existing by itself; it has the existence of a noema-correlate; its *esse* resides exactly in its *percipi*. Nothingness, the conceptual unity of negative judgments, can not have the slightest trace of reality, save that which the Stoics confer on their "lecton."[1] Can we accept this concept?

The question can be put in these terms: Is negation as the structure of the judicative proposition at the origin of nothingness? Or on the contrary is nothingness as the structure of the real, the origin and foundation of negation? Thus the problem of being had referred us first to that of the question as a human attitude, and the problem of the question now refers us to that of the being of negation.

It is evident that non-being always appears within the limits of a human expectation. It is because I expect to find fifteen hundred francs that I find only thirteen hundred. It is because a physicist *expects* a certain verification of his hypothesis that nature can tell him no. It would be in vain to deny that negation appears on the original basis of a relation of man to the world. The world does not disclose its non-beings to one who has not first posited them as possibilities. But is this to say that these non-beings are to be reduced to pure subjectivity? Does this mean to say that we ought to give them the importance and the type of existence of the Stoic "lecton," of Husserl's noema? We think not.

First it is not true that negation is only a quality of judgment. The question is formulated by an interrogative judgment, but it is not itself a judgment; it is a pre-judicative attitude. I can question by a look, by a gesture. In posing a question I stand facing being in a certain way and this relation to being is a relation of being; the judgment is only one optional expression of it. At the same time it is not necessarily a person whom the questioner questions about being; this conception of the question by making of it an intersubjective phenomenon, detaches it from the being to which it adheres and leaves it in the air as pure modality of dialogue. On the contrary, we must consider the question in dialogue to be only a particular species of the genus "question;" the being in question is not necessarily a thinking being. If my car breaks down, it is the *carburetor*, the *spark plugs*, *etc.*, that I question. If my watch stops, I can question the watchmaker about the cause of the stopping, but it is the various mechanisms of the watch that the watchmaker will in turn question. What I expect from the carburetor, what the watchmaker expects from the works of the watch, is not a judgment; it is a disclosure of being on the basis of which we can make a judgment. And if I *expect* a disclosure of being, I am prepared at the same time for the eventuality of a disclosure of a non-being. If I question the carburetor, it is because I consider it possible that "there is

[1] An abstraction or something with purely nominal existence—like space or time. Tr.

nothing there" in the carburetor. Thus my question by its nature envelops a certain pre-judicative comprehension of non-being; it is in itself a relation of being with non-being, on the basis of the original transcendence; that is, in a relation of being with being.

Moreover if the proper nature of the question is obscured by the fact that questions are frequently put by one man to other men, it should be pointed out here that there are numerous non-judicative conducts which present this immediate comprehension of non-being on the basis of being—in its original purity. If, for example, we consider *destruction*, we must recognize that it is an *activity* which doubtless could utilize judgment as an instrument but which can not be defined as uniquely or even primarily judicative. "Destruction" presents the same structure as "the question." In a sense, certainly, man is the only being by whom a destruction can be accomplished. A geological plication, a storm do not destroy—or at least they do not destroy *directly*; they merely modify the distribution of masses of beings. There is no *less* after the storm than before. There is *something else*. Even this expression is improper, for to posit otherness there must be a witness who can retain the past in some manner and compare it to the present in the form of *no longer*. In the absence of this witness, there is being before as after the storm—that is all. If a cyclone can bring about the death of certain living beings, this death will be destruction only if it is experienced as such. In order for destruction to exist, there must be first a relation of man to being—i.e., a transcendence; and within the limits of this relation, it is necessary that man apprehend one being as destructible. This supposes a limiting cutting into being by a being, which, as we saw in connection with truth, is already a process of nihilation. The being under consideration is *that* and outside of that *nothing*. The gunner who has been assigned an objective carefully points his gun in a certain direction *excluding* all others. But even this would still be nothing unless the being of the gunner's objective is revealed as *fragile*. And what is fragility if not a certain probability of non-being for a given being under determined circumstances. A being is fragile if it carries in its being a definite possibilty of non-being. But once again it is through man that fragility comes into being, for the individualizing limitation which we mentioned earlier is the condition of fragility; *one* being is fragile and not *all* being, for the latter is beyond all possible destruction. Thus the relation of individualizing limitation which man enters into with *one* being on the original basis of his relation to being causes fragility to enter into this being as the appearance of a permanent possibility of non-being. But this is not all. In order for destructibility to exist, man must determine himself in the face of this possibility of non-being, either positively or negatively; he must either take the necessary measures to realize it (destruction proper) or, by a negation of non-being, to maintain it always on the level of a simple possibility (by preventive measures). Thus it is man who renders cities destructible, precisely because he posits them as fragile and as precious and because he adopts a system of protective measures with regard to them. It is because of this ensemble of measures that an earthquake or a volcanic eruption can *destroy* these cities or these human constructions. The original meaning and aim of war are contained in the smallest building of man. It is necessary then to recognize that destruction is an essentially human thing and that it is *man* who destroys his cities through the agency of earthquakes or directly, who destroys his ships through the agency of cyclones or directly. But at the same time it is necessary to acknowledge that destruction supposes a pre-judicative comprehension of nothingness as such and a conduct in *the face of nothingness*. In addition destruction although coming into being through man, is an *objective fact* and not a thought. Fragility has been impressed upon the very being of this vase, and its destruction would be an irreversible absolute event which I could only verify. There is a transphenomenality of non-being as of being. The examination of "destruction" leads us then to the same results as the examination of "the question."

But if we wish to decide with certainty, we need only to consider an example of a negative judgment and to ask ourselves whether it causes non-being to appear at the heart of being or merely limits itself to determining a prior revelation. I have an appointment with Pierre at four o'clock. I arrive at the café a quarter of an hour late. Pierre is always punctual. Will he have waited for me? I look at the room, the patrons, and I say, "He is not here." Is there an intuition of Pierre's absence, or does negation indeed enter in only with judgment? At first sight it seems absurd to speak here of intuition since to be exact there could not be an intuition of *nothing* and since the absence of Pierre is this nothing. Popular consciousness, however, bears witness to this intuition. Do we not say, for example, "I suddenly saw that he was not there." Is this just a matter of misplacing the negation? Let us look a little closer.

It is certain that the café by itself with its patrons, its tables, its booths, its mirrors, its light, its smoky atmosphere, and the sounds of voices, rattling saucers, and footsteps which fill it—the café is a fullness of being. And all the intuitions of detail which I can have are filled by these odors, these sounds, these colors, all phenomena which have a transphenomenal being. Similarly Pierre's actual presence in a place which I do not know is also a plenitude of being. We seem to have found fullness everywhere. But we must observe that in perception there is always the construction of a figure on a ground. No one object, no group of objects is especially designed to be organized as specifically either ground or figure; all depends on the direction of my attention. When I enter this café to search for Pierre, there is formed a synthetic organization of all the objects in the café, on the ground of which Pierre is given as about to appear. This organization of the café as the ground is an original nihilation. Each element of the setting, a person, a table, a chair, attempts to isolate itself, to lift itself upon the ground constituted by the totality of the other objects, only to fall back once more into the undifferentiation of this ground; it melts into the ground. For the ground is that which is seen only in addition, that which is the object of a purely marginal attention. Thus the original nihilation of all the figures which appear and are swallowed up in the total neutrality of a ground is the necessary condition for the appearance of the principle figure, which is here the person of Pierre. This nihilation is given to my intuition; I am witness to the successive disappearance of all the objects which I look at—in particular of the faces, which detain me for an instant (Could this be Pierre?) and which as quickly decompose precisely because they "are not" the face of Pierre. Nevertheless if I should finally discover Pierre, my intuition would be filled by a solid element, I should be suddenly arrested by his face and the whole café would organize itself around him as a discrete presence.

But now Pierre is not here. This does not mean that I discover his absence in some precise spot in the establishment. In fact Pierre is absent from the whole café; his absence fixes the café in its evanescence; the café remains ground; it persists in offering itself as an undifferentiated totality to my only marginal attention; it slips into the background; it pursues its nihilation. Only it makes itself ground for a determined figure; it carries the figure everywhere in front of it, presents the figure everywhere to me. This figure which slips constantly between my look and the solid, real objects of the café is precisely a perpetual disappearance; it is Pierre raising himself as nothingness on the ground of the nihilation of the café. So that what is offered to intuition is a flickering of nothingness; it is the nothingness of the ground, the nihilation of which summons and demands the appearance of the figure, and it is the figure-nothingness which slips as a nothing to the surface of the ground. What serves as foundation for the judgment—"Pierre is not here"—is in fact the intuitive apprehension of a double nihilation. To be sure, Pierre's absence supposes an original relation between me and this café; there is an infinity of people who are without any relation with this café for want of a real expectation which establishes their absence. But, to be exact, I myself expected to see Pierre, and my expectation has caused the absence of Pierre to happen as a real event concerning this cafe. It is an objective fact at present that I have discovered this absence, and it presents itself as a synthetic relation between Pierre and the setting in which I am looking for him. Pierre absent haunts this café and is the condition of its self-nihilating organization as ground. By contrast, judg-ments which I can make subsequently to amuse myself, such as, "Wellington is not in this café, Paul Valéry is no longer here, etc."—these have a purely abstract meaning; they are pure applications of the principle of negation without real or efficacious foundation, and they never succeed in establishing a *real* relation between the cafe and Wellington or Valéry. Here the relation "is not" is merely *thought*. This example is sufficient to show that non-being does not come to things by a negative judgment; it is the negative judgment, on the contrary, which is conditioned and supported by non-being.

How could it be otherwise? How could we even conceive of the negative form of judgment if all is plenitude of being and positivity? We believed for a moment that the negation could arise from the comparison instituted between the result anticipated and the result obtained. But let us look at that comparison. Here is an original judgment, a concrete, positive psychic act which establishes a fact: "There are 1300 francs in my wallet." Then there is another which is something else, no longer it but an establishing of fact and an affirmation: "I expected to find 1500 francs." There we have real and objective facts, psychic, and positive events, affirmative judgments. Where are we to place negation? Are we to believe that it is a pure and simple application of a category? And do we wish to hold that the mind in itself possesses the *not* as a form of sorting out and separation? But in this case we remove even the slightest suspicion of negativity from the negation. If we admit that the category of the "not" which exists *in fact* in the mind and is a positive and concrete process to brace and systematize our knowledge, if we admit first that it is suddenly released by the presence in us of certain affirmative judgments and then that it comes suddenly to mark with its seal certain thoughts which result from these judgments—by these considerations we will have carefully stripped negation of all negative function. For negation is a refusal of existence. By means of it a being (or a way of being) is posited, then thrown back to nothingness. If negation is a category, if it is only a sort of stamp set indifferently on certain judgments, then how will we explain the fact that it can nihilate a being, cause it suddenly to arise, and then name it to be thrown back to non-being? If prior judgments establish fact, like those which we have taken for examples, negation must be like a free discovery, it must tear us away from this wall of positivity which encircles us. Negation is an abrupt break in continuity which can not in any case result from prior affirmations; it is an original and irreducible event. Here we are in the realm of consciousness. Consciousness moreover can not produce a negation except in the form of consciousness of negation. No category can "inhabit" consciousness and reside there in the manner of a thing. The *not*, as an abrupt intuitive discovery, appears as consciousness (of being), consciousness of the *not*. In a word, if being is everywhere, it is not only Nothingness which, as Bergson maintains, is inconceivable; for negation will never be derived from being. The necessary condition for our saying *not* is that non-being be a perpetual presence in us and outside of us, that nothingness *haunt* being.

But where does nothingness come from? If it is the original condition of the questioning attitude and more generally of all philosophical or scientific inquiry, what is the original relation of the human being to nothingness? What is the original nihilating conduct?

## III. THE DIALECTICAL CONCEPT OF NOTHINGNESS

It is still too soon for us to hope to disengage the meaning of this nothingness, against which the question has suddenly thrown us. But there are several conclusions which we can formulate even now. In particular it would be worthwhile to determine the relations between being and that non-being which haunts it. We have established a certain parallelism between the types of conduct man adopts in the face of being and those which he maintains in the face of Nothingness, and we are immediately tempted to consider being and non-being as two complementary components of the real—like dark and light. In short we would then be dealing with two strictly contemporary notions which would somehow be united in the production of existents and which it would be useless to consider in isolation. Pure being and pure non-being would be two abstractions which could be reunited only on the basis of concrete realities.

Such is certainly the point of view of Hegel. It is in the *Logic* in fact that he studies the relations of Being and Non-Being, and he calls the *Logic* "The system of the pure determinations of thought." He defines more fully by saying, "Thoughts as they are ordinarily represented, are not pure thoughts, for by a being which is thought, we understand a being of which the content is an empirical content. In logic thoughts are apprehended in such a way that they have no other content than the content of pure thought, which content is engendered by it."[2] To be sure, these determinations are "what is deepest in things" but at the same time when one considers them "in and for themselves," one deduces them from thought itself and discovers in them their truth. However the effort of Hegelian logic is to "make clear the inadequacy of the notions (which it) considers one by one and the necessity, in order to understand them, of raising each to a more complete notion which surpasses them while integrating them."[3]

One can apply to Hegel what Le Senne said of the philosophy of Hamelin: "Each of the lower terms depends on the higher term, as the abstract on the concrete which is necessary for it to realize itself." The true concrete for Hegel is the Existent with its essence; it is the Totality produced by the synthetic integration of all the abstract moments which are surpassed in it by requiring their complement. In this sense Being will be the most abstract of abstractions and the poorest, if we consider it in itself—that is, by separating

---

[2] Introduction, *Petite Logique*, E., § xxiv quoted by Lefebvre: *Morceaux choisis*.
[3] Laporte: *Le Problème de l'Abstraction*, p. 25 (Presses Universitaires, 1940).

it from its surpassing toward Essence. In fact "Being is related to Essence as the immediate to the mediate. Things in general 'are,' but their being consists in manifesting their essence. Being passes into Essence. One can express this by saying, 'Being presupposes Essence.' Although Essence appears in relation to Being as mediated, Essence is nevertheless the true origin. Being returns to its ground; Being is surpassed in Essence."[4]

Thus Being cut from Essence which is its ground becomes "mere empty immediacy." This is how the *Phenomenology of Mind* defines it by presenting pure Being "from the point of view of truth" as the immediate. If the beginning of logic is to be the immediate, we shall then find beginning in *Being*, which is "the indetermination which precedes all determination, the undetermined as the absolute point of departure."

But Being thus undetermined immediately "passes into" its opposite. "This pure Being," writes Hegel in *Logic* (of the *Encyclopaedia*) is "pure abstraction and consequently absolute negation, which taken in its immediate moment is also non-being." Is Nothingness not in fact simple identity with itself, complete emptiness, absence of determinations and of content? Pure being and pure nothingness are then the same thing. Or rather it is true to say that they are different; but "as here the difference is not yet a determined difference—for being and non-being constitute the immediate moment such as it is in them—this difference can not be named; it is only a pure opinion."[5] This means concretely that "there is nothing in heaven or on earth which does not contain in itself being and nothingness."[6]

It is still too soon for us to discuss the Hegelian concept itself; we need all the results of our study in order to take a position regarding this. It is appropriate here to observe only that being is reduced by Hegel to a signification of the existent. Being is enveloped by essence, which is its foundation and origin. Hegel's whole theory is based on the idea that a philosophical procedure is necessary in order at the outset of logic to rediscover the immediate in terms of the mediated, the abstract in terms of the concrete on which it is grounded. But we have already remarked that being does not hold the same relation to the phenomenon as the abstract holds to the concrete. Being is not one "structure among others," one moment of the object; it is the very condition of all structures and of all moments. It is the ground on which the characteristics of the phenomenon will manifest themselves. Similarly it is not admissible that the being of things "consists in manifesting their essence." For then a being of that being would be necessary. Furthermore if the being of things "consisted" in manifesting their essence, it would be hard

---

[4] *Treatise on Logic*, written by Hegel between 1808 and 1811, to serve as the basis for his course at the gymnasium at Nuremberg.
[5] Hegel: P. L., E., § Lxxxviii.          [6] Hegel: *Greater Logic*, chap. 1.

to see how Hegel could determine a pure moment of Being where we could not find at least a trace of that original structure. It is true that the understanding determines pure being, isolates and fixes it in its very determinations. But if surpassing toward essence constitutes the original character of being, and if the understanding is limited to "determining and persevering in the determinations," we can not see precisely how it does not determine being as "consisting in manifesting."

It might be said in defense of Hegel that every determination is negation. But the understanding in this sense is limited to denying that its object is *other* than it is. That is sufficient doubtless to prevent all dialectical process, but not enough to effect its disappearance at the threshold of its surpassing. In so far as being surpasses itself *toward something else*, it is not subject to the determinations of the understanding. But in so far as it surpasses *itself*—that is, in so far as it is in its very depths the origin of its own surpassing—being must on the contrary appear such as it is to the understanding which fixes it in its own determinations. To affirm that being is only what it is would be at least to leave being intact so far as it is its own surpassing. We see here the ambiguity of the Hegelian notion of "surpassing" which sometimes appears to be an upsurge from the inmost depth of the being considered and at other times an external movement by which this being is involved. It is not enough to affirm that the understanding finds in being only what it is; we must also explain how being, which is what it is, can be *only that*. Such an explanation would derive its legitimacy from the consideration of the phenomenon of being as such and not from the negating processes of the understanding.

But what needs examination here is especially Hegel's statement that being and nothingness constitute two opposites, the difference between which on the level of abstraction under consideration is only a simple "opinion."

To oppose being to nothingness as thesis and antithesis, as Hegel does, is to suppose that they are logically contemporary. Thus simultaneously two opposites arise as the two limiting terms of a logical series. Here we must note carefully that opposites alone can enjoy this simultaneity because they are equally positive (or equally negative). But non-being is not the opposite of being; it is its contradiction. This implies that logically nothingness is subsequent to being since it is being, first posited, then denied. It can not be therefore that being and non-being are concepts with the same content since on the contrary non-being supposes a irreducible mental act. Whatever may be the original undifferentiation of being, non-being is that same undifferentiation *denied*. What allows Hegel to make being pass into nothingness is that he has implicitly introduced negation into his very definition of being. This is self evident since any definition is negative, since Hegel has told us, making use of a statement of Spinoza's, that *omnis determinatio est negatio*. And does he not write, "It does not matter what the determination or content is which would distinguish being from something else; whatever would give it a content would prevent it from maintaining itself in its purity. It is pure indetermination and emptiness. Nothing can be apprehended in it."

Thus anyone who introduces negation into being from outside will discover subsequently that he makes it pass into non-being. But here we have a play on words involving the very idea of negation. For if I refuse to allow being any determination or content, I am nevertheless forced to affirm at least that it is. Thus, let anyone deny being whatever he wishes, he can not cause it not to be, thanks to the very fact that he denies that it is this or that. Negation can not touch the nucleus of being of Being, which is absolute plenitude and entire positivity. By contrast Non-being is a negation which aims at this nucleus of absolute density. Non-being is denied at the heart of Being. When Hegel writes, "(Being and nothingness) are empty abstractions, and the one is as empty as the other,"[7] he forgets that emptiness is emptiness of something.[8] Being is empty of all other determination than identity with itself, but non-being is empty of being. In a word, we must recall here against Hegel that being is and that nothingness is not.

Thus even though being can not be the support of any differentiated quality, nothingness is logically subsequent to it since it supposes being in order to deny it, since the irreducible quality of the not comes to add itself to that undifferentiated mass of being in order to release it. That does not mean only that we should refuse to put being and non-being on the same plane, but also that we must be careful never to posit nothingness as an original abyss from which being arose. The use which we make of the notion of nothingness in its familiar form always supposes a preliminary specification of being. It is striking in this connection that language furnishes us with a nothingness of things and a nothingness of human beings.[9] But the specification is still more obvious in the majority of instances. We say, pointing to a particular collection of objects, "Touch nothing," which means, very precisely, nothing of that collection. Similarly, if we question someone on well determined events in his private or public life, he may reply, "I know nothing." And this nothing includes the totality of the facts on which we questioned him. Even Socrates with his famous statement, "I know that I know nothing," designates by this nothing the totality of being considered as Truth.

If adopting for the moment the point of view of naive cosmogonies, we tried to ask ourselves what "was there" before a world existed, and if we

---

[7] P. L., E., § Lxxxvii.

[8] It is so much the more strange in that Hegel is the first to have noted that "every negation is a determined negation"; that is, it depends on a content.

[9] Ne . . . rien = "nothing" as opposed to ne . . . personne = "nobody," which are equally fundamental negative expressions. Sartre here conveniently has based his ontology on the exigencies of a purely French syntax. Tr.

replied "nothing," we would be forced to recognize that this "before" like this "nothing" is in effect retroactive. What we deny today, we who are established in being, is that there was any being before this being. Negation here springs from a consciousness which is turned back toward the beginning. If we remove from this original emptiness its characteristic of being empty of this world and of every whole taking the form of a world, as well as its characteristic of before, which presupposes an after, then the very negation disappears, giving way to a total indetermination which it would be impossible to conceive, even and especially as a nothingness. Thus reversing the statement of Spinoza, we could say that every negation is determination. This means that being is prior to nothingness and establishes the ground for it. By this we must understand not only that being has a logical precedence over nothingness but also that it is from being that nothingness derives concretely its efficacy. This is what we mean when we say that nothingness haunts being. That means that being has no need of nothingness in order to be conceived and that we can examine the idea of it exhaustively without finding there the least trace of nothingness. But on the other hand, nothingness, which is not, can have only a borrowed existence, and it gets its being from being. Its nothingness of being is encountered only within the limits of being, and the total disappearance of being would not be the advent of the reign of non-being, but on the contrary the concomitant disappearance of nothingness. Non-being exists only on the surface of being.

## IV. THE PHENOMENOLOGICAL CONCEPT OF NOTHINGNESS

There is another possible way of conceiving being and nothingness as complements. One could view them as two equally necessary components of the real without making being "pass into" nothingness—as Hegel does—and without insisting on the posteriority of nothingness as we attempted to do. We might on the contrary emphasize the reciprocal forces of repulsion which being and non-being exercise on each other, the real in some way being the tension resulting from these antagonistic forces. It is toward this new conception that Heidegger is oriented.[10]

We need not look far to see the progress which Heidegger's theory of nothingness has made over that of Hegel. First, being and non-being are no longer empty abstractions. Heidegger in his most important work has shown the legitimacy of raising the question concerning being; the latter has no longer the character of a Scholastic universal, which it still retained with

---

[10] Heidegger: Qu'est-ce que la métaphysique? (Tr. by Corbin, N.R.F. 1938). In English "What is Metaphysics?" Tr. by R.F.C. Hull and Alan Crick. From Existence and Being, ed. by Werner Brock, Henry Regnery. 1949.

Hegel. There is a meaning of being which must be clarified; there is a "pre-ontological comprehension" of being which is involved in every kind of conduct belonging to "human reality"—i.e., in each of its projects. Similarly difficulties which customarily arise as soon as a philosopher touches on the problem of Nothingness are shown to be without foundation; they are important in so far as they limit the function of the understanding, and they show simply that this problem is not within the province of the understanding. There exist on the other hand numerous attitudes of "human reality" which imply a "comprehension" of nothingness: hate, prohibitions, regret, etc. For "Dasein" there is even a permanent possibility of finding oneself "face to face" with nothingness and discovering it as a phenomenon: this possibility is anguish.

Heidegger, while establishing the possibilities of a concrete apprehension of Nothingness, never falls into the error which Hegel made; he does not preserve a being for Non-Being, not even an abstract being. Nothing is not; it nihilates itself.[11] It is supported and conditioned by transcendence. We know that for Heidegger the being of human reality is defined as "being-in-the-world." The world is a synthetic complex of instrumental realities inasmuch as they point one to another in ever widening circles, and inasmuch as man makes himself known in terms of this complex which he is. This means both that "human reality" springs forth invested with being and "finds itself" (sich befinden) in being—and also that human reality causes being, which surrounds it, to be disposed around human reality in the form of the world.

But human reality can make being appear as organized totality in the world only by surpassing being. All determination for Heidegger is surpassing since it supposes a withdrawal, a particular point of view. This passing beyond the world, which is a condition of the very rising up of the world as such, is effected by the Dasein which directs the surpassing toward itself. The characteristic of selfness (Selbstheit), in fact, is that man is always separated from what he is by all the breadth of the being which he is not. He makes himself known to himself from the other side of the world and he looks from the horizon toward himself to recover his inner being. Man is "a being of distances." In the movement of turning inward which traverses all of being, being arises and organizes itself as the world without there being either priority of the movement over the world, or the world over the movement. But this appearance of the self beyond the world—that is, beyond the totality of the real—is an emergence of "human reality" in nothingness. It is in nothingness

---

[11] Heidegger uses the by now famous expression "Das Nichts nichtet" or "Nothing nothings." I think "nihilate" is a closer equivalent to Sartre's néantise than "annihilate" because the fundamental meaning of the term is "to make nothing" rather than "to destroy or do away with." Nichtet, néantise, and nihilate are all, of course, equally without foundation in the dictionaries of the respective languages. Tr.

alone that being can be surpassed. At the same time it is from the point of view of beyond the world that being is organized into the world, which means on the one hand that human reality rises up as an emergence of being in non-being and on the other hand that the world is "suspended" in nothingness. Anguish is the discovery of this double, perpetual nihilation. It is in terms of this surpassing of the world that *Dasein* manages to realize the contingency of the world; that is, to raise the question, "How does it happen that there is something rather than nothing?" Thus the contingency of the world appears to human reality in so far as human reality has established itself in nothingness in order to apprehend the contingency.

Here then is nothingness surrounding being on every side and at the same time expelled from being. Here nothingness is given as that by which the world receives its outlines as the world. Can this solution satisfy us?

Certainly it can not be denied that the apprehension of the world qua world, is a nihilation. From the moment the world appears qua world it gives itself as *being only that*. The necessary counterpart of this apprehension then is indeed the emergence of "human reality" in nothingness. But where does "human reality" get its power of emerging thus in non-being? Without a doubt Heidegger is right in insisting on the fact that negation derives its foundation from nothingness. But if nothingness provides a ground for negation, it is because nothingness envelops the *not* within itself as its essential structure. In other words, it is not as undifferentiated emptiness or as a disguised otherness[12] that nothingness provides the ground for negation. Nothingness stands at the origin of the negative judgment because it is itself negation. It founds the negation as *an act* because it is the negation as *being*. Nothingness can be nothingness only by nihilating itself expressly as nothingness of the world; that is, in its nihilation it must direct itself expressly toward this world in order to constitute itself as refusal of the world. Nothingness carries being in its heart. But how does the emergence account for this nihilating refusal? Transcendence, which is "the project of self beyond," is far from being able to establish nothingness; on the contrary, it is nothingness which is at the very heart of transcendence and which conditions it.

Now the characteristic of Heidegger's philosophy is to describe *Dasein* by using positive terms which hide the implicit negations. *Dasein* is "outside of itself, in the world"; it is "a being of distances"; it is care; it is "its own possibilities," *etc.* All this amounts to saying that *Dasein* "is not" in itself, that it "is not" in immediate proximity to itself, and that it "surpasses" the world inasmuch as it posits itself as *not being in itself* and as *not being the world.* In this sense Hegel is right rather than Heidegger when he states that Mind is the negative. Actually we can put to each of them the same question, phrased

---

[12] What Hegel would call "immediate otherness."

slightly differently. We should say to Hegel: "It is not sufficient to posit mind as mediation and the negative; it is necessary to demonstrate negativity as the structure of being of mind. What must mind be in order to be able to constitute itself as negative?" And we can ask the same question of Heidegger in these words: "If negation is the original structure of transcendence, what must be the original structure of 'human reality' in order for it to be able to transcend the world?" In both cases we are shown a negating activity and there is no concern to ground this activity upon a negative being. Heidegger in addition makes of Nothingness a sort of intentional correlate of transcendence, without seeing that he has already inserted it into transcendence itself as its original structure.

Furthermore what is the use of affirming that Nothingness provides the ground for negation, if it is merely to enable us to form subsequently a theory of non-being which by definition separates Nothingness from all concrete negation? If I emerge in nothingness beyond the world, how can this extra-mundane nothingness furnish a foundation for those little pools of non-being which we encounter each instant in the depth of being. I say, "Pierre is not there," "I have no more money," etc. Is it really necessary to surpass the world toward nothingness and to return subsequently to being in order to provide a ground for these everyday judgments? And how can the operation be effected? To accomplish it we are not required to make the world slip into nothingness; standing within the limits of being, we simply deny an attribute to a subject. Will someone say that each attribute refused, each being denied is taken up by one and the same extra-mundane nothingness, that non-being is like the fullness of what is not, that the world is suspended in non-being as the real is suspended in the heart of possibilities? In this case each negation would necessarily have for origin a particular surpassing: the surpassing of one being toward another. But what is this surpassing, if not simply the Hegelian mediation—and have we not already and in vain sought in Hegel the nihilating ground of the mediation? Furthermore even if the explanation is valid for the simple, radical negations which deny to a determined object any kind of presence in the depth of being (e.g. Centaurs do not exist"—"There is no reason for him to be late"—"The ancient Greeks did not practice polygamy"), negations which, if need be, can contribute to constituting Nothingness as a sort of geometrical place for unfulfilled projects, all inexact representations, all vanished beings or those of which the idea is only a fiction—even so this interpretation of non-being would no longer be valid for a certain kind of reality which is in truth the most frequent: namely, those negations which include non-being in their being. How can we hold that these are at once partly within the universe and partly outside in extra-mundane nothingness?

Take for example the notion of distance, which conditions the determination of a location, the localization of a point. It is easy to see that it possesses a negative moment. Two points are distant when they are *separated* by a certain length. The length, a positive attribute of a segment of a straight line, intervenes here by virtue of the negation of an absolute, undifferentiated proximity. Someone might perhaps seek to reduce distance to *being only* the length of the segment of which the two points considered, A and B, would be the limits. But does he not see that he has changed the direction of attention in this case and that he has, under cover of the same word, given another object to intuition? The organized complex which is constituted by the segment *with* its two limiting terms can furnish actually two different objects to knowledge. We can in fact give the *segment* as immediate object of intuition, in which case this segment represents a full, concrete tension, of which the length is a positive attribute and the two points A and B appear only as a moment of the whole; that is, as they are implicated by the segment itself as its limits. Then the negation, expelled from the segment and its length, takes refuge in the two *limits*: to say that point B is a limit of the segment is to say that the segment *does not* extend beyond this point. Negation is here a secondary structure of the object. If, on the other hand, we direct our attention to the two points A and B, they arise as immediate objects of intuition on the ground of space. The segment disappears as a full, concrete object; it is apprehended in terms of two points as the emptiness, the negativity which separates them. Negation is not subject to the points, which cease to be *limits* in order to impregnate the very length of the segment with distance. Thus the total form consituted by the segment and its two limits with its inner structure of negation is capable of letting itself be apprehended in two ways. Rather there are two forms, and the condition of the appearance of the one is the disintegration of the other, exactly as in perception we constitute a particular object as a *figure* by rejecting another so as to make of it a *ground*, and conversely. In both instances we find the same quantity of negation which at one time passes into the notion of limits and at another into the notion of distance, but which in each case can not be suppressed. Will someone object that the idea of distance is psychological and that it designates only the extension which must be *cleared* in order to go from point A to point B? We shall reply that the same negation is included in this "*to clear*" since this notion expresses precisely the passive resistance of the remoteness. We will willingly admit with Heidegger that "human reality" is "remoteness-cancelling;" that is, that it rises in the world as that which creates distances and at the same time causes them to be removed (*entfernend*). But this cancelling of distances, even if it is the necessary condition in order that *there may be* remoteness in general, envelops remoteness in itself as the negative structure which must be surmounted. It will be useless to attempt to reduce distance to the simple result of a *measurement*. What has become evident in the course of the preceding discussion is that the two points and the segment which is inclosed between them have the indissoluble unity of what the Germans call a *Gestalt*. Negation is the cement which realizes this unity. It defines precisely the immediate relation which connects these two points and which presents them to intuition as the indissoluble unity of the distance. This negation can be covered over only by claiming to reduce distance to the measurement of a length, for negation is the *raison d'être* of that measurement.

What we have just shown by the examination of *distance*, we could just as well have brought out by describing realities like absence, change, otherness, repulsion, regret, distraction, *etc.* There is an infinite number of realities which are not only objects of judgment, but which are experienced, opposed, feared, etc., by the human being and which in their inner structure are inhabited by negation, as by a necessary condition of their existence. We shall call them *négatités*.[13] Kant caught a glimpse of their significance when he spoke of regulative concepts (*e.g.* the immortality of the soul), types of syntheses of negative and positive in which negation is the condition of positivity. The function of negation varies according to the nature of the object considered. Between wholly positive realities (which however retain negation as the condition of the sharpness of their outlines, as that which fixes them as what they are) and those in which the positivity is only an appearance concealing a hole of nothingness, all gradations are possible. In any case it is impossible to throw these negations back into an extra-mundane nothingness since they are dispersed in being, are supported by being, and are conditions of reality. Nothingness beyond the world accounts for absolute negation; but we have just discovered a swarm of intra-mundane beings which possess as much reality and efficacy as other beings, but which inclose within themselves non-being. They require an explanation which remains within the limits of the real. Nothingness if it is supported by being, vanishes *qua nothingness*, and we fall back upon being. Nothingness can be nihilated only on the foundation of being; if nothingness can be given, it is neither before nor after being, nor in a general way outside of being. Nothingness lies coiled in the heart of being—like a worm.

## V.  THE ORIGIN OF NOTHINGNESS

It would be well at this point to cast a glance backward and to measure the road already covered. We raised first the question of being. Then examining this very question conceived as a type of human conduct, we questioned this in turn. We next had to recognize that no question could be asked, in particular not that of being, if negation did not exist. But this negation itself when

---

[13] A word coined by Sartre with no equivalent term in English. Tr.

inspected more closely referred us back to Nothingness as its origin and foundation. In order for negation to exist in the world and in order that we may consequently raise questions concerning Being, it is necessary that in some way Nothingness be given. We perceived then that Nothingness can be conceived neither *outside* of being, nor as a complementary, abstract notion, nor as an infinite milieu where being is suspended. Nothingness must be given at the heart of Being, in order for us to be able to apprehend that particular type of realities which we have called *négatités*. But this intra-mundane Nothingness cannot be produced by Being-in-itself; the notion of Being as full positivity does not contain Nothingness as one of its structures. We can not even say that Being excludes it. Being lacks all relation with it. Hence the question which is put to us now with a particular urgency: if Nothingness can be conceived neither outside of Being, nor in terms of Being, and if on the other hand, since it is non-being, it can not derive from itself the necessary force to "nihilate itself," *where does Nothingness come from?*

If we wish to pursue the problem further, we must first recognize that we can not grant to nothingness the property of "nihilating itself." For although the expression "to nihilate itself" is thought of as removing from nothing-ness the last semblance of being, we must recognize that only *Being* can nihilate itself; however it comes about, in order to nihilate itself, it must *be*. But Nothingness *is not*. If we can speak of it, it is only because it possesses an appearance of being, a borrowed being, as we have noted above. Nothingness is not, Nothingness "is made-to-be,"[14] Nothingness does not nihilate itself; Nothingness "is nihilated." It follows therefore that there must exist a Being (this can not be the In-itself) of which the property is to nihilate Nothing-ness, to support it in its being, to sustain it perpetually in its very existence, a *being by which nothingness comes to things*. But how can this Being be related to Nothingness so that through it Nothingness comes to things? We must observe first that the being postulated can not be passive in relation to Nothing-ness, can not receive it; Nothingness could not *come* to this being except through another Being—which would be an infinite regress. But on the other hand, the Being by which Nothingness comes to the world can not *produce* Nothingness while remaining indifferent to that production—like the Stoic cause which produces its effect without being itself changed. It would be inconceivable that a Being which is full positivity should maintain and create outside itself a Nothingness or transcendent being, for there would be

---

[14] The French is *est été*, which literally means "is been," an expression as meaningless in ordinary French as in English. Maurice Natanson suggests "is-was." (*A Critique of Jean-Paul Sartre's Ontology*. University of Nebraska Studies. March 1951. p. 59.) I prefer "is made-to-be" because Sartre seems to be using *être* as a transitive verb, here in the passive voice, thus suggesting that nothingness has been subjected to an act involving being. Other passages containing this expres-sion will, I believe, bear out this interpretation. Tr.

nothing in Being by which Being could surpass itself toward Non-Being. The Being by which Nothingness arrives in the world must nihilate Nothingness in its Being, and even so it still runs the risk of establishing Nothingness as a transcendent in the very heart of immanence unless it nihilates Nothingness in its being in *connection with its own being*. The Being by which Nothingness arrives in the world is a being such that in its Being, the Nothingness of its Being is in question. *The being by which Nothingness comes to the world must be its own Nothingness*. By this we must understand not a nihilating act, which would require in turn a foundation in Being, but an ontological characteristic of the Being required. It remains to learn in what delicate, exquisite region of Being we shall encounter that Being which is its own Nothingness.

We shall be helped in our inquiry by a more complete examination of the conduct which served us as a point of departure. We must return to the question. We have seen, it may be recalled, that every question in essence posits the possibility of a negative reply. In a question we question a being about its being or its way of being. This way of being or this being is veiled; there always remains the possibility that it may unveil itself as a Nothingness. But from the very fact that we presume that an Existent can always be revealed as *nothing*, every question supposes that we realize a nihilating withdrawal in relation to the given, which becomes a simple *presentation*, fluctuating between being and Nothingness.

It is essential therefore that the questioner have the permanent possibility of dissociating himself from the causal series which constitutes being and which can produce only being. If we admitted that the question is determined in the questioner by universal determinism, the question would thereby become unintelligible and even inconceivable. A real cause, in fact, produces a real effect and the caused being is wholly engaged by the cause in positivity; to the extent that its being depends on the cause, it can not have within itself the tiniest germ of nothingness. Thus in so far as the questioner must be able to effect in relation to the questioned a kind of nihilating withdrawal, he is not subject to the causal order of the world; he detaches himself from Being. This means that by a double movement of nihilation, he nihilates the thing questioned in relation to himself by placing it in a *neutral* state, between being and non-being—and that he nihilates himself in relation to the thing questioned by wrenching himself from being in order to be able to bring out of himself the possibility of a non-being. Thus in posing a question, a certain negative element is introduced into the world. We see nothingness making the world irridescent, casting a shimmer over things. But at the same time the question emanates from a questioner who in order to motivate himself in his being as one who questions, disengages himself from being. This disengagement is then by definition a human process. Man presents himself at least in this instance as a being who causes Nothingness to arise in the world, inasmuch as he himself is affected with non-being to this end.

These remarks may serve as guiding thread as we examine the *négatités* of which we spoke earlier. There is no doubt at all that these are transcendent realities; distance, for example, is imposed on us as something which we have to take into account, which must be cleared with effort. However these realities are of a very peculiar nature; they all indicate immediately an essential relation of human reality to the world. They derive their origin from an act, an expectation, or a project of the human being; they all indicate an aspect of being as it appears to the human being who is engaged in the world. The relations of man in the world, which the *négatités* indicate, have nothing in common with the relations *à posteriori* which are brought out by empirical activity. We are no longer dealing with those relations of *instrumentality* by which, according to Heidegger, objects in the world disclose themselves to "human reality." Every *négatité* appears rather as one of the essential conditions of this relation of instrumentality. In order for the totality of being to order itself around us as instruments, in order for it to parcel itself into differentiated complexes which refer one to another and which can be *used*, it is necessary that negation rise up not as a thing among other things but as the rubric of a category which presides over the arrangement and the redistribution of great masses of being in things. Thus the rise of man in the midst of the being which "invests" him causes a world to be discovered. But the essential and primordial moment of this rise is the negation. Thus we have reached the first goal of this study. Man is the being through whom nothingness comes to the world. But this question immediately provokes another: What must man be in his being in order that through him nothingness may come to being?

Being can generate only being and if man is inclosed in this process of generation, only being will come out of him. If we are to assume that man is able to question this process—i.e., to make it the object of interrogation—he must be able to hold it up to view as a totality. He must be able to put himself *outside* of being and by the same stroke weaken the structure of the being of being. Yet it is not given to "human reality" to annihilate even provisionally the mass of being which is standing before itself. "Human reality" can only modify its *relation* with being. For man to put a particular existent out of circuit is to put himself out of circuit in relation to that existent. In this case he is not subject to it; he is out of reach; it can not act on him, for he has retired *beyond a nothingness*. Descartes following the Stoics has given a name to this possibility which human reality has to secrete a nothingness which isolates it—it is *freedom*. But freedom here is only a name. If we wish to penetrate further into the question, we must not be content with this reply and we ought to ask now, What is human freedom if through it nothingness comes into the world?

It is not yet possible to deal with the problem of freedom in all its fullness.[15] In fact the steps which we have completed up to now show clearly that freedom is not a faculty of the human soul to be envisaged and described in isolation. What we have been trying to define is the being of man in so far as he conditions the appearance of nothingness, and this being has appeared to us as freedom. Thus freedom as the requisite condition for the nihilation of nothingness is not a *property* which belongs among others to the essence of the human being. We have already noticed furthermore that with man the relation of existence to essence is not comparable to what it is for the things of the world. Human freedom precedes essence in man and makes it possible; the essence of the human being is suspended in his freedom. What we call freedom is impossible to distinguish from the *being* of "human reality." Man does not exist *first* in order to be free *subsequently*; there is no difference between the being of man and his *being-free*. This is not the time to make a frontal attack on a question which can be treated exhaustively only in the light of a rigorous elucidation of the human being. Here we are dealing with freedom in connection with the problem of nothingness and only to the extent that it conditions the appearance of nothingness.

What first appears evident is that human reality can detach itself from the world—in questioning, in systematic doubt, in sceptical doubt, in the ἐποχή, *etc.*—only if by nature it has the possibility of self-detachment. This was seen by Descartes, who is establishing doubt on freedom when he claims for us the possibility of suspending our judgments. Alain's position is similar. It is also in this sense that Hegel asserts the freedom of the mind to the degree that mind is mediation—i.e., the Negative. Furthermore it is one of the trends of contemporary philosophy to see in human consciousness a sort of escape from the self; such is the meaning of the transcendence of Heidegger. The intentionality of Husserl and of Brentano has also to a large extent the characteristic of a detachment from self. But we are not yet in a position to consider freedom as an inner structure of consciousness. We lack for the moment both instruments and technique to permit us to succeed in that enterprise. What interests us at present is a temporal operation since questioning is, like doubt, a kind of behavior; it assumes that the human being reposes first in the depths of being and then detaches himself from it by a nihilating withdrawal. Thus we are envisaging the condition of the nihilation as a relation to the self in the heart of a temporal process. We wish simply to show that by identifying consciousness with a causal sequence indefinitely continued, one transmutes it into a plenitude of being and thereby causes it to return into the unlimited totality of being—as is well illustrated by the futility of the efforts to

[15] Cf. Part IV, chap. I.

dissociate psychological determinism from universal determinism and to constitute it as a separate series.

The room of someone absent, the books of which he turned the pages, the objects which he touched are in themselves only *books, objects*; i.e., full actualities. The very traces which he has left can be deciphered as traces of him only within a situation where he has been already posited as absent. The dog-eared book with the well-read pages is not by itself a book of which Pierre has turned the pages, of which he no longer turns the pages. If we consider it as the present, transcendent motivation of my perception or even as the synthetic flux, regulated by my sensible impressions, then it is merely a volume with turned down, worn pages; it can refer only to itself or to present objects, to the lamp which illuminates it, to the table which holds it. It would be useless to invoke an association by contiguity as Plato does in the *Phaedo*, where he makes the image of the absent one appear on the margin of the perception of the lyre or of the cithara which he has touched. This image, if we consider it in itself and in the spirit of classical theories, is a definite plenitude; it is a concrete and positive psychic fact. Consequently we must of necessity pass on it a doubly negative judgment: subjectively, to signify that the image *is not* a perception; objectively, to deny that the Pierre of whom I form the image *is here* at this moment.

This is the famous problem of the characteristics of the true image, which has concerned so many psychologists from Taine to Spaier. Association, we see, does not solve the problem; it pushes it back to the level of reflection. But in every way it demands a negation; that is, at the very least, a nihilating withdrawal of consciousness in relation to the image apprehended as subjective phenomenon, in order to posit it precisely as being only a subjective phenomenon.

Now I have attempted to show elsewhere[16] that if we posit the image first *as* a renascent perception, it is radically impossible to distinguish it *subsequently* from actual perceptions. The image must enclose in its very structure a nihilating thesis. It constitutes itself qua image while positing its object as existing *elsewhere* or *not existing*. It carries within it a double negation; first it is the nihilation of the world (since the world is not offering the imagined object as an actual object of perception), secondly the nihilation of the object of the image (it is posited as not actual), and finally by the same stroke it is the nihilation of itself (since it is not a concrete, full psychic process.) In explaining how I apprehend the absence of Pierre in the room, it would be useless to invoke those famous "empty intentions" of Husserl, which are in great part constitutive of perception. Among the various perceptive intentions, indeed, there are relations of *motivation* (but motivation is not causation), and among

---

[16] *L'imagination*. Alcan, 1936.

these intentions, some are full (i.e., filled with what they aim at) and others empty. But precisely because the matter which should fill the empty intentions *does not exist*, it can not be this which motivates them in their structure. And since the other intentions are full, neither can they motivate the empty intentions inasmuch as the latter are empty. Moreover these intentions are of psychic nature and it would be an error to envisage them in the mode of things; that is, as recipients which would first be given, which according to circumstances could be emptied or filled, and which would be by nature indifferent to their state of being empty or filled. It seems that Husserl has not always escaped the materialist illusion. To be empty an intention must be conscious of itself as empty and precisely as empty of the exact matter at which it aims. An empty intention constitutes itself as empty to the exact extent that it posits its matter as non-existing or absent. In short an empty intention is a consciousness of negation which transcends itself toward an object which it posits as absent or non-existent.

Thus whatever may be the explanation which we give of it, Pierre's absence, in order to be established or realized, requires a negative moment by which consciousness in the absence of all prior determination, constitutes itself as negation. If in terms of my perceptions of the room, I conceive of the former inhabitant who is no longer in the room, I am of necessity forced to produce an act of thought which no prior state can determine nor motivate, in short to effect in myself a break with being. And in so far as I continually use *négatités* to isolate and determine existents—i.e., to think them—the succession of my "states of consciousness" is a perpetual separation of effect from cause, since every nihilating process must derive its source only from itself. Inasmuch as my present state would be a prolongation of my prior state, every opening by which negation could slip through would be completely blocked. Every psychic process of nihilation implies then a cleavage between the immediate psychic past and the present. This cleavage is precisely nothingness. At least, someone will say, there remains the possibility of successive implication between the nihilating processes. My establishment of Pierre's absence could still be determinant for my regret at not seeing him; you have not excluded the possibility of a determinism of nihilations. But aside from the fact that the original nihilation of the series must necessarily be disconnected from the prior positive processes, what can be the meaning of a motivation of nothingness by nothingness? A being indeed can *nihilate itself* perpetually, but to the extent that it nihilates itself, it foregoes being the origin of another phenomenon, even of a second nihilation.

It remains to explain what this separation is, this disengaging of consciousness which conditions every negation. If we consider the prior consciousness envisaged as motivation, we see suddenly and evidently that nothing has just slipped in between that state and the present state. There has been no break in continuity within the flux of the temporal development, for that would force us to return to the inadmissible concept of the infinite divisibility of time and of the temporal point or instant as the limit of the division. Neither has there been an abrupt interpolation of an opaque element to separate prior from subsequent in the way that a knife blade cuts a piece of fruit in two. Nor is there a *weakening* of the motivating force of the prior consciousness; it remains what it is, it does not lose anything of its urgency. What separates prior from subsequent is exactly *nothing*. This nothing is absolutely impassable, precisely because it is nothing; for in every obstacle to be cleared there is something positive which gives itself as about to be cleared. But in the case we are dealing with, it would be useless to look for a resistance to break, for an obstacle to clear. The prior consciousness is always *there* (though with the modification of "pastness"). It constantly maintains a relation of interpenetration with the present consciousness, but on the basis of this existential relation it is put out of the game, out of the circuit, between parentheses—exactly as in the eyes of one practicing the phenomenological ἐποχή, the world both is within him and outside of him.

Thus the condition on which human reality can deny all or part of the world is that human reality carry nothingness within itself as the *nothing* which separates its present from all its past. But this is still not all, for the *nothing* envisaged would not yet have the sense of nothingness; a suspension of being which would remain unnamed, which would not be consciousness of suspending being would come from outside consciousness and by reintroducing opacity into the heart of this absolute lucidity, would have the effect of cutting it in two.[17] Furthermore this nothing would by no means be negative. Nothingness, as we have seen above, is the ground of the negation because it conceals the negation within itself, because it is the negation as being. It is necessary then that conscious being constitute itself in relation to its past as separated from this past by a nothingness. It must necessarily be conscious of this cleavage in being, but not as a phenomenon which it experiences, rather as a structure of consciousness which it is. Freedom is the human being putting his past out of play by secreting his own nothingness. Let us understand indeed that this original necessity of being its own nothingness does not belong to consciousness intermittently and on the occasion of particular negations. This does not happen just at a particular moment in psychic life when negative or interrogative attitudes appear; consciousness continually experiences itself as the nihilation of its past being.

But someone doubtless will believe that he can use against us here an objection which we have frequently raised ourselves: if the nihilating consciousness exists only as consciousness of nihilation, we ought to be able

---

[17] See Introduction: III.

to define and describe a constant mode of consciousness, present *qua* consciousness, which would be consciousness of nihilation. Does this consciousness exist? Behold a new question has been raised here: if freedom is the being of consciousness, consciousness ought to exist as consciousness of freedom. What form does this consciousness of freedom assume? In freedom the human being is his own past (as also his own future) in the form of nihilation. If our analysis has not led us astray, there ought to exist for the human being, in so far as he is conscious of being, a certain mode of standing opposite his past and his future, as being both this past and this future and as not being them. We shall be able to furnish an immediate reply to this question; it is in anguish that man gets the consciousness of his freedom, or if you prefer, anguish is the mode of being of freedom as consciousness of being; it is in anguish that freedom is, in its being, in question for itself.

Kierkegaard describing anguish before the sin characterizes it as anguish in the face of freedom. But Heidegger, whom we know to have been greatly influenced by Kierkegaard,[18] considers anguish instead as the apprehension of nothingness. These two descriptions of anguish do not appear to us contradictory; on the contrary the one implies the other.

First we must acknowledge that Kierkegaard is right; anguish is distinguished from fear in that fear is fear of beings in the world whereas anguish is anguish before myself. Vertigo is anguish to the extent that I am afraid not of falling over the precipice, but of throwing myself over. A situation provokes fear if there is a possibility of my life being changed from without; my being provokes anguish to the extent that I distrust myself and my own reactions in that situation. The artillery preparation which precedes the attack can provoke fear in the soldier who undergoes the bombardment, but anguish is born in him when he tries to foresee the conduct with which he will face the bombardment, when he asks himself if he is going to be able to "hold up." Similarly the recruit who reports for active duty at the beginning of the war can in some instances be afraid of death, but more often he is "afraid of being afraid;" that is, he is filled with anguish before himself. Most of the time dangerous or threatening situations present themselves in facets; they will be apprehended through a feeling of fear or of anguish according to whether we envisage the situation as acting on the man or the man as acting on the situation. The man who has just received a hard blow—for example, losing a great part of his wealth in a crash—can have the fear of threatening poverty. He will experience anguish a moment later when nervously wringing his hands (a symbolic reaction to the action which is imposed but which remains still wholly undetermined), he exclaims to himself: "What am I going to do? But what am I going to do?" In this sense fear and anguish are

---

[18] J. Wahl: *Etudes Kierkegaardiennes*, Kierkegaard et Heidegger.

exclusive of one another since fear is unreflective apprehension of the transcendent and anguish is reflective apprehension of the self; the one is born in the destruction of the other. The normal process in the case which I have just cited is a constant transition from the one to the other. But there exist also situations where anguish appears pure; that is, without ever being preceded or followed by fear. If, for example, I have been raised to a new dignity and charged with a delicate and flattering mission, I can feel anguish at the thought that I will not be capable perhaps of fulfilling it, and yet I will not have the least fear in the world of the consequences of my possible failure.

What is the meaning of anguish in the various examples which I have just given? Let us take up again the example of vertigo. Vertigo announces itself through fear; I am on a narrow path—without a guard-rail—which goes along a precipice. The precipice presents itself to me as to be avoided; it represents a danger of death. At the same time I conceive of a certain number of causes, originating in universal determinism, which can transform that threat of death into reality; I can slip on a stone and fall into the abyss; the crumbling earth of the path can give way under my steps. Through these various anticipations, I am given to myself as a thing; I am passive in relation to these possibilities; they come to me from without; in so far as I am also an object in the world, subject to gravitation, they are not my possibilities. At this moment fear appears, which in terms of the situation is the apprehension of myself as a destructible transcendent in the midst of transcendents, as an object which does not contain in itself the origin of its future disappearance. My reaction will be of the reflective order; I will pay attention to the stones in the road; I will keep myself as far as possible from the edge of the path. I realize myself as pushing away the threatening situation with all my strength, and I project before myself a certain number of future conducts destined to keep the threats of the world at a distance from me. These conducts are my possibilities. I escape fear by the very fact that I am placing myself on a plane where my own possibilities are substituted for the transcendent probabilities where human action had no place.

But these conducts, precisely because they are my possibilities, do not appear to me as determined by foreign causes. Not only is it not strictly certain that they will be effective; in particular it is not strictly certain that they will be adopted, for they do not have existence sufficient in itself. We could say, varying the expression of Berkeley, that their "being is a sustained-being" and that their "possibility of being is only an ought-to-be-sustained."[19] Due to this fact their possibility has as a necessary condition the possibility of inconsistent conducts (not to pay attention to the stones in the road, to run, to think of something else) and the possibility of the opposite

---

[19] We shall return to possibilities in the second part of this work.

conduct (to throw myself over the precipice). The possibility which I make my concrete possibility can appear as my possibility only by raising itself on the basis of the totality of the logical possibilities which the situation allows. But these rejected possibles in turn have no other being than their "sustained-being;" it is I who sustain them in being, and inversely, their present non-being is an "ought-not-to-be-sustained." No external cause will remove them. I alone am the permanent source of their non-being, I engage myself in them; in order to cause my possibility to appear, I posit the other possibilities so as to nihilate them. This would not produce anguish if I could apprehend myself in my relations with these possibles as a cause producing its effects. In this case the effect defined as my possibility *would be strictly* determined. But then it would cease to be *possible*; it would become simply "about-to-happen." If then I wished to avoid anguish and vertigo, it would be enough if I were to consider the motives (instinct of self-preservation, prior fear, etc.), which make me reject the situation envisaged, as *determining* my prior activity in the same way that the presence at a determined point of one given mass determines the courses followed by other masses; it would be necessary, in other words, that I apprehend in myself a strict psychological determinism. But I am in anguish precisely because any conduct on my part is only *possible*, and this means that while constituting a totality of motives for pushing away that situation, I at the same moment apprehend these motives as not sufficiently effective. At the very moment when I apprehend my being as *horror* of the precipice, I am conscious of that horror as *not determinant* in relation to my possible conduct. In one sense that horror calls for prudent conduct, and it is in itself a pre-outline of that conduct; in another sense, it posits the final developments of that conduct only as possible, precisely because I do not apprehend it as the cause of these final developments but as need, appeal, *etc.*

Now as we have seen, consciousness of being is the being of consciousness. There is no question here of a contemplation which I could make after the event, of an horror already constituted; it is the very being of horror to appear to itself as "not being the cause" of the conduct it calls for. In short, to avoid fear, which reveals to me a transcendent future strictly determined, I take refuge in reflection, but the latter has only an undetermined future to offer. This means that in establishing a certain conduct as a possibility and precisely because it is *my* possibility, I am aware that *nothing* can compel me to adopt that conduct. Yet I am indeed already there in the future; it is for the sake of that being which I will be there at the turning of the path that I now exert all my strength, and in this sense there is already a relation between my future being and my present being. But a nothingness has slipped into the heart of this relation; I *am* not the self which I will be. First I am not that self because time separates me from it. Secondly, I am not that self because what I am is not the foundation of what I will be. Finally I am not that self because no actual existent can determine strictly what I am going to be. Yet as I am already what I will be (otherwise I would not be interested in any one being more than another), *I am the self which I will be, in the mode of not being it.* It is through my horror that I am carried toward the future, and the horror nihilates itself in that it constitutes the future as possible. Anguish is precisely my consciousness of being my own future, in the mode of not-being. To be exact, the nihilation of horror as a *motive*, which has the effect of reinforcing horror as a *state*, has as its positive counterpart the appearance of other forms of conduct (in particular that which consists in throwing myself over the precipice) as my possible *possibilities*. If *nothing* compels me to save my life, *nothing* prevents me from precipitating myself into the abyss. The decisive conduct will emanate from a self which I am not yet. Thus the self which I am depends on the self which I am not yet to the exact extent that the self which I am not yet does not depend on the self which I am. Vertigo appears as the apprehension of this dependence. I approach the precipice, and my scrutiny is searching for myself in my very depths. In terms of this moment, I play with my possibilities. My eyes, running over the abyss from top to bottom, imitate the possible fall and realize it symbolically; at the same time suicide, from the fact that it becomes a *possibility* possible for *me*, now causes to appear possible motives for adopting it (suicide would cause anguish to cease). Fortunately these motives in their turn, from the sole fact that they are motives of a possibility, present themselves as ineffective, as non-determinant; they can no more *produce* the suicide than my horror of the fall can *determine* me to avoid it. It is this counter-anguish which generally puts an end to anguish by transmuting it into indecision. Indecision in its turn, calls for decision. I abruptly put myself at a distance from the edge of the precipice and resume my way.

The example which we have just analyzed has shown us what we could call "anguish in the face of the future." There exists another: anguish in the face of the past. It is that of the gambler who has freely and sincerely decided not to gamble any more and who when he approaches the gaming table, suddenly sees all his resolutions melt away. This phenomenon has often been described as if the sight of the gaming table reawakened in us a tendency which entered into conflict with our former resolution and ended by drawing us in spite of this. Aside from the fact that such a description is done in materialistic terms and peoples the mind with opposing forces (there is, for example, the moralists' famous "struggle of reason with the passions"), it does not account for the facts. In reality—the letters of Dostoevsky bear witness to this—there is nothing in us which resembles an inner *debate* as if we had to weigh motives and incentives before deciding. The earlier resolution of "not playing anymore" is always *there*, and in the majority of cases the gambler when in the presence of the gaming table, turns toward it as if to ask it for help; for he does not wish to play, or rather having taken his resolution the day before, he thinks of himself still as not wishing to play anymore; he believes in the effectiveness of this resolution. But what he apprehends then in anguish is precisely the total inefficacy of the past resolution. It is there doubtless but fixed, ineffectual, surpassed by the very fact that I am conscious of it. The resolution is still *me* to the extent that I realize constantly my identity with myself across the temporal flux, but it is no longer *me*—due to the fact that it has become an object for my consciousness. I am not subject to it, it fails in the mission which I have given it. The resolution is there still, I *am* it in the mode of not-being. What the gambler apprehends at this instant is again the permanent rupture in determinism; it is nothingness which separates him from himself; I should have liked so much not to gamble anymore; yesterday I even had a synthetic apprehension of the situation (threatening ruin, disappointment of my relatives) as *forbidding me* to play. It seemed to me that I had established a *real barrier* between gambling and myself, and now I suddenly perceive that my former understanding of the situation is no more than a memory of an idea, a memory of a feeling. In order for it to come to my aid once more, I must remake it ex *nihilo* and freely. The not-gambling is only one of my possibilities, as the fact of gambling is another of them, neither more nor less. I *must rediscover* the fear of financial ruin or of disappointing my family, *etc.*, I must re-create it as experienced fear. It stands behind me like a boneless phantom. It depends on me alone to lend it flesh. I am alone and naked before temptation as I was the day before. After having patiently built up barriers and walls, after enclosing myself in the magic circle of a resolution, I perceive with anguish that *nothing* prevents me from gambling. The anguish is me since by the very fact of taking my position in existence as consciousness of being, I make myself *not to be* the past of good resolutions *which* I am.

It would be in vain to object that the sole condition of this anguish is ignorance of the underlying psychological determinism. According to such a view my anxiety would come from lack of knowing the real and effective incentives which in the darkness of the unconscious determine my action. In reply we shall point out first that anguish has not appeared to us as a proof of human freedom; the latter was given to us as the necessary condition for the question. We wished only to show that there exists a specific consciousness of freedom, and we wished to show that this consciousness is anguish. This means that we wished to establish anguish in its essential structure as consciousness of freedom. Now from this point of view the existence of a psychological determinism could not invalidate the results of our description. Either indeed anguish is actually an unrealized ignorance of this determinism—and then anguish apprehends itself in fact as freedom—or else one may claim that anguish is consciousness of being ignorant of the real causes of our acts. In the latter case anguish would come from the presentiment of monstrous motivations, hidden deep within ourselves, which would suddenly release culpable acts. But in this case we should suddenly appear to ourselves as *things in the world*; we should be to ourselves our own transcendent situation. Then anguish would disappear to give away to *fear*, for fear is a synthetic apprehension of the transcendent as dreadful.

This freedom which reveals itself to us in anguish can be characterized by the existence of that *nothing* which insinuates itself between motives and act. It is not *because* I am free that my act is not subject to the determination of motives; on the contrary, the structure of motives as ineffective is the condition of my freedom. If someone asks what this *nothing* is which provides a foundation for freedom, we shall reply that we can not describe it since it is *not*, but we can at least hint at its meaning by saying that this nothing is made-to-be by the human being in his relation with himself. The nothing here corresponds to the necessity for the motive to appear as motive only as a correlate of a consciousness of motive. In short, as soon as we abandon the hypothesis of the contents of consciousness, we must recognize that there is never a motive *in* consciousness; motives are only *for* consciousness. And due to the very fact that the motive can arise only as appearance, it constitutes itself as ineffective. Of course it does not have the externality of a temporal-spatial thing; it always belongs to subjectivity and it is apprehended as *mine*. But it is by nature transcendence in immanence, and consciousness is not subject to it because of the very fact that consciousness posits it; for consciousness has now the task of conferring on the motive its meaning and its importance. Thus the *nothing* which separates the motive from consciousness characterizes itself as transcendence in immanence. It is by arising as immanence that consciousness nihilates the nothing which makes consciousness exist for itself as transcendence. But we see that the nothingness which is the condition of all transcendent negation can be elucidated only in terms of two other original nihilations: (1) Consciousness *is not* its own motive inasmuch as it is *empty* of all content. This refers us to a nihilating structure of the pre-reflective *cogito*. (2) Consciousness confronts its past and its future as facing a self which it is in the mode of not-being. This refers us to a nihilating structure of temporality.

There can be for us as yet no question of elucidating these two types of nihilation; we do not at the moment have the necessary techniques at our disposal. It is sufficient to observe here that the definitive explanation of negation can not be given without a description of self-consciousness and of temporality.

What we should note at present is that freedom, which manifests itself through anguish, is characterized by a constantly renewed obligation to remake the *Self* which designates the free being. As a matter of fact when we showed earlier that my possibilities were filled with anguish because it depended on me alone to sustain them in their existence, that did not mean that they derived from a Me which to itself at least, would first be given and would then pass in the temporal flux from one consciousness to another consciousness. The gambler who must realize anew the synthetic apperception of a situation which would forbid him to play, must rediscover at the same time the self which can appreciate that situation, which "is in situation." This self with its a priori and historical content is the essence of man. Anguish as the manifestation of freedom in the face of self means that man is always separated by a nothingness from his essence. We should refer here to Hegel's statement: "Wesen ist was gewesen ist." Essence is what has been. Essence is everything in the human being which we can indicate by the words—that is. Due to this fact it is the totality of characteristics which explain the act. But the act is always beyond that essence; it is a human act only in so far as it surpasses every explanation which we can give of it, precisely because the very application of the formula "that is" to man causes all that is designated, to have-been. Man continually carries with him a pre-judicative comprehension of his essence, but due to this very fact he is separated from it by a nothingness. Essence is all that human reality apprehends in itself as having been. It is here that anguish appears as an apprehension of self inasmuch as its exists in the perpetual mode of detachment from what is; better yet, in so far as it makes itself exist as such. For we can never apprehend an Erlebnis as a living consequence of that nature which is ours. The overflow of our consciousness progressively constitutes that nature, but it remains always behind us and it dwells in us as the permanent object of our retrospective comprehension. It is in so far as this nature is a demand without being a recourse that it is apprehended in anguish.

In anguish freedom is anguished before itself inasmuch as it is instigated and bound by nothing. Someone will say, freedom has just been defined as a permanent structure of the human being; if anguish manifests it, then anguish ought to be a permanent state of my affectivity. But, on the contrary, it is completely exceptional. How can we explain the rarity of the phenomenon of anguish?

We must note first of all that the most common situations of our life, those in which we apprehend our possibilities as such by means of actively realizing them, do not manifest themselves to us through anguish because their very structure excludes anguished apprehension. Anguish in fact is the recognition of a possibility as my possibility; that is, it is constituted when consciousness sees itself cut from its essence by nothingness or separated from the future by its very freedom. This means that a nihilating nothing removes from me all excuse and that at the same time what I project as my future being is always nihilated and reduced to the rank of simple possibility because the future which I am remains out of my reach. But we ought to remark that in these various instances we have to do with a temporal form where I await myself in the future, where I "make an appointment with myself on the other side of that hour, of that day, or of that month." Anguish is the fear of not finding myself at that appointment, of no longer even wishing to bring myself there. But I can also find myself engaged in acts which reveal my possibilities to me at the very instant when they are realized. In lighting this cigarette I learn my concrete possibility, or if you prefer, my desire of smoking. It is by the very act of drawing toward me this paper and this pen that I give to myself as my most immediate possibility the act of working at this book; there I am engaged, and I discover it at the very moment when I am already throwing myself into it. At that instant, to be sure, it remains my possibility, since I can at each instant turn myself away from my work, push away the notebook, put the cap on my fountain pen. But this possibility of interrupting the action is rejected on a second level by the fact that the action which discovers itself to me through my act tends to crystallize as a transcendent, relatively independent form. The consciousness of man in *action* is non-reflective consciousness. It is consciousness of something, and the transcendent which discloses itself to this consciousness is of a particular nature; it is a *structure* of *exigency* in the world, and the world correlatively discloses in it complex relations of instrumentality. In the act of tracing the letters which I am writing, the whole sentence, still unachieved, is revealed as a passive exigency to be written. It is the very meaning of the letters which I form, and its appeal is not put into question, precisely because I can not write the words without transcending them toward the sentence and because I discover it as the necessary condition for the meaning of the words which I am writing. At the same time in the very framework of the act an indicative complex of instruments reveals itself and organizes itself (pen-ink-paper-lines-margin, etc.), a complex which can not be apprehended for itself but which rises in the heart of the transcendence which discloses to me as a passive exigency the sentence to be written. Thus in the quasi-generality of every day acts, I am engaged, I have ventured, and I discover my possibilities by realizing them and in the very act of realizing them as exigencies, urgencies, instrumentalities.

Of course in every act of this kind, there remains the possibility of putting this act into question—in so far as it refers to more distant, more essential ends—as to its ultimate meanings and my essential possibilities. For example, the sentence which I write is the meaning of the letters which I trace, but the whole work which I wish to produce is the meaning of the sentence. And this work is a possibility in connection with which I can feel anguish; it is truly my possibility, and I do not know whether I will continue it tomorrow; tomorrow in relation to it my freedom can exercise its nihilating power. But that anguish implies the apprehension of the work as such as my possibility. I must place myself directly opposite it and realize my relation to it. This means that I ought not only to raise with reference to it objective questions such as, "Is it necessary to write this work?" for these questions refer me simply to wider objective significations, such as, "Is it opportune to write it *at this moment*? Isn't this just a repetition of another such book? Is its material of sufficient interest? Has it been sufficiently thought through?" *etc.*—all significations which remain transcendent and give themselves as a multitude of exigencies in the world.

In order for my freedom to be anguished in connection with the book which I am writing, this book must appear in its relation with me. On the one hand, I must discover my essence as *what I have been*—I have been "wanting to write this book," I have conceived it, I have believed that it would be interesting to write it, and I have constituted myself in such a way that it is not possible to *understand me* without taking into account the fact that this book *has been* my essential possibility. On the other hand, I must discover the nothingness which separates my freedom from this essence: *I have been* "wanting to write," but *nothing*, not even what I have been, can compel me to write it. Finally, I must discover the nothingness which separates me from what I shall be: I discover that the permanent possibility of abandoning the book is the very condition of the possibility of writing it and the very meaning of my freedom. It is necessary that in the very constitution of the book as my possibility, I apprehend my freedom as being the possible destroyer in the present and in the future of what I am. That is, I must place myself on the plane of reflection. So long as I remain on the plane of action, the book to be written is only the distant and presupposed meaning of the act which reveals my possibilities to me. The book is only the implication of the action; it is not made an object and posited for itself; it does not "raise the question;" it is conceived neither as necessary nor contingent. It is only the permanent, remote meaning in terms of which I can understand what I am writing in the present, and hence, it is conceived as being; that is, only by positing the book as *the existing basis* on which my present, existing sentence emerges, can I confer a determined meaning upon my sentence.

Now at each instant we are thrust into the world and engaged there. This means that we act before positing our possibilities and that these possibilities which are disclosed as realized or in process of being realized refer to meanings which necessitate special acts in order to be put into question. The alarm which rings in the morning refers to the possibility of my going to work, which is my possibility. But to apprehend the summons of the alarm as a summons is to get up. Therefore the very act of getting up is reassuring, for it eludes the question, "Is work my possibility?" Consequently it does not put me in a position to apprehend the possibility of quietism, of refusing to work, and finally the possibility of refusing the world and the possibility of death. In short, to the extent that I apprehend the meaning of the ringing, I am already up at its summons; this apprehension guarantees me against the anguished intuition that it is I who confer on the alarm clock its exigency—I and I alone.

In the same way, what we might call everyday morality is exclusive of ethical anguish. There is ethical anguish when I consider myself in my original relation to values. Values in actuality are demands which lay claim to a foundation. But this foundation can in no way be *being*, for every value which would base its ideal nature on its being would thereby cease even to be a value and would realize the heteronomy of my will. Value derives its being from its exigency and not its exigency from its being. It does not deliver itself to a contemplative intuition which would apprehend it as *being* value and thereby would remove from it its right over my freedom. On the contrary, it can be revealed only to an active freedom which makes it exist as value by the sole fact of recognizing it as such. It follows that my freedom is the unique foundation of values and that *nothing*, absolutely nothing, justifies me in adopting this or that particular value, this or that particular scale of values. As a being by whom values exist, I am unjustifiable. My freedom is anguished at being the foundation of values while itself without foundation. It is anguished in addition because values, due to the fact that they are essentially revealed to a freedom, can not disclose themselves without being at the same time "put into question," for the possibility of overturning the scale of values appears complementarily as *my* possibility. It is anguish before values which is the recognition of the ideality of values.

Ordinarily, however, my attitude with respect to values is eminently reassuring. In fact I am engaged in a world of values. The anguished apperception of values as sustained in being by my freedom is a secondary and mediated phenomenon. The immediate is the world with its urgency; and in this world where I engage myself, my acts cause values to spring up like partridges. My indignation has given to me the negative value "baseness," my admiration has given the positive value "grandeur." Above all my obedience to a multitude of tabus, which is real, reveals these tabus to me as existing in fact. The bourgeois who call themselves "respectable citizens" do not become respectable as the result of contemplating moral values. Rather from the moment of their arising in the world they are thrown into a pattern of behavior the meaning of which is respectability. Thus respectability acquires a being; it is not put into question. Values are sown on my path as thousands of little real demands, like the signs which order us to keep off the grass.

Thus in what we shall call the world of the immediate, which delivers itself to our unreflective consciousness, we do not first appear to ourselves, to be thrown subsequently into enterprises. Our being is immediately "in situation;" that is, it arises in enterprises and knows itself first in so far as it is reflected in those enterprises. We discover ourselves then in a world peopled with demands, in the heart of projects "in the course of realization." I write. I am going to smoke. I have an appointment this evening with Pierre. I must not forget to reply to Simon. I do not have the right to conceal the truth any longer from Claude. All these trivial passive expectations of the real, all these commonplace, everyday values, derive their meaning from an original projection of myself which stands as my choice of myself in the world. But to be exact, this projection of myself toward an original possibility, which causes the existence of values, appeals, expectations, and in general a world, appears to me only beyond the world as the meaning and the abstract, logical signification of my enterprises. For the rest, there exist concretely alarm clocks, signboards, tax forms, policemen, so many guard rails against anguish. But as soon as the enterprise is held at a distance from me, as soon as I am referred to myself because I must await myself in the future, then I discover myself suddenly as the one who gives its meaning to the alarm clock, the one who by a signboard forbids himself to walk on a flower bed or on the lawn, the one from whom the boss's order borrows its urgency, the one who decides the interest of the book which he is writing, the one finally who makes the values exist in order to determine his action by their demands. I emerge alone and in anguish confronting the unique and original project which constitutes my being; all the barriers, all the guard rails collapse, nihilated by the consciousness of my freedom. I do not have nor can I have recourse to any value against the fact that it is I who sustain values in being. Nothing can ensure me against myself, cut off from the world and from my essence by this nothingness which I am. I have to realize the meaning of the world and of my essence; I make my decision concerning them—without justification and without excuse.

Anguish then is the reflective apprehension of freedom by itself. In this sense it is mediation, for although it is immediate consciousness of itself, it arises from the negation of the appeals of the world. It appears at the moment that I disengage myself from the world where I had been engaged—in order to apprehend myself as a consciousness which possesses a preontological comprehension of its essence and a pre-judicative sense of its possibilities. Anguish is opposed to the mind of the serious man who apprehends values in terms of the world and who resides in the reassuring, materialistic substantiation of values. In the serious mood I define myself in terms of the object by pushing aside a priori as impossible all enterprises in which I am not engaged at the moment; the meaning which my freedom has given to the world, I apprehend as coming from the world and constituting my obligations. In anguish I apprehend myself at once as totally free and as not being able to derive the meaning of the world except as coming from myself.

We should not however conclude that being brought on to the reflective plane and envisaging one's distant or immediate possibilities suffice to apprehend oneself in pure anguish. In each instance of reflection anguish is born as a structure of the reflective consciousness in so far as the latter considers consciousness as an object of reflection; but it still remains possible for me to maintain various types of conduct with respect to my own anguish—in particular, patterns of flight. Everything takes place, in fact, as if our essential and immediate behavior with respect to anguish is flight. Psychological determinism, before being a theoretical conception, is first an attitude of excuse, or if you prefer, the basis of all attitudes of excuse. It is reflective conduct with respect to anguish; it asserts that there are within us antagonistic forces whose type of existence is comparable to that of things. It attempts to fill the void which encircles us, to re-establish the links between past and present, between present and future. It provides us with a *nature* productive of our acts, and these very acts it makes transcendent; it assigns to them a foundation in something other than themselves by endowing them with an inertia and externality eminently reassuring because they constitute a permanent game of *excuses*. Psychological determinism denies that transcendence of human reality which makes it emerge in anguish beyond its own essence. At the same time by reducing us to *never being anything but what we are*, it reintroduces in us the absolute positivity of being-in-itself and thereby reinstates us at the heart of being.

But this determinism, a reflective defense against anguish, is not given as a reflective *intuition*. It avails nothing against the *evidence* of freedom; hence it is given as a faith to take refuge in, as the ideal end toward which we can flee to escape anguish. That is made evident on the philosophical plane by the fact that deterministic psychologists do not claim to found their thesis on the pure givens of introspection. They present it as a satisfying hypothesis, the value of which comes from the fact that it accounts for the facts—or as a necessary postulate for establishing all psychology. They admit the existence of an immediate consciousness of freedom, which their opponents hold up against them under the name of "proof by intuition of the inner sense." They merely focus the debate on the *value* of this inner revelation. Thus the intuition which causes us to apprehend ourselves as the original cause of our states and our acts has been discussed by nobody. It is within the reach of each of us to try to mediate anguish by rising above it and by *judging* it as an illusion due to the mistaken belief that we are the real causes of our acts. The problem which presents itself then is that of the degree of faith in this mediation. Is an anguish placed under judgment a disarmed anguish? Evidently not. However here a new phenomenon is born, a process of "distraction" in relation to anguish which, once again, supposes within it a nihilating power.

By itself determinism would not suffice to establish distraction since determinism is only a postulate or an hypothesis. This process of detachment is a more complete activity of flight which operates on the very level of reflection. It is first an attempt at distraction in relation to the possibles opposed to my possible. When I constitute myself as the comprehension of a possible as my possible, I must recognize its existence at the end of my project and apprehend it as myself, awaiting me down there in the future and separated from me by a nothingness. In this sense I apprehend myself as the original source of my possibility, and it is this which ordinarily we call the consciousness of freedom. It is this structure of consciousness and this alone that the proponents of free-will have in mind when they speak of the intuition of the inner sense. But it happens that I force myself at the same time to *be distracted* from the constitution of other possibilities which contradict *my possibility*. In truth I can not avoid positing their existence by the same movement which generates the chosen possibility as mine. I cannot help constituting them as *living* possibilities; that is, *as having the possibility of becoming my possibilities*. But I force myself to see them as endowed with a transcendent, purely logical being, in short, as things. If on the reflective plane I envisage the possibility of writing this book as my possibility, then between this possibility and my consciousness I cause a nothingness of being to arise which constitutes the writing of the book as a possibility and which I apprehend precisely in the permanent possibility that the possibility of not writing the book is my possibility. But I attempt to place myself on the other side of the possibility of not writing it as I might do with respect to an observable object, and I let myself be penetrated with what I wish to see there; I try to apprehend the possibility of not writing as needing to be mentioned merely as a reminder, as not concerning me. It must be an external possibility in relation to me, like movement in relation to the motionless billiard ball. If I could succeed in this, the possibilities hostile to my possibility would be constituted as logical entities and would lose their effectiveness. They would no longer be threatening since they would be "outsiders," since they would surround my possible as purely *conceivable* eventualities; that is, fundamentally, conceivable *by another or as possibles of another who might find himself in the same situation*. They would belong to the objective situation as a transcendent structure, or if you prefer (to utilize Heidegger's terminology)—I shall write this book but one could also not write it. Thus I should hide from myself the fact that the possibles are *myself* and that they are immanent conditions of the possibility of my possible. They would preserve just enough being to preserve for my possible its character as gratuitous, as a free possibility for a free being, but they would be disarmed of their threatening character. They would not *interest* me; the chosen possible would appear—due to its selection—as my only concrete possible, and consequently the nothingness which separates me from it and which actually confers on it its possibility would collapse.

But flight before anguish is not only an effort at distraction before the future; it attempts also to disarm the past of its threat. What I attempt to flee here is my very transcendence in so far as it sustains and surpasses my essence. I assert that I *am* my essence in the mode of being of the in-itself. At the same time I always refuse to consider that essence as being historically constituted and as implying my action as a circle implies its properties. I apprehend it, or at least I try to apprehend it as the original beginning of my possible, and I do not admit at all that it has in itself a beginning. I assert then that an act is free when it exactly reflects my essence. However this freedom which would disturb me if it were freedom before myself, I attempt to bring back to the heart of my essence—i.e., of my self. It is a matter of envisaging the self as a little God which inhabits me and which possesses my freedom as a metaphysical virtue. It would be no longer my being which would be free qua being but my Self which would be free in the heart of my consciousness. It is a fiction eminently reassuring since freedom has been driven down into the heart of an opaque being; to the extent that my essence is not trans-lucency, that it is transcendent in immanence, freedom would become one of its properties. In short, it is a matter of apprehending my freedom in my self as the freedom of *another*.[20] We see the principal themes of this fiction: My self becomes the origin of its acts as the other of his, by virtue of a personality already constituted. To be sure, he (the self) lives and transforms himself; we will admit even that each of his acts can contribute to transforming him. But these harmonious, continued transformations are conceived on a biological order. They resemble those which I can establish in my friend Pierre when I see him after a separation. Bergson expressly satisfied these demands for reassurance when he conceived his theory of the profound self which endures and organizes itself, which is constantly contemporary with the consciousness which I have of it and which can not be surpassed by con-sciousness, which is found at the origin of my acts not as a cataclysmic power but as a father begets his children, in such a way that the act without follow-ing from the essence as a strict consequence, without even being forseeable, enters into a reassuring relation with it, a family resemblance. The act goes farther than the self but along the same road; it preserves, to be sure, a certain irreducibility, but we recognize ourselves in it, and we find ourselves in it as a father can recognize himself and find himself in the son who continues his work. Thus by a projection of freedom—which we apprehend in ourselves— into a psychic object which is the self, Bergson has contributed to disguise our anguish, but it is at the expense of consciousness itself. What he has established and described in this manner is not our freedom as it appears to itself; it *is the freedom of the Other*.

[20] Cf. Part III, ch. I.

Such then is the totality of processes by which we try to hide anguish from ourselves; we apprehend our particular possible by avoiding considering all other possibles, which we make the possibles of an undifferentiated Other. The chosen possible we do not wish to see as sustained in being by a pure nihilating freedom, and so we attempt to apprehend it as engendered by an object already constituted, which is no other than our self, envisaged and described as if it were another person. We should like to preserve from the original intuition what it reveals to us as our independence and our responsibility but we tone down all the original nihilation in it; moreover we are always ready to take refuge in a belief in determinism if this freedom weighs upon us or if we need an excuse. Thus we flee from anguish by attempting to apprehend ourselves from without as an Other or as a thing. What we are accustomed to call a revelation of the inner sense or an original intuition of our freedom contains nothing original; it is an already constructed process, expressly designed to hide from ourselves anguish, the veritable "immediate given" of our freedom.

Do these various constructions succeed in stifling or hiding our anguish? It is certain that we can not overcome anguish, for we are anguish. As for veiling it, aside from the fact that the very nature of consciousness and its translucency forbid us to take the expression literally, we must note the particular type of behavior which it indicates. We can hide an external object because it exists independently of us. For the same reason we can turn our look or our attention away from it—that is, very simply, fix our eyes on some other object; henceforth each reality—mine and that of the object—resumes its own life, and the accidental relation which united consciousness to the thing disappears without thereby altering either existence. But if I am what I wish to veil, the question takes on quite another aspect. I can in fact wish "not to see" a certain aspect of my being only if I am acquainted with the aspect which I do not wish to see. This means that in my being I must indicate this aspect in order to be able to turn myself away from it; better yet, I must think of it constantly in order to take care not to think of it. In this connection it must be understood not only that I must of necessity perpetually carry within me what I wish to flee but also that I must aim at the object of my flight in order to flee it. This means that anguish, the intentional aim of anguish, and a flight from anguish toward reassuring myths must all be given in the unity of the same consciousness. In a word, I flee in order not to know, but I can not avoid knowing that I am fleeing; and the flight from anguish is only a mode of becoming conscious of anguish. Thus anguish, properly speaking, can be neither hidden nor avoided.

Yet to flee anguish and to be anguish can not be exactly the same thing. If I am my anguish in order to flee it, that presupposes that I can decenter myself in relation to what I am, that I can be anguish in the form of "not-being it," that I can dispose of a nihilating power at the heart of anguish itself. This nihilating power nihilates anguish in so far as I flee it and nihilates itself in so far as I *am anguish in order to flee it*. This attitude is what we call *bad faith*. There is then no question of expelling anguish from consciousness nor of constituting it in an unconscious psychic phenomenon; very simply I can make myself guilty of bad faith while apprehending the anguish which I am, and this bad faith, intended to fill up the nothingness which I *am* in my relation to myself, precisely implies the nothingness which it suppresses.

We are now at the end of our first description. The examination of the negation can not lead us farther. It has revealed to us the existence of a particular type of conduct: conduct in the face of non-being, which supposes a special transcendence needing separate study. We find ourselves then in the presence of two human ekstases: the ekstasis which throws us into being-in-itself and the ekstasis which engages us in non-being. It seems that our original problem, which concerned only the relations of man to being, is now considerably complicated. But in pushing our analysis of transcendence toward non-being to its conclusion, it is possible for us to get valuable information for the understanding of *all* transcendence. Furthermore the problem of nothingness can not be excluded from our inquiry. If man adopts any particular behavior in the face of being-in-itself—and our philosophical question is a type of such behavior—it is because he *is not* this being. We rediscover non-being as a condition of the transcendence toward being. We must then catch hold of the problem of nothingness and not let it go before its complete elucidation.

However the examination of the question and of the negation has given us all that it can. We have been referred by it to empirical freedom as the nihilation of man in the heart of temporality and as the necessary condition for the transcending apprehension of *négatités*. It remains to found this empirical freedom. It can not be both the original nihilation and the ground of all nihilation. Actually it contributes to constituting transcendences in immanence which condition all negative transcendences. But the very fact that the transcendences of empirical freedom are constituted in immanence *as transcendences* shows us that we are dealing with secondary nihilations which suppose the existence of an original nothingness. They are only a stage in the analytical regression which leads us from the examples of transcendence called "négatités" to the being which is its own nothingness. Evidently it is necessary to find the foundation of all negation in a nihilation which is exercised *in the very heart of immanence*; in absolute immanence, in the pure subjectivity of the instantaneous *cogito* we must discover the original act by which man is to himself his own nothingness. What must be the nature of consciousness in order that man in consciousness and in terms of consciousness should arise in the world as the being who is his own nothingness and by whom nothingness comes into the world?

We seem to lack here the instrument to permit us to resolve this new problem; negation directly engages only freedom. We must find in freedom itself the conduct which will permit us to push further. Now this conduct, which will lead us to the threshold of immanence and which remains still sufficiently objective so that we can objectively disengage its conditions of possibility—this we have already encountered. Have we not remarked earlier that in bad faith, we are-anguish-in-order-to-flee-anguish within the unity of a single consciousness? If bad faith is to be possible, we should be able within the same consciousness to meet with the unity of being and non-being—the being-in-order-not-to-be. Bad faith is going to be the next object of our investigation. For man to be able to question, he must be capable of being his own nothingness; that is, he can be at the origin of non-being in being only if his being—in himself and by himself—is paralyzed with nothingness. Thus the transcendences of past and future appear in the temporal being of human reality. But bad faith is instantaneous. What then are we to say that conscious-ness must be in the instantaneity of the pre-reflective *cogito*—if the human being is to be capable of bad faith?

# 2

## BAD FAITH

### I. BAD FAITH AND LIES

The human being is not only the being by whom *négatités* are disclosed in the world; he is also the one who can take negative attitudes with respect to himself. In our Introduction we defined consciousness as "a being such that in its being, its being is in question in so far as this being implies a being other than itself." But now that we have examined the meaning of "the question," we can at present also write the formula thus: "Consciousness is a being, the nature of which is to be conscious of the nothingness of its being." In a prohibition or a veto, for example, the human being denies a future transcendence. But this negation is not explicative. My consciousness is not restricted to *envisioning* a *négatité*. It constitutes itself in its own flesh as the nihilation of a possibility which another human reality projects as *its* possibility. For that reason it must arise in the world as a Not; it is as a Not that the slave first apprehends the master, or that the prisoner who is trying to escape sees the guard who is watching him. There are even men (*e.g.*, caretakers, overseers, gaolers,) whose social reality is uniquely that of the Not, who will live and die, having forever been only a Not upon the earth. Others so as to make the Not a part of their very subjectivity, establish their human personality as a perpetual negation. This is the meaning and function of what Scheler calls "the man of resentment"—in reality, the Not. But there exist more subtle behaviors, the description of which will lead us further into the inwardness of consciousness. Irony is one of these. In irony a man annihilates what he posits within one and the same act; he leads us to believe in order not to be believed; he affirms to deny and denies to affirm; he creates a positive object but it has no being other than its nothingness. Thus attitudes of negation toward the self permit us to raise a new question: What are we to say is the being of man who has the possibility of denying himself? But it is out of the question to discuss the attitude of "self-negation" in its universality. The kinds of behavior which can be ranked under this heading are too diverse; we risk retaining only the abstract form of them. It is best to choose and to examine one determined attitude which is essential to human reality and which is such that consciousness instead of directing its negation outward turns it toward itself. This attitide, it seems to me, is *bad faith* (*mauvaise foi*).

Frequently this is identified with lying. We say indifferently of a person that he shows signs of bad faith or that he lies to himself. We shall willingly grant that bad faith is a lie to oneself, on condition that we distinguish the lie to oneself from lying in general. Lying is a negative attitude, we will agree to that. But this negation does not bear on consciousness itself; it aims only at the transcendent. The essence of the lie implies in fact that the liar actually is in complete possession of the truth which he is hiding. A man does not lie about what he is ignorant of; he does not lie when he spreads an error of which he himself is the dupe; he does not lie when he is mistaken. The ideal description of the liar would be a cynical consciousness, affirming truth within himself, denying it in his words, and denying that negation as such. Now this doubly negative attitude rests on the transcendent; the fact expressed is transcendent since it does not exist, and the original negation rests on a *truth*; that is, on a particular type of transcendence. As for the inner negation which I effect correlatively with the affirmation for myself of the truth, this rests on *words*; that is, on an event in the world. Furthermore the inner disposition of the liar is positive; it could be the object of an affirmative judgment. The liar intends to deceive and he does not seek to hide this intention from himself nor to disguise the translucency of consciousness; on the contrary, he has recourse to it when there is a question of deciding secondary behavior. It explicitly exercises a regulatory control over all attitudes. As for his flaunted intention of telling the truth ("I'd never want to deceive you! This is true! I swear it!")—all this, of course, is the object of an inner negation, but also it is not recognized by the liar as *his* intention. It is played, imitated, it is the intention of the character which he plays in the eyes of his questioner, but this character, precisely because he *does not exist*, is a transcendent. Thus the lie does not put into the play the inner structure of present consciousness; all the negations which constitute it bear on objects which by this fact are removed from consciousness. The lie then does not require special ontological foundation, and the explanations which the existence of negation in general requires are valid without change in the case of deceit. Of course we have described the ideal lie; doubtless it happens often enough that the liar is more or less the victim of his lie, that he half persuades himself of it. But these common, popular forms of the lie are also degenerate aspects of it; they represent intermediaries between falsehood and bad faith. The lie is a behavior of transcendence.

The lie is also a normal phenomenon of what Heidegger calls the "Mit-sein."[1] It presupposes my existence, the existence of the Other, my existence for the Other, and the existence of the Other for me. Thus there is no difficulty in holding that the liar must make the project of the lie in entire clarity and that he must possess a complete comprehension of the lie and of the truth which he is altering. It is sufficient that an over-all opacity hide his intentions from the Other; it is sufficient that the Other can take the lie for truth. By the lie consciousness affirms that it exists by nature as hidden from the Other; it utilizes for its own profit the ontological duality of myself and myself in the eyes of the Other.

The situation can not be the same for bad faith if this, as we have said, is indeed a lie to oneself. To be sure, the one who practices bad faith is hiding a displeasing truth or presenting as truth a pleasing untruth. Bad faith then has in appearance the structure of lying. Only what changes everything is the fact that in bad faith it is from myself that I am hiding the truth. Thus the duality of the deceiver and the deceived does not exist here. Bad faith on the contrary implies in essence the unity of a single consciousness. This does not mean that it can not be conditioned by the Mit-sein like all other phenomena of human reality, but the Mit-sein can call forth bad faith only by presenting itself as a situation which bad faith permits surpassing; bad faith does not come from outside to human reality. One does not undergo his bad faith; one is not infected with it; it is not a state. But consciousness affects itself with bad faith. There must be an original intention and a project of bad faith; this project implies a comprehension of bad faith as such and a pre-reflective apprehension (of) consciousness as affecting itself with bad faith. It follows first that the one to whom the lie is told and the one who lies are one and the same person, which means that I must know in my capacity as deceiver the truth which is hidden from me in my capacity as the one deceived. Better yet I must know the truth very exactly in order to conceal it more carefully—and this not at two different moments, which at a pinch would allow us to reestablish a semblance of duality—but in the unitary structure of a single project. How then can the lie subsist if the duality which conditions it is suppressed?

To this difficulty is added another which is derived from the total trans-lucency of consciousness. That which affects itself with bad faith must be conscious (of) its bad faith since the being of consciousness is consciousness of being. It appears then that I must be in good faith, at least to the extent that I am conscious of my bad faith. But then this whole psychic system is

___
[1] A "being-with" others in the world. Tr.

annihilated. We must agree in fact that if I deliberately and cynically attempt to lie to myself, I fail completely in this undertaking; the lie falls back and collapses beneath my look; it is ruined *from behind* by the very consciousness of lying to myself which pitilessly constitutes itself well within my project as its very condition. We have here an *evanescent* phenomenon which exists only in and through its own differentiation. To be sure, these phenomena are frequent and we shall see that there is in fact an "evanescence" of bad faith, which, it is evident, vacillates continually between good faith and cynicism: Even though the existence of bad faith is very precarious, and though it belongs to the kind of psychic structures which we might call "metastable,"[2] it presents nonetheless an autonomous and durable form. It can even be the normal aspect of life for a very great number of people. A person can live in bad faith, which does not mean that he does not have abrupt awakenings to cynicism or to good faith, but which implies a constant and particular style of life. Our embarrassment then appears extreme since we can neither reject nor comprehend bad faith.

To escape from these difficulties people gladly have recourse to the unconscious. In the psychoanalytical interpretation, for example, they use the hypothesis of a censor, conceived as a line of demarcation with customs, passport division, currency control, *etc.*, to reestablish the duality of the deceiver and the deceived. Here instinct or, if you prefer, original drives and complexes of drives constituted by our individual history, make up *reality*. It is *neither true nor false* since it does not *exist for itself*. It simply *is*, exactly like this table, which is neither true nor false *in itself* but simply *real*. As for the conscious symbols of the instinct, this interpretation takes them not for appearances but for real psychic facts. Fear, forgetting, dreams exist really in the capacity of concrete facts of consciousness in the same way as the words and the attitudes of the liar are concrete, really existing patterns of behavior. The subject has the same relation to these phenomena as the deceived to the behavior of the deceiver. He establishes them in their reality and must interpret them. There is a *truth* in the activities of the deceiver; if the deceived could reattach them to the situation where the deceiver establishes himself and to his project of the lie, they would become integral parts of truth, by virtue of being lying conduct. Similarly there is a truth in the symbolic acts; it is what the psychoanalyst discovers when he reattaches them to the historical situation of the patient, to the unconscious complexes which they express, to the blocking of the censor. Thus the subject deceives himself about the *meaning* of his conduct, he apprehends it in its concrete existence but not in its *truth*, simply because he cannot derive it from an original situation and from a psychic constitution which remain alien to him.

---

[2] Sartre's own word, meaning subject to sudden changes or transitions. Tr.

By the distinction between the "id" and the "ego," Freud has cut the psychic whole into two. I *am* the ego but I *am not* the id. I hold no privileged position in relation to my unconscious psyche. I *am* my own psychic phenomena in so far as I establish them in their conscious reality. For example I am the impulse to steal this or that book from this bookstall. I am an integral part of the impulse; I bring it to light and I determine myself hand-in-hand with it to commit the theft. But I *am* not those psychic facts, in so far as I receive them passively and am obliged to resort to hypotheses about their origin and their true meaning, just as the scholar makes conjectures about the nature and essence of an external phenomenon. This theft, for example, which I interpret as an immediate impulse determined by the rarity, the interest, or the price of the volume which I am going to steal—it is in truth a process derived from self-punishment, which is attached more or less directly to an Oedipus complex. The impulse toward the theft contains a truth which can be reached only by more or less probable hypotheses. The criterion of this truth will be the number of conscious psychic facts which it explains; from a more pragmatic point of view it will be also the success of the psychiatric cure which it allows. Finally the discovery of this truth will necessitate the cooperation of the psychoanalyst, who appears as the *mediator* between my unconscious drives and my conscious life. The Other appears as being able to effect the synthesis between the unconscious thesis and the conscious antithesis. I can know myself only through the mediation of the other, which means that I stand in relation to my "id," in the position of the *Other*. If I have a little knowledge of psychoanalysis, I can, under circumstances particularly favorable, try to psychoanalyze myself. But this attempt can succeed only if I distrust every kind of intuition, only if I apply to my case *from the outside*, abstract schemes and rules already learned. As for the results, whether they are obtained by my efforts alone or with the cooperation of a technician, they will never have the certainty which intuition confers; they will possess simply the always increasing probability of scientific hypotheses. The hypothesis of the Oedipus complex, like the atomic theory, is nothing but an "experimental idea;" as Peirce said, it is not to be distinguished from the totality of experiments which it allows to be realized and the results which it enables us to foresee. Thus psychoanalysis substitutes for the notion of bad faith, the idea of a lie without a liar; it allows me to understand how it is possible for me to be lied to without lying to myself since it places me in the same relation to myself that the Other is in respect to me; it replaces the duality of the deceiver and the deceived, the essential condition of the lie, by that of the "id" and the "ego." It introduces into my deepest subjectivity the intersubjective structure of the *Mit-sein*. Can this explanation satisfy us?

Considered more closely the psychoanalytic theory is not as simple as it first appears. It is not accurate to hold that the "id" is presented as a thing in relation to the hypothesis of the psychoanalyst, for a thing is indifferent to the conjectures which we make concerning it, while the "id" on the contrary is sensitive to them when we approach the truth. Freud in fact reports resistance when at the end of the first period the doctor is approaching the truth. This resistance is objective behavior apprehended from without: the patient shows defiance, refuses to speak, gives fantastic accounts of his dreams, sometimes even removes himself completely from the psychoanalytic treatment. It is a fair question to ask what part of himself can thus resist. It can not be the "Ego," envisaged as a psychic totality of the facts of consciousness; this could not suspect that the psychiatrist is approaching the end since the ego's relation to the *meaning* of its own reactions is exactly like that of the psychiatrist himself. At the very most it is possible for the ego to appreciate objectively the degree of probability in the hypotheses set forth, as a witness of the psychoanalysis might be able to do, according to the number of subjective facts which they explain. Furthermore, this probability would appear to the ego to border on certainty, which he could not take offence at since most of the time it is he who by a *conscious* decision is in pursuit of the psychoanalytic therapy. Are we to say that the patient is disturbed by the daily revelations which the psychoanalyst makes to him and that he seeks to remove himself, at the same time pretending in his own eyes to wish to continue the treatment? In this case it is no longer possible to resort to the unconscious to explain bad faith; it is there in full consciousness, with all its contradictions. But this is not the way that the psychoanalyst means to explain this resistance; for him it is secret and deep, it comes from afar; it has its roots in the very thing which the psychoanalyst is trying to make clear.

Furthermore it is equally impossible to explain the resistance as emanating from the complex which the psychoanalyst wishes to bring to light. The complex as such is rather the collaborator of the psychoanalyst since it aims at expressing itself in clear consciousness, since it plays tricks on the censor and seeks to elude it. The only level on which we can locate the refusal of the subject is that of the censor. It alone can comprehend the questions or the revelations of the psychoanalyst as approaching more or less near to the real drives which it strives to repress—it alone because it alone *knows* what it is repressing.

If we reject the language and the materialistic mythology of psychoanalysis, we perceive that the censor in order to apply its activity with discernment must know what it is repressing. In fact if we abandon all the metaphors representing the repression as the impact of blind forces, we are compelled to admit that the censor must choose and in order to choose must be aware of so doing. How could it happen otherwise that the censor allows lawful sexual impulses to pass through, that it permits needs (hunger, thirst, sleep) to be expressed in clear consciousness? And how are we to explain that it can relax its surveillance, that it can even be deceived by the disguises of the instinct? But it is not sufficient that it discern the condemned drives; it must also apprehend them *as to be repressed*, which implies in it at the very least an awareness of its activity. In a word, how could the censor discern the impulses needing to be repressed without being conscious of discerning them? How can we conceive of a knowledge which is ignorant of itself? To know is to know that one knows, said Alain. Let us say rather: All knowing is consciousness of knowing. Thus the resistance of the patient implies on the level of the censor an awareness of the thing repressed as such, a comprehension of the end toward which the questions of the psychoanalyst are leading, and an act of synthetic connection by which it compares the *truth* of the repressed complex to the psychoanalytic hypothesis which aims at it. These various operations in their turn imply that the censor is conscious (of) itself. But what type of self-consciousness can the censor have? It must be the consciousness (of) being conscious of the drive to be repressed, but precisely *in order not be conscious of* it. What does this mean if not that the censor is in bad faith?

Psychoanalysis has not gained anything for us since in order to overcome bad faith, it has established between the unconscious and consciousness an autonomous consciousness in bad faith. The effort to establish a veritable duality and even a trinity (*Es, Ich, Ueberich* expressing themselves through the censor) has resulted in a mere verbal terminology. The very essence of the reflexive idea of hiding something from oneself implies the unity of one and the same psychic mechanism and consequently a double activity in the heart of unity, tending on the one hand to maintain and locate the thing to be concealed and on the other hand to repress and disguise it. Each of the two aspects of this activity is complementary to the other; that is, it implies the other in its being. By separating consciousness from the unconscious by means of the censor, psychoanalysis has not succeeded in dissociating the two phases of the act, since the libido is a blind conatus toward conscious expression and since the conscious phenomenon is a passive, faked result. Psychoanalysis has merely localized this double activity of repulsion and attraction on the level of the censor.

Furthermore the problem still remains of accounting for the unity of the total phenomenon (repression of the drive which disguises itself and "passes" in symbolic form), to establish comprehensible connections among its different phases. How can the repressed drive "disguise itself" if it does not include (1) the consciousness of being repressed, (2) the consciousness of having been pushed back because it is what it is, (3) a project of disguise? No mechanistic theory of condensation or of transference can explain these modifications by which the drive itself is affected, for the description of the process of disguise implies a veiled appeal to finality. And similarly how are we to account for the pleasure or the anguish which accompanies the symbolic and conscious satisfaction of the drive if consciousness does not include—beyond the censor—an obscure comprehension of the end to be attained as simultaneously desired and forbidden. By rejecting the conscious unity of the psyche, Freud is obliged to imply everywhere a magic unity linking distant phenomena across obstacles, just as sympathetic magic unites the spellbound person and the wax image fashioned in his likeness. The unconscious drive (Trieb) through magic is endowed with the character "repressed" or "condemned," which completely pervades it, colors it, and magically provokes its symbolism. Similarly the conscious phenomenon is entirely colored by its symbolic meaning although it can not apprehend this meaning by itself in clear consciousness.

Aside from its inferiority in principle, the explanation by magic does not avoid the coexistence—on the level of the unconscious, on that of the censor, and on that of consciousness—of two contradictory, complementary structures which reciprocally imply and destroy each other. Proponents of the theory have hypostasized and "reified" bad faith; they have not escaped it. This is what has inspired a Viennese psychiatrist, Stekel, to depart from the psychoanalytical tradition and to write in La femme frigide:[3] "Every time that I have been able to carry my investigations far enough, I have established that the crux of the psychosis was conscious." In addition the cases which he reports in his work bear witness to a pathological bad faith which the Freudian doctrine can not account for. There is the question, for example, of women whom marital infidelity has made frigid; that is, they succeed in hiding from themselves not complexes deeply sunk in half physiological darkness, but acts of conduct which are objectively discoverable, which they can not fail to record at the moment when they perform them. Frequently in fact the husband reveals to Stekel that his wife has given objective signs of pleasure, but the woman when questioned will fiercely deny them. Here we find a pattern of distraction. Admissions which Stekel was able to draw out inform us that these pathologically frigid women apply themselves to becoming distracted in advance from the pleasure which they dread; many for example at the time of the sexual act, turn their thoughts away toward their daily occupations, make up their household accounts. Will anyone speak of an unconscious here? Yet if the frigid woman thus distracts her consciousness from the pleasure which she experiences, it is by no means cynically and in full agreement with herself; it is in order to prove to herself that she is frigid. We have in fact to deal with a phenomenon of bad faith since the efforts taken in order not to be present to the experienced pleasure imply the recognition that the pleasure is experienced; they imply it in order to deny it. But we are no

[3] N.R.F., 1937.

longer on the ground of psychoanlysis. Thus on the one hand the explanation by means of the unconscious, due to the fact that it breaks the psychic unity, can not account for the facts which at first sight it appeared to explain. And on the other hand, there exists an infinity of types of behavior in bad faith which explicitly reject this kind of explanation because their essence implies that they can appear only in the translucency of consciousness. We find that the problem which we had attempted to resolve is still untouched.

## II. CONDUCTS OF BAD FAITH

If we wish to get out of this difficulty, we should examine more closely the patterns of bad faith and attempt a description of them. This description will permit us perhaps to fix more exactly the conditions for the possibility of bad faith; that is, to reply to the question we raised at the outset: "What must be the being of man if he is to be capable of bad faith?"

Take the example of a woman who has consented to go out with a particular man for the first time. She knows very well the intentions which the man who is speaking to her cherishes regarding her. She knows also that it will be necessary sooner or later for her to make a decision. But she does not want to realize the urgency; she concerns herself only with what is respectful and discreet in the attitude of her companion. She does not apprehend this conduct as an attempt to achieve what we call "the first approach;" that is, she does not want to see possibilities of temporal development which his conduct presents. She restricts this behavior to what is in the present; she does not wish to read in the phrases which he addresses to her anything other than their explicit meaning. If he says to her, "I find you so attractive!" she disarms this phrase of its sexual background; she attaches to the conversation and to the behavior of the speaker, the immediate meanings, which she imagines as objective qualities. The man who is speaking to her appears to her sincere and respectful as the table is round or square, as the wall coloring is blue or gray. The qualities thus attached to the person she is listening to are in this way fixed in a permanence like that of things, which is no other than the projection of the strict present of the qualities into the temporal flux. This is because she does not quite know what she wants. She is profoundly aware of the desire which she inspires, but the desire cruel and naked would humiliate and horrify her. Yet she would find no charm in a respect which would be only respect. In order to satisfy her, there must be a feeling which is addressed wholly to her personality—i.e., to her full freedom—and which would be a recognition of her freedom. But at the same time this feeling must be wholly desire; that is, it must address itself to her body as object. This time then she refuses to apprehend the desire for what it is; she does not even give it a name; she recognizes it only to the extent that it transcends itself toward admiration, esteem, respect and that it is wholly absorbed in the more refined forms which it produces, to the extent of no longer figuring anymore but as a sort of warmth and density. Now suppose he takes her hand. This act of her companion risks changing the situation by calling for an immediate decision. To leave the hand there is to consent in herself to flirt, to engage herself. To withdraw it is to break the troubled and unstable harmony which gives the hour its charm. The aim is to postpone the moment of decision as long as possible. We know what happens next; the young woman leaves her hand there, but she *does not notice* that she is leaving it. She does not notice because it happens by chance that she is at this moment all intellect. She draws her companion up to the most lofty regions of sentimental speculation; she speaks of Life, of her life, she shows herself in her essential aspect— a personality, a consciousness. And during this time the divorce of the body from the soul is accomplished; the hand rests inert between the warm hands of her companion—neither consenting nor resisting—a thing.

We shall say that this woman is in bad faith. But we see immediately that she uses various procedures in order to maintain herself in this bad faith. She has disarmed the actions of her companion by reducing them to being only what they are; that is, to existing in the mode of the in-itself. But she permits herself to enjoy his desire, to the extent that she will apprehend it as not being what it is, will recognize its transcendence. Finally while sensing profoundly the presence of her own body—to the degree of being disturbed perhaps—she realizes herself as *not being* her own body, and she contemplates it as though from above as a passive object to which events can *happen* but which can neither provoke them nor avoid them because all its possibilities are outside of it. What unity do we find in these various aspects of bad faith? It is a certain art of forming contradictory concepts which unite in themselves both an idea and the negation of that idea. The basic concept which is thus engendered, utilizes the double property of the human being, who *is* at once a *facticity* and a *transcendence*. These two aspects of human reality are and ought to be capable of a valid coordination. But bad faith does not wish either to coordinate them nor to surmount them in a synthesis. Bad faith seeks to affirm their identity while preserving their differences. It must affirm facticity as *being* transcendence and transcendence as *being* facticity, in such a way that at the instant when a person apprehends the one, he can find himself abruptly faced with the other.

We can find the prototype of formulae of bad faith in certain famous expressions which have been rightly conceived to produce their whole effect in a spirit of bad faith. Take for example the title of a work by Jacques Chardonne, *Love Is Much More than Love*.[4] We see here how unity is established

---

[4] *L'amour, c'est beaucoup plus que l'amour.*

between *present* love in its facticity—"the contact of two skins," sensuality, egoism, Proust's mechanism of jealousy, Adler's battle of the *sexes, etc.*—and love as transcendence—Mauriac's "river of fire," the longing for the infinite, Plato's *eros*, Lawrence's deep cosmic intuition, *etc.* Here we leave facticity to find ourselves suddenly beyond the present and the factual condition of man, beyond the psychological, in the heart of metaphysics. On the other hand, the title of a play by Sarment, I *Am Too Great for Myself*,[5] which also presents characters in bad faith, throws us first into full transcendence in order suddenly to imprison us within the narrow limits of our factual essence. We will discover this structure again in the famous sentence: "He has become what he was" or in its no less famous opposite: "Eternity at last changes each man into himself."[6] It is well understood that these various formulae have only the appearance of bad faith; they have been conceived in this paradoxical form explicitly to shock the mind and discountenance it by an enigma. But it is precisely this appearance which is of concern to us. What counts here is that the formulae do not constitute new, solidly structured ideas; on the contrary, they are formed so as to remain in perpetual disintegration and so that we may slide at any time from naturalistic present to transcendence and *vice versa*.

We can see the use which bad faith can make of these judgments which all aim at establishing that I am not what I am. If I were only what I *am*, I could, for example, seriously consider an adverse criticism which someone makes of me, question myself scrupulously, and perhaps be compelled to recognize the truth in it. But thanks to transcendence, I am not subject to all that I am. I do not even have to discuss the soundness of the reproach. As Suzanne says to Figaro, "To prove that I am right would be to recognize that I can be wrong." I am on a plane where no reproach can touch me since what I really am is my transcendence. I flee from myself, I escape myself, I leave my tattered garment in the hands of the fault-finder. But the ambiguity necessary for bad faith comes from the fact that I affirm here that I *am* my transcendence in the mode of being of a thing. It is only thus, in fact, that I can feel that I escape all reproaches. It is in this sense that our young woman purifies the desire of anything humiliating by pretending to consider it only as transcendence, which allows her to avoid even naming it. But inversely "I Am Too Great for Myself," while showing our transcendence changed into facticity, is the source of an infinity of excuses for our failures or our weaknesses. Similarly the young coquette maintains transcendence to the extent that the respect, the esteem manifested by the actions of her admirer are already on the plane of the transcendent. But she arrests this transcendence, she glues it down with

---

[5] *Je suis trop grand pour moi.*
[6] *Il est devenu ce qu'il était.*
*Tel qu'en lui-même enfin l'éternité le change.*

all the facticity of the present; respect is nothing other than respect, it is an arrested surpassing which no longer surpasses itself toward anything.

But although this *metastable* concept of "transcendence-facticity" is one of the most basic instruments of bad faith, it is not the only one of its kind. We can equally well use another kind of duplicity derived from human reality which we will express roughly by saying that its being-for-itself implies complementarily a being-for-others. Upon any one of my conducts it is always possible to converge two looks, mine and that of the Other. The conduct will not present exactly the same structure in each case. But as we shall see later, as each look perceives it, there is between these two aspects of my being, no difference between appearance and being—as if I were to my self the truth of myself and as if the Other possessed only a deformed image of me. The equal dignity of my being-for-others and my being-for-myself permits a perpetually disintegrating synthesis and a perpetual game of escape from the for-itself to the for-others and from the for-others to the for-itself. We have seen also the use which our young lady made of our being-in-the-midst-of-the-world—i.e., of our inert presence as a passive object among other objects—in order to relieve herself suddenly from the functions of her being-in-the-world—that is, from the being which causes there to be a world by projecting itself beyond the world toward its own possibilities. Let us note finally the confusing syntheses which play on the nihilating ambiguity of the three temporal ekstases, affirming at once that I am what I have been (the man who deliberately *arrests himself* at one period in his life and refuses to take into consideration the later changes) and that I am not what I have been (the man who in the face of reproaches or rancor dissociates himself from his past by insisting on his freedom and on his perpetual re-creation). In all these concepts, which have only a transitive role in the reasoning and which are eliminated from the conclusion, (like imaginary numbers in the calculations of physicists), we find again the same structure. We have to deal with human reality as a being which is what it is not and which is not what it is.

But what exactly is necessary in order for these concepts of disintegration to be able to receive even a pretence of existence, in order for them to be able to appear for an instant to consciousness, even in a process of evanescence? A quick examination of the idea of sincerity, the antithesis of bad faith, will be very instructive in this connection. Actually sincerity presents itself as a demand and consequently is not a *state*. Now what is the ideal to be attained in this case? It is necessary that a man be *for himself* only what he *is*. But is this not precisely the definition of the in-itself—or if you prefer—the principle of identity? To posit as an ideal the being of things, is this not to assert by the same stroke that this being does not belong to human reality and that the principle of identity, far from being a universal axiom universally applied, is only a synthetic principle enjoying a merely regional universality? Thus in order that the concepts of bad faith can put us under illusion at least for an instant, in order that the candor of "pure hearts" (cf. Gide, Kessel) can have validity for human reality as an ideal, the principle of identity must not represent a constitutive principle of human reality and human reality must not be necessarily what it is but must be able to be what it is not. What does this mean?

If man is what he is, bad faith is for ever impossible and candor ceases to be his ideal and becomes instead his being. But is man what he is? And more generally, how can he be what he is when he exists as consciousness of being? If candor or sincerity is a universal value, it is evident that the maxim "one must be what one is" does not serve solely as a regulating principle for judgments and concepts by which I express what I am. It posits not merely an ideal of knowing but an ideal of being; it proposes for us an absolute equivalence of being with itself as a prototype of being. In this sense it is necessary that we make ourselves what we are. But what are we then if we have the constant obligation to make ourselves what we are, if our mode of being is having the obligation to be what we are?

Let us consider this waiter in the café. His movement is quick and forward, a little too precise, a little too rapid. He comes toward the customers with a step a little too quick. He bends forward a little too eagerly; his voice, his eyes express an interest a little too solicitous for the order of the client. Finally there he returns, trying to imitate in his walk the inflexible stiffness of some kind of automaton while carrying his tray with the recklessness of a tight-rope-walker by putting it in a perpetually unstable, perpetually broken equilibrium which he perpetually reestablishes by a light movement of the arm and hand. All his behavior seems to us a game. He applies himself to linking his movements as if they were mechanisms, the one regulating the other; his gestures and even his voice seem to be mechanisms; he gives himself the quickness and pitiless rapidity of things. He is playing, he is amusing himself. But what is he playing? We need not watch long before we can explain it: he is playing at being a waiter in a café. There is nothing there to surprise us. The game is a kind of marking out and investigation. The child plays with his body in order to explore it, to take inventory of it; the waiter in the café plays with his condition in order to realize it. This obligation is not different from that which is imposed on all tradesmen. Their condition is wholly one of ceremony. The public demands of them that they realize it as a ceremony; there is the dance of the grocer, of the tailor, of the auctioneer, by which they endeavour to persuade their clientele that they are nothing but a grocer, an auctioneer, a tailor. A grocer who dreams is offensive to the buyer, because such a grocer is not wholly a grocer. Society demands that he limit himself to his function as a grocer, just as the soldier at attention makes himself into a soldier-thing with a straight look which does not see at all, which is no longer meant to see, since it is the rule and not the interest of the moment which determines the point he must fix his eyes on (the sight "fixed at ten paces"). There are indeed many precautions to imprison a man in what he is, as if we lived in perpetual fear that he might escape from it, that he might break away and suddenly elude his condition.

In a parallel situation, from within, the waiter in the café can not be immediately a café waiter in the sense that this inkwell is an inkwell, or the glass is a glass. It is by no means that he can not form reflective judgments or concepts concerning his condition. He knows well what it "means:" the obligation of getting up at five o'clock, of sweeping the floor of the shop before the restaurant opens, of starting the coffee pot going, *etc.* He knows the rights which it allows: the right to the tips, the right to belong to a union, etc. But all these concepts, all these judgments refer to the transcendent. It is a matter of abstract possibilities, of rights and duties conferred on a "person possessing rights." And it is precisely this person *who I have to be* (if I am the waiter in question) and who I am not. It is not that I do not wish to be this person or that I want this person to be different. But rather there is no common measure between his being and mine. It is a "representation" for others and for myself, which means that I can be he only in *representation.* But if I represent myself as him, I am not he; I am separated from him as the object from the subject, separated *by nothing,* but this nothing isolates me from him. I can not be he, I can only play at *being* him; that is, imagine to myself that I am he. And thereby I affect him with nothingness. In vain do I fulfill the functions of a café waiter. I can be he only in the neutralized mode, as the actor is Hamlet, by mechanically making the *typical gestures* of my state and by aiming at myself as an imaginary café waiter through those gestures taken as an "analogon."[7] What I attempt to realize is a being-in-itself of the café waiter, as if it were not in my power to confer value and urgency upon my duties and the rights of my position, as if it were not my free choice to get up each morning at five o'clock or to remain in bed, even though it meant getting fired. As if from the very fact that I sustain this role in existence I did not transcend it on every side, as if I did not constitute myself as one *beyond* my condition. Yet there is no doubt that I *am* in a sense a café waiter—otherwise could I not just as well call myself a diplomat or a reporter? But if I am one, this can not be in the mode of being in-itself. I am a waiter in the mode of *being what I am not.*

We are dealing with more than mere social positions; I am never any one of my attitudes, any one of my actions. The glib speaker is the one who *plays* at speaking, because he can not be *speaking.* The attentive pupil who wishes

---

[7] Cf. *L'Imaginaire,* N.R.F., 1940. Conclusion.

to be attentive, his eyes riveted on the teacher, his ears open wide, so exhausts himself in playing the attentive role that he ends up by no longer hearing anything. Perpetually absent to my body, to my acts, I am despite myself that "divine absence" of which Valéry speaks. I can not say either that I *am* here or that I *am* not here, in the sense that we say "that box of matches *is* on the table;" this would be to confuse my "being-in-the-world" with a "being-in the midst of the world." Nor that I *am* standing, nor that I *am* seated; this would be to confuse my body with the idiosyncratic totality of which it is only one of the structures. On all sides I escape being and yet—I am.

But take a mode of being which concerns only myself: I am sad. One might think that surely I am the sadness in the mode of being what I am. What is the sadness, however, if not the intentional unity which comes to reassemble and animate the totality of my conduct? It is the meaning of this dull look with which I view the world, of my bowed shoulders, of my lowered head, of the listlessness in my whole body. But at the very moment when I adopt each of these attitudes, do I not know that I shall not be able to hold on to it? Let a stranger suddenly appear and I will lift up my head, I will assume a lively cheerfulness. What will remain of my sadness except that I obligingly promise it an appointment for later after the departure of the visitor? Moreover is not this sadness itself a *conduct*? Is it not consciousness which affects itself with sadness as a magical recourse against a situation too urgent?[8] And in this case even, should we not say that being sad means first to make oneself sad? That may be, someone will say, but after all doesn't giving oneself the being of sadness mean to *receive* this being? It makes no difference from where I receive it. The fact is that a consciousness which affects itself with sadness *is* sad precisely for this reason. But it is difficult to comprehend the nature of consciousness; the being-sad is not a ready-made being which I give to myself as I can give this book to my friend. I do not possess the property of *affecting myself with being.* If I make myself sad, I must continue to make myself sad from beginning to end. I can not treat my sadness as an impulse finally achieved and put it on file without recreating it, nor can I carry it in the manner of an inert body which continues its movement after the initial shock. There is no inertia in consciousness. If I make myself sad, it is because I *am* not sad—the being of the sadness escapes me by and in the very act by which I affect myself with it. The being-in-itself of sadness perpetually haunts my consciousness (of) being sad, but it is as a value which I can not realize; it stands as a regulative meaning of my sadness, not as its constitutive modality.

---

[8] *Esquisse d'une théorie des émotions.* Hermann, Paris. In English. *The Emotions. Outline of a Theory.* Philosophical Library. 1948.

Shall we say that my consciousness at least *is*, whatever may be the object or the state of which it makes itself consciousness? But how do we distinguish my consciousness (of) being sad from sadness? Is it not all one? It is true in a way that my consciousness *is*, if one means by this that for another it is a part of the totality of being on which judgments can be brought to bear. But it should be noted, as Husserl clearly understood, that my consciousness appears originally to the Other as an absence. It is the object always present as the *meaning* of all my attitudes and all my conduct—and always absent, for it gives itself to the intuition of another as a perpetual question—still better, as a perpetual freedom. When Pierre looks at me, I know of course that he is looking at me. His eyes, things in the world, are fixed on my body, a thing in the world—that is the objective fact of which I can say: it *is*. But it is also a fact *in the world*. The meaning of this look is not a fact in the world, and this is what makes me uncomfortable. Although I make smiles, promises, threats, nothing can get hold of the approbation, the free judgment which I seek; I know that it is always beyond. I feel it in my conducts, which are no longer like those of a *worker* toward the things he uses; these conducts, to the extent I connect them to the Other, become, for myself, mere *presentations*; they await being constituted as graceful or uncouth, sincere or insincere, *etc.*, by an apprehension which is always beyond my efforts to provoke, an apprehension which will be provoked by my efforts only if of itself it lends them force (that is, only in so far as it causes itself to be provoked from the outside), *which is its own mediator with the transcendent*. Thus the objective fact of the being-in-itself of the consciousness of the Other is posited in order to disappear in negativity and in freedom: consciousness of the Other is as not-being; its being-in-itself "here and now" is not-to-be.

*Consciousness of the Other is what it is not.*

Furthermore the being of my own consciousness does not appear to me as the consciousne of the Other. It *is* because it makes itself, since its being is consciousness of being. But this means that making sustains being; consciousness has to be its own being, it is never sustained by being; it sustains being in the heart of subjectivity, which means once again that it is inhabited by being but that it is not being: *consciousness is not what it is.*

Under these conditions what can be the significance of the ideal of sincerity except as a task impossible to achieve, of which the very meaning is in contradiction with the structure of my consciousness. To be sincere, we said, is to be what one is. That supposes that I am not originally what I am. But here naturally Kant's "You ought, therefore you can" is implicitly understood. I can *become* sincere; this is what my duty and my effort to achieve sincerity imply. But we definitely establish that the original structure of "not being what one is" renders impossible in advance all movement toward being in itself or "being what one is." And this impossibility is not hidden from consciousness; on the contrary, it is the very stuff of consciousness; it is the embarrasing constraint which we constantly experience; it is our very incapacity to recognize ourselves, to constitute ourselves as being what we are. It is this necessity which means that, as soon as we posit ourselves as a certain being, by a legitimate judgment, based on inner experience or correctly deduced from *a priori* or empirical premises, then by that very positing we surpass this being—and that not toward another being but toward emptiness, toward *nothing*.

How then can we blame another for not being sincere or rejoice in our own sincerity since this sincerity appears to us at the same time to be impossible? How can we in conversation, in confession, in introspection, even attempt sincerity since the effort will by its very nature be doomed to failure and since at the very time when we announce it we have a prejudicative comprehension of its futility? Through introspection I intend to determine exactly what I am, and to be it plainly—even though it means consequently to set about searching for ways to change myself. But what does this mean if not that I am constituting myself as a thing? Shall I determine the ensemble of purposes and motivations which have pushed me to do this or that action? But this is already to postulate a causal determinism which constitutes the flow of my states of consciousness as a succession of physical states. Shall I detect in myself "drives," even though it be to affirm them in shame? But is this not deliberately to forget that these drives are realized with my consent, that they are not forces of nature but that I lend them their efficacy by a perpetually renewed decision concerning their value? Shall I pass judgment on my character, on my nature? Is this not to veil from myself at that moment what I know only too well, that I thus judge a past to which by definition my present is not subject? The proof of this is that the same man who in sincerity posits that he is what in actuality he was, is indignant at the reproach of another and tries to disarm it by asserting that he can no longer be what he was. We are readily astonished and upset when the penalties of the court affect a man who in his new freedom is *no longer* the guilty person he was. But at the same time we require of this man that he recognize himself as *being* this guilty one. What then is sincerity except precisely a phenomenon of bad faith? Have we not shown indeed that in bad faith human reality is constituted as a being which is what it is not and which is not what it is?

Let us take an example: A homosexual frequently has an intolerable feeling of guilt, and his whole existence is determined in relation to this feeling. One will readily foresee that he is in bad faith. In fact it frequently happens that this man, while recognizing his homosexual inclination, while avowing each and every particular misdeed which he has committed, refuses with all his strength to consider himself "*a paederast.*" His case is always "different," peculiar; there enters into it something of a game, of chance, of bad luck; the mistakes are all in the past; they are explained by a certain conception of the beautiful which women can not satisfy; we should see in them the results of a restless search, rather than the manifestations of a deeply rooted tendency, *etc., etc.* Here is assuredly a man in bad faith who borders on the comic since, acknowledging all the facts which are imputed to him, he refuses to draw from them the conclusion which they impose. His friend, who is his most severe critic, becomes irritated with this duplicity. The critic asks only one thing—and perhaps then he will show himself indulgent: that the guilty one recognize himself as guilty, that the homosexual declare frankly—whether humbly or boastfully matters little—"I am a paederast." We ask here: Who is in bad faith? The homosexual or the champion of sincerity?

The homosexual recognizes his faults, but he struggles with all his strength against the crushing view that his mistakes constitute for him a *destiny*. He does not wish to let himself be considered as a thing. He has an obscure but strong feeling that an homosexual is not an homosexual as this table is a table or as this red-haired man is red-haired. It seems to him that he has escaped from each mistake as soon as he has posited it and recognized it; he even feels that the psychic duration by itself cleanses him from each misdeed, constitutes for him an undetermined future, causes him to be born anew. Is he wrong? Does he not recognize in himself the peculiar, irreducible character of human reality? His attitude includes then an undeniable comprehension of truth. But at the same time he needs this perpetual rebirth, this constant escape in order to live; he must constantly put himself beyond reach in order to avoid the terrible judgment of collectivity. Thus he plays on the word *being*. He would be right actually if he understood the phrase, "I am not a paederast" in the sense of "I am not what I am." That is, if he declared to himself, "To the extent that a pattern of conduct is defined as the conduct of a paederast and to the extent that I have adopted this conduct, I am a paederast. But to the extent that human reality can not be finally defined by patterns of conduct, I am not one." But instead he slides surreptitiously towards a different connotation of the word "being." He understands "not being" in the sense of "not-being-in-itself." He lays claim to "not being a paederast" in the sense in which this table is *not* an inkwell. He is in bad faith.

But the champion of sincerity is not ignorant of the transcendence of human reality, and he knows when necessary how to appeal to it for his own advantage. He makes use of it even and brings it up in the present argument. Does he not wish, first in the name of sincerity, then of freedom, that the homosexual reflect on himself and acknowledge himself as an homosexual? Does he not let the other understand that such a confession will win indulgence for him? What does this mean if not that the man who will acknowledge himself as an homosexual will no longer be the *same* as the homosexual whom he acknowledges being and that he will escape into the region of freedom and of good will? The critic asks the man then to be what he is in order no longer to be what he is. It is the profound meaning of the saying, "A sin confessed is half pardoned." The critic demands of the guilty one that he constitute himself as a thing, precisely in order no longer to treat him as a thing. And this contradiction is constitutive of the demand of sincerity. Who can not see how offensive to the Other and how reassuring for me is a statement such as, "He's just a paederast," which removes a disturbing freedom from a trait and which aims at henceforth constituting all the acts of the Other as consequences following strictly from his essence. That is actually what the critic is demanding of his victim—that he constitute himself as a thing, that he should entrust his freedom to his friend as a fief, in order that the friend should return it to him subsequently—like a suzerain to his vassal. The champion of sincerity is in bad faith to the degree that he wants to reassure himself, while pretending to judge, to the extent that he demands that freedom as freedom constitute itself as a thing. We have here only one episode in that battle to the death of consciousnesses which Hegel calls "the relation of the master and the slave." A person appeals to another and demands that in the name of his nature as consciousness he should radically destroy himself as consciousness, but while making this appeal he leads the other to hope for a rebirth beyond this destruction.

Very well, someone will say, but our man is abusing sincerity, playing one side against the other. We should not look for sincerity in the relation of the Mit-sein but rather where it is pure—in the relations of a person with himself. But who can not see that objective sincerity is constituted in the same way? Who can not see that the sincere man constitutes himself as a thing in order to escape the condition of a thing by the same act of sincerity? The man who confesses that he is evil has exchanged his disturbing "freedom-for-evil" for an inanimate character of evil; he is evil, he clings to himself, he is what he is. But by the same stroke, he escapes from that thing, since it is he who contemplates it, since it depends on him to maintain it under his glance or to let it collapse in an infinity of particular acts. He derives a merit from his sincerity, and the deserving man is not the evil man as he is evil but as he is beyond his evilness. At the same time the evil is disarmed since it is nothing, save on the plane of determinism, and since in confessing it, I posit my freedom in respect to it; my future is virgin; everything is allowed to me.

Thus the essential structure of sincerity does not differ from that of bad faith since the sincere man constitutes himself as what he is in order not to be it. This explains the truth recognized by all that one can fall into bad faith through being sincere. As Valéry pointed out, this is the case with Stendhal. Total, constant sincerity as a constant effort to adhere to oneself is by nature a constant effort to dissociate oneself from oneself. A person frees himself from himself by the very act by which he makes himself an object for himself. To draw up a perpetual inventory of what one is means constantly to redeny oneself and to take refuge in a sphere where one is no longer anything but a pure, free regard. The goal of bad faith, as we said, is to put oneself out of reach; it is an escape. Now we see that we must use the same terms to define sincerity. What does this mean?

In the final analysis the goal of sincerity and the goal of bad faith are not so different. To be sure, there is a sincerity which bears on the past and which does not concern us here; I am sincere if I confess *having had* this pleasure or that intention. We shall see that if this sincerity is possible, it is because in his fall into the past, the being of man is constituted as a being-in-itself. But here our concern is only with the sincerity which aims at itself in present immanence. What is its goal? To bring me to confess to myself what I am in order that I may finally coincide with my being; in a word, to cause myself to be, in the mode of the in-itself, what I am in the mode of "not being what I am." Its assumption is that fundamentally I am already, in the mode of the in-itself, what I have to be. Thus we find at the base of sincerity a continual game of mirror and reflection, a perpetual passage from the being which is what it is, to the being which is not what it is and inversely from the being which is not what it is to the being which is what it is. And what is the goal of bad faith? To cause me to be what I am, in the mode of "not being what one is," or not to be what I am in the mode of "being what one is." We find here the same game of mirrors. In fact in order for me to have an intention of sincerity, I must at the outset simultaneously be and not be what I am. Sincerity does not assign to me a mode of being or a particular quality, but in relation to that quality it aims at making me pass from one mode of being to another mode of being. This second mode of being, the ideal of sincerity, I am prevented by nature from attaining; and at the very moment when I struggle to attain it, I have a vague prejudicative comprehension that I shall not attain it. But all the same, in order for me to be able to conceive an intention in bad faith, I must have such a nature that within my being I escape from my being. If I were sad or cowardly in the way in which this inkwell is an inkwell, the possibility of bad faith could not even be conceived. Not only should I be unable to escape from my being; I could not even imagine that I could escape from it. But if bad faith is possible, merely as a project, it is precisely because, so far as my being is concerned, there is no clear distinction between being and non-being.

Bad faith is possible only because sincerity is conscious of missing its goal inevitably, due to its very nature. I can try to apprehend myself as "*not being cowardly*," when I *am* so, only on condition that the "being cowardly" is itself "in question" at the very moment when it exists, on condition that it is itself *one* question, that at the very moment when I wish to apprehend it, it escapes me on all sides and annihilates itself. The condition under which I can attempt an effort in bad faith is that in one sense, I *am not* this coward which I do not wish to be. But if I *were* not cowardly in the simple mode of not-being-what-one-is-not, I would be "in good faith" by declaring that I am not cowardly. Thus this inapprehensible coward is evanescent; in order for me not to be cowardly, I must in some way also be cowardly. That does not mean that I must be "a little" cowardly, in the sense that "a little" signifies "to a certain degree cowardly—and not cowardly to a certain degree." No. I must at once both be and not be totally and in all respects a coward. Thus in this case bad faith requires that I should not be what I am; that is, that there be an imponderable difference separating being from non-being in the mode of being of human reality.

But bad faith is not restricted to denying the qualities which I possess, to not seeing the being which I am. It attempts also to constitute myself as being what I am not. It apprehends me positively as courageous when I am not so. And that is possible, once again, only if I am what I am not; that is, if non-being in me does not have being even as non-being. Of course necessarily I *am not* courageous; otherwise bad faith would not be *bad* faith. But in addition my effort in bad faith must include the ontological comprehension that even in my usual being what I *am*, I am not it really and that there is no such difference between the being of "being-sad," for example—which I *am* in the mode of not being what I am—and the "non-being" of not-being-courageous which I wish to hide from myself. Moreover it is particularly requisite that the very negation of being should be itself the object of a perpetual nihilation, that the very meaning of "non-being" be perpetually in question in human reality. If I *were not* courageous in the way in which this inkwell is not a table; that is, if I were isolated in my cowardice, stuck to it, incapable of putting it in relation to its opposite, if I were not capable of *determining* myself as cowardly—that is, to *deny* courage to myself and thereby to escape my cowardice in the very moment that I posit it—if it were not on principle *impossible* for me to coincide with my *not-being-courageous* as well as with my being-courageous—then any project of bad faith would be impossible for me. Thus in order for bad faith to be possible, sincerity itself must be in bad faith. The condition of the possibility for bad faith is that human reality, in its most immediate being, in the intrastructure of the pre-reflective *cogito*, must be what it is not and not be what it is.

## III. THE "FAITH" OF BAD FAITH

We have indicated for the moment only those conditions which render bad faith conceivable, the structures of being which permit us to form concepts of bad faith. We can not limit ourselves to these considerations; we have not yet distinguished bad faith from lying. The two-faced concepts which we have described would without a doubt be utilized by a liar to discountenance his questioner, although their two-faced quality being established on the being of man and not on some empirical circumstance, can and ought to be evident to all. The true problem of bad faith stems evidently from the fact that bad faith is *faith*. It can not be either a cynical lie or certainty—if certainty is the intuitive possession of the object. But if we take belief as meaning the adherence of being to its object when the object is not given or is given indistinctly, then bad faith is belief; and the essential problem of bad faith is a problem of belief.

How can we believe by bad faith in the concepts which we forge expressly to persuade ourselves? We must note in fact that the project of bad faith must be itself in bad faith. I am not only in bad faith at the end of my effort when I have constructed my two-faced concepts and when I have persuaded myself. In truth, I have not persuaded myself; to the extent that I could be so persuaded, I have always been so. And at the very moment when I was disposed to put myself in bad faith, I of necessity was in bad faith with respect to this same disposition. For me to have represented it to myself as bad faith would have been cynicism; to believe it sincerely innocent would have been in good faith. The decision to be in bad faith does not dare to speak its name; it believes itself and does not believe itself in bad faith; it believes itself and does not believe itself in good faith. It is this which from the upsurge of bad faith, determines the later attitude and, as it were, the *Weltanschauung* of bad faith.

Bad faith does not hold the norms and criteria of truth as they are accepted by the critical thought of good faith. What it decides first, in fact, is the nature of truth. With bad faith a truth appears, a method of thinking, a type of being which is like that of objects; the ontological characteristic of the world of bad faith with which the subject suddenly surrounds himself is this: that here being is what it is not, and is not what it is. Consequently a peculiar type of evidence appears; *non-persuasive* evidence. Bad faith apprehends evidence but it is resigned in advance to not being fulfilled by this evidence, to not being persuaded and transformed into good faith. It makes itself humble and modest; it is not ignorant, it says, that faith is decision and that after each intuition, it must decide and *will what it is*. Thus bad faith in its primitive project and in its coming into the world decides on the exact nature of its requirements. It stands forth in the firm resolution *not to demand too much*, to count itself satisfied when it is barely persuaded, to force itself in decisions to adhere to uncertain truths. This original project of bad faith is a decision in bad faith on the nature of faith. Let us understand clearly that there is no question of a reflective, voluntary *decision*, but of a spontaneous determination of our being. One puts *oneself* in bad faith as one goes to sleep and one is in bad faith as one dreams. Once this mode of being has been realized, it is as difficult to get out of it as to wake oneself up; bad faith is a type of being in the world, like waking or dreaming, which by itself tends to perpetuate itself, although its structure is of the *metastable* type. But bad faith is conscious of its structure, and it has taken precautions by deciding that the metastable structure is the structure of being and that non-persuasion is the structure of all convictions. It follows that if bad faith is faith and if it includes in its original project its own negation (it determines itself to be not quite convinced in order to convince itself that I am what I am not), then to start with, a faith which wishes itself to be not quite convinced must be possible. What are the conditions for the possibility of such a faith?

I believe that my friend Pierre feels friendship for me. I believe it in *good faith*. I believe it but I do not have for it any self-evident intuition, for the nature of the object does not lend itself to intuition. I *believe* it; that is, I allow myself to give in to all impulses to trust it; I decide to believe in it, and to maintain myself in this decision; I conduct myself, finally, as if I were certain of it—and all this in the synthetic unity of one and the same attitude. This which I define as good faith is what Hegel would call the *immediate*. It is simple faith. Hegel would demonstrate at once that the immediate calls for mediation and that belief by becoming *belief for itself*, passes to the state of non-belief. If I *believe* that my friend Pierre likes me, this means that his friendship appears to me as the meaning of all his acts. Belief is a particular consciousness of the *meaning* of Pierre's acts. But if I know that I believe, the belief appears to me as pure subjective determination without external correlative. This is what makes the very word "to believe" a term utilized indifferently to indicate the unwavering firmness of belief ("My God, I believe in you") and its character as disarmed and strictly subjective. ("Is Pierre my friend? I do not know; I believe so.") But the nature of consciousness is such that in it the mediate and the immediate are one and the same being. To believe is to know that one believes, and to know that one believes is no longer to believe. Thus to believe is not to believe any longer because that is only to believe—this in the unity of one and the same non-thetic self-consciousness. To be sure, we have here forced the description of the phenomenon by designating it with the word to know; non-thetic consciousness is not to know. But it is in its very translucency at the origin of all knowing. Thus the non-thetic consciousness (of) believing is destructive of belief. But at the same time the very law of the pre-reflective *cogito* implies that the being of believing ought to be the consciousness of believing.

Thus belief is a being which questions its own being, which can realize itself only in its destruction, which can manifest itself to itself only by denying itself. It is a being for which to be is to appear and to appear is to deny itself. To believe is not-to-believe. We see the reason for it; the being of consciousness is to exist by itself, then to make itself be and thereby to pass beyond itself. In this sense consciousness is perpetually escaping itself, belief becomes non-belief, the immediate becomes mediation, the absolute becomes relative, and the relative becomes absolute. The ideal of good faith (to believe what one believes) is, like that of sincerity (to be what one is), an ideal of being-in-itself. Every belief is a belief that falls short; one never wholly believes what one believes. Consequently the primitive project of bad faith is only the utilization of this self-destruction of the fact of consciousness. If every belief in good faith is an impossible belief, then there is a place for every impossible belief. My inability to *believe* that I am courageous will not discourage me since every belief involves not quite believing. I shall define this impossible belief as *my* belief. To be sure, I shall not be able to hide from myself that I believe in order not to believe and that I do not believe *in order to* believe. But the subtle, total annihilation of bad faith by itself can not surprise me; it exists at the basis of all faith. What is it then? At the moment when I wish to *believe* myself courageous do I know that I am a coward? And this certitude, would it come and destroy my belief? But *first*, I *am* not any more courageous than cowardly, if we are to understand this in the mode of being of the-in-itself. In the second place, I do not *know* that I am courageous; such a view of myself can be accompanied only by *belief*, for it surpasses pure reflective certitude. In the third place, it is very true that bad faith does not succeed in believing what it wishes to believe. But it is precisely as the acceptance of not believing what it believes that it is bad faith. Good faith wishes to flee the "not-believing-what-one-believes" by finding refuge in being. Bad faith flees being by taking refuge in "not-believing-what-one-believes." It has disarmed all beliefs in advance—those which it would like to take hold of and, by the same stroke, the others, those which it wishes to flee. In willing this self-destruction of belief, from which science escapes by searching for evidence, it ruins the beliefs which are opposed to it, which reveal themselves as *being only* belief. Thus we can better understand the original phenomenon of bad faith.

In bad faith there is no cynical lie nor knowing preparation for deceitful concepts. But the first act of bad faith is to flee what it can not flee, to flee what it is. The very project of flight reveals to bad faith an inner disintegration in the heart of being, and it is this disintegration which bad faith wishes to be. In truth, the two immediate attitudes which we can take in the face of our being are conditioned by the very nature of this being and its immediate relation with the in-itself. Good faith seeks to flee the inner disintegration of my being in the direction of the in-itself which it should be and is not. Bad faith seeks to flee the in-itself by means of the inner disintegration of my being. But it denies this very disintegration as it denies that it is itself bad faith. Bad faith seeks by means of "not-being-what-one-is" to escape from the in-itself which I am not in the mode of being what one is not. It denies itself as bad faith and aims at the in-itself which I am not in the mode of "not-being-what-one-is-not."[9] If bad faith is possible, it is because it is an immediate, permanent threat to every project of the human being; it is because consciousness conceals in its being a permanent risk of bad faith. The origin of this risk is the fact that the nature of consciousness simultaneously is to be what it is not and not to be what it is. In the light of these remarks we can now approach the ontological study of consciousness, not as the totality of the human being, but as the instantaneous nucleus of this being.

[9] If it is indifferent whether one is in good or in bad faith, because bad faith reapprehends good faith and creeps to the very origin of the project of good faith, that does not mean that we can not radically escape bad faith. But this supposes a self-recovery of being which was previously corrupted. This self-recovery we shall call authenticity, the description of which has no place here.

# Part II

Being-for-Itself

# 1

## IMMEDIATE STRUCTURES OF THE FOR-ITSELF

### I. PRESENCE TO SELF

Negation has referred us to freedom, freedom to bad faith, and bad faith to the being of consciousness, which is the requisite condition for the possibility of bad faith. In the light of the requirements which we have established in the preceding chapters, we must now resume the description which we attempted in the Introduction of this work; that is, we must return to the plane of the pre-reflective *cogito*. Now the *cogito* never gives out anything other than what we ask of it. Descartes questioned it concerning its functional aspect—"*I doubt, I think.*" And because he wished to pass without a conducting thread from this functional aspect to existential dialectic, he fell into the error of substance. Husserl, warned by this error, remained timidly on the plane of functional description. Due to this fact he never passed beyond the pure description of the appearance as such; he has shut himself up inside the *cogito* and deserves—in spite of his denial—to be called a phenomenalist rather than a phenomenologist. His phenomenalism at every moment borders on Kantian idealism. Heidegger, wishing to avoid that descriptive phenomenalism which leads to the Megarian, antidialectic isolation of essences, begins with the existential analytic without going through the *cogito*. But since the *Dasein* has from the start been deprived of the dimension of consciousness, it can never regain this dimension. Heidegger endows human reality with a self-understanding which he defines as an "ekstatic pro-ject" of its own possibilities. It is certainly not my intention to deny the existence of this project. But how could there be an understanding which would not in itself be the consciousness (of) being understanding? This ekstatic character of human reality will lapse into a thing-like, blind in-itself unless it arises from the consciousness of ekstasis. In truth the *cogito* must be our point of departure, but we can say of it, parodying a famous saying, that it leads us only on condition that we get out of it. Our preceding study, which concerned the conditions for the possibility of certain types of conduct, had as its goal only to place us in a position to question the *cogito* about its being and to furnish us with the dialectic instrument which would enable us to find in the *cogito* itself the means of escaping from instantaneity toward the totality of being which constitutes human reality. Let us return now to description of non-thetic self-consciousness; let us examine its results and ask what it means for consciousness that it must necessarily be what it is not and not be what it is.

"The being of consciousness," we said in the Introduction, "is a being such that in its being, its being is in question." This means that the being of consciousness does not coincide with itself in a full equivalence. Such equivalence, which is that of the in-itself, is expressed by this simple formula: being is what it is. In the in-itself there is not a particle of being which is not wholly within itself without distance. When being is thus conceived there is not the slightest suspicion of duality in it; this is what we mean when we say that the density of being of the in-itself is infinite. It is a fullness. The principle of identity can be said to be synthetic not only because it limits its scope to a region of definite being, but in particular because it masses within it the infinity of density. "A is A" means that A exists in an infinite compression with an infinite density. Identity is the limiting concept of unification: it is not true that the in-itself has any need of a synthetic unification of its being; at its own extreme limit, unity disappears and passes into identity. Identity is the ideal of "one," and "one" comes into the world by human reality. The in-itself is full of itself, and no more total plenitude can be imagined, no more perfect equivalence of content to container. There is not the slightest emptiness in being, not the tiniest crack through which nothingness might slip in.

The distinguishing characteristic of consciousness, on the other hand, is that it is a decompression of being. Indeed it is impossible to define it as coincidence with itself. Of this table I can say only that it is purely and simply *this* table. But I can not limit myself to saying that my belief is belief; my belief is the consciousness (of) belief. It is often said that the act of reflection alters the fact of consciousness on which it is directed. Husserl himself admits that the fact "of being seen" involves a total modification for each *Erlebnis*. But I believe that I have demonstrated that the first condition of all reflection is a pre-reflective *cogito*. This *cogito*, to be sure, does not posit an object; it remains within consciousness. But it is nonetheless homologous with the reflective *cogito* since it appears as the first necessity for non-reflective consciousness to be seen by itself. Originally then the *cogito* includes this nullifying characteristic of existing for a witness, although the witness for which consciousness exists is itself. Thus by the sole fact that my belief is apprehended as belief, it is *no longer only belief*; that is, it is already no longer belief, it is troubled belief. Thus the ontological judgment "belief is consciousness (of) belief" can under no circumstances be taken as a statement of identity; the subject and the attribute are radically different though still within the indissoluble unity of one and the same being.

Very well, someone will say, but at least we must say that consciousness (of) belief is consciousness (of) belief. We rediscover identity and the in-itself on this level. It was only a matter of choosing the appropriate plane on which we should apprehend our object. But that is not true: to affirm that the consciousness (of) belief is consciousness (of) belief is to dissociate consciousness from belief, to suppress the parenthesis, and to make belief an object for consciousness; it is to launch abruptly on to the plane of reflectivity. A consciousness (of) belief which would be only consciousness (of) belief would in fact have to assume consciousness (of) itself as consciousness (of) belief. Belief would become a pure transcending and noematic qualification of consciousness; consciousness would be free to determine itself as it pleased in the face of that belief. It would resemble that impassive regard which, according to Victor Cousin, consciousness casts on psychic phenomena in order to elucidate them one by one. But the analysis of methodical doubt which Husserl attempted has clearly shown the fact that only reflective consciousness can be dissociated from what is posited by the consciousness reflected-on. It is on the reflective level only that we can attempt an ἐποχή,[1] a putting between parentheses, only there that we can refuse what Husserl calls the *mitmachen*.[2] The consciousness (of) belief, while irreparably altering belief, does not distinguish itself from belief; it *exists in order* to perform the act of faith. Thus we are obliged to admit that the consciousness (of) belief is belief. At its origin we have apprehended this double game of reference: consciousness (of) belief is belief and belief is consciousness (of) belief. On no account can we say that consciousness is consciousness or that belief is belief. Each of the terms refers to the other and passes into the other, and yet each term is different from the other. We have seen that neither belief nor pleasure nor joy can exist *before* being conscious; consciousness is the measure of their being; yet it is no less true that belief, owing to the very fact that it can exist only as *troubled*, exists from the start as escaping itself, as shattering the unity of all the concepts in which one can wish to inclose it.

Thus consciousness (of) belief and belief are one and the same being, the characteristic of which is absolute immanence. But as soon as we wish to grasp this being, it slips between our fingers, and we find ourselves faced

---

[1] Correction for ἐπόχη, an obvious misprint. Tr.
[2] "To take part in," "to participate." Tr.

with a pattern of duality, with a game of reflections. For consciousness is a reflection (*reflet*), but *qua* reflection it is exactly the one reflecting (*réfléchissant*), and if we attempt to grasp it as reflecting, it vanishes and we fall back on the reflection. This structure of the reflection-reflecting (*reflet-reflétant*) has disconcerted philosophers, who have wanted to explain it by an appeal to infinity—either by positing an *idea-ideae* as Spinoza did, which requires an *idea-ideae-ideae*, etc., or by defining it in the manner of Hegel as a return upon itself, as the veritable infinite. But the introduction of infinity into consciousness, aside from the fact that it fixes the phenomenon and obscures it, is only an explicative theory expressly designed to reduce the being of consciousness to that of the in-itself. Yet if we accept the objective existence of the reflection-reflecting as it is given, we are obliged to conceive a mode of being different from that of the in-itself, not a unity which contains a duality, not a synthesis which surpasses and lifts the abstract moments of the thesis and of the antithesis, but a duality which is unity, a reflection (*reflect*) which is its own reflecting (*reflection*). In fact if we seek to lay hold on the total phenomenon (i.e., the unity of this duality or consciousness (of) belief), we are referred immediately to one of the terms, and this term in turn refers us to the unitary organization of immanence. But if on the contrary we wish to take our point of departure from duality as such and to posit consciousness and belief as a dyad, then we encounter the *idea-ideae* of Spinoza and we miss the pre-reflective phenomenon which we wished to study. This is because pre-reflective consciousness is self-consciousness. It is this same notion of *self* which must be studied, for it defines the very being of consciousness.

Let us note first that the term in-itself, which we have borrowed from tradition to designate the transcending being, is inaccurate. At the limit of coincidence with itself, in fact, the self vanishes to give place to identical being. The *self* can not be a property of being-in-itself. By nature it is a reflexive, as syntax sufficiently indicates—in particular the logical rigor of Latin syntax with the strict distinctions imposed by grammar between the uses of *ejus* and *sui*. The *self* refers, but it refers precisely to the *subject*. It indicates a relation between the subject and himself, and this relation is precisely a duality, but a particular duality since it requires particular verbal symbols. But on the other hand, the *self* does not designate being either as subject or as complement. If indeed I consider the "*se*" in "*il s'ennuie*,"[3] for example, I establish that it opens up to allow the subject himself to appear behind it. It is not the subject, since the subject without relation to himself would be condensed into the identity of the in-itself; neither is it a consistent articulation of the real, since it allows the subject to appear behind it. In fact

[3] Literally the "self" in "he bores himself" (*il s'ennuie*), a familiar construction in the many French reflexive verbs. Cf. English "he washes himself." Tr.

the *self* cannot be apprehended as a real existent; the subject can not be self, for coincidence with self, as we have seen, causes the self to disappear. But neither can it *not be* itself since the self is an indication of the subject himself. The *self* therefore represents an ideal distance within the immanence of the subject in relalation to himself, a way of *not being his own coincidence*, of escaping identity while positing it as unity—in short, of being in a perpetually unstable equilibrium between identity as absolute cohesion without a trace of diversity and unity as a synthesis of a multiplicity. This is what we shall call presence to itself. The law of being of the *for-itself*, as the ontological foundation of consciousness, is to be itself in the form of presence to itself.

This presence to itself has often been taken for a plenitude of existence, and a strong prejudice prevalent among philosophers causes them to attribute to consciousness the highest rank in being. But this postulate can not be maintained after a more thorough description of the notion of presence. Actually *presence to* always implies duality, at least a virtual separation. The presence of being to itself implies a detachment on the part of being in relation to itself. The coincidence of identity is the veritable plenitude of being exactly because in this coincidence there is left no place for any negativity. Of course the principle of identity can involve the principle of noncontradiction as Hegel has observed. The being which is what it is must be able to be the being which is not what it is not. But in the first place this negation, like all others, comes to the surface of being through human reality, as we have shown, and not through a dialectic appropriate just to being. In addition this principle can denote only the relations of being with the *external*, exactly because it presides over the relations of being with what it is not. We are dealing then with a principle constitutive of *external relations* such that they can appear to a human reality present to being-in-itself and engaged in the world. This principle does not concern the internal relations of being; these relations, inasmuch as they would posit an otherness, do not exist. The principle of identity is the negation of every species of relation at the heart of being-in-itself.

Presence to self, on the contrary, supposes that an impalpable fissure has slipped into being. If being is present to itself, it is because it is not wholly itself. Presence is an immediate deterioration of coincidence, for it supposes separation. But if we ask ourselves at this point *what it is* which separates the subject from himself, we are forced to admit that it is *nothing*. Ordinarily what separates is a distance in space, a lapse of time, a psychological difference, or simply the individuality of two co-presents—in short, a *qualified* reality. But in the case which concerns us, *nothing* can separate the consciousness (of) belief from belief, since belief is *nothing other* than the consciousness (of) belief. To introduce into the unity of a pre-reflective *cogito* a qualified element external to this *cogito* would be to shatter its unity, to destroy its translucency; there would then be in consciousness something of which it would not be conscious and which would not exist in itself as consciousness. The separation which separates belief from itself can not be grasped or even conceived in isolation. If we seek to reveal it, it vanishes. We find belief once more as pure immanence. But if, on the other hand, we wish to apprehend belief as such, then the fissure is there, appearing when we do not wish to see it, disappearing as soon as we seek to contemplate it. This fissure then is the pure negative. Distance, lapse of time, psychological difference can be apprehended in themselves and include as such elements of positivity; they have a simple negative function. But the fissure within consciousness is a nothing except by what it denies and it can have being only as we do not see it.

This negative which is the nothingness of being and the nihilating power both together, is *nothingness*. Nowhere else can we grasp it in such purity. Everywhere else in one way or another we must confer on it being-in-itself as nothingness. But the nothingness which arises in the heart of consciousness *is not*. It *is made-to-be*. Belief, for example, is not the contiguity of one being with another being; it is *its own* presence to itself, its own decompression of being. Otherwise the unity of the for-itself would dissolve into the duality of two in-itselfs.[4] Thus the for-itself must be its own nothingness. The being of consciousness qua consciousness is to exist *at a distance from itself* as a presence to itself, and this empty distance which being carries in its being is Nothingness. Thus in order for a *self* to exist, it is necessary that the unity of this being include its own nothingness as the nihilation of identity. For the nothingness which slips into belief is *its* nothingness, the nothingness of belief as belief in itself, as belief blind and full, as "simple faith." The for-itself is the being which determines itself to exist inasmuch as it can not coincide with itself.

Hence we understand how it was that by questioning the pre-reflective *cogito* without any conducting thread, we could not find nothingness anywhere. One does not *find*, one does not *disclose* nothingness in the manner in which one can find, disclose a being. Nothingness is always an *elsewhere*. It is the obligation for the for-itself never to exist except in the form of an elsewhere in relation to itself, to exist as a being which perpetually effects in itself a weakness of being. This inconsistency does not refer us to another being; it is only a perpetual reference of self to self, of the reflection to the reflecting, of the reflecting to the reflection. This reference, however, does not provoke an infinite movement in the heart of the for-itself but is given within the unity of a single act. The infinite movement belongs only to the reflective regard

---

[4] *Deux en-soi.* Ungrammatical as the expression "in-itselfs" admittedly is, it seems to me the most accurate translation. "In-themselves" would have a different meaning, for it would suggest a unity of two examples of being-in-itself, and Sartre's point here is their duality and isolation from each other. Tr.

which wants to apprehend the phenomenon as a totality and which is referred from the reflection to the reflecting, from the reflecting to the reflection without being able to stop. Thus nothingness is this hole of being, this fall of the in-itself toward the self, the fall by which the for-itself is constituted. But this nothingness can only "be made-to-be" if its borrowed existence is correlative with a nihilating act on the part of being. This perpetual act by which the in-itself degenerates into presence to itself we shall call an ontological act. Nothingness is the putting into question of being by being—that is, precisely consciousness or for-self. It is an absolute event which comes to being by means of being and which without having being, is perpetually sustained by being. Since being-in-itself is isolated in its being by its total positivity no being can produce being and nothing can happen to being through being—except for nothingness. Nothingness is the peculiar possibility of being and its unique possibility. Yet this original possibility appears only in the absolute act which realizes it. Since nothingness is nothingness of being, it can come to being only through being itself. Of course it comes to being through a particular being, which is human reality. But this being is constituted as human reality inasmuch as this being is nothing but the original project of its own nothingness. Human reality is being in so far as within its being and for its being it is the unique foundation of nothingness at the heart of being.

## II. THE FACTICITY OF THE FOR-ITSELF

Yet the for-itself is. It is, we may say, even if it is a being which is not what it is and which is what it is not. It is since whatever reefs there may be to cause it to founder, still the project of sincerity is at least conceivable. The for-itself is, in the manner of an event, in the sense in which I can say that Philip II *has been*, that my friend Pierre is or exists. The for-itself *is*, in so far as it appears in a condition which it has not chosen, as Pierre is a French bourgeois in 1942, as Schmitt was a Berlin worker in 1870; it *is* in so far as it is thrown into a world and abandoned in a "situation;" it *is* as pure contingency inasmuch as for it as for things in the world, as for this wall, this tree, this cup, the original question can be posited: "Why is this being exactly such and not otherwise?" It *is* in so far as there is in it something of which it is not the foundation—its *presence to the world*.

Being apprehends itself as not being its own foundation, and this apprehension is at the basis of every *cogito*. In this connection it is to be noted that it reveals itself immediately to the *reflective cogito* of Descartes. When Descartes wants to profit from this revelation, he apprehends himself as an imperfect being "since he doubts." But in this imperfect being, he establishes the presence of the idea of perfection. He apprehends then a cleavage between the type of being which he can conceive and the being which he is. It is this cleavage or lack of being which is at the origin of the second proof of the existence of God. In fact if we get rid of the scholastic terminology, what remains of this proof? The very clear indication that the being which possesses in itself the idea of perfection can not be its own foundation, for if it were, it would have produced itself in conformance with that idea. In other words, a being which would be its own foundation could not suffer the slightest discrepancy between what it is and what it conceives, for it would produce itself in conformance with its comprehension of being and could conceive only of what it is.

But this apprehension of being as a lack of being in the face of being is first a comprehension on the part of the *cogito* of its own contingency. I think, therefore I am. What am I? A being which is not its own foundation, which qua being, could be other than it is to the extent that it does not account for its being. This is that first intuition of our own contingency which Heidegger gives as the first motivation for the passage from the un-authentic to the authentic.[5] There is restlessness, a call of the conscience (*Ruf des Gewissens*), a feeling of guilt. In truth Heidegger's description shows all too clearly his anxiety to establish an ontological foundation for an Ethics with which he claims not to be concerned, as also to reconcile his humanism with the religious sense of the transcendent. The intuition of our contingency is not identical with a feeling of guilt. Nevertheless it is true that in our own apprehension of ourselves, we appear to ourselves as having the character of an unjustifiable fact.

Earlier, however, we apprehended ourselves as consciousness—that is, as a "being which exists by itself."[6] How within the unity of one and the same upsurge into being, can we be that being which exists by itself as not being the foundation of its being? Or in other words, since the for-itself—in so far as it is—is not its own being (i.e., is not the foundation of it), how can it as for-itself, be the foundation of its own nothingness? The answer is in the question.

While being is indeed the foundation of nothingness as the nihilation of its own being, that is not the same as saying that it is the foundation of its being. To found its own being it would have to exist at a distance from itself, and that would imply a certain nihilation of the being founded as of the being which founds—a duality which would be unity; here we should fall back into the case of the for-itself. In short, every effort to conceive of the idea of a being which would be the foundation of its being results inevitably

---

[5] I have corrected what must surely be a misprint. "From the authentic to the authentic," as the text actually reads, would make no sense. Tr.

[6] Cf. Introduction, section III.

in forming that of a being which contingent as being-in-itself, would be the foundation of its own nothingness. The act of causation by which God is *causa sui* is a nihilating act like every recovery of the self by the self, to the same degree that the original relation of necessity is a return to self, a reflexivity. This original necessity in turn appears on the foundation of a contingent being, precisely that being which is in *order to* be the the cause of itself. Leibniz' effort to define necessity in terms of possibility—a definition taken up again by Kant—is undertaken from the point of view of knowledge and not from the point of view of being. The passage from possibility to being such as Leibniz conceives it (the necessary is a being whose possibility implies its existence) marks the passage from our ignorance to knowledge. In fact since possibility precedes existence, it can be possibility only with respect to our thought. It is an external possibility in relation to the being whose possibility it is, since being unrolls from it like a consequence from a principle. But we pointed out earlier that the notion of possibility could be considered in two aspects. We can make of it a subjective indication. The statement, "It is possible that Pierre is dead," indicates that I am in ignorance concerning Pierre's fate, and in this case it is a witness who decides the possible in the presence of the world. Being has its possibility outside of itself in the pure regard which gauges its chances of being; possibility can indeed be given *to us* before being; but it is to *us* that it is given and it is in no way the possibility *of* this being. The billiard ball which rolls on the table does not possess the possibility of being turned from its path by a fold in the cloth; neither does the possibility of deviation belong to the cloth; it can be established only by a witness synthetically as an external relation. But possibility can also appear to us as an ontological structure of the real. Then it belongs to certain beings as *their* possibility; it is the possibility which they are, which they have to be. In this case being sustains its own possibilities in being; it is their foundation, and the necessity of being can not then be derived from its possibility. In a word, God, if he exists, is contingent.

Thus the being of consciousness, since this being is in itself in *order* to nihilate itself in for-itself, remains contingent; that is, it is not the role of consciousness either to give being to itself or to receive it from others. In addition to the fact that the ontological proof like the cosmological proof fails to establish a necessary being, the explanation and the foundation of my being—in so far as I am *a particular being*—can not be sought in necessary being. The premises, "Everything which is contingent must find a foundation in a necessary being. Now I am contingent," mark a desire to find a foundation and do not furnish the explicative link with a real foundation. Such premises could not in any way account for this contingency but only for the abstract idea of contingency in general. Furthermore the question here is one of value, not fact.[7] But while being in-itself is contingent, it recovers itself by degenerating into a for-itself. It *is*, in order to lose itself in a for-itself. In a word being *is* and can only be. But the peculiar possibility of being—that which is revealed in the nihilating act—is of being the foundation of itself as consciousness through the sacrificial act which nihilates being. The for-itself is the in-itself losing itself as in-itself in order to found itself as consciousness. Thus consciousness holds within itself its own being-as-consciousness, and since it is its own nihilation, it can refer only to itself; but that which is annihilated[8] in consciousness—though we can not call it the foundation of consciousness—is the contingent in-itself. The in-itself can not provide the foundation for anything; if it founds itself, it does so by giving itself the modification of the for-itself. It is the foundation of itself in so far as it is *already no longer* in-itself, and we encounter here again the origin of every foundation. If being in-itself can be neither its own foundation nor that of other beings, the whole idea of foundation comes into the world through the for-itself. It is not only that the for-itself as a nihilated in-itself is itself given a foundation, but with it foundation appears for the first time.

It follows that this in-itself, engulfed and nihilated in the absolute event which is the appearance of the foundation or upsurge of the for-itself, remains at the heart of the for-itself as its original contingency. Consciousness is its own foundation but it remains contingent *that there may be a* consciousness rather than an infinity of pure and simple in-itself. The absolute event or for-itself is contingent in its very being. If I decipher the givens of the pre-reflective *cogito*, I establish, to be sure, that the for-itself refers to itself. Whatever the for-itself may be, it is this in the mode of consciousness of being. Thirst refers to the consciousness of thirst, which it *is*, as to its foundation—and conversely. But the totality "reflected—reflecting," if it could be given, would be contingency and in-itself. But this totality can not be attained, since I can not say either that the consciousness of thirst is consciousness of thirst, or that thirst is thirst. It is there as a nihilated totality, as the evanescent unity of the phenomenon. If I apprehend the phenomenon as plurality, this plurality indicates itself as a total unity, and hence its meaning is its contingency. That is, I can ask myself, "Why am I thirsty? Why am I conscious of this glass? Of this Me?" But as soon as I consider this totality in in-itself, it nihilates itself under my regard. It is *not*; it is in order not to be, and I return to the for-itself apprehended in its suggestion of duality as the foundation of itself. I am angry because I produce myself as consciousness of anger. Suppress this self-causation which constitutes the being of the

---

[7] This reasoning indeed is explicitly based on the *exigencies* of reason.

[8] Sartre says "annihilated" here, but I feel that he must have meant "nihilated" since he has told us earlier that being cannot be annihilated. Tr.

for-itself, and you will no longer find anything, not even "anger-in-itself;" for anger exists by nature as for-itself. Thus the for-itself is sustained by a perpetual contingency for which it assumes the responsibility and which it assimilates without ever being able to suppress it. This perpetually evanescent contingency of the in-itself which, without ever allowing itself to be apprehended, haunts the for-itself and reattaches it to being-in-itself—this contingency is what we shall call the facticity of the for-itself. It is this facticity which permits us to say that the for-itself is, that it exists, although we can never realize the facticity and although we always apprehend it through the for-itself.

We indicated earlier that we can be nothing without playing at being it.[9] "If I am a café waiter," we said, "this can be only in the mode of not being one." And that is true. If I could be a café waiter, I should suddenly constitute myself as a contingent block of identity. And that I am not. This contingent being in-itself always escapes me. But in order that I may freely give a meaning to the obligations which my state involves, then in one sense at the heart of the for-itself, as a perpetually evanescent totality, being-in-itself must be given as the evanescent contingency of my situation. This is the result of the fact that while I must play at being a café waiter in order to be one, still it would be in vain for me to play at being a diplomat or a sailor, for I would not be one. This inapprehensible fact of my condition, this impalpable difference which distinguishes this drama of realization from drama pure and simple is what causes the for-itself, while choosing the meaning of its situation and while constituting itself as the foundation of itself in situation, not to choose its position. This part of my condition is what causes me to apprehend myself simultaneously as totally responsible for my being—inasmuch as I am its foundation—and yet as totally unjustifiable. Without facticity consciousness could choose its attachments to the world in the same way as the souls in Plato's Republic choose their condition. I could determine myself to "be born a worker" or to "be born a bourgeois." But on the other hand facticity can not constitute me as being a bourgeois or being a worker. It is not even strictly speaking a resistance of fact since it is only by recovering it in the substructure of the pre-reflective cogito that I confer on it its meaning and its resistance. Facticity is only one indication which I give myself of the being to which I must reunite myself in order to be what I am.

It is impossible to grasp facticity in its brute nudity, since all that we will find of it is already recovered and freely constructed. The simple fact "of being there," at that table, in that chair is already the pure object of a limiting-concept and as such can not be grasped. Yet it is contained in my "consciousness of being-there," as its full contingency, as the nihilated in-itself on the basis of which the for-itself produces itself as consciousness of

---

[9] Part One, chapter II, section ii. "Conducts of Bad Faith."

being there. The for-itself looking deep into itself as the consciousness of being there will never discover anything in itself but *motivations*; that is, it will be perpetually referred to itself and to its constant freedom. (I am there in order to . . . etc.) But the contingency which paralyzes these motivations to the same degree as they totally found themselves is the facticity of the for-itself. The relation of the for-itself, which is its own foundation qua for-itself, to facticity can be correctly termed a factual necessity. It is indeed this factual necessity which Descartes and Husserl seized upon as constituting the evidence of the *cogito*. The for-itself is necessary in so far as it provides its own foundation. And this is why it is the reflected object of an apodictic intuition. I can not doubt that I am. But in so far as this for-itself as such could also not be, it has all the contingency of a fact. Just as my nihilating freedom is apprehended in anguish, so the for-itself is conscious of its facticity. It has the feeling of its complete gratuity; it apprehends itself as being there *for nothing*, as being *de trop*.

We must not confuse facticity with that Cartesian substance whose attribute is thought. To be sure, thinking substance exists only as it thinks; and since it is a created thing, it participates in the contingency of the *ens creatum*. But it *is*. It preserves the character of being-in-itself in its integrity, although the for-itself is its attribute. This is what is called Descartes' substantialist illusion. For us, on the other hand, the appearance of the for-itself or absolute event refers indeed to the effort of an in-itself to found itself; it corresponds to an attempt on the part of being to remove contingency from its being. But this attempt results in the nihilation of the in-itself, because the in-itself can not found *itself* without introducing the *self* or a reflective, nihilating reference, into the absolute identity of its being and consequently degenerating into for-itself. The for-itself corresponds then to an expanding de-structuring of the in-itself, and the in-itself is nihilated and absorbed in its attempt to found itself. Facticity is not then a substance of which the for-itself would be the attribute and which would produce thought without exhausting itself in that very production. It simply resides in the for-itself as a memory of being, as its unjustifiable *presence in the world*. Being-in-itself can found its nothingness but not its being. In its decompression it nihilates itself in a for-itself which becomes qua for-itself its own foundation; but the contingency which the for-itself has derived from the in-itself remains out of reach. It is what *remains* of the in-itself in the for-itself as facticity and what causes the for-itself to have only a factual necessity; that is, it is the foundation of its *consciousness-of-being* or *existence*, but on no account can it found its *presence*. Thus consciousness can in no case prevent itself from being and yet it is totally responsible for its being.

## III. THE FOR-ITSELF AND THE BEING OF VALUE

Any study of human reality must begin with the *cogito*. But the Cartesian "I think" is conceived in the instantaneous perspective of temporality. Can we find in the heart of the *cogito* a way of transcending this instantaneity? If human reality were limited to the being of the "I think," it would have only the truth of an instant. And it is indeed true that with Descartes the *cogito* is an instantaneous totality, since by itself it makes no claim on the future and since an act of continuous "creation" is necessary to make it pass from one instant to another. But can we even conceive of the truth of an instant? Does the *cogito* not in its own way engage both past and future? Heidegger is so persuaded that the "I think" of Husserl is a trap for larks, fascinating and ensnaring, that he has completely avoided any appeal to consciousness in his description of Dasein. His goal is to show it immediately as *care*; that is, as escaping itself in the project of self toward the possibilities which it is. It is this projection of the self outside the self which he calls "understanding" (*Verstand*) and which permits him to establish human reality as being a "revealing-revealed." But this attempt to show first the escape from self of the Dasein is going to encounter in turn insurmountable difficulties; we cannot first suppress the dimension "consciousness," not even if it is in order to re-establish it subsequently. Understanding has meaning only if it is conscious-ness of understanding. My possibility can exist as my possibility only if it is my consciousness which escapes itself toward my possibility. Otherwise the whole system of being and its possibilities will fall into the unconscious— that is into the in-itself. Behold, we are thrown back again towards the *cogito*. We must make this our point of departure. Can we extend it without losing the benefits of reflective evidence? What has the description of the for-itself revealed to us?

First we have encountered a nihilation in which the being of the for-itself is affected in its being. This revelation of nothingness did not seem to us to pass beyond the limits of the *cogito*. But let us consider more closely.

The for-itself can not sustain nihilation without determining itself as a *lack of being*. This means that the nihilation does not coincide with a simple intro-duction of emptiness into consciousness. An external being has not expelled the in-itself from consciousness; rather the for-itself is perpetually determin-ing itself *not to be* the in-itself. This means that it can establish itself only in terms of the in-itself and against the in-itself. Thus since the nihilation is the nihilation of being, it represents the original connection between the being of the for-itself and the being of the in-itself. The concrete, real in-itself is wholly present to the heart of consciousness as that which consciousness determines itself not to be. The *cogito* must necesarily lead us to discover this total, out-of-reach presence of the in-itself. Of course the fact of this presence will be the very transcendence of the for-itself. But it is precisely the nihilation which is the origin of transcendence conceived as the original bond between the for-itself and the in-itself. Thus we catch a glimpse of a way of getting out of the *cogito*. We shall see later indeed that the profound meaning of the *cogito* is essentially to refer outside itself. But it is not yet time to describe this characteristic of the for-itself. What our ontological description has immediately revealed is that this being is the foundation of itself as a lack of being; that is, that it determines its being by means of a being which it is not.

Nevertheless there are many ways of not being and some of them do not touch the inner nature of the being which is not what it is not. If, for example, I say of an inkwell that it is not a bird, the inkwell and the bird remain untouched by the negation. This is an external relation which can be established only by a human reality acting as witness. By contrast, there is a type of negation which establishes an internal relation between what one denies and that concerning which the denial is made.[10]

Of all internal negations, the one which penetrates most deeply into being, the one which constitutes in *its being* the being concerning which it makes the denial along with the being which it denies—this negation is *lack*. This lack does not belong to the nature of the in-itself, which is all positivity. It appears in the world only with the upsurge of human reality. It is only in the human world that there can be lacks. A lack pre-supposes a trinity: that which is missing or "the lacking," that which misses what is lacking or "the existing," and a totality which has been broken by the lacking and which would be restored by the synthesis of "the lacking" and "the existing"—this is "the lacked."[11] The being which is released to the intuition of human reality is always that to which *some thing is lacking*—i.e., the existing. For example, if I say that the moon is not full and that one quarter is lacking, I base this judgment on full intuition of the crescent moon. Thus what is released to intuition is an in-itself which by itself is neither complete nor incomplete but which simply is what it *is*, without relation with other beings. In order for this in-itself to be grasped as the crescent moon, it is necessary that a human reality surpass the given toward the project of the realized totality—here the disk of the full moon—and return toward the given to constitute it as the crescent moon; that is, in order to realize it in its being in terms of the totality which becomes its foundation. In this same surpassing the lacking will be posited as

---

[10] Hegelian opposition belongs to this type of negation. But this opposition must itself be based on an original internal negation; that is, on lack. For example, if the non-essential becomes in its turn the essential, this is because it is experienced as a lack in the heart of the essential.

[11] *Le manquant*, "the lacking," *l'existant*, "the existing"; *le manqué*, "the lacked." *Le manque* is "the lack." At times when *manqué* is used as an adjective, I have translated it as "missing," *e.g.*, *l'en-soi manqué*, "the missing in-itself." Tr.

that whose synthetic addition to the existing will reconstitute the synthetic totality of the lacked. In this sense the lacking is of the same nature as the existing; it would suffice to reverse the situation in order for it to become the existing to which the lacking is missing, while the existing would become the lacking. This lacking as the complement of the existing is determined in its being by the synthetic totality of the lacked. Thus in the human world, the incomplete being which is released to intuition as lacking is constituted in its being by the lacked—that is, by what it is not. It is the full moon which confers on the crescent moon its being as crescent; what-is-not determines what-is. It is in the being of the existing, as the correlate of a human transcendence, to lead outside itself to the being which it is not—as to its meaning.

Human reality by which lack appears in the world must be itself a lack. For lack can come into being only through lack; the in-itself can not be the occasion of lack in the in-itself. In other words, in order for being to be lacking or lacked, it is necessary that a being make itself its own lack; only a being which lacks can surpass being toward the lacked.

The existence of desire as a human fact is sufficient to prove that human reality is a lack. In fact how can we explain desire if we insist on viewing it as a psychic *state*; that is, as a being whose nature is to be what it is? A being which is what it is, to the degree that it is considered as being what it is, summons nothing to itself in order to complete itself. An incomplete circle does not call for completion unless it is surpassed by human transcendence. In itself it is complete and perfectly positive as an open curve. A psychic state which existed with the sufficiency of this curve could not possess in addition the slightest "appeal to" something else; it would be itself without any relation to what is not it. In order to constitute it as hunger or thirst, an external transcendence surpassing it toward the totality "satisfied hunger" would be necessary, just as the crescent moon is surpassed toward the full moon.

We will not get out of the difficulty by making desire a *conatus* conceived in the manner of a physical force. For the *conatus* once again, even if we grant it the efficiency of a cause, can not possess in itself the character of a reaching out toward another state. The *conatus* as the *producer* of states can not be identified with desire as the *appeal* from a state. Neither will recourse to psychophysiological parallelism enable us better to clear away the difficulties. Thirst as an organic phenomenon, as a "physiological" need of water, does not exist. An organism deprived of water presents certain positive phenomena: for example, a certain coagulating thickening of the blood, which provokes in turn certain other phenomena. The ensemble is a positive state of the organism which refers only to itself, exactly as the thickening of a solution from which the water has evaporated can not be considered by itself as the solution's desire of water. If we suppose an exact correspondence between the mental and the physiological, this correspondence can be established only on the basis of ontological identity, as Spinoza has seen. Consequently the being of psychic thirst will be the being in itself of a *state*, and we are referred once again to a transcendent witness. But then the thirst will be desire for this transcendence but not for itself; it will be desire in the eyes of another. If desire is to be able to be desire to itself it must necessarily be itself transcendence; that is, it must by nature be an escape from itself toward the desired object. In other words, it must be a lack—but not an object-lack, a lack undergone, created by the surpassing which it is not; it must be its own lack of —. Desire is a lack of being. It is haunted in its inmost being by the being of which it is desire. Thus it bears witness to the existence of lack in the being of human reality. But if human reality is lack, then it is through human reality that the trinity of the existing, the lacking and the lacked comes into being. What exactly are the three terms of this trinity?

That which plays here the role of the existing is what is released to the *cogito* as the immediate of the desire; for example, it is this for-itself which we have apprehended as not being what it is and being what it is not. But how are we to define the lacked?

To answer this question, we must return to the idea of lack and determine more exactly the bond which unites the existing to the lacking. This bond can not be one of simple contiguity. If what is lacking is in its very absence still profoundly present at the heart of the existing, it is because the existing and the lacking are at the same moment apprehended and surpassed in the unity of a single totality. And that which constitutes itself as lack can do so only by surpassing itself toward one great broken form. Thus lack is appearance on the ground of a totality. Moreover it matters little whether this totality has been originally given and is now broken (*e.g.* "The arms of the Venus di Milo are now *lacking*") or whether it has never yet been realized. (*e.g.* "He lacks courage.") What is important is only that the lacking and the existing are given or are apprehended as about to be annihilated in the unity of the totality which is lacked. Everything which is lacking is lacking to − for −. What is given in the unity of a primitive upsurge is the *for*, conceived as not yet being or as not being any longer, an absence toward which the curtailed existing surpasses itself or is surpassed and thereby constitutes itself as curtailed. What is the *for* of human reality?

The for-itself, as the foundation of itself, is the upsurge of the negation. The for-itself founds itself in so far as it denies in *relation to itself* a certain being or a mode of being. What it denies or nihilates, as we know, is being-in-itself. But no matter *what* being-in-itself: human reality is before all else its own nothingness. What it denies or nihilates *in relation* to itself as for-itself can be only *itself*. The meaning of human reality as nihilated is constituted by this nihilation and this presence in it of what it nihilates; hence the self-as-being-in-itself is what human reality lacks and what makes its meaning. Since human reality in its primitive relation to itself is not what it is, its relation to itself is not primitive and can derive its meaning only from an original relation which is the *null relation* or identity. It is the self which would be what it is which allows the for-itself to be apprehended as not being what it is; the relation denied in the definition of the for-itself—which as such should be first posited—is a relation (given as perpetually absent) between the for-itself and itself in the mode of identity. The meaning of the subtle confusion by which thirst escapes and is not thirst (in so far as it is consciousness of thirst), is a thirst which would be thirst and which haunts it. What the for-itself lacks is the self—or itself as in-itself.

Nevertheless we must not confuse this missing in-itself (the lacked), with that of facticity. The in-itself of facticity in its failure to found itself is reabsorbed in pure presence in the world of the for-itself. The missing in-itself, on the other hand, is pure absence. Moreover the failure of the act to found the in-itself has caused the for-itself to rise up from the in-itself as the foundation of its own nothingness. But the meaning of the missing act of founding remains as transcendent. The for-itself in its being is failure because it is the foundation only of itself as nothingness. In truth this failure is its very being, but it has meaning only if the for-itself apprehends itself as failure *in the presence of* the being which it has failed to be; that is, of the being which would be the foundation of its being and no longer merely the foundation of its nothingness—or, to put it another way, which would be its foundation as coincidence with itself. By nature the *cogito* refers to the lacking and to the lacked, for the *cogito* is haunted by being, as Descartes well realized.

Such is the origin of transcendence. Human reality is its own surpassing toward what it lacks; it surpasses itself toward the particular being which it would be if it were what it is. Human reality is not something which exists first in order afterwards to lack this or that; it exists first as lack and in immediate, synthetic connection with what it lacks. Thus the pure event by which human reality rises as a presence in the world is apprehended by itself as *its own lack*. In its coming into existence human reality grasps itself as an incomplete being. It apprehends itself as being in so far as it is not, in the presence of the particular totality which it lacks and which it is in the form of not being it and which is what it is. Human reality is a perpetual surpassing toward a coincidence with itself which is never given. If the *cogito reaches* toward being, it is because by its very thrust it surpasses itself toward being by qualifying itself in its being as the being to which coincidence with self is lacking in order for it to be what it is. The *cogito* is indissolubly linked to being-in-itself, not as a thought to its object—which would make the in-itself relative—but as a lack to that which defines its lack. In this sense the second Cartesian proof is rigorous. Imperfect being surpasses itself toward perfect being; the being which is the foundation only of its nothingness surpasses itself toward the being which is the foundation of its being. But the being toward which human reality surpasses itself is not a transcendent God; it is at the heart of human reality; it is only human reality itself as totality.

This totality is not the pure and simple contingent in-itself of the transcendent. If what consciousness apprehends as the being toward which it surpasses itself were the pure in-itself, it would coincide with the annihilation of consciousness. But consciousness does not surpass itself toward it annihilation; it does not want to lose itself in the in-itself of identity at the limit of its surpassing. It is for the for-itself as such that the for-itself lays claim to being-in-itself.

Thus this perpetually absent being which haunts the for-itself is itself fixed in the in-itself. It is the impossible synthesis of the for-itself and the in-itself; it would be its own foundation not as nothingness but as being and would preserve within it the necessary translucency of consciousness along with the coincidence with itself of being-in-itself. It would preserve in it that turning back upon the self which conditions every necessity and every foundation. But this return to the self would be without distance; it would not be presence to itself, but identity with itself. In short, this being would be exactly the self which we have shown can exist only as a perpetually evanescent relation, but it would be this self as substantial being. Thus human reality arises as such in the presence of its own totality or self as a lack of that totality. And this totality can not be given by nature, since it combines in itself the incompatible characteristics of the in-itself and the for-itself.

Let no one reproach us with capriciously inventing a being of this kind; when by a further movement of thought the being and absolute absence of this totality are hypostasized as transcendence beyond the world, it takes on the name of God. Is not God a being who is what he is—in that he is all positivity and the foundation of the world—and at the same time a being who is not what he is and who is what he is not—in that he is self-consciousness and the necessary foundation of himself? The being of human reality is suffering because it rises in being as perpetually haunted by a totality which it is without being able to be it, precisely because it could not attain the in-itself without losing itself as for-itself. Human reality therefore is by nature an unhappy consciousness with no possibility of surpassing its unhappy state.

But what exactly is the nature of this being toward which unhappy consciousness surpasses itself? Shall we say that it does not exist? Those contradictions which we discovered in it prove only that it can not be *realized*. Nothing can hold out against this self-evident truth: consciousness can exist only as *engaged* in this being which surrounds it on all sides and which paralyzes it with its phantom presence. Shall we say that it is a being *relative* to consciousness? This would be to confuse it with the object of a *thesis*. This being is not posited through and before consciousness; there is no consciousness of this being since it haunts non-thetic self-consciousness. It points to consciousness as the meaning of its being and yet consciousness is no more conscious of it than of itself. Still it can not escape from consciousness; but inasmuch as consciousness enjoys being a consciousness (of) being, this being is there. Consciousness does not confer meaning on this being as it does for this inkwell or this pencil; but without this being, which it is in the form of not being it, consciousness would not be consciousness—i.e., lack. On the contrary, consciousness derives for itself its meaning as consciousness from this being. This being comes into the world along with consciousness, at once in its heart and outside it; it is absolute transcendence in absolute immanence. It has no priority over consciousness, and consciousness has no priority over it. They *form a dyad*. Of course this being could not exist without the for-itself, but neither could the for-itself exist without it. Consciousness in relation to this being stands in the mode of *being* this being, for this being is consciousness, but as a being which consciousness can not be. It is consciousness itself, in the heart of consciousness, and yet out of reach, as an absence, an unrealizable. Its nature is to inclose its own contradiction within itself; its relation to the for-itself is a total immanence which is achieved in total transcendence.

Furthermore this being need not be conceived as present to consciousness with only the abstract characteristics which our study has established. The concrete consciousness arises in situation, and it is a unique, individualized consciousness of this situation and (of) itself in situation. It is to this concrete consciousness that the self is present, and all the concrete characteristics of consciousness have their correlates in the totality of the self. The self is individual; it is the individual completion of the self which haunts the for-itself.

A feeling, for example, is a feeling in the presence of a norm; that is, a feeling of the same type but one which would be what it is. This norm or totality of the affective self is directly present as a lack *suffered* in the very heart of suffering. One suffers and one suffers from not suffering enough. The suffering of which we *speak* is never exactly that which we feel. What we call "noble" or "good" or "true" suffering and what moves us is the suffering which we read on the faces of others, better yet in portraits, in the face of a statue, in a tragic mask. It is a suffering which has *being*. It is presented to us as a compact, objective whole which did not await our coming in order to be and which overflows the consciousness which we have of it; it is there in the midst of the world, impenetrable and dense, like this tree or this stone; it endures; finally it is what it is. We can speak of it—that suffering there which is expressed by that set of the mouth, by that frown. It is supported and expressed by the physiognomy but not created by it. Suffering is posited upon the physiognomy; it is beyond passivity as beyond activity, beyond negation as beyond affirmation—it is. However it can be only as consciousness of self. We know well that this mask does not express the unconscious grimace of a sleeper or the rictus of a dead man. It refers to possibilities, to a situation in the world. The suffering is the conscious relation to these possibilities, to this situation, but it is solidified, cast in the bronze of being. And it is as such that it fascinates us; it stands as a degraded approximation of that suffering-in-itself which haunts our own suffering. The suffering which I experience, on the contrary, is never adequate suffering, due to the fact that it nihilates itself as in itself by the very act by which it founds itself. It escapes as suffering toward the consciousness of suffering. I can never be *surprised* by it, for it is only to the exact degree that I experience it. Its translucency removes from it all depth. I can not observe it as I observe the suffering of the statue, since I make my own suffering and since I know it. If I must suffer, I should prefer that my suffering would seize me and flow over me like a storm, but instead I must raise it into existence in my free spontaneity. I should like simultaneously to be it and to conquer it, but this enormous, opaque suffering, which should transport me out of myself, continues instead to touch me lightly with its wing, and I can not grasp it. I find only *myself*, myself who moans, myself who wails, myself who in order to realize this suffering which I am must play without respite the drama of suffering. I wring my hands, I cry in order that being-in-itselfs, their sounds, their gestures may run through the world, ridden by the suffering-in-itself which I can not be. Each groan, each facial expression of the man who suffers aims at sculpturing a statue-in-itself of suffering. But this statue will never exist save through others and for others. My suffering suffers from being what it is not and from not being what it is. At the point of being made one with itself, it escapes, separated from itself by nothing, by that nothingness of which it is itself the foundation. It is loquacious because it is not adequate, but its ideal is silence,—the silence of the statue, of the beaten man who lowers his head and veils his face without speaking. But with this man too—it is *for me* that he does not speak. In himself he chatters incessantly, for the words of the inner language are like the outlines of the "self" of suffering. It is for my eyes that he is "crushed" by suffering; in himself he feels himself responsible for that grief which he wills even while not wishing it and which he does not wish even while willing it, that grief which is haunted by a perpetual absence—the absence of the motionless, mute suffering which is the *self*, the concrete, out-of reach totality of the for-itself which suffers, the *for* of Human-Reality in suffering. We can see that my suffering never posits this suffering-in-itself which visits it. My real suffering is not an *effort* to reach to the self. But it can *be* suffering only as consciousness (of) not being enough suffering in the presence of that full and absent suffering.

Now we can ascertain more exactly what is the being of the self: it is value. Value is affected with the double character, which moralists have very inadequately explained, of both being unconditionally and not being. Qua value indeed, value has being, but this normative existent has no being precisely as reality. Its being is to be value; that is, not-to-be being. Thus the being of value qua value is the being of what does not have being. Value then appears inapprehensible. To take it as being is to risk totally misunderstanding its unreality and to make of it, as sociologists do, a requirement of fact among other facts. In this case the contingency of being destroys value. But conversely if we look only at the ideality of values, we tend to deprive them of being, and then for lack of being, they dissolve. Of course, as Scheler has shown, I can achieve an intuition of values in terms of concrete exemplifications; I can grasp nobility in a noble act. But value thus apprehended is not given as existing on the same level of being as the act on which it confers value—in the way, for example, that the essence "red" is in relation to a particular red. Value is given as a beyond of the acts confronted, as the limit, for example, of the infinite progression of noble acts. Value is beyond being. Yet if we are not to be taken in by fine words, we must recognize that this being which is beyond being possesses being in some way at least.

These considerations suffice to make us admit that human reality is that by which value comes to the world. But the meaning of the value lies in being that toward which a being surpasses its being; every value-oriented act is a wrenching away from its own being toward —. Since value is always and everywhere the beyond of all surpassings, it can be considered as the unconditioned unity of all surpassings of being. Thereby it makes a dyad with the reality which originally surpasses its being and by which surpassing comes into being—i.e., with human reality. We see also that since value is the unconditioned beyond of all surpassings, it must be originally the beyond of the very being which surpasses, for that is the only way in which value can be the original beyond of all possible surpassings. If every surpassing must be able to be surpassed, it is necessary that the being which surpasses should be a priori surpassed in so far as it is the very source of surpassings. Thus value taken in its origin, or the supreme value, is the beyond and the for of transcendence. It is the beyond which surpasses and which provides the foundation for all my surpassings but toward which I can never surpass myself, precisely because my surpassings presuppose it.

In all cases of lack value is "the lacked;" it is not "the lacking." Value is the self in so far as the self haunts the heart of the for-itself as that for which the for-itself is. The supreme value toward which consciousness at every instant surpasses itself by its very being is the absolute being of the self with its characteristics of identity, of purity, of permanence, *etc.*, and as its own foundation. This is what enables us to conceive why value can simultaneously be and not be. It is as the meaning and the beyond of all surpassing; it is as the absent in-itself which haunts being-for-itself. But as soon as we consider value, we see that it is itself a surpassing of this being-in-itself, since value *gives being to itself.* It is beyond its own being since with the type of being of coincidence with self, it immediately surpasses this being, its permanence, its purity, its consistency, its identity, its silence, by reclaiming these qualities by virtue of presence to itself. And conversely if we start by considering it as presence to itself, this presence immediately is solidified, fixed in the in-itself. Moreover it is in its being the missing totality toward which a being makes itself be. It arises for a being, not as this being is what it is in full contingency, but as it is the foundation of its own nihilation. In this sense value haunts being as being founds itself but not as being *is.* Value haunts *freedom.* This means that the relation of value to the for-itself is very particular: it is the being which has to be in so far as it is the foundation of its nothingness of being. Yet while it has to be this being, this is not because it is under the pressure of an external constraint, nor because value, like the Unmoved Mover of Aristotle, exercises over it an attraction of fact, nor is it because its being has been received; but it is because in its being it makes itself be as having to be this being. In a word the *self,* the for-itself, and their inter-relation stand within the limits of an unconditioned freedom—in the sense that *nothing* makes value exist—unless it is that freedom which by the same stroke makes me myself exist—and also within the limits of concrete factic-ity—since as the foundation of its nothingness, the for-itself can not be the foundation of its being. There is then a total contingency of being-for-value (which will come up again in connection with morality to paralyze and relativize it) and at the same time a free and absolute necessity.[12]

Value in its original upsurge is not *posited* by the for-itself; it is consubstan-tial with it—to such a degree that there is no consciousness which is not haunted by *its* value and that human-reality in the broad sense includes both

[12] One will perhaps be tempted to translate the trinity under consideration into Hegelian terms and to make of the in-itself, the thesis, of the for-itself the antithesis, and of the in-itself-for-itself or value the synthesis. But it must be noted here that while the For-itself *lacks* the In-itself, the In-itself does not *lack* the For-itself. There is then no reciprocity in the opposition. In a word, the For-itself remains non-essential and contingent in relation to the In-itself, and it is this non-essentiality which we earlier called its facticity. In addition, the synthesis or value would indeed be a return to the thesis, then a return upon itself; but as this is an unrealizable totality, the For-itself is not a moment which can be surpassed. As such its nature approaches much nearer to the "ambiguous" realities of Kierkegaard. Furthermore we find here a double play of unilateral oppositions: the For-itself in one sense lacks the In-itself, which does not lack the For-itself; but in another sense the For-itself lacks its own possibility (or the lacking For-itself), which in this case does not lack it.

the for-itself and value. If value haunts the for-itself without being posited by it, this is because value is not the object of a thesis; otherwise the for-itself would have to be a positional object to itself since value and the for-itself can arise only in the consubstantial unity of a dyad. Thus the for-itself as a non-thetic self-consciousness does not exist in the face of value in the sense that for Leibniz the monad exists "alone in the face of God." Value therefore is not known at this stage since knowledge posits the object in the face of consciousness. Value is merely given with the non-thetic translucency of the for-itself, which makes itself be as the consciousness of being. Value is everywhere and nowhere; at the heart of the nihilating relation "reflection-reflecting," it is present and out of reach, and it is simply lived as the concrete meaning of that lack which makes my present being. In order for value to become the object of a thesis, the for-itself which it haunts must also appear before the regard of reflection. Reflective consciousness in fact accomplishes two things by the same stroke; the Erlebnis reflected-on is posited in its nature as lack and value is disengaged as the out-of reach meaning of what is lacked. Thus reflective consciousness can be properly called a moral consciousness since it can not arise without at the same moment disclosing values. It is obvious that I remain free in my reflective consciousness to direct my attention on these values or to neglect them—exactly as it depends on me to look more closely at this table, my pen, or my package of tobacco. But whether they are the object of a detailed attention or not, in any case they are.

It is not necessary to conclude, however, that the reflective regard is the only one which can make value appear, nor should we by analogy project the values of our for-itself into the world of transcendence. If the object of intuition is a phenomenon of human reality but transcendent, it appears immediately with its value, for the for-itself of the Other is not a hidden phenomenon which would be given only as the conclusion of a reasoning by analogy. It manifests itself originally to my for-itself; as we shall see, the presence of the for-itself as for-others is even the necessary condition for the constitution of the for-itself as such. In this upsurge of the for-others, value is given as in the upsurge of the for-itself, although in a different mode of being. But we can not treat here the objective encounter with values in the world since we have not elucidated the nature of the for-others. We shall return to the examination of this question in the third part of this work.

## IV. THE FOR-ITSELF AND THE BEING OF POSSIBILITIES

We have seen that human reality as for-itself is a lack and that what it lacks is a certain coincidence with itself. Concretely, each particular for-itself (Erlebnis) lacks a certain particular and concrete reality, which if the for-itself were synthetically assimilated with it, would transform the for-itself into itself. It lacks *something for something else*—as the broken disc of the moon lacks that which would be necessary to complete it and transform it into a full moon. Thus the lacking arises in the process of transcendence and is determined by a return toward the existing in terms of the lacked. The lacking thus defined is transcendent and complementary in relation to the existing. They are then of the same nature. What the crescent moon lacks in order to be a full moon is precisely a fragment of moon; what the obtuse angle ABC lacks in order to make two right angles is the acute angle CBD. What the for-itself lacks in order to be made a whole with itself is the for-itself. But we are by no means dealing with a strange for-itself; that is, with a for-itself which I am not. In fact since the risen ideal is the coincidence with self, the lacking for-itself is a for-itself which I *am*. But on the other hand, if I were it in the mode of identity, the ensemble would become an in-itself. I am the lacking for-itself in the mode of having to be the for-itself which I am not, in order to identify myself with it in the unity of the self. Thus the original transcendent relation of the for-itself to the self perpetually outlines a project of identification of the for-itself with an absent for-itself which it is and which it *lacks*. What is given as the *peculiar lack* of each for-itself and what is strictly defined as lacking to precisely this for-itself and no other is the possibility of the for-itself. The possible rises on the ground of the nihilation of the for-itself. It is not conceived thematically *afterwards* as a means of reuniting the self. Rather the upsurge of the for-itself as the nihilation of the in-itself and the decompression of being causes possibility to arise as one of the aspects of this decompression of being; that is, as a way of being what one is—at a distance from the self. Thus the for-itself can not appear without being haunted by value and projected toward its own possibles. Yet as soon as it refers us to its possibles, the *cogito* drives us outside the instant toward that which it is in the mode of not being it.

In order to understand better how human reality both is and is not its own possibilities, we must return to the notion of *the possible* and attempt to elucidate it.

With the possible as with value there is the greatest difficulty in understanding its being, for it is given as prior to the being of which it is the pure possibility; and yet qua possible, at least, it necessarily must have being. Do we not say, "It *is* possible that he may come." Since Leibniz the term "possible" is usually applied to an event which is not engaged in an existing causal series such that the event can be surely determined and which involves no contradiction either with itself or with the system under consideration. Thus defined the possible is possible only with regard to knowledge since we are not in a position either to affirm or to deny the possible confronted.

Hence we may take two attitudes in the face of the possible: We can consider, as Spinoza did, that possibilities exist only in connection with our ignorance and that they disappear when our ignorance disappears. In this case the possible is only a subjective stage on the road to perfect knowledge; it has only the reality of a psychic mode; as confused or curtailed thought it has a concrete being but not as a property of the world. But it is also permissible, as Leibniz does, to make of the infinity of possibles objects of thought for the divine understanding and so confer on them a mode of absolute reality; this position reserves for the divine will the power to realize the best system among them. In this case, although the monad's chain of perceptions is strictly determined, and although in terms of the very formula of Adam's substance an all-knowing being can establish with certainty Adam's decision, it is not absurd to say: "It is possible that Adam might not pick the apple." This means only that there exists by virtue of the thought of the divine understanding another system of co-possibles such that Adam figures there as having not eaten the fruit of the Tree of Knowledge.

But is this conception so different from that of Spinoza? Actually the reality of the possible is uniquely that of the divine thought! This means that it has being as thought which has not been realized. Of course the idea of subjectivity has been here pushed to its limit, for we are dealing with a divine consciousness, not mine; and if we have first made a point of confusing subjectivity and finitude, subjectivity disappears when the understanding becomes infinite. Yet the fact remains that the possible is a thought which is only thought. Leibniz himself seems to have wished to confer an autonomy and a sort of peculiar weight on possibilities, for several of the metaphysical fragments published by Couturat show us possibles organizing themselves into systems of co-possibles in which the fullest and richest tend by themselves to be realized. But there is here only a suggestion of such a doctrine, and Leibniz has not developed it—doubtless because he could not do so. To give possibles a tendency toward being means either that the possible is already in full being and that it has the same type of being—in the sense that we grant to the bud a tendency to become a flower—or else that the possible in the bosom of the divine understanding is already an idea-force and that the maximum of idea-forces organized in a system automatically releases the divine will. But in the latter case we do not get out of the subjective. If then we define possible as non-contradictory, it can have being only as the thought of a being prior to the real world or prior to the pure consciousness of the world such as it is. In either case the possible loses its nature as possible and is reabsorbed in the subjective being of the representation.

But this represented-being of the possible can not account for its nature; on the contrary it destroys its nature. In the everyday use which we make of the possible, we can in no way apprehend it either as an aspect of our ignorance or as a non-contradictory structure belonging to a world not realized and at the margin of this world. The possible appears to us as a property of beings. After glancing at the sky I state, "It is possible that it may rain." I do not understand the "possible" here as meaning "without contradiction with the present state of the sky." This possibility belongs to the sky as a threat; it represents a surpassing on the part of these clouds, which I perceive, toward rain. The clouds carry this surpassing within themselves, which means not that the surpassing will be realized but only that the structure of being of the cloud is a transcendence toward rain. The possibility here is given as belonging to a particular being for which it is a *power*. This fact is sufficiently indicated by the way in which we say indifferently of a friend for whom we are waiting, "It is possible that he may come" or "He *can* come." Thus the possible can not be reduced to a subjective reality. Neither is it prior to the real or to the true. It is a concrete property of already existing realities. In order for the rain to be possible, there must be clouds in the sky. To suppress being in order to establish the possible in its purity is an absurd attempt. The frequently cited passage from not-being to being via possibility does not correspond to the real. To be sure, the possible state does not exist yet; but it is the possible state of a certain existent which sustains by its being the possibility and the non-being of its future state.

Certainly we are running the risk of letting these few remarks lead us to the Aristotelian "potentiality." This would be to fall from Charybdis to Scylla, to avoid the purely *logical* conception of possibility only to fall into a *magical* conception. Being-in-itself can not "be potentiality" or "have potentialities." In itself it is what it is—in the absolute plenitude of its identity. The cloud is not "potential rain;" it is, in itself, a certain quantity of water vapor, which at a given temperature and under a given pressure is strictly what it is. The in-itself is actuality. But we can conceive clearly enough how the scientific attitude in its attempt to dehumanize the world has encountered possibilities as *potentialities* and has got rid of them by making of them the pure subjective results of our logical calculation and of our ignorance. The first scientific step is correct; the possible comes into the world through human reality. These clouds can change into rain only if I surpass them towards the rain, just as the crescent moon lacks a portion of the disc only if I surpass the crescent towards the full moon. But was it necessary afterwards to make of the possible a simple given of our psychic subjectivity? Just as there can be lack in the world only if it comes to the world through a being which is its own lack, so there can be possibility in the world only if it comes through a being which is for itself in its own possibility.

But to be exact, possibility can not in essence coincide with the pure *thought* of possibilities. In fact if possibility is not first given as an objective structure of beings or of a particular being, then thought, however we consider it, can not inclose the possible within it as its thought content. If we consider possibles in the heart of the divine understanding as the content of the divine thought, beheld they become purely and simply *concrete representations*. Let us admit as a pure hypothesis—although it is impossible to understand how this negative power could come to a being wholly positive—that God has the power to deny; i.e., to bring negative judgments to bear on his representations. Even so we can not understand how he could transform these representations into *possibles*. At the very most the result of the negation would be to constitute them as "without real correspondent." But to say that the centaur does not exist is by no means to say that it is possible. Neither affirmation nor negation can confer the character of possibility on a representation. If it is claimed that this character can be given by a synthesis of negation and affirmation, still we must observe that a synthesis is not a sum and that it would be necessary to account for this synthesis as an organic totality provided with its own meaning and not in terms of the elements of which it is a synthesis. Similarly the pure subjective and negative attestation of our ignorance concerning the relation to the real of one of our ideas could not account for the character of possibility in this representation; it could only put us in a state of indifference with respect to the representation and could not confer on it that *right* over the real which is the fundamental structure of the possible. If it is pointed out that certain tendencies influence me to expect this in preference to that, we shall say that these tendencies, far from explaining transcendence, on the contrary presuppose it; they must already, as we have seen, exist as a lack. Furthermore if the possible is not given in some way, these tendencies will be able to inspire us to *hope* that my representation may adequately correspond to reality but they will not be able to confer on me a right over the real. In a word the apprehension of the possible as such supposes an original surpassing. Every effort to establish the possible in terms of a subjectivity which would be what is—that is, which would close in upon itself—is on principle doomed to failure.

But if it is true that the possible is an option on being, and if it is true that the possible can come into the world only through a being which is its own possibility, this implies for human reality the necessity of being its being in the form of an option on its being. There is possibility when instead of being purely and simply what I am, I exist as the Right to be what I am. But this very right separates me from what I have the right to be. Property right appears only when someone contests my property, when already in some respect it is no longer mine. The tranquil enjoyment of what I possess is a pure and simple fact, not a right. Thus if possibility is to exist, human reality as itself must necessarily be something other than itself. This possible is that element of the For-itself which by nature escapes it qua For-itself. The possible is a new aspect of the nihilation of the In-itself in For-itself.

If the possible can in fact come into the world only through a being which is its own possibility, this is because the in-itself, being by nature what it is, can not "have" possibilities. The relation of the in-itself to a possibility can be established only externally by a being which stands facing possibilities. The possibility of being stopped by a fold in the cloth belongs neither to the billiard ball which rolls nor to the cloth; it can arise only in the organization into a system of the ball and the cloth by a being which has a comprehension of possibles. But since this comprehension can neither come to it from with-out—i.e., from the in-itself—nor be limited to being only a thought as the subjective mode of consciousness, it must coincide with the objective struc-ture of the being which comprehends its possibles. To comprehend possibil-ity qua possibility or to be its own possibles is one and the same necessity for the being such that in its being, its being is in question. But to be its own pos-sibility—that is, to be defined by it—is precisely to be defined by that part of itself which it is not, is to be defined as an escape-from-itself towards——. In short, from the moment that I want to account for my immediate being simply in so far as it is what it is not and is not what it is, I am thrown outside it toward a meaning which is out of reach and which can in no way be confused with immanent subjective representation. Descartes apprehending himself by means of the *cogito* as *doubt* cannot hope to define this doubt as methodical doubt or even as doubt if he limits himself to what is appre-hended by pure instantaneous observation. Doubt can be understood only in terms of the always open possibility that future evidence may "remove" it; it can be grasped as doubt only in so far as it refers to possibilities of the ἐποχή[13] which are not yet realized but always open.

Strictly speaking, no fact of consciousness is this consciousness. Even if like Husserl we should quite artificially endow this consciousness with intra-structural protentions, these would have in them no way of surpassing the consciousness whose structure they are and hence would pitifully fall back on themselves—like flies bumping their noses on the window without being able to clear the glass. As soon as we wish to define a consciousness as doubt, perception, thirst, *etc.*, we are referred to the nothingness of what is not yet. Consciousness (of) reading is not consciousness (of) reading this letter or this word or this sentence, or even this paragraph; it is consciousness (of) reading *this book*, which refers me to all the pages still unread, to all the pages already read, which by definition detaches consciousness from itself. A consciousness which would be only consciousness of what it is, would be obliged to spell out each word.

Concretely, each for-itself is a lack of a certain coincidence with itself. This means that it is haunted by the presence of that with which it should coincide in order to be *itself*. But as this coincidence in Self is always coincidence with

---

[13] The French text is corrupt, reading d'χη. Obviously Sartre intended ἐποχή. Tr.

Self, the being which the For-itself lacks, the being which would make the For-itself a Self by assimilation with it—this being is still the For-itself. We have seen that the For-itself is a "presence to itself;" what this presence-to-itself lacks can fail to appear to it only as presence-to-itself. The determining relation of the for-itself to its possibility is a nihilating relaxation of the bond of presence-to-itself; this relaxation extends to transcendence since the presence-to-itself which the For-itself lacks is a presence-to-itself which is not. Thus the For-itself in so far as it is not itself is a presence-to-itself which lacks a certain presence-to-itself, and it is as a lack of this presence that it is presence-to-itself.

Every consciousness lacks something for something. But it must be understood that the lack does not come to it from without as in the case of the crescent moon as related to the full moon. The lack of the for-itself is a lack which it is. The outline of a presence-to-itself as that which is lacking to the for-itself is what constitutes the being of the for-itself as the foundation of its own nothingness. The possible is an absence constitutive of consciousness in so far as consciousness itself makes itself. Thirst—for example—is never sufficiently thirst inasmuch as it makes itself thirst; it is haunted by the presence of the Self of Thirst-itself. But in so far as it is haunted by this concrete value, it puts itself in question in its being as lacking a certain For-itself which would realize it as satisfied thirst and which would confer on it being-in-itself. This lacking For-itself is the Possible. Actually it is not exact to say that a Thirst tends toward its own annihilation as thirst; there is no consciousness which aims at its own suppression as such. Yet thirst is a lack, as we pointed out earlier. As such it wishes to be satisfied; but this satisfied thirst, which would be realized by synthetic assimilation in an act of coincidence of the For-itself-desire or Thirst with the For-itself-reflection or act of drinking, is not aimed at as the suppression of the thirst. Quite the contrary the aim is the thirst passed on to the plenitude of being, the thirst which grasps and incorporates repletion into itself as the Aristotelian form grasps and transforms matter; it becomes eternal thirst.

This point of view is very late and reflective—like that of the man who drinks to get rid of his thirst, like that of the man who goes to brothels to get rid of his sexual desire. Thirst, sexual desire, in the unreflective and naive state want to enjoy themselves; they seek that coincidence with self which is satisfaction, where thirst knows itself as thirst at the same time that the drinking satisfies it, when by the very fact of its fulfillment it loses its character as lack while making itself be thirst in and through the satisfaction. Thus Epicurus is right and wrong at the same time; in itself indeed desire is an emptiness. But no non-reflective project aims simply at suppressing this void. Desire by itself tends to perpetuate itself; man clings ferociously to his desires. What desire wishes to be is a filled emptiness but one which shapes its repletion as a mould shapes the bronze which has been poured inside it. The possible of the consciousness of thirst is the consciousness of drinking. We know moreover that coincidence with the *self* is impossible, for the for-itself attained by the realization of the Possible will make itself be as for-itself—that is, with another horizon of possibilities. Hence the constant disappointment which accompanies repletion, the famous: "Is it only this?" which is not directed at the concrete pleasure which satisfaction gives but at the evanescence of the coincidence with self. Thereby we catch a glimpse of the origin of temporality since thirst is its possible at the same time that it is *not its possible*. This nothingness which separates human reality from itself is at the origin of time. But we shall come back to this. What must be noted here is that the For-itself is separated from the Presence-to-itself which it lacks and which is its own possibility, in one sense separated by Nothing and in another sense by the totality of the existent in the world, inasmuch as the For-itself, lacking or possible, is For-itself as a *presence* to a certain state of the world. In this sense the being beyond which the For-itself projects the coincidence with itself is the world or distance of infinite being beyond which man must be reunited with his possible. We shall use the expression *Circuit of selfness* (*Circuit de ipséité*) for the relation of the for-itself with the possible which it is, and "world" for the totality of being in so far as it is traversed by the circuit of selfness.

We are now in a position to elucidate the mode of being of the possible. The possible is the *something* which the For-itself lacks *in order* to be itself. Consequently it is not appropriate to say that it is qua possible—unless by being we are to understand the being of an existent which "is made-to-be" in so far as it is made-not-to-be, or if you prefer, the appearance, at a distance, of what I am. The possible does not exist as a pure representation, not even as a denied one, but as a real lack of being which, qua lack, is beyond being. It has the being of a lack and as lack, it lacks being. The Possible is not, the possible is possibilized to the exact degree that the For-itself makes itself be; the possible determines in schematic outline a location of the nothingness which the For-itself is beyond itself. Naturally it is not at first thematically posited; it is outlined beyond the world and gives my present perception its meaning in so far as my perception is apprehension of the world in the circuit of selfness. But neither is the Possible ignored or unconscious; it outlines the limits of the non-thetic self-consciousness as a non-thetic consciousness. The non-reflective consciousness (of) thirst is the apprehension of the glass of water as desirable, without putting the Self in the centripetal position as the end of the desire. But the possible repletion appears as a non-positional correlate of the non-thetic self-consciousness on the horizon of the glass-in-the-midst-of-the-world.

## V. THE SELF AND THE CIRCUIT OF SELFNESS

In an article in Recherches Philosophiques I attempted to show that the Ego does not belong to the domain of the for-itself.[14] I shall not repeat here. Let us note only the reason for the transcendence of the Ego: as a unifying pole of Erlebnisse the Ego is in-itself, not for-itself. If it were of the nature of consciousness, in fact, it would be to itself its own foundation in the translucency of the immediate. But then we would have to say that it is what it is not and that it is not what it is, and this is by no means the mode of being of the "I." In fact the consciousness which I have of the "I" never exhausts it, and consciousness is not what causes it to come into existence; the "I" is always given as having been there before consciousness—and at the same time as possessing depths which have to be revealed gradually. Thus the Ego appears to consciousness as a transcendent in-itself, as an existent in the human world, not as of the nature of consciousness.

Yet we need not conclude that the for-itself is a pure and simple "impersonal" contemplation. But the Ego is far from being the personalizing pole of a consciousness which without it would remain in the impersonal stage; on the contrary, it is consciousness in its fundamental selfness which under certain conditions allows the appearance of the Ego as the transcendent phenomenon of that selfness. As we have seen, it is actually impossible to say of the in-itself that it is itself. It simply is. In this sense, some will say that the "I," which they wrongly hold to be the inhabitant of consciousness, is the "Me" of consciousness but not its own self. Thus through hypostasizing the being of the for-itself which is reflected-on and making it into an in-itself, these writers fix and destroy the movement of reflection upon the self; consciousness then would be a pure return to the Ego as to its self, but the Ego no longer refers to anything. The reflexive relation has been transformed into a simple centripetal relation, the center moreover, being a nucleus of opacity. We, on the contrary, have shown that the self on principle can not inhabit consciousness. It is, if you like, the reason for the infinite movement by which the reflection refers to the reflecting and this again to the reflection; by definition it is an ideal, a limit. What makes it arise as a limit is the nihilating reality of the presence of being to being within the unity of being as a type of being. Thus from its first arising, consciousness by the pure nihilating movement of reflection makes itself personal; for what confers personal existence on a being is not the possession of an Ego—which is only the sign of the personality—but it is the fact that the being exists for itself as a presence to itself.

Now this first reflective movement involves in addition a second or selfness. In selfness my possible is reflected on my consciousness and determines

[14] The article to which Sartre refers is "La transcendance de l'ego, esquisse d'une description phénoménologique," Recherches Philosophiques 6:1936–1937. pp. 85–123. Tr.

it as what it is. Selfness represents a degree of nihilation carried further than the pure presence to itself of the pre-reflective *cogito*—in the sense that the possible which I am is not pure presence to the for-itself as reflection to reflecting, but that it is *absent-presence*. Due to this fact the existence of reference as a structure of being in the for-itself is still more clearly marked. The for-itself is itself *down there*, beyond its grasp, in the far reaches of its possibilities. This free necessity of being—down there—what one is in the form of lack constitutes selfness or the second aspect of the person. In fact how can the person be defined if not as a free relation to himself?

As for the world—i.e., the totality of beings as they exist within the compass of the circuit of selfness—this can be only what human reality surpasses toward itself. To borrow Heidegger's definition, the world is "that in terms of which human reality makes known to itself what it is."[15] The possible which is my possible is a possible for-itself and as such a presence to the in-itself as consciousness of the in-itself. What I seek in the face of the world is the coincidence with a for-itself which I am and which is consciousness of the world. But this possible which is *non-thetically* an absent-present to present consciousness is not present as an object of a positional consciousness, for in that case it would be reflected-on. The satisfied thirst which haunts my actual thirst is not consciousness (of) thirst as a satisfied thirst; it is a thetic consciousness of *itself-drinking-from-a-glass* and a non-positional self-consciousness. It then causes itself to be transcended toward the glass of which it is conscious; and as a correlate of this possible non-thetic consciousness, the glass-drunk-from haunts the full glass as its possible and constitutes it as a glass to be drunk from. Thus the world by nature is *mine* in so far as it is the correlative in-itself of nothingness; that is, of the necessary obstacle beyond which I find myself as that which I am in the form "of having to be it." Without the world there is no selfness, no person; without selfness, without the person, there is no world. But the world's belonging to the *person* is never posited on the level of the pre-reflective *cogito*. It would be absurd to say that the world as it is known is known as mine. Yet this quality of "my-ness" in the world is a fugitive structure, always present, a structure which I *live*. The world (is) mine because it is haunted by possibles, and the consciousness of each of these is a possible self-consciousness which I *am*; it is these possibles as such which give the world its unity and its meaning as the world.

The examination of negating conduct and of bad faith has enabled us to approach the ontological study of the *cogito*, and the being of the *cogito* has appeared to us as being-for-itself. This being, under our observation, has been transcended toward value and possibilities; we have not been able to

---

[15] We shall see in Chapter III of this Part to what extent this definition—which we adopt provisionally—is insufficient and erroneous.

keep it within the substantial limits of the instantaneity of the Cartesian *cogito*. But precisely for this reason, we can not be content with the results which we have just obtained. If the *cogito* refuses instantaneity and if it is transcended toward its possibles, this can happen only within a temporal surpassing. It is "in time" that the for-itself is its own possibilities in the mode of "not being"; it is in time that my possibilities appear on the horizon of the world which they make mine. If, then, human reality is itself apprehended as temporal, and if the meaning of its transcendence is its temporality, we can not hope to elucidate the being of the for-itself until we have described and determined the significance of the Temporal. Only then shall we be able to approach the study of the problem which concerns us: that of the original relation of consciousness to being.

# 2

## TEMPORALITY

### I. PHENOMENOLOGY OF THE THREE TEMPORAL DIMENSIONS

Temporality is evidently an organized structure. The three so-called "elements" of time, past, present, and future, should not be considered as a collection of "givens" for us to sum up—for example, as an infinite series of "nows" in which some are not yet and others are no longer—but rather as the structured moments of an original synthesis. Otherwise we will immediately meet with this paradox: the past is no longer; the future is not yet; as for the instantaneous present, everyone knows that this does not exist at all but is the limit of an infinite division, like a point without dimension. Thus the whole series is annihilated and doubly so since the future "now," for example, is a nothingness qua future and will be realized in nothingness when it passes on to the state of a present "now." The only possible method by which to study temporality is to approach it as a totality which dominates its secondary structures and which confers on them their meaning. We will never lose sight of this fact. Nevertheless we can not launch into an examination of the being of Time without a preliminary clarification of the too often obscure meaning of the three dimensions by means of pre-ontological, phenomenological description. We must, however, consider this phenomenological description as merely a provisional work whose goal is only to enable us to attain an intuition of temporality as a whole. In particular our description must enable us to see each dimension appear *on the foundation of* temporal totality without our ever forgetting the *Unselbständigkeit* of that dimension.

## A. The past

Every theory concerning memory implies the presupposition of the being of the past. These presuppositions, which have never been elucidated, have obscured the problem of memory and that of temporality in general. Once and for all we must raise the question: what is the being of a past being? Common opinion vacillates between two equally vague conceptions. The past, it is said, is no longer. From this point of view it seems that being is to be attributed to the present alone. This ontological pre-supposition has engendered the famous theory of cerebral impressions. Since the past is no more, since it has melted away into nothingness, if the memory continues to exist, it must be by virtue of a *present* modification of our being; for example, this will be an imprint at present stamped on a group of cerebral cells. Thus everything is present: the body, the present perception, and the past as a present impression in the body—all is *actuality*; for the impression does not have a virtual existence *qua* memory; it is altogether an *actual* impression. If the memory is reborn, it is in the present as the result of a present process, as a rupture in the protoplasmic equilibrium in the cellular group under consideration. Psycho-physiological parallelism, which is instantaneous and extra-temporal, is there to explain how this physiological process is the correlate of a phenomenon strictly psychic but equally present—the appearance of the memory-image in consciousness. The more recent idea of an *engram* adds nothing except that it cloaks the theory in a pseudo-scientific terminology.

But if everything is present, how are we to explain the *pastness* (*passéité*) of the memory; that is, the fact that in its intention a consciousness which remembers transcends the present in order to aim at the event back there where it was. I have shown elsewhere that there is no way of distinguishing the image from perception if we begin by making the image a renascent perception.[1] We shall meet the same impossibilities here. But in addition we thus remove the method of distinguishing the memory from the image; neither the "feebleness" of the memory, nor its pallor, nor its incompleteness, nor the contradictions it shows with the givens of perception can distinguish it from a fiction-image since it offers the same characteristics.

Furthermore since these characteristics are *present* qualities of the memory, they can not enable us to get out of the present in order to direct ourselves toward the past. In vain will we invoke the memory's quality of belonging to me—its "myness," following Claparède, or its "intimacy," according to James. Either these characteristics manifest only a present atmosphere which envelops the memory—and then they remain present and refer to the

---

[1] *L'Imagination.* Alcan, 1936.

present, or else they are already a relation to the past as such—and then they presuppose what they must explain. Some scholars have believed they might easily get rid of the problem by reducing memory to an implied pattern of localization and this to an ensemble of intellectual operations facilitated by the existence of "social contexts of memory." No doubt these operations exist and ought to be the object of psychological investigation. But if the relation to the past is not given in some manner, these operations can not create it. In a word, if we begin by isolating man on the instantaneous island of his present, and if all his modes of being as soon as they appear are destined by nature to a perpetual present, we have radically removed all methods of understanding his original relation to the past. We shall not succeed in constituting the dimension "past" out of elements borrowed exclusively from the present any more than "geneticists" have succeeded in constituting extension from unextended elements.

Popular consciousness has so much trouble in refusing a real existence to the past that alongside the thesis just discussed it admits another conception equally unprecise, according to which the past would have a kind of honorary existence. Being past for an event would mean simply being retired, losing its efficacy without losing its being. Bergson's philosophy has made use of this idea: on going into the past an event does not cease to be; it merely ceases to act and remains "in its place" at its date for eternity. In this way being has been restored to the past, and it is very well done; we even affirm that duration is a multiplicity of interpenetration and that the past is continually organized with the present. But for all that we have not provided any reason for this organization and this interpenetration; we have not explained how the past can "be reborn" to haunt us, in short to exist for us. If it is unconscious, as Bergson claims, and if the unconscious is inactive, how can it weave itself into the woof of our present consciousness? Would it have a force of its own? But then isn't this force present since it acts on the present? How does it emanate from the past as such? Shall we reverse the question, as Husserl does, and show in the present consciousness a game of "retentions," which latch on to the consciousnesses of yesteryear, maintain them at their date, and prevent them from being annihilated? But if Husserl's *cogito* is first given as instantaneous, there is no way to get outside it. We saw in the preceding chapter how protentions[2] batter in vain on the window-panes of the present without shattering them. The same goes for retentions. Husserl for the length of his philosophical career was haunted by the idea of transcendence and surpassing. But the philosophical techniques at his disposal, in particular his idealist conception of existence, removed from him any way of accounting for that transcendence; his intentionality is only the caricature of

---

[2] "Protention" is a forward dimension of consciousness, the opposite of "retention." Tr.

it. Consciousness, as Husserl conceived it, can not in reality transcend itself either toward the world or toward the future or toward the past.

Thus we have gained nothing by conceding being to the past, for by the terms of this concession, the past must be for us as not-being. Whether the past is, as Bergson and Husserl claim, or is not any longer, as Descartes claims, is hardly of any importance if we are to begin by cutting down all bridges between it and our present.

In fact if we confer a privilege on the present by making it "a presence in the world" we must then attack the problem of the past in the perspective of intra-mundane being. People consider that we exist first as contemporary with this chair or this table, and they work out the meaning of the temporal by means of the world. But if we thus place ourselves in the midst of the world, we lose all possibility of distinguishing what no longer is from what is not. Someone may object that what no longer is must at least have been, whereas what is not has no connection of any kind with being. That is true. But the law of being of the intra-mundane instant, as we have seen, can be expressed by the simple words, "Being is," which indicate a massive plenitude of positivities where nothing which is not can be represented in any way whatsoever, not even by an impression, an emptiness, an appeal, or an "hysteresis." Being which is wholly exhausts itself in being; it has nothing to do with what is not, or with what is no longer. No negation, whether radical or subdued in a "no longer," can find a place in this absolute density. Hence the past can exist in its own way, but the bridges are cut. Being has not even "forgotten" its past, for forgetting would still be a form of connection. The past has slipped away from it like a dream.

Descartes' conception and Bergson's can be dismissed side by side because they are both subject to the same objection. Whether it be a question of annihilating the past or of preserving for it the existence of a household god, these authors have considered its condition apart, isolating it from the present. Whatever may be their concept of consciousness, they have conferred on it the existence of the in-itself; they have considered it as being what it is. There is no reason to wonder afterwards that they fail to reconnect the past to the present, for the present thus conceived will reject the past with all its strength. If they had considered the temporal phenomenon in its totality, they would have seen that "my" past is first of all mine; that is, that it exists as the function of a certain being which I am. The past is not nothing; neither is it the present; but at its very source it is bound to a certain present and to a certain future, to both of which it belongs. That "myness" of which Claparède speaks is not a subjective nuance which comes to shatter the memory; it is an ontological relation which unites the past to the present. My past never appears isolated in its "pastness;" it would be absurd even to imagine that it can *exist* as such. It is originally the past *of this* present. It is as such that it must be first elucidated.

I write that Paul in 1920 was a student at the Polytechnic School. Who is it who "was?" Paul evidently, but what Paul? The young man of 1920? But the only tense of the verb "to be" which suits Paul considered in 1920—so far as the quality of being a Polytechnic student is attributed to him—is the present. In so far as he was, we must say of him—"He is." If it is a Paul now become past who was a student at the Polytechnic School, all connection with the present is broken: the man who sustained that qualification, the subject, has remained back there with his attribute in 1920. If we want remembering to remain possible, we must on this hypothesis admit a recollecting synthesis which stems from the present in order to maintain the contact with the past. This is a synthesis impossible to conceive if it is not a mode of original being. Failing such a synthesis, we will have to abandon the past to its superb isolation. Moreover what would such a division in the personality signify? Proust, of course, admits the successive plurality of the Selves but this concept, if we take it literally, makes us fall into those insurmountable difficulties which in their time the Association School came up against.

Someone perhaps will suggest the hypothesis of a permanence in change: the one who was a pupil at the Polytechnic is this same Paul who existed in 1920 and who exists at present. It is he then of whom, after having said, "He *is* a pupil at Polytechnic," we say at present, "He is a former student at the Polytechnic." But this resort to permanence can not get us out of our difficulty. If nothing comes to turn the flow of the "nows" backward and so constitute the temporal series and permanent characteristics within this series, then permanence is nothing but a certain instantaneous content without even the density of each individual "now." It is necessary that there be a past, and consequently something or someone who was this past, in order for there to be permanence. Far from helping to constitute time, permanence presupposes it in order to reveal itself and to reveal change along with it.

We return then to what we caught a glimpse of earlier. If the existential remanence of being in the form of the past does not arise originally from my actual present, if my past of yesterday does not exist as a transcendence behind my present of today, we have lost all hope of reconnecting the past with the present. If then I say of Paul that he *was once* or that he *was for a continued period* a student at the Polytechnic, I am speaking of this same Paul who is at the present time and concerning whom I say also that he *is* now forty years old. It is not the adolescent who *was* at the Polytechnic. Concerning the latter, for so long as he was, we have to say: he *is*. It is the forty-year old who *was* the student. Actually the thirty-year old *was* the student also. But again what would this man of thirty years be without the man of forty who was he? It is at the extreme limit of his present that this man of forty "was" a student at the Polytechnic. Finally it is the very being of the *Erlebnis* which has the task of being a man of forty, a man of thirty, and an adolescent—all in the mode of *having been*. Concerning this *Erlebnis*, we say today that it *is*; we say also of the man of forty and of the adolescent in their time that they *are*; today they form a part of the past, and the past itself is in the sense that at present it *is* the past of Paul or of this *Erlebnis*. Thus the particular tenses of the perfect indicate beings who all really exist although in diverse modes of being, but of which the one *is* and at the same time *was the other*. The past is characterized as the past of something or of somebody; one has a past. It is this instrument, this society, this man who have their past. There is not first a universal past which would later be particularized in concrete pasts. On the contrary, it is *particular pasts* which we discover first. The true problem—which we shall attack in the following chapter—will be to find out by what process these individual pasts can be united so as to form *the* past.

Someone may object perhaps that we have weighted the scale by choosing an example in which the subject who "was" still exists in the present. We will cite other cases. For example, I can say of Pierre, who is dead: "He loved music." In this case, the subject like the attribute is past. There is no living Pierre in terms of which this past-being can arise. But we conceive of such a subject. We admit. What is more, we recognize that for Pierre the taste for music has never been *past*. Pierre has always been contemporary with this taste, which was *his* taste; his living personality has not survived it, nor has it survived the personality. Consequently here what is past is Pierre-loving-music. And I can pose the question which I raised earlier: *of whom* is this past Pierre the past? It can not be in relation to a universal Present which is a pure affirmation of being; it *is* then the past of my actuality. And in fact Pierre has been for-me, and I have been for-him. As we shall see, Pierre's existence has touched my inmost depths; it formed a part of a present "in-the-world, for-me and for-others" which was my present during Pierre's lifetime—a present which I have been. Thus concrete objects which have disappeared are past in so far as they form a part of the concrete past of a survivor. "The terrible thing about Death," said Malraux, "is that it transforms life into Destiny." By this we must understand that death reduces the for-itself-for-others to the state of simple for-others. Today I alone am responsible for the being of the dead Pierre, I in my freedom. Those dead who could not be transferred to the concrete past of a survivor and thus be saved are not *past*; they along with their pasts are annihilated.

There are then beings which "have" pasts. Just now we referred indifferently to an instrument, a society, a man. Was this right? Can we at the outset attribute a past to all finite existents or only to certain categories among them? This can be more easily determined if we examine more closely this very particular notion—"to have" a past. One cannot "have" a past as one "has" an automobile or a racing stable. That is, the past can not be possessed by a present being which remains strictly external to it as I remain, for example, external to my fountain pen. In short, in the sense that possession ordinarily expresses an *external* relation of the possessor to the possessed, the expression of possession is inadequate. External relations would hide an impassable abyss between a past and a present which would then be two factual givens without real communication. Even the absolute interpenetration of the present by the past, as Bergson conceives it, does not resolve the difficulty because this interpenetration, which is the organization of the past with the present, comes ultimately from the past itself and is only a relation of *habitation*. The past can indeed be conceived as being *in* the present, but by making it such we have removed all ways of presenting this immanence other than like that of a stone at the bottom of the river. The past indeed can haunt the present but it can not *be* the present; it is the present which *is* its past.

Therefore if we study the relations of the past to the present in terms of the past, we shall never establish *internal* relations between them. Consequently an in-itself, whose present is what it is, can not "have" a past. The examples cited by Chevalier in support of his thesis, and in particular the facts of hysteresis, do not allow us to establish any action by the past of matter upon its present state. There is no one of these examples, in fact, which can not be explained by the ordinary means of mechanistic determinism. Of these two nails, Chevalier tells us, the one has just been made and has never been used, the other has been bent, then straightened by strokes of the hammer; they appear absolutely similar. Yet at the first blow the one will sink straight into the wall, and the other will be bent again; this is the action of the past. According to our view, a little bad faith is needed in order to see the action of the past in this example. In place of this unintelligible explanation in terms of being which here is density, we may easily substitute the only possible explanation: the external appearances of these nails are similar, but their present molecular structures perceptibly differ. The present molecular state is at each instant the strict result of the prior molecular state, which for the scientist certainly does not mean that there is a "passage" from one instant to the next within the permanence of the past but merely an irreversible relation between the contents of two instants of physical time. Similarly, to offer as proof of this permanence of the past the remanence of magnetization in a piece of soft iron is not to prove anything worthwhile. Here we are dealing with a phenomenon which outlives its cause, not with a subsistence of the cause qua cause *in the past state*. For a long time after the stone which pierced the water has fallen to the bottom of the sea, concentric waves still pass over its surface; here nobody makes an appeal to some sort of action by the past to explain this phenomenon; the mechanism of it is almost visible. It does not seem that the facts of hysteresis or of remanence need any explanation of a different type.

In fact it is very clear that the expression "to have a past," which leads us to suppose a mode of possession in which the possessor can be passive and which as such can without violence be applied to matter, should be replaced by the expression "to be" its own past. There is a past only for a present which cannot exist without being its past—back there, behind itself; that is, only those beings have a past which are such that in their being, their past being is in question, those beings who *have to be* their past. These observations enable us to refuse *a priori* to grant a past to the in-itself (which does not mean, however, that we must confine it within the present). We shall not thus settle once and for all the question of the past of *living beings*. We shall only observe that if it were necessary—which is by no means certain—to grant a past to life, this could be done only after having proved that the being of life is such that it allows a past. In short, it would be necessary first to prove that living matter is *something other* than a physical-chemical system. The opposite attempt—that of Chevalier—which consists in putting the strongest emphasis on the past as constitutive of originality in life, is an ὕστερον πρότερον completely void of meaning. For Human Reality alone the existence of a past is manifest because it has been established that human reality has to *be what it is*. It is through the for-itself that the past arrives in the world because its "I am" is in the form of an I *am me*.

What then is the meaning of "was"? We see first of all that it is transitive. If I say, "Paul is fatigued," one might perhaps argue that the copula has an ontological value, one might perhaps want to see there only an indication of inherence. But when we say, "Paul was fatigued," the essential meaning of the "was" leaps to our eyes: the present Paul is actually responsible for having had this fatigue in the past. If he were not sustaining this fatigue with his being, he would not even have forgotten that state; there would be rather a "no-longer-being" strictly identical with a "not-being." The fatigue would be *lost*. The present being therefore is the foundation of its own past; and it is the present's character as a foundation which the "was" manifests. But we are not to understand that the present founds the past in the mode of indifference and without being profoundly modified by it. "Was" means that the present being has to be in its being the foundation of its past while *being* itself this past. What does this mean? How can the present be the past?

The crux of the question lies evidently in the term "was," which, serving as intermediary between the present and the past, is itself neither wholly present nor wholly past. In fact it can be neither the one nor the other since in either case it would be contained inside the tense which would denote its being. The term "was" indicates the ontological leap from the present into the past and represents an original synthesis of these two temporal modes. What must we understand by this synthesis?

I see first that the term "was" is a mode of being. In this sense I *am* my past.

I do not have it; I am it. A remark made by someone concerning an act which I performed yesterday or a mood which I had does not leave me indifferent; I am hurt or flattered, I protest or I let it pass; I am touched to the quick. I do not dissociate myself from my past. Of course, in time I can attempt this dissociation; I can declare that "I am no longer what I was," argue that there has been a change, progress. But this is a matter of a secondary reaction which is given as such. To deny my solidarity of being with my past at this or that particular point is to affirm it for the whole of my life. At my limit, at that infinitesimal instant of my death, I shall be no more than my past. It alone will define me. This is what Sophocles wants to express in the *Trachiniae* when he has Deianeira say, "It is a proverb current for a long time among men that one cannot pass judgment on the life of mortals and say if it has been happy or unhappy, until their death." This is also the meaning of that sentence of Malraux' which we quoted earlier. "Death changes life into Destiny." Finally this is what strikes the Believer when he realizes with terror that at the moment of death the chips are down, there remains not a card to play. Death reunites us with ourselves. Eternity has changed us into ourselves. At the moment of death we *are*; that is, we are defenceless before the judgments of others. They can decide in truth what we are; ultimately we have no longer any chance of escape from what an all knowing intelligence could do. A last hour repentance is a desperate effort to crack all this being which has slowly congealed and solidified *around us*, a final leap to dissociate ourselves from what we are. In vain. Death fixes this leap along with the rest; it does no more than to enter into combination with what has preceded it, as one factor among others, as one particular determination which is understood only in terms of the totality. By death the for-itself is changed forever into an in-itself in that it has slipped entirely into the past. Thus the past is the ever growing totality of the in-itself which we are.

Nevertheless so long as we are not dead, we are not this in-itself in the mode of identity. We *have to be* it. Ordinarily a grudge against a man ceases with his death; this is because he has been reunited with his past; he *is* it without, however, being responsible for it. So long as he lives, he is the object of my grudge; that is, I reproach him for his past not only in so far as he *is* it but in so far as he reassumes it at each instant and sustains it in being, in so far as he is *responsible* for it. It is not true that the grudge fixes the man in what he was; otherwise it would survive death. It is addressed to the living man who in his being is freely what he was. I am my past and if I were not, my past would not exist any longer either *for me* or *for anybody*. It would no longer have any relation with the present. That certainly does not mean that it would not be but only that its being would be undiscoverable. I am the one by whom my past arrives in this world. But it must be understood that I do not *give* being to it. In other words it does not exist as "my" representation. It is not because I "represent" my past that it exists. But it is because I *am* my past that it enters into the world, and it is in terms of its being-in-the-world that I can by applying a particular psychological process represent it to myself.

The past is what I have to be, and yet its nature is different from that of my possibles. The possible, which also I have to be, remains as my concrete possible, that whose opposite is equally possible—although to a less degree. The past, on the contrary, is that which is without possibility of any sort; it is that which has consumed its possibilities. *I have to be* that which no longer depends on my being-able-to-be, that which is already in itself all which it can be. The past which I am, I have to be with no possibility of not being it. I assume the total responsibility for it as if I could change it, and yet I can not be anything other than it. We shall see later that we continually preserve the possibility of changing the *meaning* of the past in so far as this is an ex-present *which has had a future*. But from the content of the past as such I can remove nothing, and I can add nothing to it. In other words the past which I *was* is what it is; it is an in-itself like the things in the world. The relation of being which I have to sustain with the past is a relation of the type of the in-itself— that *is*, an identification with itself.

On the other hand I am not my past. I *am* not it because I *was* it. The malice of others always surprises me and makes me indignant. How can they hate in the person who I am now that person who I was? The wisdom of antiquity has always insisted on this fact: I can make no pronouncement on myself which has not already become false at the moment when I pronounce it. Hegel did not disdain to employ this argument. Whatever I am doing, whatever I am saying—at the moment when I wish *to be* it, already I *was doing it, I was saying it*. But let us examine this aphorism more carefully. It amounts to saying that every judgment which I make concerning myself is already false when I make it; that is, that I have become *something else*. But what are we to understand by this *something else*? If we understand by it a mode of human reality which would enjoy the same existential type as that to which we refuse present existence, this amounts to declaring that we have committed an error in attributing a predicate to the subject and that there remains another predicate which could be attributed; it would only have been necessary to aim at it in the immediate future. In the same way a hunter who aims at a bird *there where he sees* it misses it because the bird is no longer at that place when the bullet arrives there. He will hit the bird if, on the contrary, he aims a little in advance at a point where the flying bird has not yet arrived. If the bird is no longer at this place, it is because it is *already* at another. At all events it is somewhere. But we shall see that this Eleatic concept of motion is profoundly erroneous; if we can say that the arrow *is* at A, B, *etc.*, then motion really *is* a succession of points at rest. Similarly if we conceive that there has been an infinitesimal instant no longer existing at which I was what I already no longer am, then we are constituting the "me" out of a series of fixed states which succeed each other like images from a magic lantern. If I am not what I pronounced myself to be, this is not because of a slight cleavage between judicative thought and being, not because of a retardation between the judgment and the fact, but because on principle in my immediate being in the presence of my present, I *am* not it. In short the reason why I *am* not what I was is not that there is a change, a becoming conceived as a passage to heterogeneity taking place in the homogeneity of being; on the contrary, a becoming is possible there only because on principle my being and my modes of being are heterogeneous.

The explanation of the world by means of becoming, conceived as a synthesis of being and of non-being, is easily given. But it must be noted that being in becoming could be this synthesis only if it were so to itself in an act which would establish its own nothingness. If already I am no longer what I was, it is still necessary that I have to be so in the unity of a nihilating synthesis which I myself sustain in being; otherwise I would have no relation of any sort with what I am no longer, and my full positivity would be exclusive of the non-being essential to becoming. Becoming can not be a *given*, a mode of immediate being for being; if we conceive of such a being, then being and non-being would be only juxtaposed in its heart, and no imposed or external structure could melt them into each other. The bond between being and non-being can be only internal. It is within being qua being that non-being must arise, and within non-being that being must spring up; and this relation can not be a fact, a natural law, but an upsurge of the being which is its own nothingness of being. If then I *am* not my own past, this can not be in the original mode of becoming; the truth is that I *have to be it in order not to be it* and *I have not to be it in order to be it*. This ought to clarify for us the nature of the mode "was": if I am not what I was, it is not because I have already changed, which would suppose a time already given, but because I am related to my being in the mode of an internal bond of *non-being*.

Thus it is in so far as I *am* my past that I can not-be it; it is even this very necessity of being my past which is the only possible foundation of the fact that I am not it. Otherwise at each instant, I should neither be it nor not be it save in the eyes of a strictly external witness who, moreover, would himself, have to be his past in the mode of *non-being*.

These remarks can show us that there is something inexact in that scepticism of Heraclitean origin which insists solely on the fact that I already no longer am what I say I am. Of course, no matter what someone says that I am, I am not it. But it is incorrect to affirm that I am *already* no longer it, for I have never been it if we mean here "being in itself." On the other hand, neither does it follow that I am making an error in saying that I am it, since it is very necessary that I be it in order not to be it: I am it in the mode of "was."

Thus whatever I can be said to be in the sense of being-in-itself with a full, compact density (he is quick-tempered, he is a civil servant, he is dissatisfied) is always *my past*. It is in the past that I am what I am. But on the other hand, that heavy plenitude of being is behind me; there is an absolute distance which cuts it from me and makes it fall out of my reach, without contact, without connections. If I was happy or if I have been happy, that means that I am not happy. But it does not mean that I *am* unhappy, but simply that I can be happy only in the past. It is not *because* I have a past that I thus carry my being behind me; rather the past is precisely and *only* that ontological structure which obliges me to be what I am *from behind*. This is the meaning of the "was." By definition the for-itself exists with the obligation of assuming its being, and it can be nothing except for itself. It can assume its being only by a recovery of that being, which puts it *at a distance* from that being. By the very affirmation that I *am* in the mode of the in-itself, I escape that affirmation, for in its very nature it implies a negation. Thus the for-itself is always beyond that which it is by the very fact that it is it for-itself and that it has to be it. But at the same time the being which lives behind it is indeed *its* being, and not another being. Thus we understand the meaning of the "was," which merely characterizes the type of being of the for-itself—i.e., the relation of the for-itself to its being. The past is the in-itself which I am, but I am this in-itself as *surpassed*.

It remains for us to study the specific way in which the for-itself "was" its own past. Now we know that the for-itself appears in the original act by which the in-itself nihilates itself in order to found itself. The for-itself is its own foundation in so far as it makes itself the failure of the in-itself to be *its* own foundation. But for all that the for-itself has not succeeded in freeing itself from the in-itself. The surpassed in-itself lives on and haunts the for-itself as its original contingency. The for-itself can never reach the in-itself nor apprehend itself as *being* this or that, but neither can it prevent itself from being what it is—at a distance from itself. This contingency of the for-itself, this weight surpassed and preserved in the very surpassing—this is *Facticity*. But it is also the past. "Facticity" and "Past" are two words to indicate one and the same thing. The Past, in fact, like Facticity, is the invulnerable contingency of the in-itself which I have to be without any possibility of not being it. It is the inevitability of the necessity of fact, not by virtue of necessity but by virtue of fact. It is the being of fact, which can not determine the content of my motivations but which paralyzes them with its contingency because they can neither suppress it nor change it; it is what they necessarily carry with them in order to modify it, what they preserve in order to flee it, what they have to be in their very effort not to be it; it is that in terms of which they make themselves what they are. It is this being which is responsible for the fact that each instant I *am* not a diplomat or a sailor, that I am a professor, although I can only play this being as a role and although I can never be united with it. If I can not reenter into the past, it is not because some magical power puts it beyond my reach but simply because it is in-itself and because I am for-myself. The past is what I am without being able to live it. The past is substance. In this sense the Cartesian *cogito* ought to be formulated rather: "I think; therefore I was."

What deceives us is the apparent homogeneity of the past and the present. For that shame which I experienced yesterday was part of the for-itself when I experienced it. We believe then that it has remained for-itself today; we wrongly conclude that if I can not reenter it, this is because it *no longer exists.* But we must reverse the relation in order to reach the truth. Between past and present there is an absolute heterogeneity; and if I can not enter the past, it is because the past *is.* The only way by which I could be it is for me myself to become in-itself in order to lose myself in it in the form of identification; this by definition is denied me. In fact that shame which I experienced yesterday and which was shame for itself is always shame in the present, and its essence can still be described as for-itself. But its being *is no longer* for itself since it no longer exists as reflection-reflecting. Though capable of description as for-itself, it simply *is.* The past is given as a for-itself *become* in-itself. That shame, so long as I live it, is not what it is. Now that I *was* it, I can say: it *was* shame. It has become what it was—behind me. It has the permanence and the constancy of the in-itself; it is at its date for eternity; it has the total adherence of the in-itself to itself.

In one sense then the past, which is at the same time for-itself and in-itself, *resembles* value or self, which we described in the preceding chapter; for it represents a certain synthesis of the being which is what it is not and is not what it is—with the being which is what it is. It is in this sense that we can speak of the evanescent value of the past. Hence arises the fact that memory presents to us the being which we were, accompanied by a plenitude of being which confers on it a sort of poetry. That grief which we *had*— although fixed in the past—does not cease to present the meaning of a for-itself, and yet it exists in itself with the silent fixity of the grief of another, of the grief of a statue. It no longer needs to appear before itself in order to make itself exist. On the contrary it *is* its character of for-itself; far from being the mode of being of its being, it becomes simply one way of being, a quality. Psychologists because they contemplated the psychic state *in the past* have claimed that consciousness was a quality which could affect the psychic state or not without modifying it in its being. The past psychic first is; and then it is for itself—just as Pierre is blond, as that tree is an oak.

But precisely for this reason the past which *resembles* value *is not* value. In value the for-itself becomes itself by surpassing and by founding its being; there is a recovery of the in-itself by the self. As a result, the contingency of being gives way to necessity. The past on the contrary is at the start in-itself. The for-itself is sustained in being by the in-itself; its *raison d'être* is no longer being for-itself. It has become in-itself, and as a result it appears to us in its pure contingency. There is no *reason* for our past to be this or that; it appears in the totality of its series as the pure fact for which we must account qua fact, as the *gratuitous*. In short, it is value reversed—the for-itself recovered by the in-itself and fixed by it, penetrated and blinded by the full density of the in-itself, thickened by the in-itself to the point of no longer being able to exist as a reflection for the reflecting nor as the reflecting for the reflection, but simply as an in-itself indication of the dyad reflecting-reflection. This is why the past can, if need be, be the object aimed at by a for-itself which wants to *realize* value and flee the anguish which comes to it from the perpetual absence of the self. But in essence it is radically distinct from value; it is precisely the indicative from which no imperative can be deduced; it is the unique fact for each for-itself, the contingent and unalterable fact which I was.

Thus the Past is a For-itself reapprehended and inundated by the In-itself. How can this happen? We have described the meaning of *being-past* for an event and of *having a past* for a human reality. We have seen that the Past is an ontological law of the For-itself; that is, everything which can be a For-itself must be it back there behind itself, out of reach. It is in this sense that we can accept the statement of Hegel: "*Wesen ist was gewesen ist.*" My essence is in the past; the past is the law of its being. But we have not explained why a concrete event of the For-itself *becomes* past. How does a For-itself which *was* its past become the Past which a new For-itself has to be? The passage to the past is a modification of being. What is this modification? In order to understand this we must first apprehend the relation of the *present* For-itself to being. Thus as we might have foreseen, the study of the Past refers us to that of the Present.

## B. The present

In contrast to the Past which is in-itself, the Present is for-itself. What is its being? There is a peculiar paradox in the Present: On the one hand, we willingly define it as *being*; what is present is—in contrast to the future which is not yet and to the past which is no longer. But on the other hand, a rigorous analysis which would attempt to rid the present of all which is not it—i.e., of the past and of the immediate future—would find that nothing remained but an infinitesimal instant. As Husserl remarks in his *Essays on the Inner Consciousness of Time*, the ideal limit of a division pushed to infinity is a nothingness. Thus each time that we approach the study of human reality from a new point of view we rediscover that indissoluble dyad, Being and Nothingness.

What is the fundamental meaning of the Present? It is clear that what exists in the present is distinguished from all other existence by the characteristic of *presence*. At rollcall the soldier or the pupil replies "Present!" in the sense of *adsum*. *Present* is opposed to *absent* as well as to *past*. Thus the meaning of *present* is presence to ———. It is appropriate then to ask ourselves to *what* the present is presence and *who* or *what* is present. That will doubtless enable us to elucidate subsequently the very being of the present.

My present is to be present. Present to what? To this table, to this room, to Paris, to the world, in short to being-in-itself. But can we say conversely that being-in-itself is present to me and to the being-in-itself which it is not? If that were so, the present would be a reciprocal relation of presences. But it is easy to see that it is nothing of the sort. Presence to ——— is an internal relation between the being which is present and the beings to which it is present. In any case it can not be a matter of a simple external relation of contiguity. Presence to ——— indicates existence outside oneself near to ———. Anything which can be present to ——— must be such in its being that there is in it a relation of being with other beings. I can be present to this chair only if I am united to it in an ontological relation of synthesis, only if I am there in the being of the chair as *not being* the chair. A being which is present to ——— can not be at rest "in-itself;" the in-itself cannot be present any more than it can be Past. It simply *is*. There can be no question of any kind of simultaneity between one in-itself and another in-itself except from the point of view of a being which would be co-present with two in-itselfs and which would have in it the power of presence. The Present therefore can be only the presence of the For-itself to being-in-itself. And this presence can not be the effect of an accident, of a concomitance: on the contrary it is presupposed by all concomitance, and it must be an ontological structure of the For-itself. This table must be present to that chair in a world which human reality haunts as a presence. In other words one cannot conceive of a type of existent which would be first For-itself in order *subsequently* to be present to being. But the For-itself makes itself presence to being by making itself be For-itself, and it ceases to be presence by ceasing to be for-itself. The For-itself is defined as presence to being.

To what being does the For-itself make itself presence? The answer is clear: the For-itself is presence to all of being-in-itself. Or rather the presence of the For-itself is what makes being-in-itself exist as a totality. For by this very mode of presence to being qua being, every possibility is removed whereby the For-itself might be *more present* to one privileged being than to all other beings. Even though the facticity of its existence causes it to be there rather than elsewhere, being *there* is not the same as being *present*. *Being there* determines only the perspective by which presence to the totality of the in-itself is realized. By means of the *there* the For-itself causes beings to be for one and the same presence. Beings are revealed as co-present in a world where the

For-itself unites them with its own blood by that total ekstatic sacrifice of the self which is called presence. "Before" the sacrifice of the For-itself it would have been impossible to say that beings existed either together or separated. But the For-itself is the being by which the present enters into the world; the beings of the world are co-present, in fact, just in so far as one and the same for-itself is at the same time present to all of them. Thus for the in-itselfs what we ordinarily call Present is sharply distinguished from their being although it is *nothing more* than their being. For their Present means only their co-presence in so far as a For-itself is present to them.

We know now *what is present* and *to what* the present is present. But what is *presence?*

We have seen that this can not be the pure co-existence of two existents, conceived as a simple relation of exteriority, for that would require a third term to establish the co-existence. This third term exists in the case of the co-existence of things in the midst of the world; it is the For-itself which establishes this co-existence by making itself co-present to all. But in the case of the Presence of the For-itself to being-in-itself, there can not be a third term. No witness—not even God—could *establish* that presence; even the For-itself can know it only if the presence *already is.* Nevertheless presence can not be in the mode of the in-itself. This means that originally the For-itself is presence to being in so far as the For-itself is to itself its own witness of co-existence. How are we to understand this? We know that the For-itself is the being which exists in the form of a witness of its being. Now the For-itself is present to being if it is intentionally directed outside itself upon that being. And it must adhere to being as closely as is possible without identification. This adherence, as we shall see in the next chapter, is realistic, due to the fact that the For-itself realizes its birth in an original bond with being; it is a witness to itself of itself as *not being* that being. Due to this fact it is outside that being, upon being and within being as not being that being.

In addition we can deduce the following conclusions as to the meaning of Presence: Presence to a being implies that one is bound to that being by an internal bond; otherwise no connection between Present and being would be possible. But this internal bond is a negative bond and denies, as related to the present being, that one is the being to which one is present. If this were not so, the internal bond would dissolve into pure and simple identification. Thus the For-itself's Presence to being implies that the For-itself is a witness of itself in the presence of being as not being that being; presence to being is the presence of the For-itself in so far as the For-itself is not. For the negation rests not on a difference in mode of being which would distinguish the For-itself from being but on a difference of being. This can be expressed briefly by saying that the Present is *not.*

What is meant by this non-being of the Present and of the For-itself? To grasp this we must return to the For-itself, to its mode of existing, and outline briefly a description of its ontological relation to being. Concerning the For-itself as such we should never say, "It is" in the sense that we say, for example, "It is nine o'clock;" that is, in the sense of the total equivalence of being with itself which posits and suppresses the self and which gives the external aspect of passivity. For the For-itself has the existence of an appearance coupled with a witness of a reflection which refers to a reflecting without there being any object of which the reflection would be the reflection. The For-itself does not have being because its being is always at a distance: its being is there in the reflecting, if you consider appearance, which is appearance or reflection only for the reflecting; it is there in the reflection if you consider the reflecting, which is no longer in itself anything more than a pure function of reflecting this reflection. Furthermore in itself the For-itself is not being, for it makes itself be explicitly for-itself as not being being. It is consciousness of —— as the internal negation of ——. The structure at the basis of intentionality and of selfness is the negation, which is the internal relation of the For-itself to the thing. The For-itself constitutes itself outside in terms of the thing as the negation of that thing; thus its first relation with being-in-itself is negation. It "is" in the mode of the For-itself; that is, as a separated existent inasmuch as it reveals itself as not being being. It doubly escapes being, by an internal disintegration and by express negation. The present is precisely this negation of being, this escape from being inasmuch as being is there as that from which one escapes. The For-itself is present to being in the form of flight; the Present is a perpetual flight in the face of being. Thus we have precisely defined the fundamental meaning of the Present: the Present is not. The present instant emanates from a realistic and reifying conception of the For-itself; it is this conception which leads us to denote the For-itself according to the mode of that which is and that to which it is present—for example, of that hand on the face of the clock. In this sense it would be absurd to say that it is nine o'clock for the For-itself, but the For-itself can be present to a hand pointed at nine o'clock. What we falsely call the Present is the being to which the present is presence. It is impossible to grasp the Present in the form of an instant, for the instant would be the moment when the present is. But the present is not; it makes itself present in the form of flight.

But the present is not only the For-itself's non-being making itself present. As For-itself it has its being outside of it, before and behind. Behind, it was its past; and before, it will be its future. It is a flight outside of co-present being and from the being which it was toward the being which it will be. At present it is not what it is (past) and it is what it is not (future). Here then we are referred to the Future.

## C. The future

Let us note first that the in-itself can neither be future nor contain a part of the future. The full moon is future only when I regard this crescent moon as "in the world" which is revealed to human reality: it is only by human reality that the Future arrives in the world. In itself this quarter of the moon is what it is. Nothing in it is potentiality. It is actuality. The future, like the past, does not exist as a phenomenon of that original temporality of being-in-itself. The future of the in-itself, if it existed, would exist in-itself, cut off from being—like the past. Even if we should admit with Laplace a total determinism which allowed us to foresee a future state, still it would be necessary that this future circumstance be outlined on a preliminary revelation of the future as such, on a being-to-come of the world—or else time is an illusion and chronology disguises a strictly logical order of deducibility. If the future is pre-outlined on the horizon of the world, this can be only by a being which is its own future; that is, which is to-come for itself, whose being is constituted by a coming-to-itself of its own being. Here again we discover ekstatic structures analogous to those which we have described for the Past. Only a being which has to be its being instead of simply being it can have a future.

But what exactly is meant by "being its future?" And what type of being does the future possess? We must abandon at the start the idea that the future exists as *representation*.[3] In the first place the future is seldom "represented." When it is, then as Heidegger says, it is thematized and ceases to be my future in order to become the indifferent object of my representation. Finally, if it were represented, it could not be the "content" of my representation, for content, if there were any, would have to be present. Someone may say that this present content will be animated by a "futurizing" intention. That does not make sense. Even if that intention existed, either it would itself of necessity be present—and then the problem of the future is not capable of any solution; or else the intention transcends the present in the future, and then the being of this intention is to-come, and it is necessary to recognize in the future a being different from the simple *percipi*. Moreover if the For-itself were limited within its present, how could it represent the future to itself? How could it have either knowledge of it or presentiment? No fabricated idea could furnish an equivalent for it. Once we have confined the Present to the Present, it is evident that we will never get out of it. It would be of no use to describe the Present as "pregnant with the future." Either this expression means nothing, or it denotes an actual efficacy in the present, or it indicates the law of being of the For-itself as that which is its future to itself—and in this last case it only points out what must be described and explained. The For-itself can not be "pregnant with the future" nor "expectant of the

[3] i.e., in the imagination. Tr.

future," nor can it be "a knowledge of the future" except on the basis of an original and prejudicative relation of itself to itself. We can not conceive for the For-itself the slightest possibility of a thematic foresight, not even that of determined states in a scientific universe, unless it is the being which comes to itself in terms of the future, the being which makes itself exist as having its being outside itself in the future.

Let us take a simple example. This position which I quickly assume on the tennis court has meaning only through the movement which I shall make immediately afterward with my racket in order to return the ball over the net. But I am not obeying the "clear representation" of the future motion nor the "firm will" to accomplish it. Representations and volitions are idols invented by the psychologists. It is the future motion which, without even being thematically posited, hovers in the background of the positions which I adopt, so as to clarify them, to link them, and to modify them. At one throw, as I am there on the court and returning the ball, I exist first as a lack to myself, and the intermediary positions which I adopt are only ways of uniting myself with that future state so as to merge with it; each position has meaning only through that future state. There is in my consciousness no moment which is not similarly defined by an internal relation to a future; when I write, when I smoke, when I drink, when I rest, the meaning of my conscious states is always at a distance, down there, outside. In this sense Heidegger is right in saying that the *Dasein* is "always infinitely more than it would be if we limited it to its pure present." Better yet, this limitation would be impossible, for we would then be making the Present into an In-itself. Thus finality is rightly said to be causality reversed—that is, the efficacy of the future state. But too often people have forgotten to take this formula literally.

We must not understand by the future a "now" which is not yet. If we did so, we should fall back into the in-itself, and even worse we should have to envisage time as a given and static container. The future is *what I have to be* in so far as I can not be it. Let us recall that the For-itself makes itself present before being as not being this being and as having been its own being in the past. This presence is flight. We are not dealing here with a belated presence at rest near being but with an escape outside of being towards ———. And this flight is two-fold, for in fleeing the being which it is not, Presence flees the being which it was. Toward *what* is it fleeing? We must not forget that in so far as it makes itself present to being in order to flee it the For-itself is a lack. The possible is *that which* the For-itself lacks in order to be itself or, if you prefer, the appearance of what I am—at a distance. Thus we grasp the meaning of the flight which is Presence; it is a flight toward *its being*; that is, toward the self which it will be by coincidence with what it lacks. The Future is the lack which wrenches it as lack away from the in-itself of Presence. If Presence did not lack anything, it would fall back into being and would lose *presence to being* and acquire in exchange the isolation of complete identity. It is lack as such which permits it to be presence. Because Presence is outside of itself toward something lacking which is beyond the world, it can be outside itself as presence to an in-itself which it is not.

The Future is the determining being which the For-itself has to be beyond being. There is a Future because the For-itself *has to be* its being instead of simply being it. This being which the For-itself has to be can not be in the mode of the co-present in-itselfs; for in that case it would be without being made-to-be; we could not then imagine it as a completely defined state to which presence alone would be lacking, as Kant says that existence adds nothing more to the object of the concept. But this being would no longer be able to exist, for in that case the For-itself would be only a given. This being is because the For-itself makes itself be by perpetually apprehending itself for itself as unachieved in relation to it. It is this which at a distance haunts the dyad reflection-reflecting and which causes the reflection to be apprehended by the reflecting (and conversely) as a Not-yet. But it is necessary that this lacking be given in the unity of a single upsurge with the For-itself which lacks; otherwise there would be nothing in relation to which the For-itself might apprehend itself as not-yet. The Future is revealed to the For-itself as that which the For-itself is not yet, inasmuch as the For-itself constitutes itself nonthetically for itself as a not-yet in the perspective of this revelation, and inasmuch as it makes itself be as a project of itself outside the Present toward that which it is not yet. To be sure, the Future can not be without this revelation. This revelation itself requires being revealed to itself; that is, it requires the revelation of the For-itself to itself, for otherwise the ensemble revelation-revealed would fall into the unconscious—i.e., into the In-itself. Thus only a being which is its own revealed to itself —that is, whose being is in question for itself—can have a Future. But conversely such a being can be for itself only in the perspective of a Not-yet, for it apprehends itself as a nothingness—that is, as a being whose complement of being is at a distance from itself. At a distance means beyond being. Thus everything which the For-itself is beyond being is the Future.

What is the meaning of this "beyond?" In order to understand it we must note that the Future has one essential characteristic of the For-itself: it is presence (future) to being. And it is Presence of this particular For-itself, of the For-itself for which it is the future. When I say, "I shall be happy," it is this present For-itself which will be happy; it is the actual *Erlebnis* with all which it was and which it drags behind it. It will be happy as presence to being; that is, as future Presence of the For-itself to a co-future being. So that what has been given me as the meaning of the present For-itself is ordinarily the co-future being in so far as it will be revealed to the future For-itself as that to which this For-itself will be present. For the For-itself is the thetic consciousness of the world in the form of presence and non-thetic self-consciousness. Thus what is ordinarily revealed to consciousness is the *future world* without consciousness' being aware that it is the world in so far as it will appear to a consciousness, the world in so far as it is posited as future by the presence of a For-itself to come. This world has meaning as future only in so far as I am present to it as *another* who I *will be*, in another position, physical, emotional, social, *etc.* Yet it is this which is at the end of my present For-itself and beyond being-in-itself, and this is the reason why we have a tendency first to present the future as a state of the world and to make it appear subsequently on the ground of the world. If I write, I am conscious of the words as written and as about to be written. The words alone seem to be the future which awaits me. But the very fact that they appear as *to be written* implies that writing, as a non-thetic self-consciousness, is the possibility which I am. Thus the Future as the future presence of a For-itself to a being drags being-in-itself along with it into the future. This being to which the For-itself will be present is the meaning of the in-itself co-present with the present For-itself, as the future is the meaning of the For-itself. The Future is presence to a co-future being because the For-itself can exist only outside itself at the side of being and because the future is a future For-itself. But thus through the Future a particular future arrives in the World; that is, the For-itself *is* its meaning as Presence to being which is beyond being. Through the For-itself, a Beyond of being is revealed next to which the For-itself has to be what it is. As the saying goes, "I must become what I was;" but I must become what I was—in a world that has become and in a world that has become from *the standpoint of what it is.* This means that I give to the world its own possibilities in terms of the state which I apprehend on it. Determinism appears on the ground of the futurizing project of myself. Thus the future will be distinguished from the imaginary, where similarly I am what I am not, where similarly I find my meaning in a being which I have to be but where this For-itself which I have to be emerges on the ground of the nihilation of the world, *apart from* the world of being.

But the Future is not solely the presence of the For-itself to a being situated beyond being. It is something which waits for the For-itself which I am. This something is myself. When I say that I will be happy, we understand that it is the present "I," dragging its Past after it, who will be happy. Thus the Future is "I" in as much as I await myself as presence to a being beyond being. I project myself toward the Future in order to merge there with that which I lack; that is, with that which if synthetically added to my Present would make me be what I am. Thus what the For-itself has to be as presence to being beyond being is its own possibility. The Future is the ideal point where the sudden infinite compression of facticity (Past), of the For-itself (Present), and of its possible (a particular Future) will at last cause the *Self* to arise as the existence in-itself of the For-itself. The project of the For-itself toward the future which it is is a project toward the In-itself. In this sense the For-itself has to be its future because it can be the foundation of what it is only before itself and beyond being. It is the very nature of the For-itself that it must be "an always future hollow." For this reason it will never have *become*, in the Present, what it had to be, in the Future. The entire future of the present For-itself falls into the Past as the future along with this For-itself itself. It will be the past future of a particular For-itself or a former future. This future is not *realized*. What is realized is a For-itself which is *designated* by the Future and which is constituted in connection with this future. For example, my final position on the tennis court has determined on the ground of the future all my intermediary positions, and finally it has been reunited with an ultimate position identical with what it was in the future as the meaning of my movements. But, precisely, this "reuniting" is purely ideal; it is not really operative. The future does not allow itself to be rejoined; it slides into the Past as a bygone future, and the Present For-itself in all its facticity is revealed as the foundation of its own nothingness and once again as the lack of a new future. Hence comes that ontological disillusion which awaits the For-itself at each emergence into the future. "Under the Empire how beautiful was the Republic!" Even if my present is strictly identical in its content with the future toward which I projected myself beyond being, it is not this present toward which I was projecting myself; for I was projecting myself toward the future qua future—that is, as the point of the reuniting of my being, as the place of the upsurge of the *Self*.

Now we are better able to raise the question of the being of the Future since this Future which I have to be is simply my *possibility* of presence to being beyond being. In this sense the Future is strictly opposed to the Past. The Past is, to be sure, the being which I am outside of myself, but it is the being which I am without the possibility of not being it. This is what we have defined as being its past *behind* itself. The being of the Future which I have to be, on the contrary, is such that I *can only* be it; for my freedom gnaws at its being from below. This means that the Future constitutes the meaning of my present For-itself, as the project of its possibility, but that it in no way pre-determines my For-itself which is to-come, since the For-itself is always abandoned to the nihilating obligation of being the foundation of its nothingness. The Future can only effect a pre-outline of the limits within which the For-itself will make itself be as a flight making itself present to being in the direction of another future. The future is what I would be if I were not free and what I can *have to be* only because I am free. It appears on the horizon to announce to me what I am from the standpoint of what I shall be. ("What are you doing? I *am* in the process of tacking up this tapestry, of hanging this picture on the wall"). Yet at the same time by its nature as a future present-for-itself, it is disarmed; for the For-itself which will be, will be in the mode of determining itself to be, and the Future, then become a past future as a pre-outline of this for-itself, will be able only as the past to influence it to be what it makes itself be. In a word, I am my Future in the constant perspective of the possibility of not being it. Hence that anguish which we have described above which springs from the fact that I am not sufficiently that Future which I have to be and which gives its meaning to my present: it is because I am a being whose meaning is always problematic. In vain would the For-itself long to be enchained to its Possibility, as to the being which it is outside itself but which it is *surely* outside itself. The For-itself can never be its Future except problematically, for it is separated from it by a Nothingness which it is. In short the For-itself is free, and its Freedom is to itself its own limit. To be free is to be condemned to be free. Thus the Future qua Future does not have to be. It is not *in itself*, and neither is it in the mode of being of the For-itself since it is the *meaning* of the For-itself. The Future is not, it is *possibilized*.

The Future is the continual possibilization of possibles—as the meaning of the present For-itself in so far as this meaning is problematic and as such radically escapes the present For-itself.

The Future thus defined does not correspond to a homogeneous and chronologically ordered succession of moments to come. To be sure, there is a hierarchy of my possibles. But this hierarchy does not correspond to the order of universal Temporality such as will be established on the bases of original Temporality. I *am* an infinity of possibilities, for the meaning of the For-itself is complex and cannot be contained in one formula. But a particular possibility may be more determinant for the meaning of the present For-itself than another which is nearer in universal time. For example, the possibility of going at two o'clock to see a friend whom I have not seen for two years—this is truly a possible which I am. But the nearer possibilities—the possibilities of going there in a taxi, by bus, by subway, on foot—all these at present remain undetermined. I *am not* any one of these possibilities. Also there are gaps in the series of my possibilities. In the order of knowledge the gaps will be filled by the constitution of an homogeneous time without lacuna; in the order of action they will be filled by the will—that is, by rational, thematizing choice in terms of my possibles, and of possibilities which are not and will never be my *possibilities* and which I will realize in the mode of total indifference *in order to be reunited* with a possible which I am.

## II. THE ONTOLOGY OF TEMPORALITY

### A. Static temporality

Our phenomenological description of the three temporal ekstases should enable us at present to approach temporality as a total structure organizing within it secondary ekstatic structures. But this new study must be made from two different points of view.

Temporality is often considered as an indefinable. Everybody admits however that it is before all else a succession. And succession in turn can be defined as an order in which the ordering principle is the relation before-after. A multiplicity ordered in terms of before and after is a temporal multiplicity. It is appropriate therefore to begin by considering the constitution and the requirements of the terms *before* and *after*. This is what we shall call the *static* temporal since these notions of before and after can be considered in a strictly ordinal arrangement independent of change proper. But time is not only a fixed order for a determined multiplicity; observing temporality more closely we establish the *fact* of succession; that is, the fact that a particular after *becomes* a before, that the Present *becomes* past and the future a former-future. This will be the subject of our second investigation under the name of temporal *dynamics*. It is of course in the temporal *dynamics* that we will have to look for the secret of the static constitution of time. But it is preferable to divide up the difficulties. Indeed in a sense we can say that the static temporal can be considered separately as a certain formal structure of temporality—what Kant calls the *order* of time—and that the dynamic corresponds to the material flow or—using Kantian terminology—to the *course* of time. It will be to our advantage therefore to consider separately first this order and then this course.

The order "before-after" is defined first of all by irreversibility. We call such a series successive when we can consider the terms only one at a time and only in one direction. But precisely because the terms of the series are revealed *one at a time* and because each is exclusive of the others, some people have wanted to see in the *before* and the *after* forms of separation. Actually time does separate me, for example, from the realization of my desires. If I am obliged to wait for that realization, it is because it is located *after* other events. Without the succession of the "after," I would be *immediately* what I wish to be; there would no longer be any distance between the present me and the later me, nor any separation between dream and action. Novelists and poets have insisted on time's power to separate, and they have emphasized likewise an accompanying idea, which however springs from the dynamic temporal—that every "now" is destined to become a "formerly." Time gnaws and wears away; it separates; it flies. And by virtue of separation—by separating man from his pain or from the object of his pain—time cures.

"Let time do it," said the King to Don Roderigo. In general people have been struck with the necessity for all being to be divided up into an infinite dispersion of *afters* which succeed each other. Even the *permanents*, even this table, which remains invariable while I change, must spread out and refract its being in the temporal dispersion. Time separates me from myself, from what I have been, from what I wish to be, from what I wish to do, from things, and from others. It is time which is chosen as the practical measure of distance; this town is half an hour away, that one an hour; it will take three days to finish this work, *etc.* It results from these premises that a temporal vision of the world and of man will dissolve into a crumbling of befores and afters. The unity of this crumbling, the temporal atom, will be the *instant*, which has its place *before* certain determined instants and after other instants without admitting either before or after inside its own form. The instant is indivisible and non-temporal since temporality is succession, but the world dissolves into an infinite dust of instants. And it is a problem for Descartes, for example, to learn *how* there can be a passage from one instant to another instant; for the instants are juxtaposed—i.e., separated by *nothing* and yet without communication. Similarly Proust asks how his Self can pass from one instant to another; how, for example, he discovers after a night's sleep precisely the Self of the day before rather than some other one. More radically, the empiricists after having denied the permanence of the Self try in vain to establish a semblance of transversal unity across the instants of psychic life. Thus when we consider in isolation the dissolving power of temporality, we are forced to admit that the fact of having existed at a given instant does not constitute a right to exist at the following instant, not even a mortgage or option on the future. The problem is then to explain how there is a world—i.e., connected changes and permanences in time.

Yet temporality is not solely nor even primarily separation. We can account for this by considering more precisely the notion of *before* and *after*. A, let us say, is *after* B. Now we have established an express relation of *order* between A and B which supposes therefore their unification at the heart of this very order. Even if there had been no other relation between A and B than this, it would still be sufficient to assure their connection, for it would allow thought to *go* from one to the other and to unite them in a judgment of succession. If, then, time is separation, it is at least a separation of a special type—a division which reunites. So far so good, somebody will say, but this unifying relation is preeminently an external relation. When the Association School wanted to establish that the mind's impressions were held together only by purely external bonds, did they not finally reduce all associative connections to the relation of before-after, conceived as simple "contiguity"?

Of course. But has not Kant shown that the unity of experience and hence the unification of temporal change are required in order for the slightest bond of empirical association to be even conceivable? Let us consider the association theory more carefully. It is accompanied by a monistic conception to the effect that being is everywhere being-in-itself. Each impression on the mind is in itself what it is; it is isolated in its present plenitude and does not allow any trace of the future or any lack. Hume, when he issued his famous challenge, was concerned with establishing this law, which he claimed to derive from experience: one can at will examine any impression, strong or weak; one will never find anything in it but itself so that any connection with an antecedent or a consequent, no matter how constant it may be, remains unintelligible.

Let us suppose a temporal content A existing as a being in-itself and a temporal content B, posterior to the first and existing in the same mode—that is, in the self-inclusion of identity. It should be remarked first that this self-identity obliges them to exist each without any separation from itself, without even a temporal separation, whether in eternity or in the instant—and eternity and the instant are here equivalent since the instant, not being defined internally in connection with before-after, is non-temporal. One may ask how under these circumstances the state A can be prior to the state B. It would be of no use to reply that it is not *states* which are prior or post but the *instants* which contain them, for on this theory the instants are in-itselfs, like the states. But the priority of A over B supposes in the very nature of A (instant or state) an incompleteness which points toward B. If A is prior to B, then A receives this determination in B. Otherwise neither the upsurge nor the annihilation of B isolated in its instant can confer on A isolated in its instant the slightest particular quality. In a word, if A is to be prior to B, it must be, in its very being, in B as A's future. Conversely, B, if it is to be posterior to A must linger behind itself in A, which will confer on B its sense of posteriority. If then we grant a *priori* being in-itself to A and to B, it is impossible to establish between them the slightest connection of succession. That connection in fact would be a purely external relation and as such would necessarily hang in midair, deprived of any substratum, without power to get any hold on either A or B—in a sort of non-temporal nothingness.

There remains the possibility that this relation before-after can exist only for a witness who establishes it. The difficulty is that if this witness can be simultaneously in A and in B, it is because he is himself temporal, and the problem will be raised anew for him. Or rather, on the contrary, he can transcend time by a gift of temporal ubiquity which is equivalent to non-temporality. This is the solution at which both Descartes and Kant stopped. For them temporal unity, at the heart of which is revealed the synthetic relation before-after, is conferred on the multiplicity of instants by a being who himself escapes temporality. Both of them start from the presupposition of a time which would be a form of division and which itself dissolves in pure multiplicity. Since the unity of time can not be furnished by time itself, both philosophers put an extra-temporal being in charge of it: God and his continuous creation with Descartes, the "I think" (Ich denke) and its forms of synthetic unity with Kant. For Descartes, time is unified by its material content, which is maintained in existence by a perpetual creation ex nihilo; for Kant, on the other hand the concepts of pure understanding apply to the very form of time. In both cases it is a temporal (God or "I") which is charged with providing the non-temporals (instants) with their temporality. Temporality becomes a simple external and abstract relation between non-temporal substances; there is an attempt to reconstruct it entirely with a-temporal materials.

It is evident that such a reconstruction, made first in opposition to time, can not later lead to the temporal. Either we will implicitly and surreptitiously temporalize the non-temporal; or else if we scrupulously preserve its non-temporality, time will become a pure human illusion, a dream. If time is real, then even God will have to "wait for the sugar to dissolve." He must be both down there in the future and yesterday in the past in order to effect the connection of moments, for it is necessary that he take hold of them there where they are. Thus his pseudo non-temporality hides other concepts—that of temporal infinity and that of temporal ubiquity. But these can have meaning only for a synthetic form of withdrawal from self which no longer corresponds to being in itself. If, on the contrary, we base, for example, the omniscience of God on his extra-temporality, then he does not have to wait till the sugar dissolves in order to see that it will dissolve. But then the necessity of waiting and consequently temporality can represent only an illusion resulting from human finitude; the chronological order is only the confused perception of an order which is logical and eternal. This argument can be applied without any modification to the Kantian "I think." It would be of no use to object, as Kant does, that time has a unity as such since it arises as an a priori form from the non-temporal; for the problem is not so much to account for the total unity of its upsurge as for the intra-temporal connections of before and after.

Someone may speak of a potential temporality which the unification causes to become actuality. But this potential succession is even less comprehensible than the real succession of which we spoke earlier. What is a succession which waits for unification in order to become a succession? To whom or what does it belong? Yet if it is not already given somewhere, how could the non-temporal secrete it without thereby losing all non-temporality; how could the succession even emanate from the non-temporal without shattering it? Moreover the very idea of unification is here altogether incomprehensible. We have in fact supposed two in-itselfs isolated each at its own place and date. How can we unify them? Are we dealing with a real unification? In this case either we are merely playing with words—and the unification will have no hold on the two in-itselfs isolated in their respective self-identity and completeness; or else it will be necessary to constitute a unity of a new type—namely, ekstatic unity in which each state will be outside itself, down there in order to be *before* or *after* the other. But this would necessitate shattering their being, expanding it, in a word temporalizing it, and would not merely bring them together. But how will the non-temporal unity of the "I think" as the simple faculty of thought be capable of effecting this decompression of being? Shall we say that the unification is potential; that is, that beyond impressions we have projected a type of unity roughly comparable to Husserl's *noema*? But how will a non-temporal which has to unite non-temporals conceive a unification of the type of the succession? And if as will then have to be admitted, the *esse* of time is a *percipi*, how is the *percipitur* constituted? In a word, how could a being with a-temporal structure apprehend as temporals (or intend as such) in-itselfs isolated in their non-temporality? Thus inasmuch as temporality is at once a form of separation and a form of synthesis, it does not allow itself either to be derived from a non-temporal or to be imposed from without upon non-temporals.

Leibniz in reaction against Descartes, and Bergson in reaction against Kant have in turn tried to see in temporality only a pure relation of immanence and cohesion. Leibniz considers that the problem of the passage from one instant to another and its solution, continuous creation, are a false problem and a useless solution. According to him Descartes forgot the *continuity* of time. By asserting the continuity of time, we forbid ourselves to conceive of time in the form of instants; and if there is no longer an instant, there is no longer any relation of before-after between instants. Time is a vast continuity of flow to which no original element existing in-itself may be assigned.

Leibniz has forgotten that before-after is also a form which separates. If time is a *given* continuity with an undeniable tendency to separate, one can raise Descartes' question in another form: what is the origin of the cohesive power of continuity? Of course there are no primary elements juxtaposed in a continuum. But this is precisely because there is *at the start* a unification. It is because I draw a straight line, as Kant says, that the straight line, realized in the unity of a single act, is something other than an infinite series of points. Who then *draws* time? In short this continuity is *a fact* which must be accounted for. It cannot be a solution. We may recall here the famous definition of Poincaré: a series *a*, *b*, *c*, is continuous when we can write a=b, b=c, a<c. This definition is excellent in that it gives us a foreshadowing of a type of being which is what it is not and which is not what it is. By virtue of an axiom, a=c, by virtue of continuity itself, a<c. Thus *a* is and is not equivalent to *c*. And *b*, equal to *a* and equal to *c* is different from itself inasmuch as *a* is not equal to *c*. But this ingenious definition rests on a mere playing with

words as long as we consider it in the view of the in-itself. And while it furnishes us with a type of being which at the same time is and is not, it does not furnish us with either its principles or its foundation. Everything still remains to be done. In the study of temporality in particular, we realize well what service continuity can render us by putting in between the instant $a$ and the instant $c$, no matter how close together they are, an intermediary $b$, such that, according to the formula $a=b$, $b=c$, $a<c$; in this case $b$ is at once indistinguishable from $a$ and indistinguishable from $c$, which are perfectly distinct one from the other. It is $b$ which will realize the relation before-after, it is $b$ which will be before itself inasmuch as it is indistinguishable from $a$ and from $c$. All very good! But how can such a being exist? Whence comes its ekstatic nature? How does it happen that the division which is outlined in it is not achieved? Why does it not explode into two terms, one of which would dissolve into $a$ and the other in $c$? How can we fail to see that there is here a problem concerning its unity? Perhaps a deeper examination of the conditions of the possibilities of this being would have shown us that only the For-itself could thus exist in the ekstatic unity of self. But this examination has not been attempted, and temporal cohesion, with Leibniz, hides after all the cohesion through absolute immanence of logic—i.e., identity. But if the chronological order is continuous, it could not "symbolize" with the order of identity, for the continuous is not compatible with the identical.

Similarly Bergson with his duration, which is a melodic organization and multiplicity of interpenetration, does not appear to see that an organization of multiplicity presupposes an organizing act. He is right in contrast to Descartes when he suppresses the instant; but Kant was right rather than Bergson in claiming that there is no *given* synthesis. This Past of Bergson's, which clings to the present and even penetrates it, is scarcely more than a rhetorical figure. It shows well the difficulties which Bergson encountered in his theory of memory. For if the Past, as he maintains, is inactive, it can only remain behind and will never come to penetrate the present in the form of memory unless a present being has undertaken to exist as well ekstatically in the Past. Of course, with Bergson, it is indeed one and the same being which endures. But that makes one realize all the more the need for ontological elucidations. For we do not know finally if it is the being which endures or if it is duration which is being. And if duration is being, then Bergson must tell us what is the ontological structure of duration; and if, on the contrary, it is being which endures, he must show us what it is in being which permits it to endure.

What can we conclude as the result of this discussion? First of all this: temporality is a dissolving force but it is at the center of a unifying act; it is less a real multiplicity—which could not subsequently receive any unity and which consequently would not even exist as a multiplicity—than a quasi-multiplicity, a foreshadowing of dissociation in the heart of unity. We need not try to consider either one of these two aspects separately. If we first posit temporal unity, we risk no longer being able to understand anything about irreversible succession as the *meaning* of this unity, and if we consider the disintegrating succession as the original character of time, we risk no longer being able to understand that there is *one* time. If then there is no priority of unity over multiplicity, nor of multiplicity over unity, it is necessary to conceive of temporality as a unity which multiplies *itself*; that is, temporality can be only a relation of being at the heart of this same being. We can not picture it as a container whose being would be *given*, for this would be to renounce forever the hope of understanding how this being in itself can be broken up into multiplicity or how the in-itself of the containing minima or instants can be reunited within the unity of *one* time. Temporality *is not*. Only a being of a certain structure of being can be temporal in the unity of its being. The before and after are intelligible, as we have observed, only as an internal relation. It is there in the after that the before causes itself to be determined as before and conversely. In short the before is intelligible only if it is the being which is *before* itself. This means that temporality can only indicate the mode of being of a being which is itself outside itself. Temporality must have the structure of selfness. Indeed it is only because the self in its being is there outside itself that it can be before or after itself, that there can be in general any before and after. Temporality exists only as the intra-structure of a being which has to be its own being; that is, as the intra-structure of a For-itself. Not that the For-itself has an ontological priority over temporality. But Temporality is the being of the For-itself in so far as the For-itself has to be its being ekstatically. Temporality is not, but the For-itself temporalizes itself by existing.

Conversely our phenomenological study of the Past, the Present, and the Future allows us to demonstrate that the For-itself can not be except in temporal form.

The For-itself rising into being as the nihilation of the In-itself constitutes itself simultaneously in all the possible dimensions of nihilation. From whatever point of view it is considered, it is the being which holds to itself by a single thread, or more precisely it is the being which by being causes all the possible dimensions of its nihilation to exist. In the ancient world the profound cohesion and dispersion of the Jewish people was designated by the term "Diaspora." It is this word which will serve to designate the mode of being of the For-itself; it is diasporatic. Being-in-itself has only one dimension of being, but the appearance of nothingness as that which is *made-to-be* at the heart of being complicates the existential structure by causing the appearance of the ontological mirage of the Self. We shall see later that reflection, transcendence, being-in-the-world, and being-for-others represent several dimensions of nihilation or, if you prefer, several original relations of being with the self. Thus nothingness introduces quasi-multiplicity into the heart of being. This quasi-multiplicity is the foundation of all intra-mundane multiplicities, for a multiplicity supposes an original unity at the heart of which the multiplicity is outlined. In this sense it is not true, as Meyerson claims, that the diverse creates a scandal and that the responsibility for this scandal rests with the real. The in-itself is not diversity; it is not multiplicity; and in order for it to receive multiplicity as the characteristic of its being-in-the-midst-of-the-world, a being must arise which is simultaneously present to each in-itself isolated in its own identity. It is through human reality that multiplicity comes into the world; it is the quasi-multiplicity at the heart of being-for-itself which causes number to be revealed in the world.

But what is the meaning of these multiple dimensions or quasi-multiples of the For-itself? They are various relations to its being. When something simply is what it is, it has only one way of being its being. But the moment that something is no longer its being, then various ways of being it while not being it arise simultaneously. The For-itself—if we stick to the primary ekstases (those which both indicate the original meaning of the nihilation and represent the *least* nihilation)—can and must at the same time fulfill these three requirements: (1) to not-be what it is, (2) to be what it is not, (3) to be what it is not and to not-be what it is—within the unity of a perpetual referring. Here we are dealing with three ekstatic dimensions; the meaning of the ekstasis is distance from self. It is impossible to conceive of a consciousness which would not exist in these three dimensions. And if the *cogito* discovers one of them first, that does not mean that this dimension is first but only that it is most easily disclosed. But by itself alone it is *unselbständig* and it immediately allows the other dimensions to be seen. The For-itself is a being which must simultaneously exist in all its dimensions. Here *distance*, conceived as distance from the self, is nothing real, nothing which is in a general way as in-itself; it is simply the nothing, the nothingness which "is made-to-be" as separation. Each dimension is the For-itself's way of projecting itself vainly toward the Self, of being what it is beyond a nothingness, a different way of being this fall of being, this frustration of being which the For-itself has to be. Let us consider these dimensions one by one.

In the first dimension the For-itself has to be its being, behind itself, as that which it is without being the foundation of it. Its being is there, opposite it, but a nothingness separates it from its being, the nothingness of facticity. The For-itself as the foundation of its nothingness—and as such necessary—is separated from its original contingency in that it can neither get rid of it nor merge with it. It is for itself but in the mode of the irremediable and the gratuitous. Its being is for it, but it is not for this being, because such a reciprocity of reflection-reflecting would cause the original contingency of what is to disappear. Precisely because the For-itself apprehends itself in the form of being, it is at a distance—like a game of reflection-reflecting which slipped into the in-itself and in which it is no longer the reflection which makes the reflecting exist nor the reflecting which makes the reflection exist. This being, because of the very fact that the For-itself has to be it, gives itself as something which is irretrievable precisely because the For-itself can not found it in the mode reflection-reflecting but only as it founds the connection between this being and itself. The For-itself does not found the being of this being but only the fact that this being can be *given*.

We are dealing here with an unconditional necessity: whatever the For-itself under consideration may be, it *is* in one certain sense; it *is* since it can be named, since certain characteristics may be affirmed or denied concerning it. But in so far as it is For-itself, it is never what it is. What it is is behind it as the perpetual *surpassed*. It is precisely this surpassed facticity which we call the Past. The Past then is a necessary structure of the For-itself; for the For-itself can exist only as a nihilating surpassing, and this surpassing implies something surpassed. Consequently it is impossible at any particular moment when we consider a For-itself, to apprehend it as not-yet-having a Past. We need not believe that the For-itself exists first and arises in the world in the absolute newness of a being without a past and that it then gradually constitutes a past for itself. But whatever may be the circumstances under which the For-itself arises in the world, it comes to the world in the ekstatic unity of a relation with its Past; there is no absolute beginning which without ever having a past would become past. Since the For-itself, qua For-itself, has to be its past, it comes into the world with a Past.

These few remarks may permit us to view in a somewhat different light the problem of birth. Actually it seems shocking that consciousness "appears" at a certain moment, that it comes "to inhabit" the embryo, in short that there is a moment when the living being in formation is without consciousness and a moment when a consciousness without a past is suddenly imprisoned in it. But the shock will cease if it appears that there can be no consciousness without a past. This does not mean, however, that every consciousness supposes a prior consciousness fixed in the In-itself. The relation of the present For-itself to the For-itself *become* In-itself hides from us the primitive relation of Pastness, which is a relation between the For-itself and the pure In-itself. In fact it is as the nihilation of the In-itself that the For-itself arises in the world, and it is by this absolute event that the Past as such is constituted as the original, nihilating relation between the For-itself and the In-itself. What originally constitutes the being of the For-itself is this relation to a being which *is not* consciousness, which exists in the total night of identity, and which the For-itself is nevertheless obliged to be, outside and behind itself. The For-itself, which can in no case be reduced to this being represents an absolute newness in relation to it, but the For-itself feels a profound solidarity of being with it and indicates this by the word *before*. The In-itself is what the For-itself was *before*. In this sense we can easily conceive that our past does not appear to us bounded by a fine, smooth wire, which would become actual if consciousness could spring up in the world *before* having a past; on the contrary, our past is lost in a progressive obscuration back to that darkness which is nevertheless still *ourselves*. We can conceive of the ontological meaning of this shocking solidarity with the foetus, a solidarity which we neither deny nor understand. For finally this foetus was me; it represents the factual limit for my memory but not the theoretical limit of my past.

There is a metaphysical problem concerning birth in that I can be anxious to know how I happen to have been born from *that particular* embryo; and this problem is perhaps insoluble. But it is not an ontological problem; we do not have to ask why there can be a birth of consciousness, for consciousness can appear to itself only as a nihilation of in-itself —i.e., as *being already born*. Birth as an ekstatic relation of being to the In-self which it is not and as the *a priori* constitution of pastness is a law of being for the For-itself. To be For-itself is *to be born*. But one should not next raise *metaphysical* questions concerning the In-itself from which the For-itself was born, questions such as: "How was there an In-itself *before* the birth of the For-itself? How was the For-itself born from *this* In-itself rather than from another?" *Etc.* All these questions fail to take into account the fact that it is through the For-itself that the Past in general can exist. If there is a *Before*, it is because the For-itself has arisen in the world, and it is from the standpoint of the For-itself that the past can be established. To the extent that the In-itself is made co-present with the For-itself, *a world* appears instead of isolated examples of In-itself. And in this world it is possible to effect a designation and to say *this* object, *that* object. In this sense, inasmuch as the For-itself in its coming into being causes a world of co-presences to exist, it causes also the appearance of its "before" as a co-present to the in-itselfs in a world or, if you prefer, in a state of the world which has passed.

Thus in a sense the For-itself appears as being born from the world, for the In-itself from which it is born is in the midst of the world, as a co-present past among co-present pasts; into the world and in terms of the world a For-itself arises which did not exist before and which has been born. But in another sense it is the For-itself which causes the existence of a *before* in general and the existence in this *before* of co-presents united in the unity of one past world and such that one can *designate* one or the other among them as *this* object. There is not first one universal time where a For-itself suddenly appears not yet having a Past. Rather it is in terms of *birth* as the original and *a priori* law of being for the For-itself that there is revealed a world with a universal time in which we can designate a moment when the For-itself was not yet and a moment when it appeared, beings *from which* the For-itself was not born and a being *from which* it was born. Birth is the upsurge of the absolute relation of Pastness as the ekstatic being of the For-itself in the In-itself. Through birth a Past appears in the world. We shall return to this. Here it is sufficient to note that consciousness or for-itself is a being which rises to being beyond an unalterable which it is and that this unalterable, inasmuch as it is behind the For-itself in the midst of the world, is the Past.

The Past as the unalterable being which I have to be without any possibility of not being it does not enter into the unity "reflection-reflecting" of the *Erlebnis*; it is outside. Yet neither does it exist as that *of which* there is consciousness in the sense, for example, that the perceived chair is that of which there is perceptive consciousness. In the case of the perception of the chair, there is a thesis—that is, the apprehension and affirmation of the chair as the in-itself which consciousness is not. What consciousness has to be in the mode of being of the For-itself is not-being-the-chair. For its "not-being-the-chair" is, as we shall see, in the form of the consciousness (of) not-being (*i.e.*, the appearance of not-being) for a witness who is there only to bear witness to this not-being. The negation then is explicit and constitutes the bond of being between the perceived object and the for-itself. The For-itself is nothing more than this translucent Nothing which is the negation of the thing perceived. But although the Past is *outside*, the connection here is not of the same type, for the For-itself gives itself as being the Past. Due to this fact there can not be a *thesis* of the Past, for one can posit only what one is not. Thus in the perception of the object the For-itself acknowledges itself to itself as not being the object, while in the unveiling of the Past, the For-itself acknowledges itself as *being* the Past and is separated from it only by its nature as For-itself, which can not be anything. Thus the Past is not made a *thesis*, and yet the Past is not immanent in the For-itself. It haunts the For-itself at the very moment that the For-itself acknowledges itself as not being this or that particular thing. The Past is not the object of the *look* of the For-itself. This look, translucent to itself, is directed, beyond the thing, toward the future. The Past as a thing which one *is* without positing it, as that which haunts without being observed, is behind the For-itself, outside the thematic field which is before the For-itself as that which it illuminates. The Past is "posited opposite" the For-itself and assumed as that which the For-itself has to be without being able either to affirm or deny or thematize or absorb it.

To be sure, the Past *can* be the object of a thesis for me, and indeed it is often thematized. But then it is the object of an explicit investigation, and in this case the For-itself affirms itself as *not being* this Past which it posits. The Past is no longer *behind*; it does not cease being past, but I myself cease *to be* the Past. In the primary mode I was my Past without knowing it (but by no means not without being conscious of it); in the secondary mode I know my past but I no longer was it. Someone may ask how I can be conscious of my Past if it is not in the thetic mode. Yet the Past is *there* constantly. It is the very meaning of the object which I look at and which I have already seen, of the familiar faces which surround me. It is the origin of this movement which presently is going on and which I would not be able to call circular if I were not myself—in the Past—the witness of its beginning. It is the origin and springboard of all my actions; it is that constantly given density of the world which allows me to orient myself and to get my bearings. It is myself in so far as I aim at myself as a person (there is also a structure to-come of the Ego). In short, the Past is my contingent and gratuitous bond with the world and with myself inasmuch as I constantly live it as a total abandonment. The psychologists call it *empirical knowledge* (*savoir*). But in addition to the fact that by this term they "psychologize" it, they thus remove any method of accounting for it. For empirical knowledge is everywhere and conditions everything, even memory; in a word, intellectual memory presupposes knowledge. And what is their empirical knowledge—if we are to understand by it a present fact—if it is not an intellectual memory? This supple, insinuating, changing knowledge which makes the woof of all our thoughts and which is composed of a thousand empty indications, a thousand designations which point behind us, without image, without words, without thesis—this is my concrete Past inasmuch as I was it as the unalterable background-depth of all my thoughts and all my feelings.

In its second dimension of nihilation, the For-itself apprehends itself as a certain lack. It *is* this lack and it is also the *lacking*, for it has to be what it is. To drink or to be drinking means never to have finished drinking, to have still to be drinking beyond the drinking which I am. And when "I have finished drinking," I *have drunk*: the ensemble slips into the past. While actually drinking, I am then this drinking which I have to be and which I am not; every designation of myself if it is to be heavy and full, if it is to have the density of the self-identical—every such designation escapes me into the past. If it reaches me in the Present, it is because it divides itself into the Not-yet; it is because it designates me as an unachieved totality which can not be achieved. This Not-yet is gnawed by the nihilating freedom of the For-itself. It is not only being-at-a-distance; it is the whittling down of being. Here the For-itself, which was in advance of itself in the first dimension of nihilation, is now behind itself. Before itself, behind itself: never *itself*. This is the very meaning of the two ekstases Past and Future, and this is why value in itself is by nature self-repose, non-temporality! The eternity which man is seeking is not the infinity of duration, of that vain pursuit after the self for which I am myself responsible; man seeks a repose in self, the atemporality of the absolute coincidence with himself.

Finally, in the third dimension, the For-itself, dispersed in the perpetual game of reflected-reflecting,[4] escapes itself in the unity of one and the the same flight. Here being is everywhere and nowhere: wherever one tries to seize it, it is there before one, it has escaped. It is this game of musical chairs at the heart of the For-itself which is *Presence* to being.[5]

As Present, Past, Future—all at the same time—the For-itself dispersing its being in three dimensions is temporal due to the very fact that it nihilates itself. No one of these dimensions has any ontological priority over the other; none of them can exist without the other two. Yet in spite of all this, it is best to put the accent on the present ekstasis and not on the future ekstasis as Heidegger does: for it is as a revelation to itself that the For-itself *is* its Past, as that which it has-to-be-for-itself in a nihilating surpassing; and it is as a revelation to itself that it is a lack and that it is haunted by its future—that is, by that which it is for itself down there at a distance. The Present is not ontologically "prior" to the Past and to the Future; it is conditioned by them as much as it conditions them, but it is the mould of non-being indispensible for the total synthetic form of Temporality.

Thus Temporality is not a universal time containing all beings and in particular human realities. Neither is it a law of development which is imposed on being from without. Nor is it being. But it is the intra-structure of the being which is its own nihilation—that is, the *mode of being* peculiar to being-for-itself. The For-itself is the being which has to be its being in the diasporatic form of Temporality.

## B. The dynamics of temporality

The fact that the upsurge of the For-itself is necessarily effected according to the three dimensions of Temporality teaches us nothing concerning the problem of *duration*, which falls under the heading of the dynamic of time. At first approach the problem appears twofold. Why does the For-itself undergo that modification of its being which makes it *become* Past? And why does a new For-itself arise *ex nihilo* to become the Present of this Past?

This problem has for a long time been disguised by a conception of the human being as an in-itself. It is the sinew of Kant's refutation of Berkeley's idealism and a favorite argument of Leibniz that change by itself implies permanence. Consequently if we suppose a certain non-temporal permanence which remains *across* time, temporality is reduced to being no more than the measure and order of change. Without change there is no temporality

[4] Possibly an error for the "reflection-reflecting," which Sartre has used elsewhere. Tr.

[5] I find it impossible to transfer the exact meaning from French to English. *Chassé-croisé*, literally a dancing expression, is equivalent to "set to partner." From it derives the meaning of a futile rearrangement of personnel. Tr.

since time could not get any hold on the permanent and the identical. More-over if as with Leibniz change itself is given as the logical explanation of a relation of conclusions to premises—that is, as the development of the attributes of a permanent subject—then there is no longer any real temporality.

But this conception is based on several errors. First of all, the subsistence of a permanent element *apart from* something which changes can not allow change to be constituted as such except in the eyes of a witness who would be himself united with that which changes and with that which remains. In a word the unity of change and the permanent is necessary for the constitution of change as such. But this same term unity, which Leibniz and Kant have misused, does not signify very much here. What is meant by this unity of disparate elements? Is it only a purely external attachment? Then it has no meaning. It must be a unity of *being*. But such a unity of being amounts to requiring that the permanent *be* that which changes; and hence the unity is at the start ekstatic and refers to the For-itself inasmuch as the For-itself is essentially ekstatic being; in addition the unity prevents permanence and change from existing each as in-itself. We should not say that permanence and change are taken here as phenomena and have only a *relative* being; the In-itself is not opposed to phenomena as the noumenon is. A phenomenon is in-itself, according to the very terms of our definition, when it is what it is, even if it is in relation with a subject or another phenomenon. Moreover the appearance of *relation* as determining the phenomena in connection with each other supposes antecedently the upsurge of an ekstatic being which can be what it is not in order to establish the "elsewhere" and relation in general.

Moreover resorting to permanence in order to furnish the foundation for change is completely useless. What Kant and Leibniz want to show is that an absolute change is no longer strictly speaking change since it is no longer based on *anything* which changes—or in relation to which there is change. But in fact if what changes *is* its former state in the past mode, this is sufficient to make permanence superfluous. In this case change can be absolute; we can be dealing with a metamorphosis which touches all of being; it will be consti-tuted as change in relation to a prior state just as it will be in the Past in the mode of *was*. Since this link with the past replaces the pseudo-necessity of permanence, the problem of duration can and ought to be posited in relation to absolute changes. Moreover there is no other kind even "in the world." Up to a certain threshold changes are non-existent; past this threshold, they extend to the total form—*as* the experiments of the Gestalt school have shown.

In addition when we are dealing with human reality, what is necessary is pure and absolute change, which can very well be in addition a change with *nothing* which changes and which is actual duration. Even if we admitted, for example, that the simple consciousness of a For-itself was the absolutely empty presence of this For-itself to a permanent In-itself, still the very existence of the consciousness would imply temporality since it would have to be without change what it is in the form of "having been it." There would be then not eternity but the constant necessity for the present For-itself to become the Past of a new Present and that by virtue of the very being of consciousness. And if someone should tell us that this perpetual recovery of the Present in the Past by a new Present implies an inner change in the For-itself, we should reply that then it is the temporality of the For-itself which is the foundation of the change and not the change which furnishes the foundation for temporality. Nothing can hide the following problems which at first seem insoluble: Why does the Present *become* the Past? What is this new Present which then springs forth? Where does it come from, and why does it arise? We must note that as is shown by our hypothesis of an "empty" consciousness, the question here is not the necessity for a permanence to cascade from instant to instant while remaining materially a permanence. The real question is the necessity for being, whatever it may be, to metamorphose itself completely at once—form and content, to sink into the past and to thrust itself forward at the same time *ex nihilo* toward the future.

But are these really two problems? Let us look more closely. The Present could not *pass* except by becoming the *before* of a For-itself which constitutes itself as the *after* of that Present. There is then only one phenomenon: the upsurge of a new Present which is making-past the Present which it *was*, and the Making-Past of a Present involving the appearance of a For-itself for which this Present is going to become Past. The phenomenon of temporal becoming is a global modification since a Past which would be the Past of nothing would no longer be a Past and since a Present must be necessarily the Present of this Past. This metamorphosis, moreover, affects not only the pure Present; the former Past and Future are equally affected. The Past of the Present which has undergone the modification of Pastness, becomes the Past of a Past—or a Pluperfect. So far as the Pluperfect is concerned, the heterogeneity of the Present and the Past is now suddenly suppressed since what made the Present distinct as such from the Past has now become Past. In the course of the metamorphosis the Present remains the Present of this Past, but it becomes the past Present of this Past. That means first that this present is homogeneous with the series of the Past which extends from it all the way back to its birth, second that this present is no longer its Past in the form of having to be it but in the mode of having had to be it. The connection between Past and Pluperfect is a connection which is in the mode of the In-itself, and it appears on the foundation of the present For-itself. It is this which holds the series of the Past and pluperfects welded into a single block.

The Future, on the other hand, although equally affected by the metamorphosis, does not cease to be future—that is, to remain outside the For-itself, in advance, beyond being—but it becomes the future of a past or a former future. It can enter into two kinds of relations with the new Present according to whether we are dealing with the immediate Future or the far Future. In the first case the Present is given as *being* this Future in relation to the Past: "What I was waiting for—here it is." It is the Present of its Past in the mode of the former Future of this Past. But at the same time that it is For-itself as the Future of this Past, it realizes itself as For-itself, therefore as not being what the Future promised to be. There is a split: the Present becomes the Former Future of the Past while denying that it is *this* Future. And the original Future is not realized; it is no longer future in relation to the Present, but it does not cease to be future in relation to the Past. It becomes the unrealizable co-present of the Present and preserves a total ideality. "Is this what I was waiting for?" It remains a future ideally co-present with the Present, as the unrealized Future of the Past of this Present.

When the Future is far removed, it remains future in relation to the new Present; but if the Present does not constitute itself as the lack of *this* Future, then this Future loses its character as possibility. In this case the former Future becomes an indifferent possible in relation to the new Present and not *its* Possible. In this sense it no longer possibilizes itself but qua possible it receives being-in-itself. It becomes a *given* Possible; that is, a Possible which is in-itself for a For-itself become In-itself. Yesterday it was possible—as my Possible—that I should leave next Monday for the country. Today this Possible is no longer *my* Possible; it remains the thematized object of my contemplation and has become the always future Possible *which I have been.* But its only bond with my Present is that I have to be in the mode of "was" this Present become Past for which this possible has not ceased being a possible—beyond my Present. But Future and past Present are solidified in the In-itself on the foundation of my Present. Thus the Future in the course of the temporal process, passes to the in-itself without ever losing its character as Future. In so far as it is *not* reached by the Present, it becomes simply a *given* Future. When it is reached, it is affected with the quality of *ideality*; but this ideality is ideality in-*itself*, for it presents itself as a *given* lack of a *given* past and not as the lacking which a present For-itself has to be in the mode of *not being.* When the Future is surpassed, it remains forever on the margin of the series of Pasts as a former Future—a former Future of a particular Past become Pluperfect, an ideal given Future as co-present to a Present become Past.

We have yet to examine the metamorphosis of the present For-itself into the Past with the accompanying upsurge of a new Present. It would be an error to believe that the former Present is abolished and that there arises a Present in-itself which retains an *image* of the vanished Present. In one sense it would almost be correct to reverse our terms in order to find the truth, for the making-past of the ex-present is a passage to the in-itself while the appearance of a new present is the nihilation of that in-itself. The Present is not a new In-itself; it is what it is not, that which is beyond being; it is that of which we can say "it is" only in the Past. The Past is not abolished; it is that which has become what it was; it is the Being of the Present. Finally, as we have sufficiently demonstrated, the relation of the Present to the Past is a relation of being, not of representation.

Consequently the first characteristic which strikes us is the reapprehension of the For-itself by Being, as if the For-itself no longer had the strength to sustain its own nothingness. That deep fissure which the For-itself has to be is filled up; the Nothingness which must "be made-to-be" ceases to be, is expelled with the result that Being-For-itself, made past, becomes a quality of the In-itself. If I have experienced a particular sadness in the past, it exists no longer in so far as I have made myself experience it. This sadness no longer has the exact measure of being which can be enjoyed by an appearance which makes itself its own witness. It is because it has been; being comes to it, so to speak, as an external necessity. The Past is a fatality in reverse. The For-itself can make itself what it wishes, but it can not escape from the necessity of being irremediably—for a new For-itself—what it has wished to be. Hence the Past is a For-itself which has ceased to be a transcending presence to the In-itself. Now become an in-itself, it has fallen into the midst of the world. What I have to be I am as a presence to the world which I am not but which I was; I was it in the midst of the world, just as things are, by virtue of existing within-the-world. Nevertheless this world in which the For-itself has to be what it was can not be the same as that to which it is actually present. Thus is constituted the Past of the For-itself as the past presence to a past state of the world. Even if the world has undergone no variation while the For-itself "passed" from the Present to the Past, it is at least apprehended as having undergone the same formal change which we described earlier as taking place at the heart of being-for-itself. This is a change which is only a reflection of the true internal change of consciousness. In other words, the For-itself falling into the Past as an ex-presence-to-being becomes in-itself, becomes a being "in-the-midst-of-the-world," and the world is retained in the past dimension as that in the midst of which the past For-itself is in itself. Like the Siren whose human body is completed in the tail of a fish, the extra-mundane For-itself is completed behind itself as a thing in the world. I am angry, melancholy, I have an Oedipus Complex or an inferiority complex for always, but in the past in the form of the "was" in the midst of the world—just as I am a civil servant or a man with one arm or a proletarian. In the past the world surrounds me, and I lose myself in the universal determinism; but I radically transcend my past toward the future to the same extent that I "was it."

A For-itself which has squeezed out all its nothingness and been reapprehended by the In-itself, a For-itself dissolving into the world—such is the Past which I have to be, such is the avatar of the For-itself. But this avatar is produced in unity with the appearance of a For-itself which nihilates itself as Presence to the world and which has to be the Past which it transcends. What is the meaning of this upsurge? We must guard against seeing here the appearance of a new being. Everything happens as if the Present were a perpetual hole in being—immediately filled up and perpetually reborn—as if the Present were a perpetual flight away from the snare of the "in-itself" which threatens it until that final victory of the in-itself which will drag it into a past which is no longer the past of any For-itself. It is death which is this victory, for death is the final arrest of Temporality by the making-past of the whole system, or, if you prefer, by the recapture of human Totality by the In-self.

How can we *explain* this dynamic character of temporality? If it is not—as we hope we have demonstrated—a contingent quality which is added to the being of the for-itself, we must be able to show that its dynamic is an essential structure of the For-itself conceived as the being which has to be its own nothingness. We find ourselves once more it seems, at our point of departure.

But the truth is that there is no problem. If we believe that we have met one, this is because in spite of our efforts to think of the for-itself as really for-itself, we have not been able to prevent ourselves from fixing it in the in-itself. If we start from the in-itself, the appearance of change can indeed constitute a problem: if the in-itself is what it is, how can it no longer be so. But if, on the contrary, we proceed from an adequate comprehension of the for-itself, it is no longer change which needs explaining but rather permanence—if permanence can exist. In fact if we consider our description of the *order* of time apart from everything which could come from the course of time, it is clear that a temporality reduced to its order would immediately become temporality *in-itself*. The ekstatic character of temporal being would not change anything here since this character is found in the past, not as constitutive of the for-itself but as a quality supported by the in-itself. If we imagine a Future such that it is purely and simply the Future of a for-itself, which is the for-itself of a certain past, and if we consider that change is a new problem in relation to the description of temporality as such, then we confer on the Future, conceived as *this* Future, an instantaneous immobility; we make of the for-itself a fixed quality which can be designated; and finally the ensemble becomes a *made* totality, the future and the past restrict the for-itself and constitute given limits for it. The ensemble as temporarily which *is*, is petrified around a solid nucleus, which is the present instant of the for-itself, and the problem is then indeed to explain how from this instant can arise another instant with its own cortege of past and future. We have escaped instantaneity in the sense that the instant would be the only in-itself reality limited by a nothingness of the future and a nothingness of the past, but we have fallen back into it by implicity admitting a succession of temporal totalities of which each one would be centered around an instant. In a word, we have endowed the instant with ekstatic dimensions, but we have not thereby suppressed it, which means that we cause temporal totality to be supported by the non-temporal. Time, if it is, becomes again merely a dream.

But change belongs naturally to the for-itself inasmuch as this for-itself is spontaneity. A spontaneity of which we can say: it is. Or simply: This spontaneity should be allowed to define itself; this means both that it is the foundation not only of its nothingness of being but also of its being and that simultaneously being recaptures it to fix it in the given. A spontaneity which posits itself qua spontaneity is obliged by the same stroke to refuse what it posits; otherwise its being would become an acquisition and it would be perpetuated in being as the result of being acquired. Yet this refusal itself is an acquisition which it must refuse lest it be ensnared in an inert prolongation of its existence. Someone may say that these ideas of prolongation and of acquisition already suppose temporality, and that is true. But this is because spontaneity itself constitutes the acquisition by the refusal and the refusal by the acquisition, for spontaneity can not be without temporalizing itself. Its peculiar nature is not to profit from the acquisition which it constitutes by realizing itself as spontaneity. It is impossible otherwise to conceive of spontaneity without contracting it within an instant and thereby fixing it in in-itself; that is, without supposing a transcendent time. It would be in vain to object that we cannot think of anything except in temporal form and that our account begs the question since we temporalize being in order to make time spring from it a little afterwards. It would be useless to remind us of the passages in the Critique where Kant shows that a non-temporal spontaneity is inconceivable but not contradictory. It seems to us, on the contrary, that a spontaneity which would not escape from itself and which would not escape from that very escape, of which we could say, "It is this," and which would allow itself to be inclosed in an unchangeable denomination—it seems that such a spontaneity would be precisely a contradiction and that it would ultimately be the equivalent of a particular affirmative essence, the eternal subject which is never a predicate. Moreover it is precisely its character as spontaneity which constitutes the very irreversibility of its evasions since from the moment of its appearance it is in order to refuse itself and since the order "positing-refusing" can not be reversed. The very positing is achieved in a refusing without ever attaining to an affirmative plenitude; otherwise it would be exhausted in an instantaneous in-itself, and it is only because it is refused that it passes to being in the totality of its accomplishment. The unitary series of "acquisitions-refused" has in addition an ontological priority over *change*, for change is simply the relation of the material contents of the series. But we have shown that the very irreversibility of temporalization[6] is necessary to the completely empty and *a priori* form of a spontaneity.

I have presented this thesis by using the concept of spontaneity which seemed to me more familiar to my readers. But we can now take up these ideas again in the perspective of the for-itself and with our own terminology. A for-itself which did not endure would remain of course a negation of the transcendent in-itself and a nihilation of its own being in the form of the "reflection-reflecting." But this nihilation would become a *given*; that is, it would acquire the contingency of the in-itself, and the For-itself would cease to be the foundation of its own nothingness; it would no longer be as having to be, but in the nihilating unity of the dyad reflection-reflecting, it *would be*. The flight of the for-itself is the refusal of contingency by the very act which constitutes the for-itself as being the foundation of its nothingness. But this flight establishes in contingency exactly what is fled: the for-itself which has been fled is left at its place. It can not be annihilated since I *am* it, but neither can it any longer be as the foundation of its own nothingness since it can be this only in flight. It is *accomplished*. What applies to the for-itself as presence to —— is also naturally appropriate as well to the totality of temporalization. This totality never is achieved; it is a totality which is refused and which flees from itself. It is the wrenching away from self within the unity of a single upsurge, an inapprehensible totality which at the moment when it gives itself is already beyond this gift of self.

Thus the time of consciousness is human reality which temporalizes itself as the totality which is to itself its own incompletion; it is nothingness slipping into a totality as a detotalizing ferment. This totality which runs after itself and refuses itself at the same time, which can find in itself no limit to its surpassing because it is its own surpassing and because it surpasses itself toward itself, can under no circumstance exist within the limits of an instant. There is never an instant at which we can assert that the for-itself is, precisely because the for-itself never is. Temporality, on the contrary, temporalizes itself entirely as the refusal of the instant.

## III. ORIGINAL TEMPORALITY AND PSYCHIC TEMPORALITY: REFLECTION

The for-itself endures in the form of a non-thetic consciousness (of) enduring. But I can "feel the time which flows" and apprehend myself as a unity of succession. In this case I am conscious of enduring. This consciousness is thetic and strongly resembles a knowledge just as duration which is

---

[6] Correction for *temporization*, an obvious misprint. Tr.

temporalized under my regard is roughly like an object of knowledge. What relation can exist between original temporality and this psychic temporality which I encounter as soon as I apprehend myself "in process of enduring"? This problem brings us immediately to another problem, for the consciousness of duration is a consciousness of a consciousness which endures; consequently to posit the question of the nature and laws of this thetic consciousness of duration amounts to positing that of the nature and the laws of reflection. In fact temporality in the form of psychic duration belongs to reflection, and all the processes of psychic duration belong to the consciousness reflected-on.

Before asking how a psychic duration can be constituted as the immanent object of reflection, we must try to answer this preliminary question: how is reflection possible for a being which can be only in the past? Reflection is given by Descartes and by Husserl as a type of privileged intuition because it apprehends consciousness in an act of present and instantaneous immanence. Will it keep its certitude if the being which it has to know is *past* in relation to it? And since all our ontology has its foundation in a reflective experience, does it not risk losing all its rights? Yet is it actually the past being which should make the object of reflective consciousness? If the process of reflection itself is a for-itself, ought it to be limited to an existence and certitude which are instantaneous? We can decide these questions only if we return to the reflective phenomenon and determine its structure.

Reflection is the for-itself conscious of itself. As the for-itself is already a non-thetic self-consciousness, we are accustomed to represent reflection as a new consciousness, abruptly appearing, directed on the consciousness reflected-on, and living in symbiosis with it. One recalls here the old *idea ideae* of Spinoza.

But aside from the fact that it is difficult to explain the upsurge *ex nihilo* of the reflective consciousness, it is completely impossible in this way to account for its absolute unity with the consciousness reflected-on, a unity which alone renders conceivable the rights and the certainty of the reflective intuition. We cannot here indeed say that the *esse* of that which is reflected-on is a *percipi* since its being is such that it does not need to be perceived in order to exist. And its primary relation with reflection can not be the unitary relation of a representation to a thinking subject. If the known existent is to have the same rank of being as the knowing existent, then, in short, it is in the perspective of naive realism that we must describe the relation of these two existents. But in this case we are going to encounter the major difficulty of realism: how can two isolated, independent wholes, provided with that sufficiency of being which the Germans call *Selbständigkeit*, enter into relation with each other, and in particular how can they enter into that type of internal relation which we call knowledge? If first we conceive of reflection as an autonomous consciousness, we shall never be able to reunite it later with the consciousness reflected-on. They will always be two, and if—to suppose the impossible—the reflective consciousness could be consciousness of the consciousness reflected-on, there could be only an external connection between the two consciousness; at most we could imagine that reflection isolated in itself possesses an image of the consciousness reflected-on, and we would then fall back into idealism. Reflective knowledge, and in particular the cogito would lose their certainty and would obtain in exchange only a certain probability, scarcely definable. It is agreed then that reflection must be united to that which is reflected-on by a bond of being, that the reflective consciousness must be the consciousness reflected-on.

But on the other hand, there can be no question here of a total identification of the reflective with that reflected-on, for this would suddenly suppress the phenomenon of reflection by allowing only the phantom dyad "the-reflection-reflecting"[7] to subsist. Here once again we meet that type of being which defines the for-itself: reflection—if it is to be apodictic evidence—demands that the reflective be that which is reflected-on. But to the extent that reflection is knowledge, the reflected-on must necessarily be the object for the reflective; and this implies a separation of being. Thus it is necessary that the reflective simultaneously be and not be the reflected-on. We have already discovered this ontological structure at the heart of the for-itself. But then it did not have at all the same meaning. In fact it supposed in the two terms "reflected and reflecting" a radical Unselbständigkeit on the part of the suggested duality; that is, such an inability on the part of the terms to be posited separately that the duality remained perpetually evanescent and each term, while positing itself for the other, became the other. But in the case of reflection, the case is slightly different since "the reflection-reflecting," which is reflected-on exists for a "reflection-reflecting" which is reflective. In other words, the reflected-on is an appearance for the reflective without thereby ceasing to be witness (of) itself, and the reflective is witness of the reflected-on without thereby ceasing to be an appearance to itself. It is even in so far as it is

---

[7] The translator encounters a difficulty here owing to the fact that the English word "reflection" has two different meanings which are perfectly distinct in French. In discussing the dyad "reflection-reflecting," Sartre uses reflet-reflétant. Here "reflection" means that which is reflected—like an image—and easily suggests to Sartre the idea of a game with mirrors. In the present section, however, the subject of discussion is réflexion, which mean the process of mental reflection in general and in particular introspection. As a feeble attempt to prevent confusion, I am in this section using the article with reflet, the "reflection" in the dyad, and in some cases I am giving the French as well.

A similar but less insoluble difficulty occurs with words deriving from réfléchir (to reflect in the sense of réflexion) and refléter to reflect an image. To distinguish these I am using the English expression "reflect-on" where mental action is involved. "Reflective" also indicates the mental process of reflection. Tr.

reflected in itself (se refléte en soi) that the reflected-on is an appearance for the reflective, and the reflective can be witness only in so far as it is consciousness (of) being so; that is, to the exact extent that this witness, which it is, is a reflection (reflet) for a reflecting which it is also. Reflected-on and reflective therefore each tend to the Selbständigkeit, and the nothing which separates them divides them more profoundly than the nothingness of the for-itself separates the reflection (reflet) from the reflecting.

Yet we must note two things: (1) Reflection (reflexion) as witness can have its being as witness only in and through the appearance; that is, it is profoundly affected in its being by its reflectivity and consequently can never achieve the Selbständigkeit at which it aims, since it derives its being from its function and its function from the for-itself reflected-on. (2) The reflected-on is profoundly altered by reflection (reflexion) in this sense that it is self-consciousness as the consciousness reflected-on of this or that transcendent phenomenon. The reflected-on knows itself observed. It may best be compared—to use a concrete example—to a man who is writing, bent over a table, and who while writing knows that he is observed by somebody who stands behind him. The reflected-on has then, in a way, already a consciousness (of) itself as having an outside or rather the suggestion of an outside; that is, it makes himself an object for ———, so that its meaning as reflected-on is inseparable from the reflective and exists over there at a distance from itself in the consciousness which reflects on it. In this sense the reflected-on does not possess Selbständigkeit any more than the reflective itself.

Husserl tells us that the reflected-on "gives itself as having been there before reflection." But we must not be deceived here; the Selbständigkeit of the not-reflected-on qua not-reflected-on in relation to all possible reflection does not pass into the phenomenon of reflection, for the phenomenon loses its character as not reflected-on. For a consciousness, to become reflected-on means to undergo a profound modification of its being and precisely to lose the Selbständigkeit which it possessed as the quasi-totality "the reflected-reflecting." Finally, to the extent that a nothingness separates the reflected-on from the reflective, this nothingness, which cannot derive its being from itself, must "be made-to-be." Let us understand by this that only a unitary structure of being can be its own nothingness in the form of having to be it. In fact neither the reflective nor the reflected-on can issue this separating nothingness. But reflection is one being, just like the unreflective for-itself, not an addition of being; it is a being which has to be its own nothingness. It is not the appearance of a new consciousness directed on the for-itself but an intrastructural modification which the for-itself realizes in itself; in a word it is the for-itself which makes itself exist in the mode reflective-reflected-on, instead of being simply in the mode of the dyad reflection-reflecting; furthermore, this new mode of being allows the mode of the reflection-reflecting to subsist as a primary inner structure. The one who is reflecting on me is not some sort of non-temporal look but myself, myself who am enduring engaged in the circuit of my selfness, in danger in the world, with my historicity. This historicity and this being-in-the-world and this circuit of selfness—these the for-itself which I am lives in the mode of the reflective dissociation (dédoublement).

As we have seen, the reflective is separated from the reflected-on by a nothingness. Thus the phenomenon of reflection is a nihilation of the for-itself, a nihilation which does not come to it from without but which it has to be. Where is the origin of this further nihilation? What can be its motivation?

In the upsurge of the for-itself as presence to being, there is an original dispersion: the for-itself is lost outside, next to the in-itself, and in the three temporal ekstases. It is outside of itself, and in its inmost heart this being-for-itself is ekstatic since it must look for its being elsewhere—in the reflecting (reflétant) if it makes itself a reflection (reflet), in the reflection if it posits itself as reflecting. The upsurge of the for-itself confirms the failure of the in-itself, which has not been able to be its own foundation. Reflection (reflexion) remains for the for-itself a permanent possibility, an attempt to recover being. By reflection the for-itself, which has lost itself outside itself, attempts to put itself inside its own being. Reflection is a second effort by the for-itself to found itself; that is, to be for itself what it is. Indeed if the quasi-dyad the reflection-reflecting were gathered up into a totality for a witness which would be itself, it would be in its own eyes what it is. The goal in short is to overtake that being which flees itself while being what it is in the mode of not-being and which flows on while being its own flow, which escapes between its own fingers; the goal is to make of it a given, a given which finally is what it is; the problem is to gather together in the unity of one regard this unachieved totality which is unachieved only because it is to itself its own non-achievement, to escape from the sphere of the perpetual reference which has to be a reference to itself, and—precisely because it has escaped from the chains of this reference—to make it be as a seen reference—that is, as a reference which is what it is.

But at the same time it is necessary that this being which recovers itself and establishes itself as a given—that is, which confers on itself the contingency of being in order to preserve it while founding it—this must itself be that which it recovers and founds, that which it preserves from the ekstatic scattering. The motivation of reflection (reflexion) consists in a double attempt, simultaneously an objectivation and an interiorization. To be to itself as an object-in-itself in the absolute unity of interiorization—that is what the being-of-reflection has to be.

This effort to be to itself its own foundation, to recover and to dominate within itself its own flight, finally to be that flight instead of temporalizing it as the flight which is fled—this effort inevitably results in failure; and it is precisely this failure which is reflection. In fact it is itself the being which has to recover the being which is lost, and it must be this recovery in the mode of being which is its own; that is, in the mode of the for-itself, therefore of flight. It is qua *for-itself* that the for-itself will try to be what it is or, if you prefer, it will be *for itself* what it is-for-itself. Thus reflection or the attempt to recover the for-itself by a turning back on itself results in the appearance of the for-itself for the for-itself. The being which wants to find a foundation in being is itself the foundation only of its own nothingness. The ensemble consequently remains a nihilated in-itself. At the same time the turning back of being on itself can only cause the appearance of a *distance* between what turns back and that on which it turns. This turning back upon the self is a wrenching away from self in order to return to it. It is this turning back which effects the appearance of reflective nothingness. For the necessary structure of the for-itself requires that its being can be recovered only by a being which itself exists in the form of for-itself.[8] Thus the being which effects the recovery must be constituted in the mode of the for-itself, and the being which is to be recovered must exist as for-itself. And these two beings must be the *same being*. But exactly in so far as this being recovers *itself*, it causes an absolute distance to exist between itself and itself—in the unity of being. This phenomenon of reflection is a permanent possibility of the for-itself because reflective scissiparity exists potentially in the for-itself which is reflected-on; it suffices in fact that the reflecting for-itself (reflétant) posit itself for it as a witness of the reflection (reflet) and that the for-itself (the reflection) posit itself for it as a reflection of this reflecting. Thus reflection (reflexion) as the effort of a for-itself to recover a for-itself which it is in the mode of non-being is a stage of nihilation intermediate between the pure and simple existence of the for-itself and existence *for-others*; it is an act on the part of a for-itself to recover a for-itself which it is not in the mode of non-being.[9]

Can reflection thus described be limited in its rights and its scope by the fact that the for-itself temporalizes itself? We think not.

We must distinguish two kinds of reflection if we wish to grasp the reflective phenomenon in its relations with temporality: reflection can be either pure or impure. Pure reflection, the simple presence of the reflective for-itself to the for-itself reflected-on, is at once the original form of reflection and its ideal form; it is that on whose foundation impure reflection appears, it is that

---

[8] The French says "*without* the form of," which makes no sense and must surely be a misprint. Tr.
[9] We find here again that "division of the equal to itself" which Hegel makes the peculiar trait of consciousness. But this division instead of leading to a higher integration, as in the *Phenomenology of Mind* only makes deeper and more irremediable the nothingness which separates consciousness from itself. Consciousness is Hegelian, but it is its greatest illusion.

also which is never first *given*; and it is that which must be won by a sort of katharsis. Impure or accessory reflection, of which we will speak later, includes pure reflection but surpasses it and makes further claims.

What are the titles and the rights of pure reflection to appear as evidence? Obviously the reflective *is* the reflected-on. Outside of that we should have no means of legitimizing reflection. But the reflective *is* the reflected-on in complete immanence although in the form of "not-being-in-itself." It is this which well demonstrates the fact that the reflected-on is not wholly an object but a quasi-object for reflection. Actually the consciousness reflected-on is not presented yet as something *outside* reflection—that is, as a being on which one can "take a point of view," in relation to which one can realize a withdrawal, increase or diminish the distance which separates one from it. In order for the consciousness reflected-on to be "viewed from without" and in order for reflection to be able to orient itself in relation to it, it would be necessary that the reflective should not be the reflected-on in the mode of not being what it is not: this scissiparity will be realized only in existence for-*others*.

Reflection is a knowledge; of that there is no doubt. It is provided with a positional character; it affirms the consciousness reflected-on. But every affirmation, as we shall soon see, is conditioned by a negation: to affirm this object is simultaneously to deny that I am this object. To know is to *make oneself other*. Now the reflective can not make itself wholly other than the reflected-on since it *is-in-order-to-be* the reflected-on. Its affirmation is stopped halfway because its negation is not entirely realized. It does not then detach itself completely from the reflected-on, and it can not grasp the reflected-on "from a point of view." Its knowledge is a totality; it is a lightning intuition without relief, without point of departure, and without point of arrival. Everything is given at once in a sort of absolute proximity. What we ordinarily call *knowing* supposes reliefs, levels, an order, a hierarchy. Even mathematical essences are revealed to us with an orientation in relation to other truths, to certain consequences; they are never disclosed with all their characteristics at once. But the reflection which delivers the reflected-on to us, not as a given but as the being which we have to be, in indistinction without a point of view, is a knowledge overflowing itself and without explanation. At the same time it is never surprised by itself; it does not *teach* us anything but only *posits*. In the knowledge of a transcendent object indeed there is a *revelation* of the object, and the object revealed can deceive or surprise us. But in the reflective revelation there is a positing of a being whose being was already a revelation. Reflection is limited to making this revelation exist for itself; the revealed being is not revealed as a given but with the character of the "already revealed." Reflection is recognition rather than knowledge. It implies as the original motivation of the recovery a pre-reflective comprehension of what it wishes to recover.

But if the reflective is the reflected-on, if this unity of being founds and limits the rights of reflection, it should be added that the reflected-on, itself, is its past and its future. There is then no doubt that although the totality of the reflected-on, which the reflective is in the mode of non-being, perpetually overflows the reflective, still the reflective extends its apodictic rights to that very totality which it is. Thus the reflective achievement of Descartes, the *cogito*, must not be limited to the infinitesimal instant. Moreover this conclusion could be drawn from the fact that *thought* is an act which engages the past and shapes its outline by the future. I *doubt* therefore I am, said Descartes. But what would remain of methodical doubt if it could be limited to the instant? A suspension of judgment, perhaps. But a suspension of judgment is not a doubt; it is only a necessary structure of doubt. In order for doubt to exist, it is necessary that this suspension be motivated by an insufficiency of reasons for affirming or for denying—which refers to the past—and that it be maintained deliberately until the intervention of new elements—which is already a project of the future. Doubt appears on the foundation of a pre-ontological comprehension of *knowing* and of requirements concerning truth. This comprehension and these requirements, which give all its meaning to doubt, engage the totality of human reality and its being in the world; they suppose the existence of an *object* of knowledge and of doubt—that is, of a transcendent permanence in universal time. It is then a related *conduct* which doubts the object, a conduct which represents one of the modes of the being-in-the-world of human reality. To discover oneself doubting is already to be ahead of oneself in the future, which conceals the end, the cessation, and the meaning of this doubt, and to be behind oneself in the past, which conceals the constituent motivations of the doubt and its stages of development, and to be outside of oneself in the world as presence to the object which one doubts.

These same observations would apply to any reflective statement: I read, I dream, I perceive, I act. Either they should lead us to refuse to grant apodictic evidence to reflection, and then the original knowledge which I have of myself would melt into mere probability and my very existence is only a probability (for my being-in-the-instant is not a being)—or else we must extend the laws of reflection to human totality—i.e., to the past, to the future, to presence, to the object. But if we have observed accurately, reflection is the for-itself which seeks to recover itself as a totality in perpetual incompletion. It is the affirmation of the revelation of the being which is to itself its own revelation. As the for-itself temporalizes itself, there are these results: (1) Reflection, as the mode of being of the for-itself, must be as temporalization, and it is itself its past and its future. (2) By nature reflection extends its rights and its certitude to the possibilities which I *am* and to the past which I *was*. The reflective is not the apprehension of an instantaneous reflected-on, but neither is it itself instantaneity. This does not mean that the reflective knows with its future the future of the reflected-on and with its past the past of the consciousness to be known. On the contrary it is by means of the future and the past that the reflective and the reflected-on are distinguished within the unity of their being. The future of the reflective in fact, is the ensemble of its own possibilities which the reflective has to be qua reflective. As such it could not include a consciousness of the future reflected-on. The same remarks would be valid for the reflective past although this is founded ultimately in the past of the original for-itself. But if reflection derives its meaning from its future and its past, it is already as a fleeing presence to a flight, ekstatically the whole length of this flight. In other words the for-itself, which makes itself exist in the mode of the reflective dissociation, as for-itself derives its meaning from its possibilities and from its future. In this sense reflection is a diasporatic phenomenon; but as a *presence to itself*, the for-itself is a presence present to all its ekstatic dimensions.

It remains to explain, someone may say, how this reflection, which you are claiming to be apodictic, can make so many errors with respect to just that past which you give it the capacity to know. I reply that it is free from any error to the exact extent that it apprehends the past as that which haunts the present in non-thematic form. When I say, "I read, I doubt, I hope, *etc*." as we have shown, I reach beyond my present toward the past. Now I cannot in any of these cases be mistaken. The apodictic nature of reflection allows no doubt in so far as it apprehends the past exactly as it is for the consciousness reflected-on which has to be it. On the other hand, I can make many an error when recalling to myself in the reflective mode my past feelings or my past ideas; this is because I am on the plane of memory. At that moment I no longer *am* my past but I am thematizing it. We are then no longer dealing with the reflective act.

Thus reflection is consciousness of *the three ekstatic* dimensions. It is a non-thetic consciousness (of) flow and a thetic consciousness of duration. For reflection the past and the present of the reflected-on are set in existence as *quasi-outside* in this sense: that they are not only held in the unity of a for-itself which exhausts their being in having to be it but also *for* a for-itself which is separated from them by a nothingness; they are for a for-itself which, while existing with them in the unity of a being, does not have to be their being. Through reflection also the flow reaches toward *being* as an "outside" outlined in immanence. But pure reflection still discovers temporality only in its own original non-substantiality, in its refusal to be in-itself. It discovers possibles *qua* possibles, lightened by the freedom of the for-itself. It reveals the present as transcendent; and if the past appears to it as in-itself, still the past is on the foundation of presence. Finally reflection discovers the for-itself in its detotal-ized totality as the incomparable individuality which reflection *itself is* in the mode of having to be it. It discovers the for-itself as the "reflected-on, *par excellence*," the being which is always only as itself and which is always this "self" at a distance from itself, in the future, in the past, in the world. Reflection therefore apprehends temporality and reveals it as the unique and incomparable mode of being of a selfness—that is, as historicity.

But the psychological duration which we know and which we daily make use of as successions of organized temporal forms is the opposite of historicity. It is in fact the concrete fabric of the psychic unities of the flow. This joy, for example, is an organized form which appears after a sadness, and before that there was that humiliation which I experienced yesterday. Relations of before and after are commonly established between these unities of flow, qualities, states, acts; and these are the unities which can be used for *dating*. Thus the reflective consciousness of man-in-the-world in his daily existence is found in the face of psychic objects which are what they are, which appear in the continuous woof of our temporality like the designs and motifs on a tapestry, and which succeed each other in the manner of things in the world in universal time; that is, by replacing each other without entering into any relation other than the purely external relations of succession.

We speak of a joy which I *have* or which I *had*; we say that it is my joy as if I were its support and as if it were detached from me as the finite modes of Spinoza are detached from the ground of the attribute. We even say that I *experience* this joy as if it came to imprint itself like a seal on the texture of my temporalization; or better yet, as if the presence in me of these feelings, of these ideas, of these states were a sort of *visitation*. We can not call it an illusion—this psychic duration constituted by the concrete flow of autonomous organizations; that is, in short, by the succession of psychic *facts*, of *facts* of consciousness. Indeed it is their reality which is the object of psychology. Practically it is on the level of psychic fact that concrete relations between men are established—claims, jealousies, grudges, suggestions, struggles, ruses, *etc*. Yet it is not conceivable that the unreflective for-itself, which historicizes itself[10] in its upsurge, should *be itself* these qualities, these states, and these acts. Its unity of being would dissolve into a multiplicity of existents external to one another, the ontological problem of temporality would reappear, and this time we would have removed all methods of resolving it; for while it is possible for the for-itself to be its own past, it would be absurd to require of my joy that it be the sadness which preceded it, even in the mode of "non-being."

Psychologists give a degraded representation of this ekstatic existence when they affirm that psychic facts are relative to one another and that the

---

[10] i.e., places itself in history or makes itself a history. Sartre uses *s'historialise*, which bears the same relation to French that "historicizes itself" bears to English. Tr.

thunder clap heard after a long silence is apprehended as "thunder-clap-after-a-long-silence." This observation is well made, but they have prevented themselves from explaining this relativity in succession since they have removed from it all ontological foundation. In fact if we apprehend the for-itself in its historicity, psychic duration vanishes and states, qualities, and acts disappear to give place to being-for-itself as such, which is only as the unique individuality from which the process of historization cannot be separated. It is this which flows, which calls to itself from the ground of the future, and which is heavy with the past which it was; it is this which historicizes its selfness, and we know that it is—in the primary or unreflective mode—a consciousness of the world and not of self. Thus qualities and states could not be beings in its being (in the sense that the unity of the flow of joy would be "contained" or "made" by consciousness). There exist only the internal, non-positional colorations of it; these are nothing other than itself qua for-itself, and they can not be apprehended outside of it.

Here we are then in the presence of two temporalities: the original temporality of which we *are* the temporalization, and psychic temporality which simultaneously appears as incompatible with the mode of being of our being and as an inter-subjective reality, the object of science, the goal of human acts (in the sense, for example, that I do everything possible to "*make Annie love me*," to "endow her with love for me"). This psychic temporality, which is evidently *derived*, can not stem directly from original temporality; the latter constitutes nothing other than itself. As for psychic temporality, it is incapable of constituting *itself*, for it is only a successive order of facts. Moreover psychic temporality could not appear to the unreflective for-itself, which is pure ekstatic presence to the world. Psychic temporality reveals itself to reflection, and reflection must constitute it. But how can reflection constitute it if reflection is the pure and simple discovery of the historicity which it is?

Here we must distinguish between pure reflection and impure or constituent reflection, for it is impure reflection which constitutes the succession of psychic facts or *psyche*. What is given first in daily life is impure or constituent reflection although this includes pure reflection as its original structure. But pure reflection can be attained only as the result of a modification which it effects on itself and which is in the form of a katharsis. This is not the place to describe the motivation and the structure of this katharsis. What matters to us is the description of impure reflection inasmuch as it constitutes and reveals psychic temporality.

Reflection, as we have seen, is a type of being in which the for-itself is in order to be to itself what it is. Reflection is not then a capricious upsurge into the pure indifference of being, but it arises in the perspective of a for. We have seen here that the for-itself is the being which in its being is the foundation of a for. The meaning of reflection is then its being-for. Specifically the reflective is the reflected-on nihilating itself for[11] recovering itself. In this sense the reflective in so far as it has to be the reflected-on, escapes from the for-itself which it is as reflective in the form of "having to be it." But if it were only in order to be the reflected-on which it has to be, it would escape from the for-itself in order to rediscover it; everywhere and in whatever manner it affects itself, the for-itself is condemned to be-for-itself. In fact, it is here that pure reflection is discovered.

But impure reflection, which is the first spontaneous (but not the *original*) reflective movement, is-in-order-to-be the reflected-on as in-itself. Its motivation is within it in the twofold movement, which we have already described, of interiorization and of objectivation: to apprehend the reflected-on as in-itself in order to make itself be that in-itself which is apprehended. Impure reflection then is the apprehension of the reflected-on as such only in a circuit of selfness in which reflection stands in immediate relation with an in-itself which it has to be. But on the other hand, this in-itself which reflection has to be is the *reflected-on* in so far as the reflective tries to apprehend it as being in-itself. This means that three forms exist in impure reflection: the reflective, the reflected-on, and an in-itself which the reflective has to be in so far as this in-itself would be the reflected-on, an in-itself which is nothing other than the For of the reflective phenomenon. This in-itself is pre-outlined behind the for-itself—reflected-on, by a reflection (reflexion) which traverses the reflected-on in order to recover it and to found it; it is like the projection into the in-itself on the part of the for-itself reflected-on—as a meaning: its being is not to be but to be-made-to-be, like nothingness. It is the reflected-on as a pure object for the reflective, as soon as reflection adopts a point of view on the reflective, as soon as it gets out of that lightning intuition without relief in which the reflected-on is given without a point of view for the reflective, as soon as it posits itself as *not being* the reflected-on, and as soon as it determines what the-reflected-on *is*, then reflection effects the appearance of an in-itself capable of being determined, qualified, behind the reflected-on. This transcendent in-itself or shadow cast by the reflected-on onto being is what the reflective *has to be* in so far as it is that which the reflected-on *is*.

Yet this in-itself should not be confused with the *value* of the reflected-on, which is given to reflection in a total, undifferentiated intuition—nor with the *value* which haunts the reflective as a non-thetic absence and as the For of reflective consciousness in so far as it is a non-positional self-consciousness. This in-itself is the necessary object of all reflection. In order that it may arise, it is enough that reflection confront the reflected-on as object. It is the very

---

[11] Etre-pour. In French the pour can mean either for or in order to, both of which are implied in être-pour. Tr.

decision by which reflection determines itself to consider the reflected-on as object which causes the in-itself to appear as the transcendent objectivation of the reflected-on. The act by which reflection determines itself to take the reflected-on as object is itself (1) a positing of the reflective as *not being* the reflected-on, (2) the adoption of a point of view in relation to the reflected-on. Moreover in reality these two moments make only one since the concrete negation which the reflective makes itself be in relation to the reflected-on manifests itself precisely in and *through* the fact of taking a point of view. The objectivating act, as we see, lies in the strict extensions of the reflective dissociation since this dissociation is made by the deepening of the nothingness which separates the reflection (*reflet*) from the reflecting (*reflétant*). The objectivation recovers the reflective movement as not being the reflected-on *in order that* the reflected-on may appear as an object for the reflective.

However this reflection is in bad faith. To be sure, it appears to cut the bond which unites the reflected-on to the reflective, and it seems to declare that the reflective *is not* the reflected-on in the mode of not being what one is not, at a time when in the original reflective upsurge, the reflective is not the reflected-on in the mode of what one is. But this is only *in order to* recover subsequently the affirmation of identity and to affirm concerning this in-itself that "I am it." In a word, reflection is in bad faith in so far as it constitutes itself as the revelation of *the object which I make-to-be-me*. But in the second place this more radical nihilation is not a real, metaphysical event. The real event, the third process of nihilation is the *for-others*. Impure reflection is an abortive effort on the part of the for-itself *to be another* while *remaining itself*. The transcendent object which appeared behind the for-itself-reflected-on is the only being of which the reflective can say—in this sense—that it *is not* it. But it is a mere shadow of being. It *is made-to-be* and the reflective has to be it in order not to be it. It is this shadow of being, the necessary and constant correlate of impure reflection that the psychologist studies under the name of *psychic fact*. A psychic fact is then the shadow of the reflected-on inasmuch as the reflective has to be it ekstatically in the mode of non-being. Thus reflection is impure when it gives itself as an "intuition of the for-itself in in-itself." What is revealed to it is not the temporal and non-substantial historicity of the reflected-on; beyond this reflected-on it is the very substantiality of the organized forms of the flow. The unity of these virtual beings is called *the psychic life* or *psyche*, a virtual and transcendent in-itself which underlies the temporalization of the for-itself. Pure reflection is never anything but a quasi-knowledge; but there can be a reflective knowledge of the Psyche alone. Naturally we will re-discover in each psychic object the characteristics of the real reflected-on but degraded in the In-itself. A brief *a priori* description of the Psyche will enable us to account for this In-itself.

(1) By Psyche we understand the *Ego*, its states, its qualities, and its acts.

The Ego with the double grammatical form of "I" and "Me" represents our *person* as a transcendent psychic unity. We have described it elsewhere. It is as the Ego that we are subjects in fact and subjects by statute, active and passive, voluntary agents, possible objects of a judgment concerning value of responsibility.

The qualities of the Ego represent the ensemble of virtues, latent traits, potentialities which constitute our character and our habits (in the sense of the Greek ἕξισ). The Ego is a "quality" of being angry, industrious, jealous, ambitious, sensual, etc. But we must recognize also qualities of another sort which have their origin in our history and which we call *acquired traits*: I can be *"showing my age," tired, bitter, declining, progressing*; I can appear as "having acquired assurance as the result of a success" or on the contrary as "having little by little contracted the tastes, the habits, the sexuality of an invalid" (following a long illness).

States—in contrast with qualities which exist "potentially"—give themselves as actually existing. Hate, love, jealousy are states. An illness, in so far as it is apprehended by the patient as a psycho-physiological reality, is a state. In the same way a number of characteristics which are externally attached to my person can, in so far as I live them, become *states*. Absence (in relation to a definite person), exile, dishonor, triumph are states. We can see what distinguishes the quality from the state: After my anger yesterday, my "irascibility" survives as a simple latent disposition to become angry. On the contrary, after Pierre's action and the resentment which I felt because of it, my hate survives as an *actual* reality although my thought may be currently occupied with another object. A quality furthermore is an innate or acquired disposition which contributes to *qualify* my personality. The state, on the contrary, is much more accidental and contingent; it is *something which happens to me*. There exist however intermediates between states and qualities: for example, the hatred of Pozzo di Borgo for Napoleon although existing in fact and representing an affective, contingent relation between Pozzo and Napoleon the First, was constitutive of the *person* Pozzo.

By *acts* we must understand the whole synthetic activity of the person; that is, every disposition of means as related to ends, not as the for-itself is its own possibilities but as the act represents a transcendent psychic synthesis which the for-itself must live. For example, the boxer's training is an act because it transcends and supports the For-itself, which moreover realizes itself in and through this training. The same goes for the research of the scientist, for the work of the artist, for the election campaign of the politician. In all these cases the act as a psychic being represents a transcendent existence and the objective aspect of the relation of the For-itself with the world.

(2) The "Psychic" is given solely to a special category of cognitive acts—the acts of the reflective For-itself. On the unreflective plane, in fact, the

For-itself is its own possibilities in the non-thetic mode; and since its possibilities are possible presences to the world beyond the given state of the world, what is revealed thetically but non-thematically across these possibilities is a state of the world synthetically bound with the given state. Consequently the modifications to be imposed on the world are given thetically in present things as objective potentialities which have to realize themselves by borrowing our body as the instrument of their realization. It is thus that the man who is angry sees on the face of his opponent the objective quality of asking for a punch in the nose. Hence we have such expressions as "itching to be spanked" or "asking for trouble."[12] Our body here is like a medium in a trance. Through it must be realized a certain potentiality of things (a beverage-to-be-drunk, aid-to-be-brought, dangerous-animal-to-be-killed, etc.), and reflection arising in the midst of all these apprehends the ontological relation of the For-itself to its possibilities but as an object. Thus the act rises as the virtual object of the reflective consciousness. It is then impossible for me at the same time and on the same level to be conscious of Pierre and of my friendship for him; these two existences are always separated by the breadth of the For-itself. And this For-itself is a hidden reality; in the case of consciousness not-reflected-on, the For-itself is but nonthetically, and it is effaced before the object in the world and its potentialities. In the case of the reflective upsurge the for-itself is surpassed toward the virtual object which the reflective has to be. Only a *pure* reflective consciousness can discover the For-itself reflected-on in its reality. We use the term *Psyche* for the organized totality of these virtual and transcendent existents which form a permanent cortege for impure reflection and which are the natural object of *psychological* research.

(3) The objects although virtual are not abstract; the reflective does not aim at them in emptiness; they are given as the concrete in-itself which the reflective has to be beyond the reflected-on. We shall use the term *evidence* for the immediate presence, "in person", of hate, exile, systematic doubt to the reflective For-itself. To be convinced that this presence exists, it is enough to call to mind cases in our own personal experience when we have tried to recall a dead love or a certain intellectual atmosphere which we had lived at an earlier date. On such occasions we had plainly a consciousness of aiming in emptiness at these various objects. We could form particular concepts of them, attempt a literary description of them, but we knew that they were not there. Similarly there are intermittent periods for a living love during which

---

[12] The French expressions here have no close English equivalent. "*Tête à gifles*" is a "head for slaps"; "*menton qui attire les coups*" is a "chin which attracts blows." Cf. Goneril's taunt in *King Lear*:

"Milk-liver'd man!
That bears't a cheek for blows, a head for wrongs."
(IV.ii) Tr.

we know that we love but we do not feel it. These "intermittences in the heart" have been very well described by Proust. In contrast, it is possible to grasp a love in fullness, to contemplate it. But for that is necessary a particular mode of being on the part of the For-itself reflected-on. I can apprehend my friendship for Pierre, but it is through my sympathy at the moment, which has become the reflected-on object of a reflective consciousness. In short, the only way to make-present these qualities, these states, or these acts is to apprehend them across a reflected-on consciousness of which they are the objectivation, the shadow cast onto the in-itself.

But this possibility of making-present a love proves better than any argument the transcendence of the psychic. When I abruptly discover, when I see my love, I apprehend at the same stroke that it stands before my consciousness. I can take points of view regarding it, can judge it; I am not engaged in it as the reflective is in the reflected-on. Due to this very fact I apprehend it as not being of the nature of the For-itself. It is infinitely heavier, more opaque, more solid than that absolute transparency. That is why the evidence with which the psychic gives itself to the intuition of impure reflection is not apodictic. There is a cleavage between the future of the For-itself reflected-on, which is constantly eaten away and lightened by my freedom, and the dense and menacing future of my love, a cleavage which gives to it precisely its meaning as love. If I did not apprehend in the psychic object a love with its future arrested, would it still be love? Would it not rather fall under the heading of caprice? And does not even the caprice engage the future to the extent that it is given as going to remain caprice and never to be changed into love? Thus the always nihilated future of the For-itself prevents all determination in-itself of the For-itself as the For-itself which loves or which hates; and the shadow projected by the For-itself reflected-on possesses naturally a future degraded into in-itself, one which forms an integral part of it, determining its meaning. But in correlation with the continual nihilation of Futures reflected-on, the organized psychic ensemble with its future remains only probable. And we do not mean by that an external quality which would come from a relation with my knowledge and which could be transformed if need be into certainty, but rather an ontological characteristic.

(4) The psychic object, being the shadow cast by the For-itself reflected-on, possesses in degraded form the characteristics of consciousness. In particular it appears as an achieved and probable totality where the For-itself makes itself exist in the diasporatic unity of a detotalized totality. This means that the Psychic apprehended across the three ekstatic dimensions of temporality, appears as constituted by the synthesis of a Past, a Present, and a Future. A love, an enterprise is the organized unity of these three dimensions. In fact it is not enough to say that a love "has" a future as if the future were external to the object which it characterizes; the future makes a part of the

organized form of the flow of "love," for love is given its meaning as love by its being in the future. But due to the fact that the psychic object is in-itself, its present can not be flight, nor can its future be pure possibility. In these forms of flow there is an essential priority of the Past, which is what the For-itself was and which already presupposes the transformation of the For-itself into In-itself. The reflective projects a psychic object provided with the three temporal dimensions, but it constitutes these three dimensions solely out of what the reflected-on *was*. The Future *is* already; otherwise how could my love be love? Only it is not yet *given*; it is a "now" which is not yet revealed. It loses then its character as a *possibility which-I-have-to-be*; my love, my joy *do not have to be* their future, for they *are* it in the tranquil indifference of juxtaposition, just as this fountain pen is at once a pen and—below—a cap. The Present similarly is apprehended in its real quality of *being-there*. Only this being-there is constituted in having been-there. The Present is already wholly constituted and armed from head to foot; it is a "now" which the instant brings and carries away like a costume ready made; it is a card which comes out of the game and returns to it. The passage of a "now" from the future to the present and from the present to the past does not cause it to undergo any modification since in any case, future or not, it is already past. This fact is well illustrated by the naive way in which psychologists take recourse in the unconscious in order to distinguish the three "nows" of the psychic: they call *present* the "now" which is present to the consciousness. The past and the future "now" have exactly the same characteristics, but they wait in the limbo of the unconscious; and if we take them in that undifferentiated environment, it is impossible to distinguish past from future among them. A memory which survives in the unconscious is a past "now" and at the same time, inasmuch as it awaits being evoked, it is a future "now." Thus the psychic form is not *to-be*; it is already *made*; it is already complete, past, present, future, in the mode *has been*. The "nows" which compose it have only to undergo one by one—before returning into the past—the baptism of consciousness.

The result is that the psychic form contains two co-existing contradictory modalities of being since it is *already made* and appears in the cohesive unity of an organism and since at the same time it can exist only through a succession of "nows," each one of which tends to be isolated in an in-itself. This joy, for example, passes from one instant to another because its future exists already as a terminal result and the *given* meaning of its development, not as that which it has to be, but as that which it "has been" already in the future.

Actually this inner cohesion of the psyche is nothing other than the unity of being of the For-itself hypostasized in the in-itself. A hate has no parts; it is not a sum of attitudes and of states of consciousness, but it gives itself through the attitudes and states of consciousness as the temporal unity—without parts—of their appearances. But the unity of being in the For-itself is explained by the ekstatic character of its being; it has to be in full spontaneity what it will be. The psychic, on the contrary, "is made-to-be." This means that it is by itself incapable of determining itself in existence. It is sustained in the face of the reflective by a sort of inertia; and psychologists have often insisted on its "pathological" character. It is in this sense that Descartes can speak of the "passions of the soul." Although the psychic is not on the same plane of being as the existents of the world, this inertia enables the psychic to be apprehended as related to these existents. A love is given as "aroused" by the loved object. Consequently the total cohesion of the psychic form becomes unintelligible since it does not have to be this cohesion, since it is not its own synthesis, since its unity has the character of a given. To the extent that a hatred is a given succession of "nows," all completely formed and inert, we find in it the germ of an infinite divisibility. And yet this divisibility is disguised, denied in so far as the psychic is the objectivation of the onto-logical unity of the For-itself. Hence there is a sort of magic cohesion between the successive "nows" of the hatred, which give themselves as parts only in order later to deny their exteriority.

The ambiguity is brought to light in Bergson's theory of the consciousness which endures and which is a "multiplicity of interpenetration." What Bergson is touching on here is the psychic state, not consciousness conceived as For-itself. Actually what is the meaning of "interpenetration?" It can not logically be absence of divisibility. If there is to be interpenetration, it is necessary that there be parts which interpenetrate each other. But these parts, which theoretically ought to fall back into their isolation, flow one into the other by a magic and totally unexplained cohesion; and this total fusion at present defies analysis. Bergson does not intend establishing this property of the psychic on an absolute structure of the For-itself. He establishes it as a given, a simple "intuition" which reveals to him that the psychic is an inter-iorized multiplicity. Its character as something inert, as a passive datum is accentuated by the fact that it exists without being for a consciousness, either thetic or nonthetic. It is without consciousness (of) being since a natural attitude man completely fails to recognize it and has to have recourse to intuition in order to apprehend it. Thus an object in the world is able to exist without being seen and to reveal itself after the event when we have forged the necessary instruments to disclose it. The characteristics of psychic dur-ation for Bergson are a pure contingent fact of experience; they are so because we find them so—that is all. Thus psychic temporality is an inert datum, closely akin to Bergson's duration, which undergoes its intimate cohesion with-out effecting it, which is perpetually temporalized without temporalizing itself, in which the irrational and magic interpenetration of elements that are not united by an ekstatic relation of being can be compared only to sympa-thetic magic acting from a distance—an interpenetration which hides a multiplicity of already formed "nows." These characteristics do not result from any error on the part of psychologists or from a lack of knowledge; they are constitutive of psychic temporality, which is the hypostasis of original temporality. The absolute unity of the psychic is indeed the projection of the ontological, ekstatic unity of the for-itself. But since this projection is made in the in-itself which is what it is in the distanceless proximity of self-identity, the ekstatic unity parcels itself out in an infinity of "nows" which are what they are and which, precisely for this reason, tend to isolate themselves in their self-identity. Thus participating simultaneously in the in-itself and in the for-itself, psychic temporality conceals a contradiction which is never overcome. This should not surprise us. Since psychic temporality is the product of impure reflection, it is natural that it is *made-to-be* what it is not and that it is not what it is *made-to-be*.

The foregoing will become even more perceptible by an examination of the inter-relations of psychic forms at the heart of psychic time. Let us note first of all that it is interpenetration which governs the connection between feelings, for example, at the heart of a complex psychic form. Everybody knows those feelings of affection "tinted" with envy, those hates "penetrated" despite all by admiration, those romantic friendships which novelists have often described. And so we apprehend a friendship tinted with envy like a cup of coffee clouded with cream. Admittedly this comparison is gross. Nevertheless it is certain that the amorous friendship is not given as a simple specification of the genus friendship, as the isosceles triangle is a specification of the genus triangle. The friendship is given as wholly penetrated by total love, and yet it is not love; it "does not make itself" love, for then it would lose its autonomy as friendship. But it constitutes itself as an inert object in-itself which language can scarcely name, where love, autonomous and in-itself, is magically extended through all the friendship just as the leg is extended through all the sea in the Stoic σύγχυσις.[13]

But psychic processes imply also the action from a distance of prior forms on posterior forms. We cannot conceive of this action at a distance in the mode of simple causality found, for example, in classical mechanics, which supposes the totally inert existence of a moving body enclosed in the instant. Neither can we allow the mode of physical causality conceived in the manner of John Stuart Mill, which is defined by the constant and unconditioned succession of two states where the being of each one is exclusive of the other. Inasmuch as the psychic is the objectivation of the for-itself, it possesses a degraded spontaneity which is grasped as the internal, given quality of the form of the psychic and which is inseparable from its cohesive force. This

[13] Correction for Sartre's σνγχύσις. Tr.

spontaneity can not therefore be given strictly as *produced* by the prior form. But on the other hand, neither can the spontaneity determine itself in existence since it is apprehended only as one determination among others of a *given* existent. It follows that the prior form has to effect from a distance the birth of a form of the same nature which is organized spontaneously as a form of flow. We are not dealing here with being which *has to be* its future and its past, but only with successions of past, present, and future forms which all exist in the mode of "having-been," and which at a distance influence one another. This influence will be manifested either by penetration or by motivation. If it is by penetration, the reflective apprehends as a single object two psychic objects which had at first been given separately. The result is either a new psychic object, each characteristic of which will be the synthesis of the prior two, or an object unintelligible in itself, which appears simultaneously as all one and all the other without there being any alteration in either. In motivation, on the contrary, the two objects remain each at its own place. But since a psychic object is an organized form and a multiplicity of interpenetration, it can act only simultaneously as one whole on another whole object. The result is a total action at a distance by means of a magic influence of one on the other. For example, my humiliation of yesterday is the total motive for my mood this morning, *etc.*

The fact that this action at a distance is totally magic and irrational proves better than any analysis the futility of attempts on the part of intellectualistic psychologists to remain on the level of the psychic and yet reduce this action to an intelligible causality by means of an intellectual analysis. It is thus that Proust by means of intellectualistic distinctions is perpetually trying to find bonds of rational causality between psychic states in the temporal succession of these states. But at the end of the analysis he can offer us only results such as the following:

> As soon as Swann could picture (Odette) to himself without revulsion, as soon as he thought again of the kindness in her smile, and as as soon as *the desire to take her away from everyone else was no longer added to his love by jealousy*, that love *became* again a taste for the sensations which Odette's person gave him, for the pleasure which he felt in admiring as a spectacle or in questioning as a phenomenon the lifting up of one of her glances, the formation of one of her smiles, the utterance of an intonation of her voice. And this pleasure different from all others *had ended by creating in him a need of her*, which she alone could assuage by her presence or her letters . . . Thus *by the very chemistry of his affliction*, after having *created jealousy out of his love*, he began to *manufacture tenderness*, pity for Odette.[14]

---

[14] *Du côté de chez Swann*, 37ᵉ edition, II, p. 82. My italics.

This passage is obviously concerned with the psychic. We see feelings which, individualized and separated by nature, are here acting one on the other. But Proust is trying to clarify their actions and to classify them in the hope that he may thereby make understandable the fluctuations which Swann experiences. Proust does not limit himself to describing the conclusions which he himself has been able to make (*e.g.*, the transition through "oscillation" from hate-filled jealousy to tender love); he wants to explain these findings.

What are the results of this analysis? Is the unintelligibility of the psychic removed? It is easy to see that on the contrary this somewhat arbitrary reduction of the great psychic forms to more simple elements accentuates the magic irrationality of the inter-relations which psychic objects support. How does jealousy "add" to love the "desire to take her away from everyone else?" And how does this desire once added to love (always the image of the cloud of cream "added" to the coffee) prevent it from *becoming again* "a taste for the sensations which Odette's person gave him?" And how can the pleasure *create* a need? And how does love *manufacture* that jealousy which in return *will add to love the* desire to take Odette away from everyone else? And how when freed from this desire, is it going to *manufacture* tenderness *anew*? Proust here attempts to constitute a symbolic *chemistry*, but the chemical images which he uses are capable only of disguising the motivations and irrational acts. It is an attempt to draw us toward a mechanistic interpretation of the psychic which, without being any more intelligible, would completely distort its nature. And yet Proust cannot keep from showing us between the estranged states almost interhuman relations (to create, to manufacture, to add), which would almost allow us to suppose that these psychic objects are animated agents. In his descriptions the intellectualistic analysis shows its limitations at every instant; it can effect its distinctions and its classifications only superficially and on the basis of total irrationality. It is necessary to give up trying to reduce the irrational element in psychic causality. This causality is a degradation of the ekstatic for-itself, which is its own being at a distance from itself, its degradation into magic, into an in-itself which is what it is at its own place. Magic action through influence at a distance is the necessary result of this relaxation of the bonds of being. The psychologist must describe these irrational bonds and take them as an original given of the psychic world.

Thus the reflective consciousness is constituted as consciousness of duration, and hence psychic duration appears to consciousness. This psychic temporality as a projection into the in-itself of original temporality is a virtual being whose phantom flow does not cease to accompany the ekstatic temporalization of the for-itself in so far as this is apprehended by reflection. But psychic temporality disappears completely if the for-itself remains on the un-reflective level or if impure reflection purifies itself. Psychic temporality is similar in this respect to original temporality—in that it appears as a mode of being of concrete objects and not as a limit or a pre-established rule. Psychic time is only the connected bringing together of temporal objects. But its essential difference from original temporality is that it *is* while original temporality temporalizes itself. As such psychic time can be constituted only with the past, and the future can be only as a past which will come after the present past; that is, the empty form before-after is hypostasized, and it orders the relations between objects equally past.

At the same time this psychic duration which can not be by itself must perpetually *be made-to-be*. Perpetually oscillating between the multiplicity of juxtaposition and the absolute cohesion of the ekstatic for-itself, this temporality is composed of "nows" which have been, which remain at the place which has been assigned to them, but which influence each other at a distance in their totality; it is this which renders it comparable to the magic duration of Bergson's philosophy. As soon as we enter on the plane of impure reflection—that is, of the reflection which seeks to determine the being which I am—an entire world appears which peoples this temporality. This world, a virtual presence, the probable object of my reflective intention, is the psychic world or the psyche. In one sense, its existence is purely ideal; in another it is, since it is-made-to-be, since it is revealed to consciousness. It is "my shadow;" it is what is revealed to me when I wish to see *myself*. In addition this phantom world exists as a *real situation* of the for-itself, for it can be that in terms of which the for-itself determines itself to be what it has to be. For example, I shall not go to this or that person's house "because of" the antipathy which I feel toward him. Or I decide on this or that action by taking into consideration my hate or my love. Or I refuse to discuss politics because I know my quick temper and I can not risk becoming irritated. Along with that transcendent world which is lodged in the infinite becoming of pre-historic indifference there is constituted precisely as a virtual unity of being that temporality which is called "inner" or "qualitative," which is the objectivation in in-itself of original temporality. There we find the first draft of an "outside;" the for-itself sees itself almost as bestowing an outside on its own eyes, but this outside is purely virtual. We shall see later how being-for-others *realizes* the suggestion of this "outside."

# 3

## TRANSCENDENCE

In order to arrive at as complete a description as possible of the for-itself we chose as a guiding thread the examination of negative attitudes. As we have seen, all questions which we can pose and the replies which can be made to them are conditioned by the permanent possibility of non-being, outside us and within. Our original goal, however, was not only to discover the negative structures of the for-itself. In the Introduction we encountered a problem, and it is this problem which we have wished to resolve: what is the original relation of human reality to the being of phenomena or being-in-itself? In the Introduction indeed we were obliged to reject both the realist solution and the idealist solution. It appeared to us both that transcendent being could not act on consciousness and that consciousness could not "construct" the transcendent by objectivizing elements borrowed from its subjectivity. Then we understood that the original relation to being could not be an external relation which would unite two substances originally isolated. "The relation of the regions of being is a primitive upsurge," we said, "and it forms a part of the very structure of these beings." The concrete is revealed to us as the synthetic totality of which consciousness, as well as phenomenon, are only the articulations.

But although in one sense consciousness considered in isolation is an abstraction, and although phenomena—even the phenomenon of being— are similarly abstract in so far as they cannot exist as phenomena without appearing to a consciousness, nevertheless the being of phenomena as in an in-itself which is what it is can not be considered as an abstraction. In order to be, it needs only itself; it refers only to itself. On the other hand, our description of the for-itself has shown us how this on the contrary, is removed as far as possible from a substance and from the in-itself; we have seen that it is its own nothingness and that it can exist only in the ontological unity of its ekstases. Therefore while the relation of the for-itself to the in-itself is originally constitutive of the very being which is put into the relation, we should not understand that this relation is constitutive of the in-itself but rather of the for-itself. It is in the for-itself alone that we must look for the key to that relation to being which we call, for example, knowing. The for-itself is responsible in its being for its relation with the in-itself, or if you prefer, it produces itself originally on the foundation of a relation to the in-itself. This is what we already anticipated when we defined consciousness as "a being such that in its being, its being is in question in so far as this being implies a being other than itself." But since formulating this definition we have acquired new knowledge. In particular we have grasped the profound meaning of the for-itself as the foundation of its own nothingness. It is not time now to utilize this knowledge to determine and explain that ekstatic relation of the for-itself to the in-itself on the foundation of which knowing and acting in general can appear? Are we not in a position now to reply to our original question? In order to be non-thetic self-consciousness, consciousness must be a thetic consciousness of something, as we have noted. But what we have studied hitherto is the for-itself as the original mode of being of non-thetic self-consciousness. Are we not therefore bound to describe the relations of the for-itself with the in-itself inasmuch as these are constitutive of the very being of the for-itself? Are we not able at present to find the answer to questions of the following type: Since the in-itself is what it is, how and why does the being of the for-itself have to be a knowledge of the in-itself? And what in general is knowledge?

## I. KNOWLEDGE AS A TYPE OF RELATION BETWEEN THE FOR-ITSELF AND THE IN-ITSELF

There is only intuitive knowledge. Deduction and discursive argument, incorrectly called examples of knowing, are only instruments which lead to intuition. When intuition is reached, methods utilized to attain it are effaced before it; in cases where it is not attained, reason and argument remain as indicating signs which point toward an intuition beyond reach; finally if it has been attained but is not a present mode of my consciousness, the precepts which I use remain as the results of operations formerly effected, like what Descartes called the "memories of ideas." If someone asks for a definition of intuition, Husserl will reply, in agreement with the majority of philosophers, that it is the presence of the thing (*Sache*) "in person" to consciousness. Knowledge therefore is of the type of being which we described in the preceding chapter under the title of "presence to ———." But we have established that the in-itself can never by itself be *presence*. Being-present, in fact, is an ekstatic mode of being of the for-itself. We are then compelled to reverse the terms of our definition: intuition is the presence of consciousness to the thing. Therefore we must return now to the problem of the nature and the meaning of this presence of the for-itself to being.

In the Introduction while using the still not elucidated concept of "consciousness," we proved the necessity for consciousness to be consciousness of something. In fact it is by means of that of which it is conscious that consciousness distinguishes itself in its own eyes and that it can be self-consciousness; a consciousness which would not be consciousness (of) something would be consciousness (of) nothing. But at present we have elucidated the ontological meaning of consciousness or the for-itself. We can therefore pose the problem in more precise terms and ask: What do we mean when we say that it is necessary for consciousness to-be-consciousness of something—considered on the ontological level; i.e., in the perspective of being-for-itself?

We know that the for-itself is the foundation of its own nothingness in the form of the phantom dyad—the reflection-reflecting. The reflecting exists only in order to reflect the reflection, and the reflection is a reflection only in so far as it refers to the reflecting. Thus the two terms outlined in the dyad point to each other, and each engages its being in the being of the other. But if the reflecting is nothing other than the reflecting of *this* reflection, and if the reflection can be characterized only by its "being-in-order-to-be reflected in *this* reflecting," then the two terms of the quasi-dyad support their two nothingnesses on each other, conjointly annihilating themselves. It is necessary that the reflecting reflect *something* in order that the ensemble should not dissolve into nothing. But if the reflection, on the other hand, were *something*, independent of its being-in-order-to-be-reflected, then it would necessarily be qualified not as a reflection but as an in-itself. This would be to introduce opacity into the system "the-reflection-reflecting" and, even more, to complete the suggested scissiparity. For in the for-itself the reflection *is also* the reflecting. But if the reflection is qualified, it is separated from the reflecting and its appearance is separated from its reality; the *cogito* becomes impossible. The reflection can be simultaneously "something to be reflected" and *nothing*, but only if it makes itself qualified by something other than itself or, if you prefer, if it is reflected as a relation to an outside which it is not.

What defines the reflection for the reflecting is *always that to which it is presence.* Even a joy, apprehended on the unreflective level, is only the "reflected" presence to a laughing and open world full of happy perspectives. But the few preceding comments have already informed us that non-being is an essential structure of presence. Presence incloses a radical negation as presence to that which one is not. What is present to me is what is not me. We should note furthermore that this "non-being" is implied *a priori* in every theory of knowledge. It is impossible to construct the notion of an object if we do not have originally a negative relation designating the object as that which is not consciousness. This was expressed quite well by the term "non-ego," which was in fashion for a time, although one could not detect on the part of those who employed it the slightest concern to found this "not" which originally qualified the external world. Actually neither the connection of representations, nor the necessity of certain subjective ensembles, nor temporal irreversibility, nor an appeal to infinity could serve to constitute the object as such (that is, to serve as foundation for a further negation which would separate out the non-ego and oppose it to me as such) if this negation were not given first and if it were not the *a priori* foundation of all experience.

The thing, before all comparison, before all construction, is that which is present to consciousness as *not being* consciousness. The original relation of presence as the foundation of knowledge is negative. But as negation comes to the world by means of the for-itself, and as the thing is what it is in the absolute indifference of identity, it can not be the thing which is posited as not being the for-itself. Negation comes from the for-itself. We should not conceive this negation as a type of judgment which would bear on the thing itself and deny concerning it that it is the for-itself; this type of negation could be conceived only if the for-itself were a substance already fully formed, and even in that case it could emanate only as a third being establishing from outside a negative relation between two beings. But by the original negation the for-itself constitutes itself as *not being* the thing. Consequently the definition of consciousness which we gave earlier can be formulated in the perspective of the for-itself as follows: "The for-itself is a being such that in its being, its being is in question in so far as this being is essentially a certain way of *not being* a being which it posits simultaneously as other than itself."

Knowledge appears then as a mode of being. Knowing is neither a relation established after the event between two beings, nor is it an activity of one of these two beings, nor is it a quality or a property or a virtue. It is the very being of the for-itself in so far as it is presence to ——; that is, in so far as the for-itself has to be its being by making itself not to be a certain being to which it is present. This means that the for-itself can be only in the mode of a reflection (reflet) causing itself to be reflected as not being a certain being. The "something" which must qualify the reflected in order that the dyad "reflection-reflecting" may not dissolve in nothingness is pure negation. The reflected causes itself to be qualified *outside* next to a certain being *as not being* that being. This is precisely what we mean by "to be consciousness of something."

But we must define more precisely what we understand by this original negation. Actually we should distinguish two types of negation: external negation and internal negation. The first appears as a purely external bond established between two beings by a witness. When I say, for example, "A cup is not an inkwell," it is very evident that the foundation of this negation is neither in the cup nor in the inkwell.[1] Both of these objects are what they are, and that is all. The negation stands as a categorical and ideal connection which I establish between them without modifying them in any way whatsoever, without enriching them or impoverishing them with the slightest quality; they are not even ever so slightly grazed by this negative synthesis. As it serves neither to enrich them nor to constitute them, it remains strictly external. But we can already guess the meaning of the other type of negation if we consider such expressions as "I am not rich" or "I am not handsome." Pronounced with a certain melancholy, they do not mean only that the speaker is denied a certain quality but that the denial itself comes to influence the inner structure of the positive being who has been denied the quality. When I say, "I am not handsome," I do not limit myself to denying with respect to myself taken as wholly concrete, a certain virtue which due to this fact passes into nothingness while I keep intact the positive totality of my being (as when I say, "The vase is not white, it is gray"—"The inkwell is not on the table, it is on the mantelpiece"). I intend to indicate that "not being handsome" is a certain negative virtue of my being. It characterizes me within; as negative it is a real quality of myself—that of not being handsome—and this negative quality will explain my melancholy as well as, for example, my failures in the world.

By an internal negation we understand such a relation between two beings that the one which is denied to the other qualifies the other at the heart of its essence—by absence. The negation becomes then a bond of essential being since at least one of the beings on which it depends is such that it points toward the other, that it carries the other in its heart as an absence. Nevertheless it is clear that this type of negation can not be applied to being-in-itself. By nature it belongs to the for-itself. Only the for-itself can be determined in its being by a being which it is not. And if the internal negation can appear in the world—as when we say of a pearl that it is false, of a fruit that it is not ripe, of an egg that it is not fresh, etc.—it is by the for-itself that it comes into the world—like negation in general. Knowing belongs to the for-itself alone, for the reason that only the for-itself can appear to itself as not being what it knows. And as here appearance and being are one—since the for-itself has to be its appearance—we must conclude that the for-itself includes within its being the being of the object which it is not inasmuch as the for-itself puts its own being into question as not being the being of the object.

Here we must rid ourselves of an illusion which may be formulated as

---

[1] Sartre's text reads "the foundation of this negation is neither in the table nor in the inkwell." The "table" is surely an error. Tr.

follows: in order to constitute myself as *not being* a particular being, I must have some previous knowledge of this being; for I can not judge the differences between myself and a being of which I know nothing. It is true, of course, that in our empirical existence we can not know how we differ from a Japanese or an Englishman, from a worker or a king until we have some notion of these different beings. But these empirical distinctions can not serve as a basis for us here, for we are undertaking the study of an ontological relation which must render all experience possible and which aims at establishing how in general an object can exist for consciousness. It is not possible then for me to have any experience of an object as an object which is not me until I constitute it as an object. On the contrary, what makes all experience possible is an *a priori* upsurge of the object for the subject—or since the upsurge is the original fact of the for-itself, an original upsurge of the for-itself as presence to the object which it is not. What we should do then is to invert the terms of the preceding formula and formulate it thus: the fundamental relation by which the for-itself has to be as not being this particular object to which it is present is the foundation of all knowledge of this being. But we must describe this primary relation more exactly if we want to make it understandable.

The germ of truth remaining in the statement of the intellectualist illusion pointed out in the preceding paragraph is the observation that I can not determine myself not to be an object which is originally severed from all connection with me. I can not deny that I am a particular being if I am *at a distance* from that being. If I conceive of a being entirely closed in on itself, this being in itself will be solely that which it is, and due to this fact there will be no room in it for either negation or knowledge. It is in fact in terms of the being which it is not that a being *can make known to itself* what it is not. This means in the case of an internal negation that it is within and upon the being which it is not that the for-itself appears as not being what it is not. In this sense the internal negation is a concrete ontological bond. We are not dealing here with one of those empirical negations in which the qualities denied are distinguished first by their absence or even by their non-being. In the internal negation the for-itself collapses on what it denies. The qualities denied are precisely those to which the for-itself is most present; it is from them that it derives its negative force and perpetually renews it. In this sense it is necessary to see the denied qualities as a constitutive factor of the being of the for-itself, for the for-itself must be there outside itself upon them; it must be they in order to deny that it is they. In short the term-of-origin of the internal negation is the in-itself, the thing which *is there*, and outside of it there is nothing except an emptiness, a nothingness which is distinguished from the thing only by a pure negation for which this thing furnishes the very content. The difficulty encountered by materialism in deriving knowledge from the object stems from the fact that materialism wants to produce a substance in terms of another substance. But this difficulty can not hinder us, for we affirm that there is *nothing* outside the in-itself except a reflection (*reflet*) of that nothing which is itself polarized and defined by the in-itself inasmuch as it is precisely the nothingness of *this* in-itself, the individualized nothing which is nothing only because it *is not* the in-itself. Thus in this ekstatic relation which is constitutive of the internal negation and of knowledge, it is the in-itself "in person" which is the concrete pole in its plenitude, and the for-itself is nothing other than the emptiness in which the in-itself is detached.

The for-itself is outside itself in the in-itself since it causes itself to be defined by what it is not; the first bond between the in-itself and the for-itself is therefore a bond of being. But this bond is neither a *lack* nor an *absence*. In the case of absence indeed I make myself determined by a being which I am not and which does not exist or which is not there; that is, what determines me is like a hollow in the middle of what I shall call my empirical plenitude. On the other hand, in knowledge, taken as a bond of ontological being, the being which I am not represents the absolute plenitude of the in-itself. And I, on the contrary, am the nothingness, the absence which determines itself in existence from the standpoint of this fullness. This means that in that type of being which we call knowing, the only *being* which can be encountered and which is perpetually *there* is the *known*. The knower is not; he is not apprehensible. He is nothing other than that which brings it about that there is a *being-there* on the part of the known, a presence—for by itself the known is neither present nor absent, it simply is. But this presence of the known is presence to *nothing*, since the knower is the pure reflection of a non-being; the presence appears then across the total translucency of the knower known, an *absolute* presence.

A psychological and empirical exemplification of this original relation is furnished us in the case of *fascination*. In fascination, which represents the immediate fact of *knowing*, the knower is absolutely nothing but a pure negation; he does not find or recover himself anywhere—he *is not*. The only qualification which he can support is that he *is not* precisely this particular fascinating object. In fascination there is nothing more than a gigantic object in an empty world. Yet the fascinated intuition is in no way a *fusion* with the object. In fact the condition necessary for the existence of fascination is that the object be raised in absolute relief on a background of emptiness; that is, I am precisely the immediate negation of the object and nothing but that.

We find this same pure negation at the basis of those pantheistic intuitions which Rousseau has several times described as concrete psychic events in his history. He claims that on those occasions he *melted* into the universe, that the world alone was suddenly found present as an absolute presence and unconditioned totality. And certainly we can understand this total, isolated presence of the world, its pure "being-there;" certainly we admit freely that at this privileged moment there was nothing else but the world. But this does not mean, as Rousseau claims, that there was a fusion of consciousness with the world. Such a fusion would signify the solidification of the for-itself in in-itself, and at the same stroke, the disappearance of the world and of the in-itself as presence. It is true that in the pantheistic intuition there is no longer anything but the world—save for that which causes the in-itself to be present as the world; that is, a pure negation which is a non-thetic self-consciousness as negation. Precisely because knowledge is not *absence* but *presence*, there is *nothing* which separates the knower from the known.

Intuition has often been defined as the immediate presence of the known to the knower, but it is seldom that anyone has thought about the requirements of the notion of the *immediate*. Immediacy is the absence of any mediator; that is obvious, for otherwise the mediator alone would be known and not what is mediated. But if we can not posit any intermediary, we must at the same time reject both continuity and discontinuity as a type of presence of the knower to the known. In fact we shall not admit that there is any continuity of the knower with the known, for it supposes an intermediary term which would be at once knower and known, which suppresses the autonomy of the knower in the face of the known while engaging the being of the knower in the being of the known. Then the structure of the object disappears since the object must be absolutely denied by the for-itself as the being of the for-itself. But neither can we consider the original relation of the for-itself to the in-itself as a relation of *discontinuity*. To be sure, the separation between two discontinuous elements is an emptiness—i.e., a *nothing*—but it is a *realized* nothing,—i.e., in-itself. This substantialized nothing is as such a non-conductive density; it destroys the immediacy of presence, for it has qua nothing become *something*. The presence of the for-itself to the in-itself can be expressed neither in terms of continuity nor in terms of discontinuity: it is pure *denied identity*.

To make this clearer, let us employ a comparison. When two curves are tangential to one another, they offer a type of presence without intermediaries. Nevertheless the eye grasps only a *single line* for the length of their tangency. Moreover if the two curves were hidden so that one could see only the length A B where they are tangential to each other, it would be impossible to distinguish them. Actually what separates them is *nothing*; there is neither continuity nor discontinuity but pure identity. Now suddenly uncover the two figures and we apprehend them once again as being two throughout all their length. This situation derives not from an abrupt factual separation which would suddenly be realized between them but from the fact that the two movements by which we *draw* the two curves so as to perceive them include each one a negation as a constituting act. Thus what separates the two curves at the very spot of their tangency is *nothing*, not even a distance; it is a pure negativity as the counterpart of a constituting synthesis. Such an image will enable us to understand better the relation of immediacy which originally unites the knower to the known.

Ordinarily indeed it happens that a negation depends on a "something" which exists before the negation and constitutes its matter. For example, if I say that the inkwell is not the table, then table and inkwell are objects already constituted whose being in-itself will be the support of the negative judgment. But in the case of the relation "knower-known," there is nothing on the side of the knower which can provide a support for the negation; no difference, no principle of distinction "is there" to separate *in-itself* the knower from the known. But in the total indistinction of being, there is nothing but a negation which does not even exist but which *has to be*, which does not even posit itself as a negation. Consequently knowledge and finally the knower himself are nothing except the fact "that there is" being, that being in-itself *gives* itself and raises itself in relief on the ground of this nothing. In this sense we can call knowledge *the pure solitude of the known*. It is enough to say that the original phenomenon of knowledge *adds* nothing to being and creates nothing. It does not enrich being, for knowledge is pure negativity. It only brings it about that *there* is being. But this fact "that there is" being is not an inner determination of being—which is what it is—but of negativity. In this sense every revelation of a positive characteristic of being is the counterpart of an ontological determination as pure negativity in the being of the for-itself.

For example, as we shall see later, the revelation of the spatiality of being is one with the non-positional apprehension by the for-itself of itself as *unextended*. And the unextended character of the for-itself is not a positive, mysterious virtue of spirituality which is hiding under a negative denomination; it is a natural ekstatic relation, for it is by and in the extension of the transcendent in-itself that the for-itself makes itself known to itself and realizes its own non-extension. The for-itself can not be first unextended in order later to enter into relation with an extended being, for no matter how we consider it, the concept of the unextended makes no sense by itself; it is nothing but the negation of the extended. If we could suppress—to imagine an impossibility—the extension of the revealed determinations of the in-itself, then the for-itself would remain *aspatial*; it would be neither extended nor unextended, and it could not possibly be characterized in any way whatsoever so far as extension is concerned. In this sense extension is a transcendent determination which the for-itself has to apprehend to the exact degree that it denies itself as extended. That is why the term which seems best to indicate this inner relation between knowing and being is the word *realize*, which we used earlier in its double ontological and gnostic meaning. I realize a project in so far as I give it being, but I also *realize my situation in so far as I live it and* make it be with my being. I "realize" the scope of a catastrophe, the difficulty of an undertaking. To know is to *realize* in both senses of the term. It is to cause being "to be there" while having to be the reflected negation of this being. *The real is realization.* We shall define transcendence as that inner and realizing negation which reveals the in-itself while determining the being of the for-itself.

## II. DETERMINATION AS NEGATION

To *what* being is the for-itself presence? Let us note immediately that the question is badly phrased. Being is what it is; it can not possess in itself the determination "this one" to answer the question "which?" In short the question has meaning only if it is posited in a world. Consequently the for-itself can not be present to *this* being rather than to *that* since it is the presence of the for-itself which causes the existence of a "this" rather than a "that." Our examples, however, have shown us a for-itself denying concretely that it is a *particular* being. This situation arises from the fact that, when we described the relation of knowledge, we were interested first in bringing to light its structure of negativity. In this sense, by the very fact that it was revealed in examples, that negativity was already secondary. Negativity as original transcendence is not determined in terms of a *this*; it causes a *this* to exist.

The original presence of the for-itself is *presence* to being. Shall we say then that it is presence to *all* being? That would be to fall back into our former error. For totality can come to being only by the for-itself. A totality indeed supposes an internal relation of being between the terms of a quasi-multiplicity in the same way that a multiplicity supposes—in order to be this multiplicity—an inner totalizing relation among its elements. In this sense addition itself is a synthetic act. Totality can come to beings only by a being which has to be its own totality in their presence. This is precisely the case with the for-itself, a detotalized totality which temporalizes itself in a perpetual incompleteness. It is the for-itself in its presence to being which causes there to be an *all of being*. We must understand indeed that this particular being can be called *this* only on the ground of the presence of *all* being. That does not mean that *one* being needs *all* being in order to exist but that the for-itself realizes itself as a realizing presence to this being on the original ground of a realizing presence to *all*. But conversely since totality is an internal ontological relation of "thises," it can be revealed only in and through the individual "thises." That means that the for-itself as a realizing presence to all being realizes itself as a realizing presence to the "thises," and as a realizing presence to the "thises" it realizes itself as a realizing presence to all being. In other words, the presence of the for-itself to the *world* can be realized only by its presence to one or several particular things, and conversely its presence to a particular thing can be realized only on the ground of a presence to the world. Perception is articulated only on the ontological foundation of presence to the world, and the world is revealed concretely as the ground of each individual perception. It remains to explain how the upsurge of the for-itself in being can bring it about that there is an all and "thises."

The presence of the for-itself to being as *totality* comes from the fact that the for-itself has to be—in the mode of being what it is not and of not being what it is—its own totality as a detotalized totality. In so far as the for-itself makes itself be in the unity of a single upsurge as *all* which is not being, being stands before it as *all* which the for-itself is not. The original negation, in fact, is a radical negation. The for-itself, which stands before being as its own totality, is itself the whole of the negation and hence is the negation of the whole. Thus the achieved totality of the world is revealed as constitutive of the being of the unachieved totality by which the being of totality comes into being. It is through the *world* that the for-itself makes itself known to itself as a totality detotalized, which means that by its very upsurge the for-itself is a revelation of being as a totality inasmuch as the for-itself has to be its own totality in the detotalized mode. Thus the very meaning of the for-itself is outside in being, but it is through the for-itself that the meaning of being appears. This totalization of being *adds nothing* to being; it is nothing but the manner in which being is revealed as not being the for-itself, the manner in which *there is* being. It appears *outside the for-itself*, beyond all reach, as that which determines the for-itself in its being. But the fact of revealing being as a totality does not touch being any more than the fact of counting two cups on the table touches the existence or nature of either of them. Yet it is not a purely subjective modification of the for-itself since it causes all subjectivity to be possible. But if the for-itself is to be the nothingness whereby "there is" being, then being can exist originally only as totality. Thus knowledge is the *world*. To use Heidegger's expression, the world and outside of that—*nothing*. But this "nothing" is not originally that in which human reality emerges. This *nothing* is human reality itself as the radical negation by means of which the world is revealed. Of course the very apprehension of the world as totality causes the appearance *alongside the world* of a nothingness which sustains and encompasses this totality. In fact this nothingness as the absolute nothing which is left outside the totality even determines the totality. This is why the totalization adds nothing to being, for it is only the result of the appearance of nothingness as the limit of being. But this nothingness is *not* anything except human reality apprehending itself as excluded from being and perpetually beyond being, in relationship with that "nothing". It amounts to the same thing whether we say, human reality is that by which being is revealed as totality—or, human reality is that which causes *there to be* nothing outside of being. This nothing is the possibility for there to be a beyond-the-world such that (1) this possibility reveals being as a world and (2) human reality has to be this possibility. As such, this nothing constitutes—along with the original presence to being—the circuit of selfness.

But human reality makes itself the unachieved totality of negations only in so far as it reaches beyond a concrete negation which it has to be as actual presence to being. If it were in fact a pure consciousness (of) being a syncretic and undifferentiated negation, it could not determine itself and therefore could not be a concrete totality, although detotalized, of its determinations. It is a totality only to the extent that through all its other negations it escapes the concrete negation which it is at present. Its being can be its own totality only to the extent that it is a surpassing toward the whole which it has to be, beyond the partial structure which it is. Otherwise it would simply be what it is and could in no way be considered as either a totality or a non-totality. In the sense then that a partial negative structure must appear on the ground of the undifferentiated negations which I am— and of which it forms a part—I make known to myself by means of being-in-itself a certain concrete reality which I have to not-be. The "this" is the being which I at present *am not*, in so far as it appears on the ground of the totality of being. This is what I at present am not inasmuch as I have to be nothing of being: it is what is revealed on the undifferentiated ground of being, to make known to me the concrete negation which I have to be on the totalizing ground of my negations.

This original relation between the all and the "this" is at the source of the relation between figure and ground which the "Gestalt theory" has brought to light. The "this" always appears on a ground; that is, on the undifferentiated totality of being inasmuch as the For-itself is the radical and syncretic negation of it. Yet it can always dissolve again into this undifferentiated totality when another "this" arises. But the appearance of the "this" or of the figure on the ground, since it is the correlate of the appearance of my own concrete negation on the syncretic ground of a radical negation, implies that I both am and am not that total negation or, if you prefer, that I am it in the mode of "non-being" and that I am not it in the mode of being. It is indeed only in this way that the present negation will appear on the ground of the radical negation which it is. Otherwise indeed the present negation would be entirely cut off or else it would be dissolved in the radical negation. The appearance of the *this* on the *all* is correlative with a certain way which the For-itself has of being the negation of itself. There is a *this* because I am not yet my future negations and because I am no longer my past negations. The revelation of the *this* supposes that the "accent is put" on a certain negation accompanied by the withdrawal of the others in the syncretic disappearance into the ground; that is, that the for-itself can exist only as a negation which is constituted on the withdrawal into totality of the radical negativity. The For-itself *is not* the world, spatiality, permanence, matter, in short the in-itself in general, but its manner of not-being-them is to have to not-be this table, this glass, this room on the total ground of negativity. The *this* supposes then a negation of the negation—but a negation which has to be the radical negation which it denies, which does not cease reattaching itself to it by an ontological thread, and which remains ready to dissolve in the radical negation at the upsurge of another "this." In this sense the "this" is revealed as "this" by "a withdrawal into the ground of the world" on the part of all the other "thises;" its determination, which is the origin of *all* determinations, is a negation.

We must understand that this negation—seen from the point of view of the "this"—is wholly ideal. It adds nothing to being and subtracts nothing from it. The being confronted as "this" is what it is and does not cease being it; it does not become. As such it can not be outside of itself *in* the whole as a structure of the whole, nor can it be outside of itself in the whole so as to deny its identity with the whole. Negation can come to the *this* only through a being which has to be simultaneously presence to the whole of being and to the *this*—that is, through an ekstatic being. Since it leaves the *this* intact as being in itself, since it does not effect a real synthesis of all the thises in totality, the negation constitutive of the *this* is a negation of the *external* type; the relation of the "this" to the whole is a relation of externality. Thus we see that determination appears as an external negation correlative with the radical and ekstatic internal negation which I *am*. This is the explanation of the ambiguous character of the *world*, which is revealed simultaneously as a synthetic totality and as a purely additive collection of all the "thises." In so far as the world is a totality which is revealed as that on which the For-itself has to be radically its own nothingness, the world is presented as a syncretism of undifferentiation. But in so far as this radical nihilation is always beyond a concrete and present nihilation, the world appears always ready to open like a box to allow the appearance of one or several "thises" which *already were* (there in the heart of the undifferentiation of the ground) what they are now as a differentiated figure. When we are gradually approaching a landscape which was given in great masses, we see objects appear which are given as having been there already, as elements in a discontinuous collection of "thises"; in the same way, in the experiments of the Gestalt school, the continuous background suddenly when apprehended as figure bursts into a multiplicity of discontinuous elements. Thus the world, as the correlate of a detotalized totality, appears as an evanescent totality in the sense that it is never a real synthesis but an ideal limitation—by nothing—of a collection of *thises*.

Thus the *continuous* as a formal quality of the ground allows the discontinuous to appear as a type of external relation between the *this* and the totality. It is precisely this perpetual evanescence of the totality into collection, of the continuous into the discontinuous that defines *space*. Space can not be a *being*. It is a moving relation between beings which are unrelated. It is the total independence of the in-itselfs, as it is revealed to a being which is presence to "all" the in-itself as the independence of *each one in relation to the others*. It is the unique way in which beings can be revealed as having no relation, can be thus revealed to the being through which relation comes into the world; that is, space is pure exteriority. Since this exteriority cannot belong to any one of the *thises* considered and since in addition a purely local negativity is self-destructive, it can neither be by itself nor "be made-to-be." The spatializing being is the For-itself as co-present to the whole and to the "this." Space is not the world, but it is the instability of the world apprehended as totality, inasmuch as the world can always disintegrate into external multiplicity. Space is neither the ground nor the figure but the ideality of the ground inasmuch as it can always disintegrate into figures; it is neither the continuous nor the discontinuous, but the permanent passage from continuous to discontinuous. The existence of space is the proof that the For-itself by causing being "to be there" adds *nothing* to being. Space is the ideality of the synthesis. In this sense it is at once totality to the extent that it derives its origin from the world, and at the same time *nothing* inasmuch as it results in the pullulation of the *thises*. Space does not allow itself to be apprehended by concrete intuition for it *is not*, but it is continuously spatialized. It depends on temporality and appears in temporality since it can come into the world only through a being whose mode of being is temporalization; for space is the way in which this being loses itself ekstatically in order to realize being. The spatial characteristic of the *this* is not added synthetically to the *this* but is only the "place" of the *this*; that is, its relation of exteriority to the ground inasmuch as this relation can collapse into a multiplicity of external relations with other *thises* when the ground itself disintegrates into a multiplicity of figures. In this sense it would be useless to conceive of space as a form imposed on phenomena by the *a priori* structure of our sensibility. Space can not be a form, for it is *nothing*; it is, on the contrary, the indication that nothing except the negation—and this still as a type of external relation which leaves intact what it unites—can come to the in-itself through the For-itself. As for the For-itself, if it is not space, this is because it apprehends itself precisely as not being being-in-itself in so far as the in-itself is revealed to it in the mode of exteriority which we call extension. It is precisely by denying exteriority in itself and apprehending itself as ekstatic that the For-itself spatializes space. The relation between the For-itself and the in-itself is not one of juxtaposition or indifferent exteriority. Its relation with the in-itself, which is the foundation of all relations, is the internal negation, and it is through this that being-in-itself continues in indifferent exteriority in relation to other beings existing in a world. When the exteriority of indifference is hypostasized as a substance existing in and through itself—which can be effected only at a lower stage of knowledge—it is made the object of a particular type of study under the title of geometry and becomes a pure specification of the abstract theory of multiplicities.

It remains to determine what type of being the external negation possesses since this comes to the world by the For-itself. We know that it does not belong to the *this*. This newspaper does not deny concerning itself that it is the table on which it is lying; for in that case the newspaper would be ekstatically outside itself and in the table which it denies, and its relation to the table would be an internal negation; it would thereby cease even to be in-itself and would become for-itself. The determinative relation of the *this* therefore can belong neither to the *this* nor to the *that*; it enfolds them without touching them, without conferring on them the slightest trace of new character; it leaves them for what they are. In this sense we can modify the famous statement of Spinoza, "*Omnis determinatio est negatio*," which Hegel declared to possess infinite riches; and we will claim rather that every determination which does not belong to the being which has to be its own determinations is an ideal negation. Moreover it would be inconceivable that it should be otherwise. Even if following an empirical-critical psychologism, we were to consider things as purely subjective contents, we still could not conceive that the subject would realize internal synthetic negations among these contents without *being them* in a radical ekstatic immanence which would remove all hope of any passage to objectivity.

With even more reason we can not imagine that the For-itself effects distorting synthetic negations among transcendents which it is not. In this sense the external negation constitutive of the "this" can not appear as an *objective* characteristic of the thing, if we understand by objective that which by nature belongs to the in-itself—or that which in one way or another *really* constitutes the object as it is. But we must not conclude from this that the external negation has subjective existence like the pure mode of being of the For-itself. The type of existence of the For-itself is a pure internal negation; the existence in it of an external negation would be destructive of its very existence. Consequently the external negation can not be a way of disposing and of classifying phenomena which would exist only as subjective phantoms, nor can it "subjectivize" being in so far as its revelation is constitutive of the For-itself. Its very exteriority therefore requires that it remain "in the air," exterior to the For-itself as well as to the In-itself. On the other hand, precisely because it is exteriority, it can not be by itself; it refuses all supports, it is by nature *unselbständig*, and yet it can not be referred to any substance. It is a *nothing*. In fact it is because the inkwell is not the table—nor the pipe nor the glass—that we can apprehend it as an inkwell. And yet if I say, "The inkwell is not the table," I am thinking nothing. Thus determination is a nothing which does not belong as an internal structure either to the thing or to consciousness, but its being is to-be-summoned by the For-itself across a system of internal negations in which the in-itself is revealed in its indifference to all that is not itself. In so far as the For-itself makes itself known to itself by the In-itself, which it is not—in the mode of internal negation, the indifference of the In-itself as the indifference which the For-itself has to not-be is revealed in the world as determination.

## III. QUALITY AND QUANTITY, POTENTIALITY, INSTRUMENTALITY

Quality is nothing other than the being of the this when it is considered apart from all external relation with the world or with other thises. Too often quality has been conceived as a simple subjective determination, and its quality-of-being has then been confused with the subjectivity of the psychic. The problem has then appeared to be especially to explain the constitution of an object-pole conceived as the transcendent unity of qualities. We have shown that this problem is insoluble. A quality does not objectivate itself if it is subjective. Supposing that we had projected the unity of an object-pole beyond qualities, at most each one of them would be given directly as the subjective effect of the action of things upon us. But the yellow of the lemon is not a subjective mode of apprehending the lemon; it is the lemon. And it is not true either that the object X appears as the empty form which holds together disparate qualities. In fact the lemon is extended throughout its qualities, and each of its qualities is extended throughout each of the others. It is the sourness of the lemon which is yellow, it is the yellow of the lemon which is sour. We eat the color of a cake, and the taste of this cake is the instrument which reveals its shape and its color to what we may call the alimentary intuition. Conversely if I poke my finger into a jar of jam, the sticky coldness of that jam is the revelation to my fingers of its sugary taste. The fluidity, the tepidity, the bluish color, the undulating restlessness of the water in a pool are given at one stroke, each quality through the others; and it is this total interpenetration which we call the this. This fact has been clearly shown by the experiments of painters, especially of Cézanne. Husserl is wrong in believing that a synthetic necessity unconditionally unites color and form; it is the form which is color and light. If the painter wants to vary any one of these factors, the others change as well, not because they are linked by some sort of law but because at bottom they are one and the same being.

In this sense every quality of being is all of being; the quality is the presence of the absolute contingency of being, its indifferent irreducibility. The apprehension of a quality does not add anything to being except the fact that *being is there as this*. In this sense a quality is not an external aspect of being, for being, since it has no "within," can not have a "without." But in order for there to be quality there must be being for a nothingness which by nature is *not* being. Yet being is not *in itself* a quality although it is nothing either more or less. But quality is *the whole of being* revealing itself within the limits of the "there is." It is not the "outside" of being; it is all being since there cannot be being for being but only for that which makes itself not to be being. The relation of the For-itself to quality is an ontological relation. The intuition of a quality is not the passive contemplation of a given, and the mind is not an In-itself which remains what it is in that contemplation; that is, which remains in the mode of indifference in relation to the *this* contemplated. But the For-itself makes known to itself what it is not by means of quality. For the For-itself, to perceive red as the color of this notebook is to reflect on itself as the internal negation of that quality. That is, the apprehension of quality is not a "fulfillment" (*Erfüllung*) as Husserl makes it, but the giving form to an emptiness as a determined emptiness of that quality. In this sense quality is a presence perpetually out of reach.

The description of knowledge is too often alimentary. There still remains too much of *prélogisme*[2] in epistemological philosophy, and we are not yet rid of that primitive illusion (which we must account for later) according to which to know is to eat—that is, to ingest the known object, to fill oneself with it (*Erfüllung*), and to digest it ("assimilation"). We shall best account for the original phenomenon of perception by insisting on the fact that the relation of the quality to us is that of absolute proximity (it "*is there,*" it haunts us) without either giving or refusing itself, but we must add that this proximity implies a distance. It is what is immediately out of reach, what by definition refers us to ourselves as to an emptiness. Contemplation of it can only increase our thirst for being as the sight of the food out of reach added to Tantalus' hunger. Quality is the indication of what we are not and of the mode of being which is denied to us. The perception of white is the consciousness of the impossibility on principle for the For-itself to exist as color—that is, by being what it is. In this sense not only is being not distinguished from its qualities but even the whole apprehension of quality is the apprehension of a *this*. Quality, whatever it may be, is revealed to us as a being. The odor which I suddenly breathe in with my eyes closed, even before I have referred it to an odorous object, is already an odor-being and not a subjective impression. The light which strikes my eyes in the morning

---

[2] *Prélogisme* is a term borrowed from a now discredited theory to the effect that at an earlier stage of human development, thought was not logical, in particular did not feel the necessity of avoiding contradiction. See *s.v.* "prélogique." André Lalande, *Vocabulaire technique et critique de la philosophie*. Paris. *Presses universitaires de France*. 1951. pp. 814–815. Tr.

through my closed eyelids is already a light-being. This will appear obvious if one reflects on the fact that quality *is*. As a being which is what it is, it can indeed *appear* to a subjectivity, but it can not be inserted in the woof of that subjectivity which is what it is not and which is not what it is. To say that a quality is a quality-being is not to endow it with a mysterious support analogous to substance; it is simply to observe that its mode of being is radically different from the mode of the being "for-itself." The being of whiteness or of sourness indeed could in no way be apprehended as ekstatic.

If someone should ask now how it happens that the "this" has qualities we should reply that actually the this is released as a totality on the ground of the world and that it is given as an undifferentiated unity. It is the for-itself which can deny itself from various points of view when confronting the this and which reveals the quality as a new this on the ground of the thing. For each negating act by which the freedom of the For-itself spontaneously constitutes its being, there is a corresponding total revelation of being "in profile." This profile is nothing but a relation of the thing to the For-itself, a relation realized by the For-itself. It is the absolute determination of negativity, for it is not enough that the for-itself by an original negation should not *be* being nor that it should not be this being; in order for its determination as the nothingness of being to be full, the for-itself must realize itself as a certain unique manner of not being this being.

This absolute determination, which is the determination of quality as a profile of the "this," belongs to the freedom of the For-itself. It *is not*; it is as "to-be." Anyone may see this for himself by considering how the revelation of *one* quality of the thing appears always as a factual gratuity grasped *across* a freedom. While I can not make this orange peel cease being green, it is I who am responsible for my apprehending it as a rough green or a green rough-ness. But the relation figure-ground here is rather different from that of the this to the world. For instead of the figure's appearing on an undifferentiated ground, it is wholly penetrated by the ground; it holds the ground within it as its own undifferentiated density. I apprehend the peel as green; its "brightness-roughness" is revealed as an inner undifferentiated ground and plenitude of being for the green. There is no abstraction here in the sense that abstraction separates what is united, for being always appears entire in its profile. But the realization of being conditions the abstraction, for the abstrac-tion is not the apprehension of a quality "in midair" but of a this-quality where the undifferentiation of the inner ground tends toward absolute equi-librium. The green abstracted does not lose its density of being—otherwise it would be nothing more than a subjective mode of the for-itself—but the brightness, the shape, the roughness, *etc.*, which are given across it dissolve in the nihilating equilibrium of pure and simple *massiveness*. Abstraction, how-ever, is a phenomenon of presence to being since abstract being preserves its transcendence. But it can be realized only as a presence to being beyond being; it is a surpassing. This presence to being can be realized only on the level of possibility and in so far as the For-itself has to be its own possibilities. The abstract is revealed as the meaning which quality has to be as co-present to the presence of a for-itself to-come. Thus the abstract green is the meaning-to-come of the concrete this in so far as it reveals itself to me through its profile "green-brightness-roughness." The green is the peculiar possibility of this profile in so far as it is revealed across the possibilities which I am; that is, in so far as it is made-to-be. But this brings us to instrumentality and the temporality of the world. We shall return to this point. For the moment it is sufficient to say that the abstract haunts the concrete as a possibility fixed in the in-itself, which the concrete has to be. Whatever our perception may be, as the original contact with being, the abstract is always there but to-come; I apprehend it in the future with my future. It is correlative with the peculiar possibility of my present concrete negation as the possibility of being no more than this negation. The abstract is the meaning of this in so far as it reveals itself in the future across my possibility of fixing in in-itself the negation which I have to be.

If someone should remind us here of the classic difficulties regarding abstraction, we should reply that they stem from the fact that the constitution of the "this" and the act of abstraction are taken as distinct. It is certain that if the this does not include its own abstractions, there is no possibility of deriving them from it afterward. But it is in the very constitution of the this as this that the abstraction operates as the revelation in profile of my future. The For-itself is an "abstractor," not because it could realize a psychological operation of abstraction but because it rises as a presence to being with a future—that is, a beyond being. In itself being is neither concrete nor abstract nor present nor future: it is what it is. Yet the abstraction does not enrich being; it is only the revelation of a nothingness of being beyond being. But we challenge anyone to formulate the classic objections to abstraction without deriving them implicitly from the consideration of being as a this.

The original relation of the thises to one another can be neither interaction nor causality nor even the upsurge on the same ground of the world. If we suppose that the For-itself is present to one this, the other thises exist at the same time "in the world" but by virtue of being undifferentiated; they constitute the ground on which the this confronted is raised in relief. In order to establish any relation whatsoever between one this and another this, it is necessary that the second this be revealed rising up on the ground of the world on the occasion of an express negation which the For-itself has to be. But at the same time each this must be held at a distance from the other as not being the other by a negation of a purely external type. Thus the original relation of this to that is an external negation. That appears as not being this.

And the external negation is revealed to the For-itself as a transcendent; it is outside, it is in-itself. How are we to understand it?

The appearance of the this-that can be produced first only as totality. The primary relation here is the unity of a totality capable of disintegration; the For-itself is determined en bloc to not-be "this-that" on the ground of the world. The "this-that" is my whole room in so far as I am present to it. This concrete negation will not then disappear with the disintegration of the concrete mass into this and that. On the contrary it is the very condition of the disintegration. But on this ground of presence and by means of this ground of presence, being effects the appearance of its indifferent exteriority. This exteriority is revealed to me in the fact that the negation which I am is a unity-multiplicity rather than an undifferentiated totality. My negative upsurge into being is parceled out into independent negations which have no connection other than that they are negations which I have to be; that is, they derive their inner unity from me and not from being. I am present to that table, to those chairs, and as such I constitute myself synthetically as a polyvalent negation; but this purely inner negation, in so far as it is a negation of being is paralyzed with zones of nothingness; it is nihilated by virtue of negation, it is negation detotalized. Across these striations of nothingness which I have to be as my own nothingness of negation, appears the indifference of being. But this indifference I have to realize by this nothingness of negation which I have to be, not in so far as I am originally present to the "this" but in so far as I am also present to the "that." It is in and by my presence to the table that I realize the indifference of the chair (which presently I also have to not-be) as an absence of a springboard, an arrest of my impulse toward non-being, a breakdown in the circuit. "That" appears alongside "this," in the heart of a total revelation, as that from which I can in no way profit so as to determine myself to not-be "this."

Thus cleavage comes from being, but there is cleavage and separation only through the presence of the For-itself to all of being. The negation of the unity of the negations in so far as it is a revelation of the indifference of being and in so far as it apprehends the indifference of the "this" with regard to the "that" and the "that" with regard to the "this," is a revelation of the original relation of the thises in an external negation. The "this" is not "that." This external negation within the unity of a totality capable of disintegration is expressed by the word "and." "This is not that" is written "this and that." The external negation has the double character of being-in-itself and of being pure ideality. It is in-itself in that it does not in any way belong to the For-itself; the For-itself discovers the indifference of being as exteriority across the absolute interiority of its own negation (since in aesthetic intuition I apprehend an imaginary object). Moreover we are not dealing with a negation which being has to be; this negation does not belong to any of the thises considered; it purely and simply is. It is what it is. But at the same time it is by no means a characteristic of the this, by no means one of its qualities. It is even totally independent of the thises, precisely because it does not belong to any one of them. For the indifference of being is nothing; we can not think it or even perceive it. It means simply that annihilation or the variations of the that can not engage the this at all; in this sense it is only a nothingness in-itself separating the thises, and this nothingness is the only mode in which consciousness can realize the cohesion of identity which characterizes being.

This ideal nothingness in-itself is quantity. Quantity in fact is pure exteriority; it does not depend on the terms added but is only the affirmation of their independence. To count is to make an ideal distinction inside a totality capable of disintegration and already given. The number obtained by the addition does not belong to any of the thises counted nor to the totality capable of disintegration—in so far as this is revealed as totality. If there are three men talking opposite me, it is not as I apprehend them first as a "group in conversation" that I count them; and the fact of counting them as three leaves the concrete unity of their group perfectly intact. Being a "group of three" is not a concrete property of the group. Neither is it a property of its members. We can not say of any one of them that he is three nor even that he is a third—for the quality of third is only a reflection of the freedom of the for-itself which is counting; each one of the men can be a third, but no one of them is it. The relation of quantity is therefore a relation in-itself but a purely negative and external relation. It is precisely because it does not belong either to things or to totalities that it is isolated and detached from the surface of the world as a reflection (reflet) of nothingness cast on being. As a purely exterior relation between the thises, quantity is itself exterior to them and finally exterior to itself. It is the inapprehensible indifference of being—which can appear only if there is being and which, although belonging to being, can come to it only from a for-itself, inasmuch as this indifference can be revealed only by the exteriorization to infinity of a relation of exteriority which must be exterior to being and to itself. Thus space and quantity are only one and the same type of negation. By the sole fact that this and that are revealed as having no relation to me who am my own relation, space and quantity come into the world; for each one of them is the relation of things which are unrelated or, if you prefer, the nothingness of relation apprehended as a relation by the being which is its own relation. From this we can see that what Husserl calls categories (unity-multiplicity-relation of the whole to the part—more and less—around—beside—following—first, second, etc.—one, two, three, etc.—within and without—etc.)—these are only the ideal mixing of things which leaves them wholly intact, without either enriching or impoverishing them by one iota; they merely indicate the infinite diversity of ways in which the freedom of the for-itself can realize the indifference of being.

We have treated the problem of the original relation of the for-itself to being as if the for-itself were a simple, instantaneous consciousness such as can be revealed to the Cartesian *cogito*. In truth we have already encountered the escape from self on the part of the for-itself inasmuch as this is the necessary condition for the appearance of the *thises* and of abstractions. But the ekstatic character of the for-itself was still only implicit. While we have had to proceed in this way for the sake of clarity in exposition, we should not thereby conclude that being is revealed to a being which would be first presence in order afterwards to constitute itself a future. But being-in-itself is revealed to a being which arises as about-to-come to itself. This means that the negation which the for-itself makes itself be in the presence of being has an ekstatic dimension of the future; it is in so far as I am not what I am (an ekstatic relation to my own possibilities) that I have to not-be being-in-itself as the revealing realization of the *this*. That means that I am presence to the "this" in the incompleteness of a totality detotalized. What consequence is there here for the revelation of the *this*?

Since I am always beyond what I am, about-to-come to myself, the "this" to which I am present appears to me as something which I surpass toward myself. The perceived is originally the surpassed; it is like a conductor in the circuit of selfness, and it appears within the limits of this circuit. To the extent that I make myself be the negation of the *this*, I flee this negation in the direction of a complementary negation; and the fusion of the two would effect the appearance of the in-itself which I am. There is a bond of being between the negation of the *this* and the second possible negation; the second is not just any negation but is precisely the complementary negation of my presence to the thing. But since the for-itself constitutes itself qua presence, as a non-positional self-consciousness, it makes known to itself, outside itself, through being, what it is not. It recovers its being outside in the mode "the-reflection-reflecting." The complementary negation which the for-itself is as its own possibility is then a negation-presence; that is, the for-itself has to be it as a non-thetic self-consciousness and as a thetic consciousness of being-beyond-being.

Being-beyond-being is bound to the present *this*, not by any kind of external relation but by a precise bond of complementarity which stands in exact correlation with the relation of the for-itself to its future. First of all, the *this* is revealed in the negation of a being which makes itself to not-be this, not by virtue of simple presence, but as a negation which is about-to-come to itself, which is its own possibility beyond its present. This possibility which haunts pure presence as its meaning out of reach and as that which it lacks in order to be *in-itself* exists first as a projection of the present negation by virtue of engagement. Every negation in fact which would not have beyond itself in the future the meaning of an engagement as a possibility which comes to it and toward which it flees itself, would lose all its significance as negation. What the for-itself denies, it denies "with the dimension of a future." It involves either an external negation (this is not that, that chair is not a table) or an internal negation bearing on itself. To say that "this is not that" is to posit the exteriority of the "this" in relation to the "that," whether for now and for the future or in the strict "now"; but in the latter case the negation has a *provisory* character which constitutes the future as pure exteriority in relation to the present determination "this *and* that." In both cases the meaning comes to the negation in terms of the future; all negation is ekstatic. In so far as the for-itself denies itself in the future, the *this* concerning which it makes itself a negation is revealed as coming to itself from the future. The possibility that consciousness exists non-thetically as consciousness (of) being able not to not-be this is revealed as the *potentiality* of the *this* of being what it is. The first potentiality of the object, as the correlate of the engagement, an ontological structure of the negation, is *permanence*, which perpetually comes to it on the ground of the future. The revelation of the table as table requires a permanence *of* table which comes to it from the future and which is not a purely established *given*, but a potentiality. This permanence moreover does not come to the table from a future located in temporal infinity. Infinite time does not yet exist. The table is not revealed as having the possibility of being a table indefinitely. The time concerned here is neither finite nor infinite; potentiality merely causes the dimension of the future to appear.

When we speak of the meaning-to-come of the negation, we refer to that which the negation of the for-itself lacks in order to become a negation *in itself*. In this sense the negation is, in the future, the precision[3] of the present negation. It is in the future that there is revealed the exact meaning of what I have to not-be as a correlate of the exact negation which I have to be. The polymorphic negation of the *this*, where the green is formed by a totality "roughness-light," gets its meaning only if it has to be the negation of the green; that is, of a being-green, the ground of which tends toward the equilibrium of undifferentiation. In a word, the absent-meaning of my polymorphic negation is a negation confined by a green more purely green on an undifferentiated ground. Thus the pure green comes to the "green-roughness-light" on the ground of the future as its meaning. We apprehend here the meaning of what we have called *abstraction*. The existent does not *possess* its essence as a present quality. It is even the negation of essence; the green *never is* green. But the essence comes from the ground of the future to the existent, as a meaning which is never given and which forever haunts it. It is the pure correlate of the pure ideality of my negation. In this sense there

---

[3] Used in the technical sense of "determination" or "giving an exact meaning." Tr.

is no such thing as an operation of abstraction if we mean by that a psychological affirmative act of selection effected by a constituted mind. Far from abstracting certain qualities in terms of things, we must on the contrary view abstraction as the original mode of being of the for-itself, necessary in order that there may be, in general, things and a world. The abstract is a structure of the world and is necessary for the upsurge of the concrete; the concrete is concrete only in so far as it leans in the direction of its abstraction, that it makes itself known by the abstraction which it is. The being of the for-itself is revealing-abstracting. We see that from this point of view permanence and the abstract are only one. If the table has qua table a potentiality of permanence, this is to the exact degree that it has to be a table. Permanence is pure possibility for a *this* to be consistent with its essence.

We have seen in Part Two of this work that the relation between the possible which I am and the present which I am fleeing is the same as the relation between the lacking and the one which lacks what is lacking. The ideal fusion of the lacking with the one which lacks what is lacking is an unrealizable totality which haunts the for-itself and constitutes its very being as a nothingness of being. This ideal we called the in-itself-for-itself or *value*. But on the unreflective level this value is not grasped thetically by the for-itself; it is only a condition of being. If our conclusions are accurate, this perpetual indication of an unrealizable fusion must appear not as a structure of the unreflective consciousness but as a transcendent indication of an ideal structure of the object. This structure can be easily revealed; correlative with the indication of a fusion of the polymorphic negation with the abstract negation which is its meaning, there is to be revealed a transcendent and ideal indication—that of a fusion of the existing *this* with its essence to-come. Thus fusion must be such that the abstract is the foundation of the concrete and that simultaneously the concrete is the foundation of the abstract. In other words, the concrete "flesh and blood" existence must be the essence, and the essence must itself be produced as a total concretion; that is, it must have the full richness of the concrete without however allowing us to discover in it any thing other than itself in its total purity. Or if you prefer, the form must be to itself—and totally—its own matter. And conversely the matter must be produced as absolute form.

This perpetually indicated but impossible fusion of essence and existence does not belong either to the present or the future, it indicates rather the fusion of past, present, and future, and it presents itself as a synthesis *to be effected* of temporal totality. It is value as transcendence; it is what we call *beauty*. Beauty therefore represents an ideal state of the world, correlative with an ideal realization of the for-itself; in this realization the essence and the existence of things are revealed as identity to a being who, in this very revelation, would be merged with himself in the absolute unity of the in-itself. This is precisely because the beautiful is not only a transcendent synthesis to be effected but because it can be realized only in and through a totalization of ourselves. This is precisely why we desire the beautiful and why we apprehend the universe as *lacking* the beautiful to the extent that we ourselves apprehend ourselves as a lack. But the beautiful is no more a potentiality of things than the in-itself-for-itself is a peculiar possibility of the for-itself. It haunts the world as an unrealizable. To the extent that man *realizes* the beautiful in the world, he realizes it in the imaginary mode. This means that in the aesthetic intuition, I apprehend an imaginary object across an imaginary realization of myself as a totality in-itself and for-itself. Ordinarily the beautiful, like value, is not thematically made explicit as a value-out-of-reach-of-the-world. It is implicitly apprehended on things as an absence; it is revealed implicitly across the *imperfection* of the world.

These original potentialities are not the only ones which characterize the *this*. To the extent that the for-itself has to be its being beyond its present, it is the revelation of a qualified beyond-being, which comes to the "this" on the ground of being. In so far as the for-itself is beyond the crescent moon, next to a being-beyond-being which is the future full moon the full moon becomes the potentiality of the crescent moon. In so far as the for-itself is beyond the bud, next to the flower, the flower is a potentiality of the bud. The revelation of these new potentialities implies an original relation to the past. It is in the past that the connection between the crescent moon and the full moon, between the bud and the flower, is gradually discovered. The past of the for-itself stands as empirical knowledge for the for-itself. But this knowledge does not remain as an inert given. It is behind the for-itself, of course, unrecognizable as such and out of reach. But in the ekstatic unity of its being, it is in terms of this past that the for-itself makes known to itself what it is in the future. My wisdom (*savoir*) as regards the moon escapes me as a thematic knowledge (*connaissance*). But I *am* it, and my way of being is—at least in certain cases—to cause what I no longer am to come to me in the form of what I am not yet. This negation of the *this*—which I have been—I am in two ways: in the mode of not being any longer and of not being yet. I am beyond the crescent moon as the possibility of a radical negation of the moon as a full disk; and correlative with the return of my future negation toward my presence, the full moon comes back toward the crescent in order to determine it in *this* as a negation; the full moon is what the crescent lacks; it is the lack of the full moon which makes the crescent a crescent. Thus within the unity of the same ontological negation, I attribute the dimension of the future to the crescent as crescent—in the form of permanence and essence—and I constitute it as the crescent moon by the determining return toward it of what it lacks. Thus is constituted the scale of possibilities which reaches from permanence to *potencies*. Human-reality by surpassing itself in the direction of its own possibility of negation, makes itself that by which negation through surpassing comes into the world. It is through human reality that lack comes to things in the form of "potency," of "incompletion," of "suspension," of "potentiality."

Nevertheless the transcendent being of lack can not have the nature of ekstatic lack in immanence. Let us look at it more carefully. The in-itself does not have to be its own potentiality in the mode of not-yet. The revelation of the in-itself is originally a revelation of the self-identity of indifference. The in-itself is what it is without any ekstatic dispersion of its being. It does not have to be its permanence or its essence or that which it lacks as I have to be my future. My upsurge into the world causes potentialities to arise correlatively. But these potentialities are fixed in their very arising; they are eaten away by exteriority. We shall discover here again that double aspect of the transcendent which in its very ambiguity has given birth to space: a totality which is dispersed in relations of exteriority. Potentiality on the ground of the future turns back on the *this* to determine it, but the relation between the *this* as in-itself and its potentiality is an external relation. The crescent moon is determined as *lacking* or *deprived of*—in relation to the full moon. But at the same time the crescent is revealed as being fully what it is—that concrete sign in the sky, which needs nothing in order to be what it is. The same is true for this bud or for this match, which is what it is, for which its meaning as being-a-match remains exterior, which *can* of course burst into flame but which at present is this piece of white wood with a black tip. The potentialities of the *this*, while strictly connected with it, are present as in-itselfs and are in a state of indifference in relation to it. This inkwell *can* be broken, thrown against the marble of the fireplace where it will be shattered. But this potentiality is entirely cut off from it, for it is only the transcendent correlate of my possibility of throwing the inkwell against the marble of the fireplace. In itself the inkwell is neither breakable nor unbreakable; it *is*.

That does not mean that I can consider a *this* as beyond any potentiality; from the mere fact that I am my own future, the *this* is revealed as provided with potentialities. To apprehend the match as a piece of white wood with a black tip is not to strip it of all potentiality but simply to confer on it new ones (a new permanence—a new essence). In order for the *this* to be entirely deprived of potentialities, it would be necessary that I be a pure presence, which is inconceivable. But the *this* has various potentialities which are *equivalents*—that is, in a state of equivalence in relation to it. This is because it does not have to be *them*. In addition my possibilities do not exist but are possibilized because they are eaten away from within by my freedom; that is, whatever my possible may be, its opposite is equally possible. I can shatter this inkwell but I can just as well put it in a drawer. I can aim at the full moon beyond the crescent moon, but I can just as well insist on the permanence of the crescent as such. Consequently the inkwell is found to be provided with equivalent possibilities: to be put in a drawer, to be shattered. This crescent moon can be an open curve in the sky or a disk held in suspense. Those potentialities which refer back to the *this* without being made to be by it and without having to be—those we shall call *probabilities* to indicate that they exist in the mode of being of the in-itself. We cannot say that my possibles *are*; they are possibilized. But probabilities are not "probabilized," they are each one *in itself* as probable. In this sense the inkwell *is*, but its *being-an-inkwell* is a probable; for the inkwell's having-to-be-an-inkwell is a pure appearance which is founded immediately on a relation of exteriority.

These potentialities or probabilities, which are the meaning of being beyond being, are *in-itselfs beyond being*, and precisely for this reason they are *nothings*. The essence of the inkwell is made-to-be as a correlate of the possible negation of the for-itself, but it is not the inkwell and it is not being. In so far as this essence is in-itself, it is a negation hypostasized and reified; that is, it is a nothing, it belongs to the shell of nothingness which encases and determines the world. The for-itself reveals the inkwell as an inkwell. But this revelation is made beyond the being of the inkwell, in that future which is not; all the potentialities of being, from permanence to qualified potentialities, are defined as that which being *is not yet* without ever truly having *to be them*. Here again knowledge adds nothing to being and removes nothing from it; knowledge adorns it with no new quality. It causes being to-be-there by surpassing it toward a nothingness which enters into only negative exterior relations with it. This character of pure nothingness in potentiality results in efforts on the part of science, which aims at establishing relations of simple exteriority, radically to suppress the potential (essence and potencies). But on the other hand the necessity of potentiality as a meaningful structure of perception appears clearly enough so that we need not insist on it here. Scientific knowledge, in fact, can neither overcome nor suppress the potentializing structure of perception. On the contrary science must presuppose it.

We have attempted to show how the presence of the for-itself to being reveals being as a *thing*, and for the sake of clarity in exposition we have had to show successively the various structures of the thing: the *this* and spatiality, permanence, essence and potentialities. It is evident, however, that this successive account does not correspond to a real priority of certain of these moments over others: the upsurge of the for-itself causes the thing to be revealed with the totality of its structures. Furthermore there is not one of these structures which does not imply all the others. The *this* does not have even logical priority over essence. On the contrary the *this* presupposes essence, and conversely essence is the essence of this. Similarly the *this* as the being-of-a-quality can appear only on the ground of the world, but the world is a collection of *thises*; the disintegrating relation of the world to the *thises*, of the *thises* to the world is spatiality. There is therefore no substantial form here, no principle of unity to stand *behind* the modes of appearance of the phenomenon; everything is given at one stroke without any primacy. For the same reasons, it would be incorrect to conceive of any kind of primacy as concerns the *representative*. Our descriptions have led us to put in relief *the thing in the world*, and because of this fact we might be tempted to believe that the world and the thing are revealed to the for-itself in a sort of contemplative intuition. This, however, would be an intuition after the event such that objects would be arranged one in relation to another in a practical order of instrumentality. Such an error will be avoided if we are willing to maintain that the world appears inside the circuit of selfness. It is this which separates the for-itself from itself or—to employ an expression of Heidegger's—it is this in terms of which human reality makes known to itself what it is.

This project toward self on the part of the for-itself, which constitutes selfness, is in no way a contemplative repose. It is a lack, as we have said, but not a *given* lack. It is a lack which has to be to itself its own lack. It must be understood that an *established* lack or a lack in-itself vanishes into exteriority, as we have pointed out in preceding passages. But a being which constitutes itself as lack can determine itself only there upon *that which* it lacks and *which* it is—in short, by a perpetual wrenching away from self toward the self which it has to be. This means that lack can be to itself its own lack only as a *refused lack*: the only truly inner connection between that which lacks —— and that which is lacking is the refusal. In fact to the extent that the being which lacks —— is not what it lacks, we apprehend in it a negation. But if this negation is not to slip away into pure exteriority—and along with it all possibility of negation in general—its foundation must be in the necessity for the being which lacks —— to *be* that which it lacks. Thus the foundation of the negation is negation of negation. But this negation-foundation is no more a given than the lack of which it is an essential moment; it is as having to be. The for-itself in the phantom unity "the-reflection-reflecting" makes itself be its own lack; that is, it projects itself toward its lack by refusing it. It is only as a lack *to be suppressed* that lack can be internal for the for-itself, and the for-itself can realize its own lack only by having to be it; that is, by being a project towards its suppression. Thus the relation of the for-itself to its future is never static nor given; the future comes to the present of the for-itself in order to determine it in its heart inasmuch as the for-itself is already there at the future as its suppression. The for-itself can be a lack *here* only if it is *there* a suppression of the lack, but a suppression which it has to be in the mode of non-being. It is this original relation which subsequently allows the empirical establishment of particular lacks as lacks *suffered* or *endured*. It is in general the foundation of affectivity; it is this also which some will try to explain psychologically by installing within the psyche those idols and those phantoms which we call *drives* or *appetites*. These drives or these forces, which by violence are inserted into the psyche, are not understandable in themselves, for they are given by the psychologist as in-itself existents; that is, their very character as *force* is contradicted by their inner repose of indifference, and their unity is dispersed in a pure relation of exteriority. We can apprehend them only as the result of projecting into the in-itself a relation of immanent being of the for-itself to itself and this ontological relation is precisely *lack*.

But this lack can not be grasped thetically and known by the unreflective consciousness (nor does it appear to the impure, accessory reflection which apprehends it as a psychic object—i.e., as a drive or as a feeling). It is accessible only to the purifying reflection, with which we are not here concerned. On the level of consciousness of the world, this lack can appear only in projection, as a transcendent and ideal characteristic. In fact while that which the for-itself lacks is the ideal presence to a being-beyond-being, the being-beyond-being is originally apprehended as the lacking-to-being. Thus the world is revealed as haunted by absences to be realized, and each *this* appears with a cortege of absences which point to it and determine it. These absences are not basically different from potentialities. But it is easier to grasp their meaning. Thus the absences indicate the *this* as this, and conversely the *this* points toward the absences. Since each absence is being-beyond-being—i.e., an absent-in-itself—each *this* points toward another state of its being or toward other beings. But of course this organization of indicative complexes is fixed and petrified in in-itself; hence all these mute and petrified indications, which fall back into the indifference of isolation at the same time that they arise, resemble the fixed, stony smile in the empty eyes of a statue.

The absences which appear behind things do not appear as absences *to be made present* by things. Neither can we say that they are revealed as to be realized *by me* since the "me" is a transcendent structure of the psyche and appears only to the reflective consciousness. They are pure demands which rise as "voids to be filled" in the middle of the circuit of selfness. Their character as "voids to be filled by the for-itself" is manifested to the unreflective consciousness by a direct and personal urgency which is *lived* as such without being referred to *somebody* or thematized. It is in and through the very fact of living them as claims that there is revealed what in an earlier chapter we called their selfness. They are *tasks*, and this world is a world of *tasks*. In relation to the tasks, the *this* which they indicate is both "the this of these tasks"—that is, the unique in-itself which is determined by them and which they indicate as being able to *fulfill* them—and that which does not have *to be* these tasks since it exists in the absolute unity of identity. This connection in isolation, this inert relation within the dynamic is what we call the relation of means to end. It is a being-for which is degraded, laminated by exteriority, a being-for whose transcendent ideality can be conceived only as a correlate of the being for which the for-itself has to be.

The thing, in so far as it both rests in the quiet beatitude of indifference and yet points beyond it to tasks to be performed which make known to it what it has to be, is an instrument or utensil. The original relation between things, that which appears on the foundation of the quantitative relation of the *thises*, is the relation of *instrumentality*. This instrumentality is not subsequent to or subordinate to the structures already indicated: in one sense it presupposes them; in another it is presupposed by them. The thing is not first a thing in order to be subsequently an instrument; neither is it first an instrument in order to be revealed subsequently as a thing. It is an instrumental-thing. It is true, nevertheless, that the further research of the scientist will reveal it as purely a thing—i.e., stripped of all instrumentality. But this is because the scientist is concerned only with establishing purely exterior relations. Moreover the result of this scientific research is that the thing itself, deprived of all instrumentality, finally disappears into absolute exteriority. We can see to what extent we must correct Heidegger's definition: to be sure, the world appears in the circuit of selfness; but since the circuit is non-thetic, the making known of what I am can not be thetic either. To be in the world is not to escape from the world toward oneself but to escape from the world toward a beyond-the-world which is the future world. What the world makes known to me is only "worldly." It follows that if the infinite reference of instruments never refers to a for-itself which I *am*, then the totality of instruments is the exact correlate of my possibilities; and as I *am* my possibilities, the order of instruments in the world is the image of my possibilities projected in the in-itself; i.e., the image of what I am. But I can never decipher this worldly image; I adapt myself to it in and through action, but a reflective scissiparity would be required in order for me to be able to be an object to myself.

It is not then through unauthenticity that human reality loses itself in the world. For human reality, being-in-the-world means radically to lose oneself in the world through the very revelation which causes there to be a world— that is, to be referred without respite, without even the possibility of "a purpose for which" from instrument to instrument with no recourse save the reflective revolution. It would be useless to object that the chain of "for whats" is suspended from the "for whoms" (*Worumwillen*). Of course the *Worumwillen* refers us to a structure of being which we have not yet elucidated; namely, the for-others. And the "for whom" constantly appears behind the instruments. But this "for whom," whose constitution is different from the "for what" does not break the chain. It is simply one of the links; when it is confronted in the perspective of instrumentality, it does not allow an escape from the in-itself. To be sure these workclothes are for the worker. But they are for the worker so that he can fix the roof without getting dirty. And why shouldn't he get dirty? In order not to spend most of his salary for clothes. This salary is allotted him as the minimum quantity of money which will enable him to support himself; and he "supports" himself so as to be able to apply his capacities for work at repairing roofs. And why should he repair the roof? So that it will not rain in the office where employees are working at book-keeping. Etc. This does not mean that we should always think of the Other as an instrument of a particular type, but merely that when we consider the Other in terms of the world, we do not escape even so from the infinite regress of instrumental complexes.

Thus to the extent that the for-itself is its own lack as a refusal correlative with its impulse toward self, being is revealed to the for-itself on the ground of the world as an instrumental-thing, and the world rises as the undifferentiated ground of indicative complexes of instrumentality. The ensemble of these references is void of meaning but in this sense—that the possibility of positing the problem of meaning on this level does not exist. We work to live and we live to work. The question of the *meaning* of the totality "life-work"— "Why do I work, I who am living? Why live if it is in order to work?"—this can be posited only on the reflective level since it implies a self-discovery on the part of the for-itself.

It remains to explain how as a correlate of the pure negation which I am, instrumentality can arise in the world. How does it happen that I am not a barren, indefinitely repeated negation of the *this* as pure *this*? If I am nothing but the pure nothingness which I have to be, how can this negation reveal a plurality of tasks which are my image? In order to answer this question we must recall that the for-itself is not purely and simply a future which comes to the present. It has to be also its past in the form of "was." The ekstatic involvement of the three temporal dimensions is such that while the for-itself is a being which by means of its future makes known to itself the meaning of what it was, it is also in the same upsurge a being which has to be its *will-be* within the perspectives of a certain "was" which it is fleeing. In this sense we must always look for the meaning of a temporal dimension *elsewhere*, in another dimension. This is what we have called the *diaspora*, for the unity of diasporatic being is not a pure *given* appurtenance; it is the necessity of *realizing* the diaspora by making itself conditioned there, outside, within the unity of the self.

Therefore the negation which I am and which reveals the "this" has *to be* in the mode of "was." This pure negation which as simple *presence* is not, has its being behind it, as past or facticity. As such we must recognize that it is never a negation without roots. On the contrary, it is a *qualified* negation—if by that we understand that it drags its qualification behind it as the being which it has to not-be in the form of "was." The negation arises as a non-thetic negation of the past in the mode of internal determination in so far as it makes itself a thetic negation of the this. The upsurge is effected in the unity of a double "being for," since the negation effects its existence in the mode of the-reflection-reflecting, as the negation of the this, in order to escape from the past which it is; it escapes from the past in order to disengage itself from the this by fleeing it in its being toward the future. This is what we shall call the point of view which the for-itself has on the world. This point of view, comparable to facticity, is the ekstatic qualification of the negation as the original relation to the in-itself. On the other hand, as we have seen, everything that is for-itself is so in the mode of "was" as an ekstatic appurtenance of the world. It is not in the future that I rediscover my presence since the future releases the world to me as correlative with a consciousness to-come. Rather my being appears to me in the past, although non-thematically, within the compass of being-in-itself; that is, in relief in the midst of the world. Of course this being is still consciousness of——, that is, a for-itself; but it is a for-itself fixed in in-itself, and consequently while a consciousness of the world, it is fallen into the midst of the world. The meaning of realism, of naturalism, and of materialism lies in the past; these three philosophies are descriptions of the past as if it were present.

The for-itself is then a double flight from the world; it escapes its own being-in-the-midst-of-the-world as a presence to a world which it is fleeing. The possible is the free end of the flight. The for-itself can not flee toward a transcendent which it is not, but only toward a transcendent which it is. It is this fact which removes all possibility of surcease from this perpetual flight. If I may use a down-to-earth image for the sake of making my thought clearer, picture an ass drawing behind him a cart. He attempts to get hold of a carrot which has been fastened at the end of a stick which in turn has been tied to the shaft of the cart. Every effort on the part of the ass to seize the carrot results in advancing the whole apparatus and the cart itself, which always remains at the same distance from the ass. Thus we run after a possible which our very running causes to appear, which is nothing but our running itself, and which thereby is by definition out of reach. We run toward ourselves and we are—due to this very fact—the being which can not be reunited with itself. In one sense the running is void of meaning since the goal is never given but invented and projected proportionately as we run toward it. In another sense we can not refuse to it that meaning which it rejects since in spite of everything possibility is the meaning of the for-itself. Thus there is and there is not a meaning in the flight.

Now in that very flight from the past which I am toward the future which I am, the future is prefigured in relation to the past at the same time that it confers on the past all its meaning. The future is the past surpassed as a given in-itself toward an in-itself which would be its own foundation—that is, which would be in so far as I should have to be it. My possibility is the free recovery of my past in so far as this recovery can rescue it by providing its foundation. I flee the being without foundation which I was toward the founding act which I can be only in the mode of the *I would be*. Thus the possible is the lack which the for-itself makes itself be; that is, which is lacking to the present negation in so far as it is a *qualified* negation (a negation which has its quality outside itself in the past). As such the possible is itself qualified—not by virtue of being a *given*, which would be its own quality in the world of the in-itself, but as an indication of the recovery which would found the ekstatic qualification which the for-itself *was*.

Thus thirst, for example, is three dimensional: it is a present flight from a state of emptiness which the for-itself was. This very flight confers on the *given* state its character of emptiness or lack; in the past the lack could not be lack, for the *given* can be "lacking" only if it is surpassed towards —— by a being which is its own transcendence. But this flight is a flight towards ——, and it is this "towards" which gives flight its meaning. As such flight is itself *a lack which makes itself*—that is, a constitution in the past of a given as a lack or potentiality and at the same time the free recovery of the given by a for-itself which makes itself a lack in the form, the "reflection-reflecting"—that is, as consciousness of lack. Finally *that toward which* the lack is fled, in so far as it causes itself to be conditioned in its being-a-lack by that which it lacks, is the possibility that it is to be a thirst which would be no longer a lack but a thirst-repletion. The possible is the indication of the repletion; value, as a phantom-being which surrounds and penetrates the for-itself through and through, is the indication of a thirst which would be simultaneously a *given*—as it "was it"—and a recovery—as the game of "the reflection-reflecting" constitutes it ekstatically. As one can see, we are dealing here with a plenitude which determines itself as thirst. The ekstatic relation past-present provides the outline of this plenitude with the structure "thirst" as its meaning, and the possible which I am must furnish its very density, its fleshly plenitude, as repletion.

Thus my presence to being which determines it as *this* is a negation of the "this" *in so far as* I am also *a qualified lack beside the* "this." To the extent that my possible is a possible presence to being beyond being, the qualification of my possible reveals a being-beyond-being as the being whose co-presence is a co-presence strictly linked with a repletion to-come. Thus *absence* in the world is revealed as a being to-be-realized in so far as this being is correlative with the possible-being *which I lack*. The glass of water appears as about-to-be-drunk; that is, as the correlate of a thirst grasped non-thetically and its very being as about to be satisfied. But these descriptions, which all imply a relation to the future of the world, will be clearer if we at present explain how the time of the world or universal time is revealed to consciousness on the ground of the original negation.

## IV. THE TIME OF THE WORLD

Universal time comes into the world through the For-itself. The in-itself is not adapted to temporality precisely because it is in-itself and because temporality is the mode of unitary being in a being which is perpetually at a distance from itself for itself. The For-itself, on the contrary, is temporality, but it is not consciousness of temporality except when it produces itself in the relation "reflective-reflected-on." In the unreflective mode the for-itself discovers temporality *on* being—that is, outside. Universal temporality is *objective*.

### A. The past

The "this" does not appear as a present which later will have to become past and which before that was future. This inkwell the moment I perceive it already exists in the three temporal dimensions. In so far as I apprehend it as permanence—i.e., as essence—it is already in the future although I am not present to it in my actual presence but as about-to-come-to-myself. By the same token, I can not apprehend it except as having already been there in the world inasmuch as I was already there myself as presence. In this sense there exists no "synthesis of recognition" if we mean by that a progressive operation of identification which by successive organization of the "nows" would confer a *duration* on the thing perceived. The For-itself directs the explosion of its temporality against the whole length of the revealed in-itself as though against the length of an immense and monotonous wall of which it can not see the end. I am that original negation which I have to be in the mode of *not-yet* and of *already*, beside the being which is what it is. If then we suppose a consciousness arising in a motionless world beside a unique being which is unchangeably what it is, this being will be revealed with a past and a future of immutability which will necessitate no "operation" of a synthesis and which will be one with its very revelation. The *operation* would be necessary only if the For-itself had to retain and to constitute its own past by the same stroke. But due to the mere fact that the in-itself *is* its own past as also its own future, the revelation of the in-itself can only be temporalized. The "this" is revealed temporally not because it would be refracted across an *a priori* form of inner meaning but because it is revealed to a revelation of which the very being is temporalization. Nevertheless the a-temporality of being is *represented* in its very revelation; in so far as it is grasped through and in a temporality which temporalizes itself, the *this* appears originally as temporal; but in so far as it is what it is, it refuses to be its own temporality and merely reflects time. In addition it reflects the internal ekstatic relation—which is at the source of temporality—as a purely objective relation of exteriority. Permanence, as a compromise between non-temporal identity and the ekstatic unity of temporalization, will appear therefore as the pure slipping by of in-itself instants, little nothingnesses separated one from another and reunited by a relation of simple exteriority on the surface of a being which preserves an a-temporal immutability. It is not true therefore that the non-temporality of being escapes us; on the contrary, it is given in time, it provides the foundation for the mode of being of universal time.

In so far then as the For-itself "was" what it is, the instrument or thing appears to it as having been already there. The For-itself can be presence to the this only as a presence which was; all perception is in itself, and without any "operation", a recognition. Now what is revealed through the ekstatic unity of Past and Present is an identical being. It is not apprehended as being the same in the past and in the present but as being it. Temporality is only an organ of sight. Yet this it which it is, the "this" already was. Thus the this appears as having a past. But it refuses to be this past; it only has it. Temporality in so far as it is grasped objectively is therefore a pure phantom, for it does not give itself as the temporality of the For-itself nor as the temporality which the in-itself has to be. At the same time the transcendent Past, since it is in-itself by virtue of transcendence, can not be as that which the Present has to be; the Past is isolated in a phantom of Selbständigkeit. And as each moment of the past is a "having-been Present," this isolation is pursued to the very interior of the Past. Consequently the unchangeable this is revealed across a flickering and an infinite parcelling out of phantom in-itselfs. This is how that glass or that table is revealed to me. They do not endure; they are. Time flows over them.

Of course someone will object that I merely fail to see changes in the glass or table. But this is to introduce very inappropriately a scientific point of view. Such a point of view, which nothing justifies, is contradicted by our very perception. The pipe, the pencil, all these beings which are released entire in each one of their "profiles" and whose permanence is wholly indifferent to the multiplicity of profiles, are transcendent to all temporality even though they are revealed in temporality. The "thing" exists straightway as a "form;" that is, a whole which is not affected by any of the superficial parasitic variations which we can see on it. Each this is revealed with a law of being which determines its threshold, its level of change where it will cease to be what it is in order simply not to be. This law of being, which expresses "permanence," is an immediately revealed structure of the essence of the "this;" it determines a limit-of-potentiality in the "this"—that of disappearing from the world. We shall return to this point. Thus the For-itself apprehends temporality on being, as a pure reflection which plays on the surface of being without any possibility of modifying being. The scientist will fix this absolute, spectral, nihilating quality of time in a concept under the name of homogeneity. But the transcendent apprehension on the in-itself of the ekstatic unity of the temporalizing For-itself is effected as the apprehension of an empty form of temporal unity without any being which founds that unity by being it. Thus on the plane of Present-Past, there appears that curious unity of the absolute dispersion which is external temporality. Here each before and each after is an "in-itself" isolated from others by its indifferent exteriority, and here these instants are reunited in the unity of one and the same being. And this common being or Time is nothing other than the very dispersion, conceived as necessity and substantiality. This contradictory nature could *appear* only on the double foundation of the For-itself and the In-itself. From this standpoint in so far as scientific reflection aims at hypostasizing the relation of exteriority, being will be conceived—i.e., thought of in emptiness—not as a transcendence aimed at across time but as a content which passes from instant into instant. Better yet it will be conceived as a multiplicity of contents, external to one another, and strictly *resembling* one another.

So far our description of universal temporality has been attempted under the hypothesis that nothing may come from being save its nontemporal immutability. But *something* does come from being: what, for lack of a better term, we shall call *abolitions* and *apparitions*. These apparitions and abolitions ought to be the object of a purely metaphysical elucidation, not an ontological one, for we can conceive of their necessity neither from the standpoint of the structures of being of the For-itself nor of those of the In-itself. Their existence is that of a contingent and metaphysical fact. We do not know exactly what comes from being in the phenomenon of apparition since this phenomenon is already the fact of a temporalized "this." Yet experience teaches us that there are upsurges and annihilations of the various "this." Moreover since we know that perception reveals the In-itself and outside the In-itself *nothing*, we can consider the in-itself as the foundation of these upsurges and of these annihilations. In addition we see clearly that the principle of identity as the law of being of the in-itself requires that the abolition and the apparition be totally exterior to the in-itself which has appeared or been abolished, for otherwise the in-itself would at the same time both be and not be. The abolition can not be that falling away from being which is an *end*. Only the For-itself can fall away because it is to itself its own end. Being, a quasi-affirmation in which the affirming is coated over by the affirmed, exists without any inner finitude in the peculiar tension of its "self-affirmation." Its "until then" is totally external to it. Thus the abolition does not involve the necessity of an *after*, which can be manifested only in a world and for a for-itself, but a *quasi-after*. This quasi-after can be expressed thus: being-in-itself can not effect the mediation between itself and its nothingness. Similarly apparitions are not *adventures* of the appearing being. That priority over itself which "adventure" would suppose can be found only in the For-itself, for which both apparition and end are inner adventures. Being is what it is. It is without "putting itself into being," without childhood or youth. That which has appeared is not a novelty to itself; it is from the start being without any relation to a "before" which it would have to be as pure absence. Here again we find a quasi-succession; i.e., on the part of that which has appeared, there is a complete exteriority in relation to its nothingness.

But in order for this absolute exteriority to be given in the form of the "there is," there must be already a world; that is, the upsurge of a For-itself. The absolute exteriority of the In-itself in relation to the In-itself is responsible for the fact that even the very nothingness which is the quasi-before of the apparition or the quasi-after of the abolition can find no place in the plenitude of being. It is only within the unity of a world and on the ground of a world that there can appear a *this* which *was not* or that there can be revealed that relation-of-absence-of-relation which is exteriority. The nothingness of being, which is priority in relation to an "appeared" which "was not," can come only retrospectively to a world by a For-itself which is its own nothingness and its own priority. Thus the upsurge and the annihilation of the *this* are ambiguous phenomena; here again what comes to being by the For-itself is a pure nothingness, the not-being-yet and the not-being-any-longer. The being which we are considering is not the foundation of it, nor the world as a totality apprehended *before* or *after*. On the other hand, in so far as the upsurge is revealed in the world by a For-itself which is its own *before* and its own *after*, the apparition is given first as an adventure; we apprehend the *this*, which has appeared as being already there in the world, as its own absence inasmuch as we ourselves were already present to a world from which it was absent. Thus the thing can arise from its own nothingness. Here, however, we are not dealing with a conceptual view of the mind but with an original structure of perception. The experiments of the Gestalt School show clearly that pure apparition is always grasped as a dynamic upsurge; the appearance comes on the run to being, on the ground of nothingness.

At the same time we have here the origin of the "principle of causality." The ideal of causality is not the negation of the "appeared" as such, as someone like Meyerson would make it, nor is it the assigning of a permanent bond of exteriority between two phenomena. The first causality is the apprehension of the "appeared" before it appears, as being already there in its own nothingness so as to prepare its apparition. Causality is simply the first apprehension of the temporality of the "appeared" as an ekstatic mode of being. But the *adventurous* character of the event, as the ekstatic constitution of the apparition, disintegrates in the very perception; the *before* and the *after* are fixed in its nothingness-in-itself, the "appeared" in its indifferent self-identity; the non-being of the "appeared" in that prior instant is revealed as an indifferent plenitude of the being existing at that instant; the relation of causality disintegrates into a pure relation of exteriority between the "thises" prior to the "appeared" and the "appeared" itself. Thus the ambiguity of apparition and of abolition comes from the fact that they are given, like the world, like space, like potentiality and instrumentality, like universal time itself in the form of totalities in perpetual disintegration.

Such then is the past of the world—made of homogeneous instants connected one with another by a purely external relation. By means of its Past, the For-itself founds itself in the In-itself. In the Past the For-itself, now become In-itself, is revealed as being in the midst of the world: it is; has lost its transcendence. And due to this fact its being is made past in time; there is no difference between the Past of the For-itself and the past of the world which was co-present with it except that the For-itself has to be its own past. Thus there is only *one* Past, which is the past of being or the *objective* Past in which I was. My past is past in the world, belonging to the totality of past being, which I am, which I flee. This means that there is a coincidence for one of the temporal dimensions between the ekstatic temporality which I have to be and the time of the world as a pure given nothingness. It is through the past that I belong to universal temporality; it is through the present and the future that I escape from it.

## B. The present

The Present of the For-itself is presence to being, and as such it is *not*. But it is a revelation of being. The being which appears to Presence is given *as being in the Present*. That is why the present is given paradoxically as not being at the moment when it is experienced and as being the unique measure of Being in so far as it is revealed as being what it is in the Present. Not that being does not extend beyond the present, but this superabundance of being can be grasped only through the instrument of apprehension which is the Past—that is, as that which is no longer. Thus this book on my table *is* in the present and it *was* (identical with itself) in the Past. Thus the Present is revealed through original temporality as universal being, and at the same time it is nothing— nothing more than being; it is a slipping-past alongside being, pure nothingness.

The preceding observations would seem to indicate that nothing comes from being to the present except its being. But this would be to forget that being is revealed to the For-itself either as immobile or as in motion, and that the two notions of motion and rest are in a dialectical relation. Now motion can not be derived ontologically from the nature of the For-itself nor from its fundamental relation to the In-itself, nor from what we can discover originally in the phenomenon of Being. A world without motion would be conceivable. Of course, we can not imagine the possibility of a world without change, except by virtue of a purely formal possibility, but change is not motion. Change is alteration of the quality of the *this*; it is produced, as we have seen, in a block by the upsurge or disintegration of a form. Motion, on the contrary, supposes the permanence of the quiddity. If a *this* were to be transferred from one place to another and during this transfer were to undergo a radical alteration of its being, this alteration would negate the motion since there would no longer be anything which was in motion. Motion is pure change of place affecting a *this* which remains otherwise unaltered as is shown clearly enough by our assumption of the homogeneity of space. Since motion could not be deduced from any essential characteristic of existents in presence, it was denied by the Eleatic ontology; it compelled Descartes in his ontology to take refuge in the famous "snap of the finger." Motion has the exact value of a fact; it participates wholly in the complete contingency of being and must be accepted as a given. Of course we shall soon see that a For-itself is necessary in order for motion to exist; hence it is particularly difficult to designate exactly what in pure motion comes from being. But in any case there is no doubt that the For-itself here as elsewhere *adds nothing to being.* Here as elsewhere it is pure Nothing which provides the ground on which motion raises itself in relief. But while we are forbidden by the very nature of motion to *deduce* it, it is possible and even necessary for us to *describe* it. What then are we to conclude is the *meaning* of motion?

It is believed that motion is a simple *affection* of being because *after* the motion the moving body is discovered to be just as it was before. It has so often been posited as a principle that transfer does not distort the figure transferred that it has appeared evident that motion is added to being without modifying it. It is certain, as we have seen, that the quiddity of the "this" remains unaltered. Nothing is more typical of this conception than the resistance which has been encountered by a theory like that of Fitzgerald concerning "contraction," or like Einstein's concerning "the variations of mass," because they seem particularly to attack what makes the being of the moving body. Hence evidently comes the principle of the relativity of motion, which we can easily understand if the latter is an external characteristic of being and if no intra-structural modification determines it. Motion becomes then a relation of the being to its setting so external that it amounts to saying that being is in motion and its environment at rest or conversely that the environment is in motion and the being considered is at rest. From this point of view motion appears neither as a being nor as a mode of being but as an entirely desubstantialized relation.

But the fact that the moving body is identical with itself at departure and at arrival—i.e., in the two states which encompass motion—does not pre-determine in any respect what it has been while it was in motion. It would amount to saying that the water which boils in an autoclave undergoes no transformation during the boiling, for the specious reason that it presents the same characteristics when it is cold at the start and when it is re-cooled. The fact that we can assign different successive positions to the moving body during its motion and that at each position it appears similar to itself should not deter us, for these positions define the space traversed and not motion itself. On the contrary, it is this mathematical tendency to treat the moving body as a being at rest which someone would move along a line without changing its state of rest; it is this tendency which is at the origin of the Eleatic paradoxes.

Thus the affirmation that being remains unchanged in its being, whether it be at rest or in motion, should appear to us as a simple postulate which we ought not to accept uncritically. In order to submit it to criticism let us return to the Eleatic arguments and in particular to the one concerning the arrow. The arrow, they tell us, when it passes by the position AB "is" there, exactly as if it were an arrow at rest, with the tip of its head on A and the tip of its tail on B. This appears evident if we admit that motion is superimposed on being and that consequently nothing comes to decide whether being is in motion or at rest. In a world, if motion is an accident of being, motion and rest are indistinguishable. The arguments which are usually opposed to the most famous of the Eleatic paradoxes, that of Achilles and the Tortoise, have no bearing here. What good is it to object that the Eleatics have reckoned on the infinite division of space without equally taking into account that of time? The question here concerns neither position nor the instant, but being. We approach a correct conception of the problem when we reply to the Eleatics that they have considered not motion but the space which supports motion. But we are limiting ourselves to pointing out the question without resolving it: what must be the being of the moving body in order for its quiddity to remain unchanged while in its being the moving body is distinct from a being at rest?

If we try to clarify our objections to Zeno's arguments, we establish that they originate in a certain naive conception of motion. We admit that the arrow "passes" at AB, but it does not seem to us that to pass a place is the equivalent of remaining there—i.e., of being there. Yet in this view we are guilty of serious confusion, for we consider that the moving object only passes AB (i.e., it never is there) and at the same time we continue to take for granted that in itself it is. Consequently the arrow simultaneously would be in itself and would not be at AB. This is the origin of the Eleatic Paradox: how could the arrow not be at AB since at AB it is? In other words in order to avoid the Eleatic paradox we must renounce the generally admitted postulate according to which being in motion preserves its being-in-itself. Merely to pass at AB is a being-of-passage. What does it mean to pass? It is simultaneously to be at a place and not to be there. At no moment can it be said that the being of the passage is here, without running the risk of abruptly stopping it there, but neither can it be said that it is not, or that it is *not there*, or that it is *elsewhere*. Its relation with the place is not a relation of *occupation*. But we have seen earlier that the *location* of a "this" at rest was its relation of exteriority to the ground inasmuch as this relation can collapse into a multiplicity of external relations with other "thises" when the ground itself disintegrates into a multiplicity of figures.[4] The foundation of space is therefore the reciprocal exteriority which comes to being through the For-itself and whose origin is the fact that being is what it is. In a word it is being which defines its place by revealing itself to a For-itself as indifferent to other beings. This indifference is nothing but its very identity, its absence from ekstatic reality as it is apprehended by a For-itself which is already presence to other "thises."

By the very fact therefore that the *this* is what it is, it *occupies* a place, it is in a place—that is, it is put into relation by the For-itself with other *thises as having no relation with them*. Space is the nothingness of relation apprehended as relation by the being which is its own relation. The fact of *passing by* a place, instead of being there, can therefore be interpreted only in terms of being. This means that since place is founded by being, being is no longer sufficient to found its place. It merely outlines it; its relations of exteriority with other "thises" can not be established by the For-itself because the latter must establish those relations in terms of a "this" which *is*. However these relations could not be annihilated because the being in terms of which they are established *is* not a pure nothingness. The very "now" in which they are established *is* already exterior to them; that is, simultaneously with their revelation, there are *already* revealed new relations of exteriority of which the "this" considered is the foundation and which are externally related to the first. But this continuous exteriority of spatial relations which define the place of being can find its foundation only in the fact that the *this* considered is exterior to itself. In fact to say that the *this* passes by a place means that it is already no longer there when it is still there; that is, in relation to itself it is not in an ekstatic relation of being but in a pure relation of exteriority. Thus there is "place" in so far as the "this" is revealed as exterior to other "thises." And there is a *passage* at this place in so far as being is no longer caught up in this exteriority but on the contrary is already exterior to it. Thus motion is the being of a being which is exterior to itself. The only metaphysical question which is posited on the occasion of motion is that of exteriority to self. What should we understand by that?

[4] Ch. Three, section II.

In motion being does not change in any way when it passes from A to B. This means that its quality, in so far as it represents the being which is revealed as this to the For-itself, is not transformed into another quality. Motion is in no way similar to becoming; it does not change the *essence* of the quality; neither does it *actualize* the quality. The quality remains exactly what it is; but its mode of being is changed. This red ball which rolls on the billiard table does not cease to *be* red, but the ball is not this red which it is in the same way now as it was the red when at rest. The red remains suspended between abolition and permanence. In fact in so far as it is already at B, it is exterior to what it was at A and there is an annihilation of the red; but in so far as it rediscovers itself at C, beyond B, it is exterior to that very annihilation. Thus through abolition it escapes being, and through being it escapes abolition.

Therefore a category of "thises" is encountered in the world which have the peculiar property of never being without thereby becoming nothingnesses. The only relation which the For-itself can originally apprehend on these *thises* is the relation of exteriority to self. For since the exteriority is *nothing*, a being must exist which is to itself its own relation in order that there may be "exteriority to self." In short it is impossible for us to define in the pure terms of the In-itself what is revealed to a For-itself as exteriority-to-self. That exteriority can be discovered only by a being which is already to itself *over there* what it is *here*—that is, a consciousness. This exteriority-to-self, which appears as a pure disorder of being—that is, as the impossibility which exists for certain "thises" simultaneously to be themselves and to be their own nothingness—this must be indicated by something which exists as a *nothing in the world*; that is, as a substantiated nothing. Since exteriority-to-self is in no way ekstatic, the relation of the moving body to itself is a pure relation of indifference and can be revealed only to a witness. It is an abolition which can not be completed and an apparition which can not be completed. This nothing which measures and signifies exteriority-to-self is the *trajectory*, as the constitution of exteriority in the unity of a single being. The trajectory is the line which is described—that is, an abrupt appearance of synthetic unity in space, a counterfeit which collapses immediately into the infinite multiplicity of exteriority. When the *this* is at rest, space *is*: when it is in motion space is *engendered* or *becomes*. The trajectory *never is*, since it is *nothing*; it vanishes immediately into purely external relations between different places; that is, in the simple exteriority of indifference or spatiality. Motion has no more of being; it is the least-being of a being which can neither arrive nor be abolished nor wholly be. Motion is the upsurge of the exteriority of indifference at the very heart of the in-itself. This pure vacillation of being is a contingent venture of being. The For-itself can apprehend it only across the temporal ekstasis and in an ekstatic permanent identification of the moving body with itself. This identification does not suppose any operation and in particular no "synthesis of recognition;" for the For-itself it is only the unity of ekstatic being of the Past with the Present. Thus the *temporal* identification of the moving body with itself across the constant positing of its own exteriority causes the trajectory to reveal itself—that is, to cause space to arise in the form of an evanescent becoming. By motion space is engendered in time; motion extends the line as traced from externality to self. The line vanishes at the same time as motion, and this phantom of the temporal unity of space is founded continuously in non-temporal space—that is, in the pure multiplicity of dispersion which is without becoming.

The For-itself in the present is presence to being. But the eternal identity of the permanent does not allow apprehending this presence as a reflection (*reflet*) on things since in permanence nothing comes to differentiate what is from what was. The *present* dimension of universal time would therefore be inapprehensible if there were no motion. It is motion which in the pure present determines universal time. First because universal time is revealed as *present* vacillation; already in the past it is no longer anything but an evanescent line, like the wake of a ship which fades away; in the future it is not at all, for it is unable to be its own project. It is like the steady progression of a crack in a wall. Moreover its being has the inapprehensible ambiguity of the instant, for one could not say either that it is or that it is not; in addition it no sooner appears than it is already surpassed and exterior to itself.

Therefore universal time corresponds perfectly to the Present of the For-itself: the exteriority to self of the being which can neither be or not be returns to the For-itself an image—projected on the level of the In-itself—of a being which has to be what it is not and to not-be what it is. The whole difference lies in that which separates exteriority-to-self—where being is not in order to be its own exteriority, but "is to-be," rather, through the identification of an ekstatic witness—from the pure temporalizing ekstasis where being has to be what it is not. The For-itself makes its present known to itself through that which moves; it is its own present in simultaneity with actual motion; it is motion which will be charged with *realizing* universal time, in so far as the For-itself makes known to itself its own present through the present of the moving body. This realization will give importance to the reciprocal exteriority of instants since the present of the moving body is defined—because of the very nature of motion—as exteriority to its own past and exteriority to that exteriority. The infinite division of time is founded in that absolute exteriority.

## C. The future

The original future is the possibility of that presence which I have to be beyond the real to an in-itself which is beyond the real in-itself. My future involves as a future co-presence the outline of a future world, and as we have seen, it is this future world which is revealed to the For-itself which I will be; it is not the true possibilities of the For-itself, for only the reflective regard can know these. Since my possibles are the meaning of what I am and arise straightway as a beyond the in-itself to which I am presence, the future of the in-itself which is revealed to my future is in direct, strict connection with the real to which I am presence. The future of the in-itself is the present in-itself modified, for my future is nothing other than my possibilities of presence to an in-itself which I will have modified. Thus the future of the world is revealed to my future. It is made from the scale of possibilities which runs from simple permanence and the pure essence of the thing on up to potencies. As soon as I fix the essence of the thing, as soon as I apprehend it as table or inkwell, I am already there in the future: first because its essence can only be a co-presence to my further possibility of not-being-any-more-than-this-negation, and second because the permanence and the very instrumentality of the table or inkwell refer us to the future. We have sufficiently developed these observations in preceding sections so that we need not dwell on them here. What we wish to point out is only that everything, from the moment of its appearance as an instrumental-thing, immediately houses certain of its structures and properties in the future.

From the moment of the appearance of the world and of the "thises" *there exists* a universal future. Yet we have noted earlier that every future "state" of the world remains strange to it in the full reciprocal exteriority of indifference. There are certain futures in the world which are defined by *chance* and become autonomous probables, which are not probabilized but which *are* as probables, as fully constituted *nows*, with their content well determined but not yet realized. These futures belong to each "this" or collection of "thises," but they are *outside*.

What than is the universal future? We must view it as the abstract context of that hierarchy of equivalents which are the futures, a container of reciprocal exteriorities which is itself exteriority, a sum of in-itselfs which is itself in-itself. That is, whatever may be the probable which is to prevail, there is and there will be a future. But due to this very fact, that future, indifferent and external to the present and composed of "nows," each one indifferent to the others and reunited by the substantiated relation of before-after (in so far as this relation, emptied of its ekstatic character has no longer anything but the meaning of an external negation)—this future is a series of empty containers reunited with one another in the unity of dispersion. In this sense the future sometimes appears as an urgency and a threat in so far as I strictly tie the future of a *this* to its present by the project of my own possibilities beyond the co-present. But sometimes this threat disintegrates into pure exteriority, and I no longer apprehend the future except under the aspect of a pure formal container, indifferent to what fills it and homogeneous with space, as a simple law of exteriority. And finally sometimes the future is discovered as a nothingness in-itself, inasmuch as it is pure dispersion beyond being.

Thus the temporal dimensions, across which the non-temporal *this* is given to us with its very a-temporality, assume new qualities when they appear on the object: being-in-itself, objectivity, the exteriority of indifference, absolute dispersion. Time, in so far as it is revealed to an ekstatic temporality which temporalizes itself, is everywhere a self-transcendence and a referring of the *before* to the *after* and of the *after* to the *before*. But this self-transcendence in so far as it causes itself to be apprehended on the in-itself, does not *have* to *be* it; it is made-to-be in it. The cohesion of Time is a pure phantom, the objective reflection (*reflet*) of the ekstatic project of the For-itself towards itself and the cohesion in motion of human Reality. But this cohesion has no *raison d'être* if Time is considered by itself; it immediately dissolves into an absolute multiplicity of instants which, considered separately, lose all temporal nature and are reduced purely and simply to the total a-temporality of the *this*. Thus Time is pure nothingness in-itself, which can seem to have a *being* only by the very act in which the For-itself overleaps it in order to utilize it. This being, however, is that of a particular figure which is raised on the undifferentiated ground of time and which we call the *lapse* of time. In fact our first apprehension of objective time is *practical*: it is while *being* my possibilities beyond co-present being that I discover objective time as the worldly correlate of nothingness which separates me from my possible. From this point of view time appears as a finite, organized form in the heart of an indefinite dispersion. The *lapse* of time is the result of a compression of time at the heart of an absolute decompression, and it is the project of ourselves toward our possibilities which realizes the compression. This compression of time is certainly a form of dispersion and of separation, for it expresses in the world the distance which separates me from myself. But on the other hand, since I project myself toward a possible only across an organized series of dependent possibles which are what I have to be in order to ———, and since their non-thematic and non-positional revelation is given in the non-positional revelation of the major possible toward which I project myself, time is revealed to me as an objective, temporal form, as an organized echeloning of probabilities. This objective form or *lapse* is like the *trajectory* of my act.

Thus time appears through *trajectories*. But just as spatial trajectories decompose and collapse into pure static spatiality, so the temporal trajectory collapses as soon as it is not simply lived as that which objectively implies our expectation of ourselves. In fact the probables which are revealed to me tend naturally to be isolated as in-itself *probables* and to occupy a strictly separated fraction of objective time. Then the *lapse* of time disappears, and time is revealed as the shimmer of nothingness on the surface of a strictly a-temporal being.

## V. Knowledge

This rapid outline of the revelation of the world to the For-itself enables us now to form certain conclusions. We shall grant to idealism that the being of the For-itself is knowledge of being, but we must add that this knowledge has being. The identity of the being of the For-itself and of knowledge does not come from the fact that knowledge is the measure of being but from the fact that the For-itself makes known to itself what it is, through the in-itself; that is, from the fact that in its being it is a relation to being. Knowledge is nothing other than the presence of being to the For-itself, and the For-itself is only the nothing which realizes that presence. Thus knowledge is by nature ekstatic being, and because of that fact it is confused with the ekstatic being of the For-itself. The For-itself does not exist in order subsequently to know; neither can we say that it exists only in so far as it knows or is known, for this would be to make being vanish into an infinity regulated by particular bits of know-ledge. Knowing is an absolute and primitive event; it is the absolute upsurge of the For-itself in the midst of being and beyond being, in terms of the being which it is not and as the negation of that being and a self nihilation. In a word, by a radical reversal of the idealist position, knowledge is reabsorbed in being. It is neither an attribute nor a function nor an accident of being; but there is only being. From this point of view it appears necessary to abandon the idealist position entirely, and in particular it becomes possible to hold that the relation of the For-itself to the In-itself is a fundamental ontological relation. At the end of this book we shall even be able to consider this articulation of the For-itself in relation to the In-itself as the perpetually moving outline of a quasi-totality which we can call Being. From the point of view of this totality the upsurge of the For-itself is not only the absolute event for the For-itself; it is also something which happens to the In-itself, the only possible adventure of the In-itself. In fact everything happens as if the For-itself by its very nihilation constituted itself as "consciousness of ——"; that is, as if by its very transcendence it escaped that law of the In-itself in which the affirm-ation is pasted over by the affirmed. The For-itself by its self-negation becomes the affirmation of the In-itself. The intentional affirmation is like the reverse of the internal negation; there can be affirmation only by a being which is its own nothingness and of a being which is not the affirming being. But then in the quasi-totality of Being, affirmation happens to the In-itself; it is the adventure of the In-itself to be affirmed. This affirmation which could not be effected as the affirmation of self by the In-itself without destroying its being-in-itself, happens to the In-itself as the affirmation is realized by the For-itself.

The affirmation is like a passive ekstasis of the In-itself which leaves the in-itself unchanged yet which is achieved in the in-itself and from the stand-point of the in-itself. All this happens as if the For-itself had a Passion to lose itself in order that the affirmation "world" might come to the In-itself. Of course this affirmation exists only for the For-itself; it is the For-itself itself and disappears with it. But it is not in the For-itself, for it is an ekstasis. If the For-itself is one of its terms (the affirming), then the other term, the In-itself, is *really* present in it. The world which I discover exists outside on being.

To realism, on the other hand, we shall grant that it is being which is present to consciousness in knowledge and that the For-itself adds *nothing* to the In-itself except the very fact that *there is* In-itself; that is, the affirmative negation. Indeed we have undertaken the task of showing that the world and the instrumental-thing, space and quantity, and universal time are all pure hypostasized nothingnesses which in no way modify the pure being which is revealed through them. In this sense everything is given, everything is present to me without distance and in its complete reality. Nothing of what I see comes from me; there is *nothing* outside what I see or what I could see. Being is everywhere around me; it seems that I can touch it, grasp it; *representation*, as a psychic event, is a pure invention of philosophers. But from this being which "invests me" on every side and from which *nothing* separates me, I am separated precisely by *nothing*; and this nothing because it is nothingness is impassable. "There is" being because I am the negation of being, and worldliness, spatiality, quantity, instrumentality, temporality—all come into being only because I am the negation of being. These add nothing to being but are the pure, nihilated conditions of the "there is"; they only cause the "there is" to be realized. But these conditions which *are nothing* separate me more radically from being than prismatic distortions, across which I might still hope to discover being. To say that there is being is nothing, and yet it is to effect a total metamorphosis—since *there is* being only for a For-itself. It is not in its own quality that being is *relative* to the For-itself, nor in its being, and thereby we escape from Kantian relativism. Being is relative to the for-itself in its "being there" since the For-itself in its internal negation affirms what can not be affirmed, knows being *such as* it is when the "such as it is" can not belong to being. In this sense the For-itself is immediate presence to being, and yet at the same time it slips in as an infinite distance between itself and being. This is because knowing has for its ideal being-what-one-knows and for its original structure not-being-what-is-known. Worldliness, spatiality, *etc.*, only cause this not-being to be expressed. Thus I rediscover myself everywhere between myself and being as the nothing which is not being.

The world is human. We can see the very particular position of consciousness: being is everywhere, opposite me, around me; it weighs down on me, it besieges me, and I am perpetually referred from being to being; that table which is there is being and *nothing* more; that rock, that tree, that landscape—being and *nothing* else. I want to grasp this being and I no longer find anything but *myself*. This is because knowledge, intermediate between being and non-being, refers me to absolute being if I want to make knowledge subjective and refers me to myself when I think to grasp the absolute. The very meaning of knowledge is what it is not and is not what it is; for in order to know being such as it is, it would be necessary to be that being. But there is this "such as it is" only because I am not the being which I know; and if I should become it, then the "such as it is" would vanish and could no longer even be thought. We are not dealing here either with scepticism—which supposes precisely that the *such as it is* belongs to being—nor with relativism. Knowledge puts us in the presence of the absolute, and there is a truth of knowledge. But this truth, although releasing to us nothing more and nothing less than the absolute, remains strictly human.

Perhaps some may be surprised that we have treated the problem of knowing without raising the question of the body and the senses or even once referring to it. It is not my purpose to misunderstand or to ignore the role of the body. But what is important above all else, in ontology as elsewhere, is to observe strict order in discussion. Now the body, whatever may be its function, appears first as the *known*. We can not therefore refer knowledge back to it or discuss it before we have defined knowing, nor can we derive knowing in its fundamental structure from the body in any way or manner whatsoever. Furthermore the body—our body—has for its peculiar characteristic the fact that it is essentially that which is *known by the Other*. What I know is the body of another, and the essential facts which I know concerning my own body come from the way in which others see it. Thus the nature of my body refers me to the existence of others and to my being-for-others. I discover with it for human reality another mode of existence as fundamental as being-for-itself, and this I shall call being-for-others. If I want to describe in an exhaustive manner the relation of man to being, I must now attempt the study of this new structure of my being—the For-others. Within one and the same upsurge the being of human reality must be for-itself-for-others.

# Part III

Being-for-Others

# 1

## THE EXISTENCE OF OTHERS

### I. THE PROBLEM

We have described human reality from the standpoint of negating conduct and from the standpoint of the *cogito*. Following this lead we have discovered that human reality is-for-itself. Is this *all* that it is? Without going outside our attitude of reflective description, we can encounter modes of consciousness which seem, even while themselves remaining strictly in for-itself, to point to a radically different type of ontological structure. This ontological structure is mine; it is in relation to myself as subject that I am concerned about myself, and yet this concern (for-myself) reveals to me a being which is my being without being-for-me.

Consider for example shame. Here we are dealing with a mode of consciousness which has a structure identical with all those which we have previously described. It is a non-positional self-consciousness, conscious (of) itself as shame; as such, it is an example of what the Germans call *Erlebnis*, and it is accessible to reflection. In addition its structure is intentional; it is a shameful apprehension of something and this something is *me*. I am ashamed of what I *am*. Shame therefore realizes an intimate relation of myself to myself. Through shame I have discovered an aspect of my being. Yet although certain complex forms derived from shame can appear on the reflective plane, shame is not originally a phenomenon of reflection. In fact no matter what results one can obtain in solitude by the religious *practice* of shame, it is in its primary structure shame *before somebody*. I have just made an awkward or vulgar gesture. This gesture clings to me; I neither judge it nor blame it. I simply live it. I realize it in the mode of for-itself. But now suddenly I raise my head. Somebody was there and has seen me. Suddenly I realize the vulgarity of my gesture, and I am ashamed. It is certain that my shame is not reflective, for the presence of another in my consciousness, even as a catalyst, is incompatible with the reflective attitude; in the field of my reflection I can never meet with anything but the consciousness which is mine. But the Other is the indispensable mediator between myself and me. I am ashamed of myself *as I appear* to the Other.

By the mere appearance of the Other, I am put in the position of passing judgment on myself as on an object, for it is as an object that I appear to the Other. Yet this object which has appeared to the Other is not an empty image in the mind of another. Such an image in fact, would be imputable wholly to the Other and so could not "touch" me. I could feel irritation, or anger before it as before a bad portrait of myself which gives to my expression an ugliness or baseness which I do not have, but I could not be touched to the quick. Shame is by nature *recognition*. I recognize that I *am* as the Other sees me. There is however no question of a comparison between what I am for myself and what I am for the Other as if I found in myself, in the mode of being of the For-itself, an equivalent of what I am for the Other. In the first place this comparison is not encountered in us as the result of a concrete psychic operation. Shame is an immediate shudder which runs through me from head to foot without any discursive preparation. In addition the comparison is impossible; I am unable to bring about any relation between what I am in the intimacy of the For-Itself, without distance, without recoil, without perspective, and this unjustifiable being-in-itself which I am for the Other. There is no standard here, no table of correlation. Moreover the very notion of *vulgarity* implies an inter-monad relation. Nobody can be vulgar all alone!

Thus the Other has not only revealed to me what I was; he has established me in a new type of being which can support new qualifications. This being was not in me potentially before the appearance of the Other, for it could not have found any place in the For-itself. Even if some power had been pleased to endow me with a body wholly constituted before it should be for-others, still my vulgarity and my awkwardness could not lodge there potentially; for they are meanings and as such they surpass the body and at the same time refer to a witness capable of understanding them and to the totality of my human reality. But this new being which appears for the other does not reside in the Other; I am responsible for it as is shown very well by the education system which consists in making children ashamed of what they are.

Thus shame is shame *of oneself before the Other*; these two structures are inseparable. But at the same time I need the Other in order to realize fully all the structures of my being. The For-itself refers to the For-others. Therefore if we wish to grasp in its totality the relation of man's being to being-in-itself, we can not be satisfied with the descriptions outlined in the earlier chapters of this work. We must answer two far more formidable questions: first that of the existence of the Other, then that of the relation of my *being* to the being of the Other.

## II. THE REEF OF SOLIPSISM

It is strange that the problem of Others has never truly disturbed the realists. To the extent that the realist takes everything as given, doubtless it seems to him that the Other is given. In the midst of the real what is more real than the Other? The Other is a thinking substance of the same essence as I am, a substance which will not disappear into primary and secondary qualities, and whose essential structure I find in myself. Yet for all that realism attempts to account for knowledge by an action of the world upon the thinking substance, it has not been concerned with establishing an immediate reciprocal action of thinking substances upon each other. It is through the mediacy of the world that they communicate. My body as a thing in the world and the Other's body are the necessary intermediaries between the Other's consciousness and mine. The Other's soul is therefore separated from mine by all the distance which separates first my soul from my body, then my body from the Other's body, and finally the Other's body from his soul. And if it is as yet not certain that the relation of the For-itself to the body is an external relation (we shall have to deal with this problem later), at least it is evident that the relation of my body to the Other's body is a relation of pure, indifferent exteriority. If the souls are separated by their bodies, they are distinct as this inkwell is distinct from this book; that is, we can not conceive of the immediate presence of the one in the other. And even if we admit that my soul can be immediately present to the Other's body, I still have to overcome all the density of a body before I touch his soul. Therefore if realism bases its certitude upon the presence "in person" of the spatial-temporal thing in my consciousness, it can not lay claim to the same evidence for the reality of the Other's soul since by this very admission, the Other's soul does not give itself "in person" to mine. It is an absence, a meaning; the body points to it without delivering it. In short, in a philosophy based on intuition, there is provided no intuition of the soul of the Other. But if we are not to make a mere play on words, this means that realism provides no place for the intuition of the Other. It would be of no use to say that at least the Other's body is given to us and that this body is a certain presence of the Other or of a part of the Other. It is true that the body belongs to the totality which we call "human reality" as one of its structures. But to be exact the body is the *body of a man* only in so far as it exists in the indissoluble unity of this totality, just as the organ is a living organ only in the totality of the organism. Realism in taking this position and presenting us with a body not enveloped in human totality but apart, like a stone or a tree or a piece of wax, has killed the body as surely as the physiologist who with his scalpel separates a piece of flesh from the totality of the living being. It is not the *Other's body* which is present to the realist intuition but *a body*, a body which doubtless has particular aspects and a particular ἕξις but which belongs nevertheless to the great class of bodies. If it is true that for a spiritual realism, the soul is easier to know than the body, still the body will be easier to know than the Other's soul.

To tell the truth, the realist is not much concerned with this problem; that is because he takes the existence of others as certain. This is why the realistic and positivistic psychology of the nineteenth century, taking for granted the existence of my fellow-man, occupied itself exclusively with establishing the ways by which I know this existence and read upon the body the nuances of a consciousness which is strange to me. The body, it will be said, is an object whose ἕξις demands a particular interpretation. The hypothesis which gives the best account of its behavior is that of a consciousness which is analogous to my own consciousness and whose various emotions the body reflects. It remains to explain *how* we arrive at this hypothesis. We will be told at one time that it is by analogy with what I know of myself and again that it is experience which teaches us, for example, to interpret the sudden reddening of a face as the forewarning of blows and angry cries. It will be freely admitted that this procedure can only give us a *probable* knowledge. It remains always possible[1] that the Other is only a body. If animals are machines, why shouldn't the man whom I see pass in the street be one? Why should not the radical conception of the behaviorists be the right one? What I apprehend on this face is nothing but the effect of certain muscular contractions, and they in turn are only the effect of a nervous impulse of which I know the course. Why not reduce the ensemble of these reactions to simple or conditioned reflexes? But the majority of psychologists remain convinced of the existence of the Other as a total reality of the same structure as their own. For them the existence of others is certain, and the knowledge which we have of them is probable. We can see here the sophistry of realism. Actually we ought to reverse the terms of this proposition and recognize that if the Other is accessible to us only by means of the knowledge which we have of him, and it this knowledge is only conjectural, then the existence of the Other is only conjectural, and it is the role of critical reflection to determine its exact degree of probability. Thus by a curious reversal, the realist because he has posited the reality of the external world, is forced to return to idealism when he confronts the existence of others. If the body is a real object really acting on thinking substance, the Other becomes a pure representation, whose *esse* is a simple *percipi*; that is, one whose existence is measured by the knowledge which we have of it. The more recent theories of Einfühlung, of sympathy, and of

---

[1] The French reads *probable*, which I feel certain must be an error. Tr.

forms serve only to perfect the description of our ways of making the Other present, but they do not put the debate on its true ground: that is, the Other is first *perceived* or he appears in experience as a particular form before all habitude; and in the absence of any analogous inference the fact remains that the object, signifying and perceived, the expressive form refer purely and simply to a human totality whose existence remains purely and simply conjectural.

If realism thus refers us to idealism, is it not advisable to adopt immediately the perspective of critical idealism? Since the Other is "my representation," is it not better to question this representation at the heart of a system which reduces the ensemble of objects to a connected grouping of representations and which measures all existence by the knowledge which I have of it?

We shall, however, find little help in the Kantians. In fact they, preoccupied with establishing the universal laws of subjectivity which are the same for all, never dealt with the question of *persons*. The subject is only the common essence of these persons; it would no more allow us to determine the multiplicity of persons than the essence of man, in Spinoza's system, permits one to determine that of concrete men. At first then it seems that Kant placed the problem of others among those matters which were not within the province of his critique. However let us look more closely. The Other as such is given in our experience; he is an object and a particular object. Kant adopted the point of view of the pure subject in order to determine the conditions of possibility not only for an object in general but for the various categories of objects: the physical object, the mathematical object, the beautiful or ugly object, and the one which presents teleological characteristics. In this connection Kant has been criticized for lacunas in his work, and some—following Dilthey, for example—have wished to establish the conditions of possibility for the historical object—i.e., to attempt a critique of historical reason. Similarly if it is true that the Other represents a particular type of object which is discovered to our experience, then it is necessary even within the perspective of a rigorous Kantianism to ask how the knowledge of the Other is possible; that is, to establish the conditions of possibility for the experience involving others.

Actually it would be completely erroneous to put the problem of the Other and that of noumenal realities on the same footing. Of course, if *certain* "Others" exist and if they are similar to me, the question of their intelligible existence can be posed for them as that of my noumenal existence is posed for me; to be sure also, the same reply will be valid for them and for me: this noumenal existence can only be thought, not conceived. But when I aim at the Other in my daily experience, it is by no means a noumenal reality that I am aiming at; neither do I apprehend or aim at my intelligible reality when I become aware of my emotions or of my empirical thoughts. The Other is a phenomenon which refers to other phenomena—to a phenomenon-of-anger which the Other feels toward me, to a series of thoughts which appear to him as phenomena of his inner sense. What I aim at in the Other is nothing more than what I find in myself. But these phenomena are radically distinct from all other phenomena.

In the first place the appearance of the Other in my experience is manifested by the presence of organized forms such as gestures and expression, acts and conducts. These organized forms refer to an organizing unity which on principle is located outside of our experience. The Other's anger in so far as it appears to his inner sense and is by nature refused to my apperception, gives the meaning and is perhaps the cause of the series of phenomena which I apprehend in my experience under the name of expression or gestures. The Other as the synthetic unity of his experiences and as both will and passion comes to organize my experience. It is not a question of the pure and simple action of an unknowable noumenon upon my sensibility but of the constitution of connected groups of phenomena within the field of my experience by a being who is not me. These phenomena, unlike all others, do not refer to possible experiences but to experiences which on principle are outside my experience and belong to a system which is inaccessible to me. But on the other hand, the condition of possibility for all experience is that the subject organize his impressions into a connected system. Thus we find in things "only what we have put into them." The Other therefore can not without contradiction appear to us as organizing our experience; there would be in this an over-determination of the phenomenon.

Can we make use of causality here? This question is well designed to show the ambiguous character of the Other in a Kantian philosophy. Causality could in fact link only phenomena to each other. But to be exact, the anger which the Other feels is one phenomenon, and the furious expression which I perceive is another and different phenomenon. Can there be a causal connection between them? This would conform to their phenomenal nature, and in this sense I am not prevented from considering the redness of Paul's face as the effect of his anger; this is a part of my ordinary affirmation. But on the other hand, causality has meaning only if it links the phenomena of *one and the same* experience and contributes to constituting that experience. Can it serve as a bridge between two experiences which are radically separated? Here we must note that by using causality in this capacity I shall make it lose its nature as an *ideal* unification of empirical appearances. Kantian causality is a unification of the moments of *my* time in the form of irreversibility. Now are we to admit that it will unify my time with that of the Other? What temporal relation is to be established between the decision to express himself, which is a phenomenon appearing in the woof of the Other's experience, and the expression which is a phenomenon of *my* experience? Is it simultaneity? Succession? But how can an instant of my time be in a relation of simultaneity or of succession with an instant in the Other's time? Even if a preestablished harmony (which is, however, incomprehensible in a Kantian perspective) could effect a correspondence of instant with instant in the two times considered, they would still remain two times unrelated since for each of them the unifying synthesis of moments is an act of the subject. The universality of time with Kant is only the universality of a concept; it means only that each temporality must possess a definite structure, that the conditions of possibility for a temporal experience are valid for all temporalities. But this identity of temporal essence does not prevent the incommunicable diversity of times any more than the identity of the essence of man prevents the incommunicable diversity of human consciousnesses. Thus since a relation between consciousnesses is by nature unthinkable, the concept of the Other can not constitute our experience; it must be placed along with teleological concepts among the regulative concepts. The Other therefore belongs to the category of "as if." The Other is an *a priori* hypothesis with no justification save the unity which it permits to operate in our experience, an hypothesis which can not be thought without contradiction. It is possible, so far as the pure exercise of knowledge is concerned, to conceive of the action of an intelligible reality on our sensibility, but it is not even thinkable that a phenomenon whose reality is strictly relative to its appearance in the Other's experience should *really* act on a phenomenon of *my experience*. Even if we admitted that the action of an intelligible reality should be exerted simultaneously on my experience and on that of the Other (in the sense that the intelligible reality would affect the Other to the same degree that it would affect me), it would still remain radically impossible to establish or even to postulate a parallelism and a table of correlation between two systems which are spontaneously constituted.[2] But on the other hand does the quality of a regulative concept really fit the concept of the Other? It is not a question of establishing a stronger unity between the phenomena of my experience in the manner of a purely formal concept which would only allow the discovery of details in the objects which appear to me. It is not a question of a kind of *a priori* hypothesis not extending beyond the field of my experience but inspiring new investigation within the very limits of this field. The perception of the Other-as-object refers to a coherent system of representations, and this system is not mine. This means that in my experience the Other is not a phenomenon which refers to my experience but that on principle he refers himself to phenomena located outside of all experience which is possible for me. Of course the concept of the Other allows discoveries and predictions within the heart of my system of

---

[2] Even if we adopt the Kantian metaphysics of nature and the catalogue of principles which Kant has drawn up, it would be possible to conceive of radically different types of physics based on these principles.

representations, a contraction in the web of phenomena: thanks to the hypothesis of *Others* I can anticipate *this gesture* as coming from that *expression*. But this concept does not appear as those scientific notions (imaginary numbers, for example) which intervene as instruments of calculation for the physicist, but are not presented in the empirical statement of the problem and are eliminated from the results. The concept of the Other is not purely instrumental. Far from the concepts existing *in order to* serve to unify phenomena, the truth is that certain categories of phenomena seem to exist only for the concept of the Other.

The existence of a system of meanings and experiences radically distinct from my own is the fixed skeletal framework to which diverse series of phenomena are pointing in their very flow. This framework, which on principle is external to my experience, is gradually filled in. We can never apprehend the relation of that *Other* to me and he is never given, but gradually we constitute him as a concrete object. He is *not* the instrument which serves to predict an event in my experience, but there are events in my experience which serve to constitute the Other qua Other; that is, as a system of representations out of reach, as a concrete and knowable object. What I constantly aim at *across* my experiences are the Other's feelings, the Other's ideas, the Other's volitions, the Other's character. This is because the Other is not only the one whom I see but the one *who sees* me. I aim at the Other in so far as he is a connected system of experiences out of reach in which I figure as one object among others. But to the extent that I strive to determine the concrete nature of this system of representations and the place which I occupy there as an object, I radically transcend the field of my experience. I am concerned with a series of phenomena which on principle can never be accessible to my intuition, and consequently I exceed the lawful limits of my knowledge. I seek to bind together experiences which will never be my experiences, and consequently this work of construction and unification can in no way serve for the unification of my own experience. To the extent that the Other is an absence he escapes *nature*. Therefore the Other can not be described as a regulative concept. Of course Ideas like the World, for example, also on principle escape my experience, but at least they are referred back to it and have meaning only through it. The Other, on the contrary, is presented in a certain sense as the radical negation of my experience, since he is the one for whom I am not subject but object. Therefore as the subject of knowledge I strive to determine as object the subject who denies my character as subject and who himself determines me as object.

Thus the *Other* within the perspective of idealism can be considered neither as a constitutive concept nor as a regulative concept of my knowledge. He is conceived as *real*, and yet I can not conceive of his real relation to me. I construct him as object, and yet he is never released by intuition. I posit him as *subject*, and yet it is as the object of my thoughts that I consider him. There remain then only two solutions for the idealist: either to get rid of the concept of the Other completely and prove that he is useless to the constitution of my experience, or to affirm the real existence of the Other—that is, to posit a real, extra-empirical communication between consciousnesses.

The first solution is known by the name of solipsism. Yet if it is formulated in conformity with its denomination as the affirmation of my ontological *solitude*, it is a pure metaphysical hypothesis, perfectly unjustified and gratuious; for it amounts to saying that outside of me *nothing* exists and so it *goes* beyond the limits of the field of my experience. But if it is presented more modestly as a refusal to leave the solid ground of experience and as a positive attempt not to make use of the concept of the Other, then it is perfectly logical; it remains on the level of critical positivism, and although it is opposed to the deepest inclinations of our being, it derives its justification from the contradictions of the notion of *Others* considered in the idealist perspective. A psychology which wants to be exact and objective, like the "behaviorism," of Watson, is really only solipsism as a working hypothesis. It will not try to deny within the field of my experience the presence of objects which we shall call "psychic beings" but will merely practice a sort of ἐποχη[3] with respect to the existence of systems of representations organized by a subject and located outside my experience.

Confronted with this solution, Kant and the majority of post-Kantians continue to affirm the existence of the Other. But they can refer only to common sense or to our deep-rooted tendencies to justify their affirmation. We know that Schopenhauer speaks of the solipsist as "a madman shut up up in an impregnable blockhouse." What a confession of impotence! It is in fact by this position with regard to the existence of the Other that we suddenly explode the structure of idealism and fall back into a metaphysical realism. First of all by positing a plurality of closed systems which can communicate only through the outside, we implicitly re-establish the notion of substance. Of course these systems are non-substantial since they are systems of representation. But their reciprocal exteriority is an exteriority in *itself*; it is without being known; we do not even apprehend the effects with any certainty since the solipsist hypothesis remains always possible. We are not limited to positing this nothingness in-itself as an absolute fact; indeed it is not relative to our knowledge of the Other; rather it conditions our knowledge of the Other. Therefore even if consciousnesses are only pure conceptual connections of phenomena, even if the rule of their existence is the *percipere* and the *percipi*, the fact still remains that the *multiplicity* of these relational systems is a multiplicity in-itself and that it immediately transforms them each one into a system

---

[3] Correction for ἐπόχη. Tr.

in-itself. In addition, if I posit the notion that my experience of the Other's anger has as a correlate in another system a subjective experience of anger, I reinstate the system of the true image which Kant was especially concerned to get rid of. To be sure, we are dealing with a relation of agreement between the two phenomena—the anger perceived in the gestures and signs and the anger apprehended as a phenomenal reality of inner sense—and not with a relation between a phenomenon and a thing-in-itself. But the fact remains that the criterion of truth here is the conformity of thought to its object, not the agreement of representations with each other. In fact precisely because all recourse to the noumenon is here removed, the phenomenon of the anger felt is to that of the anger established as the *objective real* is to its image. The problem is indeed one of adequate representation since there is a *real* and a mode of apprehension of this real. If we were dealing with the problem of my own anger, I could in fact consider its subjective manifestations and its physiological objectively discernible manifestations as two series of the effects of a single cause without having one of the series represent the truth of the anger or its *reality* and the other only its effect or its image. But if one of the series of the phenomena resides in the Other and the other series in me, then the one series functions as the reality of the other series, and the realist scheme of truth is the only one which can be applied here.

Thus we abandoned the realist solution of the problem only because it necessarily resulted in idealism; we deliberately placed ourselves within the idealist perspective and thereby gained nothing because, conversely, to the extent that idealism rejects the solipsistic hypothesis, it results in a dogmatic and totally unjustified realism. Let us see if we can understand this abrupt inversion of doctrines and if we can derive from this paradox some information which will facilitate a correct setting of the question.

At the origin of the problem of the existence of others, there is a fundamental presupposition: others are the Other, that is the self which is not myself. Therefore we grasp here a negation as the constitutive structure of the being-of-others. The presupposition common to both idealism and realism is that the constituting negation is an external negation. The Other is the one who is not me and the one who I am not. This *not* indicates a nothingness as a *given* element of separation between the Other and myself. Between the Other and myself *there* is a nothingness of separation. This nothingness does not derive its origin from myself nor from the Other, nor is it a reciprocal relation between the Other and myself. On the contrary, as a primary absence of relation, it is originally the foundation of all relation between the Other and me. This is because the Other appears to me empirically on the occasion of the perception of a body, and this body is an in-itself external to my body; the type of relation which unites and separates these two bodies is a spatial relation, the relation of things which have no relation among themselves, pure exteriority in so far as it is given. The realist who believes that he apprehends the Other through his body considers therefore that he is separated from the Other as one body from another body, which means that the onto-logical meaning of the negation contained in the judgment, "I am not Paul," is of the same type as that of the negation contained in the judgment, "The table is not the chair." Thus since the separation of consciousnesses is attributable to the bodies, there is a sort of original space between diverse consciousnesses; that is, precisely a given nothingness, an absolute distance passively experienced. Idealism, to be sure, reduces my body and the Other's body to objective systems of representation. For Schopenhauer my body is nothing but the "immediate object." But this view does not thereby suppress the absolute distance between consciousnesses. A total system of representa-tions—i.e., each monad—can be limited only by itself and so can not enter into relation with what is not it. The knowing subject can neither limit another subject nor cause itself to be limited by another subject. It is isolated by its positive plenitude, and consequently between itself and another equally isolated system there is preserved a *spatial* separation as the very type of exteriority. Thus it is still *space* which implicitly separates my consciousness from the Other's. Even so it must be added that the idealist without being aware of it is resorting to a "third man" in order to effect the appearance of this external negation. For as we have seen, every external relation inasmuch as it is not constituted by its very terms, requires a witness to posit it. Thus for the idealist as for the realist one conclusion is imposed: due to the fact that the Other is revealed to us in a spatial world, we are separated from the Other by a real or ideal space.

This presupposition entails a serious consequence: if my relation to the Other must in fact be in the mode of indifferent exteriority, then I can not in my being be affected by either the upsurge or the abolition of the Other any more than an In-itself can be affected by the apparition or the disappearance of another In-itself. Consequently since the Other can not act on my being by means of his being, the only way that he can reveal himself to me is by appearing as an *object* to my knowledge. But it must be understood by this that I must constitute the Other as the unification which my spontaneity imposes upon a diversity of impressions; that is, that I am the one who constitutes the Other in the field of his experience. Therefore the Other can be for me only an *image* in spite of the fact that the whole theory of knowledge which I have erected aims at rejecting this notion of image. Only a witness external both to myself and to the Other could compare the image with the model and decide whether it is a true one. Moreover this witness in order to be authorized could not in turn maintain a relation of exteriority with both the Other and myself, for otherwise he would know us only by images. Within the ekstatic unity of his being, he would have to be simultaneously *here* upon me as the *internal* negation of myself and *over there* upon the Other as the *internal* negation of the Other.

Thus the recourse to God, which we find in Leibniz, is purely and simply a recourse to the negation of interiority; this is concealed by the theological notion of creation: God at the same time is and is not both myself and the Other since he creates us. He must of necessity *be* myself in order to apprehend my reality without intermediary and with apodictic evidence, and yet it is necessary that he not be me in order that he may preserve his impartiality as witness and be able over there both to be and not be the Other. The image of creation is the most adequate here since in the creative act I look into the very heart of what I create—for what I create is me—and yet what I create opposes itself to me by closing in on itself in an affirmation of objectivity. Thus the spatializing presupposition does not leave us any choice: it must either resort to God or fall into a probabilism which leaves the door open to solipsism.

But this conception of a God who *is* his creatures makes us fall into a new dilemma: this is the difficulty presented by the problem of substances in post-Cartesian thought. If God is I and if he is the Other, then what guarantees my own existence? If creation is held to be *continuous*, I remain always suspended between a distinct existence and a pantheistic fusion with the Creator Being. If Creation is an original act and if I am shut up against God, then nothing any longer guarantees my existence to God; he is now united to me only by a relation of exteriority, as the sculptor is related to the finished statue, and once again he can know me only through images. Under these conditions the notion of God while revealing to us the internal negation as the only possible connection between consciousnesses, shows the concept's total inadequacy: God is neither necessary nor sufficient as a guarantee of the Other's existence. Furthermore God's existence as the intermediary between me and the Other already presupposes the presence of the Other to me in an internal connection; for God, being endowed with the essential qualities of a Mind, appears as the quintessence of the Other, and he must be able to maintain an internal connection with myself in order for a real foundation of the Other's existence to be valid for me. It seems therefore that a positive theory of the Other's existence must be able simultaneously to avoid solipsism and to dispense with a recourse to God if it envisages my original relation to the Other as an internal negation; that is, as a negation which posits the original distinction between the Other and myself as being such that it determines me by means of the Other and determines the Other by means of me. Is it possible to look at the question from this point of view?

## III. HUSSERL, HEGEL, HEIDEGGER

The philosophy of the nineteenth and twentieth centuries seems to have understood that once myself and the Other are considered as two separate substances, we cannot escape solipsism; any union of these substances must in fact be held to be impossible. That is why the examination of modern theories reveals to us an attempt to seize at the very heart of the consciousness a fundamental, transcending connection with the Other which would be constitutive of each consciousness in its very upsurge. But while this philosophy appears to abandon the postulate of the external negation, it nevertheless preserves its essential consequence; that is, the affirmation that my fundamental connection with the Other is realized through *knowledge*.

When Husserl in his *Cartesian Meditations* and in *Formal and Transcendental Logic* attempts to refute solipsism, he believes that he can succeed by showing that a referral to the Other is the indispensible condition for the constitution of a world. Without going into the details of his theory, we shall limit ourselves to indicating his general position. For Husserl the world as it is revealed to consciousness is inter-monadic. The Other is present in it not only as a particular concrete and empirical appearance but as a permanent condition of its unity and of its richness. Whether I consider this table or this tree or this bare wall in solitude or with companions, the Other is always there as a layer of constitutive meanings which belong to the very object which I consider; in short, he is the veritable guarantee of the object's objectivity. And since our psychophysical self is contemporary with the world, forms a part of the world, and falls with the world under the impact of the phenomenological reduction, the Other appears as necessary to the very constitution of this self. If I am to doubt the existence of my friend Pierre or of others in general, then inasmuch as this existence is on principle outside my experience, I must of necessity doubt also my concrete being, my empirical reality as a professor having this or that tendency, these habits, this particular character. There is no privilege for my self: my empirical Ego and the Other's empirical Ego appear in the world at the same time. The general meaning of "Others" is necessary to the constitution of each one of these "Egos." Thus each object far from being constituted as for Kant, by a simple relation to the *subject*, appears in my concrete experience as polyvalent; it is given originally as possessing systems of reference to an indefinite plurality of consciousnesses; it is on the table, on the wall that the Other is revealed to me as that to which the object under consideration is perpetually referred—as well as on the occasion of the concrete appearances of Pierre or Paul.

To be sure, these views show progress over the classical positions. It is undeniable that the instrumental-thing from the moment of its discovery refers to a plurality of For-itselfs. We shall have to return to this point. It is also certain that the meaning of "the Other" can not come from the experience nor from a reasoning by analogy effected on the occasion of the experience; on the contrary, it is in the light of the concept of the Other that the experience is interpreted. Does that mean that the concept of the Other is *a priori*? This we shall attempt to determine later. But in spite of these undeniable advantages Husserl's theory does not seem to us perceptibly different from Kant's. This is due to the fact that while my empirical Ego is not any more sure than the Other's, Husserl has retained the transcendental subject, which is radically distinct from the Ego and which strongly resembles the Kantian subject. Now what ought to be demonstrated is not the parallelism of the empirical "Egos" which nobody doubts but t'hat of the transcendental subjects. This is because actually the Other is *never* that empirical person who is encountered in my experience; he is the transcendental subject to whom this person by nature refers. Thus the true problem is that of the connection of transcendental subjects beyond experience. If someone replies that from the start the transcendental subject refers to other subjects *for the constitution* of the noematic whole, it is easy to reply that it refers to them as to *meanings*. The Other here would be a kind of supplementary category which would allow a world to be constituted, not a real being existing beyond this world. Of course the "category" of the Other implies in its very meaning a reference from the other side of the world to a subject, but this reference could be only hypothetical. It has the pure value of the content of a unifying concept; it is valid in and for the world. Its rights are limited to the world, and the Other is by nature outside the world. Furthermore Husserl has removed the very possibility of understanding what can be meant by the extra-mundane *being* of the Other since he defines *being* as the simple indication of an infinite series of operations to be effected. There could be no better way to measure being by knowledge. Now even admitting that knowledge in general measures being, the Other's being is measured in its reality by the knowledge which the Other has of himself, not by that which I have of him. What I must attain is the Other, not as I obtain knowledge of him, but as he obtains knowledge of himself—which is impossible. This would in fact suppose the internal identification of myself with the Other. Thus we find here again that distinction on principle between the Other and myself which does not stem from the exteriority of our bodies but from the simple fact that each of us exists in interiority and that a knowledge valid for interiority can be effected only in interiority which on principle excludes all *knowledge* of the Other as he knows himself—i.e., as he is. Moreover Husserl understood this since he says that "the Other" as he is revealed to our concrete experience is an *absence*. But within Husserl's philosophy, at least, how can one have a full intuition of an absence? The Other is the object of empty intentions, the Other on principle refuses himself to us and flees. The only reality which remains is therefore that of my intention; the Other is the empty noema which corresponds to my directing toward the Other, to the extent that he appears concretely in my experience. He is an ensemble of operations of unification and of the constitution of my experience so that he appears as a transcendental concept. Husserl replies to the solipsist that the Other's existence is as sure as that of the world, and Husserl includes in the world my psycho-physical existence. But the solipsist says the same thing: it is as sure, he will say, but no more sure. The existence of the world is measured, he will add, by the knowledge which I have of it; the case will not be otherwise for the existence of the Other.

Formerly I believed that I could escape solipsism by refuting Husserl's concept of the existence of the Transcendental "Ego."[4] At that time I thought that since I had emptied my consciousness of its subject, nothing remained there which was privileged as compared to the Other. But actually although I am still persuaded that the hypothesis of a transcendental subject is useless and disastrous, abandoning it does not help one bit to solve the question of the existence of Others. Even if outside the empirical Ego there is nothing other than the consciousness of that Ego—that is, a transcendental field without a subject—the fact remains that my affirmation of the Other demands and requires the existence beyond the world of a similar transcendental field. Consequently the only way to escape solipsism would be here again to prove that my transcendental consciousness is in its very being, affected by the extra-mundane existence of other consciousnesses of the same type. Because Husserl has reduced being to a series of meanings, the only connection which he has been able to establish between my being and that of the Other is a connection of *knowledge*. Therefore Husserl can not escape solipsism any more than Kant could.

If now instead of observing the rules of chronological succession, we are guided by those of a sort of non-temporal dialectic, we shall find that in the solution which Hegel gives to the problem in the first volume of *The Phenomenology of Mind*, he has made significant progress over Husserl. Here the appearance of the Other is indispensable not to the constitution of the world and of my empirical "Ego" but to the very existence of my consciousness as self-consciousness. In fact as self-consciousness, the Self itself apprehends itself. The equation "Myself = myself" or "I am I" is precisely the expression of this fact. At first this self-consciousness is pure self-identity, pure existence for itself. It has certitude of itself, but this certitude still lacks truth. In fact this certitude would be true only to the extent that its own existence for itself appeared to it as an independent object. Thus self-consciousness is first a syncretic relation without truth between a subject and an object, an object,

<hr />

[4] "La transcendence de l'Ego," *Recherches philosophiques*, 1937.

which is not yet objectified and which is this subject himself. Since the impulse of this consciousness is to realize its concept by becoming conscious of itself in all respects, it tends to make itself valid externally by giving itself objectivity and manifest existence. It is concerned with making the "I am I" explicit and producing itself as an object in order to attain the ultimate stage of development. This state in another sense is naturally the prime mover for the becoming of consciousness; it is self-consciousness in general, which is recognized in other self-consciousnesses and which is identical with them and with itself. The mediator is the Other. The Other appears along with myself since self-consciousness is identical with itself by means of the exclusion of every Other. Thus the primary fact is the plurality of consciousnesses, and this plurality is realized in the form of a double, reciprocal relation of exclusion. Here we are then in the presence of that connection by means of an internal negation which was demanded earlier. No external nothingness in-itself separates my consciousness from the Other's consciousness; it is by the very fact of being me that I exclude the Other. The Other is the one who excludes me by being himself, the one whom I exclude by being myself. Consciousnesses are directly supported by one another in a reciprocal imbrication of their being.

This position allows us at the same time to define the way in which the Other appears to me: he is the one who is other than I; therefore he is given as a non-essential object with a character of negativity. But this Other is also a self-consciousness. As such he appears to me as an ordinary object immersed in the being of life. Similarly it is thus that I appear to the Other: as a concrete, sensible, immediate existence. Here Hegel takes his stand on the ground not of a univocal relation which goes from me (apprehended by the *cogito*) to the Other, but of the reciprocal relation which he defines as "the self-apprehension of the one in the other." In fact it is only in so far as each man is opposed to the Other that he is absolutely for himself. Opposite the Other and confronting the Other, each one asserts his right of being individual. Thus the *cogito* itself can not be a point of departure for philosophy; in fact it can be born only in consequence of my appearance for myself as an individual, and this appearance is conditioned by the recognition of the Other. The problem of the Other should not be posited in terms of the *cogito*; on the contrary, the existence of the Other renders the *cogito* possible as the abstract moment when the self is apprehended as an object. Thus the "moment" which Hegel calls *being for the Other* is a necessary stage of the development of self-consciousness; the road of interiority passes through the Other. But the Other is of interest to me only to the extent that he is another Me, a Me-object for Me, and conversely to the extent that he reflects my Me—i.e., is, in so far as I am an object for him. Due to the fact that I must necessarily be an object for myself only over there in the Other, I must obtain from the Other the *recognition* of my being. But if another consciousness must mediate between my consciousness for *itself* and itself, then the being-for-itself of my consciousness—and consequently its being in general—depends on the Other. As I appear to the Other, so I am. Moreover since the Other is such as he appears to me and since my being depends upon the Other, the way in which I appear—that is, the moment of the development of my self-consciousness—depends on the way in which the Other appears to me. The value of the Other's recognition of me depends on the value of my recognition of the Other. In this sense to the extent that the Other apprehends me as bound to a body and immersed in *life,* I am myself only *an Other.* In order to make myself recognized by the Other, I must risk my own life. To risk one's life, in fact, is to reveal oneself as not-bound to the objective form or to any determined existence—as not-bound to life.

But at the same time I pursue the *death* of the Other. This means that I wish to cause myself to be mediated by an Other who is only other—that is, by a dependent consciousness whose essential characteristic is to exist only for another. This will be accomplished at the very moment when I risk my life, for in the struggle against the other I have made an abstraction of my sensible being by risking it. On the other hand, the Other prefers life and freedom even while showing that he has not been able to posit himself as not-bound to the objective form. Therefore he remains bound to external things in general; he appears to me and he appears to himself as *non-essential.* He is the *Slave* I am the *Master;* for him it is I who am essence. Thus there appears the famous "Master-Slave" relation which so profoundly influenced Marx. We need not here enter into its details. It is sufficient to observe that the Slave is the Truth of the Master. But this unilateral recognition is unequal and insufficient, for the truth of his self-certitude for the Master is a non-essential consciousness; therefore the Master is not certain of *being for himself as truth.* In order to attain this truth there is necessary "a moment in which the master does for himself what he does as regards the Other and when the slave does as regards the Other what he does for himself."[5] At this moment there will appear a self-consciousness in general which is recognized in other self-consciousnesses and which is identical with them and with itself.

Thus Hegel's brilliant intuition is to make me depend on the Other *in my being.* I am, he said, a being for-itself which is for-itself only through another. Therefore the Other penetrates me to the heart. I can not doubt him without doubting myself since "self-consciousness is real only in so far as it recognizes its echo (and its reflection) in another."[6] Since the very doubt implies a consciousness which exists for itself, the Other's existence conditions my

---

[5] *Phénoménologie de l'Esprit,* p. 148. Edition Lasson.
[6] *Propedeutik,* p. 20, first edition of the complete works.

attempt to doubt it just as in the work of Descartes my existence conditions systematic doubt. Thus solipsism seems to be put out of the picture once and for all. By proceeding from Husserl to Hegel, we have realized immense progress: first the negation which constitutes the Other is direct, internal, and reciprocal; second, it calls each consciousness to account and pierces it to the deepest part of its being; the problem is posited on the level of inner being, of the universal and transcendental "I;" finally in my essential being I depend on the essential being of the Other, and instead of holding that my being-for-myself is opposed to my being-for-others, I find that being-for-others appears as a necessary condition for my being-for-myself.

Yet in spite of the wide scope of this solution, in spite of the richness and profundity of the detailed insights with which the theory of the Master and the Slave is filled to overflowing, can we be satisfied with it?

To be sure, Hegel has posed the question of the being of consciousnesses. It is being-for-itself and being-for-others which he is studying, and he holds that each consciousness includes the reality of the other. Nevertheless it is certain that this ontological problem remains everywhere formulated in terms of knowledge. The mainspring of the conflict of consciousnesses is the effort of each one to transform his self-certitude into truth. And we know that this truth can be attained only in so far as my consciousness becomes as object for the Other at the same time as the Other becomes an object for my consciousness. Thus when idealism asks, "How can the Other be an object for me?" Hegel while remaining on the same ground as idealism replies: if there is in truth a Me for whom the Other is an object, this is because there is an Other for whom the Me is object. Knowledge here is still the measure of being, and Hegel does not even conceive of the possibility of a being-for-others which is not finally reducible to a "being-as-object." Thus a universal self-consciousness which seeks to disengage itself through all these dialectical phases is by its own admission reducible to a purely empty formula—the "I am I." Yet Hegel writes, "This proposition regarding self-consciousness is void of all content."[7] And in another place he says "[It is] the process of absolute abstraction which consists in surpassing all immediate existence and which results in the purely negative being of consciousness identical with itself." The limiting term of this dialectical conflict, universal self-consciousness, is not enriched in the midst of its avatars; it is on the contrary entirely denuded. It is no more than the "I know that another knows me as me." Of course this is because for idealism absolute being and knowledge are identical. But what does this identification involve?

To begin with, this "I am I," a pure, universal form of identity, has nothing in common with the concrete consciousness which we have attempted to

---

[7] Propedeutik, p. 20, first edition of the complete works.

describe in our Introduction. There we established that the being of self-consciousness could not be defined in terms of knowledge. Knowledge begins with *reflection* (reflexion) but the game of "the-reflection (reflet)-reflecting" is not a subject-object dyad, not even implicitly. Its being does not depend on any transcendent consciousness; rather its mode of being is precisely to be in question for itself. We showed subsequently in the first chapter of Part Two that the relation of the reflection to the reflecting was in no way a relation of identity and could not be reduced to the "Me = Me" or to the "I am I" of Hegel. The reflection does not make itself be the reflecting; we are dealing here with a being which nihilates itself in its being and which seeks in vain to dissolve into itself as a *self*. If it is true that this description is the only one which allows us to understand the original fact of consciousness, then we must judge that Hegel has not succeeded in accounting for this abstract doubling of the Me which he gives as equivalent to self-consciousness. Finally we succeeded in getting rid of the pure unreflective consciousness of the transcendental "I" which obscured it and we showed that selfness, the foundation of personal existence, was altogether different from an Ego or from a reference of the Ego to itself. There can be, therefore, no question of defining consciousness in terms of a transcendental ego-ology. In short, consciousness is a concrete being *sui generis*, not an abstract, unjustifiable relation of identity. It is selfness and not the seat of an opaque, useless Ego. Its being is capable of being reached by a transcendental reflection, and there is a *truth* of consciousness which does not depend on the Other; rather the very *being* of consciousness, since it is independent of knowledge, pre-exists its truth. On this plane as for naive realism, being measures truth; for the truth of a reflective intuition is measured by its conformity to being: consciousness *was there* before it was known. Therefore if consciousness is affirmed in the face of the Other, it is because it lays claim to a recognition of its being and not of an abstract truth. In fact it would be ill conceived to think that the ardent and perilous conflict between master and slave had for its sole stake the recognition of a formula as barren and abstract as the "I am I." Moreover there would be a deception in this very conflict since the end finally attained would be universal self-consciousness, "the intuition of the existing self by the self." Here as everywhere we ought to oppose to Hegel Kierkegaard, who represents the claims of the individual as such. The individual claims his achievement as an individual, the recognition of his concrete being, and of the objective specification of a universal structure. Of course the *rights* which I demand from the Other posit the universality of *self*; respect of persons demands the recognition of my person as universal. But it is my concrete and individual being which flows into this universal and fills it; it is for that *being-there* that I demand rights. The particular is here the support and foundation of the universal; the universal in this case could have no meaning if it did not exist for the purpose of the individual.

This identification of being and knowledge results in a large number of errors or impossibilities. We shall consider them here under two headings; that is we shall marshal against Hegel a twofold charge of optimism.

In the first place Hegel appears to us to be guilty of an epistemological optimism. It seems to him that the truth of self-consciousness can appear; that is, that an objective agreement can be realized between consciousnesses—by authority of the Other's recognition of me and my recognition of the Other. This recognition can be simultaneous and reciprocal: "I know that the Other knows me as himself." It produces actually and in truth the universality of self-consciousness. But the correct statement of the problem of Others renders this passage to the universal impossible. If the Other can in fact refer my "self" to me, then at least at the end of the dialectical evolution there must be a common measure between what I am for him, what he is for me, what I am for myself, what he is for himself. Of course this homogeneity does not exist at the start; Hegel agrees to this. The relation "Master-Slave" is not reciprocal. But Hegel affirms that the reciprocity must be capable of being established. Here at the outset he is creating a confusion—so easy that it seems voluntary—between *being-an-object* and *life*. The Other, he says appears to me as an object. Now the object is *Myself* in the Other. When Hegel wants to define this object-state more exactly, he distinguishes in it three elements: "This self-apprehension by one in the other is: (1) The abstract moment of self-identity. (2) Each one, however, has also this particularity, that he manifests himself to the Other as an external object, as an immediately concrete and sensible existence. (3) Each one is absolutely for himself and individual as opposed to the other."[8]

We see that the abstract moment of self-identity is given in the knowledge of the Other. It is given with two other moments of the total structure. But—a curious thing in a philosopher of Synthesis—Hegel did not ask if these three elements did not react on one another in such a way as to constitute a new form resistant to analysis. He defines his point of view in the *Phenomenology of Mind* when he declares that the Other appears first as non-essential (this is the sense of the third moment cited above) and as a "consciousness immersed in the being of life." But here we are dealing with a pure co-existence of the abstract moment and of *life*. It is sufficient therefore that I or the Other risk our life in order that in the very act of offering oneself to danger, we realize the analytical separation of life and consciousness: "What the Other is for each consciousness, each consciousness is for the Other; each consciousness in turn accomplishes in itself by means of its own activity and by means of

[8] *Propedeutik*, p. 18.

the activity of the Other, that pure abstraction of being for itself ... To present oneself as a pure abstraction of self-consciousness is to reveal oneself as a pure negation of one's objective form, to reveal oneself as not-bound to any determined existence; ... it is to reveal oneself as not-bound to life."[9] Of course Hegel will say later that by the experience of risk and of the danger of death, self-consciousness learns that life is as essential to it as pure self-consciousness; but this is from a totally different point of view, and the fact still remains that I can always separate, in the Other, the pure truth of self-consciousness from his life. Thus the slave apprehends the self-consciousness of the master; he is its truth although, as we have seen, this truth is still not adequate.[10]

But is it the same thing to say that the Other on principle appears to me as an object and to say that he appears to me as bound to a particular existence, as immersed in life? If we remain on the level of pure, logical hypotheses, we shall note first that the Other can in fact be given to a consciousness in the form of an object without that object's being precisely bound to that contingent object which we call a living body. In fact our experience presents us only with conscious, living individuals, but in theory it must be remarked that the Other is an object for me because he is the Other and not because he appears on the occasion of a body-object; otherwise we should fall back into the illusion of space which we discussed above. Thus what is essential to the Other qua Other is objectivity and not life. Moreover Hegel took this logical affirmation as his point of departure.

But if it is true that the connection between a consciousness and life does not distort the nature of the "abstract moment of self-consciousness" which remains there, immersed, always capable of being discovered, is the case the same for objectivity? In other words, since we know that a consciousness is before being known, then is not a known consciousness wholly modified by the very fact that it is known? Is "to appear as an object for a consciousness" still "to be consciousness"? It is easy to reply to this question: the very being of self-consciousness is such that in its being, its being is in question; this means that it is pure interiority. It is perpetually a reference to a self which it has to be. Its being is defined by this: that it is this being in the mode of being what it is not and of not being what it is. Its being, therefore, is the radical exclusion of all objectivity. I am the one who can not be an object for myself, the one who can not even conceive for myself of existence in the form of an object (save on the plane of the reflective dissociation—but we have seen that reflection is the drama of the being who can not be an object for himself). This is not because of the lack of detachment or because of an intellectual prejudice or of a limit imposed on my knowledge, but because objectivity

[9] Phenomenology of Mind. Ibid.    [10] Idem.

demands an explicit negation: the object is what I make myself not-be whereas I myself am what I make myself be. I pursue myself everywhere, I can not escape myself, I reapprehend myself from behind. Even if I could attempt to make myself an object, I would already be myself at the heart of that object which I am; and at the very center of that object I should have to be the subject who is looking at it. Moreover this is what Hegel hinted at when he said that the Other's existence is necessary in order for me to be an object for myself. But by holding that self-consciousness is expressed by the "I am I"—i.e., by identifying it with self-knowledge—he failed to derive the consequences of his first affirmations; for he introduced into consciousness something like an object existing potentially to be disengaged without change by the Other. But if to be an object is precisely not-to-be-me, then the fact of being an object for a consciousness radically modifies consciousness not in what it is for itself but in its appearance to the Other. The Other's consciousness is what I can simply contemplate and what because of this fact appears to me as being a pure given instead of being what has to be me. It is what is released to me in universal time (i.e. in the original dispersion of moments) instead of appearing to me within the unity of its own temporalization. For the only consciousness which can appear to me in its own temporalization is mine, and it can do so only by renouncing all objectivity. In short the for-itself as for-itself can not be known by the Other. The object which I apprehend under the name of the Other appears to me in a radically other form. The Other is not a for-itself as he appears to me; I do not appear to myself as I am for-the-Other. I am incapable of apprehending for myself the self which I am for the Other, just as I am incapable of apprehending on the basis of the Other-as-object which appears to me, what the Other is for himself. How then could we establish a universal concept subsuming under the name of self-consciousness, my consciousness for myself and (of) myself and my knowledge of the Other. But this is not all.

According to Hegel the Other is an object, and I apprehend myself as an object in the Other. But the one of these affirmations destroys the other. In order for me to be able to appear to myself as an object in the Other, I would have to apprehend the Other as subject; that is, to apprehend him in his interiority. But in so far as the Other appears to me as object, my objectivity for him can not appear to me. Of course I apprehend that the Other-as-object refers to me by means of intentions and acts, but due to the very fact that he is an object, the Other-as-a-mirror is clouded and no longer reflects anything. These intentions and these acts are things in the world and are apprehended in the Time of the World; they are established and contemplated, their meaning is an object for me. Thus I can only appear to myself as a transcendent quality to which the Other's acts and intentions refer; but since the Other's objectivity destroys my objectivity for him, it is as an internal subject that I apprehend myself as being that to which those intentions and those acts refer. It must be understood that this apprehension of myself by myself is in pure terms of consciousness, not of knowledge; by having to be what I am in form of an ekstatic self-consciousness, I apprehend the Other as an object pointing to me. Thus Hegel's optimism results in failure: between the Other-as-object and Me-as-subject there is no common measure, no more than between self-consciousness and consciousness of the Other. I can not know myself in the Other if the Other is first an object for me; neither can I apprehend the Other in his true being—that is, in his subjectivity. No universal knowledge can be derived from the relation of consciousnesses. This is what we shall call their ontological separation.

But there is in Hegel another and more fundamental form of optimism. This may be called an ontological optimism. For Hegel indeed truth is truth of the Whole. And he places himself at the vantage point of truth—i.e., of the Whole—to consider the problem of the Other. Thus when Hegelian monism considers the relation of consciousnesses, it does not put itself in any particular consciousness. Although the Whole is to be realized, it is already there as the truth of all which is true. Thus when Hegel writes that every consciousness, since it is identical with itself, is other than the Other, he has established himself in the whole, outside consciousnesses, and he considers them from the point of view of the Absolute. For individual consciousnesses are moments in the whole, moments which by themselves are *unselbständig*, and the whole is a mediator between consciousnesses. Hence is derived an ontological optimism parallel to the epistemological optimism: plurality can and must be surpassed toward the totality. But if Hegel can assert the reality of this surpassing, it is because he has already given it to himself at the outset. In fact he has forgotten his own consciousness; he is the Whole, and consequently if he so easily resolves the problem of particular consciousnesses it is because for him there never has been any real problem in this connection. Actually he does not raise the question of the relation between his own consciousness and that of the Other. By effecting completely the abstraction of his own, he studies purely and simply the relation between the consciousnesses of others—i.e. the relation of consciousnesses which are already for him objects whose nature according to him, is precisely that of being a particular type of object,—the subject-object. These consciousnesses from the totalitarian point of view which he has adopted are strictly equivalent to each other although each of them is separated from the rest by a particular privilege.

But if Hegel has forgotten himself, we can not forget Hegel. This means that we are referred back to the *cogito*. In fact, if, as we have established, the being of my consciousness is strictly irreducible to knowledge, then I can not transcend my being toward a reciprocal and universal relation in which I could see my being and that of others as equivalent. On the contrary, I must establish myself in my being and posit the problem of the Other in terms of my being. In a word the sole point of departure is the interiority of the *cogito*. We must understand by this that each one must be able by starting out from his own interiority, to rediscover the Other's being as a transcendence which conditions the very being of that interiority. This of necessity implies that the multiplicity of consciousnesses is on principle unsurpassable, for I can undoubtedly transcend myself toward a Whole, but I can not establish myself in this Whole so as to contemplate myself and to contemplate the Other. No logical or epistemological optimism could put an end to the scandal of the plurality of consciousnesses. If Hegel believed that it could, this is because he never grasped the nature of that particular dimension of being which is self-consciousness. The task which an ontology can lay down for itself is to describe this scandal and to found it in the very nature of being, but ontology is powerless to overcome it. It is possible—as we shall see better later—that we may be able to refute solipsism and show that the Other's existence is both evident and certain for us. But even if we could succeed in making the Other's existence share in the apodictic certainty of the *cogito*—i.e., of my own existence—we should not thereby "surpass" the Other toward any inter-monad totality. So long as consciousnesses exist, the separation and conflict of consciousnesses will remain; we shall simply have discovered their foundation and their true terrain.

What has this long criticism accomplished for us? Simply this: if we are to refute solipsism, then my relation to the Other is first and fundamentally a relation of being to being, not of knowledge to knowledge. We have seen Husserl's failure when on this particular level he measures being by know-ledge, and Hegel's when he identifies knowledge and being. But we have equally recognized that Hegel, although his vision is obscured by the postu-late of absolute idealism, has been able to put the discussion on its true plane.

In *Sein und Zeit* Heidegger seems to have profited by study of his predeces-sors and to have been deeply impressed with this twofold necessity: (1) the relation between "human-realities" must be a relation of being; (2) this relation must cause "human-realities" to depend on one another in their essential being. At least his theory fulfills these two requirements. In his abrupt, rather barbaric fashion of cutting Gordian knots rather than trying to untie them, he gives in answer to the question posited a pure and simple definition. He has discovered several moments—inseparable except by abstrac-tion—in "being-in-the-world," which characterizes human reality. These moments are "world," "being-in," and "being." He has described the world as "that by which human reality makes known to itself what it is;" "being-in" he has defined as *Befindlichkeit* and *Verstand*.[11] We have still to speak of being; that

---

[11] Roughly, *Befindlichkeit* is "finitude" and *Verstand* "comprehension." Tr.

is, the mode in which human reality is its being-in-the-world. Being, Heidegger tells us, is the Mit-Sein—that is, "being-with." Thus the characteristic of being of human-reality is its being with others. This does not come about by chance. I do not exist first in order that subsequently a contingency should make me encounter the Other. The question here is of an essential structure of my being. But this structure is not established from outside and from a totalitarian point of view as it was with Hegel. To be sure, Heidegger does not take his departure from the cogito in the Cartesian sense of the discovery of consciousness by itself; but the human-reality which is revealed to him and for which he seeks to fix the structures in concepts is his own. "Dasein ist je meines," he writes. It is by making explicit the preontological comprehension which I have of myself that I apprehend being-with-others as an essential characteristic of my being. In short I discover the transcendental relation to the Other as constituting my own being, just as I have discovered that being-in-the-world measures my human-reality. Henceforth the problem of the Other is a false problem. The Other is no longer first a particular existence which I encounter in the world—and which could not be indispensable to my own existence since I existed before encountering it. The Other is the ex-centric limit which contributes to the constitution of my being. He is the test of my being inasmuch as he throws me outside of myself toward structures which at once both escape me and define me; it is this test which originally reveals the Other to me.

Let us observe in addition that the type of connection with the Other has changed. With realism, idealism, Husserl, Hegel, the type of relation between consciousnesses was being-for; the Other appeared to me and even constituted me in so far as he was for me or I was for him. The problem was the mutual recognition of consciousnesses brought face to face which appeared in the world and which confronted each other. "To-be-with" has an altogether different meaning; "with" does not intend the reciprocal relation of recognition and of conflict which would result from the appearance of a human-reality other than mine in the midst of the world. It expresses rather a sort of ontological solidarity for the exploitation of this world. The Other is not originally bound to me as an ontic reality appearing in the midst of the world among "instruments" as a type of particular object; in that case he would be already degraded, and the relation uniting him to me could never take on reciprocity. The Other is not an object. In his connection with me he remains a human-reality; the being by which he determines me in my being is his pure being apprehended as "being-in-the-world." And we know that the "in" must be understood in the sense of colo, habito, not of insum; to-be-in-the-world is to haunt the world, not to be ensnared in it; and it is in my "being-in-the world" that the Other determines me. Our relation is not a frontal opposition but rather an oblique interdependence. In so far as I make a world exist as a complex of instruments which I use for the ends of my human reality, I cause myself to be determined in my being by a being who makes the world exist as a complex of instruments for the ends of his reality. Moreover it is not necessary to understand this being-with as a pure concomitance which is passively received by my being. For Heidegger, to be is to be one's own possibilities; that is, to make oneself be. It is then a mode of being which I make myself be. And it is very true that I am responsible for my being-for the Other in so far as I realize him freely in authenticity or in unauthenticity. It is in complete freedom and by an original choice that, for example, I realize my being-with in the anonymous form of "they." And if I am asked how my "being-with" can exist for-myself, I must reply that through the world I make known to myself what I am. In particular when I am in the unauthentic mode of the "they," the world refers to me a sort of impersonal reflection of my unauthentic possibilities in the form of instruments and complexes of instruments which belong to "everybody" and which belong to me in so far as I am "everybody:" ready-made clothes, common means of transportation, parks, gardens, public places, shelters made for *anyone* who may take shelter there, etc. Thus I make myself known as *anybody* by means of the indicative complex of instruments which indicate me as a *Worum-willen*. The unauthentic state—which is my ordinary state in so far as I have not realized my conversion to authenticity—reveals to me my "being-with," not as the relation of one unique personality with other personalities equally unique, not as the mutual connection of "most irreplaceable beings," but as a total interchangeability of the terms of the relation. The determination of the terms is still lacking; I am not opposed to the Other, for I am not "me;" instead we have the social unity of the *they*. To posit the problem on the level of the incommunicability of individual subjects was to commit an ὕστερον πρότερον,[12] to stand the world on its head. Authenticity and individuality have to be earned: I shall be my own authenticity only if under the influence of the call of conscience (*Ruf des Gewissens*) I launch out toward death with a resolute-decision (*Entschlossenheit*) as toward my own most peculiar possibility. At this moment I reveal myself to myself in authenticity, and I raise others along with myself toward the authentic.

The empirical image which may best symbolize Heidegger's intuition is not that of a conflict but rather a *crew*. The original relation of the Other and my consciousness is not the *you* and *me*; it is the *we*. Heidegger's being-with is not the clear and distinct position of an individual confronting another individual; it is not *knowledge*. It is the mute existence in common of one member of the crew with his fellows, that existence which the rhythm of the oars or the regular movements of the coxswain will render sensible to the rowers and

---

[12] Correction for ὕστερον πρόιηρον, obviously a misprint. Tr.

which will be made manifest to them by the common goal to be attained, the boat or the yacht to be overtaken, and the entire world (spectators, performance, etc.) which is profiled on the horizon. It is on the common ground of this co-existence that the abrupt revelation of my "being-unto-death" will suddenly make me stand out in an absolute "common solitude" while at the same time it raises the others to that solitude.

This time we have indeed been given what we asked for: a being which in its own being implies the Other's being. And yet we can not consider ourselves satisfied. First of all, Heidegger's theory offers us the indication of the solution to be found rather than that solution itself. Even if we should without reservation accept his substitution of "being-with" for "being-for," it would still remain for us a simple affirmation without foundation. Undoubtedly we shall encounter certain empirical states of our being—in particular that to which the Germans give the untranslatable name Stimmung[13]—which seem to reveal a co-existence of consciousnesses rather than a relation of opposition. But it is precisely this co-existence which must be explained. Why does it become the unique foundation of our being? Why is it the fundamental type of our relation with others? Why did Heidegger believe that he was authorized to pass from this empirical and ontic establishment of being-with to a position claiming co-existence as the ontological structure of my "being-in-the-world?" And what type of being does this co-existence have? To what extent is the negation which makes the Other an other and which constitutes him as non-essential maintained? If we suppress it entirely, are we not going to fall into a monism? And if we are to preserve it as an essential structure of the relation to the Other, then what modification must it undergo in order to lose the character of opposition which it had in being-for-others and acquire this character as a connection which creates solidarity and which is the very structure of being-with? And how shall we be able to pass from there to the concrete experience of the Other in the world, as when from my window I see a man walking in the street? To be sure it is tempting to conceive of myself as standing out on the undifferentiated ground of the human by means of the impulse of my freedom, by the choice of my unique possibilities—and perhaps this conception holds an important element of truth. But in this form at least such a view gives rise to serious objections.

First of all, the ontological point of view joins here with the abstract view of the Kantian subject. To say that human reality (even if it is my human reality) "is-with" by means of its ontological structure is to say that it is-with by nature—that is, in an essential and universal capacity. Even if this affirmation were proved, it would not enable us to explain any concrete being-with.

[13] Literally "pitch" or "tuning." Perhaps the nearest English equivalent is "sympathy" in its original Greek sense of feeling or experiencing with someone. Tr.

In other words, the ontological co-existence which appears as the structure of "being-in-the-world" can in no way serve as a foundation to an ontic being-with, such as, for example, the co-existence which appears in my friendship with Pierre or in the couple which Annie and I make. In fact it would be necessary to show that "being-with-Pierre" or "being-with-Annie" is a structure constitutive of my concreate-being. But this is impossible from the point of view which Heidegger has adopted. The Other in the relation "with," taken on the ontological level, can not in fact be concretely determined any more than the directly confronted human-reality of which it is the alter ego; it is an abstract term and hence *unselbständig*, and it does not contain the power of becoming *that* Other—Pierre or Annie. Thus the relation of the *Mit-Sein* can be of absolutely no use to us in resolving the psychological, concrete problem of the recognition of the Other. There are two incommunicable levels and two problems which demand separate solutions.

It may be said that this is only one of the difficulties which Heidegger encounters in passing in general from the ontological level to the ontic level, in passing from "being-in-the-world" in general to my relation with this particular instrument, in passing from my being-unto-death, which makes of my death my most essential possibility, to this "ontic" death which I shall experience by encountering this or that external existent. But this difficulty can be disguised, if need be, in all other cases since, for example, it is human reality which causes the existence of a world in which a threat of death to human reality is hidden. Better yet, if the world *is*, it is because it is "mortal" in the sense in which we say that a wound is mortal. But the impossibility of passing from one level to the other bursts forth when we meet the problem of the Other. In fact even if in the ekstatic upsurge of its being-in-the-world, human reality makes a world exist, one can not, for all that, say that its being-with causes another human reality to rise up. Of course I am the being by whom "there is" (*es gibt*) being. But are we to say that I am the being by whom "there is" another human-reality? If we understand by that that I am the being for whom there is *for me* another human reality, this is a pure and simple truism. If we mean that I am the being by whom *there are* in general Others, we fall back into solipsism. In fact this human reality "with whom" I am is itself "in-the-world-with-me"; it is the free foundation of a world. (How does this make it *my* world? We can not deduce from the being-with an identity of the worlds "in which" the human realities are.) Human reality is its own possibilities. It is then for itself without having to wait for me to make its being exist in the form of the "there is." Thus I can constitute a world as "mortal," but I can not constitute a human-reality as a concrete being which is its own possibilities. My being-with, apprehended from the standpoint of "my" being, can be considered only as a pure exigency founded in my being;

it does not constitute the slightest proof of the Other's existence, not the slightest bridge between me and the Other.

More precisely, this ontological relation between me and an abstract Other, due to the very fact that it defines in general my relation to others, is far from facilitating a particular ontic relation between me and Pierre; in fact it renders impossible any concrete connection between my being and a particular Other given in my experience. If my relation with the Other is *a priori*, it thereby exhausts all possibility of relation with others. Empirical and contingent relations can neither be specifications of it, nor particular cases. There can be specifications of a law only under two circumstances: either the law is derived inductively from empirical, particular facts, and that is not the case here; or else it is *a priori* and unifies experience, as the Kantian concepts do. Actually in this latter case, its scope is restricted to the limits of experience: I find in things only what I have put into them. Now the act of relating two concrete "beings-in-the world" can not belong to my experience; and it therefore escapes from the domain of *being-with*. But as the law precisely *constitutes* its own domain, it excludes *a priori* every real fact which it has not constructed. The existence of time as an *a priori* form of my sensibility would *a priori* exclude me from all connection with a noumenal time which had the characteristics of a being. Thus the existence of an ontological and hence *a priori* "being-with" renders impossible all ontic connection with a concrete human-reality which would arise *for-itself* as an absolute transcendent. The "being-with," conceived as a structure of my being, isolates me as surely as the arguments for solipsism.

The reason for this is that Heidegger's *transcendence* is a concept in bad faith: it aims, to be sure, at surpassing idealism, and it succeeds in so far as idealism presents us with a subjectivity at rest in itself and contemplating its own images. But the idealism thus surpassed is only a bastard form of idealism, a sort of empirical-critical psychologism. Undoubtedly Heidegger's human-reality "exists outside itself." But this existence outside itself is precisely Heidegger's definition of the *self*. It resembles neither the Platonic [Neo-Platonic?] ekstasis where existence is really alienation, existence in an Other, nor Malebranche's vision in God, our own conception of the ekstasis and of the internal negation. Heidegger does not escape idealism; his flight outside the self, as an *a priori* structure of his being, isolates him as surely as the Kantian reflection on the *a priori* conditions of our experience. In fact what human-reality re-discovers at the inaccessible limit of this flight outside itself is still the self: the flight outside the self is a flight toward the self, and the world appears as the pure distance between the self and the self.

Consequently it would be in vain to look in *Sein und Zeit* for a simultaneous surpassing of all idealism and of all realism. Heidegger's attempt to bring human-reality out of its solitude raises those same difficulties which idealism generally encounters when it tries to found the existence of concrete beings which are similar to us and which as such escape our experience, which even as they are being constituted do not arise from our *a priori*. He seems to escape isolation because he takes the "outside of self" sometimes as being "outside-of-self-toward-self" and sometimes as "outside-self-in-others." But the second interpretation of "outside-of-self," which Heidegger surreptitiously slides in through his devious reasoning, is strictly incompatible with the first. Human-reality at the very heart of its ekstases remains alone. It is here that we can derive a new and valid insight as the result of our critical examination of Heidegger's teaching: Human-reality remains alone because the Other's existence has the nature of a contingent and irreducible fact. We *encounter* the Other; we do not constitute him. And if this fact still appears to us in the form of a necessity, yet it does not belong with those "conditions of the possibility of our experience" or—if you prefer—with ontological necessity. If the Other's existence is a necessity, it is a "contingent necessity;" that is, it is of the same type as the *factual necessity* of the *cogito*. If the Other is to be capable of being given to us, it is by means of a direct apprehension which leaves to the encounter its character as facticity, just as the *cogito* itself leaves all its facticity to my own thought, a facticity which nevertheless shares in the apodicticity of the *cogito* itself—i.e., in its indubitability.

This long exposition of doctrine will not therefore have been useless if it enables us to formulate the necessary and sufficient conditions under which a theory of the existence of others can be valid.

(1) Such a theory can not offer a new *proof* of the existence of others, or an argument better than any other against solipsism. Actually if solipsism is to be rejected, this can be only because it is impossible or, if you prefer, because nobody is truly solipsistic. The Other's existence will always be subject to doubt, at least if one doubts the Other only in words and abstractly, in the same way that without really being able to conceive of it, I can write, "I doubt my own existence." In short the Other's existence can not be a *probability*. Probability can concern only objects which appear in our experience or from which new effects can appear in our experience. There is probability only if a validation or invalidation of it is at every moment possible. If the Other on principle and in its "For-itself" is outside my experience, the probability of his existence as *Another Self* can never be either validated or invalidated; it can neither increase nor decrease, it can not even be measured; it loses therefore its very being as probability and becomes a pure fictional conjecture. In the same way M. Lalande[14] has effectively shown that an hypothesis concerning the existence of living beings on the planet Mars will remain purely conjectural with no chance of being either true or false so

[14] *Les théories de l'induction et de l'expérimentation.*

long as we do not have at our disposal instruments or scientific theories enabling us to produce facts validating or invalidating this hypothesis. But the structure of the Other is on principle such that no new experiment will ever be able to be conceived, that no new theory will come to validate or invalidate the hypothesis of his existence, that no instrument will come to reveal new facts inspiring me to affirm or to reject this hypothesis. Therefore if the Other is not immediately present to me, and if his existence is not as sure as my own, all conjecture concerning him is entirely lacking in meaning. But I do not conjecture about the existence of the Other: I affirm it. A theory of the Other's existence must therefore simply question me in my being, must make clear and precise the meaning of that affirmation; in particular, far from inventing a proof, it must make explicit the very foundation of that certainty. In other words Descartes has not *proved* his existence. Actually I have always known that I existed, I have never ceased to practice the *cogito*. Similarly my resistance to solipsism—which is as lively as any I should offer to an attempt to doubt the *cogito*—proves that I have always known that the Other existed, that I have always had a total though implicit *comprehension* of his existence, that this "pre-ontological" comprehension comprises a surer and deeper understanding of the nature of the Other and the relation of his being to my being than all the theories which have been built outside my comprehension. If the Other's existence is not a vain conjecture, a pure fiction, this is because there is a sort of *cogito* concerning it. It is this *cogito* which we must bring to light by specifying its structures and determining its scope and its laws.

(2) On the other hand, Hegel's failure has shown us that the only point of departure possible is the Cartesian *cogito*. Moreover the *cogito* alone establishes us on the ground of that factual necessity which is the necessity of the Other's existence. Thus what for lack of a better term we called the *cogito* of the Other's existence is merged with my own *cogito*. The *cogito* examined once again, must throw me outside it and onto the Other, just as it threw me outside upon the In-itself; and this must be done not by revealing to me an *a priori* structure of myself which would point toward an equally *a priori* Other but by disclosing to me the concrete, indubitable presence of a particular, concrete Other, just as it has already revealed to me my own incomparable, contingent but necessary, and concrete existence. Thus we must ask the For-itself to deliver to us the For-others; we must ask absolute immanence to throw us into absolute transcendence. In my own inmost depths I must find not *reasons for believing* that the Other exists but the Other himself as not being me.

(3) What the *cogito* must reveal to us is not the-Other-as-object. For a long time now it must have been obvious that what is called an *object* is said to be *probable*. If the Other is an object for me, he refers me to probability. But probability is founded solely on the congruity of our representations to

infinity. Since the Other is neither a representation nor a system of representations nor a necessary unity of our representations, he can not be probable: he can not *at first* be an object. Therefore if he is *for us*, this can be neither as a constitutive factor of our knowledge of the world nor as a constitutive factor of our knowledge of the self, but as one who "interests" our being, and that not as he contributes *a priori* to constitute our being but as he interests it concretely and "ontically" in the empirical circumstances of our facticity.

(4) If we attempt somehow regarding the Other what Descartes attempted to do for God with that extraordinary "proof by the idea of perfection" which is wholly animated by the intuition of transcendence, then for our apprehension of the Other qua Other we are compelled to reject a certain type of negation which we have called an external negation. The Other must appear to the *cogito* as *not being* me. This negation can be conceived in two ways: either it is a pure, external negation, and it will separate the Other from myself as one substance from another substance—and in this case all apprehension of the Other is by definition impossible; or else it will be an internal negation, which means a synthetic, active connection of the two terms, each one of which constitutes itself by denying that it is the other. This negative relation will therefore be reciprocal and will possess a two fold interiority: This means first that the multiplicity of "Others" will not be a *collection* but a *totality* (in this sense we admit that Hegel is right) since each Other finds his being in the Other.[15] It also means that this Totality is such that it is on principle impossible for us to adopt "the point of view of the whole." In fact we have seen that no abstract concept of consciousness can result from the comparison of my being-for-myself with my object-state for the Other. Furthermore this totality—like that of the For-itself—is a detotalized totality; for since existence-for-others is a radical refusal of the Other, no totalitarian and unifying synthesis of "Others" is possible.

It is in the light of these few observations that we in turn shall now approach the question of The Other.

## IV. THE LOOK

This woman whom I see coming toward me, this man who is passing by in the street, this beggar whom I hear calling before my window, all are for me *objects*—of that there is no doubt. Thus it is true that at least one of the modalities of the Other's presence to me is *object-ness*. But we have seen that if this relation of object-ness is the fundamental relation between the Other and myself, then the Other's existence remains purely conjectural. Now it is not only conjectural but *probable* that this voice which I hear is that of a man and

---

[15] *Chaque autrui trouve son être en l'autre.* Tr.

not a song on a phonograph; it is infinitely *probable* that the passerby whom I see is a man and not a perfected robot. This means that without going beyond the limits of probability and indeed because of this very probability, my apprehension of the Other as an object essentially refers me to a fundamental apprehension of the Other in which he will not be revealed to me as an object but as a "presence in person." In short, if the Other is to be a probable object and not a dream of an object, then his object-ness must of necessity refer not to an original solitude beyond my reach, but to a fundamental connection in which the Other is manifested in some way other than through the knowledge which I have of him. The classical theories are right in considering that every perceived human organism *refers* to something and that this to which it refers is the foundation and guarantee of its probability. Their mistake lies in believing that this reference indicates a separate existence, a consciousness which would be behind its perceptible manifestations as the noumenon is behind the Kantian *Empfindung*. Whether or not this consciousness exists in a separate state, the face which I see does not refer to it; it is not this consciousness which is the truth of the probable object which I perceive. In actual fact the reference to a twin upsurge in which the Other is presence for me is to a "being-in-a-pair-with-the-Other," and this is given outside of knowledge proper even if the latter be conceived as an obscure and unexpressible form on the order of intuition. In other words, the problem of Others has generally been treated as if the primary relation by which the Other is discovered is object-ness; that is, as if the Other were first revealed—directly or indirectly—to our perception. But since this perception by its very nature *refers* to something other than to itself and since it can refer neither to an infinite series of appearances of the same type—as in idealism the perception of the table or of the chair does—nor to an isolated entity located on principle outside my reach, its essence must be to refer to a primary relation between my consciousness and the Other's. This relation, in which the Other must be given to me directly as a subject although in connection with me, is the fundamental relation, the very type of my being-for-others.

Nevertheless the reference here cannot be to any mystic or ineffable experience. It is in the reality of everyday life that the Other appears to us, and his probability refers to everyday reality. The problem is precisely this: there is in everyday reality an original relation to the Other which can be constantly pointed to and which consequently can be revealed to me outside all reference to a religious or mystic unknowable. In order to understand it I must question more exactly this ordinary appearance of the Other in the field of my perception; since this appearance refers to that fundamental relation, the appearance must be capable of revealing to us, at least as a reality aimed at, the relation to which it refers.

I am in a public park. Not far away there is a lawn and along the edge of that lawn there are benches. A man passes by those benches. I see this man; I apprehend him as an object and at the same time as a man. What does this signify? What do I mean when I assert that this object *is a man?*

If I were to think of him as being only a puppet, I should apply to him the categories which I ordinarily use to group temporal-spatial "things." That is, I should apprehend him as being "beside" the benches, two yards and twenty inches from the lawn, as exercising a certain pressure on the ground, *etc.* His relation with other objects would be of the purely additive type; this means that I could have him disappear without the relations of the other objects around him being perceptibly *changed.* In short, no new relation would appear *through him* between those things in my universe: grouped and synthesized *from my point of view* into instrumental complexes, they would from *his* disintegrate into multiplicities of indifferent relations. Perceiving him as a *man,* on the other hand, is not to apprehend an additive relation between the chair and him; it is to register an organization *without distance* of the things in my universe around that privileged object. To be sure, the lawn remains two yards and twenty inches away from him, but it is also *as a lawn* bound to him in a relation which at once both transcends distance and contains it. Instead of the two terms of the distance being indifferent, interchangeable, and in a reciprocal relation, the distance *is unfolded starting from* the man whom I see and *extending up to* the lawn as the synthetic up-surge of a univocal relation. We are dealing with a relation which is without *parts,* given at one stroke, inside of which there unfolds a spatiality which is not *my* spatiality; for instead of a grouping *toward me* of the objects, there is now an orientation *which flees from me.*

Of course this relation without distance and without parts is in no way that original relation of the Other to me which I am seeking. In the first place, it concerns only the man and the things in the world. In addition it is still an object of knowledge; I shall express it, for example, by saying that this man sees the lawn, or that in spite of the prohibiting sign he is preparing to walk on the grass, *etc.* Finally it still retains a pure character of probability: First, it is *probable* that this object is a man. Second, even granted that he is a man, it remains only probable that he *sees* the lawn at the moment that I perceive him; it is possible that he is dreaming of some project without exactly being aware of what is around him, or that he is blind, *etc., etc.* Nevertheless this new relation of the object-man to the object-lawn has a particular character; it is simultaneously given to me as a whole, since it is there in the world as an object which I can know (it is, in fact, an objective relation which I express by saying: Pierre has glanced at this watch, Jean has looked out the window, *etc.*), and at the same time it entirely escapes me. To the extent that the man-as-object is the fundamental term of this relation, to the extent that the relation *reaches toward him,* it escapes me. I can not put myself at the center of it. The distance which unfolds between the lawn and the man through the synthetic upsurge of this primary relation is a negation of the distance which I establish—as a pure type of external negation—between these two objects. The distance appears as a pure *disintegration* of the relations which I apprehend between the objects of my universe. It is not I who realize this disintegration; it appears to me as a relation which I aim at emptily across the distances which I originally established between things. It stands as a background of things, a background which on principle escapes me and which is conferred on them from without. Thus the appearance, among the objects of my universe, of an element of disintegration in that universe is what I mean by the appearance of a man in my universe.

The Other is first the permanent flight of things toward a goal which I apprehend as an object at a certain distance from me but which escapes me inasmuch as it unfolds about itself its own distances. Moreover this disintegration grows by degrees; if there exists between the lawn and the Other a relation which is without distance and which creates distance, then there exists necessarily a relation between the Other and the statue which stands on a pedestal in the middle of the lawn, and a relation between the Other and the big chestnut trees which border the walk; there is a total space which is grouped around the Other, and this space is made with my space; there is a regrouping in which I take part but which escapes me, a regrouping of all the objects which people my universe. This regrouping does not stop there. The grass is something qualified; it is this green grass which exists for the Other; in this sense the very quality of the object, its deep, raw green is in direct relation to this man. This green turns toward the Other a face which escapes me. I apprehend the relation of the green to the Other as an objective relation, but I can not apprehend the green as it appears to the Other. Thus suddenly an object has appeared which has stolen the world from me. Everything is in place; everything still exists for me; but everything is traversed by an invisible flight and fixed in the direction of a new object. The appearance of the Other in the world corresponds therefore to a fixed sliding of the whole universe, to a decentralization of the world which undermines the centralization which I am simultaneously effecting.

But the Other is still an object for me. He belongs to my distances; the man is there, twenty paces from me, he is turning his back on me. As such he is again two yards, twenty inches from the lawn, six yards from the statue; hence the disintegration of my universe is contained within the limits of this same universe; we are not dealing here with a flight of the world toward nothingness or outside itself. Rather it appears that the world has a kind of drain hole in the middle of its being and that it is perpetually flowing off through this hole. The universe, the flow, and the drain hole are all once again recovered, reapprehended, and fixed as an object. All this is there for me as a partial structure of the world, even though the total disintegration of the universe is involved. Moreover these disintegrations may often be contained within more narrow limits. There, for example, is a man who is reading while he walks. The disintegration of the universe which he represents is purely virtual; he has ears which do not hear, eyes which see nothing except his book. Between his book and him I apprehend an undeniable relation without distance of the same type as that which earlier connected the walker with the grass. But this time the form has closed in on itself. There is a full object for me to grasp. In the midst of the world I can say "man-reading" as I could say "cold stone," "fine rain." I apprehend a closed "Gestalt" in which the *reading* forms the essential quality; for the rest, it remains blind and mute, lets itself be known and perceived as a pure and simple temporal-spatial thing, and seems to be related to the rest of the world by a purely indifferent externality. The quality "man-reading" as the relation of the man to the book is simply a little particular crack in my universe. At the heart of this solid, visible form he makes himself a particular emptying. The form is massive only in appearance; its peculiar meaning is to be—in the midst of my universe, at ten paces from me, at the heart of that massivity—a closely consolidated and localized flight.

None of this enables us to leave the level on which the Other is an *object*. At most we are dealing with a particular type of objectivity akin to that which Husserl designated by the term *absence* without, however, his noting that the Other is defined not as the absence of a consciousness in relation to the body which I see but by the absence of the world which I perceive, an absence discovered at the very heart of my perception of this world. On this level the Other is an object in the world, an object which can be defined by the world. But this relation of flight and of absence on the part of the world in relation to me is only probable. If it is this which defines the objectivity of the Other, then to what original presence of the Other does it refer? At present we can give this answer: if the Other-as-object is defined in connection with the world as the object which *sees* what I see, then my fundamental connection with the Other-as-subject must be able to be referred back to my permanent possibility of *being seen* by the Other. It is in and through the revelation of my being-as-object for the Other that I must be able to apprehend the presence of his being-as-subject. For just as the Other is a probable object for me-as-subject, so I can discover myself in the process of becoming a probable object for only a certain subject. This revelation can not derive from the fact that *my universe is an object for the Other-as-object*, as if the Other's look after having wandered over the lawn and the surrounding objects came following a definite path to turn toward me. I have observed that I can not be an object for an object. A radical conversion of the Other is necessary if he is to escape objectivity. Therefore I can not consider the look which the Other directs on me as one of the possible manifestations of his objective being; the Other can not look at *me* as he looks at the grass. Furthermore my objectivity can not itself derive for me from the objectivity of the world since I am precisely the one by whom there is a world; that is, the one who on principle can not be an object for himself.

Thus this relation which I call "being-seen-by-another," far from being merely one of the relations signified by the word man, represents an irreducible fact which can not be deduced either from the essence of the Other-as-object, or from my being-as-subject. On the contrary, if the concept of the Other-as-object is to have any meaning, this can be only as the result of the conversion and the degradation of that original relation. In a word, my apprehension of the Other in the world as probably being a man refers to my permanent possibility of being-seen-by-him; that is, to the permanent possibility that a subject who sees me may be substituted for the object seen by me. "Being-seen-by-the-Other" is the truth of "seeing-the-Other." Thus the notion of the Other can not under any circumstances aim at a solitary, extra-mundane consciousness which I can not even think. The man is defined by his relation to the world and by his relation to myself. He is that object in the world which determines an internal flow of the universe, an internal hemor-rhage. He is the subject who is revealed to me in that flight of myself toward objectivation. But the original relation of myself to the Other is not only an absent truth aimed at across the concrete presence of an object in my universe; it is also a concrete, daily relation which at each instant I experience. At each instant the Other is looking at me. It is easy therefore for us to attempt with concrete examples to describe this fundamental connection which must form the basis of any theory concerning the Other. If the Other is on principle the one who looks at me, then we must be able to explain the meaning of the Other's look.

Every look directed toward me is manifested in connection with the appearance of a sensible form in our perceptive field, but contrary to what might be expected, it is not connected with any determined form. Of course what most often manifests a look is the convergence of two ocular globes in my direction. But the look will be given just as well on occasion when there is a rustling of branches, or the sound of a footstep followed by silence, or the slight opening of a shutter, or a light movement of a curtain. During an attack men who are crawling through the brush apprehend as a look to be avoided, not two eyes, but a white farm-house which is outlined against the sky at the top of a little hill. It is just probable, of course, that the object thus constituted still manifests the look. It is only probable that behind the bush which has just moved there is someone hiding who is watching me. But this probability need not detain us for the moment; we shall return to this point later. What is important first is to define the look in itself. Now the bush, the farmhouse are not the look; they only represent the eye, for the eye is not at first appre-hended as a sensible organ of vision but as the support for the look. They never refer therefore to the actual eye of the watcher hidden behind the curtain, behind a window in the farmhouse. In themselves they are already eyes. On the other hand neither is the look one quality among others of the object which functions as an eye, nor is it the total form of that object, nor a "worldly" relation which is established between that object and me. On the contrary, far from perceiving the look on the objects which manifest it, my apprehension of a look turned toward me appears on the ground of the destruction of the eyes which "look at me." If I apprehend the look, I cease to perceive the eyes; they are there, they remain in the field of my perception as pure *presentations*, but I do not make any use of them; they are neutralized, put out of play; they are no longer the object of a thesis but remain in that state of "disconnection"[16] in which the world is put by a consciousness practicing the phenomenological reduction prescribed by Husserl. It is never when eyes are looking at you that you can find them beautiful or ugly, that you can remark on their color. The Other's look hides his eyes; it seems to *go in front of them*. This illusion stems from the fact that eyes as objects of my perception remain at a precise distance which unfolds from me to them (in a word, I am present to the eyes without distance, but they are distant from the place where I "find myself") whereas the look is upon me without distance while at the same time it holds me at a distance—that is, its immediate presence to me unfolds a distance which removes me from it. I can not therefore direct my attention on the look without at the same stroke causing my perception to decompose and pass into the background. There is produced here something analogous to what I attempted to show elsewhere in connection with the subject of the imagination.[17] We can not, I said then, perceive and imagine simultaneously; it must be either one or the other. I should willingly say here: we can not perceive the world and at the same time apprehend a look fastened upon us; it must be either one or the other. This is because to perceive is to *look at*, and to apprehend a look is not to apprehend a look-as-object in the world (unless the look is not directed upon us); it is to be conscious of *being looked at*. The look which the *eyes* manifest, no matter what kind of eyes they are is a pure reference to myself. What I apprehend immediately when I hear the branches crackling behind me is not that *there is someone there*; it is that I am vulnerable, that I have a body which can be hurt, that I occupy a place and that I can not in any case escape from the space in which I am without defense—in short, that I *am seen*. Thus the look is first an intermediary which refers from me to myself. What is the nature of this intermediary? What does *being seen* mean for me?

Let us imagine that moved by jealousy, curiosity, or vice I have just glued

---

[16] Literally, "put out of circuit" (*mise hors circuit*). Tr.

[17] *L'Imaginaire*. N.R.F., 1940. In English, *The Psychology of the Imagination*. Philosophical Library, 1948.

my ear to the door and looked through a keyhole. I am alone and on the level of a non-thetic self-consciousness. This means first of all that there is no self to inhabit my consciousness, nothing therefore to which I can refer my acts in order to qualify them. They are in no way known; I *am my acts* and hence they carry in themselves their whole justification. I am a pure consciousness of things, and things, caught up in the circuit of my selfness, offer to me their potentialities as the proof of my non-thetic consciousness (of) my own possibilities. This means that behind that door a spectacle is presented as "to be seen," a conversation as "to be heard." The door, the keyhole are at once both instruments and obstacles; they are presented as "to be handled with care;" the keyhole is given as "to be looked through close by and a little to one side," *etc.* Hence from this moment "I do what I have to do." No transcending view comes to confer upon my acts the character of a *given* on which a judgment can be brought to bear. My consciousness sticks to my acts, it is my acts; and my acts are commanded only by the ends to be attained and by the instruments to be employed. My attitude, for example, has no "outside"; it is a pure process of relating the instrument (the keyhole) to the end to be attained (the spectacle to be seen), a pure mode of losing myself in the world, of causing myself to be drunk in by things as ink is by a blotter in order that an instrumental-complex oriented toward an end may be synthetically detached on the ground of the world. The order is the reverse of causal order. It is the end to be attained which organizes all the moments which precede it. The end justifies the means; the means do not exist for themselves and outside the end.

Moreover the ensemble exists only in relation to a free project of my possibilities. Jealousy, as the possibility which I *am*, organizes this instrumental complex by transcending it toward itself. But I *am* this jealousy; I do not know it. If I contemplated it instead of making it, then only the worldly complex of instrumentality could teach it to me. This ensemble in the world with its double and inverted determination (there is a spectacle to be seen behind the door only because I am jealous, but my jealousy is nothing except the simple objective fact that *there is* a sight to *be seen* behind the door)—this we shall call *situation*. This situation reflects to me at once both my facticity and my freedom; on the occasion of a certain objective structure of the world which surrounds me, it refers my freedom to me in the form of tasks to be freely done. There is no constraint here since my freedom eats into my possibles and since correlatively the potentialities of the world indicate and offer only themselves. Moreover I can not truly define myself as *being* in a situation: first because I am not a positional consciousness of myself; second because I am my own nothingness. In this sense—and since I am what I am not and since I am not what I am—I can not even define myself as truly *being* in the process of listening at doors. I escape this provisional definition of myself by means of all my transcendence. There as we have seen is the origin of bad faith. Thus not only am I unable to know myself, but my very being escapes—although I am that very escape from my being—and I am absolutely nothing. There is nothing there but a pure nothingness encircling a certain objective ensemble and throwing it into relief outlined upon the world, but this ensemble is a real system, a disposition of means in view of an end.

But all of a sudden I hear footsteps in the hall. Someone is looking at me! What does this mean? It means that I am suddenly affected in my being and that essential modifications appear in my structure—modifications which I can apprehend and fix conceptually by means of the reflective *cogito*.

First of all, I now exist as *myself* for my unreflective consciousness. It is this irruption of the self which has been most often described: I see *myself* because *somebody* sees me—as it is usually expressed. This way of putting it is not wholly exact. But let us look more carefully. So long as we considered the for-itself in its isolation, we were able to maintain that the unreflective consciousness can not be inhabited by a self; the self was given as an object only for the reflective consciousness. But here the self comes to haunt the unreflective consciousness. Now the unreflective consciousness is a consciousness of the world. Therefore for the unreflective consciousness the self exists on the level of objects in the world; this role which devolved only on the reflective consciousness—the making-present of the self—belongs now to the unreflective consciousness. Only the reflective consciousness has the self directly for an object. The unreflective consciousness does not apprehend the *person* directly or as *its* object; the person is presented to consciousness *in so far as the person is an object for the Other*. This means that all of a sudden I am conscious of myself as escaping myself, not in that I am the foundation of my own nothingness but in that I have my foundation outside myself. I am for myself only as I am a pure reference to the Other.

Nevertheless we must not conclude here that the object is the Other and that the *Ego* present to my consciousness is a secondary structure or a meaning of the Other-as-object; the Other is not an object here and can not be an object, as we have shown, unless by the same stroke my self ceases to be an object-for-the-Other and vanishes. Thus I do not aim at the Other as an object nor at my *Ego* as an object for myself; I do not even direct an empty intention toward that *Ego* as toward an object presently out of my reach. In fact it is separated from me by a nothingness which I can not fill since I apprehend it *as not being for me* and since on principle it exists for the *Other*. Therefore I do not aim at it as if it could someday be given me but on the contrary in so far as it on principle flees from me and will never belong to me. Nevertheless I *am that Ego*; I do not reject it as a strange image, but it is present to me as a self which I *am* without knowing it; for I discover it in shame and, in other instances, in pride. It is shame or pride which reveals to me the Other's look and myself at the end of that look. It is the shame or pride which makes me live, not know the situation of being looked at.

Now, shame, as we noted at the beginning of this chapter, is shame of self; it is the recognition of the fact that I am indeed that object which the Other is looking at and judging. I can be ashamed only as my freedom escapes me in order to become a given object. Thus originally the bond between my unreflective consciousness and my Ego, which is being looked at, is a bond not of knowing but of being. Beyond any knowledge which I can have, I am this self which another knows. And this self which I am—this I am in a world which the Other has made alien to me, for the Other's look embraces my being and correlatively the walls, the door, the keyhole. All these instrumental-things in the midst of which I am, now turn toward the Other a face which on principle escapes me. Thus I am my Ego for the Other in the midst of a world which flows toward the Other. Earlier we were able to call this internal hemorrhage the flow of my world toward the Other-as-object. This was because the flow of blood was trapped and localized by the very fact that I fixed as an object in my world that Other toward which this world was bleeding. Thus not a drop of blood was lost; all was recovered, surrounded, localized although in a being which I could not penetrate. Here on the contrary the flight is without limit; it is lost externally; the world flows out of the world and I flow outside myself. The Other's look makes me be beyond my being in this world and puts me in the midst of the world which is at once this world and beyond this world. What sort of relations can I enter into with this being which I am and which shame reveals to me?

In the first place there is a relation of being. I am this being. I do not for an instant think of denying it; my shame is a confession. I shall be able later to use bad faith so as to hide it from myself, but bad faith is also a confession since it is an effort to flee the being which I am. But I am this being, neither in the mode of "having to be" nor in that of "was;" I do not found it in its being; I can not produce it directly. But neither is it the indirect, strict effect of my acts as when my shadow on the ground or my reflection in the mirror is moved in correlation with the gestures which I make. This being which I am preserves a certain indetermination, a certain unpredictability. And these new characteristics do not come only from the fact that I can not know the Other; they stem also and especially from the fact that the Other is free. Or to be exact and to reverse the terms, the Other's freedom is revealed to me across the uneasy indetermination of the being which I am for him. Thus this being is not my possible; it is not always in question at the heart of my freedom. On the contrary, it is the limit of my freedom, its "backstage" in the sense that we speak of "behind the scenes." It is given to me as a burden which I carry without ever being able to turn back to know it, without even being able to realize its weight. If it is comparable to my shadow, it is like a shadow which is projected on a moving and unpredictable material such that no table of reference can be provided for calculating the distortions resulting from these movements. Yet we still have to do with my being and not with an image of my being. We are dealing with my being as it is written in and by the Other's freedom. Everything takes place as if I had a dimension of being from which I was separated by a radical nothingness; and this nothingness is the Other's freedom. The Other has to make my being-for-him *be* in so far as he has to be his being. Thus each of my free conducts engages me in a new environment where the very stuff of my being is the unpredictable freedom of another. Yet by my very shame I claim as mine that freedom of another. I affirm a profound unity of consciousnesses, not that harmony of monads which has sometimes been taken as a guarantee of objectivity but a unity of being; for I accept and wish that others should confer upon me a being which I recognize.

Shame reveals to me that I *am* this being, not in the mode of "was" or of "having to be" but *in-itself*. When I am alone, I can not realize my "being-seated;" at most it can be said that I simultaneously both am it and am not it. But in order for me to be what I am, it suffices merely that the Other look at me. It is not for myself, to be sure; I myself shall never succeed at realizing this being-seated which I grasp in the Other's look. I shall remain forever a consciousness. But it is for the Other. Once more the nihilating escape of the for-itself is fixed, once more the in-itself closes in upon the for-itself. But once more this metamorphosis is effected *at a distance*. For the Other *I am seated as this inkwell is on the table*; for the Other, *I am leaning over* the keyhole as this tree *is bent* by the wind. Thus for the Other I have stripped myself of my transcendence. This is because my transcendence becomes for whoever makes himself a witness of it (i.e., determines himself *as not being* my transcendence) a purely established transcendence, a given-transcendence; that is, it acquires a nature by the sole fact that the Other confers on it an outside. This is accomplished, not by any distortion or by a refraction which the Other would impose on my transcendence through his categories, but by his very being. If there is an Other, whatever or whoever he may be, whatever may be his relations with me, and without his acting upon me in any way except by the pure upsurge of his being—then I have an outside, I have a *nature*. My original fall is the existence of the Other. Shame—like pride—is the apprehension of myself as a nature although that very nature escapes me and is unknowable as such. Strictly speaking, it is not that I perceive myself losing my freedom in order to become a thing, but my nature is—over there, outside my lived freedom—as a given attribute of this being which I am for the Other.

I grasp the Other's look at the very center of my *act* as the solidification and alienation of my own possibilities. In fear or in anxious or prudent anticipation, I perceive that these possibilities which I *am* and which are the condition of my transcendence are given also to another, given as about to be transcended in turn by his own possibilities. The Other as a look is only that—my transcendence transcended. Of course I still *am* my possibilities in the mode of non-thetic consciousness (of) these possibilities. But at the same time the look alienates them from me. Hitherto I grasped these possibilities thetically on the world and in the world in the form of the potentialities of instruments: the dark corner in the hallway referred to me the possibility of hiding—as a simple potential quality of its shadow, as the invitation of its darkness. This quality or instrumentality of the object belonged to it alone and was given as an objective, ideal property marking its real belonging to that complex which we have called *situation*. But with the Other's look a new organization of complexes comes to superimpose itself on the first. To apprehend myself as seen is, in fact, to apprehend myself as seen *in the world* and from the standpoint of the world. The look does not carve me out in the universe; it comes to search for me at the heart of my situation and grasps me only in irresolvable relations with instruments. If I am seen as seated, I must be seen as "seated-on-a-chair," if I am grasped as bent over, it is as "bent-over-the-keyhole," *etc.* But the alienation of myself, which is the fact of being-looked-at, involves at once the alienation of the world which I organize. I am seen as seated on this chair with the result that I do not see it at all, that it is impossible for me to see it, that it escapes me so as to organize itself into a new and differently oriented complex—with other relations and other distances in the midst of other objects which similarly have for me a secret face.

Thus I, who in so far as I am my possibles, am what I am not and am not what I am—behold now I *am* somebody! And the one who I am—and who on principle escapes me—I am he *in the midst of the world* in so far as he escapes me. Due to this fact my relation to an object or the potentiality of an object decomposes under the Other's look and appears to me in the world as my possibility of utilizing the object, but only as this possibility on principle escapes me; that *is*, in so far as it is surpassed by the Other toward his own possibilities. For example, the potentiality of the dark corner becomes a given possibility of hiding in the corner by the sole fact that the Other[18] can pass beyond it toward his possibility of illuminating the corner with his flashlight. This possibility is there, and I apprehend it but as absent, *as in the Other*; I apprehend it through my anguish and through my decision to give up that hiding place which is "*too risky*." Thus my possibilities are present to my unreflective consciousness in so far as the Other is *watching me*. If I see him ready for anything, his hand in his pocket where he has a weapon, his finger

[18] The French has *l'auteur*, "the author," which I feel sure must be a misprint for *l'autrui*, "the Other." Tr.

placed on the electric bell and ready "at the slightest movement on my part" to call the police, I apprehend my possibilities from outside and through him at the same time that I *am* my possibilities, somewhat as we objectively apprehend our thought through language at the same time that we think it *in order to* express it in language. This inclination to run away, which dominates me and carries me along and which I *am*—this I read in the Other's watchful look and in that other look—the gun pointed at me. The Other apprehends this inclination in me in so far as he has anticipated it and is already prepared for it. He apprehends it in me in so far as he surpasses it and disarms it. But I do not grasp the actual surpassing; I grasp simply the death of my possibility. A subtle death: for my possibility of hiding still remains *my* possibility; inasmuch as I *am* it, it still lives; and the dark corner does not cease to signal me, to refer its potentiality to me. But if instrumentality is defined as the fact of "being able to be surpassed towards ———," then my very possibility becomes an instrumentality. My possibility of hiding in the corner becomes the fact that the Other can surpass it toward his possibility of pulling me out of concealment, of identifying me, of arresting me. *For the Other* my possibility is at once an obstacle and a means as all instruments are. It is an obstacle, for it will compel him to certain new acts (to advance toward me, to turn on his flashlight). It is a means, for once I am discovered in this cul-de-sac, I "am caught." In other words every act performed against the Other can on principle be for the Other an instrument which will serve him against me. And I grasp the Other not in the clear vision of what he can make out of my act but in a fear which *lives* all my possibilities as ambivalent. The Other is the hidden death of my possibilities in so far as I live that death as hidden in the midst of the world. The connection between my possibility and the instrument is no more than between two instruments which are adjusted to each other outside in view of an end which escapes me. *Both* the obscurity of the dark corner and my possibility of hiding there are surpassed by the Other when, before I have been able to make a move to take refuge there, he throws the light on the corner. Thus in the shock which seizes me when I apprehend the Other's look, this happens—that suddenly I experience a subtle alienation of all my possibilities, which are now associated with objects of the world, far from me in the midst of the world.

Two important consequences result. The first is that my possibility becomes a *probability* which is outside me. In so far as the Other grasps it as eaten away by a freedom which he is not, in so far as he makes himself a witness of it and calculates its results, it is a pure indetermination in the game of possibles, and it is precisely thus that I guess at it. Later when we are in direct connection with the Other by language and when we gradually learn what he thinks of us, this is the thing which will be able at once to fascinate us and fill us with horror.

"I swear to you that I will do it."

"Maybe so. You tell me so. I want to believe you. It is indeed possible that you will do it."

The sense of this dialogue implies that the Other is originally placed before my freedom as before a given property of indetermination and before my possibles as before my probables. This is because originally I perceive myself to be over there *for the Other*, and this phantom-outline of my being touches me to the heart. For in shame and anger and fear I do not cease to assume myself as such. Yet I assume myself in blindness since I *do not know* what I assume. I simply am it.

On the other hand, the ensemble "instrument-possibility," made up of myself confronting the instrument, appears to me as surpassed and organized into a world by the Other. With the Other's look the "situation" escapes me. To use an everyday expression which better expresses our thought, I *am no longer master of the situation*. Or more exactly, I remain master of it, but it has one real dimension by which it escapes me, by which unforeseen reversals cause it *to be* otherwise than it appears for me. To be sure it can happen that in strict solitude I perform an act whose consequences are completely opposed to my anticipations and to my desires; for example I gently draw toward me a small platform holding this fragile vase, but this movement results in tipping over a bronze statuette which breaks the vase into a thousand pieces. Here, however, there is nothing which I could not have foreseen if I had been more careful, if I had observed the arrangement of the objects, *etc.—nothing which on principle escapes me*. The appearance of the Other, on the contrary, causes the appearance in the situation of an aspect which I did not wish, of which I am not master, and which on principle escapes me since it is *for the Other*. This is what Gide has appropriately called "the devil's part." It is the unpredictable but still real *reverse side*.

It is this unpredictability which Kafka's art attempts to describe in *The Trial* and *The Castle*. In one sense everything which K. and the Surveyor are doing belongs strictly to them in their own right, and in so far as they act upon the world the results conform strictly to anticipations; they are successful acts. But at the same time the truth of these acts constantly escapes them; the acts have on principle a meaning which is their *true meaning* and which neither K. nor the Surveyor will ever know. Without doubt Kafka is trying here to express the transcendence of the divine; it is for the divine that the human act is constituted in truth. But God here is only the concept of the Other pushed to the limit. We shall return to this point. That gloomy, evanescent atmosphere of *The Trial*, that ignorance which, however, is lived as ignorance, that total opacity which can only be felt as a presentiment across a total trans-lucency —this is nothing but the description of our being-in-the-midst-of-the-world-for-others.

In this way therefore the situation in and through its surpassing for the Other is fixed and organized around me into a *form*, in the sense in which the Gestaltists use that term. A given synthesis is there of which I am the essential structure, and this synthesis at once possesses both ekstatic cohesion and the character of the in-itself. My bond with those people who are speaking and whom I am watching is suddenly given outside me as an unknowable substratum of the bond which I myself establish. In particular my own *look* or my connection without distance with these people is stripped of its transcendence by the very fact that it is a *look-looked-at*. I am fixing the people whom I *see* into objects; I am in relation to them as the Other is in relation to me. In looking at them I measure my power. But if the Other sees them and sees me, then my look loses its power; it can not transform those people into objects for *the Other* since they are already the objects of his look. My look simply manifests a relation in the midst of the world, a relation of myself-as-object to the object-looked-at—something like the attraction which two masses exert over one another at a distance. On the one hand, the objects are ordered around this look: the distance between me and those looked at *exists* at present, but it is contracted, circumscribed, and compressed by my look so that the ensemble "distance-objects" is like a ground on which the look is detached in the manner of a "this" on the ground of the world. On the other hand, my attitudes are ordered around the look and are given as a series of means employed in order to "maintain" the look. In this sense I constitute an organized whole which *is* the look, I am a look-as-object; that is, an instrumental complex which *is* endowed with an inner finality and which can dispose itself in a relation of means and end in order to realize a presence to a particular other object beyond the distance. But the distance *is given to me*. In so far as I am looked at, I do not unfold the distance, I am limited to *clearing* it. The Other's look confers spatiality upon me. To apprehend oneself as looked-at is to apprehend oneself as a spatializing-spatialized.

But the Other's look is not only apprehended as spatializing; it is also *temporalizing*. The appearance of the Other's look is manifested for me through an *Erlebnis* which was on principle impossible for me to get in solitude—that of simultaneity. A world for a single for-itself could not comprehend simultaneity but only co-presences, for the for-itself is lost outside itself everywhere in the world, and it links all beings by the unity of its single presence. But simultaneity supposes the temporal connection of two existents which are not bound by any other relation. Two existents which exercise a reciprocal action on one another are not simultaneous because they belong to the same system. Simultaneity therefore does not belong to the existents of the world, it supposes the co-presence to the world of two presents considered as *presences-to*. Pierre's presence *to the* world is simultaneous *with* my presence. In this sense the original phenomenon of simultaneity is the fact that this glass is for Paul *at the same time* that it is for me. This supposes therefore a foundation for all simultaneity which must of necessity be the presence of an Other who is temporalized by my own temporalization. But to be exact, in so far as the other temporalizes *himself*, he temporalizes *me* with him; in so far as he launches out toward his own time, I appear to him in universal time. The *Other's look* in so far as I apprehend it comes to give to my time a new dimension. My presence, in so far as it is a present grasped by another as my present, has an outside; this presence which makes-itself-present *for me* is alienated for me in a present to which the Other makes himself present. I am thrown into the universal present in so far as the Other makes himself be a presence to me. But the universal present in which I come to take my place is a pure alienation of my universal present; physical time flows toward a pure and free temporalization which I am not; what is outlined on the horizon of that simultaneity which I live is an absolute temporalization from which I am separated by a nothingness.

As a temporal-spatial object in the world, as an essential structure of a temporal-spatial situation in the world, I offer myself to the Other's appraisal. This also I apprehend by the pure exercise of the *cogito*. To be looked at is to apprehend oneself as the unknown object of unknowable appraisals—in particular, of value judgments. But at the same time that in shame or pride I recognize the justice of these appraisals, I do not cease to take them for what they are—a free surpassing of the given toward possibilities. A judgment is the transcendental act of a free being. Thus being-seen constitutes me as a defenseless being for a freedom which is not my freedom. It is in this sense that we can consider ourselves as "slaves" in so far as we appear to the Other. But this slavery is not a historical result—capable of being surmounted—of a life in the abstract form of consciousness. I am a slave to the degree that my being is dependent at the center of a freedom which is not mine and which is the very condition of my being. In so far as I am the object of values which come to qualify me without my being able to act on this qualification or even to know it, I am enslaved. By the same token in so far as I am the instrument of possibilities which are not my possibilities, whose pure presence beyond my being I can not even glimpse, and which deny my transcendence in order to constitute me as a means to ends of which I am ignorant—I am in *danger*. This danger is not an accident but the permanent structure of my being-for-others.

This brings us to the end of our description. Yet before we can make use of it to discover just what the Other is, we must note that this description *has been worked out entirely on the level of the cogito*. We have only made explicit the meaning of those subjective reactions to the Other's look which are fear (the feeling of being in danger before the Other's freedom), pride, or shame (the feeling of being finally what I am but elsewhere, over there for the Other), the recognition of my slavery (the feeling of the alienation of all my possibilities). Besides, this specification is in no way a conceptual fixing of bits of *knowledge* more or less obscure. Let each one refer to his own experience. There is no one who has not at some time been surprised in an attitude which was guilty or simply ridiculous. The sudden modification then experienced was in no way provoked by the irruption of knowledge. It is rather in itself a solidification and an abrupt stratification of myself which leaves intact my possibilities and my structures "for-myself," but which suddenly pushes me into a new dimension of existence—the dimension of the *unrevealed*. Thus the appearance of the look is apprehended by me as the upsurge of an ekstatic relation of being, of which one term is the "me" as for-itself which is what it is not and which is not what it is, and of which other term is still the "me" but outside my reach, outside my action, outside my knowledge. This term, since it is directly connected with the infinite possibilities of a free Other, is itself an infinite and inexhaustible synthesis of unrevealed properties. Through the Other's look I *live* myself as fixed in the midst of the world, as in danger, as irremediable. But I *know* neither what I am nor what is my place in the world, not what face this world in which I am turns toward the Other.

Now at last we can make precise the meaning of this upsurge of the Other in and through his look. The Other is in no way given to us as an object. The objectivation of the Other would be the collapse of his being-as-a-look. Furthermore as we have seen, the Other's look is the disappearance of the Other's eyes as objects which manifest the look. The Other can not even be the object aimed at emptily at the horizon of my being for the Other. The objectivation of the Other, as we shall see, is a defence on the part of my being which, precisely by conferring on the Other a being for-me, frees me from my being-for the Other. In the phenomenon of the look, the Other is on principle that which can not be an object. At the same time we see that he can not be a *limiting term* of that relation of myself to myself which makes me arise for myself as the *unrevealed*. Neither can the Other be the goal of my *attention*; if in the upsurge of the Other's look, I *paid attention* to the look or to the Other, this could be only as to objects, for attention is an intentional direction toward objects. But it is not necessary to conclude that the Other is an abstract condition, a conceptual structure of the ekstatic relation; there is here in fact no object really thought, of which the Other could be a universal, formal structure. The Other is, to be sure, the condition of my being-unrevealed. But he is the concrete, particular condition of it. He is not engaged in my being in the midst of the world as one of its integral parts since he is precisely that which transcends this world in the midst of which I am as non-revealed; as such he can therefore be neither an object nor the formal, constituent element of an object. He can not appear to me, as we have seen, as a unifying or regulative category of my experience since he comes to me through an encounter. Then what is the Other?

In the first place, he is the being toward whom I do not turn my attention. He is the one who looks at me and at whom I am not yet looking, the one who delivers me to myself as *unrevealed* but without revealing himself, the one who is present to me as directing at me but never as the object of my direction; he is the concrete pole (though out of reach) of my flight, of the alienation of my possibles, and of the flow of the world toward another world which is the *same* world and yet lacks all communication with it. But he can not be distinct from this same alienation and flow; he is the meaning and the direction of them; he haunts this flow not as a *real or categorial* element but as a presence which is fixed and made part of the world if I attempt to "make-it-present" and which is never more present, more urgent than when I am not aware of it. For example if I am wholly engulfed in my shame, the Other is the immense, invisible presence which supports this shame and embraces it on every side; he is the supporting environment of my being-unrevealed. Let us see what it is which the Other manifests as *unrevealable* across my lived experience of the unrevealed.

First, the *Other's look* as the necessary condition of my objectivity is the destruction of all objectivity for me. The Other's look touches me across the world and is not only a transformation of myself but a total metamorphosis of the *world*. I am looked-at in a world which is looked-at. In particular the Other's look, which is a look-looking and not a look-looked-at, denies my distances from objects and unfolds its own distances. This look of the Other is given immediately as that by which distance comes to the world at the heart of a presence without distance. I withdraw; I am stripped of my distanceless presence to my world, and I am provided with a distance from the Other. There I am fifteen paces from the door, six yards from the window. But the Other comes searching for me so as to constitute me at a certain distance from him. As the Other constitutes me as at six yards from him, it is necessary that he be present to me without distance. Thus within the very experience of my distance from things and from the Other, I experience the distanceless presence of the Other to me.

Anyone may recognize in this abstract description that immediate and burning presence of the Other's look which has so often filled him with shame. In other words, in so far as I experience myself as looked-at, there is realized for me a trans-mundane presence of the Other. The Other looks at me not as he is "in the midst of" my world but as he comes toward the world and toward me from all his transcendence; when he looks at me, he is separated from me by no distance, by no object of the world—whether real or ideal—by no body in the world, but the sole fact of his nature as Other. Thus the appearance of the Other's look is not an appearance in the world—neither in "mine" nor in the "Other's"—and the relation which unites me to the Other can not be a relation of exteriority inside the world. By the Other's look I effect the concrete proof that there is a "beyond the world." The Other is present to me without any intermediary as a transcendence which is not mine. But this presence is not reciprocal. All of the world's density is necessary in order that I may myself be present to the Other. An omnipresent and inapprehensible transcendence, posited upon me without intermediary as I am my being-unrevealed, a transcendence separated from me by the infinity of being, as I am plunged by this look into the heart of a world complete with its distances and its instruments—such is the Other's look when first I experience it as a look.

Furthermore by fixing my possibilities the Other reveals to me the impossibility of my being an object except for another freedom. I can not be an object for myself, for I am what I am; thrown back on its own resources, the reflective effort toward a dissociation results in failure; I am always reapprehended by myself. And when I naively assume that it is possible for me to be an objective being without being responsible for it, I thereby implicitly suppose the Other's existence; for how could I be an object if not for a subject. Thus for me the Other is first the being for whom I am an object; that is, the being through whom I gain my objectness. If I am to be able to conceive of even one of my properties in the objective mode, then the Other is already given. He is given not as a being of my universe but as a pure subject. Thus this pure subject which by definition I am unable to know—i.e., to posit as object—is always there out of reach and without distance whenever I try to grasp myself as object. In experiencing the look, in experiencing myself as an unrevealed object-ness, I experience the inapprehensible subjectivity of the Other directly and with my being.

At the same time I experience the Other's infinite freedom. It is for and by means of a freedom and only for and by means of it that my possibles can be limited and fixed. A material obstacle can not fix my possibilities; it is only the occasion for my projecting myself toward other possibles and can not confer upon them an outside. To remain at home because it is raining and to remain at home because one has been forbidden to go out are by no means the same thing. In the first case I myself determine to stay inside in consideration of the consequences of my acts; I surpass the obstacle "rain" toward myself and I make an instrument of it. In the second case it is my very possibilities of going out of or staying inside which are presented to me as surpassed and fixed and which a freedom simultaneously foresees and prevents. It is not mere caprice which causes us often to do very naturally and without annoyance what would irritate us if another commanded it. This is because the order and the prohibition cause us to experience the Other's freedom across our own slavery. Thus in the look the death of my possibilities causes me to experience the Other's freedom. This death is realized only at the heart of that freedom; I am inaccessible to myself and yet myself, thrown, abandoned at the heart of the Other's freedom. In connection with this experience my belonging to universal time can appear to me only as contained and realized by an autonomous temporalization; only a for-itself which temporalizes itself can throw me into time.

Thus through the look I experience the Other concretely as a free, conscious subject who causes there to be a world by temporalizing himself toward his own possibilities. That subject's presence without intermediary is the necessary condition of all thought which I would attempt to form concerning myself. The Other is that "myself" from which nothing separates me, absolutely nothing except his pure and total freedom; that is, that indetermination of himself which he has to be for and through himself.

We know enough at present to attempt to explain that unshakable resistance which common sense has always opposed to the solipsistic argument. This resistance indeed is based on the fact that the Other is given to me as a concrete evident presence which I can in no way derive from myself and which can in no way be placed in doubt nor made the object of a phenomenological reduction or of any other ἐποχή.[19]

If someone looks at me, I am conscious of being an object. But this consciousness can be produced only in and through the existence of the Other. In this respect Hegel was right. However that other consciousness and that other freedom are never given to me; for if they were, they would be known and would therefore be an object, which would cause me to cease being an object. Neither can I derive the concept or the representation of them from my own background. First because I do not "conceive" them nor "represent" them to myself; expressions like these would refer us again to "knowing," which on principle is removed from consideration. In addition every concrete proof of freedom which I can effect by myself is a proof of my freedom; every concrete apprehension of a consciousness is consciousness (of) my consciousness; the very notion of consciousness makes reference only to my possible consciousnesses. Indeed we established in our Introduction that the existence of freedom and of consciousness precedes and conditions their essence; consequently these essences can subsume only concrete exemplifications of my consciousness or of my freedom. In the third place the Other's freedom and consciousness can not be categories serving for the unification of my representations. To be sure, as Husserl has shown, the ontological structure of "my" world demands that it be also a world for others. But to the extent that the Other confers a particular type of objectivity on the objects of my world, this is because he is already in this world in the capacity of an object. If it is

[19] Correction for ἐπόχή. Tr.

correct that Pierre, who is reading before me, gives a particular type of objectivity to the face of the book which is turned toward him, then this objectivity is conferred on a face which on principle I can see (although as we have said, it escapes me in so far as it is read), on a face which belongs to the world where I am and which consequently by a magic bond is connected beyond distance to Pierre-as-object. Under these conditions the concept of the Other can in fact be fixed as an empty form and employed constantly as a reinforcement of objectivity for the world which is mine. But the Other's presence in his look-looking can not contribute to reinforce the world, for on the contrary it undoes the world by the very fact that it causes the world to escape me. The escape of the world from me when it is *relative* and when it is an escape toward the Other-as-object, reinforces objectivity. The escape of the world and of my self from me when it is absolute and when it is effected toward a freedom which is not mine, is a dissolution of my knowledge. The world disintegrates in order to be reintegrated over there as a world; but this disintegration is not given to me; I can not know it nor even think it. The presence to me of the Other-as-a-look is therefore neither a knowledge nor a projection of my being nor a form of unification nor a category. It *is* and I can not derive it from me.

At the same time I can not make it fall beneath the stroke of the phenomenological ἐποχή. The latter indeed has for its goal putting the world within brackets so as to reveal transcendental consciousness in its absolute reality. Whether in general this operation is possible or not is something which is not for us to decide here. But in the case which concerns us the Other can not be put out of consideration since as a look-looking he definitely does not belong to the world. I am ashamed of myself *before* the Other, we said. The phenomenological reduction must result in removing from consideration the object of shame in order better to make shame itself stand out in its absolute subjectivity. But the Other is not the *object* of the shame; the object is my act or my situation in the world. They alone can be strictly "reduced." The Other is not even an objective condition of my shame. Yet he is as the very-being of it. Shame is the revelation of the Other not in the way in which a consciousness reveals an object but in the way in which one moment of consciousness implies on the side another moment as its motivation. If we should have attained pure consciousness by means of the *cogito*, and if this pure consciousness were only a consciousness (of being) shame, the Other's consciousness would still haunt it as an inapprehensible presence and would thereby escape all reduction. This demonstrates sufficiently that it is not in the world that the Other is first to be sought but at the side of consciousness as a consciousness in which and by which consciousness makes itself be what it is. Just as my consciousness apprehended by the *cogito* bears indubitable witness of itself and of its own existence, so certain particular consciousnesses—

for example, "shame-consciousness"—bear indubitable witness to the *cogito* both of themselves and of the existence of the Other.

But, someone may object, is this not simply because of the Other's look as *meaning* of my objectivity-for-myself. If so, we shall fall back into solipsism; when I integrate myself as an object in the concrete system of representations, the meaning of this objectivation would be projected outside me and hypostasized as *the Other.*

But we must note the following:

(1) My object-ness for myself is in no way a specification of Hegel's *Ich bin Ich.* We are not dealing with a formal identity, and my being-as-object or being-for-others is profoundly different from my being-for-myself. In fact the notion of *objectivity*, as we observed in Part One, requires an explicit negation. The object is that which is not my consciousness; consequently it is that which does not have the characteristics of consciousness since the only existent which has for me the characteristics of consciousness is the consciousness which is *mine.* Thus the Me-as-object-for-myself is a Me which *is not* Me; that is, which does not have the characteristics of consciousness. It is a *degraded* consciousness; objectivation is a radical metamorphosis. Even if I could see myself clearly and distinctly as an object, what I should see would not be the adequate representation of what I am in myself and for myself, of that "incomparable monster preferable to all," as Malraux puts it, but the apprehension of my being-outside-myself, for the Other; that is, the objective apprehension of my being-other, which is radically different from my being-for-myself, and which does not refer to myself at all.

To apprehend myself as *evil*, for example, could not be to refer myself to what I am for myself, for I am not and can not be evil for myself for two reasons. In the first place, I *am* neither evil, for myself, nor a civil servant or a physician. In fact I am in the mode of not being what I am and of being what I am not. The qualification "evil," on the contrary, characterizes me as an in-itself. In the second place, if I were *to be* evil for myself, I should of necessity be so in the mode of *having* to be so and would have to apprehend myself and will myself as evil. But this would mean that I must discover myself as willing what appears to myself as the opposite of my Good and precisely because it is the Evil or the opposite of my Good. It is therefore expressly necessary that I will the contrary of what I desire at one and the same moment and in the same relation; that is, I would have to hate myself precisely as I am myself. If on the level of the for-itself I am to realize fully this essence of evil, it would be necessary for me to assume myself as evil; that is, I would have to approve myself by the same act which makes me blame myself. We can see that this notion of evil can in no way derive its origin from me in so far as I am Me. It would be in vain for me to push the ekstasis to its extreme limits or to effect a detachment from self which would constitute me for myself; I shall never succeed in conferring evil on myself or even in conceiving it for myself if I am thrown on my own resources.

This is because I *am* my own detachment from myself, I *am* my own nothingness; simply because I am my own mediator between Me and Me, all objectivity disappears. I can not *be* this nothingness which separates me from me-as-object, for there must of necessity be a *presentation* to me of the object which I am. Thus I can not confer on myself any quality without mediation or an objectifying power which is not my own power and which I can neither pretend nor forge. Of course this has been said before; it was said a long time ago that the Other teaches me who I am. But the same people who uphold this thesis affirm on the other hand that I derive the concept of the Other from myself by reflecting on my own powers and by projection or analogy. Therefore they remain at the center of a vicious circle from which they can not get out. Actually the Other can not be the meaning of my objectivity; he is the concrete, transcending condition of it. This is because such qualities as "evil," "jealous," "sympathetic" or "antipathetic" and the like are not empty imaginings; when I use them to qualify the Other, I am well aware that I want to touch him in his being. Yet I can not live them as my own realities. If the Other confers them on me, they are admitted by what I am for-myself; when the Other describes my character, I do not "recognize" myself and yet I know that "it is me." I accept the responsibility for this stranger who is presented to me, but he does not cease to be a stranger. This is because he is neither a simple unification of my subjective representations, not a "Me" which I am in the sense of the *Ich bin Ich*, nor an empty image which the Other makes of me for himself and for which he alone bears the responsibility. This Me, which is not to be compared to the Me which I have to be, is still Me but metamorphosed by a new setting and adapted to that setting; it is a being, my being but with entirely new dimensions of being and new modalities. It is Me separated from Me by an impassible nothingness, for I *am* this me but I am not this nothingness which separates me from myself. It is the Me which I am by an ultimate ekstasis which transcends all *my ekstases* since it is not the ekstasis which I have to be. My being for-others is a fall through absolute emptiness toward objectivity. And since this fall is an *alienation*, I can not make myself be for myself as an object; for in no case can I ever alienate myself from myself.

(2) Furthermore the Other does not constitute me as an object for myself but for him. In other words he does not serve as a regulative or constitutive concept for the pieces of knowledge which I may have of myself. Therefore the Other's presence does not cause me-as-object to "appear." I apprehend nothing but an escape from myself toward ———. Even when language has revealed that the Other considers me evil or jealous, I shall never have a concrete intuition of my evil or of my jealousy. These will never be more than

fleeting notions whose very nature will be to escape me. I shall not apprehend my evil, but in relation to this or that particular act I shall escape myself, I shall feel my alienation or my flow towards . . . a being which I shall only be able to think emptily as evil and which nevertheless I shall *feel that I am*, which I shall live at a distance through shame or fear.

Thus myself-as-object is neither knowledge nor a unity of knowledge but an uneasiness, a lived wrenching away from the ecstatic unity of the for-itself, a limit which I can not reach and which yet I am. The Other through whom this Me *comes to me* is neither knowledge nor category but *the fact* of the presence of a strange freedom. In fact my wrenching away from myself and the upsurge of the Other's freedom are one; I can feel them and live them only as an ensemble; I cannot even try to conceive of one without the other. The fact of the Other is incontestable and touches me to the heart. I realize him through *uneasiness*; through him I am perpetually in *danger* in a world which is *this* world and which nevertheless I can only glimpse. The Other does not appear to me as a being who is constituted first so as to encounter me later; he appears as a being who arises in an original relation of being with me and whose indubitability and *factual necessity* are those of my own consciousness.

A number of difficulties remain. In particular there is the fact that through shame we confer on the Other an indubitable presence. Now as we have seen, it is only *probable* that the Other is looking at me. That farm at the top of the hill *seems* to be looking at the commandos, and it is certain that the house is occupied by the enemy. But it is not certain that the enemy soldiers are at present watching through the windows. It is not certain that the man whose footstep I hear behind me is looking at me; his face could be turned away, his look fixed on the ground or on a book. Finally in general it is not sure that those eyes which are fixed on me are eyes; they could be only "artificial ones" resembling real eyes. In short must we not say that in turn the look becomes *probable* because of the fact that I can constantly believe that I am looked at without actually being so? As a result does not our certainty of the Other's existence take on a purely hypothetical character?

The difficulty can be expressed in these terms: On the occasion of certain appearances in the world which seem to me to manifest a look, I apprehend in myself a certain "being-looked-at" with its own structures which refer me to the Other's real existence. But it is possible that I am mistaken; perhaps the objects of the world which I took for eyes were not eyes; perhaps it was only the wind which shook the bush behind me; in short perhaps these concrete objects did not *really* manifest a look. In this case what becomes of my certainty that I *am looked-at*? My shame was in fact *shame before somebody*. But nobody is there. Does it not thereby become *shame before nobody*? Since it has posited somebody where there was nobody, does it not become a false shame?

This difficulty should not keep us for long, and we should not even have mentioned it except that actually it can help us in our investigation by indicating more purely the nature of our being-for-others. There is indeed a confusion here between two distinct orders of knowledge and two types of being which can not be compared. We have always known that the object-in-the-world can be only probable. This is due to its very character as object. It is probable that the passerby is a man; if he turns his eyes toward me, then although I immediately experience and with certainty the fact of *being-looked-at*, I can not make this certainty pass into my experience of the Other-as-object. In fact it reveals to me only the Other-as-subject, a transcending presence to the world and the real condition of my being-as-object. In any case, it is impossible to transfer my certainty of the Other-as-subject to the Other-as-object which was the occasion of that certainty, and conversely it is impossible to invalidate the evidence of the appearance of the Other-as-subject by pointing to the constitutional probability of the Other-as-object. Better yet, the *look*, as we have shown, appears on the ground of the destruction of the object which manifests it. If this gross and ugly passerby shuffling along toward me suddenly looks at me, then there is nothing left of his ugliness, his obesity, and his shuffling. During the time that I feel myself looked-at he is a pure mediating freedom between myself and me. The fact of being-looked-at can not therefore *depend* on the object which manifests the look. Since my shame as an *Erlebnis* which is reflectively apprehensible is a witness for the Other for the same reason as it is its own witness, I am not going to put it in question on the occasion of an object of the world which can on principle be placed in doubt. This would amount to doubting my own existence, just because the perceptions which I have of my own body (when I see my hand, for example) are subject to error. Therefore if the being-looked-at, in its pure form, is not bound to the *Other's body* any more than in the pure realization of the *cogito* my consciousness of being a consciousness is bound to *my own body*, then we must consider the appearance of certain objects in the field of my experience—in particular the convergence of the Other's eyes in my direction—as a pure *monition*, as the pure occasion of realizing my *being-looked-at*. In the same way for Plato the contradictions of the sensible world are the occasion of effecting a philosophical conversion. In a word what is certain is that I *am* looked-at: what is only probable is that the look is bound to this or that intra-mundane presence. Moreover there is nothing here to surprise us since as we have seen, it is never eyes which look at us; it is the Other-as-subject.

Nevertheless, someone will say, the fact remains that I can discover that I have been mistaken. Here I am bent over the keyhole; suddenly I hear a footstep. I shudder as a wave of shame sweeps over me. Somebody has seen me. I straighten up. My eyes run over the deserted corridor. It was a false alarm. I breathe a sigh of relief. Do we not have here an experience which is self-destructive?

Let us look more carefully. Is it actually my being-as-object for the Other which has been revealed as an error? By no means. The Other's existence is so far from being placed in doubt that this false alarm can very well result in making me give up my enterprise. If, on the other hand, I persevere in it, I shall feel my heart beat fast, and I shall detect the slightest noise, the slightest creaking of the stairs. Far from disappearing with my first alarm, the Other is present everywhere, below me, above me, in the neighboring rooms, and I continue to feel profoundly my being-for-others. It is even possible that my shame may not disappear; it is my red face as I bend over the keyhole. I do not cease to *experience* my being-for-others; my possibilities do not cease to "die," nor do the distances cease to unfold toward me in terms of the stairway where somebody "could" be, in terms of this dark corner where a human presence "could" hide. Better yet, if I tremble at the slightest noise, if each creak announces to me a look, this is because I am already in the state of being-looked-at. What then is it which falsely appeared and which was self-destructive when I discovered the false alarm? It is not the Other-as-subject, nor is it his presence to me. It is the Other's *facticity*; that is, the contingent connection between the Other and an object-being in my world. Thus what is doubtful is not the Other himself. It is the Other's *being-there*; i.e., that concrete, historical event which we can express by the words, "There is someone in this room."

These observations may enable us to proceed further. The Other's presence in the world can not be derived analytically from the presence of the Other-as-subject to me, for this original presence is transcendent—i.e., being-beyond-the-world. I believed that the Other was present in the room, but I was mistaken. He was not *there*. He was "absent." What then is *absence*?

If we take the expression "absence" in its empirical and everyday usage, it is clear that I do not use it to indicate just any kind of "not-being-there." In the first place, if I do not find my package of tobacco in its usual spot, I do not say that it is *absent* even though I could declare that it "ought to be there." This is because the place of a material *object* or of an instrument, even though sometimes it may be precisely assigned, does not derive from the nature of the object or instrument. To be exact, its nature can barely bestow on it a location but it is through me that the *place* of an instrument is realized. Human-reality is the being which causes a *place* to come to objects. Human reality alone, in so far as it is its own possibilities, can originally take a place. On the other hand I shall not say that Aga-Khan or the Sultan of Morocco is absent from this apartment, but I say that Pierre, who usually lives here, is absent for a quarter of an hour. In short, absence is defined as a mode of being of human-reality in relation to locations and places which it has itself determined by its presence. Absence is not a nothingness of connections with a place; on the contrary, I determine Pierre in relation to a determined place by declaring that he is absent from it. Finally I shall not speak of Pierre's absence in relation to a natural location even if he often passes by there. On the other hand, I shall be able to lament his absence from a picnic which "took place" in a part of the country where he has never been. Pierre's absence is defined in relation to a place where he might himself determine himself to be, but this place itself is delimited as a place, not by the site nor even by the solitary relations of the location to Pierre himself, but by the presence of other human-realities. It is in relation to *other* people that Pierre is absent. Absence is Pierre's concrete mode of being in relation to Thérèse; it is a bond between human-realities, not between human-reality and the world. It is in relation to Thérèse that Pierre is absent *from this location*. Absence therefore is a bond of being between two or several human-realities which necessitates a fundamental presence of these realities one to another and which, moreover, is only one of the particular concretizations of this presence. For Pierre to be absent in relation to Thérèse is a particular way of his being present. In fact absence has meaning only if all the relations of Pierre with Thérèse are preserved: he loves her, he is her husband, he supports her, *etc.* In particular, absence supposes the maintenance of the *concrete* existence of Pierre: death is not an absence. Due to this fact the *distance* from Pierre to Thérèse in no way changes the fundamental fact of their reciprocal presence. In fact if we consider this presence from the point of view of Pierre, we see that it means *either* that Thérèse is existing in the midst of the world as the-Other-as-object, *or else* that he feels that he exists for Thérèse as for the-Other-as-subject. In the first case the distance is made contingent and signifies nothing in relation to the fundamental fact that Pierre is the one by whom "there is" a world as a Totality and that Pierre is present without distance to this world as the one through whom the distance exists. In the second case Pierre feels himself existing for Thérèse without distance: she is *at a distance* from him to the extent that she is removed and unfolds a distance between her and him; the entire world separates him from her. But for her he is without distance inasmuch as he is an object in the world which she makes come into being. Consequently in neither case can removal modify these essential relations. Whether the distance is small or great, between Pierre-as-object and Thérèse-as-subject, between Thérèse-as-object and Pierre-as-subject there is the infinite density of a world. Between Pierre-as-subject and Thérèse-as-object, and again between Thérèse-as-subject and Pierre-as-object there is no distance at all. Thus the empirical concepts of absence and of presence are two specifications of a fundamental presence of Pierre to Thérèse and of Thérèse to Pierre. They are only different ways of expressing the presence and have meaning only through it. At London, in the East Indies, in

THE EXISTENCE OF OTHERS

America, on a desert island, Pierre is present to Thérèse who remains in Paris; he will cease to be present to her only at his death.

This is because a being is not *situated* in relation to locations by means of degrees of longitude and latitude. He is situated in a human space—between "the Guermantes side" and "Swann's side," and it is the immediate presence of Swann and of the Duchesse de Guermantes which allows the unfolding of the "hodological"[20] space in which he is situated. Now this presence has a location in transcendence; it is the presence-to-me in transcendence of my cousin in Morocco which allows me to enfold between him and me this road which situates-me-in-the-world and which can be called the road to Morocco. This road, indeed, is nothing but the distance between the Other-as-object which I could *perceive* in connection with my "being-for" and the Other-as-subject who is present to me without distance. Thus I am situated by the infinite diversity of the roads which lead me to the object of my world in correlation with the immediate presence of transcendent subjects. And as the world is given to me all at once with all its beings, these roads represent only the ensemble of instrumental complexes which allow me to cause an Other-as-object to appear as a "this" on the ground of the world, an Other-as-object who is already implicitly and really contained there.

But these remarks can be generalized; it is not only Pierre, René, Lucien, who are absent or present in relation to me on the ground of original presence, for they are not alone in contributing to situate me; I am situated also as a European in relation to Asiatics, or to Negroes, as an old man in relation to the young, as a judge in relation to delinquents, as a bourgeois in relation to workers, *etc.* In short it is in relation to every living man that every human reality is present or absent on the ground of an original presence. This original presence can have meaning only as a being-looked-at or as a being-looking-at; that is, according to whether the Other is an object for me or whether I myself am an object-for-the-Other. Being-for-others is a constant fact of my human reality, and I grasp it with its factual necessity in every thought, however slight, which I form concerning myself. Wherever I go, whatever I do, I only succeed in changing the distances between me and the Other-as-object, only avail myself of paths toward the Other. To withdraw, to approach, to discover this particular Other-as-object is only to effect empirical variations on the fundamental theme of my being-for-others. The Other is present to me everywhere as the one through whom I become an object. Hence I can indeed be mistaken concerning the empirical presence of an Other-as-object whom I happen to encounter on my path. I can indeed

---

[20] An expression borrowed from Lewin and explained by Sartre in *The Emotions*, pp. 57 and 65. It refers to a map or spatial organization of our environment in terms of our acts and needs. "The Guermantes side" and "Swann's side" are references to Proust's *Remembrance of Things Past*. Tr.

believe that it is Annie who is coming toward me on the road and discover that it is an unknown person; the fundamental presence of Annie to me is not thereby changed. I can indeed believe that it is a man who is watching me in the half light and discover that it is a trunk of a tree which I took for a human being; my fundamental presence to all men, the presence of all men to myself is not thereby altered. For the appearance of a man as an object in the field of my experience is not what informs me that there are men. My certainty of the Other's existence is independent of these experiences and is, on the contrary, that which makes them possible.

What appears to me then about which I can be mistaken is not the Other nor the real, concrete bond between the Other and Me; it is a this which can represent a man-as-object as well as not represent one. What is only probable is the distance and the real proximity of the Other; that is, his character as an object and his belonging to the world which I cause to be revealed are not doubtful inasmuch as I make an Other appear by my very upsurge. However this objectivity dissolves in the world as the result of the Other's being "an Other somewhere in the world." The Other-as-object is certain as an appearance correlative with the recovery of my subjectivity, but it is never certain that the Other is that object. Similarly the fundamental fact, my being-as-object for a subject is accompanied by evidence of the same type as reflective evidence, but the case is not the same for the fact that at this precise moment and for a particular Other, I am detached as "this" on the ground of the world rather than remaining drowned in the indistinction of the ground. It is indubitable that at present I exist as an object for some German or other. But do I exist as a Frenchman, as a Parisian in the indifferentiation of these collectivities or in my capacity as this Parisian around whom the Parisian population and the French collectivity are suddenly organized to serve for him as ground? On this point I shall never obtain anything but bits of probable knowledge although they can be infinitely probable.

We are able now to apprehend the nature of the look. In every look there is the appearance of an Other-as-object as a concrete and probable presence in my perceptive field; on the occasion of certain attitudes of that Other I determine myself to apprehend—through shame, anguish, etc.—my being-looked-at. This "being-looked-at" is presented as the pure probability that I am at present this concrete this—a probability which can derive its meaning and its very nature as probable, only from a fundamental certainty that the Other is always present to me inasmuch as I am always for-others. The experience of my condition as man, as an object for all other living men, as thrown in the arena beneath millions of looks and escaping myself millions of times—this experience I realize concretely on the occasion of the upsurge of an object into my universe if this object indicates to me that I am probably an object at present functioning as a differentiated this for a consciousness. The whole phenomenon, we call it the *look*. Each look makes us feel concretely—and in the indubitable certainty of the *cogito*—that we exist for all living men; that is, that there are (some) consciousnesses for whom I exist. We put "some" between parentheses to indicate that the Other-as-subject present to me in this look is not given in the form of plurality any more than as unity (save in its concrete relation to *one* particular Other-as-object). Plurality, in fact, belongs only to objects; it comes into being through the appearance of a world-making For-itself. The being-looked-at, by causing (some) subjects to arise for us, puts us in the presence of an unnumbered reality.

By contrast, as soon as I *look at* those who are looking at me, the *other* consciousnesses are isolated in multiplicity. On the other hand if I turn away from the look as the occasion of concrete proof and seek to think *emptily* of the infinite indistinction of the human presence and to unify it under the concept of the infinite subject which is never an object, then I obtain a purely formal notion which refers to an infinite series of mystic experiences of the presence of the Other, the notion of God as the omnipresent, infinite subject *for whom* I exist. But these two objectivations, the concrete, enumerating objectivation and the unifying, abstract objectivation, both lack proved reality—that is, the prenumerical presence of the Other.

These few remarks will become more concrete if we recall an experience familiar to everybody: if we happen to appear "in public" to act in a play or to give a lecture, we never lose sight of the fact that we are looked at, and we execute the ensemble of acts which we have come to perform *in the presence of* the look; better yet we attempt to constitute a being and an ensemble of objects for this look. But it remains unnumbered. While we are speaking, attentive only to the ideas which we wish to develop, the Other's presence remains undifferentiated. It would be wrong to unify it under the headings *class, audience, etc.* In fact we are not conscious of a concrete and individualized being with a collective consciousness; these are images which will be able to serve after the event to translate our experience and which will more than half betray it. But neither do we apprehend a plural look. It is a matter rather of an intangible reality, fleeting and omnipresent, which realizes our unrevealed Me confronting us and which collaborates with us in the production of this Me which escapes us. If on the other hand, I want to verify that my thought has been well understood and if in turn I look at the audience, then I shall suddenly see heads and eyes appear. When objectivized the prenumerical reality of the Other is decomposed and pluralized. But the look has disappeared as well. It is for this prenumerical concrete reality that we ought to reserve the term "they" rather than for human reality's state of unauthenticity. Wherever I am, *they* are perpetually looking at me. The *they* can never be apprehended as an object, for it immediately disintegrates.

Thus the look has set us on the track of our being-for-others and has revealed to us the indubitable existence of this Other for whom we are. But it can not lead us any further. What we must examine next is the fundamental relation of the Me to the Other as he has been revealed to us. Or if you prefer, we must at present make explicit and fix thematically everything which is included within the limits of this original relation and ask what is the *being* of this being-for-others.

There is one consideration which may be drawn from the preceding remarks and which will be of help to us. This is the fact that being-for-others is not an ontological structure of the For-itself. We can not think of deriving being-for-others from a being-for-itself as one would derive a consequence from a principle, nor conversely can we think of deriving being-for-itself from being-for-others. Of course our human-reality must of necessity be simultaneously for-itself and for-others, but our present investigation does not aim at constituting an anthropology. It would perhaps not be impossible to conceive of a For-itself which would be wholly free from all For-others and which would exist without even suspecting the possibility of being an object. But this For-itself simply would not be "man." What the *cogito* reveals to us here is just factual necessity: it is found—and this is indisputable—that our being along with its being-for-itself is also for-others; the being which is revealed to the reflective consciousness is for-itself-for-others. The Cartesian *cogito* only makes an affirmation of the absolute truth of a *fact*—that of my existence. In the same way the *cogito* a little expanded as we are using it here, reveals to us as a fact the existence of the Other and my existence for the Other. That is all we can say. It is also true that my being-for-others as the upsurge of my consciousness into being has the character of an absolute event. Since this event is at once an historization—for I temporalize myself as presence to others—and a condition of all history, we shall call it a pre-historic historization. It is as a prehistoric temporalization of simultaneity that we shall consider it here. By prehistoric we do not mean that it is in a time prior to history—which would not make sense—but that it is a part of that original temporalization which historicizes itself while making history possible. It is as fact—as a primary and perpetual fact—not as an *essential* necessity that we shall study being-for-others.

We have seen previously the difference which separates the internal type of negation from the external negation. In particular we have noted that the foundation of all knowledge of a determined being is the original relation by which in its very upsurge the For-itself has to be *as* not being this being. The negation which the For-itself thus realizes is an internal negation; the For-itself realizes it in its full freedom. Better yet, the for-itself *is* this negation in so far as it chooses itself as finitude. But the negation binds the For-itself indissolubly to the being which it is not, and we have been able to state that the For-itself includes in its being the being of the object which it is not, inasmuch as its being is in question as not being this being.

These observations are applicable without any essential change to the primary relation of the For-itself with the Other. If in general there is an Other, it is necessary above all that I be the one who is not the Other, and it is in this very negation effected by me upon myself that I make myself be and that the Other arises as the Other. This negation which constitutes my being and which, as Hegel said, makes me appear as the Same confronting the Other, constitutes me on the ground of a non-thetic selfness as "Myself." We must not understand by this that a Self comes to dwell in our consciousness but that selfness is reinforced by arising as a negation of another selfness and that this reinforcement is positively apprehended as the continuous choice of selfness by itself as the *same* selfness and as *this very selfness*. A for-itself which would have to be a self without being *itself* would be conceivable. The For-itself which I am simply has to be what it is in the form of a refusal of the Other; that is, as itself. Thus by utilizing the formulae applied to the knowledge of the Not-me in general, we can say that the For-itself as itself includes the being of the Other in its being in so far as its being is in question as not being the Other. In other words, in order for a consciousness to be able to not-be the Other and therefore in order that *there may be an Other* without making this non-being, which is the condition of the self of consciousness, become purely and simply the object of the establishment of a "third man" as witness, two things are necessary: consciousness must have to be itself and must spontaneously have to be this non-being; consciousness must freely disengage itself from the Other and wrench itself away by choosing itself as a nothingness which is simply Other than the Other and thereby must be reunited in "itself." This very detachment, which is the being of the For-itself, causes there to be an Other. This does not mean that it gives being to the Other but simply that it gives to the Other its being-other or the essential condition of the "there is." It is evident that for the For-itself the mode of being-what-is-not-the-Other is wholly paralyzed by Nothingness; the For-itself is what is not the Other in the nihilating mode of "the-reflection-reflecting." The not-being-the-Other is never *given* but perpetually chosen in a perpetual resurrection: consciousness can not-be the Other only in so far as it is consciousness (of) itself as not being the Other. Thus the internal negation, here as in the case of presence to the world, is a unitary bond of being. It is necessary that the Other be present to consciousness in every part and even that it penetrate consciousness completely in order that consciousness precisely by *being nothing* may escape that Other who threatens to ensnare it. If consciousness were abruptly to be something, the distinction between itself and the Other would disappear at the heart of a total undifferentiation.

This description, however, allows an essential addition which will radically modify its implications. When consciousness realized itself as not being a particular *this* in the world, the negative relation was not reciprocal. The *this* confronted did not make itself not-be consciousness; it was determined in and through consciousness not to be consciousness; its relation to consciousness remained that of pure indifferent exteriority. This is because the "this" preserved its nature as *in-itself*, and it was as *in-itself* that it was revealed to consciousness in the very negation by which the For-itself made itself be by denying that it was in-itself. But with regard to the Other, on the contrary, the internal negative relation is a relation of reciprocity. The being which consciousness has to not-be is defined as a being which has to not-be this consciousness. This is because at the time of the perception of the *this* in the world, consciousness differed from the *this* not only by its own individuality but also in its mode of being. It was *For-itself* confronting the *In-itself*. In the upsurge of the Other, however, consciousness is in no way different from the Other so far as its mode of being is concerned. The Other is what consciousness is. The Other is For-itself and consciousness, and he refers to possibles which are his possibles; he is himself by excluding the Other. There can be no question of viewing this opposition to the Other in terms of a pure numerical determination. We do not have *two* or *several* consciousnesses here; numbering supposes an external witness and is the pure and simple establishment of exteriority. There can be an *Other* for the For-itself only in a spontaneous and prenumerical negation. The Other exists for consciousness only as a *refused self*. But precisely because the Other is a self, he can himself be refused for and through me only insofar as it is his self *which refuses me*. I can neither apprehend nor conceive of a consciousness which does not apprehend me. The only consciousness which exists without apprehending me or refusing me and which I myself can conceive is not a consciousness isolated somewhere outside the world; it is my own. Thus the Other whom I recognize in order to refuse to be him is before all *else the one for whom my For-itself is*. Not only do I make myself not-be this other being by denying that he is me, I make myself not-be a being who is making himself not-be me.

This double negation, however, is in a sense self-destructive. One of two things happens: Either I make myself not-be a certain being, and then he is an object for me and I lose my object-ness for him; in this case the Other ceases to be the Other-Me—that is, the subject who makes me be an object by refusing to be me. Or else this being is indeed the Other and makes himself not-be me, in which case I become an object for him and he loses his own object-ness. Thus originally the Other is the Not-Me-not-object. Whatever may be the further steps in the dialectic of the Other, if the Other is to be at the start the Other, then on principle he can not be revealed in the same upsurge by which I deny being him. In this sense my fundamental negation can not be direct, for there is nothing on which it can be brought to bear.

What I refuse to be can be nothing but this refusal to be the Me by means of which the Other is making me an object. Or, if you prefer, I refuse my refused Me; I determine myself as Myself by means of the refusal of the Me-refused; I posit this refused Me as an alienated-Me in the same upsurge in which I wrench myself away from the Other. But I thereby recognize and affirm not only the Other but the existence of my Self-for-others. Indeed this is because I can not not-be the Other unless I assume my being-as-object for the Other. The disappearance of the alienated Me would involve the disappearance of the Other through the collapse of Myself. I escape the Other by leaving him with my alienated Me in his hands. But as I choose myself as a tearing away from the Other, I assume and recognize as mine this alienated Me. My wrenching away from the Other—that is, my Self—is by its essential structure an assumption as *mine* of this Me which the Other refuses; we can even say that it is *only that*.

Thus this Me which has been alienated and refused is simultaneously my bond with the Other and the symbol of our absolute separation. In fact to the extent that I am The One who makes there be an Other by means of the affirmation of my selfness, the Me-as-object is mine and I claim it; for the separation of the Other and of myself is never given; I am perpetually responsible for it in my being. But in so far as the Other is co-responsible for our original separation, this Me escapes me since it is what the Other makes himself not-be. Thus I claim as *mine* and for me a Me which escapes me. And since I make myself not-be the Other, in so far as the Other is a spontaneity identical with mine, it is precisely as Me-escaping-myself that I claim this Me-as-object. This Me-as-object is the Me *which I am* to the exact extent that it escapes me; in fact I should refuse it as mine if it could coincide with myself in a pure selfness.

Thus my being-for-others—i.e., my Me-as-object—is not an image cut off from me and growing in a strange consciousness. It is a perfectly real being, my being as the condition of my selfness confronting the Other and of the Other's selfness confronting me. It is my *being-outside*—not a being passively submitted to which would itself have come to me from outside, but an outside assumed and recognized as *my* outside. In fact it is possible for me to deny that the Other is me only in so far as the Other is himself a *subject*. If I immediately refused the Other as pure object—that is, as existing in the midst of the world—it would not be the Other which I refused but rather an object which on principle had nothing in common with subjectivity. I should remain defenseless before a total assimilation of myself to the Other for failing to take precautions within the true province of the Other—subjectivity—which is also *my* province. I can keep the Other at a distance only if I accept a limit to my subjectivity. But this limit can neither come from me nor be thought by me, for I can not limit myself; otherwise I should be a finite totality. On the other hand, in Spinoza's terms, thought can be limited only by thought. Consciousness can be limited only by consciousness. Now we can grasp the nature of my Self as-object: it is the limit between two consciousnesses as it is produced by the limiting consciousness and assumed by the limited consciousness. And we must understand it in the two senses of the word "limit." On the side of the limiting, indeed, the limit is apprehended as the container which contains me and surrounds me, the shell of emptiness which excludes me as a totality while putting me out of play; on the side of the limited, it is wholly a phenomenon of selfness and is as the mathematical limit is to the series which progresses toward it without ever reaching it. Every being which I have to be is at its limit like an asymptotic curve to a straight line. Thus I am a detotalized and indefinite totality, contained within a finite totality which surrounds me at a distance and which I am outside myself without ever being able either to realize it or even to touch it.

A good comparison for my efforts to apprehend myself and their futility might be found in that sphere described by Poincaré in which the temperature decreases as one goes from its center to its surface. Living beings attempt to arrive at the surface of this sphere by setting out from its center, but the lowering of temperature produces in them a continually increasing contraction. They tend to become infinitely flat proportionately to their approaching their goal, and because of this fact they are separated from the surface by an infinite distance. Yet this limit beyond reach, the Self-as-object, is not ideal; it is a real being. This being is not in-itself, for it is not produced in the pure exteriority of indifference. But neither is it for-itself, for it is not the being which I have to be by nihilating myself. It is precisely my being-for-others, this being which is divided between two negations with opposed origins and opposite meanings. For the Other is not this Me of which he has an intuition and I do not have the intuition of this Me which I am. Yet this Me, produced by the one and assumed by the other, derives its absolute reality from the fact that it is the only separation possible between two beings fundamentally identical as regards their mode of being and immediately present one to the other; for since consciousness alone can limit consciousness, no other mean is conceivable between them.

In view of this presence of the Other-as-subject to me in and through my assumed object-ness, we can see that my making an object out of the Other must be the second moment in my relation to him. In fact the Other's presence beyond my unrevealed limit can serve as motivation for my reapprehension of myself as a free selfness. To the extent that I deny that I am the Other and as the Other is first manifested, he can be manifested only as the Other; that is, as a subject beyond my limit, as the one who limits me. In fact nothing can limit me except the Other. Therefore he appears as the one who in his full freedom and in his free projection toward his possibles puts me out of play and strips me of my transcendences by refusing to "*join in*" (in the sense of the German *mit-machen*). Thus at first I must grasp only that one of the two negations for which I am not responsible, the one which does not come to me through myself. But in the very apprehension of this negation there arises the consciousness (of) myself as myself; that is, I can obtain an explicit self-consciousness inasmuch as I am also responsible for a negation of the Other which is my own possibility. This is the process of making explicit the second negation, the one which proceeds from me to the Other. In truth it was already there but hidden by the other negation since it was lost in order to make the other appear. But the other negation is the reason for the appearance of the new one; for if there is an Other who puts me out of play by positing my transcendence as purely contemplated, this is because I wrench myself away from the Other by assuming my limit. The consciousness (of) this wrenching away of the consciousness of (being) the same in relation to the Other is the consciousness (of) my free spontaneity. By this very wrenching away which puts the Other in possession of my limit, I am already putting the Other out of play. Therefore in so far as I am conscious (of) myself as of one of my free possibilities and in so far as I project myself toward myself in order to realize this selfness, to that extent I am responsible for the existence of the Other. It is I who by the very affirmation of my free spontaneity cause there to be an Other and not simply an infinite reference of consciousness to itself. The Other then finds himself put out of play; he is now what it depends on me to not-be, and thereby his transcendence is no longer a transcendence which *transcends me* toward himself but a purely contemplated transcendence, simply a *given* circuit of selfness. Since I can not realize both negations at once, the new negation, although it has the other negation for its motivation, in turn disguises it. The Other appears to me as a degraded presence. This is because the Other and I are in fact co-responsible for the Other's existence, but it is by two negations such that I can not experience the one without immediately disguising the second. Thus the Other becomes now what I limit in my very projection toward not-being-the-Other.

Naturally it is necessary to realize here that the motivation of this passage is of the affective order. For example, nothing would prevent me from remaining fascinated by this Unrevealed with its beyond if I did not realize this Unrevealed specifically in fear, in shame, or in pride. It is precisely the affective character of these motivations which accounts for the empirical contingency of these changes in point of view. But these feelings themselves are nothing more than our way of affectively experiencing our being-for-others. Fear in fact implies that I appear to myself as threatened by virtue of my being a presence in the world, not in my capacity as a For-itself which causes a world to exist. It is the object which I am which is in danger in the world and which as such, because of its indissoluble unity of being with the being which I have to be, can involve in its own ruin the ruin of the For-itself which I have to be. Fear is therefore the discovery of my being-as-object on the occasion of the appearance of another object in my perceptive field. It refers to the origin of all fear, which is the fearful discovery of my pure and simple object-state in so far as it is surpassed and transcended by possibles which are not my possibles. It is by thrusting myself toward my possibles that I shall escape fear to the extent that I shall consider my object-ness as non-essential. This can happen only if I apprehend myself as being responsible for the Other's being. The Other becomes then *that which I make myself not-be*, and his possibilities are possibilities which I refuse and which I can simply contemplate—hence dead-possibilities. Therefore I surpass my present possibilities in so far as I consider them as always able to be surpassed by the Other's possibilities, but I also surpass the Other's possibilities by considering them from the point of view of the only quality which he has which is not his own possibility—his very character as Other inasmuch as I cause there to be an Other. I surpass the Other's possibilities by considering them as possibilities of surpassing me which I can always surpass toward new possibilities. Thus by one and the same stroke I have regained my being-for-itself through my consciousness (of) myself as a perpetual center of infinite possibilities, and I have transformed the Other's possibilities into dead-possibilities by affecting them all with the character of *"not-lived-by-me"*—that is as *simply given*.

Similarly shame is only the original feeling of having my being *outside*, engaged in another being and as such without any defense, illuminated by the absolute light which emanates from a pure subject. Shame is the consciousness of being irremediably what I always was: "in suspense"—that is, in the mode of the "not-yet" or of the "already-no-longer." Pure shame is not a feeling of being this or that guilty object but in general of being *an* object; that is, of *recognizing myself* in this degraded, fixed, and dependent being which I am for the Other. Shame is the feeling of an *original fall*, not because of the fact that I may have committed this or that particular fault but simply that I have "fallen" into the world in the midst of things and that I need the mediation of the Other in order to be what I am.

Modesty and in particular the fear of being surprised in a state of nakedness are only a symbolic specification of original shame; the body symbolizes here our defenseless state as objects. To put on clothes is to hide one's object-state; it is to claim the right of seeing without being seen; that is, to be pure subject. This is why the Biblical symbol of the fall after the original sin is the fact that Adam and Eve "know that they are naked." The reaction to shame will consist exactly in apprehending as an object the one who apprehended my own object-state.

In fact from the moment that the Other appears to me as an object, his subjectivity becomes a simple *property* of the object considered. It is degraded and is defined as "an ensemble of *objective* properties which on principle elude me." The-Other-as-Object "has" a subjectivity as this hollow box has "an inside." In this way I *recover* myself, for I can not be *an object for an object*. I certainly do not deny that the Other remains connected with me "inside him," but the consciousness which he has of me, since it is consciousness-as-an-object, appears to me as pure interiority without efficacy. It is just one property among others of that "inside," something comparable to a sensitized plate in the closed compartment of a camera. In so far as I make there be an Other, I apprehend myself as the free source of the knowledge which the Other has of me, and the Other appears to me as *affected* in his being by that knowledge which he has of my being inasmuch as I have *affected* him with the character of Other. This knowledge takes on then a *subjective* character in the new sense of "relative;" that is, it remains in the subject-as-object as a quality *relative* to the being-other with which I have affected him. It no longer *touches* me; it is an image of *me in* him. Thus subjectivity is degraded into interiority, free consciousness into a pure absence of principles, possibilities into properties, and the knowledge by which the Other touches me in my being, into a pure *image* of me in the Other's "consciousness." Shame motivates the reaction which surpasses and overcomes the shame inasmuch as the reaction incloses within it an implicit and non-thematized comprehension of being-able-to-be-an-object on the part of the subject for whom I am an object. This implicit comprehension is nothing other than the consciousness (of) my "being-myself;" that is, of my selfness reinforced. In fact in the structure which expresses the experience "I am ashamed of myself," shame supposes a me-as-object for the Other but *also* a selfness which is ashamed and which is imperfectly expressed by the "I" of the formula. Thus shame is a unitary apprehension with three dimensions: "I am ashamed of *myself* before the Other."

If any one of these dimensions disappears, the shame disappears as well. If, however, I conceive of the "they" as a subject before whom I am ashamed, as he can not become an object without being scattered into a plurality of Others, if I posit it as the absolute unity of the subject which can in no way become an object, I thereby posit the eternity of my being-as-object and so perpetuate my shame. This is shame before God; that is, the recognition of my being-an-object before a subject which can never become an object. By the same stroke I *realize* my object-state in the absolute and hypostasize it. The positing of God is accompanied by a reification of my object-ness. Or better yet, I posit my being-an-object-for-God as more real than my For-itself; I exist alienated and I cause myself to learn from outside what I must be. This is the origin of fear before God. Black masses, desecration of the host, demonic associations, *etc.*, are so many attempts to confer the character of object on the absolute Subject. In desiring Evil for Evil's sake I attempt to contemplate the divine transcendence—for which Good is the peculiar possibility—as a purely given transcendence and one which I transcend toward Evil. Then I "make God suffer," I "irritate him," *etc.* These attempts, which imply the absolute *recognition* of God as a subject who can not be an object, carry their own contradiction within them and are always failures.

Pride does not exclude original shame. In fact it is on the ground of fundamental shame or shame of being an object that pride is built. It is an ambiguous feeling. In pride I recognize the Other as the subject through whom my being gets its object-state, but I recognize as well that I myself am also responsible for my object-ness. I emphasize my responsibility and I assume it. In one sense therefore pride is at first resignation; in order to be proud of *being that,* I must of necessity first resign myself to *being only that.* We are therefore dealing with a primary reaction to shame, and it is already a reaction of flight and of bad faith; for without ceasing to hold the Other as a subject, I try to apprehend myself as *affecting* the Other by my object-state. In short there are two authentic attitudes: that by which I recognize the Other as the subject through whom I get my object-ness—this is shame; and that by which I apprehend myself as the free object by which the Other gets his being-other—this is arrogance or the affirmation of my freedom confronting the Other-as-object. But pride—or vanity—is a feeling without equilibrium, and it is in bad faith. In vanity I attempt in my capacity as Object to act upon the Other. I take this beauty or this strength or this intelligence which he confers on me—in so far as he constitutes me as an object—and I attempt to make use of it in a return shock so as to affect him passively with a feeling of admiration or of love. But at the same time I demand that this feeling as the sanction of my being-as-object should be entertained by the Other in his capacity as subject—i.e., as a freedom. This is, in fact, the only way of conferring an absolute object-ness on my strength or on my beauty. Thus the feeling which I demand from the other carries within itself its own contradiction since I must affect the Other with it in so far as he is free. The feeling is entertained in the mode of bad faith, and its internal development leads it to disintegration. In fact as I play my assumed role of my being-as-object, I attempt to recover it *as an object.* Since the Other is the key to it, I attempt to lay hold of the Other so that he may release to me the secret of my being. Thus vanity impels me to get hold of the Other and to constitute him as an object in order to burrow into the heart of this object to discover there my own object-state. But this is to kill the hen that lays the golden eggs. By constituting the Other as object, I constitute myself as an image at the heart of the Other-as-object; hence the disillusion of vanity. In that image which I wanted to grasp in order to recover it and merge it with my own being, I no longer recognize myself. I must willy-nilly impute the image to the Other as one of his own subjective properties. Freed in spite of myself from my object-state, I remain alone confronting the Other-as-object in my unqualifiable selfness which I have to be forever without relief.

Shame, fear, and pride are my original reactions; they are only various ways by which I recognize the Other as a subject beyond reach, and they include within them a comprehension of my selfness which can and must serve as my motivation for constituting the Other as an object.

This Other-as-object who suddenly appears to me does not remain a purely objective abstraction. He rises before me with his particular meanings. He is not only the object which possesses freedom as a *property*, as a tran-scended transcendence. He is also "angry" or "joyful," or "attentive;" he is "amiable" or "disagreeable;" he is "greedy," "quick-tempered," etc. This is because while apprehending myself as myself, I make the Other-as-object exist in the midst of the world. I recognize his transcendence, but I recognize it not as a transcendence transcending, but as a transcendence transcended. It appears therefore as a surpassing of instruments toward ends to the exact extent that in my unitary projection of myself I surpass these ends, these instruments, and the Other's surpassing of the instruments, toward ends. This is because I never apprehend myself abstractly as the pure possibility of being myself, but I live my selfness in its concrete projection toward this or that particular end. I exist only as *engaged*.[21] and I am conscious (of) being only *as engaged*. Thus I apprehend the Other-as-object only in a concrete and *engaged* surpassing of his transcendence. But conversely the Other's engagement, which is his mode of being, appears to me, in so far as it is transcended by my transcendence, as a *real* engagement, as a *taking root*. In short, so far as I exist for-*myself*, my "engagement" in a situation must be understood in the sense in which we say: "I am engaged to a particular person, I am engaged to return that money," *etc.* It is this engagement which characterizes the Other-as-subject since he is another self like me. But when I grasp the Other as an object, his objectivized engagement is degraded and becomes an engage-ment-as-object in the sense in which we say, "The knife is deeply engaged in the wound." Or, "The army was engaged in a narrow pass." It must be understood that the being-in-the-midst-of-the-world which comes to the Other *through me* is a real being. It is not at all a purely subjective necessity which makes me know him as existing in the midst of the world. Yet on the other hand the Other did not by himself lose himself in the world. I make him lose himself in the world which is mine by the sole fact that he is for me the one who I have to not-be; that is, by the sole fact that I hold him outside

---

[21] Somewhat unhappy I have decided to use the English words "engage" and "engagement" for Sartre's *engager* and *engagement* simply because there is no one English word which conveys all the meaning of the French. In French *engager* includes the ideas of "commitment," of "involvement," of "immersion," and even of "entering," as well as the English sense of "engagement." Tr.

myself as a purely contemplated reality surpassed toward my own ends. Thus objectivity is not the pure refraction of the Other across my consciousness; it comes through me to the Other as a real qualification: I make the Other be in the midst of the world.

Therefore what I apprehend as real characteristics of the Other is a being-in-situation. In fact I organize him in the midst of the world in so far as he organizes the world toward himself; I apprehend him as the objective unity of instruments and of obstacles. In Part Two of this work we explained that the totality of instruments is the exact correlate of my possibilities.[22] Since I am my possibilities, the order of instruments in the world is the image of my possibilities projected into the in-itself; that is, the image of what I am. But this mundane image I can never decipher; I adapt myself to it in and through action. The Other inasmuch as he is a subject is found similarly *engaged in his image*. On the other hand, in so far as I grasp him as object, it is this mundane image which leaps to my eyes. The Other becomes the instrument which is defined by his relation with all other instruments; he is an order of my instruments which is included in the order which I impose on these instruments. To apprehend the Other is to apprehend this enclave-order and to refer it back to a central absence or "interiority;" it is to define this absence as a fixed flow of the objects of my world toward a definite object of my universe. And the meaning of this flow is furnished to me by those objects themselves. The arrangement of the hammer and nails, of the chisel and marble, the arrangement which I surpass without being its foundation defines the meaning of this internal hemorrhage in the world.

Thus the world announces the Other to me in his totality and as a totality. To be sure, the announcement remains ambiguous. But this is because I grasp the order of the world toward the Other as an undifferentiated totality on the ground of which certain explicit structures appear. If I could make explicit all the instrumental complexes as they are turned toward the Other (that is, if I could grasp not only the place which the hammer and the nails occupy in this complex of instrumentality but also the street, the city, the nation, *etc.*), I should have defined explicitly and totally the being of the Other as object. If I am mistaken concerning an intention of the Other, this is not because I refer his gesture to a subjectivity beyond reach; this subjectivity in itself and by itself has no common measure with the gesture, for it is transcendence for itself, an unsurpassable transcendence. But I am mistaken because I organize the entire world around this gesture differently than it is organized in fact. Thus by the sole fact that the Other appears as object, he is given to me on principle as a totality; he is extended across the whole world as a mundane power for the synthetic organization of this world. I can not make this

---

[22] Part Two, ch. III, Section iii.

synthetic organization explicit any more than I can make the world itself explicit in so far as it is my world. The difference between the Other-as-subject—i.e., between the Other such as he is for-himself—and the Other-as-object is not a difference between the whole and the part or between the hidden and the revealed. The Other-as-object is on principle a whole co-extensive with subjective totality; nothing is hidden and in so far as objects refer to other objects, I can increase indefinitely my knowledge of the Other by indefinitely making explicit his relations with other instruments in the world. The ideal of knowledge of the Other remains the exhaustive specification of the meaning of the flow of the world. The difference of principle between the Other-as-object and the Other-as-subject stems solely from this fact: that the Other-as-subject can in no way be known nor even conceived as such. There is no problem of the knowledge of the Other-as-subject, and the objects of the world do not refer to his subjectivity; they refer only to his object-state in the world as the meaning—surpassed toward my selfness—of the intra-mundane flow.

Thus the Other's presence to me as the one who produces my object-state is experienced as a subject-totality. If I turn toward this presence in order to grasp it, I apprehend the Other once more as totality: an object-totality co-extensive with the totality of the world. This apprehension is made all of a sudden; it is from the standpoint of the entire world that I arrive at the Other-as-object. But it is never anything but particular relations which come out in relief like figures on the ground of the world. Around this man whom I do not know and who is reading in the subway, the entire world is present. It is not his body only—as an object in the world—which defines him in his being; it is his identity card, it is the direction of the particular train which he has boarded, it is the ring which he wears on his finger. Not as the signs of what he is—this notion of a sign, in fact, would refer us to a subjectivity which I can not even conceive and in which he is precisely nothing, strictly speaking, since he is what he is not and is not what he is—but by virtue of real characteristics of his being. Yet if I know that he is in the midst of the world, in France, in Paris, in the process of reading, still for lack of seeing his identity card, I can only suppose that he is a foreigner (which means: to suppose that he is subject to special regulations, that he figures on some official register, that I must speak to him in Dutch, or in Italian in order to obtain from him this or that particular gesture, that the international post directs toward him by this or that route letters bearing this or that stamp, etc.). Yet this identity card is on principle given to me in the midst of the world. It does not escape me—from the moment that it was created, it has been set to existing for me. It exists in an implicit state like each point of the circle which I see as a completed form. And it would be necessary to change the present totality of my relations to the world in order to make the identity card appear as an explicit *this* on the ground of the universe. In the same way the anger of the Other-as-object as it is manifested to me across his cries, his stamping, and his threatening gestures is not the *sign* of a subjective and hidden anger; it refers to nothing except to other gestures and to other cries. It defines the Other, it is the Other. To be sure, I can be mistaken and can take for true anger what is only a pretended irritation. But it is only in relation to other gestures and to other *objectively* apprehensible acts that I can be mistaken. I am mistaken if I apprehend the motion of his hand as a *real* intention to hit me. That is, I am mistaken if I interpret it as the function of an objectively discernible gesture which will not take place. In a word the anger objectively apprehended is a disposition of the world around an intra-mundane presence-absence.

Does this mean that we must grant that the Behaviorists are right? Certainly not. For although the Behaviorists interpret man in terms of his situation, they have lost sight of his characteristic principle, which is transcendence-transcended. In fact if the Other is the object which can not be limited to himself, he is also the object which is understood only in terms of his end. Of course the hammer and the saw are not understood any differently. Both are apprehended through their function; that is, through their end. But this is exactly because they are already human. I can understand them only in so far as they refer me to an instrumental-organization in which the Other is the center, only in so far as they form a part of a complex wholly transcended toward an end which I in turn transcend. If then we can compare the Other to a machine, this is because the machine as a human fact presents already the trace of a transcendence-transcended, just as the looms in a mill are explained only by the fabrics which they produce. The Behaviorist point of view must be reversed, and this reversal, moreover, will leave the Other's objectivity intact. For that which first of all is objective—what we shall call *signification* after the fashion of French and English psychologists, *intention* according to the Phenomenologists, *transcendence* with Heidegger, or *form* with the Gestalt School—this is the fact that the Other can be defined only by a total organization of the world and that he is the key to this organization. If therefore I return from the world to the Other in order to define him, this is not because the world would make me understand the Other but because the Other-as-object is nothing but a center of autonomous and intra-mundane reference in my world.

Thus the objective fear which we can apprehend when we perceive the Other-as-object is not the ensemble of the physiological manifestations of disorder which we see or which we measure with sphygmograph or a stethoscope. Fear is a flight; it is a fainting. These phenomena themselves are not released to us as a pure series of *movements* but as transcendence-transcended: the flight or the fainting is not only that desperate running through the brush, nor that heavy fall on the stones of the road; it is the total upheaval of the instrumental-organization which had the Other for its center. This soldier who is fleeing formerly had the Other-as-enemy at the point of his gun. The distance from him to the enemy was measured by the trajectory of his bullet, and I too could apprehend and transcend that distance as a distance organized round the "soldier" as center. But behold now he throws his gun in the ditch and is trying to save himself. Immediately the presence of the enemy surrounds him and presses in upon him; the enemy, who had been held at a distance by the trajectory of the bullets, leaps upon him at the very instant when the trajectory collapses; at the same time that land in the background, which he was defending and against which he was leaning as against a wall, suddenly opens fan-wise and becomes the foreground, the welcoming horizon toward which he is fleeing for refuge. All this I establish objectively, and it is precisely this which I apprehend as fear. Fear is nothing but a magical conduct tending by incantation to suppress the frightening objects which we are unable to keep at a distance.[23] It is precisely through its results that we apprehend fear, for it is given to us as a new type of internal hemorrhage in the world—the passage from the world to a type of magical existence.

We must be careful however to remember that the Other is a qualified object for me only to the extent that I can be one for him. Therefore he will be objectivized as a non-individualized portion of the "they" or as purely "absent" represented by his letters and his written accounts of himself or as this man present in fact, according to whether I shall have been myself an element for him of the "they" or a "dear absent one" or a concrete "this man." What decides in each case the type of objectivation of the Other and of his qualities is both my situation in the world and his situation; that is, the instrumental complexes which we have each organized and the various thises which appear to each one of us on the ground of the world. All this naturally brings us to facticity. It is my facticity and the Other's facticity which decide whether the Other can see me and whether I can see this particular Other. But the problem of facticity is beyond the scope of this general exposition. We shall consider it in the course of the next chapter.

Thus I experience the Other's presence as a quasi-totality of subjects in my being-an-object-for-Others, and on the ground of this totality I can experience more particularly the presence of a concrete subject without however being able to specify it as that particular Other. My defensive reaction to my object-state will cause the Other to appear before me in the capacity of this or that object. As such he will appear to me as a "this-one;" that is, his subjective quasi-totality is degraded and becomes a totality-as-object co-extensive with the totality of the World. This totality is revealed to me without

---

[23] Cf. The Emotions.

reference to the Other's subjectivity. The relation of the Other-as-subject to the Other-as-object is in no way comparable to that which we usually establish, for example, between the physical object and the object of perception. The Other-as-object is revealed to me for what he is, he refers only to himself. The Other-as-object is simply such as he appears to me on the plane of object-ness in general and in his being-as-object; it is not even conceivable that I should refer back any knowledge which I have of him to his subjectivity such as I experience it on the occasion of the look. The Other-as-object is only an object, but my apprehension of him includes the comprehension of the fact that I could always and on principle produce from him another *experience* by placing myself on another plane of being. This comprehension is constituted on the one hand by the *empirical knowledge* of my past experience—which is moreover as we have seen, the pure past (out of reach and what I have to be) of this experience, and on the other hand it is constituted by an implicit apprehension of the dialectic of the Other. The Other is at present what I make myself not-be. But although for the instant I am rid of him and escape him, there remains around him the permanent possibility that he may *make himself* other. Nevertheless this possibility, foreseen in the embarrassment and constraint which forms the specific quality of my attitude confronting the Other-as-object, is strictly speaking *inconceivable*: first because I can not conceive of a possibility which is not *my* possibility nor can I apprehend transcendence except by transcending it—that is, by grasping it as a transcendence-transcended; secondly because this anticipated possibility is not the possibility of the Other-as-object—the possibilities of the Other-as-object are dead-possibilities which refer to other objective aspects of the Other. The peculiar possibility of apprehending myself as an object is the possibility belonging to the Other-as-subject and hence is not for a me a living possibility; it is an absolute possibility—which derives its source only from itself—that on the ground of the total annihilation of the Other-as-object, there may occur the upsurge of an Other-as-subject which I shall experience across my objectivity-for-him.

Thus the Other-as-object is an explosive instrument which I handle with care because I foresee around him the permanent possibility that *they* are going to make it explode and that with this explosion I shall suddenly experience the flight of the world away from me and the alienation of my being. Therefore my constant concern is to contain the Other within his objectivity, and my relations with the Other-as-object are essentially made up of ruses designed to make him remain an object. But one look on the part of the Other is sufficient to make all these schemes collapse and to make me experience once more the transfiguration of the Other. Thus I am referred from transfiguration to degradation and from degradation to transfiguration without ever being able either to get a total view of the ensemble of these two modes of being on the part of the Other—for each of them is self-sufficient and refers only to itself—or to hold firmly to either one of them—for each has its own instability and collapses in order for the other to rise from its ruins. Only the dead can be perpetually objects without every becoming subjects—for to die is not to lose one's objectivity in the midst of the world; all the dead are there in the world around us. But to die is to lose all possibility of revealing oneself as subject to an Other.

At this point in our investigation now we have elucidated the essential structures of being-for-others, there is an obvious temptation to raise the metaphysical question: "Why are there Others?" As we have seen, the existence of Others is not a consequence which can derive from the ontological structure of the for-itself. It is a primary event, to be sure, but of a *metaphysical* order; that is, it results from the contingency of being. The question "why" is essentially connected with these metaphysical existences.

We know very well that the answer to the "why" can only refer us to an original contingency, but still it is necessary to prove that the metaphysical phenomenon which we are considering is an irreducible contingency. In this sense ontology appears to us capable of being defined as the specification of the structures of being of the existent taken as a totality, and we shall define metaphysics rather as raising the question of the existence of the existent. This is why in view of the absolute contingency of the existent, we are convinced that any metaphysics must conclude with a "that is"—i.e., in a direct intuition of that contingency.

Is it possible to pose the question of the existence of Others? Is this existence an irreducible fact, or is it to be derived from a fundamental contingency? Such are the preliminary questions which we can in turn pose to the metaphysician who questions us concerning the existence of Others.

Let us examine more closely the possibility of the metaphysical question. What appears to us first is the fact that the being-for-others represents the third ekstasis of the for-itself. The first ekstasis is indeed the tridimensional projection on the part of the for-itself toward a being which it has to be in the mode of non-being. It represents the first fissure, the nihilation which the for-itself has to be, the wrenching away on the part of the for-itself from everything which it is, and this wrenching away is constitutive of its being. The second ekstasis or reflective ekstasis is the wrenching away from this very wrenching away. The reflective scissiparity corresponds to a vain attempt to take a point of view on the nihilation which the for-itself has to be, in order that this nihilation as a simply given phenomenon may be a nihilation which is. But at the same time reflection wants to recover this wrenching away, which it attempts to contemplate as a pure given, by affirming concerning itself that it is this nihilation which is. This is a flagrant contradiction: in order to be able to apprehend my transcendence, I should have to transcend it. But my own transcendence can only transcend. I *am* my own transcendence; I can not make use of it so as to constitute it as a transcendence-transcended. I am condemned to be forever my own nihilation. In short reflection (*reflexion*) *is* the reflected-on.

The reflective nihilation, however, is pushed further than that of the pure for-itself as a simple self-consciousness. In self-consciousness, in fact, the two terms of the dyad "reflected-reflecting" (*reflété-reflétant*) were so incapable of presenting themselves separately that the duality remained perpetually evanescent and each term while positing itself for the other *became* the other. But with reflection the case is different since the "reflection-reflecting" which is reflected-on exists for a "reflection-reflecting" which is reflective. Reflected-on and reflective, therefore, each tend toward independence, and the *nothing* which separates them tends to divide them more profoundly than the *nothingness* which the For-itself has to be separates the reflection from the reflecting. Yet neither the reflective nor the reflected-on can secrete this separating nothingness, for in that case reflection (*reflexion*) would be an autonomous for-itself coming to direct itself on the reflected-on, which would be to suppose an external negation as the preliminary condition of an internal negation. There can be no reflection if it is not entirely a *being*, a being which has to be its own nothingness.

Thus the reflective ekstasis is found on the path to a more radical ekstasis—the being-for-others. The final term of the nihilation, the ideal pole should be in fact the external negation—that is, a scissiparity in-itself or the spatial exteriority of indifference. In relation to this external negation the three ekstases are ranked in the order which we have just presented, but the goal is never achieved. It remains on principle ideal; in fact the for-itself—without running the risk of ceasing by the same stroke to be-for-itself—can not by itself realize in relation to any being a negation which would be in-itself. The constitutive negation of being-for-others is therefore *an internal negation*; it is a nihilation which the for-itself has to be, just like the reflective nihilation. But here the scissiparity attacks the very negation; it is no longer only the negation which divides being into reflected and reflecting and in turn divides the dyad reflected-reflecting into (reflected-reflecting) reflected and (reflected-reflecting) reflecting. Here the negation is divided into two internal and opposed negations; each is an internal negation, but they are nevertheless separated from one another by an inapprehensible external nothingness. In fact since each of them is exhausted in denying that one for-itself is the other and since each negation is wholly engaged in that being which it has to be, it is no longer in command of itself so as to deny concerning itself that it is the opposite negation. Here suddenly appears the *given*, not as the result of an identity of being-in-itself but as a sort of phantom of exteriority which neither of the negations has to be and which yet separates them. Actually in the reflective being we have already found the beginning of this negative inversion. In fact the reflective as a witness is profoundly affected in its being by its reflectivity, and consequently in so far as it makes itself reflective, it aims at not being the reflected-on. But reciprocally the reflected-on is self-consciousness as the reflected-on consciousness of this or that transcendent phenomenon. We said of it that it knows itself looked-at. In this sense it aims on its part at not-being the reflective since every consciousness is defined by its negativity. But this tendency to a double schism was recovered and stifled by the fact that in spite of everything the reflective had to be the reflected-on and that the reflected-on had to be the reflective. The double negation remained evanescent.

In the case of the third ekstasis we behold a reflective scissiparity pushed further. The results may surprise us: on the one hand, since the negations are effected in interiority, the Other and myself can not come to one another from the outside. It is necessary that there be a *being* "I-and-the-Other" which has to be the reciprocal scissiparity of the for-others just as the totality "reflective-reflected-on" is a being which has to be its own nothingness; that is, my selfness and that of the Other are structures of one and the same totality of being. Thus Hegel appears to be right: the point of view of the totality is the point of view of being, the *true* point of view. Everything happens as if my selfness confronting that of the Other were produced and maintained by a totality which would push its own nihilation to the extreme; being-for-others appears to be the prolongation of the pure reflective scissiparity. In this sense everything happens as if the Other and myself indicated the vain effort of a totality of for-itself to reapprehend itself and to envelop what it *has to be* in the pure and simple mode of the in-itself. This effort to reapprehend itself as object is pushed here to the limit—that is, well beyond the reflective division—and would produce a result precisely the reverse of the end toward which this totality would project itself. By its effort to be self-consciousness the totality-for-itself would be constituted in the face of the self as a self-as-consciousness which has to not-be the self of which it is consciousness. Conversely the self-as-object in order to *be* would have to experience itself as made-to-be by and for a consciousness which it has to not-be if it wishes to be. Thus would be born the schism of the for-others, and this dichotomic division would be repeated to infinity in order to constitute a plurality of consciousnesses as fragments of a radical explosion. "There would be" numerous *Others* as the result of a failure the reverse of the reflective failure. In reflection in fact if I do not succeed in apprehending myself as an object but only as a quasi-object, this is because I am the object which I wish to grasp; I have to be the nothingness which separates me from myself. I can escape my selfness neither by taking a point of view on myself (for thus I do not succeed in realizing myself as being) nor by apprehending myself in the form of the "there is" (here the recovery fails because the recoverer is to himself the recovered). In the case of being-for-others, on the contrary, the scissiparity is pushed further; the (reflection-reflecting) reflected is radically distinct from the (reflection-reflecting) reflecting and thereby can be an object for it. But this time the recovery fails because the recovered is *not* the one recovering. Thus the totality which is not what it is but which is what it is not, would—as the result of a radical attempt at wrenching away from self— everywhere produce its being as an "elsewhere." The scattering of being-in- itself of a shattered totality, always elsewhere, always at a distance, never in itself, but always maintained in being by the perpetual explosion of this totality—such would be the being of others and of myself as other.

But on the other hand, *simultaneously* with my negation of myself, the Other denies concerning himself that he is me. These two negations are equally indispensible to being-for-others, and they can not be reunited by any syn- thesis. This is not because an external nothingness would have separated them at the start but rather because the in-itself would recapture each one in relation to the other by the mere fact that each one is *not* the other without having to not-be the other. There is here a kind of limit of the for-itself which stems from the for-itself itself but which qua limit is independent of the for- itself. We rediscover something like facticity and we can not conceive how the totality of which we were speaking earlier would have been able at the very heart of the most radical wrenching away to produce in its being a nothing- ness which it in no way has to be. In fact it seems that this nothingness has slipped into this totality in order to shatter it just as in the atomism of Leucippus non-being slips into the Parmenidean totality of being and makes it explode into atoms. Therefore it represents the negation of any synthetic totality in terms of which one might claim to understand the plurality of consciousnesses. Of course it is inapprehensible since it is produced neither by the Other nor by myself, nor by any intermediary, for we have established that consciousnesses experience one another without intermediary. Of course where we direct our sight, we encounter as the object of our descrip- tion only a pure and simple internal negation. Yet it is there in the irreducible fact that there is a *duality* of negations. It is not, to be sure, the *foundation* of the multiplicity of consciousnesses, for if it existed before this multiplicity, it would make all *being-for* others impossible. On the contrary, we must conceive of it as the expression of this multiplicity; it appears with this multiplicity. But since there is *nothing* which can found it, neither a particular conscious- ness nor a totality exploding into consciousnesses, it appears as a pure, irreducible contingency. It is *the fact that my denial that I am the Other is not sufficient to make the Other exist, but that the Other must simultaneously with my own negation deny that he is me.* It is the facticity of being-for-others.

Thus we arrive at this contradictory conclusion: being-for-others can be only if it is *made-to-be* by a totality which is lost so that being-for-others may arise, a position which would lead us to postulate the existence and passion of the mind. But on the other hand, this being-for-others can exist only if it involves an inapprehensible and external non-being which no totality, not even the mind, can produce or found. In one sense the existence of a plurality of consciousnesses can not be a primary fact and it refers us to an original fact of a wrenching away from self, a fact of the mind. Thus the question "Why is there a plurality of consciousnesses?" could receive an answer. But in another sense the facticity of this plurality seems to be irreducible; and if the mind is considered from the standpoint of the *fact* of the plurality, it vanishes. Then the metaphysical question no longer has meaning; we have encountered a fundamental contingency, and we can answer only by "So it is." Thus the original ekstasis is deepened; it appears that we can not assign to the nothingness its share. The for-itself has appeared to us as a being which exists in so far as it is not what it is and is what it is not. The ekstatic totality of the mind is not simply a totality detotalized; it appears to us as a shattered being concerning which we can neither say that it exists or that it does not exist. Thus our description has enabled us to satisfy the preliminary conditions which we have posited for any theory about the existence of the Other. The multiplicity of consciousnesses appears to us as a *synthesis* and not as a *collection*, but it is a synthesis whose totality is inconceivable.

Is this to say that the antinomic nature of the totality is itself an irreducible? Or from a higher point of view can we make it disappear? Ought we to posit that the mind is the *being which is and is not* just as we posited that the for-itself is what it is not and is not what it is? The question has no meaning. It is supposing that it is possible for us to *take a point of view* on the totality; that is, to consider it from outside. But this is impossible precisely because I exist as myself on the foundation of this totality and to the extent that I am engaged in it. No consciousness, not even God's, can "see the underside"—that is, apprehend the totality as such. For if God is consciousness, he is integrated in the totality. And if by his nature, he is a being *beyond consciousness* (that is, an in-itself which would be its own foundation) still the totality can appear to him only as *object* (in that case he lacks the totality's internal disintegration as the subjective effort to reapprehend the self) or as *subject* (then since God is not this subject, he can only experience it without knowing it.) Thus no point of view on the totality is conceivable; the totality has no "outside," and the very question of the meaning of the "underside" is stripped of meaning. We cannot go further.

Here we have arrived at the end of this exposition. We have learned that the Other's existence was experienced with evidence in and through the fact of my objectivity. We have seen also that my reaction to my own alienation for the Other was expressed in my grasping the Other as an object. In short, the

Other can exist for us in two forms: if I experience him with evidence, I fail to know him; if I know him, if I act upon him, I only reach his being-as-object and his probable existence in the midst of the world. No synthesis of these two forms is possible. But we can not stop here. This object which the Other is for me and this object which I am for him are manifested each *as a body*. What then is my body? What is the body of the Other?

# 2

## THE BODY

The problem of the body and its relations with consciousness is often obscured by the fact that while the body is from the start posited as a certain thing having its own laws and capable of being defined from outside, consciousness is then reached by the type of inner intuition which is peculiar to it. Actually if after grasping "my" consciousness in its absolute interiority and by a series of reflective acts, I then seek to unite it with a certain living object composed of a nervous system, a brain, glands, digestive, respiratory, and circulatory organs whose very matter is capable of being analyzed chemically into atoms of hydrogen, carbon, nitrogen, phosphorus, etc., then I am going to encounter insurmountable difficulties. But these difficulties all stem from the fact that I try to unite my consciousness not with my body but with the body of others. For the body which I have just described is not my body such as it is for me. I have never seen and never shall see my brain nor my endocrine glands. But because I who am a man have seen the cadavers of men dissected, because I have read articles on physiology, I conclude that my body is constituted exactly like all those which have been shown to me on the dissection table or of which I have seen colored drawings in books. Of course the physicians who have taken care of me, the surgeons who have operated on me, have been able to have direct experience with the body which I myself do not know. I do not disagree with them, I do not claim that I lack a brain, a heart, or a stomach. But it is most important to choose the order of our bits of knowledge. So far as the physicians have had any experience with my body, it was with my body in the midst of the world and as it is for others. My body as it is for me does not appear to me in the midst of the world. Of course during a radioscopy I was able to see the picture of my vertebrae on a screen, but I was outside in the midst of the world.

I was apprehending a wholly constituted object as a this among other thises, and it was only by a reasoning process that I referred it back to being mine; it was much more my property than my being.

It is true that I see and touch my legs and my hands. Moreover nothing prevents me from imagining an arrangement of the sense organs such that a living being could see one of his eyes while the eye which was seen was directing its glance upon the world. But it is to be noted that in this case again I am the Other in relation to my eye. I apprehend it as a sense organ constituted in the world in a particular way, but I can not "see the seeing;" that is, I can not apprehend it in the process of revealing an aspect of the world to me. Either it is a thing among other things, or else it is that by which things are revealed to me. But it can not be both at the same time. Similarly I see my hand touching objects, but do not know it in its act of touching them. This is the fundamental reason why that famous "sensation of effort" of Maine de Biran does not really exist. For my hand reveals to me the resistance of objects, their hardness or softness, but not itself. Thus I see my hand only in the way that I see this inkwell. I unfold a distance between it and me, and this distance comes to integrate itself in the distances which I establish among all the objects of the world. When a doctor takes my wounded leg and looks at it while I, half raised up on my bed, watch him do it, there is no essential difference between the visual perception which I have of the doctor's body and that which I have of my own leg. Better yet, they are distinguished only as different structures of a single global perception; there is no essential difference between the doctor's perception of my leg and my own present perception of it. Of course when I touch my leg with my finger, I realize that my leg is touched. But this phenomenon of double sensation is not essential: cold, a shot of morphine, can make it disappear. This shows that we are dealing with two essentially different orders of reality. To touch and to be touched, to feel that one is touching and to feel that one is touched—these are two species of phenomena which it is useless to try to reunite by the term "double sensation." In fact they are radically distinct, and they exist on two incommunicable levels. Moreover when I touch my leg or when I see it, I surpass it toward my own possibilities. It is, for example, in order to pull on my trousers or to change a dressing on my wound. Of course I can at the same time arrange my leg in such a way that I can more conveniently "work" on it. But this does not change the fact that I transcend it toward the pure possibility of "curing myself" and that consequently I am present to it without its being me and without my being it. What I cause to exist here is the thing "leg;" it is not the leg as the possibility which I am of walking, running, or of playing football.

Thus to the extent that my body indicates my possibilities in the world, seeing my body or touching it is to transform these possibilities of mine into dead-possibilities. This metamorphosis must necessarily involve a complete *thisness* with regard to the body as a living possibility of running, of dancing, *etc.* Of course, the discovery of my body as an object is indeed a revelation of its being. But the being which is thus revealed to me is its *being-for-others*. That this confusion may lead to absurdities can be clearly seen in connection with the famous problem of "inverted vision." We know the question posed by the physiologists: "How can we set upright the objects which are painted upside down on our retina?" We know as well the answer of the philosophers: "There is no problem. An object is upright or inverted in relation to the rest of the universe. To perceive the whole universe inverted means nothing, for it would have to be inverted in relation to something." But what particularly interests us is the origin of this false problem. It is the fact that people have wanted to link my consciousness of objects to the body of the Other. Here are the candle, the crystalline lens, the inverted image on the screen of the retina. But to be exact, the retina enters here into a physical system; it is a *screen* and only that; the crystalline lens is a *lens* and only a lens; both are homogeneous in their being with the candle which completes the system. Therefore we have deliberately chosen the physical point of view— i.e., the point of view of the outside, of exteriority—in order to study the problem of vision; we have considered a dead eye in the midst of the visible world in order to account for the visibility of this world. Consequently, how can we be surprised later when consciousness, which is absolute interiority, refuses to allow itself to be bound to this object? The relations which I establish between the Other's body and the external object are *really* existing relations, but they have for their being the being of the for-others; they suppose a center of intra-mundane flow in which knowledge is a *magic* property such as, "action at a distance." From the start they are placed in the perspective of the Other-as-object.

If then we wish to reflect on the nature of the body, it is necessary to establish an order of our reflections which conforms to the order of being: we can not continue to confuse the ontological levels, and we must in succession examine the body first as being-for-itself and then as being-for-others. And in order to avoid such absurdities as "inverted vision," we must keep constantly in mind the idea that since these two aspects of the body are on different and incommunicable levels of being, they can not be reduced to one another. Being-for-itself must be wholly body and it must be wholly consciousness; it can not be *united* with a body. Similarly being-for-others is wholly body; there are no "psychic phenomena" there to be united with the body. There is nothing *behind* the body. But the body is wholly "psychic." We must now proceed to study these two modes of being which we find for the body.

## I. THE BODY AS BEING-FOR-ITSELF: FACTICITY

It appears at first glance that the preceding observations are opposed to the givens of the Cartesian *cogito*. "The soul is easier to know than the body," said Descartes. Thereby he intended to make a radical distinction between the facts of thought, which are accessible to reflection, and the facts of the body, the knowledge of which must be guaranteed by divine Providence. It appears at first that reflection reveals to us only pure facts of consciousness. Of course on this level we encounter phenomena which appear to include within themselves some connection with the body; "physical" pain, the uncomfortable, pleasure, *etc.* But these phenomena are no less *pure facts of consciousness*. There is a tendency therefore to make *signs* out of them, affections of consciousness occasioned by the body, without realizing that one has thereby irremediably driven the body out of consciousness and that no bond will ever be able to reunite this body, which is already a body-for-others, with the consciousness which, it is claimed, makes the body manifest.

That is why we ought not to take this as our point of departure but rather our primary relation to the in-itself: our being-in-the-world. We know that there is not a for-itself on the one hand and a world on the other as two closed entities for which we must subsequently seek some explanation as to how they communicate. The for-itself is a relation to the world. The for-itself, by denying that it is being, makes there be a world, and by surpassing this negation toward its own possibilities it reveals the "thises" as instrumental-things.

But when we say that the for-itself is-in-the-world, that consciousness is consciousness of the world, we must understand that the world exists in front of consciousness as an indefinite multiplicity of reciprocal relations which consciousness flies over without perspective and contemplates without a point of view. For *me* this glass is to the left of the decanter and a little behind it; for *Pierre*, it is to the right and a little in front. It is not even conceivable that a consciousness could fly over the world in such a way that the glass should be *simultaneously* given to it at the right and at the left of the decanter, in front of it and behind it. This is by no means the consequence of a strict application of the principle of identity but because this fusion of right and left, of before and behind, would result in the total disappearance of "*thises*" at the heart of a primitive indistinction. Similarly if the table leg hides the designs in the rug from my sight, this is not the result of some finitude and some imperfection in my visual organs, but it is because a rug which would not be hidden by the table, a rug which would not be either under it or above it or to one side of it, would not have any relation of any kind with the table and would no longer belong to the "world" in which there is the table. The in-itself which is made manifest in the form of the *this* would return to its indifferent self-identity. Even space as a purely external relation would disappear. The constitution of space as a multiplicity of reciprocal relations can be effected only from the abstract point of view of science; it can not be lived, it can not even be represented. The triangle which I trace on the blackboard so as to help me in abstract reasoning is necessarily to the right of the circle tangent to one of its sides, necessarily to the extent that it is on the blackboard. And my effort is to surpass the concrete characteristics of the figure traced in chalk by not including its relation to me in my calculations any more than the thickness of the lines or the imperfection of the drawing.

Thus by the mere fact that there is a world, this world can not exist without a univocal orientation in relation to me. Idealism has rightly insisted on the fact that relation makes the world. But since idealism took its position on the ground of Newtonian science, it conceived this relation as a relation of reciprocity. Thus it attained only abstract concepts of pure exteriority, of action and reaction, etc., and due to this very fact it missed the world and succeeded only in making explicit the limiting concept of absolute objectivity. This concept in short amounted to that of a "*desert world*" or of "a world without men;" that is, to a contradiction, since it is through human reality that there is a world. Thus the concept of objectivity, which aimed at replacing the in-itself of dogmatic truth by a pure relation of reciprocal agreement between representations, is self-destructive if pushed to the limit.

Moreover the progress of science has led to rejecting this notion of absolute objectivity. What Broglie is led to call "experience" is a system of univocal relations from which the observer is not excluded. If microphysics must reintegrate the observer into the heart of the scientific system, this is not pure subjectivity—this notion would have no more meaning than that of pure objectivity—but as an original relation to the world, as a place, as that toward which all envisaged relations are oriented. Thus, for example, Heisenberg's principle of indeterminacy can not be considered either as an invalidation or a validation of the determinist postulate. Instead of being a pure connection between things, it includes within itself the original relation of man to things and his place in the world. This is sufficiently demonstrated, for example, by the fact that we cannot make the dimensions of bodies in motion increase in proportionate quantities without changing their relative speed. If I examine the movement of one body toward another first with the naked eye and then with the microscope, it will appear to me a hundred times faster in the second case; for although the body in motion approaches no closer to the body toward which it is moving, it has in the same time traversed a space a hundred times as large. Thus the notion of speed no longer means anything unless it is speed in relation to given dimensions of a body in motion. But it is we ourselves who decide these dimensions by our very upsurge into the world and it is very necessary that we decide them, for otherwise they *would not be* at all. Thus they are relative not to the knowledge which we get of them but to our primary engagement at the heart of the world.

This fact is expressed perfectly by the theory of relativity: an observer placed at the heart of a system can not determine by any experiment whether the system is at rest or in motion. But this relativity is not a "relativism;" it has nothing to do with *knowledge*; better yet, it implies the dogmatic postulate according to which knowledge releases to us *what is*. The relativity of modern science aims at *being*. Man and the world *are* relative beings, and the principle of their being *is* the relation. It follows that the first relation proceeds from human-reality to the world. To come into existence, for me, is to unfold my distances from things and thereby to cause things "to be there." But consequently things are precisely "things-which-exist-at-a-distance-from-me." Thus the world refers to me that univocal relation which is my being and by which I cause it to be revealed.

The point of view of pure knowledge is contradictory; there is only the point of view of *engaged* knowledge. This amounts to saying that knowledge and action are only two abstract aspects of an original, concrete relation. The real space of the world is the space which Lewin calls "hodological." A pure knowledge in fact would be a knowledge without a point of view; therefore a knowledge of the world but on principle located outside the world. But this makes no sense; the knowing being would be only knowledge since he would be defined by his object and since his object would disappear in the total indistinction of reciprocal relations. Thus knowledge can be only an engaged upsurge in a determined point of view which one *is*. For human reality, to be is to-be-there; that is, "there in that chair," "there at that table," "there at the top of that mountain, with these dimensions, this orientation, *etc.*" It is an ontological necessity.

This point must be well understood. For this necessity appears between two contingencies; on the one hand, while it is necessary that I be in the form of being-there, still it is altogether contingent that I be, for I am not the foundation of my being; on the other hand, while it is necessary that I be engaged in this or that point of view, it is contingent that it should be precisely in this view to the exclusion of all others. This twofold contingency which embraces a necessity we have called the *facticity* of the for-itself. We have described it in Part Two. We showed there that the nihilated in-itself, engulfed in the absolute event which is the appearance of the foundation or the upsurge of the for-itself, remains at the heart of the for-itself as its original contingency. Thus the for-itself is supported by a perpetual contingency for which it becomes responsible and which it assimilates without ever being able to suppress it. Nowhere can the for-itself find this contingency anywhere within itself; nor can the for-itself anywhere apprehend and know it—not even by the reflective *cogito*. The for-itself forever surpasses this contingency toward its own possibilities, and it encounters in itself only the nothingness which it has to be. Yet facticity does not cease to haunt the foritself, and it is facticity which causes me to apprehend myself simultaneously as totally responsible for my being and as totally unjustifiable.

But the world refers to me the image of this unjustifiability in the form of the synthetic unity of its univocal relations to me. It is absolutely necessary that the world appear to me *in order*. And in this sense this order *is me*; it is that image of me which we described in the last chapter of Part Two. But it is wholly contingent that it should be *this* order. Thus it appears as the necessary and totally unjustifiable arrangement of the totality of being. This absolutely necessary and totally unjustifiable order of the things of the world, this order which is myself in so far as I am neither the foundation of my being nor the foundation of a *particular* being—this order is the body as it is on the level of the for-itself. In this sense we could define the body as the *contingent form which is assumed by the necessity of my contingency*. The body is nothing other than the foritself; it is not an in-itself in the for-itself, for in that case it would solidify everything. But it is the fact that the for-itself is not its own foundation, and this fact is expressed by the necessity of existing as an engaged, contingent being among other contingent beings. As such the body is not distinct from the *situation* of the for-itself since for the for-itself, to exist and to be situated are one and the same; on the other hand the body is identified with the whole world inasmuch as the world is the total situation of the for-itself and the measure of its existence.

But a situation is not a pure contingent given. Quite the contrary, it is revealed only to the extent that the for-itself surpasses it toward itself. Consequently the body-for-itself is never a given which I can know. It is there everywhere as the surpassed; it exists only in so far as I escape it by nihilating myself. The body is what I nihilate. It is the in-itself which is surpassed by the nihilating for-itself and which reapprehends the for-itself in this very surpassing. It is the fact that I am my own motivation without being my own foundation, the fact that I am nothing without having to be what I am and yet in so far as I have to be what I am, I am without having to be. In one sense therefore the body is a necessary characteristic of the for-itself; it is not true that the body is the product of an arbitrary decision on the part of a demiurge nor that the union of soul and body is the contingent bringing together of two substances radically distinct. On the contrary, the very nature of the foritself demands that it be body; that is, that its nihilating escape from being should be made in the form of an engagement in the world. Yet in another sense the body manifests my contingency; we can even say that it is only this contingency. The Cartesian rationalists were right in being struck with this characteristic; in fact it represents the individualization of my engagement in the world. And Plato was not wrong either in taking the body as *that which individualizes the soul*. Yet it would be in vain to suppose that the soul can detach itself from this individualization by separating itself from the body at death or by pure thought, for the soul is the body inasmuch as the for-itself is its own individualization.

We shall understand the bearing of these remarks better if we try to apply them to the problem of sense knowledge.

The problem of sense knowledge is raised on the occasion of the appearance in the midst of the world of certain objects which we call the *senses*. First we established that the Other had eyes; later as physiologists dissected cadavers, they learned the structure of these objects; they distinguished the cornea from the crystalline lens and the lens from the retina. They established that the object, crystalline lens, was classed in a family of particular objects— lenses—and that they could apply to the object of their study those laws of geometric optics which concern lenses. More precise dissections effected progressively as surgical instruments were perfected, have taught us that a bundle of nerves leave the retina and end up in the brain. With the microscope we have examined the nerves of cadavers and have determined exactly their trajectory, their point of departure, and their point of arrival. The totality of these pieces of knowledge concerned therefore a certain spatial object called the eye; they implied the existence of space and of the world. In addition they implied that we could *see* this eye, and touch it; that is, we are ourselves provided with a sensible point of view on things. Finally between our knowledge of the eye and the eye itself are interposed all our technical knowledge (the art of making our scalpels, our lancets) and our scientific skills (*e.g.*, geometric optics, which enables us to construct and use microcopes). In short, between me and the eye which I dissect there is interposed the whole world such as I make it appear by my very upsurge. Later a more thorough examination has enabled us to establish the existence of various nerve endings on the surface of our body. We have even succeeded in acting separately on certain of these endings and performing experiments on living subjects. We then found ourselves in the presence of two objects in the world: on the one hand the stimulant; on the other hand, the sensitive cell or the free nerve ending which we stimulated. The stimulant was a physical-chemical object, an electric current, a mechanical or chemical agent whose properties we knew with precision and which we could vary in intensity or in duration in a definite way. Therefore we were dealing with two mundane objects, and their intra-mundane relation could be established by our own senses or by means of instruments. The knowledge of this relation once again supposed a whole system of scientific and technical skills, in short, the existence of a world and our original upsurge into the world. Our empirical information enabled us, furthermore, to conceive a relation between "the inside" of the

Other-as-object and the ensemble of these objective establishments. We learned in fact that by acting on certain senses we "provoked a modification" in the Other's consciousness. We learned this *through language*—that is, through the meaningful and objective reactions of the Other. A physical object (the stimulant), a physiological object (sense), a psychic object (the Other), objective manifestations of meaning (language): such are the terms of the objective relation which we wished to establish. But not one of them could enable us to get out of the world of objects.

On occasion I have served as subject for the research work of physiologists or psychologists. If I volunteered for some experiment of this kind, I found myself suddenly in a laboratory where I perceived a more or less illuminated screen, or else felt tiny electric shocks, or I was brushed by an object which I could not exactly determine but whose global presence I grasped as in the midst of the world and over against me. Not for an instant was I isolated from the world; all these events happened for me in a laboratory in the middle of Paris, in the south building of the Sorbonne. I remained in the Other's presence, and the very meaning of the experiment demanded that I could communicate with him through language. From time to time the experimenter asked me if the screen appeared to me more or less illuminated, if the pressure exerted on my hand seemed to me stronger or weaker, and I replied; that is, I gave objective information concerning things which appeared in the midst of my world. Sometimes an inept experimenter asked me if "my sensation of light was stronger or weaker, more or less intense." Since I was in the midst of objects and in the process of observing these objects, his phrase would have had no meaning for me if I had not long since learned to use the expression "sensation of light" for objective light as it appeared to me in the world at a given instant. I replied therefore that the sensation of light was, for example, less intense, but I meant by this that the screen was *in my opinion* less illuminated. Since I *actually* apprehended the screen as less illuminated, the phrase "in my opinion" corresponded to nothing real except to an attempt not to confuse the objectivity of the world-for-me with a stricter objectivity, which is the result of experimental measures and of the agreement of minds with each other. What I could not *know* in any case was a certain object which the experimenter observed during this time and which was my visual organ or certain tactile endings. Therefore the result obtained at the end of the experiment could be only the relating of two series of *objects*: those which were revealed to me during the experiment and those which were revealed during the same period to the experimenter. The illumination of the screen belonged to my world; my eyes as objective organs belonged to the world of the experimenter. The connection of these two series was held to be like a bridge between two worlds; under no circumstances could it be a table of correlation between the subjective and the objective.

Why indeed should we use the term "subjectivity" for the ensemble of luminous or heavy or odorous objects such as they appeared to me in this laboratory at Paris on a day in February, etc. And if despite all we are to consider this ensemble as subjective, then why should we recognize objectivity in the system of objects which were revealed simultaneously to the experimenter, in this laboratory, this same day in February? We do not have two weights or two measures here; we do not encounter anywhere anything which is given as purely felt, as experienced for me without objectivation. Here as always I am conscious of the world, and on the ground of the world I am conscious of certain transcendent objects. As always I surpass what is revealed to me toward the possibility which I have to be—for example, toward that of replying correctly to the experimenter and of enabling the experiment to succeed. Of course these comparisons can give certain objective results: for example, I can establish that the warm water appears cold to me when I put my hand in it after having first plunged my hand in hot water. But this establishment which we pompously call "the law of relativity of sensations" has nothing to do with sensations. Actually we are dealing with a quality of the object which is revealed to me: the warm water is cold when I submerge my heated hand in it. A comparison of this objective quality of the water to equally objective information which the thermometer gives me simply reveals to me a contradiction. This contradiction motivates on my part a free choice of true objectivity. I shall give the name subjectivity to the objectivity which I have not chosen. As for the reasons for the "relativity of sensations," a further examination will reveal them to me in certain objective, synthetic structures which I shall call forms (Gestalt). The Müller-Lyer's illusion, the relativity of the senses, etc., are so many names given to objective laws concerning the structures of these forms. These laws teach us nothing about appearances, but they concern synthetic structures. I intervene here only to the extent that my upsurge into the world gives birth to this putting into relation of objects with each other. As such they are revealed as forms. Scientific objectivity consists in considering the structures separately by isolating them from the whole; hence they appear with other characteristics. But in no case do we get out of an existing world. In the same way we might show that what is called the "threshold of sensation" or the specificity of the senses is referred back to pure determinations of objects as such.

Yet some have claimed that this objective relation of the stimulant to the sense organ is itself surpassed toward a relation of the objective (stimulant-sense organ) to the subjective (pure sensation) and that this subjective is defined by the action exercised on us by the stimulant through the intermediary of the sense organ. The sense organ appears to us to be affected by the stimulant; the protoplasmic and physical-chemical modifications which appear in the sense organ are not actually produced by that organ; they come to it *from* the outside. At least we assert this in order to remain faithful to the principle of inertia which constitutes all nature as exteriority. Therefore when we establish a correlation between the objective system (stimulant-sensory organ) which we presently perceive, and the subjective system which for us is the ensemble of the internal properties of the other-object, then we are compelled to admit that the new modality which has just appeared in this subjectivity in connection with the stimulation of the sense is also produced by something other than itself. If it were produced spontaneously, in fact, it would immediately be cut off from all connection with the organ stimulated, or if you prefer, the relation which could be established between them would be *anything whatsoever*. Therefore we shall conceive of an objective unity corresponding to even the tiniest and shortest of perceptible stimulations, and we shall call it sensation. We shall endow this unity with *inertia*; that is, it will be pure exteriority since, conceived in terms of the "*this*," it will participate in the exteriority of the in-itself. This exteriority which is projected into the heart of the sensation touches it almost in its very existence; its reason for being and the occasion of its existence are outside of it. It is therefore an *exteriority to itself*. At the same time its *raison d'être* does not reside in any "internal" fact of the same nature as it but in a real object (the stimulant) and in the change which affects another real object (the sense organ). Nevertheless as it remains inconceivable that a certain being existing on a certain level of being and incapable of being supported in being by itself alone can be determined to exist by an existent standing on a plane of being which is radically distinct, I must in order to support the sensation and in order to furnish it with being, conceive of an environment which is homogeneous with it and constituted likewise in exteriority. This environment I call *mind* or sometimes even *consciousness*. But I conceive of this consciousness as an Other's consciousness—that is, as an object. Nonetheless as the relations which I wish to establish between the sense organ and the sensation must be universal, I posit that the consciousness thus conceived must be also my consciousness, not *for the other* but in itself. Thus I have determined a sort of internal space in which certain figures called sensations are formed on the occasion of external stimulations. Since this space is pure passivity, I declare that it *suffers* its sensations. But I do not thereby mean only that it is the internal environment which serves as matrix for them. I am inspired at present with a biological vision of the world which I borrow for my objective conception of the sensory organ considered, and I claim that this internal space *lives* its sensation. Thus *life* is a magical connection which I establish between a passive environment and a passive mode of this environment. The mind does not produce its own sensations and hence they remain *exterior* to it; but on the other hand, it appropriates them to itself by living them. The unity of the "lived" and the "living" is no longer indeed a spatial juxtaposition nor a relation of content to container; it is a magical inherence. The mind *is* its own sensations while remaining distinct from them. Thus sensation becomes a particular type of object—inert, passive, and simply lived. Behold us now obliged to bestow on it absolute subjectivity. But the word "subjectivity" must be correctly understood. It does not mean here the belonging to a subject; that is, to a selfness which spontaneously motivates itself. The subjectivity of the psychologist is of an entirely different sort; on the contrary, it manifests inertia and the absence of all transcendence. That is subjective which can not get out of itself. And precisely to the extent that sensation, since it is pure exteriority, can be only an impression in the mind, precisely to the extent that it is only itself, only this figure which is formed by an eddy in psychic space, it is not transcendence; it is purely and simply that which is suffered, the simple determination of our receptivity. It is subjectivity because it is neither presentative nor representative. The subjective quality of the Other-as-object is purely and simply a closed box. Sensation is inside the box.

Such is the notion of sensation. We can see its absurdity. First of all, it is pure fiction. It does not correspond to anything which I experience in myself or with regard to the Other. We have apprehended only the objective universe; all our personal determinations suppose the world and arise as relations to the world. Sensation supposes that man is already in the world since he is provided with sense organs, and it appears in him as the pure cessation of his relations with the world. At the same time this pure "subjectivity" is given as the necessary basis on which all these transcendent relations which its appearance has just caused to disappear will have to be reconstructed. Thus we meet with these three moments of thought:

(1) In order to establish sensation we must proceed on the basis of a certain realism; thus we take as valid our perception of the Other, the Other's senses, and inductive instruments.

(2) But on the level of sensation all this realism disappears; sensation, a modification which one suffers, gives us information only about ourselves; it belongs with the "lived."

(3) Nevertheless it is sensation which I give as the basis of my knowledge of the external world. This basis could not be the foundation of a real contact with things; it does not allow us to conceive of an intentional structure of the mind.

We are to use the term *objectivity* not for an immediate connection with being but for certain combinations of sensations which will present more permanence or more regularity or which will accord better with the ensemble of our representations. In particular it is thus that we shall have to define our perception of the Other, the Other's sense organs, and inductive instruments. We are dealing with subjective formations of a particular coherence—that is all. On this level there can be no question of explaining my sensation by the sense organ as I perceive it in the Other or in myself; quite the contrary, it is the sense organ which I explain as a certain association of my sensations. We can see the inevitable circle. My perception of the Other's senses serves me as a foundation for an explanation of sensations and in particular of my sensations, but reciprocally my sensations thus conceived constitute the only *reality* of my perception of the Other's senses. In this circle the same object—the Other's sense organ—maintains neither the same nature nor the same truth throughout each of its appearances. It is at first *reality*, and then because it is reality it founds a doctrine which contradicts it. In *appearance* the structure of the classical theory of sensation is exactly that of the Cynic argument of the Liar in that it is precisely because the Cretan tells the truth that he is found to be lying. But in addition, as we have just seen, a sensation is pure subjectivity. How are we supposed to construct an object out of subjectivity? No synthetic grouping can confer an objective quality on what is on principle of the nature of what is lived. If there is to be perception of objects in the world, it is necessary that from the time of our very upsurge we should be in the presence of the world and of objects. Sensation, a hybrid notion between the subjective and the objective, conceived from the standpoint of the object and applied subsequently to the subject, a bastard existence concerning which we can not say whether it exists in fact or in theory—sensation is a pure daydream of the psychologist. It must be deliberately rejected by any serious theory concerning the relations between consciousness and the world.

But if sensation is only a word, what becomes of the senses? No doubt one will recognize that we never in ourselves encounter that phantom and strictly subjective impression which is sensation. One will admit that I apprehend only *the green* of this notebook, of this foliage and never the sensation of green nor even the "quasi-green" which Husserl posits as the hyletic material which the intention animates into green-as-object. One will declare that he is easily convinced of the fact that on the supposition that the phenomenological reduction is possible—which remains to be proved—it will put us face to face with objects put within brackets as the pure correlates of positional acts but not of impressional residues. Nonetheless it is still true that the senses remain. I *see* the green, *touch* this cold, polished marble. An accident can deprive me of a whole sense; I can lose my sight, become deaf, *etc.* What then is a sense which does not give us sensation?

The answer is easy. Let us establish first that *senses* are everywhere and yet everywhere inapprehensible. This inkwell on the table is given to me immediately in the form of a *thing*, and yet it is given to me *by sight*. This means that its presence is a visible presence and that I am conscious that it is present to me as visible—that is, I am conscious (of) seeing it. But at the same time that sight is *knowledge* of the inkwell, sight slips away from all knowledge;

there is no knowledge of sight. Even reflection will not give us this know-ledge. My reflective consciousness will give to me indeed a knowledge of my reflected-on consciousness of the inkwell but not that of a sensory activity. It is in this sense that we must take the famous statement of Auguste Comte: "The eye can not see itself." It would be admissible, indeed, that another organic structure, a contingent arrangement of our visual apparatus would enable a third eye to *see* our two eyes while they were seeing. Can I not see and touch my hand while it is touching? But then I shall be assuming the point of view of the Other with regard to my senses. I should be seeing eyes-as-objects; I can not see the eye seeing; I can not touch my hand as it is touching. Thus any sense in so far as it is-for-me is an inapprehensible; it is not the infinite collection of my sensations since I never encounter anything but objects in the world. On the other hand if I assume a reflective point of view on my consciousness, I shall encounter my consciousness of this or that thing-in-the-world, not my visual or tactile sense; finally if I can see or touch my sense organs, I have the revelation of pure objects in the world, not of a revealing or constructive activity. Nevertheless the senses are there. *There is* sight, touch, hearing.

On the other hand, if I consider the system of *seen* objects which appear to me, I establish that they are not presented to me in just any order; they are *oriented*. Therefore since a sense can not be defined either by an apprehensible act or by a succession of lived states, it remains for us to attempt to define it by its objects. If sight is not the sum of visual sensations, can it not be the system of seen objects? In this case it is necessary to return to that idea of *orientation* which we indicated earlier and to attempt to grasp its significance.

In the first place let us note that orientation is a constitutive structure of the thing. The object appears on the ground of the world and manifests itself in a relation of exteriority with other "thises" which have just appeared. Thus its revelation implies the complementary constitution of an undifferentiated ground which is the total perceptive field or the world. The formal structure of this relation of the figure to the ground is therefore necessary. In a word, the existence of a visual or tactile or auditory field is a necessity; silence, for example, is the resonant field of undifferentiated noises against which the particular sound we pay attention to stands out. But the material connection of a *particular* "this" to the ground is both chosen and given. It is chosen in so far as the upsurge of the for-itself is an explicit and internal negation of a *particular* "this" on the ground of the world: I *look* at the cup or the inkwell. It is given in the sense that my choice operates in terms of an original distribution of the *thises* which manifests the very facticity of my upsurge. It is necessary that the book appear to me on the right or on the left side of the table. But it is contingent that the book appears to me specifically on the left, and finally I am free to look at *the book* on the table or at *the table* supporting the book. It is this contingency between the necessity and the freedom of my choice that we call *sense*. It means that an object *must always appear to me all at once*—it is *the cube, the inkwell, the cup* which I see—but that this appearance always takes place in a particular perspective which expresses its relations to the ground of the world and to other *thises*. It is always *the note of the violin* which I hear. But it is necessary that I hear it *through a door* or *by the open window* or *in a concert hall*. Otherwise the object would no longer be in the midst of the world and would no longer be manifested to an existent-rising-up-in-the-world.

On the other hand while it is very true that all the *thises* can not appear *at once* on the ground of the world and that the appearance of certain among them results in the fusion of certain others with the ground, while it is true that each *this* can manifest itself only in one way *at a time* although there exists for it an infinity of ways of appearing, still these rules of appearance should not be considered as subjective and psychological. They are strictly objective and derive from the nature of things. If the inkwell hides a portion of the table from me, this does not stem from the nature of my senses but from the nature of the inkwell and of light. If the object gets smaller when moving away, we must not explain this by some kind of illusion in the observer but by the strictly external laws of perspective. Thus by these objective laws a strictly objective center of reference is defined.

For example, in a perspective scheme the eye is the point toward which all the objective lines converge. Thus the perceptive field refers to a center objectively defined by that reference and located *in the very field* which is oriented around it. Only we do not see this center as the structure of the perceptive field considered; *we are the center*. Thus the order of the objects in the world perpetually refers to us the image of an object which on principle can not be an object *for us* since it is what we have to be. The structure of the world demands that we can not see without *being visible*. The intra-mundane references can be made only to objects in the world, and the seen world perpetually defines a visible object to which its perspectives and its arrangements refer. This object appears in the midst of the world and at the same time as the world. It is always given as an addition to some grouping of objects since it is defined by the orientation of these objects; without it there would be no orientation since all orientations would be equivalent. It is the contingent upsurge of one orientation among the infinite possibilities of orienting the world; it is *this* orientation raised to the absolute. But on this level this object exists for us only in the capacity of an abstract indication; it is what everything indicates to me and what on principle I can not apprehend since it is what I *am*. In fact what I am can not on principle be an object for me inasmuch as I *am* it. The object which the things of the world indicate and which they include in their radius is for itself and on principle a non-object. But the upsurge of my being, by unfolding distances *in terms of a center*, by the very act of this unfolding determines an object which is itself in so far as it causes itself to be indicated by the world; and I could have no intuition of it as object because I am it, I who am presence to myself as the being which is its own nothingness. Thus my being-in-the-world, by the sole fact that it *realizes* a world, causes itself to be indicated to itself as a being-in-the-midst-of-the-world by the world which it realizes. The case could not be otherwise, for my being has no other way of entering into contact with the world except *to be in the world*. It would be impossible for me to realize a world in which I was not and which would be for me a pure object of a surveying contemplation. But on the contrary it is necessary that I lose myself in the world in order for the world to exist and for me to be able to transcend it. Thus to say that I have entered into the world, "come to the world," or that there is a world, or that I have a body is one and the same thing. In this sense my body is everywhere-in the world; it is over there in the fact that the lamp-post hides the bush which grows along the path, as well in the fact that the roof up there is above the windows of the sixth floor or in the fact that a passing car swerves from right to left behind the truck or that the woman who is crossing the street seems smaller than the man who is sitting on the sidewalk in front of the café. My body is co-extensive with the world, spread across all things, and at the same time it is condensed into this single point which all things indicate and which I am without being able to know it. This explanation should allow us to understand the meaning of the senses.

A sense is not given *before* sensible objects. For is it not capable indeed of appearing as an object to the Other? Neither is it given *after* sensible objects; for in that case it would be necessary to suppose a world of incommunicable images, simple copies of reality the mechanism of whose appearance was inconceivable. The senses are contemporaneous with objects; they are things "in person" as they are revealed to us in perspective. They represent simply an objective rule of this revelation. Thus sight does not *produce* visual *sensations*; neither is it affected by light rays. It is the collection of all visible objects in so far as their objective and reciprocal relations all refer to certain chosen sizes—submitted to all at once—as measures, and to a certain center of perspective. From this point of view the senses must in no way be identified with subject-ivity. In fact all variations which can be registered in a perceptive field are *objective* variations. In particular, the fact that one can cut off vision by "closing the eyelids" is an *external* fact which does not refer to the subjectivity of the apperception. The eyelid, in fact, is merely one object perceived among other objects, an object which hides other objects from me as the result of its objective relation with them. *No longer* to see the objects in my room because I have closed my eyes is *to see* the curtain of my eyelids. In the same way if I put my gloves on the tablecloth, then *no longer* to see a particular design in the cloth is precisely to *see the gloves*. Similarly the *accidents* which affect a sense belong to the province of objects. "I see yellow" because I have jaundice or because I am wearing yellow glasses. In each case the reason for the phenomenon is not found in a subjective modification of the sense nor even in an organic chage but in an objective relation between objects in the world; in each case I see "through" something, and the truth of my vision is objective. Finally if in one way or another the center of visual reference is destroyed (since destruction can come only from the development of the world according to its own laws—i.e., expressing in a certain way my facticity), visible objects are not by the same stroke annihilated. They continue to exist for me, but they exist without any center of reference, as a visible totality without the appearance of any particular this; that is, they exist in the absolute reciprocity of their relations. Thus it is the upsurge of the for-itself in the world which by the same stroke causes the world to exist as the totality of things and causes senses to exist as the objective mode in which the qualities of things are presented. What is fundamental is my relation to the world, and this relation at once defines the world and the senses according to the point of view which is adopted. Blindness, Daltonism, myopia originally represent the way in which there is a world for me; that is, they define my visual sense in so far as this is the facticity of my upsurge. This is why I can know and objectively define my senses but only emptily, in terms of the world; all that is necessary is that my rational and universalizing thought should prolong in the abstract the indications which things give to myself about my sense and that it reconstitute the sense in terms of these signs as the historian reconstitutes an historical personality according to the evidence indicating it. But in this case I have reconstructed the world on the ground of pure rationality by abstracting myself from the world through thought. I fly over the world without attaching myself to it; I place myself in an attitude of absolute objectivity, and each sense becomes one object among objects, a center of relative reference and one which itself supposes co-ordinates. But thereby I establish in thought the absolute equivalence of all centers of reference. I destroy the world's quality of being a world—without my even being aware of it. Thus the world by perpetually indicating the senses which I am and by inviting me to reconstitute it impels me to eliminate the personal equation which I am by reinstating in the world the center of mundane reference in relation to which the world is arranged. But by the same stroke I escape—through abstract thought—from the senses which I am; that is, I cut my bonds with the world. I place myself in a state of simple surveying, and the world disappears in the absolute equivalence of its infinite possible relations. The senses indeed are our being-in-the-world in so far as we have to be it in the form of being-in-the-midst-of-the-world.

These observations can be generalized; they can be applied in toto to my body inasmuch as it is the total center of reference which things indicate. In particular our body is not only what has long been called "the seat of the five senses;" it is also the instrument and the end of our actions. It is impossible to distinguish "sensation" from "action" even if we use the terms of classical psychology: this is what we had in mind when we made the observation that reality is presented to us neither as a thing nor as an instrument but as an instrumental-thing. This is why for our study of the body as a center of action we shall be able to take as a guiding thread the reasoning which has served us to reveal the true nature of the senses.

As soon as we formulate the problem of action, we risk falling into a confusion with grave consequences. When I take this pen and plunge it into the inkwell I am acting. But if I look at Pierre who at that same instant is drawing up a chair to the table, I establish also that he is acting. Thus there is here a very distinct risk of committing the mistake which we denounced a propos of the senses; that is, of interpreting my action as it is-for-me in terms of the Other's action. This is because the only action which I can know at the same time that it is taking place is the action of Pierre. I see his gesture and at the same time I determine his goal: he is drawing a chair up to the table in order to be able to sit down at the table and to write the letter which he told me he wished to write. Thus I can apprehend all the intermediate positions of the chair and of the body which moves it as instrumental organizations; they are ways to achieve his purpose. The Other's body appears to me here as one instrument in the midst of other instruments, not only as a tool to make tools but also as a tool to handle tools, in a word as a tool-machine. If I interpret the role of my body in relation to my action, in the light of the knowledge I have gained of the Other's body, I shall then consider myself as disposing of a certain instrument which I can dispose of at my whim and which in turn will dispose of other instruments all functioning toward a certain end which I pursue.

Thus we are brought back to the classical distinction between the soul and the body; the soul utilizes the tool which is the body. The parallel with the theory of sensation is perfect. We have seen indeed that the latter started from the knowledge of the Other's senses and that subsequently it endowed me with senses exactly similar to the sensible organs which I perceived in the Other. We have seen also the difficulty which such a theory immediately encountered: this is because I then perceive the world and particularly the Other's sense organs through my own sense, a distorting organ, a refracting environment which can give me information only on its own affections. Thus the consequences of the theory ruin the objectivity of the very principle which has served to establish them. The theory of action, since it has an analogous structure, encounters analogous difficulties. In fact if I start with the Other's body, I apprehend it as an instrument and in so far as I myself make use of it as an instrument. I can utilize it in order to arrive at ends which I could not attain alone; I *command* its acts through orders or supplications; I can also provoke its act by my own acts. At the same time I must take precautions with respect to a tool which is particularly delicate and dangerous to handle. In relation to it I stand in the complex attitude of the worker with respect to his tool-machine when simultaneously he directs its movements and avoids being caught by it. Once again in order to utilize the Other's body to my best interests I need an instrument which is my own body just as in order to perceive the Other's sense organs I need other sense organs which are my own. Therefore if I conceive of my body in the image of the Other's body, it is an instrument in the world which I must handle delicately and which is like a key to the handling of other tools. But my relations with this privileged instrument can themselves be only technical, and I need an instrument in order to handle this instrument—which refers us to infinity. Thus if I conceive of my sense organs as like those of the Other, they require a sense organ in order to perceive them; and if I apprehend my body as an instrument like the Other's body, it demands an instrument to manage it; and if we refuse to conceive of this recourse to infinity, then we must of necessity admit that paradox of a physical instrument *handled* by a soul, which, as we know, causes us to fall into inextricable aporias.

Let us see whether we can attempt here as with the problem of sensations to restore to the body its nature-for-us. Objects are revealed to us at the heart of a complex of instrumentality in which they occupy a determined *place*. This place is not defined by pure spatial co-ordinates but in relation to axes of practical reference. "*The glass is* on the coffee table;" this means that we must be careful not to upset the glass if we move the table. The package of tobacco *is on* the mantle piece; this means that we must clear a distance of three yards if we want to go from the pipe to the tobacco while avoiding certain obstacles—end tables, foot-stools, *etc.*—which are placed between the mantle piece and the table. In this sense perception is in no way to be distinguished from the practical organization of existents into a *world*. Each instrument refers to other instruments, to those which are its *keys* and to those for which it is the *key*. But these references could not be grasped by a purely contemplative consciousness. For such a consciousness the hammer would not refer to the nails but would be alongside them; furthermore the expression "alongside" loses all meaning if it does not outline a path which goes from the hammer to the nail and which *must be* cleared. The space which is originally revealed to me is hodological space; it is furrowed with paths and highways; it is instrumental and it is the *location* of tools. Thus the world from the moment of the upsurge of my For-itself is revealed as the indication of acts to be performed; these acts refer to other acts, and those to others, and so on. It is to be noted however that if from this point of view perception and action are indistinguishable, action is nevertheless presented as a future efficacy which surpasses and transcends the pure and simple perceived. Since the perceived is that to which my For-itself is presence, it is revealed to me as co-presence; it is immediate contact, present adherence, it brushes lightly over me. But as such it is offered without my being able *at present* to grasp it. The thing perceived is full of promises; it touches me lightly in passing, and each of the properties which it promises to reveal to me, each surrender silently consented to, each meaningful reference to other objects engages the future.

Thus I am *in the presence* of things which are only promises beyond an ineffable *presence* which I can not possess and which is the pure "being-there" of things; that is, the "mine," my facticity, my body. The cup is there on the saucer; it is presently given to me with its bottom side which is there, which everything indicates but which I do not see. And if I wish to see the bottom side—i.e., to make it explicit, to make it "appear-on-the-bottom-of-the-cup"—it is necessary for me to grasp the cup by the handle and turn it upside down. The bottom of the cup is at the end of my projects, and it amounts to the same thing whether I say that the other structures of the cup indicate it as an indispensable element of the cup or that they indicate it to me as the action which will best *appropriate* the cup for me with its meaning. Thus the world as the correlate of the possibilities which I *am* appears from the moment of my upsurge as the enormous skeletal outline of all my possible actions. Perception is naturally surpassed toward action; better yet, it can be revealed only in and through projects of action. The world is revealed as an "always future hollow," for we are always future to ourselves.[1]

Yet it must be noted that this future of the world which is thus revealed to us is strictly objective. The instrumental-things indicate other instruments or objective ways of making use of them: the nail is "to be pounded in" this way or that, the hammer is "to be held by the handle," the cup is "to be picked up by its handle," etc. All these properties of things are immediately revealed, and the Latin gerundives perfectly translate them. Of course they are correlates of non-thetic projects which we are, but they are revealed only as structures of the world: potentialities, absences, instrumentalities. Thus the world appears to me as objectively articulated; it never refers to a creative subjectivity but to an infinity of instrumental complexes.

Nevertheless while each instrument refers to another instrument and this to another, all end up by indicating an instrument which stands as the *key* for all. This center of reference is necessary, for otherwise all the instrumentalities would become equivalent and the world would vanish due to the total undifferentiation of gerundives. Carthage is "*delenda*" for the Romans but "*servanda*" for the Carthaginians. Without relation to its centers Carthage is no

---

[1] "*Creux toujours futur.*" There is a suggestion here of a mould to be filled but, of course, with no idea of a determined future. Tr.

longer anything; it falls into the indifference of the in-itself, for the two gerundives annihilate each other. Nevertheless we must of necessity see that the *key* is never *given* to me but only indicated by a sort of gap.[2] What I objectively apprehend in action is a world of instruments which encroach on one another, and each of them as it is apprehended in the very act by which I adapt myself to it and surpass it, refers to another instrument which must enable me to utilize this one. In this sense the nail refers to the hammer and the hammer refers to the hand and the arm which utilizes it. But it is only to the extent that I cause the nails to be pounded in by the Other that the hand and the arm become in turn instruments which I utilize and which I surpass toward their potentiality. In this case the Other's hand refers me to the instrument which will allow me to utilize this hand (to threats-promises-salary, *etc.*) The first term is present everywhere but it is only *indicated*. I do not apprehend *my* hand in the act of writing but only the pen which is writing; this means that I use my pen in order to form letters but not my *hand* in order to hold the pen. I am not in relation to my hand in the same utilizing attitude as I am in relation to the pen; I *am* my hand. That is, my hand is the arresting of references and their ultimate end. The hand is only the utilization of the pen. In this sense the hand is at once the unknowable and non-utilizable term which the last instrument of the series indicates ("book to be read— characters to be formed on the paper—pen") and at the same time the orientation of the entire series (the printed book itself refers back to the hand). But I can apprehend it—at least in so far as it is acting—only as the perpetual, evanescent reference of the whole series. Thus in a duel with swords or with quarter-staffs, it is the quarter-staff which I watch with my eyes and which I handle. In the act of writing it is the point of the pen which I look at in synthetic combination with the line or the square marked on the sheet of paper. But my hand has vanished; it is lost in the complex system of instrumentality in order that this system may exist. It is simply the meaning and the orientation of the system.

Thus, it seems, we find ourselves before a double and contradictory necessity: since every instrument is utilizable and even apprehensible only by means of another instrument, the universe is an indefinite, objective reference from tool to tool. In this sense the structure of the world implies that we can insert ourselves into the field of instrumentality only by being ourselves an instrument, that we can not *act* without being *acted on*. Yet on the other hand, an instrumental complex can be revealed only by the determination of a cardinal meaning of this complex, and this determination is itself practical and active—to pound a nail, to sow seed. In this case the very existence of the complex immediately refers to a center. Thus this center is at once a tool

---

[2] *Indiquée en creux*; literally, "indicated in a hollow (or mould)." Tr.

objectively defined by the instrumental field which refers to it and at the same time the tool which we can not utilize since we should thus be referred to infinity. We do not use this instrument, for we *are* it. It is given to us in no other way than by the instrumental order of the world, by hodological space, by the univocal or reciprocal relations of machines, but it can not be *given* to my action. I do not have to adapt myself to it nor to adapt another tool to it, but it is my very adaptation to tools, the adaptation which I am.

This is why if we reject the analogical reconstruction of my body according to the body of the Other, there remain two ways of apprehending the body: First, it is *known* and objectively defined in terms of the world but emptily; for this view it is enough that rationalizing thought reconstitute the instrument which I am from the standpoint of the indications which are given by the instruments which I utilize. In this case, however, the fundamental tool becomes a relative center of reference which itself supposes other tools to utilize it. By the same stroke the instrumentality of the world disappears, for in order to be revealed it needs a reference to an absolute center of instrumentality; the world of action becomes the world *acted upon* of classical science; consciousness surveys a universe of exteriority and can no longer in any way *enter into the* world. Secondly the body is *given concretely* and fully as the very arrangement of things in so far as the For-itself surpasses it towards a new arrangement. In this case the body is present in every action although invisible, for the act reveals the hammer and the nails, the brake and the change of speed, not the foot which brakes or the hand which hammers. The body is *lived* and not *known*. This explains why the famous "sensation of effort" by which Maine de Biran attempted to reply to Hume's challenge is a psychological myth. We never have any sensation of our effort, but neither do we have peripheral sensations from the muscles, bones, tendons, or skin, which have been suggested to replace the sensation of effort. We perceive the *resistance* of things. What I perceive when I want to lift this glass to my mouth is not my effort but the *heaviness of the glass*—that is, its resistance to entering into an instrumental complex which I have made appear in the world.

Bachelard rightly reproaches phenomenology for not sufficiently taking into account what he calls the "coefficient of adversity" in objects.[3] The accusation is just and applies to Heidegger's transcendence as well as to Husserl's intentionality. But we must understand that the instrumentality is primary: it is in relation to an original instrumental complex that things reveal their resistance and their adversity. The bolt is revealed as too big to be screwed into the nut; the pedestal too fragile to support the weight which I want to hold up, the stone too heavy to be lifted up to the top of the wall, *etc.* Other objects will appear as threatening to an instrumental complex already

[3] Bachelard, *L'Eau et les Rêves*, 1942. Editions José Corti.

established—the storm and the hail threatening to the harvest, the phyloxera to the vine, the fire to the house. Thus step by step and across the instrumental complexes already established, their threat will extend to the center of reference which all these instruments indicate, and in turn it will indicate this center through them. In this sense every *means* is simultaneously favorable and adverse but within the limits of the fundamental project realized by the upsurge of the For-itself in the world. Thus my body is indicated originally by instrumental complexes and secondarily by destructive devices. I live my body in danger as regards menacing machines as for manageable instruments. My body is everywhere: the bomb which destroys my house also damages my body in so far as the house was already an indication of my body. This is why my body always extends across the tool which it utilizes: it is at the end of the cane on which I lean and against the earth; it is at the end of the telescope which shows me the stars; it is on the chair, in the whole house; for it is my adaptation to these tools.

Thus at the end of this account sensation and action are rejoined and become one. We have given up the idea of first endowing ourselves with a body in order to study *second* the way in which we apprehend or modify the world through the body. Instead we have laid down as the foundation of the revelation of the body as such our original relation to the world—that is, our very upsurge into the midst of being. Far from the body being first for us and revealing things to us, it is the instrumental-things which in their original appearance indicate our body to us. The body is not a screen between things and ourselves; it manifests only the individuality and the contingency of our original relation to instrumental-things. In this sense we defined the senses and the sense organs in general as our being-in-the-world in so far as we have to be it in the form of being-in-the-midst-of-the-world. Similarly we can define *action* as our being-in-the-world in so far as we have to be it in the form of being-an-instrument-in-the-midst-of-the-world. But if I am in the midst of the world, this is because I have caused the world to-be-there by transcending being toward myself. And if I am an instrument in the world, this is because I have caused instruments in general to-be-there by the projection of myself toward my possibles. It is only in a world that there can be a body, and a primary relation is indispensible in order that this world may exist. In one sense the body is what I immediately am. In another sense I am separated from it by the infinite density of the world; it is given to me by a reflux of the world toward my facticity, and the condition of this reflux of the world toward my facticity is a perpetual surpassing.

We are now able to define our body's *nature-for-us*. The preceding observations have allowed us to conclude that the body is perpetually the *surpassed*. The body as a sensible center of reference is that *beyond* which I am in so far as I am immediately present to the glass or to the table or to the distant tree which I perceive. Perception, in fact, can be accomplished only at the very place where the object is perceived and *without distance*. But at the same time it unfolds the distances, and that in relation to which the perceived object indicates its distance as an absolute property of its being is the body. Similarly as an instrumental center of instrumental complexes the body can be only the *surpassed*; it is that which I surpass toward a new combination of complexes and which I shall perpetually have to surpass whatever may be the instrumental combination at which I arrive; for every combination from the moment that my surpassing fixes it in its being indicates the body as the center of reference for its own fixed immobility. Thus the body, since it is surpassed, is the Past. It is the immediate presence to the For-itself of "sensible" things in so far as this presence indicates a center of reference and is *already surpassed* either toward the appearance of a new *this* or toward a new combination of instrumental-things. In each project of the For-itself, in each perception the body is there; it is the immediate Past in so far as it still touches on the Present which flees it. This means that it is at once *a point of view and a point of departure*—a point of view, a point of departure which I *am* and which at the same time I surpass toward what I have to be.

This point of view which is perpetually surpassed and which is perpetually reborn at the heart of the surpassing, this point of departure which I do not cease to leave and which is myself remaining behind me—this is the necessity of my contingency. It is doubly necessary. First it is necessary because it is the continual reapprehension of the For-itself by the In-itself and the ontological fact that the For-itself can be only as the being which is not its own foundation. To have a body is to be the foundation of one's own nothingness and not to be the foundation of one's being; I *am* my body to the extent that I am; I *am* not my body to the extent that I am not what I am. It is by my nihilation that I escape it. But I do not thereby make an object of it, for what I am is what I perpetually escape. The body is necessary again as the obstacle to be surpassed in order to be in the world; that is, the obstacle which I am to myself. In this sense it is not different from the absolute order of the world, this order which I cause to arrive in being by surpassing it toward a being-to-come, toward being-beyond-being. We can clearly grasp the unity of these two necessities: being-for-itself is to surpass the world and to cause there to be a world by surpassing it. But to surpass the world is not to survey it but to be engaged in it in order to emerge from it; it is necessary always that a *particular* perspective of surpassing be effected. In this sense *finitude* is the necessary condition of the original project of the For-itself. The necessary condition for me to be what I am not and to not-be what I am—beyond a world which I cause to come into being—this condition is that at the heart of the infinite pursuit which I am there should be perpetually an inapprehensible given. This given which I am without having to be it—except in the mode of non-being—this I can neither grasp nor know, for it is everywhere recovered and surpassed, utilized for my assumed projects. On the other hand everything indicates it to me, every transcendent outlines it in a sort of hollow by its very transcendence without my ever being able to turn back on that which it indicates since I *am* the being indicated. In particular we must not understand the indicated-given as a pure center of reference of a static order of instrumental-things. On the contrary their dynamic order, whether it depends on my action or not, refers to it according to rules, and thereby the center of reference is defined in its change as in its identity. The case could not be otherwise since it is by denying that I am being that I make the world come into being and since it is from the standpoint of my past—i.e., in projecting myself beyond my own being—that I can deny that I am this or that particular being. From this point of view the body—i.e., this inapprehensible given—is a necessary condition of my action. In fact if the ends which I pursue could be attained by a purely arbitrary wish, if it were sufficient to hope in order to obtain, and if definite rules did not determine the use of instruments, I could never distinguish within me desire from will, nor dream from act, nor the possible from the real. No project of myself would be possible since it would be enough to conceive of it in order to realize it. Consequently my being-for-myself would be annihilated in the indistinction of present and future. A phenomenology of action would in fact show that the act supposes a break in continuity between the simple conception and the realization—that is, between a universal and abstract thought such as "A carburetor must not *be clogged*" and a technical and concrete thought directed upon this particular carburetor as it appears to me with its absolute dimensions and its absolute position. The condition of this technical thought, which is not distinguished from the act which it directs, is my finitude, my contingency, finally my facticity.

Now, to be exact, I am in *fact* in so far as I have a past, and this immediate past refers to the primary in-itself on the nihilation of which I arise through birth. Thus the body as facticity is the past as it refers originally to a birth; that is, to the primary nihilation which causes me to arise from the In-itself which I am in fact without having to be it. Birth, the past, contingency, the necessity of a point of view, the factual condition for all possible action on the world—such is the body, such it is for me. It is therefore in no way a contingent addition to my soul; on the contrary it is a permanent structure of my being and the permanent condition of possibility for my consciousness as consciousness of the world and as a transcendent project toward my future. From this point of view we must recognize both that it is altogether contingent and absurd that I am a cripple, the son of a civil servant or of a laborer, irritable and lazy, and that it is nevertheless *necessary that* I be *that* or something else, French or German or English, *etc.*, a proletarian or bourgeois or aristocrat, *etc.*, weak and sickly or vigorous, irritable or of amiable disposition—precisely because I can not fly over the world without the world disappearing. My birth as it conditions the way in which objects are revealed to me (objects of luxury or of basic necessity are more or less *accessible*, certain social realities appear to me as *forbidden*, there are barriers and obstacles in my hodological space); *my race* as it is indicated by the Other's attitude with regard to me (these attitudes are revealed as scornful or admiring, as trusting or distrusting); *my class* as it is disclosed by the revelation of the social community to which I belong inasmuch as the places which I frequent refer to it; *my nationality*; my physiological structure as instruments imply it by the very way in which they are revealed as resistant or docile and by their very coefficient of adversity; *my character*; *my past*, as everything which I have experienced is indicated as my point of view on the world by the world itself: all this in so far as I surpass it in the synthetic unity of my being-in-the-world is my body as the necessary condition of the existence of a world and as the contingent realization of this condition.

Now at last we can grasp clearly the definition which we gave earlier of the body in its being-for-us: the body is the contingent form which is taken up by the necessity of my contingency. We can never apprehend this contingency as such in so far as our body is *for us*; for we are a choice, and for us, to be is to choose ourselves. Even this disability from which I suffer I have assumed by the very fact that I live; I surpass it toward my own projects, I make of it the necessary obstacle for my being, and I can not be crippled without choosing myself as crippled. This means that I choose the way in which I constitute my disability (as "unbearable," "humiliating," "to be hidden," "to be revealed to all," "an object of pride," "the justification for my failures," *etc.*). But this inapprehensible body is precisely the necessity that *there be a choice*, that I do not exist *all at once*. In this sense my finitude is the condition of my freedom, for there is no freedom without choice; and in the same way that the body conditions consciousness as pure consciousness of the world, it renders consciousness possible even in its very freedom.

It remains for us to achieve a conception of what the body is for me; for precisely because the body is inapprehensible, it does not belong to the objects in the world—i.e., to those objects which I know and which I utilize. Yet on the other hand since I can be nothing without being the consciousness of what I am, the body must necessarily be in some way given to my consciousness. In one sense, to be sure, the body is what is indicated by all the instruments which I grasp, and I apprehend the body without knowing it in the very indications which I perceive on the instruments. But if we limit ourselves to this observation, we shall not be able to distinguish, for example, between the body and the telescope through which the astronomer looks at the planets. In fact if we define the body as a contingent point of view on the world, we must recognize that the notion of a point of view supposes a double relation: a relation with the things on which the body is a point of view and a relation with the observer for whom the body is a point of view. When we are dealing with the body-as-a-point-of-view, this second relation is radically different from the first; it is not truly distinct when we are dealing with a point of view in the world (spectacles, a look-out point, a magnifying glass, etc.) which is an objective instrument distinct from the body. A traveler contemplating the landscape from a belvedere sees the belvedere as well as the landscape; he sees the trees between the columns of the belvedere, the roof of the belvedere hides the sky from him, etc. Nevertheless the "distance" between him and the belvedere is by definition less great than that between his eyes and the panorama. The point of view can approach the body to the point of almost being dissolved in it, as we see, for example in the case of glasses, pince-nez, monocles, etc., which become, so to speak, a supplementary sense organ. At its extreme limit—if we conceive of an absolute point of view—the distance between it and the one for whom it is a point of view is annihilated. This means that it would become impossible to withdraw in order to "give oneself plenty of room" and to constitute a new point of view on the point of view. It is precisely this fact, as we have seen, which characterizes the body. It is the instrument which I can not use in the way I use any other instrument, the point of view on which I can no longer take a point of view. This is why on the top of that hill which I call a "good viewpoint," I take a point of view at the very instant when I look at the valley, and this point of view on the point of view is my body. But I can not take a point of view on my body without a reference to infinity. Therefore the body can not be for me transcendent and known; the spontaneous, unreflective consciousness is no longer the consciousness of the body. It would be best to say, using "exist" as a transitive verb—that consciousness exists its body. Thus the relation between the body-as-point-of-view and things is an objective relation, and the relation of consciousness to the body is an existential relation. What do we mean by an existential relation?

First of all, it is evident that consciousness can exist its body only as consciousness. Therefore my body is a conscious structure of my consciousness. But precisely because the body is the point of view on which there can not be a point of view, there is on the level of the unreflective consciousness no consciousness of the body. The body belongs then to the structures of the non-thetic self-consciousness. Yet can we identify it purely and simply with this non-thetic consciousness? That is not possible either, for non-thetic consciousness is self-consciousness as the free project toward a possibility which is its own; that is, in so far as it is the foundation of its own nothingness. Non-positional consciousness is consciousness (of the) body as being that which it surmounts and nihilates by making itself consciousness—i.e., as being something which consciousness is without having to be it and which it *passes over* in order to be what it has to be. In short, consciousness (of) the body is lateral and retrospective; the body is the *neglected*, the "*passed by in silence.*" And yet the body is what this consciousness *is*; it is not even anything except body. The rest is nothingness and silence.

Consciousness of the body is comparable to the consciousness of a *sign*. The sign moreover is on the side of the body; it is one of the essential structures of the body. Now the consciousness of a sign exists, for otherwise we should not be able to understand its meaning. But the sign is that which is *surpassed toward meaning*, that which is neglected for the sake of the meaning, that which is never apprehended for itself, that beyond which the look is perpetually directed. Consciousness (of) the body is a lateral and retrospective consciousness of what consciousness is without having to be it (i.e., of its inapprehensible contingency, of that in terms of which consciousness makes itself a choice) and hence it is a non-thetic consciousness of the manner in which it is *affected*. Consciousness of the body is often confused with original affectivity. Again it is very important to grasp the meaning of this affectivity; and for this we must make a further distinction. Affectivity as introspection reveals it to us is in fact already a *constituted* affectivity; it is consciousness of the world. All hate is hate *of* someone; all anger is apprehension of someone as hateful or unjust or faulty; to have sympathy for someone is to "find him sympathetic," *etc.* In these various examples a transcendent "intention" is directed toward the world and apprehends it as such. Already therefore there is a surpassing, an internal negation; we are on the level of transcendence and choice. But Scheler has effectively demonstrated that this "intention" must be distinguished from pure affective qualities. For example, if I have a "headache" I can discover within me an intentional affectivity directed toward my pain so as to "suffer" it, to accept it with resignation, or to reject it, to evaluate it (as unjust, as deserved, as purifying, as humiliating, etc.) so as to escape it. Here it is the very intention which is the affection; it is pure act and already a project, a pure consciousness of something. This cannot be what we should consider consciousness (of) the body.

In reality this intention can not be the whole of affectivity. Since affectivity is a surpassing, it pre-supposes a surpassed. Moreover this is proved by the existence of what Baldwin incorrectly calls "emotional abstracts." Baldwin has indeed established that we can realize affectively within us certain emotions without feeling them concretely. For example, if someone tells me of a particular painful event which has just darkened the life of Pierre, I shall exclaim, "How he must have suffered!" I do not know this suffering and I do not actually *feel* it. These intermediaries between pure knowledge and true affection Baldwin calls "abstracts." But the mechanism of such an abstraction remains very obscure. Who abstracts? If following M. Laporte's definition we say that to abstract is to think of structures in *isolation* which can not *exist* separately, it is necessary either that we identify emotional abstracts with pure abstract concepts of emotions or else that we recognize that these abstracts can *exist* as such as real modalities of consciousness. In actuality these so-called "emotional abstracts" are empty intentions, pure projects of emotion. That is, we direct ourselves towards pain and shame, we strain toward them, consciousness transcends itself—but *emptily*. Grief is there, objective and transcendent, but it lacks concrete existence. It would be better to give to these insubstantial significations the name of affective *images*. Their importance of artistic creation and psychological understanding is undeniable. But the important thing here is the fact that what separates them from real shame, for example, is the absence of the quality of being *lived*.

There exist therefore pure affective qualities which are surpassed and transcended by affective projects. We shall not make of them as Scheler did, some kind of "hyle" borne upon the flux of consciousness. For us it is simply a matter of the way in which consciousness *exists* its contingency; it is the very texture of consciousness in so far as it surpasses this texture toward its own possibilities; it is the manner in which consciousness *exists* spontaneously and in the non-thetic mode, that which it *constitutes* thetically but implicitly as a point of view on the world. This can be pure grief, but it can also be a mood, an affective, non-thetic tonality, the pure agreeable, the pure disagreeable. In a general way, it is what is called *coenesthesia*. This "coenesthesia" rarely appears without being surpassed toward the world by a transcendent project on the part of the For-itself; as such it can only with difficulty be studied in isolation. Yet there exist some privileged experiences in which it can be apprehended in its purity, in particular what we call "physical" pain. Therefore we shall now examine this experience in order to fix conceptually the structures of the consciousness (of) the body.

My eyes are hurting but I should finish reading a philosophical work this evening. I am reading. The object of my consciousness is the book and across the book the truths which it points out. The body is in no way apprehended for itself; it is a point of view and a point of departure. The words slip by one after the other before me; I *make them slip by; those* at the bottom of the page which I have not yet read still belong to a relative ground or "the-page-as-ground" which is organized upon the "book-as-ground" and on the absolute ground or ground of the world. But from the ground of their indistinction they are calling to me; they already possess the character of a *friable totality*; they are given as "to be made to slip by under my sight." In all this the body is given only *implicitly*; the movement of my eyes belongs only to an observer's glance. For myself I apprehend thetically only this fixed upsurge of the words one after the other. Yet the succession of the words in objective time is given and known through my own temporalization. Their motionless movement is given across a "movement" of my consciousness; and this "movement" of consciousness, a pure metaphor which designates a temporal progression, is for me exactly the movement of my eyes. It is impossible for me to distinguish the movement of my eyes from the synthetic progression of my states of consciousness without resorting to the point of view of the Other. Yet at the very moment that I am reading *my eyes hurt*. Let us note first that this pain can itself be *indicated* by objects of the world; *i.e.*, by the book which I read. It is with more difficulty that the words are detached from the undifferentiated ground which they constitute; they may tremble, quiver; their meaning may be derived only with effort, the sentences which I have just read twice, three times may be given as "not understood," as "to be re-read." But these same indications can be lacking—for example, in the case when my reading "absorbs me" and when I "forget" my pain (which does not mean that it has disappeared since if I happen to gain knowledge of it in a later *reflective* act, it will be given as having always been there). In any case this is not what interests us; we are looking for the way in which consciousness *exists* its pain. But at the start someone will ask, how is the pain given as pain *in the eyes*? Is there not there an intentional reference to a transcendent object, to my body precisely in so far as it exists outside in the world? It is undeniable that pain contains information about itself; it is impossible to confuse pain in the eyes with pain in the finger or the stomach. Nevertheless pain is totally void of intentionality. It must be understood that if pain is given as pain "in the eyes," there is no mysterious "local sign" there nor any knowledge either. Pain *is precisely the eyes* in so far as consciousness "exists them." As such it is distinguished from other pain by its very existence, not by a criterion nor by anything added on. To be sure, the expression pain *in the eyes* supposes a whole constitutive work which we shall have to describe. But at this stage in the argument, there is not as yet any reason to consider this, for it is not made. Pain is not considered from a reflective point of view; it is not referred back to a body-for-others. It is the-eyes-as-pain or vision-as-pain; it is not distinguished from my way of apprehending transcendent words. We ourselves have called it pain in the eyes for the sake of clarity; but it is not named in consciousness, for it is not *known*. Pain in the eyes is distinguished from other possible pains inexpressibly and by its very being.

This pain however does not exist anywhere among the actual objects of the universe. It is not to the right or to the left of the book nor among the truths which are revealed through the book nor in my body-as-object (the body which the other sees and which I can always partially touch and partially see), nor in my body-as-a-point-of-view as the latter is implicitly indicated by the world. Neither must we say that the pain is an "overprint" or that it is like a harmonic "superimposed" on the things which I see. Those are images which have no meaning. Pain then is not in space. But neither does it belong

to objective time; it temporalizes itself, and it is in and through this temporalization that the time of the world can appear. What then is this pain?
Simply the translucent matter of consciousness, its *being-there*, its attachment to
the world, in short the peculiar contingency of the act of reading. The pain
exists beyond all attention and all knowledge since it slips into each act of
attention and of knowledge, since it is this very act in so far as the act is
without being the foundation of its being.

Yet even on this plane of pure being, pain as a contingent attachment to the
world can be existed non-thetically by consciousness only if it is surpassed.
Pain-consciousness is an internal negation of the world; but at the same time
it exists its pain—i.e., itself—as a wrenching away from self. Pure pain as the
simple "lived" can not be reached; it belongs to the category of indefinables
and indescribables which are what they are. But pain-consciousness is a project toward a further consciousness which would be empty of all pain; that is,
to a consciousness whose contexture, whose being-there would be not painful. But this *lateral* escape, this wrenching away from self which characterizes
pain-consciousness does not constitute pain as a psychic object. It is a non-
thetic project of the For-itself; we apprehend it only through the world. For
example, it is given in the way in which the book appears as "having to be
read in a hurried, jerky rhythm" where the words press against each other in
an infernal, fixed round, where the whole universe is pierced with *anxiety*. In
addition—and this is the characteristic of corporal existence—the inexpressible which one wishes to flee reappears at the heart of this very wrenching
away; it is this which is going to constitute the consciousnesses which surpass
it; it is the very contingency and the being of the flight which wishes to
flee it. Nowhere else shall we come closer to touching that nihilation of the
In-itself by the For-itself and that re-apprehension of the For-itself by
the In-itself which nourishes the very nihilation.

Granted, someone may say. But you are weighting the scales by choosing a
case where pain is specifically pain in a functioning organ, pain in the eye
while it is looking, in the hand while it is grasping. But I can suffer from a
wound in my finger while I am reading. In this case it would be difficult to
maintain that my pain is the very contingency of my "act of reading."

Let us note first that no matter how absorbed I am in my reading, I do not
for all that cease making the world come into being. Better yet, my reading is
an act which implies in its very nature the existence of the world as a necessary ground. This certainly does not mean that I have a weaker consciousness
of the world but that I am conscious of it as a *ground*. I do not lose sight of the
colors, the movements which surround me, I do not cease to hear sounds;
they are simply lost in the undifferentiated totality which serves as the background for my reading. Correlatively my body does not cease to be indicated
by the world as the total point of view on mundane totality, but it is the

world as ground which indicates it. Thus my body does not cease to be existed in totality as it is the total contingency of my consciousness. It is what the totality of the world as ground indicates, and at the same time it is the totality which I exist affectively in connection with the objective apprehension of the world. But to the extent that a particular this detaches itself as figure on the ground of the world, it correlatively points toward a functional specification of the corporal totality, and by the same stroke my consciousness exists a corporal form which arises on the body-as-totality which it exists. The book is read, and to the extent that I exist and that I surpass the contingency of vision—or if you prefer of reading—the eyes appear as figure on the ground of the corporal totality. On this plane of existence the eyes certainly are not the sensory organ seen by the Other but rather the very contexture of my consciousness of seeing inasmuch as this consciousness is a structure of my larger consciousness of the world. To be conscious is always to be conscious of the world, and the world and body are always present to my consciousness although in different ways. But this total consciousness of the world is consciousness of the world as ground for a particular this; thus just as consciousness specifies itself in its very act of nihilation, there is the presence of a particular structure of the body on the total ground of corporeality. When I am in the process of reading, I do not cease to be a body seated in a particular arm chair three yards from the window under given conditions of pressure and temperature. And I do not cease to exist this pain in my left index finger any more than I cease to exist my body in general. However I exist the pain in such a way that it disappears in the ground of corporeality as a structure subordinated to the corporal totality. The pain is neither absent nor unconscious; it simply forms a part of that distance-less existence of positional consciousness for itself. If a little later I turn the pages of the book, the pain in my finger, without becoming thereby an object of knowledge, will pass to the rank of existed contingency as a figure on a new organization of my body as the total ground of contingency. Moreover these statements are in agreement with the empirical observation that this is because it is easier when reading to "be distracted" from a pain in the finger or in the lower back then from pain in the eyes. For pain in the eyes is precisely my reading, and the words which I read refer me to it every instant, whereas the pain in my finger or back is the apprehension of the world as ground and hence is itself lost as a partial structure in the body as the fundamental apprehension of the ground of the world.

But now suppose that I suddenly cease to read and am at present absorbed in apprehending my pain. This means that I direct a reflective consciousness on my present consciousness or consciousness-as-vision. Thus the actual texture of my consciousness reflected-on—in particular my pain—is apprehended and posited by my reflective consciousness. We must recall here what we said concerning reflection: it is a total grasp without a point of view; it is a knowledge which overflows itself and which tends to be objectivized, to project the known at a distance so as to be able to contemplate it and to think it. The first movement of reflection is therefore to transcend the pure quality of consciousness in pain toward a pain-as-object. Thus if we restrict ourselves to what we have called an accessory reflection, reflection tends to make of pain something *psychic*.

The psychic object apprehended through pain is *illness*.[4] This object has all the characteristics of pain, but it is transcendent and passive. It is a reality which has its own time, not the time of the external universe nor that of consciousness, but psychic time. The psychic object can then support evaluations and various determinations. As such it is distinct even from consciousness and appears through it; it remains permanent while consciousness develops, and it is this very permanence which is the condition of the opacity and the passivity of illness. But on the other hand, this illness in so far as it is apprehended through consciousness has all the characteristics of unity, interiority, and spontaneity which consciousness possesses—but in degraded form. This degradation confers psychic individuality upon it. That is, first of all, the illness has an absolute cohesion without parts. In addition it has its own duration since it is outside consciousness and possesses a past and a future. But this duration which is only the projection of the original temporalization, is a multiplicity of interpenetration. The illness is "penetrating," "caressing," *etc.* And these characteristics aim only at rendering the way in which this illness is outlined in duration; they are melodic qualities. A pain which is given in twinges followed by lulls is not apprehended by reflection as the pure alteration of painful and non-painful consciousnesses. For organizing reflection the brief respites are a part of the illness just as silences are a part of a melody. The ensemble constitutes the rhythm and the *behavior* of the illness. But at the same time that it is a passive object, illness as it is seen through an absolute spontaneity which is consciousness, is a projection of this spontaneity into the In-itself. As a passive spontaneity it is magical; it is given as extending itself, as entirely the master of its temporal form. It appears and disappears differently than spatial-temporal objects. If I no longer see the table, this is because I have turned my head, but if I no longer feel my illness, it is because it "has left." In fact there is produced here a phenomenon analogous to that which psychologists of form call the stroboscopic illusion. The disappearance of the illness by frustrating the projects of the reflective for-itself is given as a movement of withdrawal, almost as will. There is an animism of illness; it is given as a living thing which has its form,

---

[4] In this passage the reader should bear in mind that Sartre uses the word *mal*, which can refer both to a specific disease or to evil in general. Both ideas are involved in his discussion. Tr.

its own duration, its habits. The sick maintain sort of intimacy with it. When it appears, it is not as a new phenomenon; it is, the sick man will say, "my afternoon crisis." Thus reflection does not join together the moments of the same crisis, but passing over an entire day it links the crises together. Nevertheless this synthesis of recognition has a special character; it does not aim at constituting an object which would remain existing even when it would not be given to consciousness (in the manner of a hate which remains "dormant" or stays "in the unconscious"). In fact when the illness goes away it disappears for good. "Nothing is left of it." But the curious consequence follows that when the illness reappears, it rises up in its very passivity by a sort of spontaneous generation. For example, one can feel its "gentle overtures." It is "coming back again." "This is it." Thus the first pains just like the rest are not apprehended for themselves as a simple, bare texture of the consciousness reflected-on; they are the "announcements" of the illness or rather the illness itself which is born slowly—like a locomotive which gradually gets under way. On the other hand it is very necessary to understand that I constitute the illness with the pain. This does not mean that I apprehend the illness as the cause of the pain but rather that each concrete pain is like a note in a melody: it is at once the whole melody and a "moment" in the melody. Across each pain I apprehend the entire illness and yet it transcends them all, for it is the synthetic totality of all the pains, the theme which is developed by them and through them. But the matter of the illness does not resemble that of a melody. In the first place it is something purely lived; there is no distance between the consciousness reflected-on and the pain nor between the reflective consciousness and the consciousness reflected-on. The result is that the illness is transcendent but without distance. It is outside my consciousness as a synthetic totality and already close to being elsewhere. But on the other hand it is in my consciousness, it fastens on to consciousness with all its teeth, penetrates consciousness with all its notes; and these teeth, these notes are my consciousness.

What has become of the body on this level? There has been, we noted, a sort of scission from the moment of the reflective projection: for the unreflective consciousness pain was the body; for the reflective consciousness the illness is distinct from the body, it has its own form, it comes and goes. On the reflective level where we are taking our position—i.e., before the intervention of the for-others—the body is not explicitly and thematically given to consciousness. The reflective consciousness is consciousness of the illness. However while the illness has a form which is peculiar to it and a melodic rhythm which confers on it a transcending individuality, it adheres to the for-itself by means of its matter since it is revealed through the pain and as the unity of all my pains of the same type. The illness is mine in this sense that I give to it its matter. I apprehend it as sustained and nourished by a certain passive environment in which the passivity is precisely the projection into the in-itself of the contingent facticity of the pains. It is *my* passivity. This passive environment is not apprehended for itself except as the matter of the statue is apprehended when I perceive its form, and yet it is there. *The illness feeds on this passivity* and magically derives new strength from it just as Antaeus was nour-ished by the earth. It is my body on a new plane of existence; that is, as the pure noematic correlate of a reflective consciousness. We shall call it a *psychic body*. It is not yet known in any way, for the reflection which seeks to appre-hend the pain-consciousness is not yet cognitive. This consciousness is affect-ivity in its original upsurge. It apprehends the illness as an object but as an affective object. One directs oneself first toward one's pain so as to hate it, to endure it with patience, to apprehend it as unbearable, sometimes to love it, to rejoice in it (if it foretells a release, a cure), to evaluate it in some way. Naturally it is the illness which is evaluated or rather which rises up as the necessary correlate of the evaluation. The illness is therefore not known; it is *suffered*, and similarly the body is revealed by the illness and is likewise suf-fered by consciousness. In order to add cognitive structures to the body as it has been given to reflection, we will have to resort to the Other. We can not discuss this point at present, for it is necessary first to bring to light the structures of the body-for-others.

At present, however, we can note that this psychic body since it is the projection on the plane of the in-itself of the intra-contexture of conscious-ness, provides the implicit matter of *all* the phenomena of the psyche. Just as the original body was existed by each consciousness as its own contingency, so the psychic body is suffered as the contingency of hate or of love, of acts and qualities, but this contingency has a new character. In so far as it was existed by consciousness it was the recapture of consciousness by the in-itself;—in so far as it is suffered by reflection in the illness or the hate or the enterprise, it is *projected into* the in-itself. Hence it represents the tendency of each psychic object beyond its magical cohesion to be parcelled out in exter-iority; it represents beyond the magical relations which unite psychic objects to each other, the tendency of each one of them to be isolated in an insularity of indifference. It is therefore a sort of implicit space supporting the melodic duration of the psychic. In so far as the body is the contingent and indifferent matter of all our psychic events, the body determines a *psychic space*. This space has neither high nor low, neither left nor right; it is without parts in as much as the magical cohesion of the psychic comes to combat its tendency towards a division in indifference. This is nonetheless a *real* characteristic of the psy-che—not that the psyche is *united* to a body but that under its melodic organ-ization the body is its substance and its perpetual condition of possibility. It is this which appears as soon as we *name* the psychic. It is this which is at the basis of the mechanistic and chemical metaphors which we use to classify and to explain the events of the psyche. It is this which we aim at and which we form into images (image-making consciousnesses) which we produce in order to aim at absent feelings and make them present. It is this, finally, which motivates and to some degree justifies psychological theories like that of the unconscious, problems like that of the preservation of memories.

It goes without saying that we have chosen physical pain for the sake of an example and that there are thousands of other ways, themselves contingent, to exist our contingency. In particular we must note that when no pain, no specific satisfaction or dissatisfaction is "existed" by consciousness, the for-itself does not thereby cease to project itself beyond a contingency which is pure and so to speak unqualified. Consciousness does not cease "to have" a body. Coenesthetic affectivity is then a pure, non-positional apprehension of a contingency without color, a pure apprehension of the self as a factual existence. This perpetual apprehension on the part of my for-itself of an insipid taste which I cannot place, which accompanies me even in my efforts to get away from it, and which is my taste—this is what we have described else-where under the name of Nausea. A dull and inescapable nausea perpetually reveals my body to my consciousness. Sometimes we look for the pleasant or for physical pain to free ourselves from this nausea; but as soon as the pain and the pleasure are existed by consciousness, they in turn manifest its factic-ity and its contingency; and it is on the ground of this nausea that they are revealed. We must not take the term nausea as a metaphor derived from our physiological disgust. On the contrary, we must realize that it is on the foundation of this nausea that all concrete and empirical nauseas (nausea caused by spoiled meat, fresh blood, excrement, etc.) are produced and make us vomit.

## II. THE BODY-FOR-OTHERS

We have just described the being of my body for-me. On this ontological plane my body is such as we have described it and it is only that. It would be useless to look there for traces of a physiological organ, of an anatomical and spatial constitution. Either it is the center of reference indicated emptily by the instrumental-objects of the world or else it is the contingency which the for-itself exists. More exactly, these two modes of being are complementary. But the body knows the same avatars as the for-itself; it has other planes of existence. It exists also for-others. We must now study it in this new ontological perspec-tive. To study the way in which my body appears to the Other or the way in which the Other's body appears to me amounts to the same thing. In fact we have established that the structures of my being-for-the-Other are identical to those of the Other's being-for-me. It is then in terms of the Other's being-for-me that—for the sake of convenience—we shall establish the nature of the body-for-others (that is, of the Other's body).

We showed in the preceding chapter that the body is not that which first manifests the Other to me. In fact if the fundamental relation of my being to that of the Other were reduced to the relation of my body to the Other's body, it would be a purely external relation. But my connection with the Other is inconceivable if it is not an internal negation. I must apprehend the Other first as the one for whom I exist as an object; the reapprehension of my selfness causes the Other to appear as an object in a second moment of prehistoric historization. The appearance of the Other's body is not therefore the primary encounter; on the contrary, it is only one episode in my relations with the Other and in particular in what we have described as making an object of the Other. Or if you prefer, the Other exists for me first and I apprehend him in his body *subsequently*. The Other's body is for me a secondary structure.

In the fundamental phenomenon of making an object of the Other, he appears to me as a transcendence-transcended. That is, by the mere fact that I project myself toward my possibilities, I surpass and transcend the Other's transcendence. It is put out of play; it is a transcendence-as-object. I apprehend this transcendence in the world, and originally, as a certain arrangement of the instrumental-things of my world inasmuch as they indicate *in addition* a secondary center of reference which is in the midst of the world and which is not me. These indications—unlike the indications which *indicate* me—are not constitutive of the indicating thing; they are lateral properties of the object. The Other, as we have seen, can not be a constitutive concept of the world. These indications all have therefore an original contingency and the character of an *event*. But the center of reference which they indicate is indeed *the Other* as a transcendence simply contemplated or transcended. The secondary arrangement of objects refers me to the Other as to the organizer or to the beneficiary of this arrangement, in short to an instrument which disposes of instruments in view of an end which it itself produces. But in turn I surpass this end and utilize it; it is in the midst of the world and I can make use of it for my own ends. Thus the Other is at first indicated by things as an instrument. Things also indicate me too as an instrument, and I am a body precisely in so far as I make myself be indicated by things. Therefore it is the Other-as-body whom things indicate by their lateral and secondary arrangements. The fact is that I actually do not know instruments which do not refer secondarily to the Other's body.

Earlier we pointed out that I could not take any point of view on my body in so far as it was designated by things. The body is, in fact, the point of view on which I can take no point of view, the instrument which I can not utilize in the way I utilize any other instrument. When by means of universalizing thought I tried to think of my body emptily as a pure instrument in the midst of the world, the immediate result was the collapse of the world as such. On the other hand, because of the mere fact that I *am not the Other*, his body appears to me originally as a point of view on which I can take a point of view, an instrument which I can utilize with other instruments. The Other's body is indicated by the round of instrumental-things, but in turn it indicates other objects; finally it is integrated with my world, and it indicates my body. Thus the Other's body is radically different from my body-for-me; it is the tool which I am not and which I utilize (or which resists me, which amounts to the same thing). It is presented to me originally with a certain objective coefficient of utility and of adversity. The Other's body is therefore the Other himself as a transcendence-instrument.

These same remarks apply to the Other's body as the synthetic ensemble of sense organs. We do not *discover* in and through the Other's body the possibility which the Other has of knowing us. This is revealed fundamentally in and through my *being-as-object for the Other*; that is, it is the essential structure of our original relation with the Other. And in this original relation the flight of my world toward the Other is equally given. By the reapprehension of my selfness I transcend the Other's transcendence inasmuch as this transcendence is the permanent possibility of apprehending myself as an object. Due to this fact it becomes a purely given transcendence surpassed toward my own goals, a transcendence which simply "is-there," and the knowledge which the Other has of me and of the world becomes knowledge-as-an-object. This means that it is a given property of the Other, a property which in turn I can know. In truth this knowledge which I get of it remains empty in this sense that I shall never know *the act of knowing*; this act, since it is pure transcendence can be apprehended only by itself in the form of non-thetic consciousness or by the reflection issuing from it. What I know is only knowledge as *being-there* or, if you like, *the being-there of knowledge*. Thus this relativity of the sensory organ which is revealed to my universalizing reason but which can not be thought, so far as my own sense is concerned, without determining the collapse of the world—this I apprehend first when I apprehend the Other-as-object. I apprehend it *without danger*; for since the Other forms part of my universe, his relativity can not determine the collapse of this universe. The senses of the Other are *senses known as knowing*.

We can see here the explanation of the error of psychologists who define *my senses* by the Other's senses and who give to the sense organ as it is for me a relativity which belongs to its being-for-others. We can see also how this error becomes truth if we place it on its proper level of being after we have determined the true order of being and of knowing. Thus the objects of my world indicate laterally an object-center-of-reference which is the Other. But this center in turn appears to me from a point-of-view-without-a-point-of-view which is mine, which is my body or my contingency. In short, to employ an inaccurate but common expression, *I know the Other through the senses*. Just as the Other is the instrument which I utilize in the manner of the instrument which I am and which no instrument can any longer utilize, so he is the ensemble of sense organs which are revealed to my *sense knowledge*; that is, he is a facticity which appears to a facticity. Thus there can be in its true place in the order of knowing and of being, a study of the Other's sense organs as they are known through the senses by me. This study will attach the greatest importance to the function of these sense organs—*which is to know*. But this knowledge in turn will be a pure object for me; here, for example, belongs the false problem of "inverted vision." In reality the sensory organ of the Other originally is in no way an instrument of knowledge for him; it is simply the Other's knowledge, his pure act of knowing in so far as this knowledge exists in the mode of an object in my universe.

Nevertheless we have as yet defined the Other's body only in so far as it is indicated laterally by the instrumental-things of my universe. Actually this by no means gives us his being-there in "flesh and blood." To be sure, the Other's body is everywhere present in the very indication which instrumental-things give of it since they are revealed as utilized by him and as known by him. This room in which I wait for the master of the house reveals to me in its totality the body of its owner: this easy chair is a chair-where-he-sits, this desk is a desk-at-which-he-writes, this window is a window through which there enters the light-which-illuminates-the-objects-which-he-sees. Thus he is outlined everywhere, and this outline is an outline-of-an-object; an object may come at every instant to fill the outline with content. But still the master of the house "is not there." He is *elsewhere*; he is *absent*.

Now we have seen that absence is a structure of *being-there*. To be absent is to-be-elsewhere-in-my-world; it is to be already given for me. As soon as I receive a letter from my cousin in Africa, his being-elsewhere is concretely given to me by the very indications of this letter, and this being-elsewhere is a being-somewhere; it is already his body. We can in no other way explain why a mere letter from a beloved woman sensually affects her lover; all the body of the beloved is present as an absence in these lines and on this paper. But since the being-elsewhere is a *being-there* in relation to a concrete ensemble of instrumental-things in a *concrete situation*, it is already facticity and contingency. It is not only the *encounter* which I have today with Pierre which defines his contingency and mine; his absence yesterday similarly defined our contingencies and our facticities. And this facticity of the absent is implicitly given in these instrumental-things which indicate it; his abrupt appearance does not add anything. Thus the Other's body is his *facticity* as an instrument and as a synthesis of sense organs as it is revealed to my facticity. It is given to me as soon as the Other exists for me in the world; the presence or absence of the Other changes nothing.

But look! Now Pierre appears. He is entering my room. This appearance changes nothing in the fundamental structure of my relation to him; it is contingency but so was his absence contingency. Objects indicate him to me: the door which he pushes indicates a human presence when it *opens* before him, the same with the chair when he sits down, etc.

But the objects did not cease to indicate him during his absence. Of course I exist for him, he speaks to me. But I existed equally yesterday when he sent me that telegram, which is now on my table, to tell me of his coming. Yet there is something new. This is the fact that he appears at present on the ground of the world as a this which I can look at, apprehend, and utilize directly. What does this mean? First of all, the facticity of the Other—that is, the contingency of his being—is now *explicit* instead of being implicitly contained in the lateral indications of instrumental-things. This facticity is precisely what the Other *exists*—in and through his for-itself; it is what the other perpetually lives in nausea as a non-positional apprehension of a contingency which he is, as a pure apprehension of self as a factual existence. In a word, it is his *coenesthesia*. The Other's appearance is the revelation of the taste of his being as an immediate existence. I, however, do not grasp this taste as he does. Nausea for him is not knowledge; it is the non-thetic apprehension of the contingency which he is. It is the surpassing of this contingency toward the unique possibilities of the for-itself. It is an existed contingency, a contingency submitted to and refused. It is this same contingency, and no other, which I presently grasp. But I *am not* this contingency. I surpass it toward my own possibilities, but this surpassing is the transcendence of *an Other*. It is given to me in entirety and without appeal; it is irremediable. The Other's for-itself wrenches itself away from this contingency and perpetually surpasses it. But in so far as I transcend the Other's transcendence, I fix it. It is no longer a resource against facticity; quite the contrary, it participates in turn in facticity, it emanates from facticity. Thus nothing comes to interpose itself between the Other's pure contingency *as a taste for himself* and my consciousness. Indeed I apprehend this taste as it is existed. However, from the very fact of my otherness, this taste appears as a known and given this in the midst of the world. The Other's body is given to me as the pure in-itself of his being—an in-itself among in-itselfs and one which I surpass toward my possibilities. The Other's body is revealed therefore with two equally contingent characteristics: it is here and could be elsewhere; that is, instrumental-things could be arranged otherwise in relation to it, could indicate it otherwise; the distance between the chair and this body could be different; the body is like this and could be otherwise—i.e., I grasp its original contingency in the form of an objective and contingent configuration. But in reality these two characteristics are only one. The second only makes the first present, only makes it explicit for me. The Other's body is the pure fact of the Other's presence in my world as a being-there which is expressed by a being-as-this. Thus the Other's very existence as the Other-for-me implies that he is revealed as a tool possessing the property of knowing and that this property of knowing is bound to some objective existence. This is what we shall call the necessity for the Other to be contingent for me.

From the moment that there is an Other, it must be concluded that he is an instrument provided with certain sense organs. But these considerations only serve to show the abstract necessity for the Other to have a body. This body of the Other as I encounter it is the revelation as object-for-me of the contingent form assumed by the necessity of this contingency. Every Other must have sense organs but not necessarily these sense organs, not any particular face and finally not this face. But face, sense organs, presence—all that is nothing but the contingent form of the Other's necessity to exist himself as belonging to a race, a class, an environment, etc., in so far as this contingent form is surpassed by a transcendence which does not have to exist it. What for the Other is his taste of himself becomes for me the Other's flesh. The flesh is the pure contingency of presence. It is ordinarily hidden by clothes, make-up, the cut of the hair or beard, the expression, etc. But in the course of long acquaintance with a person there always comes an instant when all these disguises are thrown off and when I find myself in the presence of the pure contingency of his presence. In this case I achieve in the face or the other parts of a body the pure intuition of the flesh. This intuition is not only knowledge; it is the affective apprehension of an absolute contingency, and this apprehension is a particular type of nausea.

The Other's body is then the facticity of transcendence transcended as it refers to my facticity. I never apprehend the Other as body without at the same time in a non-explicit manner apprehending my body as the center of reference indicated by the Other. But all the same we can not perceive the Other's body as flesh, as if it were an isolated object having purely external relations with other thises. That is true only for a corpse. The Other's body as flesh is immediately given as the center of reference in a situation which is synthetically organized around it, and it is inseparable from this situation. Therefore we should not ask how the Other's body can be first body for me and subsequently enter into a situation. The Other is originally given to me as a body in situation. Therefore there is not, for example, first a body and later action. But the body is the objective contingency of the Other's action. Thus once again we find on another plane an ontological necessity which we pointed out in connection with the existence of my body for me: the contingency of the for-itself, we said, can be existed only in and through a transcendence; it is the reapprehension—perpetually surpassed and perpetually reapprehending—of the for-itself, the reapprehension of the for-itself by the in-itself on the ground of the primary nihilation. Similarly here the Other's body as flesh can not be inserted into a situation preliminarily defined. The Other's body is precisely that in terms of which there is a situation. Here also it can exist only in and through a transcendence. Now, however, this transcendence is at the start transcended; it is itself an object. Thus Pierre's body is not first a hand which could subsequently take hold of this glass; such a conception would tend to put the corpse at the origin of the living body. But his body is the complex hand-glass, since the flesh of the hand marks the original contingency of this complex.

Far from the relation of the body to objects being a problem, we never apprehend the body outside this relation. Thus the Other's body is meaningful. Meaning is nothing other than a fixed movement of transcendence. A body is a body as this mass of flesh which it is is defined by the table which the body looks at, the chair in which it sits, the pavement on which it walks, etc. But to proceed further, there could be no question of exhausting the meanings which constitute the body—by means of reference to concerted actions, to the rational utilization of instrumental-complexes. The body is the totality of meaningful relations to the world. In this sense it is defined also by reference to the air which it breathes, to the water which it drinks, to the food which it eats. The body in fact could not appear without sustaining meaningful relations with the totality of what is. Like action, life is a transcended transcendence and a meaning. There is no difference in nature between action and life conceived as a totality. Life represents the ensemble of meanings which are transcended toward objects which are not posited as thises on the ground of the world. Life is the Other's body-as-ground in contrast to the body-as-figure inasmuch as this body-as-ground can be apprehended, not by the Other's for-itself and as something implicit and non-positional, but precisely, explicitly, and objectively by me. His body appears then as a meaningful figure on the ground of the universe but without ceasing to be a ground for the Other and precisely as a ground. But here we should make an important distinction: the Other's body actually appears "to my body." This means that there is a facticity in my point of view on the Other. In this sense we must not confuse my possibility of apprehending an organ (an arm, a hand) on the ground of the corporal totality and, on the other hand, my explicit apprehension of the Other's body or of certain structures of this body in so far as they are lived by the Other as the body-as-ground. It is only in the second case that we apprehend the Other as life. In the first instance it can happen that we apprehend as ground that which is figure for him. When I look at his hand, the rest of his body is united into ground. But it is perhaps his forehead or his thorax which for him exists non-thetically as figure on a ground in which his arms and his hands are dissolved.

The result, of course, is that the being of the Other's body is for me a synthetic totality. This means: (1) I can never apprehend the Other's body except in terms of a total situation which indicates it. (2) I can not perceive any organ of the Other's body in isolation, and I always cause each single organ to be indicated to me in terms of the totality of the flesh or of life. Thus my perception of the Other's body is radically different from my perception of things.

(1) The Other moves within limits which appear in immediate connection with his movements and which are the terms within which I cause the meaning of these movements to be indicated to myself. These limits are both spatial and temporal. Spatially it is the glass placed *at a distance* from Pierre which is the meaning of his actual gesture. Thus in my perception I go from the ensemble "table-glass-bottle, *etc.*," to the movement of the arm in order to make known to myself what it is. If the arm is visible and if the glass is hidden, I perceive Pierre's movement in terms of the pure idea of *situation* and in terms of the goal aimed at emptily beyond the objects which hide the glass from me, and this is the meaning of the gesture.

Pierre's gesture which is revealed to me in the present I always apprehend temporally from the standpoint of the future goals toward which he is reaching. Thus I make known to myself the present of the body by means of its future and still more generally, by means of the future of the world. We shall never be able to understand anything about the psychological problem of the perception of the Other's body if we do not grasp first this essential truth—that the Other's body is perceived wholly differently than other bodies: for in order to perceive it we always move to it from what is outside of it, in space and in time; we apprehend its gesture "against the current" by a sort of inversion of time and space. To perceive the Other is to make known to oneself what he is by means of the world.

(2) I never perceive an arm raised alongside a motionless body. I perceive Pierre-who-raises-his-hand. This does not mean that by an act of judgment I relate the movement of the hand to a "consciousness" which instigated it; rather I can apprehend the movement of the hand or of the arm only as a temporal structure of the whole body. Here it is the whole which determines the order and the movement of its parts. In order to prove that we are dealing here with an original perception of the Other's body, we need only recall the horror we feel if we happen to see an arm which looks "as if it did not belong to any body," or we may recall any one of those rapid perceptions in which we see, for example, a hand (the arm of which is hidden) crawl like a spider up the length of the doorway. In such cases there is a disintegration of the body, and this disintegration is apprehended as extraordinary. In addition, we know the positive proofs the Gestalt psychology has often advanced. It comes as a shock when a photograph registers an enormous enlargement of Pierre's hands as he holds them forward (because the camera grasps them in

their own dimension and without synthetic connection with the corporal totality), for we perceive that these same hands appear without enlargement if we look at them with the naked eye. In this sense the body appears within the limits of the situation as a synthetic totality of *life* and *action*.

Following these observations, it is evident that Pierre's body is in no way to be distinguished from Pierre-for-me. The Other's body with its various meanings exists only for me: to be an object-for-others or to-be-a-body are two ontological modalities which are strictly equivalent expressions of the being-for-others on the part of the for-itself. Thus the meanings do not refer to a mysterious psychism; they are this psychism in so far as it is a transcendence-transcended. Of course there is a psychic cryptography; certain phenomena are "hidden." But this certainly does not mean that the meanings refer to something "beyond the body." They refer to the world and to themselves. In particular these emotional manifestations or, more generally, the phenomena erroneously called the phenomena of *expression*, by no means *indicate* to us a hidden affection lived by some psychism which would be the immaterial object of the research of the psychologist. These frowns, this redness, this stammering, this slight trembling of the hands, these downcast looks which seem at once timid and threatening—these do not *express* anger; they *are* the anger. But this point must be clearly understood. In itself a clenched fist is nothing and means nothing. But also we never perceive a *clenched fist*. We perceive a man who in a certain situation clenches his fist. This meaningful act considered in connection with the past and with possibles and understood in terms of the synthetic totality "body in situation" is the anger. It refers to nothing other than to actions in the world (to strike, insult, etc.); that is, to new meaningful attitudes of the body. We can not get away from the fact that the "psychic object" is entirely given to perception and is inconceivable outside corporeal structures.

If this fact has not been taken into account hitherto or if those who have supported it, like the Behaviorists, have not themselves very well understood what they wanted to say and have shocked the world with their pronouncements, this is because people too readily believe that all perceptions are of the same kind. Actually perception must give to us immediately the spatial-temporal object. Its fundamental structure is the internal negation, and it gives to me the object *as it is*, not as an empty image of some reality beyond reach. But precisely for this reason a new structure of perception corresponds to each type of reality. The body is the psychic object *par excellence*—*the only psychic object*. But if we consider that the body is a transcended transcendence, then the perception of it can not *by nature* be of the same type as that of inanimate objects. We must not understand by this that the perception is progressively enriched but that originally it is of another structure. Thus it is not necessary to resort to habit or reason by analogy in order to explain how we *understand* expressive conduct. This conduct is originally given to perception as understandable; its meaning is part of its being just as the color of the paper is part of the being of the paper. It is therefore no more necessary to refer to other conduct in order to understand a particular conduct than to refer to the color of the table, or of another paper or of foliage in order to perceive the color of the folio which is placed before me.[5]

The Other's body, however, is given to us immediately as what the Other is. In this sense we apprehend it as that which is perpetually surpassed toward an end by each particular meaning. Take for example a man who is walking. From the start I understand his walking in terms of a spatial-temporal ensemble (alley-street-sidewalk-shops-cars, *etc.*) in which certain structures represent the meaning-to-come of the walking. I perceive this walking by going from the future to the present—although the future in which there is a question belongs to universal time and is a pure "now" which is not yet. The walking itself, a pure, inapprehensible, and nihilating becoming is the *present*. But this present is a surpassing toward a future goal on the part of *something* which is walking; beyond the pure and inapprehensible present of the movement of the arm we attempt to grasp the substratum of the movement. This substratum, which we never apprehend as it is except in the corpse, is yet always there as the surpassed, *the past*. When I speak of an arm-in-motion, I consider this arm which *was at rest* as the substance of the motion. We pointed out in Part Two that such a conception can not be supported. What moves can not be the motionless arm; motion is a disorder of being. It is nonetheless true that the psychic movement refers to two limits—the future terminus of its *result*, and the past terminus—the motionless organ which it alters and surpasses. I perceive the movement-of-the-arm as a perpetual, inapprehensible reference toward a past-being. This past-being (the arm, the leg, the whole body at rest) I do not see at all; I can never catch sight of it except *through* the movement which surpasses it and to which I am a presence—just as one gets a glimpse of a pebble at the bottom of the stream through the movement of the water. Yet this immobility of being which is always *surpassed and never realized*, to which I perpetually refer in order to say *what is* in motion—this is pure facticity, pure flesh, the pure in-itself as the past of a transcended transcendence which is perpetually being made past.

This pure in-itself, which exists only by virtue of being *surpassed* and in and through this surpassing, falls to the level of the *corpse* if it ceases to be simultaneously revealed and hidden by the transcendence-transcended. As a *corpse*—i.e., as the *pure past of a life*, as simply the *remains*—it is still truly understandable only in terms of the surpassing which no longer surpasses it: it is

[5] If Sartre did not intend to pun on the words *feuillage* and *feuille*, then I apologize for my feeble attempt with "foliage" and "folio." Tr.

*that which has been surpassed toward situations perpetually renewed.* On the other hand, in so far as it appears at present as a pure in-itself, it exists in relation to other "thises" in the simple relation of indifferent exteriority: the corpse is *no longer in situation.* At the same time it collapses into itself in a multiplicity of sustaining beings, each maintaining purely external relations with the others. The study of exteriority, which always implies facticity since this exteriority is never perceptible except on the corpse, is *anatomy.* The synthetic reconstitution of the living person from the standpoint of corpses, is *physiology.* From the outset physiology is condemned to understand nothing of life since it conceives life simply as a particular modality of death, since it sees the infinite divisibility of the corpse as primary, and since it does not know the synthetic unity of the "surpassing towards" for which infinite divisibility is the pure and simple *past.* Even the study of life in the living person, even vivisection, even the study of the life of protoplasm, even embryology or the study of the egg can not rediscover life; the organ which is observed is living, but it is not established in the synthetic unity of *a particular* life; it is understood in terms of anatomy—*i.e.,* in terms of death. There is therefore an enormous error in believing that the Other's body, which is originally revealed to us, is the body of anatomical-physiology. The fault here is as serious as that of confusing our senses "for ourselves" with our sensory organs for others. The Other's body is the facticity of the transcendence-transcended as this facticity is perpetually a *birth*; that is, as it refers to the indifferent exteriority of an in-itself perpetually surpassed.

These considerations enable us to explain what is called *character.* It should be noted in fact that character has distinct existence only in the capacity of an object of knowledge for the Other. Consciousness does not know its own character—unless in determining itself reflectively from the standpoint of another's point of view. It exists its character in pure indistinction nonthematically and non-thetically in the proof which it effects of its own contingency and in the nihilation by which it recognizes and surpasses its facticity. This is why pure introspective self-description does not give us character. Proust's hero "does not have" a directly apprehensible character; he is presented first as being conscious of himself as an ensemble of general reactions common to all men ("mechanisms" of passion, emotions, a certain order of memories, *etc.*) in which each man can recognize himself. This is because these reactions belong to the general "nature" of the psychic. If (as Abraham attempted in his book on Proust) we succeed in determining the character of Proust's hero (for example, his weakness, his passivity, his particular way of linking love and money), this is because we are interpreting brute givens. We adopt an external point of view regarding them; we compare them and we attempt to disengage from them permanent, objective relations. But this necessitates detachment. So long as the reader using the usual optic process of reading identifies himself with the hero of the novel, the character of "Marcel" escapes him; better yet it does not exist on this level. It appears only if I break the complicity which unites me to the writer, only if I consider the book no longer as a confidant but as a confidence, still better as a *document*. This character exists therefore only on the plane of the for-others, and that is the reason why the maxims and the descriptions of "moralists" (that is, those French authors who have undertaken an objective, social psychology) never coincide with the lived experience of the subject.

But if character is essentially *for others*, it can not be distinguished from the body as we have described it. To suppose, for example, that temperament is the *cause* of character, that the "sanguine temperament" is the *cause* of irascibility is to posit character as a psychic entity presenting all the aspects of objectivity and yet subjective and *suffered* by the subject. Actually the Other's irascibility is known from the outside and is from the start transcended by my transcendence. In this sense it is not to be distinguished from the "sanguine temperament." In both instances we apprehend the apoplectic redness, the same corporeal aspects, but we transcend these givens differently according to our projects. We shall be dealing with *temperament* if we consider this redness as the manifestation of the *body-as-ground*; that is, by cutting all that binds it to the situation. If we try to understand it *in terms of the corpse*, we shall be able to conduct a physiological and medical study of it. If on the contrary, we consider it by approaching it in terms of the global situation, it will be anger itself or again a promise of anger, or rather an anger in promise—that is, a permanent relation with instrumental-things, a potentiality. Between temperament and character there is therefore only a difference of principle, and character is identical with the body. This is what justifies the attempts of numerous authors to instate a physiognomy as the basis of the studies of character and in particular the fine research of Kretschmer on character and the structure of the body. The character of the Other, in fact, is immediately given to intuition as a synthetic ensemble. This does not mean that we can immediately *describe* it. It would take time to make the differentiated structures appear, to make explicit certain givens which we have immediately apprehended affectively, to transform the global indistinction which is the Other's body into organized form. We can be deceived. It is permissible also to resort to general and discursive knowledge (laws empirically or statistically established in connection with other subjects) in order to *interpret* what we see. But in any case the problem will be only to make explicit and to organize the content of our first intuition in terms of foresight and action. This is without a doubt what is meant by people who insist that "first impressions are not mistaken." In fact from the moment of the first encounter the Other is given entirely and immediately without any veil or mystery. Here to learn is to understand, to develop, and to appreciate.

Nevertheless as the Other is thus given, he is given in what he *is*. Character is not different from facticity—that is, from original contingency. We apprehend the Other as *free*, and we have demonstrated above that *freedom* is an objective quality of the Other as the unconditioned power of modifying situations. This power is not to be distinguished from that which originally constitutes the Other and which is the power to make a situation exist in general. In fact, to be able to modify a situation is precisely to make a situation exist. The Other's objective freedom is only transcendence-transcended; it is, as we have established, freedom-as-object. In this sense the Other appears as the one who must be understood from the standpoint of a situation perpetually modified. This is why his body is always the *past*. In this sense the Other's character is released to us as the *surpassed*. Even irascibility as the promise of anger is always a surpassed promise. Thus character is given as the Other's facticity as it is accessible to my intuition but also in so far as it is only in order to be surpassed. In this sense to "get angry" is already to surpass the irascibility by the very fact that one consents to it; it is to give irascibility a meaning. Anger will appear therefore as the recovery of irascibility by freedom-as-object. This does not mean that we are hereby referred to a subjectivity but only that what we transcend here is not only the Other's facticity but his transcendence, not only his being (i.e., his past) but his present and his future. Although the Other's anger appears to me always as a free-anger (which is evident by the very fact that I *pass judgment* on it) I can always transcend it—i.e., stir it up or calm it down; better yet it is by transcending it and only by transcending it that I apprehend it. Thus since the body is the facticity of the transcendence-transcended, it is always the body-which-points-beyond-itself; it is at once in space (it is the situation) and in time (it is freedom-as-object). The body for-others is the magic object *par excellence*. Thus the Other's body is always "a body-more-than-body" because the Other is given to me totally and without intermediary in the perpetual surpassing of its facticity. But this surpassing does not refer me to a subjectivity; it is the objective fact that the body—whether it be as organism, as character, or as tool—never appears to me without *surroundings*, and that the body must be determined in terms of these surroundings. The Other's body must not be confused with his objectivity. The Other's objectivity is his transcendence as transcended. The body is the facticity of this transcendence. But the Other's corporeality and objectivity are strictly inseparable.

## III. THE THIRD ONTOLOGICAL DIMENSION OF THE BODY

I exist my body: this is its first dimension of being. My body is utilized and known by the Other: this is its second dimension. But in so far as I *am for others*, the Other is revealed to me as the subject for whom I am an object. Even there the question, as we have seen, is of my fundamental relation with the Other. I exist therefore for myself as known by the Other—in particular in my very facticity. I exist for myself as a body known by the Other. This is the third ontological dimension of my body. This is what we are going to study next; with it we shall have exhausted the question of the body's modes of being.

With the appearance of the Other's look I experience the revelation of my being-as-object; that is, of my transcendence as transcended. A me-as-object is revealed to me as an unknowable being, as the flight into an Other which I am with full responsibility. But while I can not know nor even conceive of this "Me" in its reality, at least I am not without apprehending certain of its formal structures. In particular I feel myself touched by the Other in my factual existence; it is my being-there-for-others for which I am responsible. This *being-there* is precisely the body. Thus the encounter with the Other does not only touch me in my transcendence: in and through the transcendence which the Other surpasses, the facticity which my transcendence nihilates and transcends exists for the Other; and to the extent that I am conscious of existing for the Other I apprehend my own facticity, not only in its non-thetic nihilation, not only in *the existent*, but in its flight towards a being-in-the-midst-of-the-world. The shock of the encounter with the Other is for me a revelation in emptiness of the existence of my body outside as an in-itself for the Other. Thus my body is not given merely as that which is purely and simply lived; rather this "lived experience" becomes—in and through the contingent, absolute fact of the Other's existence—extended outside in a dimension of flight which escapes me. My body's depth of being is for me this perpetual "outside" of my most intimate "inside."

To the extent that the Other's omnipresence is the fundamental fact, the objectivity of my being-there is a constant dimension of my facticity; I exist my contingency in so far as I surpass it toward my possibles and in so far as it surreptitiously flees me toward an irremediable. My body is there not only as the point of view which I am but again as a point of view on which are actually brought to bear points of view which I could never take; my body escapes me on all sides. This means first that this ensemble of *senses*, which themselves can not be apprehended, is given as apprehended elsewhere and by others. This apprehension which is thus emptily manifested does not have the character of an ontological necessity; its existence can not be derived even from my facticity, but it is an evident and absolute fact. It has the character of a factual necessity. Since my facticity is pure contingency and is revealed to me non-thetically as a factual necessity, the being-for-others of this facticity comes to increase the contingency of this facticity, which is lost and flees from me in an infinity of contingency which escapes me. Thus at the very moment when I live my senses as this inner point of view on which I can take no point of view, their being-for-others haunts me: they *are*. For the Other, my senses are as this table or as this tree is for me. They are in the midst of *a world*; they are in and through the absolute flow of *my* world toward the Other. Thus the relativity of my senses, which I can not think abstractly without destroying my world, is at the same time perpetually made present to me through the Other's existence; but it is a pure and inapprehensible appresentation.

In the same way my body is for me the instrument which I am and which can not be utilized by any instrument. But to the extent that the Other in the original encounter transcends my being-there toward his possibilities, this instrument which I am is made-present to me as an instrument submerged in an infinite instrumental series, although I can in no way view this series by "surveying" it. My body as alienated escapes me toward a being-a-tool-among-tools, toward a being-a-sense-organ-apprehended-by-sense-organs, and this is accompanied by an alienating destruction and a concrete collapse of my world which flows toward the Other and which the Other will reapprehend in his world. When, for example, a doctor listens to my breathing, I *perceive his ear*. To the extent that the objects of the world indicate me as an absolute center of reference, this perceived ear indicates certain structures as forms which I exist on my body-as-a-ground. These structures—in the same upsurge with my being—belong with the purely lived; they are that which I exist and which I nihilate. Thus we have here in the first place the original connection between designation and the lived. The things perceived designate that which I subjectively exist. But I apprehend—on the collapse of the sense object "ear"—the doctor as listening to the sounds in my body, feeling my body with his body, and immediately the lived-designated becomes designated as *a thing outside my subjectivity*, in the midst of a world which is not mine. My body is designated as alienated.

The experience of my alienation is made in and through affective structures such as, for example, *shyness*.[6] To "feel oneself blushing," to "feel oneself sweating," etc., are inaccurate expressions which the shy person uses to describe his state; what he really means *is* that he is vividly and constantly conscious of his body not as it is for him but as it is *for the Other*. This constant uneasiness, which is the apprehension of my body's alienation as irremediable, can determine psychoses such as ereutophobia (a pathological fear of blushing); these are nothing but the horrified metaphysical apprehension of the existence of my body for the Others. We often say that the shy man is

---

[6] In French, *timidité*, which carries also the idea of timidity. Tr.

"embarrassed by his own body." Actually this expression is incorrect; I can not be embarrassed by my own body as I exist it. It is my body as it is for the Other which may embarrass me. Yet there too the expression is not a happy one, for I can be embarrassed only by a concrete thing which is present inside my universe and which hinders me as I try to use other tools. Here the embarrassment is more subtle, for what constrains me is absent. I never encounter my body-for-the-Other as an obstacle; on the contrary, it is because the body is never there, because it remains inapprehensible that it can be *constraining*. I seek to reach it, to master it, by making use of it as an instrument—since it is also given as an *instrument in a world*—in order to give it the form and the attitude which are appropriate. But it is on principle out of reach, and all the acts which I perform in order to appropriate it to myself escape me in turn and are fixed at a distance from me as my body-for-the-Other. Thus I forever act "blindly," shoot at a venture without ever knowing the results of my shooting. This is why the effort of the shy man after he has recognized the uselessness of these attempts will be to suppress his body-for-the-Other. When he longs "not to have a body anymore," to be "invisible," *etc.*, it is not his body-for-himself which he wants to annihilate, but this inapprehensible dimension of the body-alienated.

The explanation here is that we in fact attribute to the body-for-the-Other as much reality as to the body-for-us. Better yet, the body-for-the-Other *is* the body-for-us, but inapprehensible and alienated. It appears to us then that the Other accomplishes for us a function of which we are incapable and which nevertheless is incumbent on us: to *see ourselves as we are*. Language by revealing to us abstractly the principle structures of our body-for-others (even though the existed body is ineffable) impels us to place our alleged mission wholly in the hands of the Other. We resign ourselves to seeing ourselves through the Other's eyes; this means that we attempt to learn our being through the revelations of language. Thus there appears a whole system of verbal correspondence by which we cause our body to be designated for us as it is for the Other by utilizing these designations to denote our body as it is for us. It is on this level that there is effected the analogical identification of the Other's body with mine. It is indeed necessary—if I am to be able to think that "my body is for the Other as the Other's body is for me"—that I have met the Other first in his object-making subjectivity and then as object. If I am to judge the Other's body as an object similar to my body then it is necessary that he has been given to me as an object and that my body has for its part revealed itself to me as possessing an object-dimension. Analogy or resemblance can never at the start constitute the Other's body-as-object and the objectivity of my body; on the contrary, these two object-states must exist beforehand in order that an analogical principle may be brought into play.

Here therefore it is language which teaches me my body's structures for the Other.

Nevertheless it is necessary to realize that it is not on the unreflective plane that language with its meanings can slip in between my body and my consciousness which exists it. On this plane the alienation of the body toward the Other and its third dimension of being can only be experienced emptily; they are only an extension of the lived facticity. No concept, no cognitive intuition can be attached to it. The object-state of my body for the Other is not an object for me and can not constitute my body as an object; it is experienced as the flight of the body which I exist. In order that any knowledge which the Other has of my body and which he communicates to me by language may give to my body-for-me a structure of a particular type, it is necessary that this knowledge be applied to an object and that my body already be an object for me. It is therefore on the level of the reflective consciousness that the Other's knowledge can be brought into play; it will not qualify facticity as the pure *existed* of the non-thetic consciousness but rather facticity as the quasi-object apprehended by reflection. It is this conceptual stratum which by inserting itself between the quasi-object and the reflective consciousness will succeed in making an object of the psychic quasi-body. Reflection, as we have seen, apprehends facticity and surpasses it toward an unreal whose *esse* is a pure *percipi* and which we have named *psychic*. This psychic is constituted. The conceptual pieces of knowledge which we acquire in our history and which all come from our commerce with the Other are going to produce a stratum constitutive of the psychic body. In short, so far as we suffer our body reflectively we constitute it as a quasi-object by means of an accessory reflection—thus observation comes from ourselves. But as soon as we know the body—i.e., as soon as we apprehend it in a purely cognitive intuition—we constitute it by that very intuition with the Other's knowledge (i.e., as it would never be for us by itself). The knowable structures of our psychic body therefore simply indicate emptily its perpetual alienation. Instead of living this alienation we constitute it emptily by surpassing the lived facticity toward this quasi-object which is the psychic-body and by once again surpassing this quasi-object which is *suffered* toward characters of being which on principle can not be given to me and which are simply signified.

Let us return, for example, to our description of "physical" pain. We have seen how reflection while "suffering" physical pain constitutes it *as* Illness. But we had to stop midway in our description because we lacked the means to proceed further. Now, however, we can pursue the point. The Illness which I suffer I can aim at in its In-itself; that is, precisely in its being-for-others. At this moment I know it; that is, I aim at it in its dimension of being which escapes me, at the face which it turns toward Others, and my aim is impregnated with the wisdom which language has brought to me;—i.e., I utilize instrumental concepts which come to me from the Other, and which I should in no case have been able to form by myself or think of directing upon my body. It is by means of the Other's concepts that I *know* my body. But it follows that even in reflection I assume the Other's point of view on my body; I try to apprehend it as if I were the Other in relation to it. It is evident that the categories which I then apply to the Illness constitute it *emptily*; that is, in a dimension which escapes me. Why speak then of *intuition*? It is because despite all, the *body which is suffered* serves as a nucleus, as matter for the alienating means which surpass it. The body is this *Illness* which escapes me toward new characteristics which I establish as limits and empty schemata of organization. It is thus, for example, that my *Illness*, suffered as psychic, will appear to me reflectively as sickness in my *stomach*. Let us understand, of course, that pain "in the stomach" is the stomach itself as painfully lived. As such before the intervention of the alienating, cognitive stratum, the pain is neither a local sign nor identification. Gastralgia is the stomach present to consciousness as the pure quality of pain. As we have seen, the Illness as such is distinguished from all other pain and from any other illness—and by itself without an intellectual operation of identification or of discrimination. At this level, how ever, "the stomach" is an inexpressible; it can be neither named nor thought. It is only this suffered figure which is raised on the ground of the body-existed. Objectivating empirical knowledge, which presently surpasses the Illness suffered toward the *stomach* named, is the knowing of a certain objective nature possessed by the stomach. I know that it has the shape of a bagpipe, that is is a sack, that it produces juices, and enzymes, that it is inclosed by a muscular tunica with smooth fibres, *etc.* I can also know—because a physician has told me—that the stomach has an ulcer, and again I can more or less clearly picture the ulcer to myself. I can imagine it as a redness, a slight internal putrescence; I can conceive of it by means of analogy with abscesses, fever blisters, pus, canker sores, *etc.* All this on principle stems from bits of knowledge which I have acquired from Others or from such knowledge as Others have of me. In any case all this can constitute my Illness, not as I enjoy possession of it, but as it escapes me. The stomach and the ulcer become directions of flight, perspectives of alienation from the object which I possess.

At this point a new layer of existence appears: we have surpassed the lived pain toward the suffered illness; now we surpass the illness toward the *Disease*.[7] The Disease as *psychic* is of course very different from the disease known

---

[7] Sartre in this and in the earlier related passage is contrasting three things—pain, illness, disease. "Pain" refers to the specific aches and twinges, "illness" to the familiar recurrent pattern of these, "disease" to a totality which includes along with pain and illness the cause of them both and which can be diagnosed and named by the physician. The French words are *douleur, mal, and maladie.* Tr.

and described by the physician; it is a state. There is no question here of bacteria or of lesions in tissue, but of a synthetic form of destruction. This form on principle escapes me; at times it is revealed to the Other by the "twinges" of pain, by the "crises" of my Illness, but the rest of the time it remains out of reach without disappearing. It is then objectively discernible for Others. Others have informed me of it, Others can diagnose it; it is present for Others even though I am not conscious of it. Its true nature is therefore a pure and simple being-for-others. When I am not suffering, I speak of it, I conduct myself with respect to it as with respect to an object which on principle is out of reach, for which others are the depositories. If I have hepatitis, I avoid drinking wine so as not to arouse pains in my liver. But my precise goal—not to arouse pains in my liver—is in no way distinct from that other goal—to obey the prohibitions of the physician who revealed the pain to me. Thus another is responsible for my disease.

Yet this object which comes to me through others preserves characteristics of a degraded spontaneity deriving from the fact that I apprehend it through my Illness. It is not our intention to describe this new object nor to dwell on its characteristics—its magical spontaneity, its destructive finality, its evil potentiality—on its familiarity with me, and on its concrete relations with my being (for it is before all else, my disease). We wish only to point out that in the disease itself the body is a given: by the very fact that it was the support of the Illness, it is at present the substance of the disease, that which is destroyed by the disease, that across which this destructive form is extended. Thus the injured stomach is present through the gastralgia as the very matter out of which this gastralgia is made. The stomach is there; it is present to intuition and I apprehend it with its characteristics through the suffered pain. I grasp it as that which is gnawed at, as a "sack in the shape of a bagpipe," etc. I do not see it, to be sure, but I know that it is my pain. Hence the phenomena which are incorrectly called "endoscopy." In reality the pain itself tells me nothing about my stomach—contrary to what Sollier claims. But in and by means of the pain, my practical knowledge of it constitutes a stomach-for-others, which appears to me as a concrete and definite absence with exactly those objective characteristics which I have been able to know in it. But on principle the object thus defined stands as the pole of alienation of my pain; it is, on principle, that which I am without having to be it and without being able to transcend it toward anything else. Thus in the same way that a being-for-others haunts my facticity (which is non-thetically lived), so a being-an-object-for-others haunts—as a dimension of escape from my psychic body—the facticity constituted as a quasi-object for an accessory reflection. In the same way pure nausea can be surpassed toward a dimension of alienation; it will then present to me my body-for-others in its "shape," its "bearing," its physiognomy;" it will be given then as disgust with my face, disgust with my too-white flesh, with my too-grim expression, *etc*. But we must reverse the terms. I am not disgusted *by* all this. Nausea *is* all this as non-thetically existed. My knowledge extends my nausea toward that which it is for others. For it is the Other who grasps my nausea, precisely as *flesh* and with the nauseous character of all flesh.

We have not with these observations exhausted the description of the appearances of my body. It remains to describe what we shall call an *aberrant* type of appearance. In actuality I can see my hands, touch my back, smell the odor of my sweat. In this case my hand, for example, appears to me as one object among other objects. It is no longer *indicated* by the environment as a center of reference. It is organized with the environment, and like it indicates my body as a center of reference. It forms a part of the world. In the same way my hand is no longer the instrument which I can not handle along with other instruments; on the contrary, it forms a part of the utensils which I discover in the midst of the world; I can *utilize* it by means of my other hand—for example, when I hold an almond or walnut in my left fist and then pound it with my right hand. My hand is then integrated with the infinite system of utensils-utilized. There is nothing in this new type of appearance which should disturb us or make us retract the preceding statements. Nevertheless this type of appearance must be mentioned. It can be easily explained on condition that we put it *in its proper place* in the order of the appearances of the body; that is, on condition that we examine it last and as a "curiosity" of our constitution. This appearance of my hand means simply that in certain well-defined cases we can adopt with regard to our own body the Other's point of view or, if you like, that our own body can appear to us as the body of the Other. Scholars who have made this appearance serve as a basis for a general theory of the body have radically reversed the terms of the problem and have shown themselves up as understanding nothing about the question. We must realize that this possibility of *seeing* our body is a pure factual given, absolutely contingent. It can be deduced neither from the necessity on the part of the for-itself "to have" a body nor from the factual structures of the body-for-others. One could easily conceive of bodies which could not take any view on themselves; it even appears that this is the case for certain insects which, although provided with a differentiated nervous system and with sense organs, can not employ this system and these organs to know themselves. We are dealing therefore with a particularity of structure which we must mention without attempting to deduce it. To have hands, to have hands which can touch each other—these are two facts which are on the same plane of contingency and which as such fall in the province of either pure anatomical description or metaphysics. We can not take them for the foundation of a study of corporeality.

We must note in addition that this appearance of the body does not give us the body as it acts and perceives but only as it is acted on and perceived. In short, as we remarked at the beginning of this chapter, it would be possible to conceive of a system of visual organs such that it would allow one eye to see the other. But the seen eye would be seen as a thing, not as a being of reference. Similarly the hand which I grasp with my other hand is not apprehended as a hand which is grasping but as an apprehensible object. Thus the nature of our body for us entirely escapes us to the extent that we can take upon it the Other's point of view. Moreover it must be noted that even if the arrangement of sense organs allows us to see the body as it appears to the Other, this appearance of the body as an instrumental-thing is very late in the child; it is in any case later than the consciousness (of) the body proper and of the world as a complex of instrumentality; it is later than the perception of the body of the Other. The child has known for a long time how to grasp, to draw toward himself, to push away, and to hold on to something before he first learns to pick up his hand and to look at it. Frequent observation has shown that the child of two months does not see his hand as his hand. He considers it, and if it is outside his visual field, he turns his head and looks around for his hand as if it did not depend on him to bring it back within his sight. It is by a series of psychological operations and of syntheses of identification and recognition that the child will succeed in establishing tables of reference between the body-existed and the body-seen. Moreover, it is necessary that the child begin the learning process with the Other's body. Thus the perception of my body is placed chronologically after the perception of the body of the Other.

Considered at its proper place and time and in its original contingency, this appearance of the body does not seem to be capable of giving rise to new problems. The body is the instrument which I am. It is my facticity of being "in-the-midst-of-the-world" in so far as I surpass this facticity toward my being-in-the-world. It is, of course, radically impossible for me to take a global point of view on this facticity, for then I should cease to be it. But why should we be surprised that certain structures of my body, without ceasing to be a center of reference for the objects of the world, get organized from a radically different point of view from other objects in such a way that along with the objects they point to one of my sense organs as a partial center of reference and stand out as a figure against the body-as-ground? That my eye should see itself is by nature impossible. But why is it astonishing that my hand touches my eyes? If this seems surprising to us, it is because we have apprehended the necessity for the for-itself to arise as a concrete point of view on the world as if it were an ideal obligation strictly reducible to knowable relations between objects and to simple rules for the development of my achieved knowledge. But instead we ought to see here the necessity of a concrete and contingent existence in the midst of the world.

# 3

## CONCRETE RELATIONS
## WITH OTHERS

Up to this point we have described only our fundamental relation with the Other. This relation has enabled us to make explicit our body's three dimensions of being. And although the original bond with the Other arises before the relation between my body and the Other's body, it seemed clear to us that the knowledge of the nature of the body was indispensable to any study of the particular relations of my being with that of the Other. These particular relations, in fact, on both sides presuppose facticity; that is, our existence as body in the midst of the world. Not that the body is the instrument and the cause of my relations with others. But the body constitutes their meaning and marks their limits. It is as body-in-situation that I apprehend the Other's transcendence-transcended, and it is as body-in-situation that I experience myself in my alienation for the Other's benefit. Now we can examine these concrete relations since we are cognizant of what the body is. They are not simple specifications of the fundamental relation. Although each one of them includes within it the original relation with the Other as its essential structure and its foundation, they are entirely new modes of being on the part of the for-itself. In fact they represent the various attitudes of the for-itself in a world where there are Others. Therefore each relation in its own way presents the bilateral relation: for-itself-for-others, in-itself. If then we succeed in making explicit the structures of our most primitive relations with the Other-in-the-world, we shall have completed our task. At the beginning of this work, we asked, "What are the relations of the for-itself with the in-itself?" We have learned now that our task is more complex. There is a relation of the for-itself with the in-itself *in the presence of the Other.* When we have described this concrete fact, we shall be in a position to form conclusions concerning the fundamental relations of the three modes of being, and we shall perhaps be able to attempt a metaphysical theory of being in general.

The for-itself as the nihilation of the in-itself temporalizes itself as a *flight toward*. Actually it surpasses its facticity (i.e., to be either *given* or past or body) toward the in-itself which it would be if it were able to be its own foundation. This may be translated into terms already psychological—and hence inaccurate although perhaps clearer—by saying that the for-itself attempts to escape its factual existence (i.e., its being there, as an in-itself for which it is in no way the foundation) and that this flight takes place toward an impossible future always pursued where the for-itself would be an in-itself-for-itself—i.e., an in-itself which would be to itself its own foundation. Thus the for-itself is both a flight and a pursuit; it flees the in-itself and at the same time pursues it. The for-itself is a pursued-pursuing. But in order to lessen the danger of a psychological interpretation of the preceding remarks, let us note that the for-itself is not *first* in order to attempt *later* to attain being; in short we must not conceive of it as an existent which would be provided with tendencies as this glass is provided with certain particular qualities. This pursuing flight is not given which is added on to the being of the for-itself. The for-itself *is* this very flight. The flight is not to be distinguished from the original nihilation. To say that the for-itself is a pursued-pursuing, or that it is in the mode of having to be its being, or that it is not what it is and is what it is not—each of these statements is saying the same thing. The for-itself is not the in-itself and can not be it. But it is a relation to the in-itself. It is even the sole relation possible to the in-itself. Cut off on every side by the in-itself, the for-itself can not escape it because the for-itself is *nothing* and it is separated from the in-itself by *nothing*. The for-itself is the foundation of all negativity and of all relation. *The for-itself is relation.*

Such being the case, the upsurge of the Other touches the for-itself in its very heart. By the Other and for the Other the pursuing flight is fixed in in-itself. Already the in-itself was progressively recapturing it; already it was at once a radical negation of fact, an absolute positing of value and yet wholly paralyzed with facticity. But at least it was escaping by temporalization; at least its character as a totality detotalized conferred on it a perpetual "elsewhere." Now it is this very totality which the Other makes appear before him and which he transcends toward his own "elsewhere." It is this totality which is totalized. For the Other I am irremediably what I am, and my very freedom is a given characteristic of my being. Thus the in-self recaptures me at the threshold of the future and fixes me wholly in my very flight, which becomes a flight foreseen and contemplated, a *given* flight. But this fixed flight is never the flight which I am for myself; it is fixed *outside*. The objectivity of my flight I experience as an alienation which I can neither transcend nor know. Yet by the sole fact that I experience it and that it confers on my flight that in-itself which it flees, I must turn back toward it and assume *attitudes* with respect to it.

Such is the origin of my concrete relations with the Other; they are wholly governed by my attitudes with respect to the object which I am for the Other. And as the Other's existence reveals to me the being which I am without my being able either to appropriate that being or even to conceive it, this existence will motivate two opposed attitudes: First—The Other *looks* at me and as such he holds the secret of my being, he knows what I *am*. Thus the profound meaning of my being is outside of me, imprisoned in an absence. The Other has the advantage over me. Therefore in so far as I am fleeing the in-itself which I am without founding it, I can attempt to deny that being which is conferred on me from outside; that is, I can turn back upon the Other so as to make an object out of him in turn since the Other's object-ness destroys my object-ness for him. But on the other hand, in so far as the Other as freedom is the foundation of my being-in-itself, I can seek to recover that freedom and to possess it without removing from it its character as freedom. In fact if I could identify myself with that freedom which is the foundation of my being-in-itself, I should be to myself my own foundation. To transcend the Other's transcendence, or, on the contrary, to incorporate that transcendence within me without removing from it its character as transcendence—such are the two primitive attitudes which I assume confronting the Other. Here again we must understand the words exactly. It is not true that I first am and then later "seek" to make an object of the Other or to assimilate him; but to the extent that the upsurge of my being is an upsurge in the presence of the Other, to the extent that I am a pursuing flight and a pursued-pursuing, I am—at the very root of my being—the project of assimilating or making an object of the Other. I am the proof of the Other. That is the original fact. But this proof of the Other is in itself an attitude toward the Other; that is, I can not *be in the presence of the Other* without being that "in-the-presence" in the form of having to be it. Thus again we are describing the for-itself's structures of being although the Other's presence in the world is an absolute and self-evident fact, but a contingent fact—that is, a fact impossible to deduce from the ontological structures of the for-itself.

These two attempts which I am are opposed to one another. Each attempt is the death of the other; that is, the failure of the one motivates the adoption of the other. Thus there is no dialectic for my relations toward the Other but rather a circle—although each attempt is enriched by the failure of the other. Thus we shall study each one in turn. But it should be noted that at the very core of the one the other remains always present, precisely because neither of the two can be held without contradiction. Better yet, each of them is in the Other and engenders the death of the other. Thus we can never get outside the circle. We must not forget these facts as we approach the study of these fundamental attitudes toward the Other. Since these attitudes are produced and destroyed in a circle, it is as arbitrary to begin with the one as with the other. Nevertheless since it is necessary to choose, we shall consider first the conduct in which the for-itself tries to assimilate the Other's freedom.

## I. FIRST ATTITUDE TOWARD OTHERS: LOVE, LANGUAGE, MASOCHISM

Everything which may be said of me in my relations with the Other applies to him as well. While I attempt to free myself from the hold of the Other, the Other is trying to free himself from mine; while I seek to enslave the Other, the Other seeks to enslave me. We are by no means dealing with unilateral relations with an object-in-itself, but with reciprocal and moving relations. The following descriptions of concrete behavior must therefore be envisaged within the perspective of *conflict*. Conflict is the original meaning of being-for-others.

If we start with the first revelation of the Other as a *look*, we must recognize that we experience our inapprehensible being-for-others in the form of a *possession*. I am possessed by the Other; the Other's look fashions my body in its nakedness, causes it to be born, sculptures it, produces it as it is, sees it as I shall never see it. The Other holds a secret—the secret of what I am. He makes me be and thereby he possess me, and this possession is nothing other than the consciousness of possessing me. I in the recognition of my object-state have proof that he has this consciousness. By virtue of consciousness the Other is for me simultaneously the one who has stolen my being from me and the one who causes "there to be" a being which is my being. Thus I have a comprehension of this ontological structure: I am responsible for my being-for-others, but I am not the foundation of it. It appears to me therefore in the form of a contingent given for which I am nevertheless responsible; the Other founds my being in so far as this being is in the form of the "there is." But he is not responsible for my being although he founds it in complete freedom—in and by means of his free transcendence. Thus to the extent that I am revealed to myself as responsible for my being, I *lay claim to* this being which I am; that is, I wish to recover it, or, more exactly, I am the project of the recovery of my being. I want to stretch out my hand and grab hold of this being which is presented to me as *my being* but at a distance—like the dinner of Tantalus; I want to found it by my very freedom. For if in one sense my being-as-object is an unbearable contingency and the pure "possession" of myself by another, still in another sense this being stands as the indication of what I should be obliged to recover and found in order to be the foundation of myself. But this is conceivable only if I assimilate the Other's freedom.

Thus my project of recovering myself is fundamentally a project of absorbing the Other.

Nevertheless this project must leave the Other's nature intact. Two consequences result: (1) I do not thereby cease to assert the Other—that is, to deny concerning myself that I am the Other. Since the Other is the foundation of my being, he could not be dissolved in me without my being-for-others disappearing. Therefore if I project the realization of unity with the Other, this means that I project my assimilation of the Other's Otherness as my own possibility. In fact the problem for me is to make myself be by acquiring the possibility of taking the Other's point of view on myself. It is not a matter of acquiring a pure, abstract faculty of knowledge. It is not the pure *category* of the Other which I project appropriating to myself. This category is not conceived nor even conceivable. But on the occasion of concrete experience with the Other, an experience suffered and realized, it is this concrete Other as an absolute reality whom in his otherness I wish to incorporate into myself. (2) The Other whom I wish to assimilate is by no means the Other-as-object. Or, if you prefer, my project of incorporating the Other in no way corresponds to a recapturing of my for-itself as myself and to a surpassing of the Other's transcendence toward my own possibilities. For me it is not a question of obliterating my object-state by making an object of the Other, which would amount to *releasing* myself from my being-for-others. Quite the contrary, I want to assimilate the Other as the Other-looking-at-me, and this project of assimilation includes an augmented recognition of my being-looked-at. In short, in order to maintain before me the Other's freedom which is looking at me, I identify myself totally with my being-looked-at. And since my being-as-object is the only possible relation between me and the Other, it is this being-as-object which alone can serve me as an instrument to effect my assimilation of the *other freedom*.

Thus as a reaction to the failure of the third ekstasis, the for-itself wishes to be identified with the Other's freedom as founding its own being-in-itself. To be other to oneself—the ideal always aimed at concretely in the form of being *this Other* to oneself—is the primary value of my relations with the Other. This means that my being-for-others is haunted by the indication of an absolute-being which would be itself as other and other as itself and which by freely giving to itself its being-itself as other and its being-other as itself, would be the very being of the ontological proof—that is, God. This ideal can not be realized without my surmounting the original contingency of my relations to the Other; that is, by overcoming the fact that there is no relation of internal negativity between the negation by which the Other is made other than I and the negation by which I am made other than the Other. We have seen that this contingency is insurmountable; it is the *fact* of my relations with the Other, just as my body is the *fact* of my being-in-the-world. Unity with the Other is therefore in fact unrealizable. It is also unrealizable in theory, for the assimilation of the for-itself and the Other in a single transcendence would necessarily involve the disappearance of the characteristic of otherness in the Other. Thus the condition on which I project the identification of myself with the Other is that I persist in denying that I am the Other. Finally this project of unification is the source of *conflict* since while I experience myself as an object for the Other and while I project assimilating him in and by means of this experience, the Other apprehends me as an object in the midst of the world and does not project identifying me with himself. It would therefore be necessary—since being-for-others includes a double internal negation—to act upon the internal negation by which the Other transcends my transcendence and makes me exist for the Other; that is, *to act upon the Other's freedom*.

This unrealizable ideal which haunts my project of myself in the presence of the Other is not to be identified with love in so far as love is an enterprise; i.e., an organic ensemble of projects toward my own possibilities. But it is the ideal of love, its motivation and its end, its unique value. Love as the primitive relation to the Other is the ensemble of the projects by which I aim at realizing this value.

These projects put me in direct connection with the Other's freedom. It is in this sense that love is a conflict. We have observed that the Other's freedom is the foundation of my being. But precisely because I exist by means of the Other's freedom, I have no security; I am in danger in this freedom. It moulds my being and *makes me be*, it confers values upon me and removes them from me; and my being receives from it a perpetual passive escape from self. Irresponsible and beyond reach, this protean freedom in which I have engaged myself can in turn engage me in a thousand different ways of being. My project of recovering my being can be realized only if I get hold of this freedom and reduce it to being a freedom subject to my freedom. At the same time it is the only way in which I can act on the free negation of interiority by which the Other constitutes me as an Other; that is the only way in which I can prepare the way for a future identification of the Other with me. This will be clearer perhaps if we study the problem from a purely psychological aspect. Why does the lover want to be *loved*? If Love were in fact a pure desire for physical possession, it could in many cases be easily satisfied. Proust's hero, for example, who installs his mistress in his home, who can see her and possess her at any hour of the day, who has been able to make her completely dependent on him economically, ought to be free from worry. Yet we know that he is, on the contrary, continually gnawed by anxiety. Through her consciousness Albertine escapes Marcel even when he is at her side, and that is why he knows relief only when he gazes on her while she sleeps. It is certain then that the lover wishes to capture a "consciousness." But why does he wish it? And how?

The notion of "ownership," by which love is so often explained, is not actually primary. Why should I want to appropriate the Other if it were not precisely that the Other makes me be? But this implies precisely a certain mode of appropriation; it is the Other's freedom as such that we want to get hold of. Not because of a desire for power. The tyrant scorns love, he is content with fear. If he seeks to win the love of his subjects, it is for political reasons; and if he finds a more economical way to enslave them, he adopts it immediately. On the other hand, the man who wants to be loved does not desire the enslavement of the beloved. He is not bent on becoming the object of passion which flows forth mechanically. He does not want to possess an automaton, and if we want to humiliate him, we need only try to persuade him that the beloved's passion is the result of a psychological determinism. The lover will then feel that both his love and his being are cheapened. If Tristan and Isolde fall madly in love because of a love potion, they are less interesting. The total enslavement of the beloved kills the love of the lover. The end is surpassed; if the beloved is transformed into an automaton, the lover finds himself alone. Thus the lover does not desire to possess the beloved as one possesses a thing; he demands a special type of appropriation. He wants to possess a freedom as freedom.

On the other hand, the lover can not be satisfied with that superior form of freedom which is a free and voluntary engagement. Who would be content with a love given as pure loyalty to a sworn oath? Who would be satisfied with the words, "I love you because I have freely engaged myself to love you and because I do not wish to go back on my word." Thus the lover demands a pledge, yet is irritated by a pledge. He wants to be loved by a freedom but demands that this freedom as freedom should no longer be free. He wishes that the Other's freedom should determine itself to become love—and this not only at the beginning of the affair but at each instant—and at the same time he wants this freedom to be captured by itself, to turn back upon itself, as in madness, as in a dream, so as to will its own captivity. This captivity must be a resignation that is both free and yet chained in our hands. In love it is not a determinism of the passions which we desire in the Other nor a freedom beyond reach; it is a freedom which plays the role of a determinism of the passions and which is caught in its own role. For himself the lover does not demand that he be the cause of this radical modification of freedom but that he be the unique and privileged occasion of it. In fact he could not want to be the cause of it without immediately submerging the beloved in the midst of the world as a tool which can be transcended. That is not the essence of love. On the contrary, in Love the Lover wants to be "the whole World" for the beloved. This means that he puts himself on the side of the world; he is the one who assumes and symbolizes the world; he is a this which includes all other thises. He is and consents to be an object. But on the other hand, he wants to be the object in which the Other's freedom consents to lose itself, the object in which the Other consents to find his being and his *raison d'être* as his second facticity—the object-limit of transcendence, that toward which the Other's transcendence transcends all other objects but which it can in no way transcend. And everywhere he desires the circle of the Other's freedom; that is, at each instant as the Other's freedom accepts this limit to his transcendence, this acceptance is *already* present as the motivation of the acceptance considered. It is in the capacity of an end already chosen that the lover wishes to be chosen as an end. This allows us to grasp what basically the lover demands of the beloved; he does not want to *act* on the Other's freedom but to exist *a priori* as the objective limit of this freedom; that is, to be given at one stroke along with it and in its very upsurge as the limit which the freedom must accept in order to be free. By this very fact, what he demands is a liming, a gluing down of the Other's freedom by itself; this limit of structure is in fact a *given*, and the very appearance of the given as the limit of freedom means that the freedom *makes itself exist* within the given by being its own prohibition against surpassing it. This prohibition is envisaged by the lover *simultaneously* as something lived—that is, something suffered (in a word, as a facticity) and as something freely consented to. It must be freely consented to since it must be effected only with the upsurge of a freedom which chooses itself as freedom. But it must be only what is lived since it must be an impossibility always present, a facticity which surges back to the heart of the Other's freedom. This is expressed psychologically by the demand that the free decision to love me, which the beloved formerly has taken, must slip in as a magically determining motivation *within* his present free engagement.

Now we can grasp the meaning of this demand: the facticity which is to be a factual limit for the Other in my demand to be loved and which is to result in being *his own* facticity—this is *my* facticity. It is in so far as I am the object which the Other makes come into being that I must be the inherent limit to his very transcendence. Thus the Other by his upsurge into being makes me be as unsurpassable and absolute, not as a nihilating For-itself but as a being-for-others-in-the-midst-of-the-world. Thus to want to be loved is to infect the Other with one's own facticity; it is to wish to compel him to recreate you perpetually as the condition of a freedom which submits itself and which is engaged; it is to wish both that freedom found fact and that fact have pre-eminence over freedom. If this end could be attained, it would result in the first place in my being *secure* within the Other's consciousness. First because the motive of my uneasiness and my shame is the fact that I apprehend and experience myself in my being-for-others as that which can always be surpassed towards something else, that which is the pure object of a value judgment, a pure means, a pure tool. My uneasiness stems from the fact that I assume necessarily and freely that being which another makes me be in an absolute freedom. "God knows what I am for him! God knows what he thinks of me!" This means "God knows what he makes me be." I am haunted by this being which I fear to encounter someday at the turn of a path, this being which is so strange to me and which is yet *my being* and which I know that I shall never encounter in spite of all my efforts to do so. But if the Other loves me then I become the *unsurpassable*, which means that I must be the absolute end. In this sense I am saved from *instrumentality*. My existence in the midst of the world becomes the exact correlate of my transcendence-for-myself since my independence is absolutely safeguarded. The object which the Other must make me be is an object-transcendence, an absolute center of reference around which all the instrumental-things of the world are ordered as pure *means*. At the same time, as the absolute limit of freedom—i.e., of the absolute source of all values —I am protected against any eventual devaloriza-tion. I am the absolute value. To the extent that I assume my being-for-others, I assume myself as value. Thus to want to be loved is to want to be placed beyond the whole system of values posited by the Other and to be the condition of all valorization and the objective foundation of all values. This demand is the usual theme of lovers' conversations, whether as in *La Porte Etroite*, the woman who wants to be loved identifies herself with an ascetic morality of self-surpassing and wishes to embody the ideal limit of this surpassing—or as more usually happens, the lover demands that the beloved in his acts should sacrifice traditional morality for him and is anxious to know whether the beloved would betray his friends for him, "would steal for him," "would kill for him," *etc.*

From this point of view, my being must escape the *look* of the beloved, or rather it must be the object of a look with another structure. I must no longer be seen on the ground of the world as a "this" among other "thises," but the world must be revealed in terms of me. In fact to the extent that the upsurge of freedom makes a world exist, I must be, as the limiting-condition of this upsurge, the very condition of the upsurge of a world. I must be the one whose function is to make trees and water exist, to make cities and fields and other men exist, in order to give them later to the Other who arranges them into a world, just as the mother in matrilineal communities receives titles and the family name not to keep them herself but to transfer them immediately to her children. In one sense if I am to be loved, I am the object through whose procuration the world will exist for the Other; in another sense I am the world. Instead of being a "this" detaching itself on the background-world, I am the object-as-ground on which the world detaches itself. Thus I am reassured; the Other's look no longer paralyzes me with finitude. It no longer fixes my being in *what I am*. I can no longer be *looked at* as ugly, as small, as cowardly, since these characteristics necessarily represent a factual limitation of my being and an apprehension of my finitude as finitude. To be sure, my possibles remain transcended possibilities, dead-possibilities; but I possess all possibles. I am all the dead-possibilities in the world; hence I cease to be the being who is understood from the standpoint of other beings or of its acts. In the loving intuition which I demand, I am to be given as an absolute totality in terms of which all its peculiar acts and all beings are to be understood. One could say, slightly modifying a famous pronouncement of the Stoics, that "the beloved can fail in three ways."[1] The ideal of the sage and the ideal of the man who wants to be loved actually coincide in this that both want to be an object-as-totality accessible to a global intuition which will apprehend the beloved's or the sage's actions in the world as partial structures which are interpreted in terms of the totality. Just as wisdom is proposed as a state to be attained by an absolute metamorphosis, so the Other's freedom must be absolutely metamorphosed in order to allow me to attain the state of being loved.

Up to this point our description would fall into line with Hegel's famous description of the Master and Slave relation. What the Hegelian Master is for the Slave, the lover wants to be for the beloved. But the analogy stops here, for with Hegel the master demands the Slave's freedom only laterally and, so to speak, implicitly, while the lover wants the beloved's freedom first and foremost. In this sense if I am to be loved by the Other, this means that I am to be freely chosen as beloved. As we know, in the current terminology of love, the beloved is often called the chosen one. But this choice must not be relative and contingent. The lover is irritated and feels himself cheapened when he thinks that the beloved has chosen him from among others. "Then if I had not come into a certain city, if I had not visited the home of so and so, you would never have known me, you wouldn't have loved me?" This thought grieves the lover; his love becomes one love among others and is limited by the beloved's facticity and by his own facticity as well as by the contingency of encounters. It becomes love in the world, an object which presupposes the world and which in turn can exist for others. What he is demanding he expresses by the awkward and vitiated phrases of "fatalism." He says, "We were made for each other," or again he uses the expression "soul mate." But we must translate all this. The lover knows very well that "being made for each other" refers to an original choice. This choice can be God's, since he is the being who is absolute choice, but God here represents only the farthest possible limit of the demand for an absolute. Actually what the lover demands is that the beloved should make of him an absolute choice. This means that the beloved's being-in-the-world must be a being-as-loving. The upsurge of the beloved must be the beloved's free choice of the lover. And since the Other is the foundation of my being-as-object, I demand of him that the free upsurge

[1] Literally, "can tumble three times." Tr.

of his being should have his choice of me as his unique and absolute end; that is, that he should choose to be for the sake of founding my object-state and my facticity.

Thus my facticity is *saved*. It is no longer this unthinkable and insurmountable given which I am fleeing; it is that for which the Other freely makes himself exist; it is as an end which he has given to himself. I have infected him with my facticity, but as it is in the form of freedom that he has been infected with it, he refers it back to me as a facticity taken up and consented to. He is the foundation of it in order that it may be his end. By means of this love I then have a different apprehension of my alienation and of my own facticity. My facticity—as for-others—is no longer a fact but a right. My existence *is* because it is required. That existence, in so far as I assume it, becomes pure generosity. I am because I give myself away. These beloved veins on my hands exist by kindness. How good I am to have eyes, hair, eyebrows and to lavish them away tirelessly in an overflow of generosity to this tireless desire which the Other freely makes himself be. Whereas before being loved we were uneasy about that unjustified, unjustifiable protuberance which was our existence, whereas we felt ourselves "*de trop*," we now feel that our existence is taken up and willed even in its tiniest details by an absolute freedom which at the same time our existence conditions and which we ourselves will with our freedom. This is the basis for the joy of love when there is joy: we feel that our existence is justified.

By the same token if the beloved can love us, he is wholly ready to be assimilated by our freedom; for this being-loved which we desire is already the ontological proof applied to our being-for-others. Our objective essence implies the existence of the Other, and conversely it is the Other's freedom which founds our essence. If we could manage to interiorize the whole system, we should be our own foundation.

Such then is the real goal of the lover in so far as his love is an enterprise — i.e., a project of himself. This project is going to provoke a conflict. The beloved in fact apprehends the lover as one Other-as-object among others; that is, he perceives the lover on the ground of the world, transcends him, and utilizes him. The beloved is *a look*. He can not therefore employ his transcendence to fix an ultimate limit to his surpassings, nor can he employ his freedom to captivate itself. The beloved can not will to love. Therefore the lover must seduce the beloved, and his love can in no way be distinguished from the enterprise of seduction. In seduction I do not try to reveal my subjectivity to the Other. Moreover I could do so only by *looking at* the other; but by this look I should cause the Other's subjectivity to disappear, and it is exactly this which I want to assimilate. To seduce is to risk assuming my object-state completely for the Other; it is to put myself beneath his look and to make him look at me; it is to risk the danger of *being-seen* in order to effect a new departure and to appropriate the Other in and by means of my object-ness. I refuse to leave the level on which I make proof of my object-ness; it is on this level that I wish to engage in battle by making myself a *fascinating object*. In Part Two we defined fascination as a *state*. It is, we said, the non-thetic consciousness of being *nothing* in the presence of being. Seduction aims at producing in the Other the consciousness of his state of nothingness as he confronts the seductive object. By seduction I aim at constituting myself as a fullness of being and at making myself *recognized as such*. To accomplish this I constitute myself as a meaningful object. My acts must *point* in two directions: On the one hand, toward that which is wrongly called subjectivity and which is rather a depth of objective and hidden being; the act is not performed for itself only, but it points to an infinite, undifferentiated series of other real and possible acts which I give as constituting my objective, unperceived being. Thus I try to guide the transcendence which transcends me and to refer it to the infinity of my dead-possibilities precisely in order to be the unsurpassable and to the exact extent to which the only unsurpassable is the infinite. On the other hand, each of my acts tries to point to the great density of possible-world and must present me as bound to the vastest regions of the world, whether I present the world to the beloved and try to constitute myself as the necessary intermediary between him and the world, whether I manifest by my acts infinitely varied examples of my power over the world (money, position, "connections," etc.). In the first case I try to constitute myself as an infinity of depth, in the second case to identify myself with the world. Through these different procedures I propose myself as unsurpassable. This proposal could not be sufficient in itself; it is only a besieging of the Other. It can not take on value as fact without the consent of the Other's freedom, which I must capture by making it recognize itself as nothingness in the face of my plenitude of absolute being.

Someone may observe that these various attempts at expression *presuppose* language. We shall not disagree with this. But we shall say rather that they *are* language or, if you prefer, a fundamental mode of language. For while psy-chological and historical problems exist with regard to the existence, the learning and the use of *a particular* language, there is no special problem concerning what is called the discovery or invention of language. Language is not a phenomenon added on to being-for-others. It *is* originally being-for-others; that is, it is the fact that a subjectivity experiences itself as an object for the Other. In a universe of pure objects language could under no circum-stances have been "invented" since it presupposes an original relation to another subject. In the intersubjectivity of the for-others, it is not necessary to invent language because it is already given in the recognition of the Other. I *am* language. By the sole fact that whatever I may do, my acts freely conceived and executed, my projects launched toward my possibilities have outside of them a meaning which escapes me and which I experience. It is in this sense—and in this sense only—that Heidegger is right in declaring that I am what I say.[2] Language is not an instinct of the constituted human creature, nor is it an invention of our subjectivity. But neither does it need to be referred to the pure "being-outside-of-self" of the Dasein. It forms part of the human condition; it is originally the proof which a for-itself can make of its being-for-others, and finally it is the surpassing of this proof and the utilization of it toward possibilities which are my possibilities; that is, toward my possibilities of being this or that for the Other. Language is therefore not distinct from the recognition of the Other's existence. The Other's upsurge confronting me as a look makes language arise as the condition of my being. This primitive language is not necessarily seduction; we shall see other forms of it. Moreover we have noted that there is no primitive attitude facing the Other and that the two succeed each other in a circle, each implying the other. But conversely seduction does not presuppose any earlier form of language; it is the complete realization of language. This means that language can be revealed entirely and at one stroke by seduction as a primitive mode of being of expression. Of course by language we mean all the phenomena of expression and not the articulated word, which is a derived and secondary mode whose appearance can be made the object of an historical study. Especially in seduction language does not aim at giving to be known but at causing to experience.

But in this first attempt to find a fascinating language I proceed blindly since I am guided only by the abstract and empty form of my object-state for the Other. I can not even conceive what effect my gestures and attitudes will have since they will always be taken up and founded by a freedom which will surpass them and since they can have a meaning only if this freedom confers one on them. Thus the "meaning" of my expressions always escapes me. I never know exactly if I signify what I wish to signify nor even if I am signifying anything. It would be necessary that at the precise instant I should read in the Other what on principle is inconceivable. For lack of knowing what I actually express for the Other, I constitute my language as an incomplete phenomenon of flight outside myself. As soon as I express myself, I can only guess at the meaning of what I express—i.e., the meaning of what I am—since in this perspective to express and to be are one. The Other is always there, present and experienced as the one who gives to language its

---

[2] This formulation of Heidegger's position is that of A. de Waehlens. La philosophie de Martin Heidegger. Louvain, 1942, p. 99. Cf. also Heidegger's text, which he quotes: "Diese Bezeugung meint nicht hier einen nachträglichen und beiherlaufenden Ausdruck des Menschseins, sonder sie macht das Dasein des Menschen mit usw. (Hölderlin und das Wesen der Dichtung, p. 6.)

("This affirmation does not mean here an additional and supplementary expression of human existence, but it does in the process make plain the existence of man." Douglas Scott's translation. Existence and Being, Chicago: Henry Regnery. 1949, p. 297.)

meaning. Each expression, each gesture, each word is on my side a concrete proof of the alienating reality of the Other. It is not only the psychopath who can say, "someone has stolen my thought"—as in cases of psychoses of influence, for example.[3] The very fact of expression is a stealing of thought since thought needs the cooperation of an alienating freedom in order to be constituted as an object. That is why this first aspect of language—in so far as it is I who employ it for the Other—is *sacred*. The sacred object is an object which is in the world and which points to a transcendence beyond the world. Language reveals to me the freedom (the transcendence) of the one who listens to me in silence.

But at the same moment I remain for the Other a meaningful object—as I have always been. There is no path which departing from my object-state can lead the Other to my transcendence. Attitudes, expressions, and words can only indicate to him other attitudes, other expressions, and other words. Thus language remains for him a simple property of a magical object—and this magical object itself. It is an action at a distance whose effect the Other exactly knows. Thus the word is *sacred* when I employ it and *magic* when the Other hears it. Thus I do not know my language any more than I know my body for the Other. I can not hear myself speak nor see myself smile. The problem of language is exactly parallel to the problem of bodies, and the description which is valid in one case is valid in the other.

Fascination, however, even if it were to produce a state of being-fascinated in the Other could not by itself succeed in producing love. We can be fascinated by an orator, by an actor, by a tightrope-walker, but this does not mean that we love him. To be sure we can not take our eyes off him, but he is still raised on the ground of the world, and fascination does not posit the fascinating object as the ultimate term of the transcendence. Quite the contrary, fascination is transcendence. When then will the beloved become in turn the lover?

The answer is easy: when the beloved projects being loved. By himself the Other-as-object never has enough strength to produce love. If love has for its ideal the appropriation of the Other qua Other (i.e., as a subjectivity which is looking at an object) this ideal can be projected only in terms of my encounter with the Other-as-subject, not with the Other-as-object. If the Other tries to seduce me by means of his object-state, then seduction can bestow upon the Other only the character of a *precious* object "to be possessed." Seduction will perhaps determine me to risk much to conquer the Other-as-object, but this desire to appropriate an object in the midst of the

---

[3] Furthermore the psychosis of influence, like the majority of psychoses, is a special experience translated by myths, of a great metaphysical fact—here the fact of alienation. Even a madman in his own way realizes the human condition.

world should not be confused with love. Love therefore can be born in the beloved only from the experience which he makes of his alienation and his flight toward the Other. Still the beloved, if such is the case, will be transformed into a lover only if he projects being loved; that is, if what he wishes to overcome is not a body but the Other's subjectivity as such. In fact the only way that he could conceive to realize this appropriation is to make himself be loved. Thus it seems that to love is in essence the project of making oneself be loved. Hence this new contradiction and this new conflict: each of the lovers is entirely the captive of the Other inasmuch as each wishes to make himself loved by the Other to the exclusion of anyone else; but at the same time each one demands from the other a love which is not reducible to the "project of being-loved." What he demands in fact is that the Other without originally seeking to make himself be loved should have at once a contemplative and affective intuition of his beloved as the objective limit of his freedom, as the ineluctable and chosen foundation of his transcendence, as the totality of being and the supreme value. Love thus exacted from the other could not *ask* for anything; it is a pure engagement without reciprocity. Yet this love can not exist except in the form of a demand on the part of the lover.

The lover is held captive in a wholly different way. He is the captive of his very demand since love is the demand to be loved; he *is* a freedom which wills itself a body and which demands an outside, hence a freedom which imitates the flight toward the Other, a freedom which qua freedom lays claim to its alienation. The lover's freedom, in his very effort to make himself be loved as an object by the Other, is alienated by slipping into the body-for-others; that is, it is brought into existence with a dimension of flight toward the Other. It is the perpetual refusal to posit itself as pure selfness, for this affirmation of self as itself would involve the collapse of the Other as a look and the upsurge of the Other-as-object—hence a state of affairs in which the very possibility of being loved disappears since the Other is reduced to the dimension of objectivity. This refusal therefore constitutes freedom as dependent on the Other; and the Other as subjectivity becomes indeed an unsurpassable limit of the freedom of the for-itself, the goal and supreme end of the for-itself since the Other holds the key to its being. Here in fact we encounter the true ideal of love's enterprise: alienated freedom. But it is the one who wants to be loved who by the mere fact of wanting someone to love him alienates his freedom.

My freedom is alienated in the presence of the Other's pure subjectivity which founds my objectivity. It can never be alienated before the Other-as-object. In this form in fact the beloved's alienation, of which the lover dreams, would be contradictory since the beloved can found the being of the lover only by transcending it on principle toward other objects of the world; therefore this transcendence can not constitute the object which it surpasses both as a transcended object and as an object limit of all transcendence. Thus each one of the lovers wants to be the object for which the Other's freedom is alienated in an original intuition; but this intuition which would be love in the true sense is only a contradictory ideal of the for-itself. Each one is alienated only to the exact extent to which he demands the alienation of the other. Each one wants the other to love him but does not take into account the fact that to love is to want to be loved and that thus by wanting the other to love him, he only wants the other to want to be loved in turn. Thus love relations are a system of indefinite reference—analogous to the pure "reflection-reflected" of consciousness—under the ideal standard of the *value* "love;" that is, in a fusion of consciousnesses in which each of them would preserve his otherness in order to found the other. This state of affairs is due to the fact that consciousnesses are separated by an insurmountable nothingness, a nothingness which is both the internal negation of the one by the other and a factual nothingness between the two internal negations. Love is a contradictory effort to surmount the factual negation while preserving the internal negation. I demand that the Other love me and I do everything possible to realize my project; but if the Other loves me, he radically deceives me by his very love. I demanded of him that he should found my being as a privileged object by maintaining himself as pure subjectivity confronting me; and as soon as he loves me he experiences me as subject and is swallowed up in his objectivity confronting my subjectivity.

The problem of my being-for-others remains therefore without solution. The lovers remain each one for himself in a total subjectivity; nothing comes to relieve them of their duty to make themselves exist each one for himself; nothing comes to relieve their contingency nor to save them from facticity. At least each one has succeeded in escaping danger from the Other's freedom— but altogether differently than he expected. He escapes not because the Other makes him be as the object-limit of his transcendence but because the Other experiences him as subjectivity and wishes to experience him only as such. Again the gain is perpetually compromised. At the start, each of the consciousnesses can at any moment free itself from its chains and suddenly comtemplate the other as an *object*. Then the spell is broken; the Other becomes one mean among means. He is indeed an object for-others as the lover desires but an object-as-tool, a perpetually transcended object. The illusion, the game of mirrors which makes the concrete reality of love, suddenly ceases. Later in the experience of love each consciousness seeks to shelter its being-for-others in the Other's freedom. This supposes that the Other is beyond the world as pure subjectivity, as the absolute by which the world comes into being. But it suffices that the lovers should be *looked at* together by a third person in order for each one to experience not only his own objectivation but that of the other as well. Immediately the Other is no longer for me the absolute transcendence which founds me in my being; he is a transcendence-transcended, not by me but by another. My original relation to him—i.e., my relation of being the beloved for my lover, is fixed as a dead-possibility. It is no longer the experienced relation between a limiting object of all transcendence and the freedom which founds it; it is a love-as-object which is wholly alienated toward the third. Such is the true reason why lovers seek solitude. It is because the appearance of a third person, whoever he may be, is the destruction of their love. But factual solitude (*e.g.* we are alone in my room) is by no means a theoretical solitude. Even if nobody sees us, we exist for *all* consciousnesses and we are conscious of existing for all. The result is that love as a fundamental mode of being-for-others holds in its being-for-others the seed of its own destruction.

We have just defined the triple destructibility of love: in the first place it is, in essence, a deception and a reference to infinity since to love is to wish to be loved, hence to wish that the Other wish that I love him. A preontological comprehension of this deception is given in the very impulse of love—hence the lover's perpetual dissatisfaction. It does not come, as is so often said, from the unworthiness of being loved but from an implicit comprehension of the fact that the amorous intuition is, as a fundamental-intuition, an ideal out of reach. The more I am loved, the more I lose my *being*, the more I am thrown back on my own responsibilities, on my own power to be. In the second place the Other's awakening is always possible; at any moment he can make me appear as an object—hence the lover's perpetual insecurity. In the third place love is an absolute which is perpetually *made relative* by others. One would have to be alone in the world with the beloved in order for love to preserve its character as an absolute axis of reference—hence the lover's perpetual shame (or pride—which here amounts to the same thing).

Thus it is useless for me to have tried to lose myself in objectivity; my passion will have availed me nothing. The Other has referred me to my own unjustifiable subjectivity—either by himself or through others. This result can provoke a total despair and a new attempt to realize the identification of the Other and myself. Its ideal will then be the opposite of that which we have just described; instead of projecting the absorbing of the Other while preserving in him his otherness, I shall project causing myself to be absorbed by the Other and losing myself in his subjectivity in order to get rid of my own. This enterprise will be expressed concretely by the *masochistic* attitude. Since the Other is the foundation of my being-for-others, if I relied on the Other to make me exist, I should no longer be anything more than a being-in-itself founded in its being by a freedom. Here it is my own subjectivity which is considered as an obstacle to the primordial act by which the Other would found me in my being. It is my own subjectivity which above all must be denied by *my own freedom*. I attempt therefore to engage myself wholly in my being-as object. I refuse to be anything more than an object. I rest upon the Other, and as I experience this being-as-object in shame, I will and I love my shame as the profound sign of my objectivity. As the Other apprehends me as object by means of *actual desire*, I wish to be desired, I make myself in shame an object of desire.[4]

This attitude would resemble that of love if instead of seeking to exist for the Other as the object-limit of his transcendence, I did not rather insist on making myself be treated as one object among others, as an instrument to be used. Now it is my transcendence which is to be denied, not his. This time I do not have to project capturing his freedom; on the contrary I hope that this freedom may *be* and will itself to be radically free. Thus the more I shall feel myself surpassed toward other ends, the more I shall enjoy the abdication of my transcendence. Finally I project being nothing more than an *object*; that is, radically an *in-itself*. But inasmuch as a freedom which will have absorbed mine will be the foundation of this in-itself, my being will become again the foundation of itself. Masochism, like sadism, is the assumption of guilt.[5] I am guilty due to the very fact that I am an object, I am guilty toward myself since I consent to my absolute alienation. I am guilty toward the Other, for I furnish him with the occasion of being guilty—that is, of radically missing my freedom as such. Masochism is an attempt not to fascinate the Other by means of my objectivity but to cause myself to be fascinated by my objectivity-for-others; that is, to cause myself to be consti- tuted as an object by the Other in such a way that I non-thetically apprehend my subjectivity as a *nothing* in the presence of the in-itself which I represent to the Other's eyes. Masochism is characterized as a kind of vertigo, vertigo not before a precipice of rock and earth but before the abyss of the Other's subjectivity.

But masochism is and must be itself a failure. In order to cause myself to be fascinated by my self-as-object, I should necessarily have to be able to realize the intuitive apprehension of this object such as it is *for the Other*, a thing which is on principle impossible. Thus I am far from being able to be fascin- ated by this alienated Me, which remains on principle inapprehensible. It is useless for the masochist to get down on his knees, to show himself in ridiculous positions, to cause himself to be used as a simple lifeless instru- ment. It is *for the Other* that he will be obscene or simply passive, for the Other that he will *undergo* these postures; for himself he is forever condemned to *give them to himself*. It is in and through his transcendence that he disposes of himself as a being to be transcended. The more he tries to taste his objectiv- ity, the more he will be submerged by the consciousness of his subjectivity— to the point of anguish. Even the masochist who pays a woman to whip him

---

[4] Cf. following section.    [5] Cf. following section.

is treating her as an instrument and by this very fact posits himself in transcendence in relation to her.

Thus the masochist ultimately treats the Other as an object and transcends him toward his own objectivity. Recall, for example, the tribulations of Sacher Masoch, who in order to make himself scorned, insulted, reduced to a humiliating position, was obliged to make use of the great love which women bore toward him; that is, to act upon them just in so far as they experienced themselves as an object for him. Thus in every way the masochist's objectivity escapes him, and it can even happen—in fact usually does happen—that in seeking to apprehend his own objectivity he finds the Other's objectivity, which in spite of himself frees his own subjectivity. Masochism therefore is on principle a failure. This should not surprise us if we realize that masochism is a "vice" and that vice is, on principle, the love of failure. But this is not the place to describe the structures peculiar to vice. It is sufficient here to point out that masochism is a perpetual effort to *annihilate* the subject's subjectivity by causing it to be assimilated by the Other; this effort is accompanied by the exhausting and delicious consciousness of failure so that finally it is the failure itself which the subject ultimately seeks as his principal goal.[6]

## II. SECOND ATTITUDE TOWARD OTHERS: INDIFFERENCE, DESIRE, HATE, SADISM

The failure of the first attitude toward the Other can be the occasion for my assuming the second. But of course neither of the two is really first; each of them is a fundamental reaction to being-for-others as an original situation. It can happen therefore that due to the very impossibility of my identifying myself with the Other's consciousness through the intermediacy of my object-ness for him, I am led to turn deliberately toward the Other and look at him. In this case to look at the Other's look is to posit oneself in one's own freedom and to attempt on the ground of this freedom to confront the Other's freedom. The meaning of the conflict thus sought would be to bring out into the open the struggle of two freedoms confronted as freedoms. But this intention must be immediately disappointed, for by the sole fact that I assert myself in my freedom confronting the Other, I make the Other a transcendence-transcended—that is, an object. It is the story of that failure which we are about to investigate. We can grasp its general pattern. I direct my look upon the Other who is looking at me. But a look can not be looked

---

[6] Consistent with this description, there is at least one form of exhibitionism which ought to be classed among masochistic attitudes. For example, when Rousseau exhibits to the washerwomen "not the obscene object but the ridiculous object." Cf. *Confessions*, book III.

at. As soon as I look in the direction of the look it disappears, and I no longer see anything but eyes. At this instant the Other becomes a being which I possess and which recognizes my freedom. It seems that my goal has been achieved since I possess the being who has the key to my object-state and since I can cause him to make proof of my freedom in a thousand different ways. But in reality the whole structure has collapsed, for the being which remains within my hands is an Other-as-object. As such he has lost the key to my being-as-object, and he possesses a pure and simple image of me which is nothing but one of its objective affects and which no longer touches me. If he experiences the effects of my freedom, if I can act upon his being in a thousand different ways and transcend his possibilities with all my possibilities, this is only in so far as he is an object in the world and as such is outside the state of recognizing my freedom. My disappointment is complete since I seek to appropriate the Other's freedom and perceive suddenly that I can act upon the Other only in so far as this freedom has collapsed beneath my look. This disappointment will be the result of my further attempts to seek again for the Other's freedom across the object which he is for me and to find privileged attitudes or conduct which would appropriate this freedom across a total appropriation of the Other's body. These attempts, as one may suspect, are on principle doomed to failure.

But it can happen also that "to look at the look" is my original reaction to my being-for-others. This means that in my upsurge into the world, I can choose myself as looking at the Other's look and can build my subjectivity upon the collapse of the subjectivity of the Other. It is this attitude which we shall call *indifference toward others*. Then we are dealing with a kind of *blindness* with respect to others. But the term "blindness" must not lead us astray. I do not suffer this blindness as a state. I *am* my own blindness with regard to others, and this blindness includes an implicit comprehension of being-for-others; that is, of the Other's transcendence as a look. This comprehension is simply what I myself determine to hide from myself. I practice then a sort of factual solipsism; others are those forms which pass by in the street, those magic objects which are capable of acting at a distance and upon which I can act by means of specific conducts. I scarcely notice them; I act as if I were alone in the world. I brush against "people" as I brush against a wall; I avoid them as I avoid obstacles. Their freedom-as-object is for me only their "co-efficient of adversity." I do not even imagine that they can *look at* me. Of course they have some knowledge of me, but this knowledge does not touch me. It is a question of pure modifications of their being which do not pass from them to me and which are tainted with what we call a "suffered-subjectivity" or "subjectivity-as-object;" that is, they express what they are, not what I am, and they are the effect of my action upon them. Those "people" are functions: the ticket-collector is only the function of collecting tickets; the café waiter is nothing but the function of serving the customers. From this point of view they will be most useful if I know their *keys* and those "master-words" which can release their mechanisms. Hence is derived that "realist" psychology which the seventeenth century in France has given us; hence those treatises of the eighteenth century, *How to Succeed* (*Le Moyen de parvenir*) by Beroalde de Verville, *Dangerous Connections* (*Les Liaisons dangereuses*) by Laclos, *Treatise on Ambition* (*Traité de l'ambition*) by Hérault de Séchelles, all of which give to us a *practical* knowledge of the Other and the art of acting upon him. In this state of blindness I concurrently ignore the Other's absolute subjectivity as the foundation of my being-in-itself and my being-for-others, in particular of my "body for others." In a sense I am reassured, I am self-confident; that is, I am in no way conscious of the fact that the Other's look can fix my possibilities and my body. I am in a state the very opposite of what we call *shyness* or timidity. I am at ease; I am not embarrassed by myself, for I am not *outside*; I do not feel myself alienated. This state of *blindness* can be maintained for a long time, as long as my fundamental bad faith desires; it can be extended—with relapses—over several years, over a whole life; there are men who die without—save for brief and terrifying flashes of illumination—ever having suspected what the *Other is*.

But even if one is entirely immersed in this state, one does not thereby cease to experience its inadequacy. And like all bad faith it is the state itself which furnishes us with the motives for getting out of it; for blindness as concerns the Other concurrently causes the disappearance of every lived apprehension of my *objectivity*. Nevertheless the Other as freedom and my objectivity as my alienated-self *are there*, unperceived, not thematized, but given in my very comprehension of the world and of my being in the world. The conductor, even if he is considered as a *pure* function, refers me by his very function to a being-outside—even though this being-outside is neither apprehended nor apprehensible. Hence a perpetual feeling of lack and of uneasiness. This is because my fundamental project toward the Other—whatever may be the attitude which I assume—is twofold: first there is the problem of protecting myself against the danger which is incurred by my being-outside-in-the-Other's-freedom, and second there is the problem of utilizing the Other in order finally to totalize the detotalized totality which I am, so as to close the open circle, and finally to be my own foundation. But on the one hand the Other's disappearance as look throws me back into my unjustifiable subjectivity and reduces my being to this perpetual pursued-pursuit toward an inapprehensible In-itself-for-itself. Without the Other I apprehend fully and nakedly this terrible necessity of being free which is my lot; that is, the fact that I can not put the responsibility for making-myself-be off onto anyone but myself even though I have not chosen to be and although I have been *born*. On the other hand although the *blindness* toward the Other does in appearance release me from the fear of being in danger in the Other's freedom, it includes despite all an implicit comprehension of this freedom. It therefore places me at the extreme degree of objectivity at the very moment when I can believe myself to be an absolute and unique subjectivity since I am seen without being able to experience the fact that I am seen and without being able by means of the same experience to defend myself against my "being-seen." I am possessed without being able to turn toward the one who possesses me. In making direct proof of the Other as a look, I defend myself by putting the Other to the test, and the possibility remains for me to trans-form the Other into an object. But if the Other is an object for me while *he is looking at me*, then I am in danger without knowing it. Thus my *blindness* is anxiety because it is accompanied by the consciousness of a "wandering and inapprehensible" look, and I am in danger of its alienating me behind my back. This uneasiness can occasion a new attempt to get possession of the Other's freedom. But this will mean that I am going to turn back upon the Other-as-object which has been merely brushing against me and attempt now to utilize him as an instrument in order to touch his freedom. But precisely because I address myself to the *object* "Other" I can not ask him to account for his transcendence, and since I am myself on the level where I make an object of the Other, I can not even conceive of what I wish to appropriate. Thus I am in an irritating and contradictory attitude with respect to this object which I an considering: not only can I not obtain from him what I wish, but in addition this quest provokes a disappearance of the practical knowledge pertaining to what I wish. I engage myself in a desperate pursuit of the Other's freedom and midway I find *myself engaged* in a pursuit which has lost its meaning. All my efforts to bring back meaning to the pursuit result only in making me lose it further and provoking my bewilder-ment and my uneasiness—just as when I attempt to recover the memory of a dream and this memory melts between my fingers leaving me with a vague and irritating impression of a total knowledge but with no object, or just as when I attempt to make explicit the content of a false recollection and the very explanation causes it to melt away in translucency.

My original attempt to get hold of the Other's free subjectivity through his objectivity-for-me is *sexual desire*. Perhaps it will come as a surprise to see a phenomenon which is usually classified among "psycho-physiological reac-tions" now mentioned on the level of primary attitudes which manifest our original mode of realizing Being-for-Others. For the majority of psycholo-gists indeed, desire, as a fact of consciousness, is in strict correlation with the nature of our sexual organs, and it is only in connection with an elaborate study of these that sexual desire can be understood. But since the differenti-ated structure of the body (mammalian, viviparous, *etc.*) and consequently the particular sexual structure (uterus, Fallopian tubes, ovaries, *etc.*) are in the domain of absolute contingency and in no way derive from the ontology of "consciousness" or of the "Dasein," it seems that the same must be true for sexual desire. Just as the sex organs are a contingent and particular formation of our body, so the desire which corresponds to them would be a contingent modality of our psychic life; that is, it would be described only on the level of an empirical psychology based on biology. This is indicated sufficiently by the term *sex instinct*, which is reserved for desire and all the psychic structures which refer to it. The term "instinct" always in fact qualifies contingent formations of psychic life which have the double character of being co-extensive with all the duration of this life—or in any case of not deriving from our "history"—and of nevertheless not being such that they can not be deduced as belonging to the very essence of the psychic. This is why existential philosophies have not believed it necessary to concern themselves with sexuality. Heidegger, in particular, does not make the slightest allusion to it in his existential analytic with the result that his "Dasein" appears to us as asexual. Of course one may consider that it is contingent for "human reality" to be specified as "masculine" or "feminine"; of course one may say that the problem of sexual differentiation has nothing to do with that of *Existence* (*Existenz*) since man and woman equally exist.

These reasons are not wholly convincing. That sexual differentiation lies within the domain of facticity we may eventually accept. But does this mean that the For-itself is sexual "accidentally," by the pure contingency of having this particular body? Can we admit that this tremendous matter of the sexual life comes as a kind of addition to the human condition? Yet it appears at first glance that desire and its opposite, sexual repulsion, are fundamental structures of being-for-others. It is evident that if sexuality derives its origin from sex as a physiological and contingent determination of man, it can not be indispensable to the being of the For-Others. But do we not have the right to ask whether the problem is not perchance of the same order as that which we encountered apropos of sensations and sense organs? Man, it is said, is a sexual being because he possesses genitals. And if the reverse were true? If genitals were only the instrument and, so to speak, the *image* of a fundamental sexuality? If man possessed genitals only because he is originally and fundamentally a sexual being as a being who exists in the world in relation with other men? Infantile sexuality precedes the physiological maturation of the sex organs. Men who have become eunuchs do not thereby cease to feel desire. Nor do many old men. The fact of being able to *make use* of a sex organ fit to fertilize and to procure enjoyment represents only one phase and one aspect of our sexual life. There is one mode of sexuality "with the possibility of satisfaction," and the developed genitals represent and make concrete this possibility. But there are other modes of sexuality of the type which can not get satisfaction, and if we take these modes into account we are forced to recognize that sexuality appears with birth and disappears only with death. Moreover neither the tumescence of the penis nor any other physiological phenomenon can ever explain or provoke sexual desire—no more than the vaso-constriction or the dilation of the pupils (or the mere consciousness of these physiological modifications) will be able to explain or to provoke fear. In one case as in the other although the body plays an important role, we must—in order to understand it—refer to being-in-the-world and to being-for-others. I desire a human being, not an insect or a mollusk, and I desire him (or her) as he is and as I am in situation in the world and as he is an Other for me and as I am an Other for him.

The fundamental problem of sexuality can therefore be formulated thus: is sexuality a contingent accident bound to our physiological nature, or is it a necessary structure of being-for-itself-for-others? From the sole fact that the question can be posited in these terms, we see that we must go back to ontology to decide it. Moreover ontology can decide this question only by determining and fixing the meaning of sexual existence for-the-Other. To have sexual organs means—in accordance with the description of the body which we attempted in the preceding chapter—to exist sexually for an Other who exists sexually for me. And it must be well understood that at first this Other is not necessarily for me—nor I for him—a *heterosexual* existent but only a sexed being. Considered from the point of view of the For-itself, this apprehension of the Other's sexuality could not be the pure disinterested contemplation of his primary or secondary sexual characteristics. My first apprehension of the Other as sexed does not come when I conclude from the distribution of his hair, from the coarseness of his hands, the sound of his voice, his strength that he is of the masculine sex. We are dealing there with derived conclusions which refer to an original state. The first apprehension of the Other's sexuality in so far as it is lived and suffered can be only *desire*; it is by desiring the Other (or by discovering myself as incapable of desiring him) or by apprehending his desire for me that I discover his being-sexed. Desire reveals to me simultaneously *my* being-sexed and *his* being-sexed, *my* body as sex and *his* body. Here therefore in order to decide the nature and ontological position of sex we are referred to the study of desire. What therefore is desire? And first, desire *of what*?

We must abandon straight off the idea that desire is the desire of pleasure or the desire for the cessation of a pain. For we can not see how the subject could get out of this state of immanence so as to "attach" his desire to an object. Every subjectivist and immanentist theory will fail to explain how we desire a particular woman and not simply our sexual satisfaction. It is best therefore to define desire by its transcendent object. Nevertheless it would be wholly inaccurate to say that desire is a desire for "physical possession" of the desired object—if by "possess" we mean here "to make love to." Of course the sexual act for a moment frees us from desire, and in certain cases it can be posited explicitly as the hoped-for issue of the desire—when desire, for example, is painful and fatiguing. But in this case it is necessary that the desire itself be the object which is posited as "to be overcome," and this can be accomplished only by means of a reflective consciousness. But desire by itself is non-reflective; therefore it could never posit itself as an object to be overcome. Only a roué represents his desire to himself, treats it as an object, excites it, "turns it off," varies the means of assuaging it, *etc.* But in this case, we must observe, it is the desire itself which becomes the desirable. The error here stems from the fact that we have learned that the sexual act suppresses the desire. We have therefore added on a bit of knowledge to the desire and from outside we have added pleasure as desire's normal satisfaction—for reasons external to the essence of desire (*e.g.*, procreation, the sacred character of maternity, the exceptional strength of the pleasure provoked by ejaculation, the symbolic value attached to the sexual act). Thus the average man through mental sluggishness and desire to conform can conceive of no other goal for his desire than ejaculation. This is what has allowed people to conceive of desire as an instinct whose origin and end are strictly physiological since in man, for example, it would have as its cause the erection and as its final limit the ejaculation. But desire by itself by no means implies the sexual act; desire does not thematically posit it, does not even suggest it in outline, as one sees when it is a question of the desire of very young children or of adults who are ignorant of the "technique" of love. Similarly desire is not a desire of any special amorous practice; this is sufficiently proved by the diversity of sexual practices, which vary with social groups. In a general way desire is not a desire of *doing*. The "doing" is after the event, is added on to the desire from outside and necessitates a period of apprenticeship; there is an amorous technique which has its own ends and means. Therefore since desire can not posit its suppression as its supreme end nor single out for its ultimate goal any particular act, it is purely and simply the desire of a transcendent object. Here again we find that affective intentionality of which we spoke in preceding chapters and which Scheler and Husserl have described.

But what is the object of desire? Shall we say that desire is the desire of a *body*? In one sense this can not be denied. But we must take care to understand this correctly. To be sure it is the body which disturbs us: an arm or a half-exposed breast or perhaps a foot. But we must realize at the start that we desire the arm or the uncovered breast only on the ground of the presence of the whole body as an organic totality. The body itself as totality may be hidden. I may see only a bare arm. But the body is there. It is from the standpoint of the body that I apprehend the arm as an arm. The body is as much present, as adherent to the arm which I see as the designs of the rug, which are hidden by the feet of the table, are present and adherent to those designs which I see.

And my desire is not mistaken; it is addressed not to a sum of physiological elements but to a total form—better yet, to a form *in situation*. A particular attitude, as we shall see later, does much to provoke desire. Now along with the attitude the surroundings are given and finally the world. But here suddenly we are at the opposite pole from a simple physiological pruritus; desire posits the world and desires the body in terms of the world and the beautiful hand in terms of the body. It follows exactly the process which we described in the preceding chapter, that by which we apprehended the Other's body from the standpoint of his situation in the world. Moreover there is nothing in this which should surprise us since desire is nothing but one of the great forms which can be assumed by the revelation of the Other's body. Yet precisely for this reason we do not desire the body as a purely material object; a purely material object is not *in situation*. Thus this organic totality which is immediately present to desire is desirable only in so far as it reveals not only life but also an appropriate consciousness. Nevertheless, as we shall see, the Other's being-in-situation which desire reveals is of an entirely original type. Furthermore the consciousness here considered is still only one *property* of the desired object; that is, it is nothing but the sense of flow of the objects in the world, precisely in so far as this flow is cut off, localized, and made a part of my world. To be sure, one can desire a woman who is asleep, but one desires her in so far as this sleep appears on the ground of consciousness. Consciousness therefore remains always at the horizon of the desired body; it makes the meaning and the unity of the body. A living body as an organic totality in situation with consciousness at the horizon: such is the object to which desire *is addressed*. What does desire wish from this object? We can not determine this until we have answered a preliminary question: *Who* is the one who desires?

The answer is clear. I *am* the one who desires, and desire is a particular mode of my subjectivity. Desire is consciousness since it can *be* only as a non-positional consciousness of itself. Nevertheless we need not hold that the desiring consciousness differs from the cognitive consciousness, for example, only in the nature of its object. For the For-itself, to choose itself as desire is not to produce a desire while remaining indifferent and unchanged—as the Stoic cause produces its effect. The For-itself puts itself on a certain plane of existence which is not the same, for example, as that of a For-itself which chooses itself as a metaphysical being. Every consciousness, as we have seen, supports a certain relation with its own facticity. But this relation can vary from one mode of consciousness to another. The facticity of a pain-consciousness, for example, is a facticity discovered in a perpetual flight. The case is not the same for the facticity of desire. The man who desires *exists* his body in a particular mode and thereby places himself on a particular level of existence. In fact everyone will agree that desire is not only *longing*, a clear and translucent *longing* which directs itself through our body toward a certain object. Desire is defined as *trouble*. The notion of "trouble" can help us better to determine the nature of desire. We contrast troubled water with transparent water, a troubled look with a clear look. Troubled water remains water; it preserves the fluidity and the essential characteristics of water; but its translucency is "troubled" by an inapprehensible presence which makes one with it, which is everywhere and nowhere, and which is given as a clogging of the water by itself. To be sure, we can explain the troubled quality by the presence of fine solid particles suspended in the liquid, but this explanation is that of the *scientist*. Our original apprehension of the troubled water is given us as changed by the presence of an invisible *something* which is not distinct from this water and which is manifested as a pure factual resistance. If the desiring consciousness is *troubled*, it is because it is analogous to the troubled water.

To make this analogy precise, we should compare sexual desire with another form of desire—for example, with hunger. Hunger, like sexual desire, supposes a certain state of the body, defined here as the impoverishment of the blood, abundant salivary secretion, contractions of the tunica, *etc.* These various phenomena are described and classified from the point of view of the Other. For the For-itself they are manifested as pure facticity. But this facticity *does not compromise* the nature of the For-itself, for the For-itself immediately flees it toward its possibles; that is, toward a certain state of satisfied-hunger which, as we have pointed out in Part Two, is the In-itself-for-itself of hunger. Thus hunger is a pure surpassing of corporal facticity; and to the extent that the For-itself becomes conscious of this facticity in a non-thetic form, the For-itself becomes conscious of it as a surpassed facticity. The body here is indeed the *past, the passed-beyond*. In sexual desire, to be sure, we can find that structure common to all appetites—a state of the body. The Other can note various physiological modifications (the erection of the penis, the turgescence of the nipples of the breasts, changes in the circulatory system, rise in temperature, *etc.*) The desiring consciousness exists this facticity; it is *in terms of this facticity*—we could even say *through it*—that the desired body appears as desirable. Nevertheless if we limited ourselves to this description, sexual desire would appear as a *distinct and clear desire*, comparable to the desire of eating and drinking. It would be a pure flight from facticity toward other possibles. Now everyone is aware that there is a great abyss between sexual desire and other appetites. We all know the famous saying, "Make love to a pretty woman when you want her just as you would drink a glass of cold water when you are thirsty." We know also how unsatisfactory and even shocking this statement is to the mind. This is because when we do desire a woman, we do not keep ourselves wholly outside the desire; the desire *compromises* me; I am the accomplice of my desire. Or rather the desire has fallen wholly into complicity with the body. Let any man consult his own experience; he knows how consciousness is clogged, so to speak, by sexual desire; it seems that one is invaded by facticity, that one ceases to flee it and that one slides toward a *passive* consent to the desire. At other moments it seems that facticity invades consciousness in its very flight and renders consciousness opaque to itself. It is like a yeasty tumescence of *fact*.

The expressions which we use to designate desire sufficiently show its specificity. We say that it *takes hold of* you, that it *overwhelms* you, that it *paralyzes* you. Can one imagine employing the same words to designate hunger? Can one think of a hunger which "would overwhelm" one? Strictly speaking, this would be meaningful only when applied to impressions of emptiness. But, on the contrary, even the feeblest desire is already overwhelming. One can not hold it at a distance as one can with hunger and "think of something else" while keeping desire as an undifferentiated tonality of non-thetic consciousness which would be desire and which would serve as a sign of the body-as-ground. But *desire is consent to desire*. The heavy, fainting consciousness slides toward a languor comparable to sleep. Every one has been able to observe the appearance of desire in another. Suddenly the man who desires becomes a heavy tranquillity which is frightening; his eyes are fixed and appear half-closed, his movements are stamped with a heavy and sticky sweetness; many seem to be falling asleep. And when one "struggles against desire," it is precisely this languor which one resists. If one succeeds in resisting it, the desire before disappearing will become wholly distinct and clear, like hunger. And then there will be "an awakening." One will feel that one is lucid but with heavy head and beating heart. Naturally all these descriptions are inexact; they show rather the way in which we interpret desire. However they indicate the primary fact of desire: in desire consciousness chooses to exist its facticity on another plane. It no longer flees it; it attempts to subordinate itself to its own contingency—as it apprehends another body—i.e., another contingency—as desirable. In this sense desire is not only the revelation of the Other's body but the revelation of my own body. And this, not in so far as this body *is an instrument* or a *point of view*, but in so far as it is pure facticity; that is, a simple contingent form of the necessity of my contingency. I feel my skin and my muscles and my breath, and I feel them not in order to transcend them *toward* something as in emotion or appetite but as a living and inert datum, not simply as the pliable and discrete instrument of my action upon the world but as a *passion* by which I am engaged in the world and in danger in the world. The For-itself *is not* this contingency; it continues to exist but it experiences the vertigo of its own body. Or, if you prefer, this vertigo is precisely its way of existing its body. The non-thetic consciousness allows itself to go over to the body, *wishes to be* the body and to be only body. In desire the body instead of being only the contingency which the For-itself flees toward possibles which are peculiar to it, becomes at the same time the most immediate possible of the For-itself. Desire is not only the desire of the Other's body; it is—within the unity of a single act—the non-thetically lived project of being swallowed up in the body. Thus the final state of sexual desire can be swooning as the final stage of consent to the body. It is in this sense that desire can be called the desire of one body for another body. It is in fact an appetite directed toward the Other's body, and it is lived as the vertigo of the For-itself before its own body. The being which desires is consciousness making itself body.

But granted that desire is a consciousness which makes itself body in order to appropriate the Other's body apprehended as an organic totality in situation with consciousness on the horizon—what then is the meaning of desire? That is, why does consciousness make itself body—or vainly attempt to do so—and what does it expect from the object of its desire? The answer is easy if we realize that in desire I make myself flesh in the presence of the Other in order to appropriate the Other's flesh. This means that it is not merely a question of my grasping the Other's shoulders or thighs or of my drawing a body over against me: it is necessary as well for me to apprehend them with this particular instrument which is the body as it produces a clogging of consciousness. In this sense when I grasp these shoulders, it can be said not only that my body is a means for touching the shoulders but that the Other's shoulders are a means for my discovering my body as the fascinating revelation of facticity—that is, as flesh. Thus desire is the desire to appropriate a body as this appropriation reveals to me my body as flesh. But this body which I wish to appropriate, I wish to appropriate as flesh. Now at first the Other's body is not flesh for me; it appears as a synthetic form in action. As we have seen, we can not perceive the Other's body as pure flesh; that is, in the form of an isolated object maintaining external relations with other thises. The Other's body is originally a body in situation; flesh on the contrary, appears as the pure contingency of presence. Ordinarily it is hidden by cosmetics, clothing, etc.; in particular it is hidden by movements. Nothing is less "in the flesh" than a dancer even though she is nude. Desire is an attempt to strip the body of its movements as of its clothing and to make it exist as pure flesh; it is an attempt to incarnate the Other's body.

It is in this sense that the caress is an appropriation of the Other's body. It is evident that if caresses were only a stroking or brushing of the surface, there could be no relation between them and the powerful desire which they claim to fulfill; they would remain on the surface like looks and could not appropriate the Other for me. We know well the deceptiveness of that famous expression, "The contact of two epidermises." The caress does not want simple contact; it seems that man alone can reduce the caress to a contact, and then he loses its unique meaning. This is because the caress is not a simple stroking; it is a *shaping.* In caressing the Other I cause her[7] flesh to be born beneath my caress, under my fingers. The caress is the ensemble of those rituals which *incarnate* the Other. But, someone will object, was the Other not already incarnated? To be precise, *no.* The Other's flesh did not exist explicitly for me since I grasped the Other's body in situation; neither did it exist for her since she transcended it toward her possibilities and toward the object. The caress causes the Other to be born as flesh for me and for herself. And by flesh we do not mean a *part* of the body such as the dermis, the connective tissues or, specifically, epidermis; neither need we assume that the body will be "at rest" or dozing although often it is thus that its flesh is best revealed. But the caress reveals the flesh by stripping the body of its action, by cutting it off from the possibilities which surround it; the caress is designed to uncover the web of inertia beneath the action—i.e., the pure "being-there"—which sustains it. For example, by *clasping* the Other's hand and *caressing* it, I discover underneath the act of *clasping,* which this hand is *at first,* an extension of flesh and bone which can be grasped; and similarly my look caresses when it discovers underneath this leaping which is at first the dancer's legs, the curved extension of the thighs. Thus the caress is in no way distinct from the desire: to caress with the eyes and to desire are one and the same. *Desire is expressed by the caress as thought is by language.* The caress reveals the Other's flesh as flesh to myself *and to the Other.* But it reveals this flesh in a very special way. To take hold of the Other reveals to her her inertia and her passivity as a transcendence-transcended; but this is not to caress her. In the caress it is not my body as a synthetic form in action which caresses the Other; it is my body as flesh which causes the Other's flesh to be born. The caress is designed to cause the Other's body to be born, through pleasure, for the Other—and for myself—as a *touched* passivity in such a way that my body is made flesh in order to touch the Other's body with its own passivity; that is, by caressing itself with the Other's body rather than by caressing her. This is why amorous gestures have a languidness which could almost be said to be deliberate; it is not a question so much of taking hold of a part of the Other's body as of placing one's own body against the Other's body. Not so much to push or to touch in the active sense but to place against. It seems that I lift my own arm as an inanimate object and that I *place* it against the flank of the desired woman, that my fingers which I run over her arm are inert at the end of my hand. Thus the revelation of the Other's flesh is made through my own flesh; in desire and in the caress which expresses desire, I incarnate myself in order to realize the incarnation of the Other. The caress by *realizing* the Other's incarnation reveals

---

[7] The pronouns in French are masculine because they refer to *autrui* (the Other) which may stand for either man or woman but which, grammatically, is masculine. The feminine sounds more natural in English. Tr.

to me my own incarnation; that is, I make myself flesh in order to impel the Other to realize *for-herself* and *for me* her own flesh, and my caresses cause my flesh to be born for me in so far as it is for the Other *flesh causing her to be born as flesh*. I make her enjoy my flesh through her flesh in order to compel her to feel herself flesh. And so possession truly appears as a *double reciprocal incarnation*. Thus in desire there is an attempt at the incarnation of consciousness (this is what we called earlier the clogging of consciousness, a troubled consciousness, *etc.*) in order to realize the incarnation of the Other.

It remains to determine what is the *motive* of desire—or if you prefer, its meaning. For anyone who has so far followed the descriptions which we have here attempted will have understood long before this that for the For-itself, to be is to choose its way of being on the ground of the absolute contingency of its being-there. Desire therefore does not *come* to consciousness as heat *comes to* the piece of iron which I hold near the flame. Consciousness chooses itself as desire. For this, of course, there must be a motive; I do not desire just anything at any time. But as we showed in Part One of this book, the motive is raised in terms of the past, and consciousness by *turning back upon* it, confers on the motive its weight and its value. There is therefore no difference between the choice of the motive of the desire and the meaning of the upsurge—in the three ekstatic dimensions of duration—of a consciousness which makes itself desiring. Desire—like emotions or the imagining attitude or in general all the attitudes of the For-itself—has a meaning which constitutes it and surpasses it. The description which we have just attempted would hold no interest if it did not lead us to pose a further question: why does consciousness nihilate itself in the form of desire?

One or two preliminary observations will help us in replying to this question. In the first place we must note that the desiring consciousness does not desire its object on the ground of a world which is unchanged. In other words, it is not a question of causing the desirable to appear as a certain "this" on the ground of a world which would preserve its instrumental relations with us and its organization in complexes of instrumentality. The same is true of desire as of emotion. We have pointed out elsewhere that emotion is not the apprehension of an exciting object in an unchanged world; rather since it corresponds to a global modification of consciousness and of its relations to the world, emotion expresses itself by means of a radical alteration of the world.[8] Similarly sexual desire is a radical modification of the For-itself; since the For-itself makes itself be on another plane of being, it determines itself to exist its body differently, to make itself be clogged by its facticity. Correlatively the world must come into being for the For-itself in a new way. There is a world of desire. If my body is no longer felt

---

[8] Cf. *The Emotions.*

as the instrument which can not be utilized by any instrument—i.e., as the synthetic organization of my acts in the world—if it is lived as flesh, then it is as a reference to my flesh that I apprehend the objects in the world. This means that I make myself passive in relation to them and that they are revealed to me from the point of view of this passivity, in it and through it (for passivity is the body, and the body does not cease to be a point of view). Objects then become the transcendent ensemble which reveals my incarnation to me. A contact with them is a *caress*; that is, my perception is not the *utilization* of the object and the surpassing of the present in view of an end, but to perceive an object when I am in the desiring attitude is to caress myself with it. Thus I am sensitive not so much to the form of the object and to its instrumentality, as to its matter (gritty, smooth, tepid, greasy, rough, *etc.*). In my desiring perception I discover something like a *flesh* of objects. My shirt rubs against my skin, and I feel it. What is ordinarily for me an object most remote becomes the immediately sensible; the warmth of air, the breath of the wind, the rays of sunshine, *etc.*; all are present to me in a certain way, as posited upon me without distance and revealing my flesh by means of their flesh. From this point of view desire is not only the clogging of a consciousness by its facticity; it is correlatively the ensnarement of a body by the world. The world is made *ensnaring*; consciousness is engulfed in a body which is engulfed in the world.[9] Thus the ideal which is proposed here is being-in-the-midst-of-the-world; the For-itself attempts to realize a being-in-the-midst-of-the-world as the ultimate project of its being-in-the-world; that is why sensual pleasure is so often linked with death—which is also a metamorphosis or "being-in-the-midst-of-the-world." There is, for example, the theme of "pseudo-death" so abundantly treated in all literatures.

But desire is not first nor primarily a relation to the world. The world here appears only as the ground for explicit relations with the Other. Usually it is on the occasion of the Other's *presence* that the world is revealed as the world of desire. Accessorily it can be revealed as such on the occasion of the *absence* of a particular Other or even on occasion of the absence of *all* Others. But we have already observed that absence is a concrete existential relation between the Other and me, which appears on the original ground of Being-for-others. I can, of course, by discovering my body in solitude, abruptly realize myself as flesh, "suffocate" with desire, and experience the world as "suffocating." But this solitary desire is an appeal to either a particular Other or the presence of the undifferentiated Other. I desire to be revealed as flesh by means of and for

---

[9] Naturally it is necessary to take into account here as everywhere the coefficient of adversity in things. These objects are not only "caressing." But within the general perspective of the caress, they can appear also as "anti-caresses"; that is, with a rudeness, a cacophony, a harshness which—precisely because we are in the state of desire—offend us in a way that is unbearable.

another flesh. I try to cast a spell over the Other and make him appear; and the world of desire indicates by a sort of prepared space the *Other* whom I am calling. Thus desire is by no means a physiological accident, an itching of our flesh which may fortuitously direct us on the Other's flesh. Quite the contrary, in order for my flesh to exist and for the Other's flesh to exist, consciousness must necessarily be preliminarily shaped in the mould of desire. This desire is a primitive mode of our relations with the Other which constitutes the Other as desirable flesh on the ground of a world of desire.

We are now in a position to make explicit the profound meaning of desire. In the primordial reaction to the Other's look I constitute myself as a look. But if I look at his look in order to defend myself against the Other's freedom and to transcend it as freedom, then both the freedom and the look of the Other collapse. I see eyes; I see a being-in-the-midst-of-the-world. Henceforth the Other escapes me. I should like to act upon his freedom, to appropriate it, or at least, to make the Other's freedom recognize my freedom. But this freedom is dead; it is no longer in the world in which I encounter the Other-as-object, for its characteristic is to be transcendent to the world. To be sure, I can grasp the Other, grab hold of him, knock him down. I can, providing I have the power, compel him to perform this or that act, to say certain words. But everything happens as if I wished to get hold of a man who runs away and leaves only his coat in my hands. It is the coat, it is the outer shell which I possess. I shall never get hold of more than a body, a psychic object in the midst of the world. And although all the acts of this body can be interpreted in terms of freedom, I have completely lost the key to this interpretation; I can act only upon a facticity. If I have preserved my *awareness* of a transcendent freedom in the Other, this awareness irritates me in vain by indicating a reality which is on principle beyond my reach and by revealing to me every instant the fact that I *am missing* it, that everything which I do is done "blindly" and takes on a meaning elsewhere in a sphere of existence from which I am on principle excluded. I can make the Other beg for mercy or ask my pardon, but I shall always be ignorant of what this submission means for and in the Other's freedom.

Moreover at the same time my *awareness* is altered; I lose the exact comprehension of *being-looked-at*, which is, as we know, the only way in which I can make proof of the Other's freedom. Thus I am engaged in an enterprise the meaning of which I have forgotten. I am bewildered confronting this Other as I see him and touch him but am at a loss as to what to do with him. I have barely preserved the vague memory of a certain *Beyond* which is beyond what I see and what I touch, a Beyond concerning which I know that this is precisely what I want to appropriate. It is now that I *make myself desire*. Desire is a conduct of enchantment. Since I can grasp the Other only in his objective facticity, the problem is to ensnare his freedom within this facticity. It is necessary that his freedom be "caught" in it as the cream is caught up by a person skimming milk. So the Other's For-itself must come to play on the surface of his body, and be extended all through his body; and by touching this body I should finally touch the Other's free subjectivity. This is the true meaning of the word *possession*. It is certain that I want to *possess* the Other's body, but I want to possess it in so far as it is itself a "possessed"; that is, in so far as the Other's consciousness is identified with his body. Such is the impossible ideal of desire: to possess the Other's transcendence as pure transcendence and at the same time as *body*, to reduce the Other to his simple *facticity* because he is then in the midst of my world but to bring it about that this facticity is a perpetual appresentation of his nihilating transcendence.

But in truth the Other's facticity (his pure being-there) can not be given to my intuition without a profound modification of my own unique being. In so far as I surpass my personal facticity toward my own possibilities, so far as I exist my facticity in an impulse of flight, I surpass as well not only the Other's facticity but also the pure *existence of things*. In my very upsurge I cause them to emerge in instrumental existence; their pure and simple being is hidden by the complexity of indicative references which constitute their *manageability* and their *instrumentality*. To pick up a fountain pen is already to surpass my being-there toward the possibility of writing, but it is also to surpass the pen as a simple existent toward its potentiality and once again to surpass this potentiality toward certain future existents which are the "words-about-to-be-formed" and finally the "book-about-to-be-written." This is why the being of existents is ordinarily veiled by their function. The same is true for the being of the Other. If the Other appears to me as a servant, as an employee, as a civil servant, or simply as the passerby whom I must avoid or as this voice which is speaking in the next room and which I try to *understand* (or on the other hand, which I want to forget because it "keeps me from sleeping"), it is not only the Other's extramundane transcendence which escapes me but also his "being-there" as a pure contingent existence in the midst of the world. This is because it is exactly in so far as I treat him as a servant, or as an office clerk, that I surpass his potentialities (transcendence-transcended, dead-possibilities) by the very project by which I surpass and nihilate my own facticity. If I want to return to his simple presence and taste it *as presence*, it is necessary for me to reduce myself to my own presence. Every surpassing of my being-there is in fact a surpassing of the Other's being-there. And if the world is around me as the situation which I surpass toward myself, then I apprehend the Other in terms of *his* situation; that is, already as a center of reference.

Of course the desired Other must also be apprehended in situation: I desire a woman *in the world*, standing *near a table*, lying naked *on a bed*, or seated *at my side*. But if the desire flows back from the situation upon the being who is in situation, it is in order to dissolve the situation and to corrode the Other's relations in the world. The movement of desire which goes from the surrounding "environment" to the desired person is an isolating movement which destroys the environment and cuts off the person in question in order to effect the emergence of his pure facticity. But this is possible only if each object which refers me to the person is fixed in its pure contingency at the same time that it indicates him to me; consequently this return movement to the Other's being is a movement of return to myself as pure being-there. I destroy my possibilities in order to destroy those of the world and to constitute the world as a "world of desire"; that is, as a destructured world which has lost its meaning, a world in which things jut out like fragments of pure matter, like brute qualities. Since the For-itself is a choice, this is possible only if I project myself toward a new possibility: that of being "absorbed by my body as ink is by a blotter," that of being reduced to my pure being-there. This project, inasmuch as it is not simply conceived and thematically posited but rather lived—that is, inasmuch as its realization is not distinct from its conception—is "disturbance" or "trouble." Indeed we must not understand the preceding descriptions as meaning that I deliberately put myself in a state of disturbance with the purpose of rediscovering the Other's pure "being-there." Desire is a lived project which does not suppose any preliminary deliberation but which includes within itself its meaning and its interpretation. As soon as I throw myself toward the Other's facticity, as soon as I wish to push aside his acts and his functions so as to touch him in his flesh, I incarnate myself, for I can neither wish nor even conceive of the incarnation of the Other except in and by means of my own incarnation. Even the empty outline of a desire (as when one absentmindedly "undresses a woman with one's look") is an empty outline of troubled disturbance, for I desire only with my trouble, and I disrobe the Other only by disrobing myself; I foreshadow and outline the Other's flesh only by outlining my own flesh.

But my incarnation is not only the preliminary condition of the appearance of the Other as flesh to my eyes. My goal is to cause him to be incarnated as flesh in his own eyes. It is necessary that I drag him onto the level of pure facticity; he must be reduced for himself to being only flesh. Thus I shall be reassured as to the permanent possibilities of a transcendence which can at any instant transcend me on all sides. This transcendence will be no more than this; it will remain inclosed within the limits of an object; in addition and because of this very fact, I shall be able to touch it, feel it, possess it. Thus the other meaning of my incarnation—that is, of my troubled disturbance—is that it is a magical language. I make myself flesh so as to fascinate the Other by my nakedness and to provoke in her the desire for my flesh—exactly because this desire will be nothing else in the Other but an incarnation similar to mine. Thus desire is an invitation to desire. It is my flesh alone which knows how to find the road to the Other's flesh, and I lay my flesh next to her flesh so as to awaken her to the meaning of flesh. In the caress when I slowly lay my inert hand against the Other's flank, I am making that flank feel my flesh, and this can be achieved only if it renders itself inert. The shiver of pleasure which it feels is precisely the awakening of its consciousness as flesh. If I extend my hand, remove it, or clasp it, then it becomes again body in action; but by the same stroke I make my hand disappear as flesh. To let it run indifferently over the length of her body, to reduce my hand to a soft brushing almost stripped of meaning, to a pure existence, to a pure matter, slightly silky, slightly satiny, slightly rough—this is to give up for oneself being the one who establishes references and unfolds distances; it is to be made pure mucous membrane. At this moment the communion of desire is realized; each consciousness by incarnating itself has realized the incarnation of the other; each one's disturbance has caused disturbance to be born in the Other and is thereby so much enriched. By each caress I experience my own flesh and the Other's flesh through my flesh, and I am conscious that this flesh which I feel and appropriate through my flesh is flesh-realized-by-the-Other. It is not by chance that desire while aiming at the body as a whole attains it especially through masses of flesh which are very little differentiated, grossly nerveless, hardly capable of spontaneous movement, through breasts, buttocks, thighs, stomach: these form a sort of image of pure facticity. This is why also the true caress is the contact of two bodies in their mostly fleshy parts, the contact of stomachs and breasts; the caressing hand is too clever, too much like a perfected instrument. But the full pressing together of the flesh of two people against one another is the true goal of desire.

Nevertheless desire is itself doomed to failure. As we have seen, coitus, which ordinarily terminates desire, is not its essential goal. To be sure, several elements of our sexual structure are the necessary expression of the nature of desire, in particular the erection of the penis and the clitoris. This is nothing else in fact but the affirmation of the flesh by the flesh. Therefore it is absolutely necessary that it should not be accomplished *voluntarily*; that is, that we can not use it as an instrument but that we are dealing with a biological and autonomous phenomenon whose autonomous and involuntary expression accompanies and signifies the submerging of consciousness in the body. It must be clearly understood that no fine, prehensile organ provided with striated muscles can be a sex organ, a sex. If sex were to appear as an organ, it could be only one manifestation of the vegetative life. But contingency reappears if we consider that there are sexes and *particular* sexes. Consider especially the penetration of the female by the male. This does, to be sure, conform to that radical incarnation which desire wishes to be. (We may in fact observe the organic passivity of sex in coitus. It is the whole body which advances and withdraws, which *carries* sex forward or withdraws it. Hands help to introduce the penis; the penis itself appears as an instrument which one manages, which one makes penetrate, which one withdraws, which one utilizes. And similarly the opening and the lubrication of the vagina can not be obtained voluntarily.) Yet coitus remains a perfectly contingent modality of our sexual life. It is as much a pure contingency as sexual pleasure proper. In truth the ensnarement of consciousness in the body normally has its own peculiar result—that is, a sort of particular ecstasy in which consciousness is no more than consciousness (of) the body and consequently a reflective consciousness of corporeality. Pleasure in fact—like too keen a pain—motivates the appearance of reflective consciousness which is "*attention to pleasure.*"

But pleasure is the death and the failure of desire. It is the death of desire because it is not only its fulfillment but its limit and its end. This, moreover, is only an organic contingency: it *happens that* the incarnation is manifested by erection and that the erection ceases with ejaculation. But in addition pleasure closes the sluice to desire because it motivates the appearance of a reflective consciousness of pleasure, whose object becomes a reflective enjoyment; that is, it is *attention to the incarnation of the For-itself which is reflected-on* and by the same token it is forgetful of the Other's incarnation. Here we are no longer within the province of contingency. Of course it remains contingent that the passage to the fascinated reflection should be effected on the occasion of that particular mode of incarnation which is pleasure (although there are numerous cases of passage to the reflective without the intervention of pleasure), but there is a permanent danger for desire in so far as it is an attempt at incarnation. This is because consciousness by incarnating itself loses sight of the Other's incarnation, and its own incarnation absorbs it to the point of becoming the ultimate goal. In this case the pleasure of caressing is transformed into the pleasure of being caressed; what the For-itself demands is to feel within it its own body expanding to the point of nausea. Immediately there is a rupture of contact and desire misses its goal. It happens very often that this failure of desire motivates a passage to masochism; that is, consciousness apprehending itself in its facticity demands to be apprehended and transcended as body-for-the-Other by means of the Other's consciousness. In this case the Other-as-object collapses, the Other-as-look appears, and my consciousness is a consciousness swooning in its flesh beneath the Other's look.

Yet conversely desire stands at the origin of its own failure inasmuch as it is a desire of *taking* and of *appropriating*. It is not enough merely that troubled disturbance should effect the Other's incarnation; desire is the desire to appropriate this incarnated consciousness. Therefore desire is naturally continued not by *caresses* but by acts of taking and of penetration. The caress has for its goal only to impregnate the Other's body with consciousness and freedom. Now it is necessary to take this saturated body, to seize it, to enter into it. But by the very fact that I now attempt to seize the Other's body, to pull it toward me, to grab hold of it, to bite it, my own body *ceases* to be flesh and becomes again the synthetic instrument *which I am*. And by the same token the *Other ceases* to be an incarnation; she becomes once more an instrument in the midst of the world which I apprehend in terms of its situation. Her consciousness, which played on the surface of her flesh and which I tried to *taste* with my flesh,[10] disappears under my sight; she remains no more than an *object* with object-images inside her. At the same time my disturbance disappears. This does not mean that I cease to desire but that desire has lost its matter; it has become *abstract*; it is a desire to handle and to take. I insist on taking the Other's body but my very insistence makes my incarnation disappear. At present I surpass my body anew toward my own possibilities (here the possibility of taking), and similarly the Other's body which is surpassed toward its potentialities falls from the level of *flesh* to the level of pure object. This situation brings about the rupture of that reciprocity of incarnation which was precisely the unique goal of desire. The Other may remain troubled; she may remain flesh *for herself*, and I can understand it. But it is a flesh which I no longer apprehend through my flesh, a flesh which is no longer anything but the *property* of an Other-as-object and not the incarnation of an Other-as-consciousness. Thus I *am body* (a synthetic totality in situation) confronting a *flesh*. I find myself in almost the same situation as that from which I tried to escape by means of desire; that is, I try to utilize the Other-as-object in order to call her to account for her transcendence, and precisely because she is *all* object she escapes me with *all* her transcendence. Once again I have even lost the precise comprehension of what I seek and yet I am engaged in the search. I take and discover myself in the process of taking, but what I take in my hands is *something else* than what I wanted to take. I feel this and I suffer from it but without being capable of saying what I wanted to take; for along with my troubled disturbance the very comprehension of my desire escapes me. I am like a sleeper who wakens to find himself in the process of gripping the edge of the bed while he cannot recall the nightmare which provoked his gesture. It is this situation which is at the origin of *sadism*.

Sadism is passion, dryness, and relentlessness. It is relentlessness because it is the state of a For-itself which apprehends itself as engaged without understanding *in what* it is engaged and which persists in its engagement without having a clear consciousness of the goal which it has set for itself or a precise recollection of the value which it has attached to this engagement. It is dryness because it appears when desire is emptied of its trouble. The sadist

---

[10] Doña Prouhèze (*Soulier de Satin, 11ᵉ journée*): "*Il ne connaîtra pas le goût que j'ai.*" (He will not know the taste which I have.)

has reapprehended his body as a synthetic totality and center of action; he has resumed the perpetual flight from his own facticity. He experiences himself in the face of the Other as pure transcendence. He has a horror of troubled disturbance for *himself* and considers it a humiliating state; it is possible also that he simply can not *realize* it in himself. To the extent that he coldly persists, that he is at once relentlessness and dryness the sadist is impassioned. His goal, like that of desire, is to seize and to make use of the Other not only as the Other-as-object but as a pure incarnated transcendence. But in sadism the emphasis is put on the instrumental appropriation of the incarnated-Other. The "moment" of sadism in sexuality is the one in which the incarnated For-itself surpasses its own incarnation in order to appropriate the incarnation of the Other. Thus sadism is a refusal to be incarnated and a flight from all facticity and at the same time an effort to get hold of the Other's facticity. But as the sadist neither can nor will realize the Other's incarnation by means of his own incarnation, as due to this very fact he has no resource except to treat the Other as an instrumental-object, he seeks to utilize the Other's body as a tool to make the Other realize an incarnated existence. Sadism is an effort to incarnate the Other through violence, and this incarnation "by force" must be already the appropriation and utilization of the Other. Sadism like desire seeks to strip the Other of the acts which hide him. It seeks to reveal the flesh beneath the action. But whereas the For-itself in desire loses itself in its own flesh in order to reveal to the Other that he too is flesh, the sadist refuses his own flesh at the same time that he uses instruments to reveal by force the Other's flesh to him. The object of sadism is immediate appropriation. But sadism is a blind alley, for it not only enjoys the possession of the Other's flesh but at the same time in direct connection with this flesh, it enjoys its own non-incarnation. It *wants* the non-reciprocity of sexual relations, it enjoys being a free appropriating power confronting a freedom captured by flesh. That is why the sadist wants to make the flesh present to the Other's con-sciousness *differently*. He wants to make it present by treating the Other as an instrument; he makes it present in pain. In pain facticity invades conscious-ness, and ultimately the reflective consciousness is fascinated by the facticity of the unreflective consciousness. There is then indeed an incarnation through pain. But at the same time the pain is procured *by means of instruments*. The body of the torturing For-itself is no longer anything more than an instrument for giving pain. Thus from the start the For-itself can give itself the illusion of getting hold of the Other's freedom instrumentally; that is, of plunging this freedom into flesh without ceasing to be the one who *provokes*, who grabs hold, who seizes, *etc*.

As for the type of incarnation which sadism would like to realize, this is precisely what is called the Obscene. The obscene is a *species* of Being-for-Others which belongs to the *genus* of the ungraceful. But not everything which is ungraceful is obscene. In *grace* the body appears as a psychic being in situation. It reveals above all its transcendence as a transcendence-transcended; it is in act and is understood in terms of the situation and of the end pursued. Each movement therefore is apprehended in a perceptive process which is in the present is based on the future. For this reason the graceful act has on the one hand the precision of a finely perfected machine and on the other hand the perfect unpredictability of the psychic since, as we have seen, the psychic is for others the *unpredictable object*. Therefore the graceful act is at each instant perfectly understandable in so far as one considers that in it which has *elapsed*. Better yet, that part of the act which has elapsed is implied by a sort of aesthetic necessity which stems from its perfect adaptation. At the same time the goal to come illuminates the act in its totality. But all the future part of the act remains unpredictable although upon the very body of the act it is felt that the future will appear as necessary and adapted once it too has elapsed. It is this moving image of necessity and of freedom (as the property of the Other-as-object) which, strictly speaking, constitutes grace. Bergson has given a good description of it. In grace the body is the instrument which manifests freedom. The graceful act in so far as it reveals the body as a precision instrument, furnishes it at each instant with its justification for existing; the hand is in order to grasp and manifests at the start its being-in-order-to-grasp. In so far as it is apprehended in terms of a situation which requires grasping, the hand appears as itself *required* in its being, as summoned. And in so far as it manifests its freedom through the unpredictability of its gesture, it appears at the origin of its being. It seems that the hand is itself produced as the result of a justifying appeal from the situation. Grace therefore forms an objective image of a being which would be the *foundation of itself in order to* ——. Facticity then is clothed and disguised by grace; the nudity of the flesh is wholly present, but it can not be seen. Therefore the supreme coquetry and the supreme challenge of grace is to exhibit the body unveiled with no clothing, with no veil except grace itself. The most graceful body is the naked body whose acts inclose it with an invisible visible garment while entirely disrobing its flesh, while the flesh is totally present to the eyes of the spectators.

The ungraceful, on the contrary, appears when one of the elements of grace is thwarted in its realization. A movement may become *mechanical*. In this case the body always forms part of an ensemble which justifies it but in the capacity of a pure instrument; its transcendence-transcended disappears, and along with it the *situation* disappears as the lateral over-determination of the instrumental-objects of my universe. It can happen also that the actions are abrupt and violent; in this case it is the adaptation of the situation which collapses; the situation remains but an hiatus slips in like an emptiness between it and the *Other* in situation. In this case the Other remains free, but this freedom is apprehended only as pure unpredictability; it resembles the *clinamen* of Epicurean atoms, in short an indeterminism. At the same time the end remains posited, and it is always in terms of the future that we perceive the Other's gesture. But the fall from adaptation involves this consequence, that the perceptive interpretation by means of the future is always too broad or too narrow; it is an approximate interpretation. Consequently the justification of the gesture and the being of the Other is imperfectly realized. In the final analysis the awkward is unjustifiable; all its facticity, which was engaged in the situation, is absorbed by it, flows back upon it. The awkward one frees his facticity inopportunely and suddenly places it beneath our sight; hence where we expected to seize a key to the situation, spontaneously emanating from the very situation, we suddenly encounter the unjusifiable contingency of an unadapted presence; we are put face to face with the existence of an existent.

Nevertheless if the body is wholly within the act, the facticity is not yet flesh. The *obscene* appears when the body adopts postures which entirely strip it of its acts and which reveal the inertia of its flesh. The sight of a naked body from behind is not obscene. But certain involuntary waddlings of the rump are obscene. This is because then it is only the legs which are acting for the walker, and the rump is like an isolated cushion which is carried by the legs and the balancing of which is a pure obedience to the laws of weight. It can not be justified by the situation; on the contrary, it is entirely destructive of any situation since it has the passivity of a thing and since it is made to rest like a thing upon the legs. Suddenly it is revealed as an unjustifiable facticity; it is *de trop* like every contingent. It is isolated in the body for which the present meaning is walking; it is naked even if material covers it, for it no longer shares in the transcendence-transcended of the body in action. Its movement of balancing instead of being interpreted in terms of what is to come is interpreted and known as a physical fact in terms of the past. These remarks naturally can apply to cases in which it is the whole body which is made flesh, either by some sort of flabbiness in its movements, which can not be interpreted by the situation, or by a deformity in its structure (for example the proliferation of the fat cells) which exhibits a super-abundant facticity in relation to the effective presence which the situation demands. This revealed flesh is specifically obscene when it is revealed to someone who is not in a state of desire and *without exciting his desire*. A particular lack of adaptation which destroys the situation at the very moment when I apprehend it and which releases to me the inert expanding of flesh as an abrupt appearance beneath the thin clothing of the movements which cover it (when I am not in a state of desire for this flesh): this is what I shall call the obscene.

Now we can see the meaning of the sadist's demand: grace reveals freedom as a property of the Other-as-object and refers obscurely—just as do the contradictions in the sensible world in the case of Platonic recollection—to a transcendent Beyond of which we preserve only a confused memory and which we can reach only by a radical modification of our being; that is, by resolutely assuming our being-for-others. Grace both unveils and veils the Other's flesh, or if you prefer, it unveils the flesh in order immediately to veil it; in grace flesh is the inaccessible Other. The sadist aims at destroying grace in order *actually* to constitute another synthesis of the Other. He wants to make the Other's flesh appear; and in its very appearance the flesh will destroy grace, and facticity will reabsorb the Other's freedom-as-object. This reabsorption is not annihilation; for the sadist it is the Other-as-free who is manifested as flesh. The identity of the Other-as-object is not destroyed through these avatars, but the relations between flesh and freedom are reversed. In grace freedom contained and veiled facticity; in the new synthesis to be effected it is facticity which contains and hides freedom. The sadist aims therefore at making the flesh appear abruptly and by compulsion; that is, by the aid not of his own flesh but of his body as instrument. He aims at making the Other assume attitudes and positions such that his body appears under the aspect of the *obscene*; thus the sadist himself remains on the level of instrumental appropriation since he causes flesh to be born by exerting force upon the Other, and the Other becomes an instrument in his hands. The sadist handles the Other's body, leans on the Other's shoulders so as to bend him toward the earth and to make his haunches stick up, *etc.* On the other hand, the goal of this instrumental utilization is immanent in the very utilization; the sadist treats the Other as an instrument in order to make the Other's flesh appear. The sadist is the being who apprehends the Other as the instrument whose function is his own incarnation. The ideal of the sadist will therefore be to achieve the moment when the Other will be already flesh without ceasing to be an instrument, flesh to cause the birth of flesh, the moment at which the thighs, for example, already offer themselves in an obscene expanding passivity, and yet are instruments which are managed, which are pushed aside, which are bent so as to make the buttocks stick out in order in turn to incarnate them. But let us not be deceived here. What the sadist thus so tenaciously seeks, what he wants to knead with his hands and bend under his wrists is the Other's freedom. The freedom is there in that flesh; it is freedom which is this flesh since there is a facticity of the Other. It is therefore this freedom which the sadist tries to appropriate.

Thus the sadist's effort is to ensnare the Other in his flesh by means of violence and pain, by appropriating the Other's body in such a way that he treats it as flesh so as to cause flesh to be born. But this appropriation surpasses the body which it appropriates, for its purpose is to possess the body only in so far as the Other's freedom has been ensnared within it. This is why the sadist will want manifest proofs of this enslavement of the Other's freedom through the flesh. He will aim at making the Other ask for pardon, he will use torture and threats to force the Other to humiliate himself, to deny what he holds most dear. It is often said that this is done through the will to dominate or thirst for power. But this explanation is either vague or absurd. It is the will to dominate which should be explained first. This can not be prior to sadism as its foundation, for in the same way and on the same plane as sadism, it is born from anxiety in the face of the Other. In fact, if the sadist is pleased upon obtaining a denial by means of torture, this is for a reason analogous to that which allows us to interpret the meaning of Love. We have seen in fact that Love does not demand the abolition of the Other's freedom but rather his enslavement as freedom; that is, freedom's self-enslavement. Similarly the sadist does not seek to suppress the freedom of the one whom he tortures but to force this freedom freely to identify itself with the tortured flesh. This is why the moment of pleasure for the torturer is that in which the victim betrays or humiliates himself.

In fact no matter what pressure is exerted on the victim, the abjuration remains free; it is a spontaneous production, a response to a situation; it manifests human-reality. No matter what resistance the victim has offered, no matter how long he has waited before begging for mercy, he would have been able despite all to wait ten minutes, one minute, one second longer. He has *determined* the moment at which the pain became unbearable. The proof of this is the fact that he will later live out his abjuration in remorse and shame. Thus he is entirely responsible for it. On the other hand the sadist for his part considers himself entirely the cause of it. If the victim resists and refuses to beg for mercy, the game is only that much more pleasing. One more turn of the screw, one extra twist and the resistence will finally give in. The sadist posits himself as "having all the time in the world." He is calm, he does not hurry. He uses his instruments like a technician; he tries them one after another as the locksmith tries various keys in a keyhole. He enjoys this ambiguous and contradictory situation. On the one hand indeed he is the one who patiently at the heart of universal determinism employs means in view of an end which will be *automatically* attained—just as the lock will automatically open when the locksmith finds the "right" key; on the other hand, this determined end can be realized only with the Other's free and complete cooperation. Therefore until the last the end remains both predictable and unpredictable. For the sadist the object realized is ambiguous, contradictory, without equilibrium since it is both the strict consequence of a technical utilization of determinism and the manifestation of an unconditioned freedom. The spectacle which is offered to the sadist is that of a freedom which struggles against the expanding of the flesh and which finally freely chooses to be submerged in the flesh. At the moment of the abjuration the result sought is attained: the body is wholly flesh, panting and obscene; it holds the position which the torturers have given to it, not that which it would have assumed by itself; the cords which bind it hold it as an inert thing, and thereby it has ceased to be the object which moves spontaneously. In the abjuration a freedom chooses to be wholly identified with this body; this distorted and heaving body is the very image of a broken and enslaved freedom.

These few remarks do not aim at exhausting the problem of sadism. We wanted only to show that it is as a seed in desire itself, as the failure of desire; in fact as soon as I seek to take the Other's body, which through my incarnation I have induced to incarnate itself, I break the reciprocity of incarnation, I surpass my body toward its own possibilities, and I orient myself in the direction of sadism. Thus sadism and masochism are the two reefs on which desire may founder—whether I surpass my troubled disturbance toward an appropriation of the Other's flesh or, intoxicated with my own trouble, pay attention only to my flesh and ask nothing of the Other except that he should be the look which aids me in realizing my flesh. It is because of this inconstancy on the part of desire and its perpetual oscillation between these two perils that "normal" sexuality is commonly designated as "sadistic-masochistic."

Nevertheless sadism too—like blind indifference and like desire—bears within itself the cause of its own failure In the first place there is a profound incompatibility between the apprehension of the body as flesh and its instrumental utilization. If I make an instrument out of flesh, it refers me to other instruments and to potentialities, in short to a future; it is partially justified in its being-there by the situation which I create around myself, just as the presence of nails and of a picture to be nailed on the wall justifies the existence of the hammer. Suddenly the body's character as flesh—that is, its unutilizable facticity—gives way to that of an instrumental-thing. The complex "flesh-as-instrument" which the sadist has attempted to create disintegrates. This profound disintegration can be hidden so long as the flesh is the instrument to reveal flesh, for in this way I constitute an instrument with an immanent end. But when the incarnation is achieved, when I have indeed before me a panting body, then I no longer know how to utilize this flesh. No goal can be assigned to it, precisely because I have effected the appearance of its absolute contingency. It is there, and it is there for nothing. As such I can not get hold of it as flesh; I can not integrate it in a complex system of instrumentality without its materiality as flesh, its "fleshliness" immediately escaping me. I can only remain disconcerted before it in a state of contemplative astonishment or else incarnate myself in turn and allow myself again to be troubled, so as to place myself once more at least on the level where flesh is revealed to flesh in its entire "fleshliness." Thus sadism at the very moment when its goal is going to be attained gives way to desire. Sadism is the failure of desire, and desire is the failure of sadism. One can get out of the circle only by means of satiation and so-called "physical possession." In this a new synthesis of sadism and of desire is given. The tumescence of sex manifests incarnation, the fact of "entering into" or of being "penetrated" symbolically realizes the sadistic and masochistic attempt to appropriate. But if pleasure enables us to get out of the circle, this is because it kills both the desire and the sadistic passion without satisfying them.

At the same time and on a totally different level sadism harbors a new motive for failure. What the sadist seeks to appropriate is in actuality the transcendent freedom of the victim. But this freedom remains on principle out of reach. And the more the sadist persists in treating the other as an instrument, the more this freedom escapes him. He can act upon the freedom only by making it an objective property of the Other-as-object; that is, on freedom in the midst of the world with its dead-possibilities. But since the sadist's goal is to recover his being-for-others, he misses it on principle, for the only Other with whom he has to do is the Other in the world who has only "images in his head" of the sadist assaulting him.

The sadist discovers his error when his victim *looks at* him; that is, when the sadist experiences the absolute alienation of his being in the Other's freedom; he realizes then not only that he has not recovered his *being-outside* but also that the activity by which he seeks to recover it is itself transcended and fixed in "sadism" as an *habitus* and a property with its cortège of dead-possibilities and that this transformation takes place through and for the Other whom he wishes to enslave. He discovers then that he can not act on the Other's freedom even by forcing the Other to humiliate himself and to beg for mercy, for it is precisely in and through the Other's absolute freedom that there exists a world in which there are sadism and instruments of torture and a hundred pretexts for being humiliated and for forswearing oneself. Nobody has better portrayed the power of the victim's look at his torturers than Faulkner has done in the final pages of *Light in August*. The "good citizens" have just hunted down the Negro, Christmas, and have castrated him. Christmas is at the point of death:

> "But the man on the floor had not moved. He just lay there, with his eyes open and empty of everything save consciousness, and with something, a shadow, about his mouth. For a long moment he looked up at them with peaceful and unfathomable and unbearable eyes. Then his face, body, all, seemed to collapse, to fall in upon itself and from out the slashed garments about his hips and loins the pent black blood seemed to rush like a released breath. It seemed to rush out of his pale body like the rush of sparks from a rising rocket; upon that black blast the man seemed to rise soaring into their memories forever and ever. They are not to lose it, in whatever peaceful

valleys, beside whatever placid and reassuring streams of old age, in the mirroring face of whatever children they will contemplate old disasters and newer hopes. *It will be there, musing, quiet, steadfast, not fading and not particularly threatful, but of itself alone serene, of itself alone triumphant.* Again from the town, deadened a little by the walls, the scream of the siren mounted toward its unbelievable crescendo, passing out of the realm of hearing."[11]

Thus this explosion of the Other's look in the world of the sadist causes the meaning and goal of sadism to collapse. The sadist discovers that it was that freedom which he wished to enslave, and at the same time he realizes the futility of his efforts. Here once more we are referred from the being-in-the-act-of-looking to the being-looked-at; we have not got out of the circle.

We have not thought by these few remarks to exhaust the problem of sex, still less that of possible attitudes toward the Other. We have wished simply to show that the sexual attitude is a primary behavior towards the Other. It goes without saying that this behavior necessarily includes within it the original contingency of being-for-others and that of our own facticity. But we can not admit that this behavior is subject from the start to a physiological and empirical constitution. As soon as "there is" the body and as soon as "there is" an Other, we react by desire, by Love, and by the derived attitudes which we have mentioned. Our physiological structure only causes the symbolic expression, on the level of absolute contingency, of the fact that we are the permanent possibility of assuming one or the other of these attitudes. Thus we shall be able to say that the For-itself is sexual in its very upsurge in the face of the Other and that through it sexuality comes into the world.

Obviously we do not claim that all attitudes toward the Other are reducible to those sexual attitudes which we have just described. If we have dealt with them at considerable length, it is for two reasons: first because they are fundamental, and second because all of men's complex patterns of conduct toward one another are only enrichments of these two original attitudes (and of a third—hate—which we are going to describe next). Of course examples of concrete conduct (collaboration, conflict, rivalry, emulation, engagement, obedience, etc.)[12] are infinitely more delicate to describe, for they depend on the historic situation and the concrete particularities of each relation of the For-itself with the Other; but they all include as their skeleton—so to speak—sexual relations. This is not because of the existence of a certain libido which

---

[11] The italics are Sartre's. I have quoted directly from Faulkner rather than translating back into English from the French translation which Sartre used. Tr. William Faulkner, *Light in August*. New York: Modern Library. p. 407. Tr.

[12] Also maternal love, pity, kindness, etc.

would slip in everywhere but simply because the attitudes which we have described are the fundamental projects by which the For-itself *realizes* its being-for-others and tries to transcend this factual situation.

This is not the place to show what of love and desire can be contained in pity, admiration, disgust, envy, gratitude, *etc.* But each man will be able to determine it by referring to his own experience, as well as to the eidetic intuition of these various essences. Naturally this does not mean that these different attitudes are simply disguises borrowed by sexuality. But it must be understood that sexuality is integrated in them as their foundation and that they include and surpass it just as the notion of a circle includes and surpasses that of a rotating line segment, one of whose extremities is fixed. These fundamental-attitudes can remain hidden just as a skeleton is veiled by the flesh which surrounds it; in fact this is what usually happens. The contingency of bodies, the structure of the original project which I am, the history which I historicize can usually determine the sexual attitude to remain implicit, inside more complex conduct. For example, it is only seldom that one explicitly desires an Other "of the same sex." But behind the prohibitions of morality and the taboos of society the original structure remains, at least in that particular form of "trouble" which is called sexual disgust. And it is not necessary to understand this permanence of the sexual project as if it dwelt "within us" in the unconscious state. A project of the For-itself can exist only in conscious form. It exists as integrated with a particular structure in which it is dissolved. This is what psychoanalysts have had in mind when they have made of sexual affectivity a "tabula rasa" deriving all its determinations from the individual history. Only it is not necessary to hold that sexuality at its origin is underdetermined; in fact it includes all its determinations from the moment of the upsurge of the For-itself into a world where "there are" Others. What is undetermined and what must be fixed by each one's history is the particular type of relation with the Other in which the sexual attitude (desire-love, masochism-sadism) will be manifested in its explicit purity.

It is precisely because these attitudes are original that we have chosen them in order to demonstrate the *circle* of relations with the Other. Since these attitudes are in fact integrated in *all* attitudes toward Others, they involve in their circularity the integrality of all conduct toward the Other. Just as Love finds its failure within itself and just as Desire arises from the death of Love in order to collapse in turn and give way to Love, so all the patterns of conduct toward the Other-as-object include within themselves an implicit and veiled reference to an Other-as-subject, and this reference is their death. Upon the death of a particular conduct toward the Other-as-object arises a new attitude which aims at getting hold of the Other-as-subject, and this in turn reveals its instabiliy and collapses to give way to the opposite conduct. Thus we are indefinitely referred from the Other-as-object to the Other-as-subject and *vice versa*. The movement is never arrested, and this movement with its abrupt reversals of direction constitutes our relation with the Other. At whatever moment a person is considered, he is in one or the other of these attitudes— unsatisfied by the one as by the other. We can maintain ourselves for a greater or less length of time in the attitude adopted depending on our bad faith or depending on the particular circumstances of our history. But never will either attitude be sufficient in itself; it always points obscurely in the direction of its opposite. This means that we can never hold a consistent attitude toward the Other unless he is simultaneously revealed to us as subject and as object, as transcendence-transcending and as transcendence-transcended— which is on principle impossible. Thus ceaselessly tossed from being-a-look to being-looked-at, falling from one to the other in alternate revolutions, we are always, no matter what attitude is adopted, in a state of instability in relation to the Other. We pursue the impossible ideal of the simultaneous apprehension of his freedom and of his objectivity. To borrow an expression from Jean Wahl, we are—in relation to the Other—sometimes in a state of *trans-descendence* (when we apprehend him as an object and integrate him with the world), and sometimes in a state of *trans-ascendence* (when we experience him as a transcendence which transcends us). But neither of these two states is sufficient in itself, and we shall never place ourselves concretely on a plane of equality; that is, on the plane where the recognition of the Other's freedom would involve the Other's recognition of our freedom.

The Other is on principle inapprehensible; he flees me when I seek him and possesses me when I flee him. Even if I should want to act according to the precepts of Kantian morality and take the Other's freedom as an unconditioned end, still this freedom would become a transcendence-transcended by the mere fact that I make it my goal. On the other hand, I could act for his benefit only by utilizing the Other-as-object as an instrument in order to realize this freedom. It would be necessary, in fact, that I apprehend the Other in situation as an object-instrument, and my sole power would be then to modify the situation in relation to the Other and the Other in relation to the situation. Thus I am brought to that paradox which is the perilous reef of all liberal politics and which Rousseau has defined in a single word: I must "force" the Other to be free. Even if this force is not always nor even very frequently exercised in the form of violence, nevertheless it still governs the relations of men with each other. If I offer comfort and reassurance, it is in order to disengage the Other's freedom from the fears or griefs which darken it; but consolation or reassuring argument is the organization of a system of means to an end and is designed to *act* upon the Other and consequently to integrate him in turn as an instrumental-thing in the system. Furthermore the comforter effects an arbitrary distinction between the freedom which he is identifying with the use of Reason and the pursuit of the

Good, on the one hand, and the affliction which appears to him the result of a psychic determinism. Therefore the problem is to separate the freedom from the affliction as one separates out each of two components of a chemical product. By the sole fact that the comforter is considering freedom as capable of being separated out, he transcends it and does violence to it, and he can not on the level where he is placed apprehend this truth: that it is freedom itself which *makes itself* the affliction and that consequently to act so as to free freedom from affliction is to act against freedom.

It does not follow, however, that an ethics of "*laisser-faire*" and tolerance would respect the Other's freedom any better. From the moment that I exist I establish a factual limit to the Other's freedom. I *am* this limit, and each of my projects traces the outline of this limit around the Other. Charity, *laisser-faire*, tolerance—even an attitude of abstention—are each one a project of myself which engages me and which engages the Other in his acquiescence. To realize tolerance with respect to the Other is to cause the Other to be thrown forcefully into a tolerant world. It is to remove from him on principle those free possibilities of courageous resistance, of perseverance, of self-assertion which he would have had the opportunity to develop in a world of intolerance. This fact is made still more manifest if we consider the problem of education: a severe education treats the child as an instrument since it tries to bend him by force to values which he has not admitted, but a liberal education in order to make use of other methods nevertheless chooses *a priori* principles and values in the name of which the child will be trained. To train the child by persuasion and gentleness is no less to compel him. Thus respect for the Other's freedom is an empty word; even if we could assume the project of respecting this freedom, each attitude which we adopted with respect to the Other would be a violation of that freedom which we claimed to respect. The extreme attitude which would be given as a total indifference toward the Other is not a solution either. We are already thrown in the world in the face of the Other; our upsurge is a free limitation of his freedom and nothing—not even suicide—can change this original situation. Whatever our acts may be, in fact, we must accomplish them in a world where there are already others and where I am *de trop* in relation to others.

It is from this singular situation that the notion of guilt and of sin seems to be derived. It is before the Other that I am *guilty*. I am guilty first when beneath the Other's look I experience my alienation and my nakedness as a fall from grace which I must assume. This is the meaning of the famous line from Scripture: "They knew that they were naked." Again I am guilty when in turn I look at the Other, because by the very fact of my own self-assertion I constitute him as an object and as an instrument, and I cause him to experience that same alienation which he must now assume. Thus original sin is my upsurge in a world where there are others; and whatever may be my further relations with others, these relations will be only variations on the original theme of my guilt.

But this guilt is accompanied by helplessness without this helplessness ever succeeding in cleansing me of my guilt. Whatever I may do for the Other's freedom, as we have seen, my efforts are reduced to treating the Other as an instrument and to positing his freedom as a transcendence-transcended. But on the other hand, no matter what compelling power I use, I shall never touch the Other save in his being-as-object. I shall never be able to accomplish anything except to furnish his freedom with occasions to manifest itself without my ever succeeding in increasing it or diminishing it, in directing it or in getting hold of it. Thus I am guilty toward the Other in my very being because the upsurge of my being, in spite of itself, bestows on the Other a new dimension of being; and on the other hand I am powerless either to profit from my fault or to rectify it.

A for-itself which by historicizing itself has experienced these various avatars can determine with full knowledge of the futility of its former attempts, to pursue the death of the Other. This free determination is called hate. It implies a fundamental resignation; the for-itself abandons its claim to realize any union with the Other; it gives up using the Other as an instrument to recover its own being-in-itself. It wishes simply to rediscover a freedom without factual limits; that is, to get rid of its own inapprehensible being-as-object-for-the-Other and to abolish its dimension of alienation. This is equivalent to projecting the realization of a world in which the Other does not exist. The for-itself which hates consents to being only for-itself; instructed by its various experiences of the impossibility of making use of its being-for-others, it prefers to be again only a free nihilation of its being, a totality detotalized, a pursuit which assigns to itself its own ends. The one who hates projects no longer being an object; hate presents itself as an absolute positing of the freedom of the for-itself before the Other. This is why hate does not abase the hated object, for it places the dispute on its true level. What I hate in the Other is not this appearance, this fault, this particular action. What I hate is his existence in general as a transcendence-transcended. This is why hate implies a recognition of the Other's freedom. But this recognition is abstract and negative; hate knows only the Other-as-object and attaches itself to this object. It wishes to destroy this object in order by the same stroke to overcome the transcendence which haunts it. This transcendence is only dimly sensed as an inaccessible beyond, as the perpetual possibility of the alienation of the for-itself which hates. It is therefore never *apprehended for itself*; moreover it could not be so without becoming an object. I experience it as a perpetually fleeing character in the Other-as-object, as a "not-given," "undeveloped" aspect of his most accessible empirical qualities, as a sort of perpetual threat which warns me that "I am missing the point."

This is why one hates *right through* the revealed psychic but not the psychic itself; this is why also it is indifferent whether we hate the Other's transcendence through what we empirically call his vices or his virtues. What I hate is the whole psychic-totality in so far as it refers me to the Other's transcendence. I do not lower myself to hate any particular objective detail. Here we find the distinction between hating and despising. And hate does not necessarily appear on the occasion of my being subjected to something evil. On the contrary, it can arise when one would theoretically expect gratitude—that is, on the occasion of a kindness. The occasion which arouses hate is simply an act by the Other which puts me in the state of *being subject to* his freedom. This act is in itself humiliating; it is humiliating as the concrete revelation of my instrumental object-ness in the face of the Other's freedom. This revelation is immediately obscured, is buried in the past and becomes opaque. But it leaves in me the feeling that there is "something" to be destroyed if I am to free myself. This is the reason, moreover, why gratitude is so close to hate; to be grateful for a kindness is to recognize that the Other was entirely free in acting as he has done. No compulsion, not even that of duty, has determined him in it. He is wholly responsible for his act and for the values which have presided over its accomplishment. I, myself, have been only the excuse for it, the matter on which his act has been exercised. In view of this recognition the for-itself can project love or hate as it chooses; it can no longer ignore the Other.

The second consequence of these observations is that hate is the hate of all Others in one Other. What I want to attain symbolically by pursuing the death of a particular Other is the general principle of the existence of others. The Other whom I hate actually represents all Others. My project of suppressing him is a project of suppressing others in general; that is, of recapturing my non-substantial freedom as for-itself. In hate there is given an understanding of the fact that my dimension of being-alienated is a real enslavement which comes to me through others. It is the suppression of this enslavement which is projected. That is why hate is a *black* feeling; that is, a feeling which aims at the suppression of an Other and which qua project is consciously projected against the disapproval of others. I disapprove of the hate which one person bears toward another; it makes me uneasy and I seek to suppress it because although it is not explicitly aimed at me, I know that it concerns me and that it is realized against me. And in fact it aims at destroying me not in so far as it would seek to suppress me but in so far as it principally lays claim to my disapproval in order to pass beyond it. Hate demands to be hated—so that to hate is equivalent to an uneasy recognition of the freedom of the one who hates.

But hate too is in turn a failure. Its initial project is to suppress other consciousnesses. But even if it succeeded in this—i.e., if it could at this moment abolish the Other—it could not bring it about that the Other had not been. Better yet, if the abolition of the Other is to be lived as the triumph of hate, it implies the explicit recognition that the Other *has existed*. Immediately my being-for-others by slipping into the past becomes an irremediable dimension of myself. It is what I have to be as having-been-it. Therefore I can not free myself from it. At least, someone will say, I escape it for the present, I shall escape it in the future. But no. He who has once been for-others is contaminated in his being for the rest of his days even if the Other should be entirely suppressed; he will never cease to apprehend his dimension of being-for-others as a permanent possibility of his being. He can never recapture what he has alienated; he has even lost all hope of acting on this alienation and turning it to his own advantage since the destroyed Other has carried the key to this alienation along with him to the grave. What I was for the Other is fixed by the Other's death, and I shall irremediably be it in the past. I shall be it also and in the same way in the present if I persevere in the attitude, the projects, and the mode of life which have been judged by the Other. The Other's death constitutes me as an irremediable object exactly as my own death would do. Thus the triumph of hate is in its very upsurge transformed into failure. Hate does not enable us to get out of the circle. It simply represents the final attempt, the attempt of despair. After the failure of this attempt nothing remains for the for-itself except to re-enter the circle and allow itself to be indefinitely tossed from one to the other of the two fundamental attitudes.[13]

## III. "BEING-WITH" (*MITSEIN*) AND THE "WE"

One could probably point out to us that our description is incomplete since it leaves no place for certain concrete experiences in which we discover ourselves not in conflict with the Other but in community with him. And it is true that we frequently use the word "we." The very existence and use of this grammatical form necessarily refers us to a real experience of the *Mitsein*. "We" can be subject and in this form it is identical with the plural of the "I." To be sure, the parallel between grammar and thought is in many cases more than doubtful; in fact, the question should be revised completely and the relation of language to thought studied from an entirely new approach. Yet it is nonetheless true that the "we" subject does not appear even conceivable unless it refers at least to the thought of a plurality of subjects which would simultaneously apprehend one another as subjectivities, that is, as transcendences-transcending and not as transcendences-transcended. If the word "we" is not simply a *flatus vocis*, it denotes a concept subsuming an

---

[13] These considerations do not exclude the possibility of an ethics of deliverance and salvation. But this can be achieved only after a radical conversion which we can not discuss here.

infinite variety of possible experiences. And these experiences appear *a priori* to contradict the experience of my being-as-object for the Other and the experience of the Other's being-as-object for me. In the "we," nobody is the object. The "we" includes a plurality of subjectives which recognize one another as subjectivities. Nevertheless this recognition is not the object of an explicit thesis; what is explicitly posited is a common action or the object of a common perception. "We" resist, "we" advance to the attack, "we" condemn the guilty, "we" look at this or that spectacle. Thus the recognition of subjectivities is analogous to that of the self-recognition of the non-thetic consciousness. More precisely, it must be effected *laterally* by a non-thetic consciousness whose thetic object is this or that spectacle in the world.

The best example of the "we" can be furnished us by the spectator at a theatrical performance whose consciousness is exhausted in apprehending the imaginary spectacle, in foreseeing the events through anticipatory schemes, in positing imaginary beings as the hero, the traitor, the captive, *etc.*, a spectator, who, however, in the very upsurge which makes him a consciousness of the spectacle is constituted non-thetically as consciousness (of) being a *co-spectator* of the spectacle. Everyone knows in fact that unavowed embarrassment which grips us in an auditorium half empty and, on the other hand, that enthusiasm which is let loose and is reinforced in a full and enthusiastic hall. Moreover it is certain that the experience of the we-as-subject can be manifested in any circumstance whatsoever. I am sitting in front of a café; I observe the other customers and I know myself to be observed. We remain here in the most ordinary case of conflict with others (the Other's being-as-object for me, my being-as-object for the Other). But suddenly some incident occurs in the street; for example, a slight collision between a carrier tricycle and a taxi. Immediately at the very instant when I become a spectator of the incident, I experience my self non-thetically as engaged in "we." The earlier rivalries, the slight conflicts have disappeared, and the consciousnesses which furnished the matter of the "we" are precisely those of all the patrons: "we" look at the event, "we" take part. It is this unanimity which Romains wanted to describe in *Vie unanime* or in *Vin blanc de la Villette*. Here we are brought back again to Heidegger's *Mitsein*. Was it worth while then to criticize it earlier?[14]

We shall only remark here that we had no intention of casting doubt on the *experience* of the "we." We limited ourselves to showing that this experience could not be the foundation of our consciousness of the Other. It is clear, in fact, that it could not constitute an ontological structure of human-reality; we have proved that the existence of the for-itself in the midst of others was at its

[14] Part III, ch. I.

origin a metaphysical and contingent fact. In addition it is clear that the "we" is not an inter-subjective consciousness nor a new being which surpasses and encircles its parts as a synthetic whole in the manner of the collective consciousness of the sociologists. The "we" is experienced by a particular consciousness; it is not necessary that *all* the patrons at the café should be conscious of being "we" in order for me to experience myself as being engaged in a "we" with them. Everyone is familiar with this pattern of everyday dialogue: "We are very dissatisfied." "But no, my dear, speak for yourself." This implies that there are aberrant consciousnesses of the "we"—which as such are nevertheless perfectly normal consciousnesses. If this is the case, then in order for a consciousness to get the consciousness of being engaged in a "we," it is necessary that the other consciousnesses which enter into community with it should be first given in some other way; that is, either in the capacity of a transcendence-transcending or as a transcendence-transcended. The "we" is a certain particular experience which is produced in special cases on the foundation of being-for-others in general. The being-for-others precedes and founds the *being-with-others*.

Furthermore the philosopher who wants to study the "we" must take precautions and know of what he speaks. There is not only a We-as-subject; grammar teaches us that there is also a We-as-complement—i.e., a We-as-object.[15] Now from all which has been said up till now it is easy to understand that the "we" in "We are looking at them" can not be on the same ontological plane as the "us" in "They are looking at us." There is no question here of subjectivities qua subjectivities. In the sentence, "They are looking at *me*," I want to indicate that I experience myself as an object for others, as an alienated Me, as a transcendence-transcended. If the sentence, "They are looking at us," is to indicate a real experience, it is necessary that in this experience I make proof of the fact that I am engaged with others in a community of transcendences-transcended, of alienated "Me's." The "Us" here refers to an experience of *being-objects in common*. Thus there are two radically different forms of the experience of the "we," and the two forms correspond exactly to the being-in-the-act-of-looking and the being-looked-at which constitute the fundamental relations of the For-itself with the Other. It is these two forms of the "we" which must be studied next.

## A. The Us-object

We shall begin by examining the second of these experiences; its meaning can be grasped more easily and it will perhaps serve as a means of approach

---

[15] Here the difference between English and French presents a certain difficulty for the translator since *nous* in French is used for both subject and object—i.e., "we" and "us." Tr.

to the study of the Other. First we must note that the Us-object precipitates us into the world; we experience it in shame as a community alienation. This is illustrated by that significant scene in which convicts choke with anger and shame when a beautiful, elegantly dressed woman comes to visit their ship, sees their rags, their labor, and their misery. We have here a common shame and a common alienation. How then is it possible to experience oneself as an object in a community of objects? To answer this we must return to the fundamental characteristics of our being-for-others.

Hitherto we have considered the simple case in which I am alone confronting the Other who is also alone. In this case I look at him or he looks at me. I seek to transcend his transcendence or I experience my own as transcended; and I feel my possibilities as dead-possibilities. We form a *pair* and we are in *situation* each one in relation to the Other. But this situation has objective existence only for the one or the Other. There is no *reverse side* to our reciprocal relation. In our description we have not yet taken into account the fact that my relation with the Other appears on the infinite ground of my relation and of *his* relation to *all Others*; that is, to the quasi-totality of consciousnesses. As a result my relation to *this* Other, which I experienced earlier as the foundation of my being-for-others, or the relation of the Other to me can at each instant and according to the motives which intervene be experienced as *objects for Others*. This will be manifested clearly in the case of the appearance of a *third person*. Suppose, for example, that the Other is looking at me. At this moment I experience myself as wholly *alienated*, and I assume myself as such. Now the Third comes on the scene. If he looks at me, I experience them as forming a community, as "They" (they-subject) through my alienation. This "they" tends, as we know, toward the impersonal "somebody" or "one" (on). It does not alter the fact that I am looked at; it does not strengthen (or barely strengthens) my original alienation. But if the Third looks at the Other who is looking at me, the problem is more complex. I can in fact apprehend the Third *not directly* but upon the Other, who becomes the Other-looked-at (by the Third). Thus the third transcendence transcends the transcendence which transcends me and thereby contributes to disarming it. There is constituted here a metastable state which will soon decompose depending upon whether I ally myself to the Third so as to look at the Other who is then transformed into *our* object—and here I experience the We-as-subject of which we will speak later—or whether I look at the Third and thus transcend this third transcendence which transcends the Other. In the latter case the Third becomes an object in my universe, his possibilities are dead-possibilities, he can not deliver me from the Other. Yet he looks at the Other who is looking at me. There follows a situation which we shall call indeterminate and inconclusive since I am an object for the Other who is an object for the Third who is an object for me. Freedom alone by insisting on one or the other of these relations can give a structure to this situation.

But it can just as well happen that the Third looks at the Other *at whom I am looking*. In this case I can look at both of them and thus disarm the look of the Third. The Third and the Other will appear to me then as They-as-objects or "Them." I can also grasp upon the Other the look of the Third so that without seeing the Third I apprehend upon the Other's behavior the fact that he knows himself to be looked-at. In this case I *experience upon the Other and apropos of the Other* the Third's transcendence-transcending. The Third experiences it as a radical and absolute alienation of the Other. The Other flees away from my world; he no longer belongs to me; he is an object for another transcendence. Therefore he does not lose his character as an object, but he becomes ambiguous; he escapes me not by means of his own transcendence but through the transcendence of the Third. Whatever I can apprehend upon him and concerning him at present, he is always Other, as many times Other as there are Others to perceive him and think about him. In order for me to reappropriate the Other for myself, it is necessary for me to look at the Third and to confer an object-state upon him. But in the first place, this is not always possible; moreover the Third can be himself looked at by other Thirds; that is, can be indefinitely the Other whom I do not see. There results an original instability in the Other-as-object and an infinite pursuit by the For-itself which seeks to reappropriate this object-state. This is the reason, as we have seen, why lovers seek solitude.

It is possible also for me to experience myself as looked-at by the Third while I look at the Other. In this case I experience my alienation non-positionally at the same time that I posit the alienation of the Other. My possibilities of utilizing the Other as an instrument are experienced by me as dead-possibilities, and my transcendence which prepares to transcend the Other toward my own ends falls back into transcendence-transcended. I let go my hold. The Other does not thereby become a subject, but I no longer feel myself qualified to keep him in an object-state. He becomes a *neutral*; something which is purely and simply there and with which I have nothing to do. This will be the case, for example, if I am surprised in the process of beating and humiliating a man helpless to defend himself. The appearance of the Third "disconnects" me. The helpless man is no longer either "to be beaten" or "to be humiliated"; he is nothing more than a pure existence. He is nothing more, he is no longer even "a helpless man." Or if he becomes so again, this will be through the Third serving as interpreter; I *shall learn from the Third* that the Other was a helpless man ("Aren't you ashamed? You have attacked one who is helpless," *etc.*). The quality of helplessness will in my eyes be conferred on the Other by the Third; it will no longer be part of my world but of a universe in which I am with the helpless man for the Third.

This brings us finally to the case with which we are primarily concerned: I am engaged in a conflict with the Other. The Third comes on the scene and embraces both of us with his look. Correlatively I experience my alienation and my object-ness. For the Other I am outside as an object in the midst of a world which is not "mine." But the Other whom I was looking at or who was looking at me undergoes the same modification, and I discover this modification of the Other simultaneously with that which I experience. The Other is an object in the midst of the world of the Third. Moreover this object-state is not a simple modification of his being which is *parallel* with that which I undergo, but the two object-states come to me and to the Other in a global modification of the situation in which I am and in which the Other finds himself. Before the look of the Third appeared there were two situations, one circumscribed by the possibilities of the Other in which I was as an instrument, and a reverse situation circumscribed by my own possibilities and including the Other. Each of these situations was the death of the Other and we could grasp the one only by objectivizing the other. Now at the appearance of the Third I suddenly experience the alienation of my possibilities, and I discover by the same token that the possibilities of the Other are dead-possibilities. The situation does not thereby disappear, but it flees outside both my world and the Other's world; it is constituted in objective form in the midst of a third world. In this third world it is seen, judged, transcended, utilized, but suddenly there is effected a leveling of the two opposed situations; there is no longer any structure of priority which goes from me to the Other or conversely from the Other to me since our possibilities are equally dead-possibilities *for the Third*. This means that I suddenly experience the existence of an objective situation-form in the world of the Third in which the Other and I shall figure as *equivalent* structures in *solidarity* with each other. Conflict does not arise, in this objective situation, from the free upsurge of our transcendences, but it is established and transcended by the Third as a factual given which defines us and holds us together. The Other's possibility of striking me and my possibility of defending myself, far from being exclusive of one another, are now complementary to each other, imply one another, and involve one another for the Third by virtue of their being dead-possibilities, and this is precisely what I experience non-thetically and without having any *knowledge* of it. Thus what I experience is a being-outside in which I am organized with the Other in an indissoluble, objective whole, a whole in which I am fundamentally *no longer distinct* from the Other but which I agree in solidarity with the Other to constitute. And to the extent that on principle I assume my being-outside for the Third, I must similarly assume the Other's being-outside; what I assume is a community of equivalence by means of which I exist engaged in a form which like the Other I agree to constitute. In a word

I assume myself as engaged outside in the Other, and I assume the Other as engaged outside in me.

I carry the fundamental assumption of this engagement before me without apprehending it; it is this free recognition of my responsibility as including the responsibility for the Other which is the experience of the Us-object. Thus the Us-object is never known in the sense that reflection gives to us the knowledge of our Self, for example; it is never felt in the sense that a feeling reveals to us a particular concrete object as antipathetic, hateful, troubling, etc. Neither is it simply experienced, for what is experienced is the pure situation of solidarity with the Other. The Us-object is revealed to us only by my assuming the responsibility for this situation; that is, because of the internal reciprocity of the situation, I must of necessity—in the heart of my free assumption—assume also the Other. Thus in the absence of any Third person I can say, "I am fighting against the Other." But as soon as the Third appears, the Other's possibilities and my own are leveled into dead-possibilities and hence the relation becomes reciprocal; I am compelled to experience the fact that "we are fighting each other." For the statement, "I fight him and he fights me" would be plainly inadequate. Actually I fight him because he fights me and reciprocally. The project of combat has germinated in his mind as in mine, and for the Third it is united into a single project common to that they-as-object which he embraced with his look and which even constitutes the unifying synthesis of this "Them." Therefore I must assume myself as apprehended by the Third as an integral part of the "Them." And this "Them" which is assumed by a subjectivity as its meaning-for-others becomes the "Us."

Reflective consciousness can not apprehend this "Us." Its appearance coincides on the contrary with the collapse of the "Us"; the For-itself disengages itself and posits its selfness against Others. In fact it is necessary to conceive that originally the belonging to the Us-object is felt as a still more radical alienation on the part of the For-itself since the latter is no longer compelled only to assume what it is for the Other but to assume also a totality which it is not although it forms an integral part of it. In this sense the Us-object is an abrupt experience of the human condition as engaged among Others as an objectively established fact. The Us-object although experienced on the occasion of a concrete solidarity and centered in this solidarity (I shall be ashamed precisely because we have been caught in the act of fighting one another) has a meaning which surpasses the particular circumstance in which it is experienced and which aims at including my belonging as an object to the human totality (minus the pure consciousness of the Third) which is equally apprehended as an object. Therefore it corresponds to an experience of humiliation and impotence; the one who experiences himself as constituting an Us with other men feels himself trapped among an infinity of strange existences; he is alienated radically and without recourse.

Certain situations appear more likely than others to arouse the experience of the Us. In particular there is communal work: when several persons experience themselves as apprehended by the Third while they work in solidarity to produce the same object, the very meaning of the manufactured object refers to the working collectivity as to an "Us." The movement which I make and which is required by the assembling to be realized has meaning only if it is preceded by this movement on the part of my neighbor and followed by that movement on the part of that other workman. There results a form of the "Us" more easily accessible since it is the requirement of the object itself and its potentialities and its coefficient of adversity which refer to us workmen as an Us-object. We have therefore experienced ourselves as apprehended as an "Us" through a material object "to be created." Materiality puts its seal on our interdependent community, and we appear to ourselves as an instrumental disposition and technique of means, each one having a particular place assigned by an end.

But if some situations thus appear empirically more favorable to the upsurge of the "Us," we must not lose sight of the fact that *every* human situation since it is an engagement in the midst of others, is experienced as "Us" as soon as the Third appears. If I am walking in the street behind this man and see only his back, I have with him the minimum of technical and practical relations which can be conceived. Yet once the Third looks at me, looks at the road, looks at the Other, I am bound to the Other by the solidarity of the "Us": we are walking one behind the Other on *la rue Blomet* on a July morning. There is always a point of view from which diverse for-itselfs can be united in an "Us" by a look. Conversely just as the look is only the concrete manifestation of the original fact of my existence for others, just as therefore I experience myself existing for the Other outside any individual appearance of a look, so it is not necessary that a concrete look should penetrate and transfix us in order for us to be able to experience ourselves as integrated outside in an "Us." So long as the detotalized-totality "humanity" exists, it is possible for some sort of plurality of individuals to experience itself as "Us" in relation to all or part of the rest of men, whether these men are present "in flesh and blood" or whether they are real but *absent*. Thus whether in the presence or in the absence of the Third I can always apprehend myself either as pure selfness or as integrated in an "Us." This brings us to certain special forms of the "Us," in particular to that which we call "class consciousness."

Class consciousness is evidently the assuming of a particular "Us" on the occasion of a collective situation more plainly structured than usual. It matters little here how we define this situation; what interests us is only the nature of the "Us" which is assumed. If a society, so far as its economical or political structure is concerned, is divided into oppressed classes and oppressing classes, the situation of the oppressing classes presents the oppressed classes with the image of a perpetual Third who considers them and transcends them by his freedom. It is not the hard work, the low living standard, or the privations endured which will constitute the oppressed collectivity as a class. The solidarity of work, in fact, could (as we shall see in the following section) constitute the laboring collectivity as a "We-subject" in so far as this collectivity—whatever may be the coefficient of adversity of *things*—makes proof of itself as transcending the intra-mundane objects towards its own ends. The living standard is a wholly relative thing, and appreciation of it will vary according to circumstances (it can be simply *endured* or *accepted* or *demanded* in the name of a common ideal). The privations if considered in themselves have the result of isolating the persons who suffer them rather than of uniting them and are in general sources of conflict. Finally, the pure and simple comparison which the members of the oppressed collectivity can make between the harshness of their conditions and the privileges enjoyed by the oppressing classes can not in any case suffice to constitute a class consciousness; at most it will provoke individual jealousies or particular despairs; it does not possess the possibility of unifying and of making each one assume the responsibility for the unification. But the ensemble of these characteristics as it constitutes the *condition* of the oppressed class is not simply endured or accepted. It would be equally erroneous, however, to say that from the beginning it is apprehended by the oppressed class as *imposed* by the oppressing class. On the contrary, a long time is necessary to construct and spread a theory of oppression. And this theory will have only an *explicative* value. The primary fact is that the member of the oppressed collectivity, who as a simple person is engaged in fundamental conflicts with other members of this collectivity (love, hate, rivalry of interests, *etc.*), apprehends his condition and that of other members of this collectivity as looked-at and thought about by consciousnesses which escape him.

The "master," the "feudal lord," the "bourgeois," the "capitalist" all appear not only as powerful people who command but in addition and above all as *Thirds*; that is, as those who are outside the oppressed community and *for whom* this community exists. It is therefore *for* them and *in their freedom* that the reality of the oppressed class is going to exist. They cause it to be born by their look. It is to them and through them that there is revealed the identity of my condition and that of the others who are oppressed; it is for them that I exist in a situation organized with others and that my possibles as dead-possibles are strictly equivalent with the possibles of others; it is for them that I am a worker and it is through and in their revelation as the Other-as-a-look that I experience myself as one among others. This means that I discover the

"Us" in which I am integrated or "the class" *outside*, in the look of the Third, and it is this collective alienation which I assume when saying "Us." From this point of view the privileges of the Third and "our" burdens, "our" miseries have value at first only as a *signification*; they signify the independence of the Third in relation to "Us"; they present our alienation to us more plainly. Yet as they are none the less *endured, as in particular our work, our fatigue are none the less suffered*, it is across this endured suffering that I experience my being-looked-at-as-a-thing-engaged-in-a-totality-of-things. It is in terms of my suffering, of my misery that I am collectively apprehended with others by the Third; that is, in terms of the adversity of the world, in terms of the facticity of my condition. Without the Third, no matter what might be the adversity of the world, I should apprehend myself as a triumphant transcendence; with the appearance of the Third, "I" experience "Us" as apprehended in terms of things and as things overcome by the world.

Thus the oppressed class finds its class unity in the knowledge which the oppressing class has of it, and the appearance among the oppressed of class consciousness corresponds to the assumption in shame of an Us-object. We shall see in the following section what "class consciousness" can be for a member of the oppressing class. What is important for us here in any case and what is sufficiently illustrated by the example which we have just chosen is that the experience of the Us-object presupposes that of the being-for-others, of which it is only a more complex modality. Therefore by virtue of being a particular case it falls within the compass of our preceding descriptions. Moreover it incloses within itself a power of disintegration since it is experienced through shame and since the "Us" collapses as soon as the for-itself reclaims its selfness in the face of the Third and looks at him in turn. This individual claim of selfness is moreover only one of the possible ways of suppressing the Us-object. The assumption of the "Us" in certain strongly structured cases, as, for example, class consciousness, no longer implies the project of freeing oneself from the "Us" by an individual recovery of selfness but rather the project of freeing the whole "Us" from the object-state by transforming it into a We-subject.

At bottom we are dealing with a variation of the project already described of transforming the one who is looking into the one who is looked-at; it is the usual passage from one to the other of the two great fundamental attitudes of the for-others. The oppressed class can, in fact, affirm itself as a We-subject only in relation to the oppressing class and at the latter's expense; that is, by transforming it in turn into "they-as-objects" or "Them." The person who is engaged objectively in the class aims at involving the whole class in and by means of his project of reversal. In this sense the experience of the Us-object refers to that of the We-subject just as the experience of my being-an-object-for-others refers me to the experience of being-an-object-for-others-for-me. Similarly we shall find in what is called "mob psychology" collective crazes (*Boulangism*, etc.) which are a particular form of love. The person who says "Us" then reassumes in the heart of the crowd the original project of love, but it is no longer on his own account; he asks a Third to save the whole collectivity in its very object-state so that he may sacrifice his freedom to it. Here as above disappointed love leads to masochism. This is seen in the case in which the collectivity rushes into servitude and asks to be treated as an object. The problem involves here again multiple individual projects of men in the crowd; the crowd has been constituted *as a crowd* by the look of the leader or the speaker; its unity is an object-unity which each one of its members reads in the look of the Third who dominates it, and each one then forms the project of losing himself in this object-ness, of wholly abandoning his selfness in order to be no longer anything but an instrument in the hands of the leader. But this instrument in which he wants to be dissolved is no longer his pure and simple personal for-others; it is the totality, objective-crowd. The monstrous materiality of the crowd and its profound reality (although only experienced) are fascinating for each of its members; each one demands to be submerged in the crowd-instrument by the look of the leader.[16]

In these various instances we have seen that the Us-object is always constituted in terms of a concrete situation in which one part of the detotalized-totality "humanity" is immersed to the exclusion of another part. We are "Us" only in the eyes of Others, and it is in terms of the Others' look that we assume ourselves as "Us." But this implies that there can exist an abstract, unrealizable project of the for-itself toward an absolute totalization of itself and of *all* Others. This effort at recovering the human totality can not take place without positing the existence of a Third, who is on principle distinct from humanity and in whose eyes humanity is wholly object. This unrealizable Third, is simply the object of the limiting-concept of otherness. He is the one who is Third in relation to all possible groups, the one who in no case can enter into community with any human group, the Third in relation to whom no other can constitute himself as a third. This concept is the same as that of the being-who looks-at and who can never be looked-at; that is, it is one with the idea of God. But if God is characterized as radical absence, the effort to realize humanity as *ours* is forever renewed and forever results in failure. Thus the humanistic "Us"—the Us-object—is proposed to each individual consciousness as an ideal impossible to attain although everyone keeps the illusion of being able to succeed in it by progressively enlarging the circle of communities to which he does belong. This humanistic "Us" remains an

---

[16] Cf. the numerous cases of a refusal of selfness. The for-itself *refuses to emerge in anguish outside the* "Us."

empty concept, a pure indication of a possible extension of the ordinary usage of the "Us." Each time that we use the "Us" in this sense (to designate suffering humanity, sinful humanity, to determine an objective historical meaning by considering man as an object which is developing its potentialities) we limit ourselves to indicating a certain concrete experience to be undergone in the presence of the absolute Third; that is, of God. Thus the limiting-concept of humanity (as the totality of the Us-object) and the limiting-concept of God imply one another and are correlative.

## B. The we-subject

It is the world which makes known to us our belonging to a subject-community, especially the existence in the world of manufactured objects. These objects have been worked on by men for they-subjects; that is, for a non-individualized and unnumbered transcendence which coincides with the undifferentiated look which we called earlier the "They." The worker—servile or not—works in the presence of an undifferentiated and absent transcendence and can only outline the free possibilities of this transcendence in a vacuum—so to speak—upon the object on which he is working. In this sense the worker, whoever he may be, experiences in work his being-an-instrument for others. Work, when it is not strictly destined for the ends of the worker himself, is a mode of alienation. The alienating transcendence is here the consumer; that is, the "They" whose projects the worker is limited to anticipating. As soon as I use a manufactured object, I meet upon it the outline of my own transcendence; it indicates to me the movement to be made; I am to turn, push, draw, or lean. Moreover we are dealing here with an hypothetical imperative; it refers me to an end which is equally in the world: if I want to sit down, if I want to open the box, etc. And this end itself has been anticipated in the constitution of the object as an end posited by some transcendence. It belongs at present to the object as its most peculiar potentiality. Thus it is true that the manufactured object makes me known to myself as "they"; that is, it refers to me the image of my transcendence as that of any transcendence whatsoever. And if I allow my possibilities to be channeled by the instrument thus constituted, I experience myself as any transcendence: to go from the subway station at "Trocadéro" to "Sèvres-Babylon," "They" change at "La Motte-Picquet." This change is foreseen, indicated on maps, etc.; if I change routes at La Motte-Picquet, I am the "They" who change. To be sure, I differentiate myself by each use of the subway as much by the individual upsurge of my being as by the distant ends which I pursue. But these final ends are only on the horizon of my act. My immediate ends are the ends of the "They," and I apprehend myself as interchangeable with any one of my neighbors. In this sense we lose our real individuality, for the project which we are is precisely the project which others are. In this subway corridor there is only one and the same project, inscribed a long time ago in matter, where a living and undifferentiated transcendence comes to be absorbed. To the extent that I realize myself in solitude as any transcendence, I have only the experience of undifferentiated-being (e.g., if alone in my room I open a bottle of preserves with the proper bottle opener). But if this undifferentiated transcendence projects its projects, whatever they are, in connection with other transcendences experienced as real presences similarly absorbed in projects identical with my projects, then I realize my project as one among thousands of identical projects projected by one and the same undifferentiated transcendence. Then I have the experience of a common transcendence directed toward a unique end of which I am only an ephemeral particularization; I insert myself into the great human stream which from the time that the subway first existed has flowed incessantly into the corridors of the station "La Motte-Picquet-Grenelle." But we must note the following:

(1) This experience is of the psychological order and not ontological. It in no way corresponds to a real unification of the for-itselfs under consideration. Neither does it stem from an immediate experience of their transcendence as such (as in being-looked-at), but it is motivated rather by the double objectivizing apprehension of the object transcended in common and of the bodies which surround mine. In particular the fact that I am engaged with others in a common rhythm which I contribute to creating is especially likely to lead me to apprehend myself as engaged in a We-subject. This is the meaning of the cadenced march of soldiers; it is the meaning also of the rhythmic work of a crew. It must be noted, however, that in this case the rhythm emanates freely from me; it is a project which I realize by means of my transcendence; it synthesizes a future with a present and a past within a perspective of regular repetition; it is I who produce this rhythm. But at the same time it melts into the general rhythm of the work or of the march of the concrete community which surrounds me. It gets its meaning only through this general rhythm; this is what I experience, for example, when the rhythm which I adopt is *contre-temps*. Yet the enveloping of my rhythm by the rhythm of the Other is apprehended "laterally." I do not utilize the collective rhythm as an instrument; neither do I contemplate it—in the sense in which for example, I might contemplate dancers on a stage. It surrounds me and involves me without being an *object* for me. I do not transcend it toward my own possibilities; but I slip my transcendence into its transcendence, and my own end—to accomplish a particular work, to arrive at a particular place—is an end of the "They" which is not distinct from the peculiar end of the collectivity. Thus the rhythm which I cause to be born is born in connection with me and laterally as the collective rhythm; it is *my* rhythm to the extent

that it is their rhythm and conversely. There precisely is the motive for the experience of the We-subject; it is finally our rhythm.

Yet we can see that this can be only if by the earlier acceptance of a common end and of common instruments I constitute myself as an undifferentiated transcendence by rejecting my personal ends beyond the collective ends at present pursued. Thus whereas in the experience of being-for-others the upsurge of a dimension of real and concrete being is the condition for the very experience, the experience of the We-subject is a pure psychological, subjective event in a single consciousness; it corresponds to an inner modification of the structure of this consciousness but does not appear on the foundation of a concrete ontological relation with others and does not realize any *Mitsein*. It is a question only of a way of feeling myself in the midst of others. Of course this experience can be looked on as the symbol of an absolute, metaphysical unity of all transcendences; it seems, in fact, that it overcomes the original conflict of transcendences by making them converge in the direction of the world. In this sense the ideal We-subject would be the "we" of a humanity which would make itself master of the earth. But the experience of the "we" remains on the ground of individual psychology and remains a simple symbol of the longed-for unity of transcendences. It is, in fact, in no way a lateral, real apprehension of subjectivities as such by a single subjectivity; the subjectivities remain out of reach and radically separated. But it is things and bodies, it is the material channeling of my transcendence which disposes me to apprehend it as extended and supported by the other transcendences without my getting out of my self and without the others getting out of themselves. I apprehend through the world that I form a part of "we."

This is why my experience of the We-subject in no way implies a similar and correlative experience in others; this is why also it is so unstable; for it depends on particular organizations in the midst of the world and it disappears with those organizations. In truth, there is in the world a host of formations which indicate me as *anybody*: first of all, all instrumental formations from tools proper to buildings with their elevators, their water or gas pipes, their electricity, not to mention means of transportation, shops, etc. Every shop window, each plate of glass refers to me my image as an undifferentiated transcendence. In addition professional and technical relations with others make me known to myself as anybody: for the waiter I am any patron, for the ticket collector, I am any user of the subway. Finally the chance incident which suddenly takes place in front of the pavement of the café where I am sitting indicates me as an anonymous spectator and as a pure "look which *makes this incident exist*—as an outside." Similarly it is the anonymity of the spectator which is indicated by the theatrical performance which I am attending or the exhibition of pictures which I visit. And of course I make myself anybody when I try on shoes or uncork a bottle or go into an elevator or laugh in the theater. But the experience of this undifferentiated transcendence is an inner and contingent event which concerns only me. Certain particular circumstances which come from the world can add to my impression of being part of the "we." But in every instance we are dealing with only a purely subjective impression which engages only me.

(2) The experience of the We-subject can not be primary; it can not constitute an original attitude toward others since, on the contrary, it must in order to be realized presuppose a twofold preliminary recognition of the existence of others. In the first place, the manufactured object is such only if it refers to the producers who have made it and to rules for its use which have been fixed by others. Confronting an inanimate thing which has not been worked on, for which I myself fix its mode of use and to which I myself assign a new use (if, for example, I use a stone as a hammer), I have a non-thetic consciousness of my self as a *person*; that is, of my selfness, of my own ends, and of my free inventiveness. The rules for using, the "methods of employing" manufactured objects are both rigid and ideal like *taboos* and by their essential structure put me in the presence of the Other; it is because the Other treats me as an undifferentiated transcendence that I can realize myself as such.

For a ready example, take those big signs which are above the portals of a station or in a waiting room and which bear the words "Exit" or "Entrance"; or again the directing hands on signboards which indicate a building or a direction. Here we are dealing once more with hypothetical imperatives. But here the formulation of the imperative clearly allows the Other to show through, the Other who is speaking and addressing himself directly to me. It is indeed to me that the printed sentence is directed; it represents in fact an immediate communication from the Other to me: I am *aimed at*. But if the Other aims at me, it is in so far as I am an undifferentiated transcendence. As soon as I avail myself of the opening marked "Exit" and go out through it, I am not using it in the absolute freedom of my *personal* projects. I am not constituting a tool by means of *invention*; I do not surpass the pure materiality of the thing toward my possibles. But between the object and me there has already slipped in a human transcendence which guides my transcendence. The object is already *humanized*; it signifies "human kindom." The "Exit"— considered as a pure opening out onto the street—is strictly equivalent to the "Entrance"; neither its coefficient of adversity nor its visible utility designates it as an exit. I do not submit to the object itself when I use it as an "Exit"; I adapt myself to the human order. By my very act I *recognize* the Other's existence; I set up a dialogue with the Other.

All this Heidegger has said and very well. But the conclusion which he neglects to derive from it is that in order for the object to appear as manufactured, it is necessary that the Other be first given in some other way. A person who had not already experienced the Other would in no way be able to distinguish the manufactured object from the pure materiality of a thing which has not been worked on. Even if he were to utilize it according to the method foreseen by the manufacturer, he would be reinventing this method and would thus realize a free appropriation of a natural thing. To go out by the passage marked "Exit" without having read the writing or without knowing the language is to be like the Stoic madman who in broad daylight says, "It is day," not as the consequence of an objective establishment but by virtue of inner resources of his madness. If therefore the manufactured object refers to Others and thereby to my undifferentiated transcendence, this is because I already know Others. Thus the experience of the We-subject is based on the original experience of the Other and can be only a secondary and subordinate experience.

Furthermore, as we have seen, to apprehend oneself as an undifferentiated transcendence—that is, basically, as a pure exemplification of the "human species"—is not yet to apprehend oneself as the partial structure of a We-subject. For that, in fact, one must discover oneself as *any body* in the center of some human stream. Therefore it is necessary to be surrounded by others. We have seen also that the others are in no way experienced as subjects in this experience, but neither are they apprehended as objects. They are not posited *at all*. Of course, I proceed on the basis of their factual existence in the world and of the perception of their acts. But I do not apprehend their facticity or their movements *positionally*; I have a lateral and non-positional consciousness of their bodies as correlative with my body, of their acts as unfolding in connection with my acts in such a way that I can not determine whether it is my acts which give birth to their acts or their acts which give birth to mine. A few observations will suffice to make clear that the experience of the "We" can not enable me originally to know as Others the Others who make part of the We. Quite the contrary, it is necessary that first there should be some awareness of what the Other is in order for an experience of my relations with Others to be realized in the form of the *Mitsein*. The *Mitsein* by itself would be *impossible* without a preliminary recognition of what the Other is: "I am with ——." Very well. But with *whom*? In addition even if this experience were ontologically primary, one cannot see how one could pass, without a radical modification of this experience, from a totally undifferentiated transcendence to the experience of particular persons. If the Other were not given elsewhere, the experience of the "We" when broken up would give birth only to the apprehension of pure object-instruments in the world circumscribed by my transcendence.

These few remarks do not claim to exhaust the question of the "We." They aim only at indicating that the experience of the We-subject has no value as a metaphysical revelation; it depends strictly on the various forms of the for-others and is only an empirical enrichment of certain of these forms. It is to this fact evidently that we should attribute the extreme instability of this experience. It comes and disappears capriciously, leaving us in the face of others-as-objects or else of a "They" who look at us. It appears as a provisional appeasement which is constituted at the very heart of the conflict, not as a definitive solution of this conflict. We should hope in vain for a human "we" in which the intersubjective totality would obtain consciousness of itself as a unified subjectivity. Such an ideal could be only a dream produced by a passage to the limit and to the absolute on the basis of fragmentary, strictly psychological experiences. Furthermore this ideal itself implies the recognition of the conflict of transcendences as the original state of being-for-others.

This fact explains an apparent paradox: since the unity of the oppressed class stems from the fact that it is experienced as an Us-object in the face of an undifferentiated "They" which is the Third or the oppressing class, one might be tempted to believe that by a sort of symmetry the oppressing class apprehends itself as a We-subject in the face of the oppressed class. But the weakness of the oppressing class lies in the fact that although it has at its disposal precise and rigorous means for coercion, it is within itself profoundly anarchistic. The "bourgeois" is not only defined as a certain *homo œconomicus* disposing of a precise power and privilege in the heart of a society of a certain type; he is described inwardly as a consciousness which does not recognize its belonging to a class. His situation, in fact, does not allow him to apprehend himself as engaged in an Us-object in community with the other members of the bourgeois class. But on the other hand, the very nature of the We-subject implies that it is made up of only fleeting experiences without metaphysical bearing. The "bourgeois" commonly denies that there are classes; he attributes the existence of a proletariat to the action of agitators, to awkward incidents, to injustices which can be repaired by particular measures; he affirms the existence of a solidarity of interests between capital and labor; he offers instead of class solidarity a larger solidarity, natural solidarity, in which the worker and the employer are integrated in a *Mitsein* which suppresses the conflict. The question here is not, as so often said, one of maneuvers or of a stupid refusal to see the situation in its true light; rather the member of the oppressing class sees the totality of the oppressed class confronting him as an objective ensemble of "they-subjects" without his correlatively realizing his community of being with the other members of the oppressing class. The two experiences are in no way complementary; in fact one may be alone in the face of an oppressed collectivity and still be able to grasp it as an object-instrument and apprehend oneself as the internal-negation of this collectivity; i.e., simply as the impartial Third. It is only when the oppressed class by revolution or by a sudden increase of its power posits itself as "they-who-look-at" in the face of members of the oppressing class, it is only then that the oppressors experience themselves as "Us." But this will be in fear and shame and as an Us-object.

Thus there is no symmetry between the making proof of the Us-object and the experience of the We-subject. The first is the revelation of a dimension of real existence and corresponds to a simple enrichment of the original proof of the for-others. The second is a psychological experience realized by an historic man immersed in a worked up universe and in a society of a definite economic type. It reveals nothing particular; it is a purely subjective *Erlebnis*.

It appears therefore that the experience of the "We" and the "Us" although real, is not of a nature to modify the results of our prior investigations. As for the Us-object, this is directly dependent on the Third—i.e., on my being-for-others—and it is constituted on the foundation of my being-outside-for-others. And as for the We-subject, this is a psychological experience which supposes one way or another that the Other's existence as such has been already revealed to us. It is therefore useless for human-reality to seek to get out of this dilemma: one must either transcend the Other or allow oneself to be transcended by him. The essence of the relations between consciousnesses is not the *Mitsein*; it is conflict.

At the end of this long description of the relations of the for-itself with others we have then achieved this certainty: the for-itself is not only a being which arises as the nihilation of the in-itself which it is and the internal negation of the in-itself which it is not. This nihilating flight is entirely reapprehended by the in-itself and fixed in in-itself as soon as the Other appears. The for-itself when alone transcends the world; it is the nothing by which there are things. The Other by rising up confers on the for-itself a being-in-itself-in-the-midst-of-the-world as a thing among things. This petrifaction in in-itself by the Other's look is the profound meaning of the myth of Medusa.

We have therefore advanced in our pursuit: we wanted to determine the original relation of the for-itself to the in-itself. We learned first that the for-itself was the nihilation and the radical negation of the in-itself; at present we establish that it is also—by the sole fact of meeting with the Other and without any contradiction—totally in-itself, present in the midst of the in-itself. But this second aspect of the for-itself represents its *outside*; the for-itself by nature is the being which can not coincide with its being-in-itself.

These remarks can serve as the basis for a general theory of being, which is the goal toward which we are working. Nevertheless it is still too soon for us to attempt this theory. Actually it is not sufficient to describe the for-itself as simply projecting its possibilities beyond being-in-itself. This project of its possibilities does not statically determine the configuration of the world; it changes the world at every instant. If we read Heidegger, for example, we are struck, from this point of view, with the inadequacy of his hermeneutic descriptions. Adopting his terminology, we shall say that he has described the *Dasein* as the existent which surpasses existents toward *their being*. And being, here, signifies the meaning or the mode of being of the existent. It is true that the for-itself is the being by which existents reveal their mode of being. But Heidegger passes over in silence the fact that the for-itself is not only the being which constitutes an ontology of existents but that it is also the being by whom ontic modifications supervene for the existent qua existent. This perpetual possibility of *acting*—that is, of modifying the in-itself in its ontic materiality, in its "flesh"—must evidently be considered as an essential characteristic of the for-itself. As such this possibility must find its foundation in an original relation of the for-itself to the in-itself, a relation which we have not yet brought to light. What does it mean *to act*? Why does the for-itself act? How *can* it act? Such are the questions to which we must reply at present. We have all the elements for a reply: nihilation, facticity and the body, being-for-others, the peculiar nature of the in-itself. We must question them once more.

# Part IV

## Having, Doing, and Being

"Having," "doing," and "being"[1] are the cardinal categories of human reality. Under them are subsumed all types of human conduct. *Knowing*, for example, is a modality of *having*. These categories are not without connection with one another, and several writers have emphasized these ties. Denis de Rougemont is throwing light on this kind of relation when he writes in his article on Don Juan, "He was not enough to have." Again a similar connection is indicated when a moral agent is represented as doing in order to "do himself" and "doing himself" in order to be.

However since the reaction against the doctrine of substance has won out in modern philosophy, the majority of thinkers have attempted to do on the ground of human conduct what their predecessors have done in physics—to replace substance by simple motion. For a long time the aim of ethics was to provide man with a way of *being*. This was the meaning of Stoic morality or of Spinoza's Ethics. But if the being of man is to be reabsorbed in the succession of his acts, then the purpose of ethics will no longer be to raise man to a higher ontological dignity. In this sense the Kantian morality is the first great ethical system which substitutes doing for being as the supreme value of

---

[1] *Avoir, faire, être.* It is difficult to know how to translate *faire* since Sartre gives to it all of the twofold significance of *doing* and *making* which the word carries in French. On the whole "doing" seems closer, especially since such expressions as "to do a book" or "to do a play" carry the same double meaning and make sense in English even though they are admittedly awkward. Tr.

action. The heroes of *L'Espoir* are for the most part on the level of *doing*, and Malraux shows us the conflict between the old Spanish democrats who still try to *be* and the Communists whose morality results in a series of precise, detailed obligations, each of these obligations aiming at a particular *doing*. Who is right? Is the supreme value of human activity a *doing* or a *being*? And whichever solution we adopt, what is to become of *having*? Ontology should be able to inform us concerning this problem; moreover it is one of ontology's essential tasks if the for-itself is the being which is defined by *action*. Therefore we must not bring this work to a close without giving a broad outline for the study of action in general and of the essential relations of *doing*, of *being*, and of *having*.

# 1

# BEING AND DOING: FREEDOM

## I. FREEDOM: THE FIRST CONDITION OF ACTION

It is strange that philosophers have been able to argue endlessly about determinism and free-will, to cite examples in favor of one or the other thesis, without ever attempting first to make explicit the structures contained in the very idea of *action*. The concept of an act contains, in fact, numerous subordinate notions which we shall have to organize and arrange in a hierarchy: to act is to modify the *shape* of the world; it is to arrange means in view of an end; it is to produce an organized instrumental complex such that by a series of concatenations and connections the modification effected on one of the links causes modifications throughout the whole series and finally produces an anticipated result. But this is not what is important for us here. We should observe first that an action is on principle *intentional*. The careless smoker who has through negligence caused the explosion of a powder magazine has not *acted*. On the other hand the worker who is charged with dynamiting a quarry and who obeys the given orders has acted when he has produced the expected explosion; he knew what he was doing or, if you prefer, he intentionally realized a conscious project.

This does not mean, of course, that one must foresee all the consequences of his act. The emperor Constantine when he established himself at Byzantium, did not foresee that he would create a center of Greek culture and language, the appearance of which would ultimately provoke a schism in the Christian Church and which would contribute to weakening the Roman Empire. Yet he performed an act just in so far as he realized his project of creating a new residence for emperors in the Orient. Equating the result with the intention is here sufficient for us to be able to speak of action. But if this is the case, we establish that the action necessarily implies as its condition the recognition of a "desideratum"; that is, of an objective lack or again of a *négatité*. *The intention* of providing a rival for Rome can come to Constantine only through the apprehension of an objective lack: Rome lacks a counter-weight; to this still profoundly pagan city ought to be opposed a Christian city which at the moment is missing. Creating Constantinople is understood as an *act* only if first the conception of a new city has preceded the action itself or at least if this conception serves as an organizing theme for all later steps. But this conception can not be the pure representation of the city as *possible*. It apprehends the city in its essential characteristic, which is to be a *desirable* and not yet realized possible.

This means that from the moment of the first conception of the act, consciousness has been able to withdraw itself from the full world of which it is consciousness and to leave the level of being in order frankly to approach that of non-being. Consciousness in so far as it is considered exclusively in its being, is perpetually referred from being to being and can not find in being any motive for revealing non-being. The imperial system with Rome as its capital functions positively and in a certain real way which can be easily discovered. Will someone say that the taxes are collected badly, that Rome is not secure from invasions, that it does not have the geographical location which is suitable for the capital of a Mediterranean empire which is threatened by barbarians, that its corrupt morals make the spread of the Christian religion difficult? How can anyone fail to see that all these considerations are *negative*; that is, that they aim at what is not, not at what is. To say that sixty per cent of the anticipated taxes have been collected can pass, if need be for a positive appreciation of the situation *such as it is*. To say that they are *badly* collected is to consider the situation across a situation which is posited as an absolute end but which precisely *is not*. To say that the corrupt morals at Rome hinder the spread of Christianity is not to consider this diffusion for what it is; that is, for a propagation at a rate which the reports of the clergy can enable us to determine. It is to posit the diffusion in itself as insufficient; that is, as suffering from a secret nothingness. But it appears as such only if it is surpassed toward a limiting-situation posited *a priori* as a value (for example, toward a certain rate of religious conversions, toward a certain mass morality). This limiting-situation can not be conceived in terms of the simple consideration of the real state of things; for the most beautiful girl in the world can offer only what she *has*, and in the same way the most miserable situation can by itself be designated only as it is without any reference to an ideal nothingness.

In so far as man is immersed in the historical situation, he does not even succeed in conceiving of the failures and lacks in a political organization or determined economy; this is not, as is stupidly said, because he "is accustomed to it," but because he apprehends it in its plenitude of being and because he does not even imagine that things can be otherwise. For it is necessary here to reverse common opinion and to admit that the harshness of a situation or the sufferings which it imposes, are not sufficient motives for conceiving of another state of affairs in which things would be better for everybody. It is on the day that we can conceive of a different state of affairs that a new light falls on our troubles and our suffering and that we *decide* that these are unbearable. A worker in 1830 is capable of revolting if his salary is lowered, for he easily conceives of a situation in which his wretched standard of living would be not as low as the one which is about to be imposed on him. But he does not represent his sufferings to himself as unbearable; he adapts himself to them not through resignation but because he lacks the education and reflection necessary for him to conceive of a social state in which these sufferings would not exist. Consequently *he does not act.* Having gained control of Lyon after a riot, the workers at Croix-Rousse do not know what to do with their victory; they return home bewildered, and the regular army has no trouble in overcoming them. Their misfortunes do not appear to them "habitual" but rather *natural*; they *are*, that is all, and they constitute the worker's condition. They are not detached; they are not seen in the clear light of day, and consequently they are integrated by the worker with his being. He suffers without considering his suffering and without conferring value upon it. To suffer and to *be* are one and the same for him. His suffering is the pure affective tenor of his non-positional consciousness, but he does not *contemplate* it. Therefore this suffering can not be in itself a *motive*[1] for his acts. Quite the contrary, it is after he has formed the project of changing the situation that it will appear intolerable to him. This means that he will have had to give himself room, to withdraw in relation to it, and will have to have effected a double nihilation: on the one hand, he must posit an ideal state of affairs as a pure *present* nothingness; on the other hand, he must posit the actual situation as nothingness in relation to this state of affairs. He will have to conceive of a happiness attached to his class as a pure possible—that is, presently as a certain nothingness—and on the other hand, he will return to the present situation in order to illuminate it in the light of this nothingness and in order to nihilate it in turn by declaring: "I *am not* happy."

Two important consequences result. (1) No factual state whatever it may be (the political and economic structure of society, the psychological "state," *etc.*) is capable by itself of motivating any act whatsoever. For an act is a

---

[1] In this and following sections Sartre makes a sharp distinction between *motif* and *mobile*. The English word "motive" expresses sufficiently adequately the French *mobile*, which refers to an inner subjective fact or attitude. For *motif* there is no true equivalent. Since it refers to an external fact or situation, I am translating it by "cause." The reader must remember, however, that this carries with it no idea of determinism. Sartre emphatically denies the existence of any cause in the usual deterministic sense. Tr.

projection of the for-itself toward what is not, and what is can in no way determine by itself what is not. (2) No factual state can determine consciousness to apprehend it as a négatitè or as a lack. Better yet no factual state can determine consciousness to define it and to circumscribe it since, as we have seen, Spinoza's statement, "Omnis determinatio est negatio," remains profoundly true. Now every action has for its express condition not only the discovery of a state of affairs as "lacking in ——," i.e., as a négatitè—but also, and before all else, the constitution of the state of things under consideration into an isolated system. There is a factual state—satisfying or not—only by means of the nihilating power of the for-itself. But this power of nihilation can not be limited to realizing a simple withdrawal in relation to the world. In fact in so far as consciousness is "invested" by being, in so far as it simply suffers what is, it must be included in being. It is the organized form—worker-finding-his-suffering-natural—which must be surmounted and denied in order for it to be able to form the object of a revealing contemplation. This means evidently that it is by a pure wrenching away from himself and the world that the worker can posit his suffering as unbearable suffering and consequently can make of it the motive for his revolutionary action. This implies for consciousness the permanent possibility of effecting a rupture with its own past, of wrenching itself away from its past so as to be able to consider it in the light of a non-being and so as to be able to confer on it the meaning which it has in terms of the project of a meaning which it does not have. Under no circumstances can the past in any way by itself produce an act; that is, the positing of an end which turns back upon itself so as to illuminate it. This is what Hegel caught sight of when he wrote that "the mind is the negative," although he seems not to have remembered this when he came to presenting his own theory of action and of freedom. In fact as soon as one attributes to consciousness this negative power with respect to the world and itself, as soon as the nihilation forms an integral part of the positing of an end, we must recognize that the indispensable and fundamental condition of all action is the freedom of the acting being.

Thus at the outset we can see what is lacking in those tedious discussions between determinists and the proponents of free will. The latter are concerned to find cases of decision for which there exists no prior cause, or deliberations concerning two opposed acts which are equally possible and possess causes (and motives) of exactly the same weight. To which the determinists may easily reply that there is no action without a cause and that the most insignificant gesture (raising the right hand rather than the left hand, etc.) refers to causes and motives which confer its meaning upon it. Indeed the case could not be otherwise since every action must be intentional; each action must, in fact, have an end, and the end in turn is referred to a cause. Such indeed is the unity of the three temporal ekstases; the end or temporalization of my future implies a cause (or motive); that is, it points toward my past, and the present is the upsurge of the act. To speak of an act without a cause is to speak of an act which would lack the intentional structure of every act; and the proponents of free will by searching for it on the level of the act which is in the process of being performed can only end up by rendering the act absurd. But the determinists in turn are weighting the scale by stopping their investigation with the mere designation of the cause and motive. The essential question in fact lies beyond the complex organization "cause-intention-act-end"; indeed we ought to ask how a cause (or motive) can be constituted as such.

Now we have just seen that if there is no act without a cause, this is not in the sense that we can say that there is no phenomenon without a cause. In order to be a *cause*, the *cause* must be *experienced* as such. Of course this does not mean that it is to be thematically conceived and made explicit as in the case of deliberation. But at the very least it means that the for-itself must confer on it its value as cause or motive. And, as we have seen, this constitution of the cause as such can not refer to another real and positive existence; that is, to a prior cause. For otherwise the very nature of the act as engaged intentionally in non-being would disappear. The motive is understood only by the end; that is, by the non-existent. It is therefore in itself a négatité. If I accept a niggardly salary it is doubtless because of fear; and fear is a motive. But it is *fear of dying from starvation*; that is, this fear has meaning only outside itself in an end ideally posited, which is the preservation of a life which I apprehend as "in danger." And this fear is understood in turn only in relation to the *value* which I implicitly give to this life; that is, it is referred to that hierarchal system of ideal objects which are values. Thus the motive makes itself understood as what it is by means of the ensemble of beings which "are not," by ideal existences, and by the future. Just as the future turns back upon the present and the past in order to elucidate them, so it is the ensemble of my projects which turns back in order to confer upon the *motive* its structure as a motive. It is only because I escape the in-itself by nihilating myself toward my possibilities that this in-itself can take on value as cause or motive. Causes and motives have meaning only inside a projected ensemble which is precisely an ensemble of non-existents. And this ensemble is ultimately myself as transcendence; it is Me in so far as I have to be myself outside of myself.

If we recall the principle which we established earlier—namely that it is the apprehension of a revolution as possible which gives to the work-man's suffering its value as a motive—we must thereby conclude that it is by fleeing a situation toward our possibility of changing it that we organize this situation into complexes of causes and motives. The nihilation by which we achieve a withdrawal in relation to the situation is the same as the ekstasis by which we project ourselves toward a modification of this situation. The result is that it is in fact impossible to find an act without a motive but that this does not mean that we must conclude that the motive causes the act; the motive is an integral part of the act. For as the resolute project toward a change is not distinct from the act, the motive, the act, and the end are all constituted in a single upsurge. Each of these three structures claims the two others as its meaning. But the organized totality of the three is no longer explained by any particular structure, and its upsurge as the pure temporalizing nihilation of the in-itself is one with freedom. It is the act which decides its ends and its motives, and the act is the expression of freedom.

We cannot, however, stop with these superficial considerations; if the fundamental condition of the act is freedom, we must attempt to describe this freedom more precisely. But at the start we encounter a great difficulty. Ordinarily, to describe something is a process of making explicit by aiming at the structures of a particular essence. Now freedom has no essence. It is not subject to any logical necessity; we must say of it what Heidegger said of the *Dasein* in general: "In it existence precedes and commands essence." Freedom makes itself an act, and we ordinarily attain it across the act which it organizes with the causes, motives, and ends which the act implies. But precisely because this act has an essence, it appears to us *as constituted*; if we wish to reach the constitutive power, we must abandon any hope of finding it an essence. That would in fact demand a new constitutive power and so on to infinity. How then are we to describe an existence which perpetually makes itself and which refuses to be confined in a definition? The very use of the term "freedom" is dangerous if it is to imply that the word refers to a concept as words ordinarily do. Indefinable and unnamable, is freedom also indescribable?

Earlier when we wanted to describe nothingness and the being of the phenomenon, we encountered comparable difficulties. Yet they did not deter us. This is because there can be descriptions which do not aim at the essence but at the existent itself in its particularity. To be sure, I could not describe a freedom which would be common to both the Other and myself; I could not therefore contemplate an essence of freedom. On the contrary, it is freedom which is the foundation of all essences since man reveals intra-mundane essences by surpassing the world toward his own possibilities. But actually the question is of my freedom. Similarly when I described consciousness, I could not discuss a nature common to certain individuals but only *my* particular consciousness, which like my freedom is beyond essence, or—as we have shown with considerable repetition—for which *to be* is to have been. In order to reach this consciousness in its very existence, I had at my disposal a particular experience—the *cogito*. Husserl and Descartes, as Gaston Berger has shown, demand that the *cogito* release to them a *truth as essence*: with Descartes we achieve the connection of two simple natures; with Husserl we grasp the eidetic structure of consciousness.[2] But if in consciousness its existence must precede its essence, then both Descartes and Husserl have committed an error. What we can demand from the *cogito* is only that it discover for us a factual necessity. It is also to the *cogito* that we appeal in order to determine freedom as the freedom which is *ours*, as a pure factual necessity; that is, as a contingent existent but one which I *am not able* not to experience. I am indeed an existent who *learns* his freedom through his acts, but I am also an existent whose individual and unique existence temporalizes itself as freedom. As such I am necessarily a consciousness (of) freedom since nothing exists in consciousness except as the non-thetic consciousness of existing. Thus my freedom is perpetually in question in my being; it is not a quality added on or a *property* of my nature. It is very exactly the stuff of my being; and as in my being, my being is in question, I must necessarily possess a certain comprehension of freedom. It is this comprehension which we intend at present to make explicit.

In our attempt to reach to the heart of freedom we may be helped by the few observations which we have made on the subject in the course of this work and which we must summarize here. In the first chapter we established the fact that if negation comes into the world through human-reality, the latter must be a being who can realize a nihilating rupture with the world and with himself; and we established that the permanent possibility of this rupture is the same as freedom. But on the other hand, we stated that this permanent possibility of nihilating what I am in the form of "having-been" implies for man a particular type of existence. We were able then to determine by means of analyses like that of bad faith that human reality is its own nothingness. For the for-itself, to be is to nihilate the in-itself which it is. Under these conditions freedom can be nothing other than this nihilation. It is through this that the for-itself escapes its being as its essence; it is through this that the for-itself is always something other than what can be *said* of it. For in the final analysis the For-itself is the one which escapes this very denomination, the one which is already beyond the name which is given to it, beyond the property which is recognized in it. To say that the for-itself has to be what it is, to say that it is what it is not while not being what it is, to say that in it existence precedes and conditions essence or inversely according to Hegel, that for it "Wesen its was gewesen ist"—all this is to say one and the same thing: to be aware that man is free. Indeed by the sole fact that I am conscious of the causes which inspire my action, these causes are already transcendent objects for my consciousness; they are outside. In vain shall I seek to catch hold of them; I escape them by my very existence. I am condemned to exist forever beyond my essence, beyond the causes and motives

[2] Gaston Berger: *Le Cogito chez Husserl et chez Descartes*, 1940.

of my act. I am condemned to be free. This means that no limits to my freedom can be found except freedom itself or, if you prefer, that we are not free to cease being free. To the extent that the for-itself wishes to hide its own nothingness from itself and to incorporate the in-itself as its true mode of being, it is trying also to hide its freedom from itself.

The ultimate meaning of determinism is to establish within us an unbroken continuity of existence in itself. The motive conceived as a psychic fact—i.e., as a full and given reality—is, in the deterministic view, articulated without any break with the decision and the act, both of which are equally conceived as psychic givens. The in-itself has got hold of all these "data"; the motive provokes the act as the physical cause its effect; everything is real, everything is full. Thus the refusal of freedom can be conceived only as an attempt to apprehend oneself as being-in-itself; it amounts to the same thing. Human reality may be defined as a being such that in its being its freedom is at stake because human reality perpetually tries to refuse to recognize its freedom. Psychologically in each one of us this amounts to trying to take the causes and motives as things. We try to confer permanence upon them. We attempt to hide from ouselves that their nature and their weight depend each moment on the meaning which I give to them; we take them for constants. This amounts to considering the meaning which I gave to them just now or yesterday—which is irremediable because it is past—and extrapolating from it a character fixed still in the present. I attempt to persuade myself that the cause is as it was. Thus it would pass whole and untouched from my past consciousness to my present consciousness. It would inhabit my consciousness. This amounts to trying to give an essence to the for-itself. In the same way people will posit ends as transcendences, which is not an error. But instead of seeing that the transcendences there posited are maintained in their being by my own transcendence, people will assume that I encounter them upon my surging up in the world; they come from God, from nature, from "my" nature, from society. These ends ready made and pre-human will therefore define the meaning of my act even before I conceive it, just as causes as pure psychic givens will produce it without my even being aware of them.

Cause, act, and end constitute a continuum, a plenum. These abortive attempts to stifle freedom under the weight of being (they collapse with the sudden upsurge of anguish before freedom) show sufficiently that freedom in its foundation coincides with the nothingness which is at the heart of man. Human-reality is free because it is not enough. It is free because it is perpetually wrenched away from itself and because it has been separated by a nothingness from what it is and from what it will be. It is free, finally, because its present being is itself a nothingness in the form of the "reflection-reflecting." Man is free because he is not himself but presence to himself. The being which is what it is can not be free. Freedom is precisely the nothingness which is made-to-be at the heart of man and which forces human-reality to make itself instead of to be. As we have seen, for human reality, to be is to choose oneself; nothing comes to it either from the outside or from within which it can receive or accept. Without any help whatsoever, it is entirely abandoned to the intolerable necessity of making itself be—down to the slightest detail. Thus freedom is not a being; it is the being of man—i.e., his nothingness of being. If we start by conceiving of man as a plenum, it is absurd to try to find in him afterwards moments or psychic regions in which he would be free. As well look for emptiness in a container which one has filled beforehand up to the brim! Man can not be sometimes slave and sometimes free; he is wholly and forever free or he is not free at all.

These observations can lead us, if we know how to use them, to new discoveries. They will enable us first to bring to light the relations between freedom and what we call the "will." There is a fairly common tendency to seek to identify free acts with voluntary acts and to restrict the deterministic explanation to the world of the passions. In short the point of view of Descartes. The Cartesian will is free, but there are "passions of the soul." Again Descartes will attempt a physiological interpretation of these passions. Later there will be an attempt to instate a purely psychological determinism. Intellectualistic analyses such as Proust, for example, attempts with respect to jealousy or snobbery can serve as illustrations for this concept of the passional "mechanism." In this case it would be necessary to conceive of man as simultaneously free and determined, and the essential problem would be that of the relations between this unconditioned freedom and the determined processes of the psychic life: how will it master the passions, how will it utilize them for its own benefit? A wisdom which comes from ancient times—the wisdom of the Stoics—will teach us to come to terms with these passions so as to master them; in short it will counsel us how to conduct ourselves with regard to affectivity as man does with respect to nature in general when he obeys it in order better to control it. Human reality therefore appears as a free power besieged by an ensemble of determined processes. One will distinguish wholly free acts, determined processes over which the free will has power, and processes which on principle escape the human-will.

It is clear that we shall not be able to accept such a conception. But let us try better to understand the reasons for our refusal. There is one objection which is obvious and which we shall not waste time in developing; this is that such a trenchant duality is inconceivable at the heart of the psychic unity. How in fact could we conceive of a being which could be one and which nevertheless on the one hand would be constituted as a series of facts determined by one another—hence existents in exteriority—and which on the other hand would be constituted as a spontaneity determining itself to be and revealing only itself? *A priori* this spontaneity would be capable of no action on a determinism already constituted. On what could it act? On the object itself (the present psychic fact)? But how could it modify an in-itself which by definition is and can be only what it is? On the actual law of the process? This is self-contradictory. On the antecedents of the process? But it amounts to the same thing whether we act on the present psychic fact in order to modify it in itself or act upon it in order to modify its consequences. And in each case we encounter the same impossibility which we pointed out earlier. Moreover, what instrument would this spontaneity have at its disposal? If the hand can clasp, it is because it can be clasped. Spontaneity, since by definition it is *beyond reach* can not in turn *reach*; it can produce only itself. And if it could dispose of a special instrument, it would then be necessary to conceive of this as of an intermediary nature between free will and determined passions— which is not admissible. Conversely, the passions could get no hold upon the will. Indeed it is impossible for a determined process to act upon a spontaneity, exactly as it is impossible for objects to act upon consciousness. Thus any synthesis of two types of existents is impossible; they are not homogeneous; they will remain each one in its incommunicable solitude. The only bond which a nihilating spontaneity could maintain with mechanical processes would be the fact that it *produces itself by an internal negation directed toward these existents*. But then the spontaneity will exist precisely only in so far as it denies concerning itself that it is these passions. Henceforth the ensemble of the determined πάθος will of necessity be apprehended by spontaneity as a pure transcendent; that is, as what is necessarily *outside*, as what *is not* it.[3] This internal negation would therefore have for its effect only the dissolution of the πάθος in the world, and the πάθος would exist as some sort of object in the midst of the world for a free spontaneity which would be simultaneously will and consciousness. This discussion shows that two solutions and only two are possible: either man is wholly determined (which is inadmissible, especially because a determined consciousness—i.e., a consciousness externally motivated—becomes itself pure exteriority and ceases to be consciousness) or else man is wholly free.

But these observations are still not our primary concern. They have only a negative bearing. The study of the will should, on the contrary, enable us to advance further in our understanding of freedom. And this is why the fact which strikes us first is that if the will is to be autonomous, then it is impossible for us to consider it as a given psychic fact; that is, in-itself. It can not belong to the category defined by the psychologist as "states of consciousness." Here as everywhere else we assert that the state of consciousness is a pure idol of a positive psychology. If the will *is* to be freedom, then it is of

---

[3] I.e., is not spontaneity. Tr.

necessity negativity and the power of nihilation. But then we no longer can see why autonomy should be preserved for the will. In fact it is hard to conceive of those holes of nihilation which would be the volitions and which would surge up in the otherwise dense and full web of the passions and of the πάθος in general. If the will is nihilation, then the ensemble of the psychic must likewise be nihilation. Moreover—and we shall soon return to this point—where do we get the idea that the "fact" of passion or that pure, simple desire is not nihilating? Is not passion first a project and an enterprise? Does it not exactly posit a state of affairs as intolerable? And is it not thereby forced to effect a withdrawal in relation to this state of affairs and to nihilate it by isolating it and by considering it in the light of an end—i.e., of a non-being? And does not passion have its own ends which are recognized precisely at the same moment at which it posits them as non-existent? And if nihilation is precisely the being of freedom, how can we refuse autonomy to the passions in order to grant it to the will?

But this is not all: the will, far from being the unique or at least the privileged manifestation of freedom, actually—like every event of the for-itself—must presuppose the foundation of an original freedom in order to be able to constitute itself as will. The will in fact is posited as a reflective decision in relation to certain ends. But it does not create these ends. It is rather a mode of being in relation to them: it decrees that the pursuit of these ends will be reflective and deliberative. Passion can posit the same ends. For example, if I am threatened, I can run away at top speed because of my fear of dying. This passional fact nevertheless posits implicitly as a supreme end the value of life. Another person in the same situation will, on the contrary, understand that he must remain at his post even if resistance at first appears more dangerous than flight; he "will stand firm." But his goal, although better understood and explicitly posited, remains the same as in the case of the emotional reaction. It is simply that the methods of attaining it are more clearly conceived; certain of them are rejected as dubious or inefficacious, others are more solidly organized. The difference here depends on the choice of means and on the degree of reflection and of making explicit, not on the end. Yet the one who flees is said to be "passionate," and we reserve the term "voluntary" for the man who resists. Therefore the question is of a difference of subjective attitude in relation to a transcendent end. But if we wish to avoid the error which we denounced earlier and not consider these transcendent ends as pre-human and as an *a priori* limit to our transcendence, then we are indeed compelled to recognize that they are the temporalizing projection of our freedom. Human reality can not receive its ends, as we have seen, either from outside or from a so-called inner "nature." It chooses them and by this very choice confers upon them a transcendent existence as the external limit of its projects. From this point of view—and if it is understood that the existence of the *Dasein* precedes and commands its essence—human reality in and through its very upsurge decides to define its own being by its ends. It is therefore the positing of my ultimate ends which characterizes my being and which is identical with the sudden thrust of the freedom which is mine. And this thrust is an *existence*; it has nothing to do with an essence or with a property of a being which would be engendered conjointly with an idea.

Thus since freedom is identical with my existence, it is the foundation of ends which I shall attempt to attain either by the will or by passionate efforts. Therefore it can not be limited to voluntary acts. Volitions, on the contrary, like passions are certain subjective attitudes by which we attempt to attain the ends posited by original freedom. By original freedom, of course, we should not understand a freedom which would be prior to the voluntary or passionate act but rather a foundation which is strictly contemporary with the will or the passion and which these *manifest*, each in its own way. Neither should we oppose freedom to the will or to passion as the "profound self" of Bergson is opposed to the superficial self; the for-itself is wholly selfness and can not have a "profound self," unless by this we mean certain transcendent structures of the psyche. Freedom is nothing but the *existence* of our will or of our passions in so far as this existence is the nihilation of facticity; that is, the existence of a being which is its being in the mode of having to be it. We shall return to this point. In any case let us remember that the will is determined within the compass of motives and ends already posited by the for-itself in a transcendent projection of itself toward its possibles. If this were not so, how could we understand deliberation, which is an evaluation of means in relation to already existing ends?

If these ends are already posited, then what remains to be decided at each moment is the way in which I shall conduct myself with respect to them; in other words, the attitude which I shall assume. Shall I act by volition or by passion? Who can decide except me? In fact, if we admit that circumstances decide for me (for example, I can act by volition when faced with a minor danger but if the peril increases, I shall fall into passion), we thereby suppress all freedom. It would indeed be absurd to declare that the will is autonomous when it appears but that external circumstances strictly determine the moment of its appearance. But, on the other hand, how can it be maintained that a will which does not yet exist can suddenly decide to shatter the chain of the passions and suddenly stand forth on the fragments of these chains? Such a conception would lead us to consider the will as a *power* which sometimes would manifest itself to consciousness and at other times would remain hidden, but which would in any case possess the permanence and the existence "in-itself" of a property. This is precisely what is inadmissible. It is, however, certain that common opinion conceives of the moral life as a struggle between a will-thing and passion-substances. There is here a sort of psychological Manichaeism which is absolutely insupportable.

Actually it is not enough to will; it is necessary to will to will. Take, for example, a given situation: I can react to it emotionally. We have shown elsewhere that emotion is not a physiological tempest;[4] it is a reply adapted to the situation; it is a type of conduct, the meaning and form of which are the object of an intention of consciousness which aims at attaining a particular end by particular means. In fear, fainting and cataplexie[5] aim at suppressing the danger by suppressing the consciousness of the danger. There is an intention of losing consciousness in order to do away with the formidable world in which consciousness is engaged and which comes into being through consciousness. Therefore we have to do with magical behavior provoking the symbolic satisfactions of our desires and revealing by the same stroke a magical stratum of the world. In contrast to this conduct voluntary and rational conduct will consider the situation scientifically, will reject the magical, and will apply itself to realizing determined series and instrumental complexes which will enable us to resolve the problems. It will organize a system of means by taking its stand on instrumental determinism. Suddenly it will reveal a technical world; that is, a world in which each instrumental-complex refers to another larger complex and so on. But what will make me decide to choose the magical aspect or the technical aspect of the world? It can not be the world itself, for this in order to be manifested waits to be discovered. Therefore it is necessary that the for-itself in its project must choose being the one by whom the world is revealed as magical or rational; that is, the for-itself must as a free project of itself give to itself magical or rational existence. It is responsible for either one, for the for-itself can be only if it has chosen itself. Therefore the for-itself appears as the free foundation of its emotions as of its volitions. My fear is free and manifests my freedom; I have put all my freedom into my fear, and I have chosen myself as fearful in this or that circumstance. Under other circumstances I shall exist as deliberate and courageous, and I shall have put all my freedom into my courage. In relation to freedom there is no privileged psychic phenomenon. All my "modes of being" manifest freedom equally since they are all ways of being my own nothingness.

This fact will be even more apparent in the description of what we called the "causes and motives" (les motifs et le mobiles) of action. We have outlined that description in the preceding pages; at present it will be well to return to it and take it up again in more precise terms. Did we not say indeed that

---

[4] Esquisse d'une théorie phénoménologique des émotions, Hermann, 1939.

In English, The Emotions: Outline of a Theory. Tr. by Bernard Frechtman. Philosophical Library, 1948.

[5] A word invented by Preyer to refer to a sudden inhibiting numbness produced by any shock. Tr.

passion is the *motive* of the act—or again that the passional act is that which has passion for its motive? And does not the will appear as the decision which follows deliberation concerning causes and motives? What then is a cause? What is a motive?

Generally by cause we mean the *reason* for the act; that is, the ensemble of rational considerations which justify it. If the government decides on a conversion of Government bonds, it will give the causes for its act: the lessening of the national debt, the rehabilitation of the Treasury. Similarly it is by *causes* that historians are accustomed to explain the acts of ministers or monarchs; they will seek the *causes* for a declaration of war: the occasion is propitious, the attacked country is disorganized because of internal troubles; it is time to put an end to an economic conflict which is in danger of lasting interminably. If Clovis is converted to Catholicism, then inasmuch as so many barbarian kings are Arians, it is because Clovis sees an opportunity of getting into the good graces of the episcopate which is all powerful in Gaul. And so on. One will note here that the cause is characterized as an objective appreciation of the situation. The cause of Clovis' conversion is the political and religious state of Gaul; it is the relative strengths of the episcopate, the great landowners, and the common people. What motivates the conversion of the bonds is the state of the national debt. Nevertheless this objective appreciation can be made only in the light of a presupposed end and within the limits of a project of the for-itself toward this end. In order for the power of the episcopate to be revealed to Clovis as the cause of his conversion (that is, in order for him to be able to envisage the objective consequences which this conversion could have) it is necessary first for him to posit as an end the conquest of Gaul. If we suppose that Clovis has other ends, he can find in the situation of the Church causes for his becoming Arian or for remaining pagan. It is even possible that in the consideration of the Church he can even find no cause for acting in any way at all; he will then discover nothing in relation to this subject; he will leave the situation of the episcopate in the state of "unrevealed," in a total obscurity. We shall therefore use the term *cause* for the objective apprehension of a determined situation as this situation is revealed in the light of a certain end as being able to serve as the means for attaining this end.

The motive, on the contrary, is generally considered as a subjective fact. It is the ensemble of the desires, emotions, and passions which urge me to accomplish a certain act. The historian looks for motives and takes them into account only as a last resort when the causes are not sufficient to explain the act under consideration. Ferdinand Lot, for example, after having shown that the reasons which are ordinarily given for the conversion of Constantine are insufficient or erroneous, writes: "Since it is established that Constantine had everything to lose and apparently nothing to gain by embracing Christianity, there is only one conclusion possible—that he yielded to a sudden impulse, pathological or divine as you prefer."[6] Lot is here abandoning the explanation by causes, which seems to him unenlightening, and prefers to it an explanation by motives. The explanation must then be sought in the psychic state—even in the "mental" state—of the historical agent. It follows naturally that the event becomes wholly contingent since another individual with other passions and other desires would have acted differently. In contrast to the historian the psychologist will by preference look for motives; usually he supposes, in fact, that they are "contained in" the state of consciousness which has provoked the action. The ideal rational act would therefore be the one for which the motives would be practically nil and which would be uniquely inspired by an objective appreciation of the situation. The irrational or passionate act will be characterized by the reverse proportion.

It remains for us to explain the relation between causes and motives in the everyday case in which they exist side by side. For example, I can join the Socialist party because I judge that this party serves the interests of justice and of humanity or because I believe that it will become the principal historical force in the years which will follow my joining: these are causes. And at the same time I can have motives: a feeling of pity or charity for certain classes of the oppressed, a feeling of shame at being on the "good side of the barricade," as Gide says, or again an inferiority complex, a desire to shock my relatives, *etc.* What can be meant by the statement that I have joined the Socialist party for these causes *and* these motives? Evidently we are dealing with two radically distinct layers of meaning. How are we to compare them? How are we to determine the part played by each of them in the decision under consideration? This difficulty, which certainly is the greatest of those raised by the current distinction between causes and motives, has never been resolved; few people indeed have so much as caught a glimpse of it. Actually under a different name it amounts to positing the existence of a conflict between the will and the passions. But if the classic theory is discovered to be incapable of assigning to cause and motive their proper influence in the simple instance when they join together to produce a single decision, it will be wholly impossible[7] for it to explain or even to conceive of a conflict between causes and motives, a conflict in which each group would urge its individual decision. Therefore we must start over again from the beginning.

To be sure, the cause is objective; it is the state of contemporary things as it is revealed to a consciousness. It is *objective* that the Roman plebs and aristocracy were corrupted by the time of Constantine or that the Catholic Church is ready to favor a monarch who at the time of Clovis will help it triumph over Arianism. Nevertheless this state of affairs can be revealed only

[6] Ferdinand Lot: *La fin du monde antique et le début du moyen âge*, p. 35. *Renaissance du Livre*, 1927.
[7] Sartre says "wholly possible" (*tout à fait possible*) which I feel sure is a misprint. Tr.

to a for-itself since in general the for-itself is the being by which "there is" a world. Better yet, it can be revealed only to a for-itself which chooses itself in this or that particular way—that is, to a for-itself which has made its own individuality. The for-itself must of necessity have projected itself in this or that way in order to discover the instrumental implications of instrumental-things. Objectively the knife is an instrument made of a blade and a handle. I can grasp it objectively as an instrument to slice with, to cut with. But lacking a hammer, I can just as well grasp the knife as an instrument to hammer with. I can make use of its handle to pound in a nail, and this apprehension is no less *objective*. When Clovis appreciates the aid which the Church can furnish him, it is not certain that a group of prelates or even one particular priest has made any overtures to him, nor even that any member of the clergy has clearly thought of an alliance with a Catholic monarch. The only strictly objective facts, those which any for-itself whatsoever can establish, are the great power of the Church over the people of Gaul and the anxiety of the Church with regard to the Arian heresy. In order for these established facts to be organized into a cause for conversion, it is necessary to isolate them from the ensemble—and thereby to nihilate them—and it is necessary to transcend them toward a particular potentiality: the Church's potentiality objectively apprehended by Clovis will be to give its support to a converted king. But this potentiality can be revealed only if the situation is surpassed toward a state of things which does not yet exist—in short, towards a nothingness. In a word the world gives counsel only if one questions it, and one can question it only for a well determined end.

Therefore the cause, far from determining the action, appears only in and through the project of an action. It is in and through the project of imposing his rule on all of Gaul that the state of the Western Church appears objectively to Clovis as a cause for his conversion. In other words the consciousness which carves out the cause in the ensemble of the world has already its own structure; it has given its own ends to itself, it has projected itself toward its possibles, and it has its own manner of hanging on to its possibilities: this peculiar manner of holding to its possibles is here affectivity. This internal organization which consciousness has given to itself in the form of non-positional self-consciousness is strictly correlative with the carving out of causes in the world. Now if one reflects on the matter, one must recognize that the internal structure of the for-itself by which it effects in the world the upsurge of causes for acting is an "irrational" fact in the historical sense of the term. Indeed we can easily understand rationally the technical usefulness of the conversion of Clovis under the hypothesis by which he would have projected the conquest of Gaul. But we can not do the same with regard to his project of conquest. It is not "self-explanatory." Ought it to be interpreted as a result of Clovis' *ambition*? But precisely what is the ambition if not the purpose of conquering? How could Clovis' ambition be distinguished from the precise project of conquering Gaul? Therefore it would be useless to conceive of this original project of conquest as "incited" by a pre-existing motive which would be ambition. It is indeed true that the ambition is a motive since it is wholly subjectivity. But as it is not distinct from the project of conquering, we shall say that this first project of his possibilities in the light of which Clovis discovers a cause for being converted is precisely the *motive*. Then all is made clear and we can conceive of the relations of these three terms: causes, motives, ends. We are dealing here with a particular case of being-in-the-world: just as it is the upsurge of the for-itself which causes there to be a world, so here it is the very being of the for-itself—in so far as this being is a pure project toward an end—which causes there to be a certain objective structure of the world, one which deserves the name of cause in the light of this end. The for-itself is therefore the consciousness of this cause. But this positional consciousness of the cause is on principle a non-thetic consciousness of itself as a project toward an end. In this sense it is a motive; that is, it experiences itself non-thetically as a project, more or less keen, more or less passionate, toward an end at the very moment at which it is constituted as a revealing consciousness of the organization of the world into causes.

Thus cause and motive are correlative, exactly as the non-thetic self-consciousness is the ontological correlate of the thetic consciousness of the object. Just as the consciousness of something is self-consciousness, so the motive is nothing other than the apprehension of the cause in so far as this apprehension is self-consciousness. But it follows obviously that the cause, the motive, and the end are the three indissoluble terms of the thrust of a free and living consciousness which projects itself toward its possibilities and makes itself defined by these possibilities.

How does it happen then that the motive appears to the psychologist as the affective content of a fact of consciousness as this content determines another fact of consciousness or a decision? It is because the motive, which is nothing other than a non-thetic self-consciousness, slips into the past with this same consciousness and along with it ceases to be living. As soon as a consciousness is made-past, it is what I have to be in the form of the "was." Consequently when I turn back toward my consciousness of yesterday, it preserves its intentional significance and its meaning as subjectivity, but, as we have seen, it is fixed; it is outside like a thing, since the past is in-itself. The motive becomes then that of which there is consciousness. It can appear to me in the form of "empirical knowledge"; as we saw earlier, the dead past haunts the present in the aspect of a *practical knowing*. It can also happen that I turn back toward it so as to make it explicit and formulate it while guiding myself by the knowledge which it is for me in the present. In this case it is an object of consciousness; it is this very consciousness of which I am *conscious*. It appears therefore—like my memories in general—simultaneously as *mine* and as transcendent. Ordinarily we are surrounded by these motives which we "no longer enter," for we not only have to decide concretely to accomplish this or that act but also to accomplish actions which we decided upon the day before or to pursue enterprises in which we are engaged. In a general way consciousness at whatever moment it is grasped is apprehended as engaged and this very apprehension implies a practical knowing of the motives of the engagement or even a thematic and positional explanation of these causes. It is obvious that the apprehension of the motive refers at once to the cause, its correlate, since the motive, even when made-past and fixed in in-itself, at least maintains as its meaning the fact that it has been a consciousness of a cause; i.e., the discovery of an objective structure of the world. But as the motive is *in-itself* and as the cause is objective, they are presented as a dyad without ontological distinction; we have seen, indeed, that our past is lost in the midst of the world. That is why we put them on the same level and why we are able to speak of the causes *and* of the motives of an action as if they could enter into conflict or both concur in determined proportion in a decision.

Yet if the motive is transcendent, if it is only the irremediable being which we have to be in the mode of the "was," if like all our past it is separated from us by a breadth of nothingness, then it can act only if it is *recovered*; in itself it is without force. It is therefore by the very thrust of the engaged consciousness that a value and a weight will be conferred on motives and on prior causes. What they have been does not depend on consciousness, but consciousness has the duty of maintaining them in their existence in the past. I have willed this or that: here is what remains irremediable and which even constitutes my essence, since my essence is what I have been. But the meaning held for me by this desire, this fear, these objective considerations of the world when presently I project myself toward my futures—this must be decided by me alone. I determine them precisely and only by the very act by which I project myself toward my ends. The recovery of former motives—or the rejection or new appreciation of them—is not distinct from the project by which I assign new ends to myself and by which in the light of these ends I apprehend myself as discovering a supporting cause in the world. Past motives, past causes, present motives and causes, future ends, all are organized in an indissoluble unity by the very upsurge of a freedom which is beyond causes, motives, and ends.

The result is that a voluntary deliberation is always a deception. How can I evaluate causes and motives on which I myself confer their value before all deliberation and by the very choice which I make of myself? The illusion here stems from the fact that we endeavor to take causes and motives for entirely transcendent things which I balance in my hands like weights and which possess a weight as a permanent property. Yet on the other hand we try to view them as contents of consciousness, and this is self-contradictory. Actually causes and motives have only the weight which my project—i.e., the free production of the end and of the known act to be realized—confers upon them. When I deliberate, the chips are down.[8] And if I am brought to the point of deliberating, this is simply because it is a part of my original project to realize motives by means of *deliberation* rather than by some other form of discovery (by passion, for example, or simply by action, which reveals to me the organized ensemble of causes and of ends as my language informs me of my thought). There is therefore a choice of deliberation as a procedure which will make known to me what I project and consequently what I am. And *the choice* of deliberation is organized with the ensemble motives-causes and end by free spontaneity. When the will intervenes, the decision is taken, and it has no other value than that of making the announcement.

The voluntary act is distinguished from involuntary spontaneity in that the latter is a purely unreflective consciousness of causes across the pure and simple project of the act. As for the motive, in the unreflective act it is not an object for itself but a simple non-positional self-consciousness. The structure of the voluntary act, on the other hand, requires the appearance of a reflective consciousness which apprehends the motive as a quasi-object or which even intends it as a psychic object across the consciousness reflected-on. For the latter, the cause, since it is grasped by the intermediary of the consciousness reflected-on, is as separated. To adopt Husserl's famous expression, simple voluntary reflection by its structure as reflectivity practices the ἐποχή with regard to the cause; it holds the cause in suspense, puts it within parentheses. Thus it can build up a semblance of appreciative deliberation by the fact that a more profound nihilation separates the reflective consciousness from the consciousness reflected-on or motive and by the fact that the cause is suspense. Nevertheless, as we know, although the result of the reflection is to widen the gap which separates the for-itself from itself, such is not its *goal*. The goal of the reflective scissiparity is, as we have seen, to *recover* the reflected-on so as to constitute that unrealizable totality "In-itself-for-itself," which is the fundamental value posited by the for-itself in the very upsurge of its being. If, therefore, the will is in essence reflective, its goal is not so much to decide what end is to be attained since in any case the chips are down; the profound intention of the will bears rather on the *method* of attaining this end already posited. The for-itself which exists in the voluntary mode wishes to recover itself in so far as it decides and acts. It does not wish merely to be carried toward an end, nor to be the one which chooses itself as carried toward a particular end; it wishes again to recover itself as a spontaneous

---

[8] *Les jeux sont faits.* Sartre has written a scenario by this title. Tr.

project toward this or that particular end. The ideal of the will is to be an "in-itself-for-itself" as a project toward a certain end.

This is evidently a reflective ideal and it is the meaning of the satisfaction which accompanies a judgment such as, "I have done what I wished to do." But it is evident that the reflective scissiparity in general has its foundation in a project more profound than itself, a project which for lack of a better term we called "motivation" in Part Two, Chapter III. Now that we have defined cause and motive, it is necessary to give to this project which underlies reflection the name *intention*. To the extent therefore that the will is an instance of reflection, the fact of its being placed so as to act on the voluntary level demands for its foundation a more profound intention. It is not enough for the psychologist to describe a particular subject as realizing his project in the mode of voluntary reflection; the psychologist must also be capable of releasing to us the *profound intention* which makes the subject realize his project in this mode of volition rather than in a wholly different mode. Moreover, it must be clearly understood that any mode of consciousness whatsoever may have produced the same realization once the ends are posited by an original project. Thus we have touched on a more profound freedom than the will, simply by showing ourselves to be more *exacting* than the psychologists; that is, by raising the question "Why?" whereas they limit themselves to establishing the mode of consciousness as volitional.

This brief study does not attempt to exhaust the question of the will; on the contrary, it would be desirable to attempt a phenomenological description of the will for itself. But this is not our goal; we hope simply that we have shown that the will is not a privileged manifestation of freedom but that it is a psychic event of a peculiar structure which is constituted on the same plane as other psychic events and which is supported, neither more nor less than the others, by an original, ontological freedom.

By the same token freedom appears as an unanalyzable totality; causes, motives, and ends, as well as the mode of apprehending causes, motives, and ends, are organized in a unity within the compass of this freedom and must be understood in terms of it. Does this mean that one must view freedom as a series of capricious jerks comparable to the Epicurean clinamen? Am I free to will anything whatsoever at any moment whatsoever? And must I at each instant when I wish to explain this or that project encounter the irrationality of a free and contingent choice? Inasmuch as it has seemed that the recognition of freedom had as its consequence these dangerous conceptions which are completely contradictory to experience, worthy thinkers have turned away from a belief in freedom. One could even state that determinism—if one were careful not to confuse it with fatalism—is "more human" than the theory of free will. In fact while determinism throws into relief the strict conditioning of our acts, it does at least give the *reason* for each of them. And if it is strictly limited to the psychic, if it gives up looking for a conditioning in the ensemble of the universe, it shows that the reason for our acts is in ourselves: we act as we are, and our acts contribute to making us.

Let us consider more closely however the few certain results which our analysis has enabled us to attain. We have shown that freedom is actually one with the being of the For-itself; human reality is free to the exact extent that it has to be its own nothingness. It has to be this nothingness, as we have seen, in multiple dimensions: first, by temporalizing itself—i.e., by being always at a distance from itself, which means that it can never let itself be determined by its past to perform this or that particular act; second, by rising up as consciousness of something and (of) itself—i.e., by being presence to itself and not simply self, which implies that nothing exists in consciousness which is not consciousness of existing and that consequently nothing external to consciousness can motivate it; and finally, by being transcendence—i.e., not something which would first be in order subsequently to put itself into relation with this or that end, but on the contrary, a being which is originally a project—i.e., which is defined by its end.

Thus we do not intend here to speak of anything arbitrary or capricious. An existent which as consciousness is necessarily separated from all others because they are in connection with it only to the extent that they are for it, an existent which decides its past in the form of a tradition in the light of its future instead of allowing it purely and simply to determine its present, an existent which makes known to itself what it is by means of something other than it (that is, by an end which it is not and which it projects from the other side of the world)—this is what we call a free existent. This does not mean that I am free to get up or to sit down, to enter or to go out, to flee or to face danger —if one means by freedom here a pure capricious, unlawful, gratuitous, and incomprehensible contingency. To be sure, each one of my acts, even the most trivial, is entirely free in the sense which we have just defined; but this does not mean that my act can be anything whatsoever or even that it is unforeseeable. Someone, nevertheless may object and ask how if my act can be understood neither in terms of the state of the world nor in terms of the ensemble of my past taken as an irremediable thing, it could possibly be anything but gratuitous. Let us look more closely.

Common opinion does not hold that to be free means only to choose oneself. A choice is said to be free if it is such that it could have been other than what it is. I start out on a hike with friends. At the end of several hours of walking my fatigue increases and finally becomes very painful. At first I resist and then suddenly I let myself go, I give up, I throw my knapsack down on the side of the road and let myself fall down beside it. Someone will reproach me for my act and will mean thereby that I was free—that is, not only was my act not determined by any thing or person, but also I could have succeeded in resisting my fatigue longer, I could have done as my companions did and reached the resting place before relaxing. I shall defend myself by saying that I was *too* tired. Who is right? Or rather is the debate not based on incorrect premises? There is no doubt that I could have done otherwise, but that is not the problem. It ought to be formulated rather like this: could I have done otherwise without perceptibly modifying the organic totality of the projects which I am; or is the fact of resisting my fatigue such that instead of remaining a purely local and accidental modification of my behavior, it could be effected only by means of a radical transformation of my being-in-the-world—a transformation, moreover, which is *possible?* In other words: I could have done otherwise. Agreed. But *at what price?*

We are going to reply to this question by first presenting a *theoretical* description which will enable us to grasp the principle of our thesis. We shall see subsequently whether the concrete reality is not shown to be more complex and whether without contradicting the results of our theoretical inquiry, it will not lead us to enrich them and make them more flexible.

Let us note first that the fatigue by itself could not provoke my decision. As we saw with respect to physical pain, fatigue is only the way in which I exist my body. It is not at first the object of a positional consciousness, but it is the very facticity of my consciousness. If then I hike across the country, what is revealed to me is the surrounding world; this is the object of my consciousness, and this is what I transcend toward possibilities which are my own—those, for example, of arriving this evening at the place which I have set for myself in advance. Yet to the extent that I apprehend this countryside with my eyes which unfold distances, my legs which climb the hills and consequently cause new sights and new obstacles to appear and disappear, with my back which carries the knapsack—to this extent I have a non-positional consciousness (of) this body which rules my relations with the world and which signifies my engagement in the world, in the form of fatigue. Objectively and in correlation with this non-thetic consciousness the roads are revealed as interminable, the slopes as *steeper*, the sun as more burning, etc. But I do not yet *think* of my fatigue; I apprehend it as the quasi-object of my reflection. Nevertheless there comes a moment when I do seek to consider my fatigue and to recover it. We really ought to provide an interpretation for this same intention; however, let us take it for what it is. It is not at all a contemplative apprehension of my fatigue; rather, as we saw with respect to pain, I *suffer* my fatigue. That is, a reflective consciousness is directed upon my fatigue in order to live it and to confer on it a value and a practical relation to myself. It is only on this plane that the fatigue will appear to me as bearable or intolerable. It will never be anything in itself, but it is the reflective For-itself which rising up suffers the fatigue as intolerable.

Here is posited the essential question: my companions are in good health—like me; they have had practically the same training as I so that although it is not possible to *compare* psychic events which occur in different subjectivities, I usually conclude—and witnesses after an objective consideration of our bodies-for-others conclude—that they are for all practical purposes "as fatigued as I am." How does it happen therefore that they suffer their fatigue differently? Someone will say that the difference stems from the fact that I am a "sissy" and that the others are not. But although this evaluation undeniably has a practical bearing on the case and although one could take this into account when there arose a question of deciding whether or not it would be a good idea to take me on another expedition, such an evaluation can not satisfy us here. We have seen that to be ambitious is to project conquering a throne or honors; it is not a *given* which would incite one to conquest; it is this conquest itself. Similarly to be a "sissy" can not be a factual given and is only a name given to the way in which I suffer my fatigue. If therefore I wish to understand under what conditions I can suffer a fatigue as unbearable, it will not help to address oneself to so-called factual givens, which are revealed as being only a choice; it is necessary to attempt to examine this choice itself and to see whether it is not explained within the perspective of a larger choice in which it would be integrated as a secondary structure. If I question one of my companions, he will explain to me that he is fatigued, of course, but that he *loves* his fatigue; he gives himself up to it as to a bath; it appears to him in some way as the privileged instrument for discovering the world which surrounds him, for adapting himself to the rocky roughness of the paths, for discovering the "mountainous" quality of the slopes. In the same way it is this light sunburn on the back of his neck and this slight ringing in his ears which will enable him to realize a direct contact with the sun. Finally the feeling of effort is for him that of fatigue overcome. But as his fatigue is nothing but the passion which he endures so that the dust of the highways, the burning of the sun, the roughness of the roads may exist to the fullest, his effort (i.e., this sweet familiarity with a fatigue which he loves, to which he abandons himself and which nevertheless he himself directs) is given as a way of appropriating the mountain, of suffering it to the end and being victor over it. We shall see in the next chapter what is the meaning of the word *having* and to what extent *doing* is a method of *appropriating*. Thus my companion's fatigue is lived in a vaster project of a trusting abandon to nature, of a passion consented to in order that it may exist at full strength, and at the same time the project of sweet mastery and appropriation. It is only in and through this project that the fatigue will be able to be understood and that it will have meaning for him.

But this meaning and this vaster, more profound project are still by themselves *unselbständig*. They are not self-sufficient. For they precisely presuppose a particular relation of my companion to his body, on the one hand, and to things, on the other. It is easy to see, indeed, that there are as many ways of existing one's body as there are For-itselfs although naturally certain original structures are invariable and in each For-itself constitute human-reality. We shall be concerned elsewhere with what is incorrectly called the relation of the individual to species and with the conditions of a universal truth. For the moment we can conceive in connection with thousands of meaningful events that there is, for example, a certain type of flight before facticity, a flight which consists precisely in abandoning oneself to this facticity; that is, in short, in trustingly reassuming it and loving it in order to try to recover it. This original project of recovery is therefore a certain choice which the For-itself makes of itself in the presence of the problem of being. Its project remains a nihilation, but this nihilation turns back upon the in-itself which it nihilates and expresses itself by a particular valorization of facticity. This is expressed especially by the thousands of behavior patterns called *abandon*. To abandon oneself to fatigue, to warmth, to hunger, to thirst, to let oneself fall back upon a chair or a bed with sensual pleasure, to relax, to attempt to let oneself be drunk in by one's own body, not now beneath the eyes of others as in masochism but in the original solitude of the For-itself—none of these types of behavior can ever be confined to itself. We perceive this clearly since in another person they irritate or attract. Their condition is an initial project of the recovery of the body; that is, an attempt at a solution of the problem of the absolute (of the In-itself-for-itself).

This initial form can itself be limited to a profound acceptance of facticity; the project of "making oneself body" will mean then a happy abandon to a thousand little passing gluttonies, to a thousand little desires, a thousand little weaknesses. One may recall from Joyce's *Ulysses* Mr. Bloom satisfying his natural needs and inhaling with favor "the intimate odor rising from beneath him." But it is also possible (and this is the case with my companion) that by means of the body and by compliance to the body, the For-itself seeks to recover the totality of the non-conconscious—that is, the whole universe as the ensemble of material things. In this case the desired synthesis of the in-itself with the for-itself will be the quasi pantheistic synthesis of the totality of the in-itself with the for-itself which recovers it. Here the body is the instrument of the synthesis; it loses itself in fatigue, for example, in order that this in-itself may exist to the fullest. And since it is the body which the for-itself exists as its own, this passion of the body coincides for the for-itself with the project of "making the in-itself exist." The ensemble of this attitude—which is that of one of my companions—can be expressed by the dim feeling of a kind of mission: he is going on this expedition because the mountain which he is going to climb and the forests which he is going to cross *exist*; his mission is to be the one by whom their meaning will be made manifest. Therefore he attempts to be the one who founds them in their very existence.

We shall return in the next chapter to this appropriative relation between the for-itself and the world, but we do not yet have at hand the elements necessary to elucidate it fully. In any case it is evident following our analysis that the way in which my companion *suffers* his fatigue necessarily demands— if we are to understand it—that we undertake a regressive analysis which will lead us back to an initial project. Is this project we have outlined finally *selbständig?* Certainly—and it can be easily proved to be so. In fact by going further and further back we have reached the original relation which the for-itself chooses with its facticity and with the world. But this original relation is nothing other than the for-itself's being-in-the-world inasmuch as this being-in-the-world is a choice—that is, we have reached the original type of nihilation by which the for-itself has to be its own nothingness. No interpretation of this can be attempted, for it would implicitly suppose the being-in-the-world of the for-itself just as all the demonstrations attempted by Euclid's Postulate implicitly suppose the adoption of this postulate.

Therefore if I apply this same method to interpret the way in which I suffer my fatigue, I shall first apprehend in myself a distrust of my body—for example, a way of wishing not "to have anything to do with it," wanting not to take it into account, which is simply one of numerous possible modes in which I can *exist my body*. I shall easily discover an analogous distrust with respect to the in-itself and, for example, an original project for recovering the in-itself which I nihilate *through the intermediacy of others*, which project in turn refers me to one of the initial projects which we enumerated in our preceding discussion. Hence my fatigue instead of being suffered "flexibly" will be grasped "sternly" as an importunate phenomenon which I want to get rid of—and this simply because it incarnates my body and my brute contingency in the midst of the world at a time when my project is to preserve my body and my presence in the world by means of the looks of others. I am referred to myself as well as to my original project; that is, to my being-in-the-world in so far as this being is a choice.

We are not attempting to disguise how much this method of analysis leaves to be desired. This is because everything remains still to be done in this field. The problem indeed is to disengage the meanings implied by an act—by every act—and to proceed from there to richer and more profound meanings until we encounter the meaning which does not imply any other meaning and which refers only to itself. This ascending dialectic is practiced spontaneously by most people; it can even be established that in knowledge of oneself or of another there is given a spontaneous comprehension of this hierarchy of interpretations. A gesture refers to a *Weltanschauung* and we *sense* it. But nobody has attempted a systematic disengagement of the meanings implied by an act. There is only one school which has based its approach on the same original evidence as we, and that is the Freudian. For Freud as for us an act can not be limited to itself; it refers immediately to more profound structures. And psychoanalysis is the method which enables us to make these structures explicit. Freud like us asks: under what conditions is it possible that this particular person has performed this particular act? Like us he refuses to interpret the action by the antecedent moment—i.e., to conceive of a horizontal psychic determinism. The act appears to him symbolic; that is, it seems to him to express a more profound desire which itself could be interpreted only in terms of an initial determination of the subject's libido. Freud, however, aims at constituting a vertical determinism. In addition because of this bias his conception necessarily is going to refer to the subject's past. Affectivity for Freud is at the basis of the act in the form of psycho-physiological drives. But this affectivity is originally in each of us a *tabula rasa*; for Freud the external circumstances and, so to speak, the *history* of the subject will decide whether this or that drive will be fixed on this or that object. It is the child's situation in the family which will determine in him the birth of the Oedipus complex; in other societies composed of families of another type (such as, for example, among primitive peoples on the Coral Islands in the Pacific) this complex could not be formed. Furthermore it is again external circumstances which will decide whether at the age of puberty this complex will be "resolved" or, on the contrary, will remain the pole of the sexual life. Consequently through the intermediacy of history Freud's vertical determinism remains axised on an horizontal determinism. To be sure, a particular symbolic act expresses an underlying, contemporaneous desire just as this desire manifests a more profound complex and all this within the unity of a single psychic process; but the complex nonetheless pre-exists its symbolic manifestation. It is the past which has constituted it such as it is and in accordance with the classic connections, transfer, condensation, *etc.*, which we find mentioned not only in psychoanalysis but in all attempts at a deterministic reconstruction of the psychic life. Consequently the dimension of the future does not exist for psychoanalysis. Human reality loses one of its ekstases and must be interpreted solely by a regression toward the past from the standpoint of the present. At the same time the fundamental structures of the subject, which are signified by its acts, are not so signified *for him* but for an objective witness who uses discursive methods to make these meanings explicit. No pre-ontological comprehension of the meaning of his acts is granted to the subject. And this is just, since in spite of everything his acts are only a result of the past, which *is* on principle out of reach, instead of seeking to inscribe their goal in the future.

Thus we should restrict ourselves to taking the psychoanalytic *method* as our inspiration; that is, we should attempt to disengage the meanings of an act by proceeding from the principle that every action, no matter how trivial, is not the simple effect of the prior psychic state and does not result from a linear determinism but rather is integrated as a secondary structure in global structures and finally in the totality which I am. Otherwise, in fact, I should have to understand myself either as a horizontal flux of phenomena, each one of which is externally conditioned by the preceding—or as a supporting substance for a flow, a substance deprived of the meaning of its modes. Both these conceptions would lead us to confuse the for-itself with the in-itself.

But if we accept the method of psychoanalysis—and we shall discuss this at length in the following chapter—we must apply it in *a reverse sense*. Actually we conceive of every act as a *comprehensible* phenomenon, and we do not admit any deterministic "chance" as Freud does. But instead of understanding the considered phenomenon in terms of the past, we conceive of the comprehensive act as a turning back of the future toward the present. The way in which I suffer my fatigue is in no way dependent on the chance difficulty of the slope which I am climbing or on the more or less restless night which I have spent; these factors can contribute to constituting my fatigue itself but not to the way in which I suffer it. But we refuse to view this as one of Adler's disciples would, as an expression of an inferiority complex, for example, in the sense that this complex would be a prior formation. That a certain passionate and tense way of struggling against the fatigue can express what is called an inferiority complex we shall not deny. But the inferiority complex itself is a project of my own for-itself in the world in the presence of the Other. As such it is always transcendence, as such again it is a way of choosing myself. This inferiority which I struggle against and which nevertheless I recognize, this I *have chosen* from the start. No doubt it is indicated by my various "patterns of failure behavior"; but to be exact it is nothing other than the organized totality of my failure behavior, as a projected plan, as a general device of my being, and each attitude of failure is itself transcendence since each time I surpass the real toward my possibilities. To give in to fatigue, for example, is to transcend the path by causing it to constitute in itself the meaning of "a path too difficult to traverse." It is impossible seriously to consider the feeling of inferiority without determining it in terms of the future and of my possibilities. Even assertions such as "I am ugly," "I am stupid," *etc.* are by nature anticipations. We are not dealing here with the pure establishment of my ugliness but with the apprehension of the coefficient of adversity which is presented by women or by society to my enterprises. And this can be discovered only through and in the choice of these enterprises. Thus the inferiority complex is a free and global project of myself as inferior before others; it is the way in which I choose to assume my being-for-others, the free solution which I give to the Other's existence, that insuperable scandal. Thus it is necessary to understand my reactions of inferiority and my failure behavior in terms of the free outline of my inferiority as a choice of myself in the world.

We grant to the psychoanalysts that every human reaction is *a priori* comprehensible. But we reproach them for having misunderstood just this initial "comprehensibility" as is shown by their trying to explain the reaction under consideration by means of a prior reaction, which would reintroduce causal mechanism; comprehension must be otherwise defined. Every action is comprehensible as a project of oneself toward a possible. It is comprehensible first in so far as it offers a rational content which is immediately apprehensible—I place my knapsack on the ground *in order to* rest for a moment. This means that we immediately apprehend the possible which it projects and the end at which it aims. In the second place it is comprehensible in that the possible under consideration refers to other possibles, these to still others, and so on to the ultimate possibility which I am. The comprehension is effected in two opposed senses: by a regressive psychoanalysis one ascends back from the considered act to my ultimate possible; and by a synthetic progression one redescends from this ultimate possible to the considered act and grasps its integration in the total form.

This form which we call our ultimate possibility is not just *one* possible among others—not even though it be, as Heidegger claims, the possibility of dying or of "no longer realizing any presence in the world." Every particular possibility, in fact, is articulated in an ensemble. It is necessary to conceive of this ultimate possibility as the unitary synthesis of all our actual possibles; each of these possibles resides in an undifferentiated state in the ultimate possibility until a particular circumstance comes to throw it into relief without, however, thereby suppressing its quality of belonging to the totality. Indeed we pointed out in Part Two that the perceptive apprehension of any object whatsoever is effected on the *ground of the world*.[9] By this we meant that what the psychologists are accustomed to call "perception" can not be limited to objects which are strictly "seen" or "understood" *etc.* at a certain instant but that the objects considered refer by means of implications and various significations to the totality of the existent in-itself *from the standpoint of which* they are apprehended. Thus it is not true that I proceed by degrees from that table to the room where I am and then going out pass from there to the hall, to the stairway, to the street in order finally to conceive as the result of a passage to the limit, the world as the sum of all existents. Quite the contrary, I can not perceive any instrumental thing whatsoever unless it is in terms of the absolute existence of all existents, for my first being is being-in-the-world.

Thus we find that for man in so far as "*there are*" things, there is in things a

[9] Part II, chapter III.

perpetual appeal toward the integration which makes us apprehend things by descending from the total integration which is immediately realized down to this particular structure which is interpreted only in relation to this totality. But on the other hand if *there is a world*, it is because we rise up into the world suddenly and in totality. We have observed, in fact, in that same chapter devoted to transcendence, that the in-itself by itself alone is not capable of any unity as a world. But our upsurge is a passion in this sense that we lose ourselves in nihilation in order that a world may exist. Thus the first phenomenon of being in the world is the original relation between the totality of the in-itself or world and my own totality detotalized; I choose myself as a whole in the world which is a whole. Just as I come from the world to a particular "this," so I come from myself as a detotalized totality to the outline of one of my particular possibilities since I can apprehend a particular "this" on the ground of the world only on the occasion of a particular project of myself. But in this case just as I can apprehend a particular "this" only on the ground of the world by surpassing it toward this or that possibility, so I can project myself beyond the "this" toward this or that possibility only on the ground of my ultimate and total possibility. Thus my ultimate and total possibility, as the original integration of all my particular possibles, and the world as the totality which comes to existents by my upsurge into being are two strictly correlative notions. I can perceive the hammer (i.e., outline a plan of "hammering" with it) only on the ground of the world; but conversely I can outline this act of "hammering" only on the ground of the totality of myself and in terms of that totality.

Thus the fundamental act of freedom is discovered; and it is this which gives meaning to the particular action which I can be brought to consider. This constantly renewed act is not distinct from my being; it is a choice of myself in the world and by the same token it is a discovery of the world. This enables us to avoid the perilous reef of the unconscious which psychoanalysis meets at the start. If nothing is in consciousness which is not a consciousness of being, some will say to us by way of objection that then this fundamental choice must of necessity be a *conscious* choice. They will ask, "Can you maintain that when you yield to fatigue, you are conscious of all the implications which this fact supposes?" We shall reply that we are perfectly conscious of them. Only this consciousness itself must have for its limit the structure of consciousness in general and of the choice which we are making.

So far as the latter is concerned, we must insist on the fact that the question here is not of a deliberate choice. This is not because the choice is *less* conscious or *less* explicit than a deliberation but rather because it is the foundation of all deliberation and because, as we have seen, a deliberation requires an interpretation in terms of an original choice. Therefore it is necessary to defend oneself against the illusion which would make of original freedom a *positing* of causes and motives as objects, then a decision from the standpoint of these causes and these motives. Quite the contrary, as soon as there are cause and motive (that is, an appreciation of things and of the structures of the world) there is already a positing of ends and consequently a choice. But this does not mean that the profound choice is thereby unconscious. It is simply one with the consciousness which we have of ourselves. This consciousness, as we know, can be only non-positional; it is we-as-consciousness since it is not distinct from our being. And as our being is precisely our original choice, the consciousness (of) the choice is identical with the self-consciousness which we have. One must be conscious in order to choose, and one must choose in order to be conscious. Choice and consciousness are one and the same thing. This is what many psychologists have felt when they declared that consciousness was "selection." But because they have not traced this selection back to its ontological foundation, they have remained on a level in which the selection appeared as a gratuitous function of a consciousness in other respects substantial. This reproach may in particular be leveled against Bergson. But if it has been well established that consciousness is a nihilation, the conclusion is that to be conscious of ourselves and to choose ourselves are one and the same. This is the explanation of the difficulties which moralists like Gide have met when they wanted to define the purity of the feelings. What difference is there, Gide asked, between a willed feeling and an *experienced* feeling?[10] Actually there is no difference. "To will to love" and to love are one since to love is to choose oneself as loving by assuming consciousness of loving. If the πάθος is free, it is a choice.

We have remarked sufficiently—in particular in the chapter concerning Temporality—that the Cartesian *cogito* must be extended. In fact, as we have seen, to assume self-consciousness never means to assume a consciousness of the instant; for the instant is only one view of the mind and even if it existed, a consciousness which would apprehend itself in the instant would no longer apprehend *anything*. I can assume consciousness of myself only as a particular man engaged in this or that enterprise, anticipating this or that success, fearing this or that result, and by means of the ensemble of these anticipations, outlining his whole figure. Indeed it is thus that I am apprehending myself at this moment when I am writing; I am not the simple perceptive consciousness of my hand which is making marks on the paper. I am well in advance of this hand all the way to the completion of the book and to the meaning of this book—and of philosophical activity in general—in my life. It is within the compass of this project (i.e., within the compass of what I am) that there are inserted certain projects toward more restricted possibilities such as that of presenting this or that idea in this or that way or of ceasing to

---

[10] *Journal des faux monnayeurs.* (Diary of *The Counterfeiters.*)

write for a moment or of paging through a volume in which I am looking for this or that reference, *etc.* Nevertheless it would be an error to believe that there is an analytical and differentiated consciousness corresponding to this global choice. My ultimate and initial project—for these are but one—is, as we shall see, always the outline of a solution of the problem of being. But this solution is not first conceived and then realized; we *are* this solution. We make it exist by means of our very engagement, and therefore we shall be able to apprehend it only by living it. Thus we are always wholly present to ourselves; but precisely because we are wholly present, we can not hope to have an analytical and detailed consciousness of what we are. Moreover this consciousness can be only non-thetic.

On the other hand, the world by means of its very articulation refers to us exactly the image of what we are. Not, as we have seen so many times, that we can decipher this image—i.e., break it down and subject it to analysis—but because the world necessarily appears to us as we are. In fact, it is by surpassing the world toward ourselves that we make it appear such as it is. We choose the world, not in its contexture as in-itself but in its meaning, by choosing ourselves. Through the internal negation by denying that we are the world, we make the world appear as world, and this internal negation can exist only if it is at the same time a projection toward a possible. It is the very way in which I entrust myself to the inanimate, in which I abandon myself to my body (or, on the other hand, the way in which I resist either one of these) which causes the appearance of both my body and the inanimate world with their respective value. Consequently there also I enjoy a full consciousness of myself and of my fundamental projects, and this time the consciousness is positional. Nevertheless, precisely because it is positional, what it releases to me is the transcendent image of what I am. The value of things, their instrumental role, their proximity and real distance (which have no relation to their spatial proximity and distance) do nothing more than to outline my image—that is, my choice. My clothing (a uniform or a lounge suit, a soft or a starched shirt) whether neglected or cared for, carefully chosen or ordinary, my furniture, the street on which I live, the city in which I reside, the books with which I surround myself, the recreation which I enjoy, everything which is mine (that is, finally, the world of which I am perpetually conscious, at least as a meaning implied by the object which I look at or use): all this informs me of my choice—that is, my being. But such is the structure of the positional consciousness that I can trace this knowledge back to a subjective apprehension of myself, and it refers me to other objects which I produce or which I dispose of in connection with the order of the preceding without being able to perceive that I am thus more and more sculpturing my figure in the world. Thus we are fully conscious of the choice which we are. And if someone objects that in accordance with these observations it would be necessary to be conscious not of our *being-chosen* but of *choosing* ourselves, we shall reply that this consciousness is expressed by the two-fold "feeling" of anguish and of responsibility. Anguish, abandonment, responsibility, whether muted or full strength, constitute the *quality* of our consciousness in so far as this is pure and simple freedom.

Earlier we posed a question: I have yielded to fatigue, we said, and doubtless I *could have* done otherwise but *at what price?* At present we are in a position to answer this. Our analysis, in fact, has just shown us that this act was not *gratuitous*. To be sure, it was not explained by a motive or a cause conceived as the content of a prior state of consciousness, but it had to be interpreted in terms of an original project of which it formed an integral part. Hence it becomes evident that we can not suppose that the act could have been modified without at the same time supposing a fundamental modification of my original choice of myself. This way of yielding to fatigue and of letting myself fall down at the side of the road expresses a certain initial stiffening against my body and the inanimate in-itself. It is placed within the compass of a certain view of the world in which difficulties can appear "not worth the trouble of being tolerated"; or, to be exact, since the motive is a pure non-thetic consciousness and consequently an initial project of itself toward an absolute end (a certain aspect of the in-itself-for-itself), it is an apprehension of the world (warmth, distance from the city, uselessness of effort, *etc.*) as the cause of my ceasing to walk. Thus this *possible*—to stop—*theoretically* takes on its meaning only in and through the hierarchy of the possibles which I am in terms of the ultimate and initial possible. This does not imply that I *must necessarily* stop but merely that I can refuse to stop only by a radical conversion of my being-in-the-world; that is, by an abrupt metamorphosis of my initial project—i.e., by another choice of myself and of my ends. Moreover this modification is always possible.

The anguish which, when this possibility is revealed, manifests our freedom to our consciousness is witness of this perpetual modifiability of our initial project. In anguish we do not simply apprehend the fact that the possibles which we project are perpetually eaten away by our freedom-to-come; in addition we apprehend our choice—i.e., ourselves—as *unjustifiable*. This means that we apprehend our choice as not deriving from any prior reality but rather as being about to serve as foundation for the ensemble of significations which constitute reality. Unjustifiability is not only the subjective recognition of the absolute contingency of our being but also that of the interiorization and recovery of this contingency on our own account. For the choice—as we shall see—issues from the contingency of the in-itself which it nihilates and transports it to the level of the gratuitous determination of the for-itself by itself. Thus we are perpetually engaged in our choice and perpetually conscious of the fact that we ourselves can abruptly invert this choice and "reverse steam"; for we project the future by our very being, but our existential freedom perpetually eats it away as we make known to ourselves what we are by means of the future but without getting a grip on this future which remains always possible without ever passing to the rank of the *real*. Thus we are perpetually *threatened* by the nihilation of our actual choice and perpetually threatened with choosing ourselves—and consequently with becoming—other than we are. By the sole fact that our choice is absolute, it is *fragile*; that is, by positing our freedom by means of it, we posit by the same stroke the perpetual possibility that the choice may become a "here and now" which has been made-past in the interests of a "beyond" which I shall be.

Nevertheless let us thoroughly understand that our present choice is such that it furnishes us with no *motive* for making it past by means of a further choice. In fact, it is this present choice which originally creates all causes and all motives which can guide us to partial actions; it is this which arranges the world with its meaning, its instrumental-complexes, and its coefficient of adversity. The absolute change which threatens us from our birth until our death remains perpetually unpredictable and incomprehensible. Even if we envisage other fundamental attitudes as *possible*, we shall never consider them except from outside, as the behavior of Others. And if we attempt to refer our conduct to them, they shall not for all that lose their character as external and as transcended-transcendences. To "understand" them in fact would be already to have chosen them. We are going to return to this point.

In addition we must not think of the original choice as "producing itself from one instant to the next"; this would be to return to the instantaneous conception of consciousness from which Husserl was never able to free himself. Since, on the contrary, it is consciousness which temporalizes itself, we must conceive of the original choice as unfolding time and being one with the unity of the three ekstases. To choose ourselves is to nihilate ourselves; that is, to cause a future to come to make known to us what we are by conferring a meaning on our past. Thus there is not a succession of instants separated by nothingnesses—as with Descartes—such that my choice at the instant t can not act on my choice of the instant t1. To choose is to effect the upsurge along with my engagement of a certain finite extension of concrete and continuous duration, which is precisely that which separates me from the realization of my original possibles. Thus freedom, choice, nihilation, temporalization are all one and the same thing.

Yet the *instant* is not an empty invention of philosophers. To be sure, there is no subjective instant when I am engaged in my task. At this moment, for example, when I am writing and trying to grasp my ideas and put them in order, there is no instant for me, there is only a perpetual pursued-pursuit of myself toward the ends which define me (the making explicit of ideas which are to form the basis of this work). And yet we are perpetually threatened by the instant. That is, we are such, by the very choice of our freedom, that we can always cause the instant to appear as the rupture of our ekstatic unity. What then is the instant? In the process of temporalization the instant can not be cut off from a concrete project; we have just shown this. But neither can it be identified with the initial term or with the final term (if it is to exist) of this process. For both of these terms are incorporated in the totality of the process and are an integral part of it. Therefore neither term has the characteristics of the instant. The initial term is incorporated in the process of which it is the initial term in that it is the process' beginning. But on the other hand, it is limited by a prior nothingness in that it is a beginning. The final term is incorporated in the process which it terminates in that it is the process' end; the last note belongs to the melody. But it is followed by a nothingness which limits it in that it is an end. The instant if it is to be able to exist, must be limited by a double nothingness. This is in no way conceivable if it is to be given ahead of time to all the processes of temporalization—as we have shown. But in the very development of our temporalization, we can produce instants if certain processes arise on the collapse of prior processes. The instant will be then both a beginning and an end. In short, if the end of one project coincides with the beginning of another project, an ambiguous, temporal reality will arise which will be limited by a prior nothingness in that it is a beginning and limited by a posterior nothingness in that it is an end. But this temporal structure will be concrete only if the beginning is itself given as the end of the process which it is making-past. A beginning which is given as the end of a prior project—such must be the instant. It will exist therefore only if we are a beginning and an end to ourselves within the unity of a single act.

Now it is precisely this which is produced in the case of a radical modification of our fundamental project. By the free choice of this modification, in fact, we temporalize a project which we are, and we make known to ourselves by a future the being which we have chosen; thus the pure present belongs to the new temporalization as a beginning, and it receives from the future which has just arisen its own nature as a beginning. It is the future alone, in fact, which can turn back on the pure present in order to qualify it as a beginning; otherwise this present would be merely any sort of present whatsoever. Thus the present of the choice belongs already, as an integral structure, to the newly begun totality. But on the other hand, it is not possible for this choice not to determine itself in connection with the past which it has to be. The choice is even, on principle, a decision to apprehend as past the choice for which it is substituted. A converted atheist is not simply a believer; he is a believer who has for himself rejected atheism, who has made past within him the project of being an atheist. Thus the new choice is given as a beginning in so far as it is an end and as an end in so far as it is a beginning; it is limited by a double nothingness, and as such it realizes a break in the ekstatic unity of our being. However the instant is by itself only a nothingness, for where-ever we cast our view, we apprehend only a continuous temporalization which will be in accordance with the direction in which we look: either the completed and closed series which has just passed dragging its final term with it—or else the living temporalization which is beginning and whose initial term is caught and dragged along by the future possibility.

Thus every fundamental choice defines the direction of the pursued-pursuit at the same time that it temporalizes itself. This does not mean that it *gives an initial thrust* or that there is something settled—which I can exploit to my profit so long as I hold myself within the limits of this choice. On the contrary, the nihilation is pursued continuously, and consequently the free and continuous recovery of the choice is obligatory. This recovery, however, is not made from *instant to instant* while I freely reassume my choice. This is because there is no instant. The recovery is so narrowly joined to the ensemble of the process that it has no instantaneous meaning and can not have any. But precisely because it is free and perpetually recovered by freedom, my choice is limited by freedom itself; that is, it is haunted by the specter of the instant. In so far as I *shall reassume* my choice, the making-past of the process will be effected in perfect ontological continuity with the present. The process which is made-past remains organized with the present nihilation in the form of a *practical knowing*; that is, meaning which is lived and interiorized without ever being an *object* for the consciousness which projects itself toward its own ends. But precisely because I am free I always have the possibility of positing my immediate past as an object. This means that even though my prior consciousness was a pure non-positional consciousness (of) the past while it constituted itself as an internal negation of the co-present real and made its meaning known to itself by its ends posited as "re-assumed," now at the time of the new choice, consciousness posits its own past as an object; that is, it *evaluates* its past and takes its bearings in relation to it. This act of objectivizing the immediate past is the same as the new choice of other ends; it contributes to causing the instant to spring forth as the nihilating rupture of the temporalization.

It will be easier for the reader to understand the results obtained by this analysis if we compare them to another theory of freedom—for example, to that of Leibniz. For Leibniz as for us, when Adam took the apple it would have been *possible* for him not to take it. But for Leibniz as for us the implications of this gesture are so numerous and so ramified that ultimately to declare that it would have been possible for Adam not to take the apple amounts to saying that another Adam would have been possible. Thus Adam's contingency is the same as his freedom since this contingency means that this *real* Adam is surrounded by an infinity of possible Adams, each one of whom as compared to the real Adam is characterized by a slight or profound alteration of all his attributes; that is, ultimately, of his substance. For Leibniz, then, the freedom claimed by human reality is as the organization of three different notions: that man is free who (1) determines himself rationally to perform an act; (2) is such that this act is understood fully by the very nature of the one who has committed it; (3) is contingent—that is, exists in such a way that other persons committing other acts in connection with the same situation would have been possible. But because of the necessary connection of possibles, another gesture of Adam would have been possible only for and by another Adam, and the existence of another Adam implies that of another world. We recognize along with Leibniz that Adam's gesture engages his whole person and that another gesture could be understood only in the light of and within the compass of another personality in Adam. But Leibniz falls into a necessitarianism completely opposed to the idea of freedom when at the outset he establishes the assertion of the substance of Adam as a premise which will bring in the act of Adam as one of its partial conclusions; that is, when he reduces the chronological order to being only a symbolic expression of the logical order. The result is that on the one hand, the act is strictly necessitated by the very essence of Adam; also the contingency which according to Leibniz makes freedom possible is found wholly contained within the essence of Adam. And this essence is not chosen by Adam himself but by God. Thus it is true that the act committed by Adam necessarily derives from Adam's essence and that it thereby depends on Adam himself and on no other, which, to be sure, is one condition of freedom. But Adam's essence is for Adam himself a *given*; Adam has not chosen it; he could not choose to be Adam. Consequently he does not support the responsibility for his being. Hence once he himself has been given, it is of little importance that one can attribute to him the relative responsibility for his act.

For us, on the contrary, Adam is not defined by an essence since for human reality essence comes after existence. Adam is defined by the choice of his ends; that is, by the upsurge of an ekstatic temporalization which has nothing in common with the logical order. Thus Adam's contingency expresses the finite choice which he has made of himself. But henceforth what makes his *person* known to him is the future and not the past; he chooses to learn what he is by means of ends toward which he projects himself—that is, by the totality of his tastes, his likes, his hates, *etc.* inasmuch as there is a thematic organization and an inherent *meaning* in this totality. Thus we can avoid the objection which we offered to Leibniz when we said, "To be sure, Adam chose to take the apple, but he did not choose to be Adam." For us, indeed, the problem of freedom is placed on the level of Adam's choice of himself— that is, on the determination of essence by existence. In addition we recognize with Leibniz that another gesture of Adam, implying another Adam, implies another world; but by "another world" we do not mean a particular organization of co-possibles such that the other possible Adam finds his place there, rather that the revelation of another face of the world will correspond to another being-in-the-world of Adam.

Finally for Leibniz since the possible gesture of the other Adam is organized in another possible world, it pre-exists for all eternity—as possible—the realization of the contingent, real Adam. Here again essence precedes existence for Leibniz, and the chronological order depends on the eternal order of logic. For us, on the contrary, the possible is only a pure and unformed possibility of another being such that it is not *existed* as possible by a new project of Adam toward new possibilities. Thus the possible of Leibniz remains eternally an abstract possible whereas for us the possible appears only by possibilizing itself; that is, by coming to announce to Adam what he is. Consequently the order of psychological explanation in the work of Leibniz goes from past to present to the same extent that this succession expresses the eternal order of essences; everything is finally fixed in a logical eternity, and the only contingency is that of principle, which means that Adam is a postulate of the divine understanding. For us, on the contrary, the order of interpretation is strictly *chronological*; it does not seek to *reduce* time to a purely logical concatenation (*reason*) or a chronological-logical (*cause*, determinism). It is interpreted therefore from the standpoint of the future.

But what we must especially insist on is that our preceding analysis is purely *theoretical. In theory only*, another gesture of Adam is possible and only within the limits of the total overthrow of the ends by which Adam chooses himself as Adam. We have presented things in this way—and hence we have been able to seem like Leibnizians—so as to present our view first with the maximum of simplicity. In actual fact reality is far more complex. This is because in reality the order of interpretation is purely chronological and not logical; the understanding of an act in terms of the original ends posited by the freedom of the for-itself is not an *intellection*. And the descending hierarchy of possibles from the final and initial possible to the derived possible which we are trying to understand has nothing in common with the deductive series which goes from a principle to its consequence. First of all, the connection between the derived possible (to resist fatigue or to give into it) and the fundamental possible is not a connection of *deductibility*. It is the connection between a totality and a partial structure. The view of the total project enables one to "understand" the particular structure considered. But the Gestalt School has shown us that the *prägnanz* of the total forms does not exclude the variability of certain secondary structures. There are certain lines which I can add to or subtract from a given figure without altering its specific character. There are others, on the contrary, which cannot be added without involving the immediate disappearance of the figure and the appearance of another figure. The same thing is true with regard to the relation between the secondary possibles and the fundamental possible or the formal totality of my possibles. The meaning of the secondary possible considered refers always, to be sure, to the total meaning which I am. But other possibles could have replaced this one without altering the total meaning; that is, they could always and just as well have indicated this totality as the form which enables them to be understood—or in the ontological order of realization they could just as well have been projected as the means of attaining the totality and in the light of this totality. In short the act of understanding is the interpretation of a factual connection and not the apprehension of a necessity.

Thus the psychological interpretation of our acts must frequently return to the Stoic notion of "indifferents." To relieve my fatigue, it is indifferent whether I sit down on the side of the road or whether I take a hundred steps more in order to stop at the inn which I see from a distance. This means that the apprehension of the complex, global form which I have chosen as my ultimate possible *does not suffice* to account for the choice of one possible rather than another. There is not here an act deprived of *motives* and *causes* but rather a spontaneous invention of *motives* and *causes*, which placed within the compass of my fundamental choice thereby enriches it. In the same way each "this" must appear on the background-world and in the perspective of my facticity, but neither my facticity nor the world allows us to understand why I presently grasp this glass rather than this inkwell as a figure raising itself on the background. In relation to these indifferents our freedom is entire and unconditioned. This fact of choosing one indifferent possible and then abandoning it for another will not cause the *instant* to surge up as the rupture of duration; on the contrary, these free choices are all integrated—even if they are successive and contradictory—in the unity of my fundamental project. This does not mean that they are to be apprehended as gratuitous. In fact whatever they may be, they will always be interpreted in terms of the original choice; and to the extent that they enrich this choice and make it concrete, they will always bring with them their motive—that is, the consciousness of their cause or, if you prefer, the apprehension of the situation as articulated in this or that way.

Another thing which will render the strict appreciation of the connection between the secondary possible and the fundamental possible particularly delicate is the fact that there exists no *a priori* "ready-reckoner" to which one can refer in order to determine this connection. On the contrary, it is the for-itself which chooses to consider the secondary possible as indicative of the fundamental possible. Just where we have the impression that the free subject is turning his back on his fundamental goal, we often introduce the observer's coefficient of error; that is, we use our own scales to weigh the relation between the act considered and the final ends. But the for-itself in its freedom invents not only primary and secondary ends; by the same stroke it invents the whole system of interpretation which allows their interconnections. In no case can there be a question of establishing a system of universal understanding of the secondary possibles in terms of the primary possibles: in every instance the subject himself must furnish his touchstone and his personal criteria.

Finally the for-itself can make voluntary decisions which are opposed to the fundamental ends which it has chosen. These decisions can be only voluntary—that is, reflective. In fact they can derive only from an error committed either in good faith or in bad faith against the ends which I pursue, and this error can be committed only if the ensemble of *motives* which I am are discovered in the capacity of an object by the reflective consciousness. Since the unreflective consciousness is a spontaneous self-projection toward its possibilities, it can never be deceived about itself; one must take care not to hold it responsible for making a mistake regarding itself when the error is actually a false evaluation of the objective situation—an error which can bring into the world consequences absolutely opposed to those which the unreflective consciousness wanted to effect, without however there having been any misunderstanding of its proposed ends. The reflective attitude, on the contrary, involves a thousand possibilities of error, not in that it apprehends the pure *motive*—i.e., the consciousness reflected-on—as a quasi-object but in so far as it aims at constituting across that consciousness reflected-on veritable psychic objects which are only probable objects, as we have seen in Part II, chapter III, and which can even be false objects. It is therefore possible for me as regards errors concerning myself to impose upon myself reflectively—i.e., on the voluntary plane—projects which contradict my initial project without, however, fundamentally modifying the initial project. Thus, for example, if my initial project aims at choosing myself as inferior in the midst of others (what is called the inferiority complex), and if stuttering, for example, is a behavior which is understood and interpreted in terms of the primary project, I can for social reasons and through a misunderstanding of my own choice of inferiority decide to cure myself of stuttering. I can even *succeed in it*, yet without having ceased to feel myself and to will myself to be inferior. In fact I can obtain a result by using merely technical methods. This is what we usually call a voluntary self-reform. But these results will only *displace* the infirmity from which I suffer; another will arise in its place and will in its own way express the total end which I pursue. As this profound inefficacy of a voluntary act directed on itself may surprise us, we are going to analyze the chosen example more closely.

It should be observed first of all that the choice of total ends although totally free is not necessarily nor even frequently made in joy. We must not confuse our necessity of choosing with the will to power. The choice can be effected in resignation or uneasiness; it can be a flight; it can be realized in bad faith. We can choose ourselves as fleeing, as inapprehensible, as indecisive, etc. We can even choose not to choose ourselves. In these various instances, ends are posited beyond a factual situation, and the responsibility for these ends falls on us. Whatever our being may be, it is a choice; and it depends on us to choose ourselves as "great" or "noble" or "base" and "humiliated." If we have chosen humiliation as the very stuff of our being, we shall realize ourselves as humiliated, embittered, inferior, etc. We are not dealing here with *givens* with no further meaning. But the man who realizes himself as humiliated thereby constitutes himself as a *means* of attaining certain ends: the humiliation chosen can be, for example, identified like masochism with an instrument designed to free us from existence-for-itself; it be a project of getting rid of our anguishing freedom to the advantage of others; our project can be to cause our being-for-itself to be entirely absorbed by our being-for-others. At all events the "inferiority complex" can arise only if it is founded on a free apprehension of our being-for-others. This being-for-others as a *situation* will act in the capacity of a cause, but all the same it must be discovered by a *motive* which is nothing but our free project. Thus the inferiority which is felt and lived is the chosen instrument to make us comparable to a *thing*; that is, to make us exist as a pure outside in the midst of the world. But it is evident that it must be lived in accordance with the *nature* which we confer on it by this choice—i.e., in shame, anger, and bitterness. Thus to *choose* inferiority does not mean to be sweetly contented with an *aurea mediocritas*; it is to produce and to assume the rebellion and despair which constitute the revelation of this inferiority. For example, I can persist in manifesting myself in a certain kind of employment *because* I am inferior in it, whereas in some other field I could without difficulty show myself equal to the average. It is this fruitless effort which I have chosen, simply because it is fruitless—either because I prefer to be the last rather than to be lost in the mass or because I have chosen discouragement and shame as the best means of attaining *being*.

It is obvious, however, that I can *choose as* a field of action the province in which I am inferior only if this choice implies the reflective will to be superior there. To choose to be an inferior artist is of necessity to *wish* to be a great artist; otherwise the inferiority would be neither suffered nor recognized. To choose to be a modest artisan in no way implies the pursuit of inferiority; it is a simple example of the choice of finitude. On the contrary, the choice of inferiority implies the constant realization of a *gap* between the end pursued by the will and the end obtained. The artist who wishes to be great and who chooses to be inferior intentionally maintains this gap; he is like Penelope and destroys by night what he makes by day. Thus with his artistic realizations he maintains himself constantly on the *voluntary* level and hence displays a desperate energy. But his very will is in *bad faith*; that is, it flees the recognition of the true ends chosen by the spontaneous consciousness, and it constitutes false psychic objects as *motives* in order to be able to deliberate concerning these motives and to determine itself in terms of them (the love of glory; the love of the beautiful, *etc.*). The will here is by no means opposed to the fundamental choice; quite the contrary it is understood in its ends and in its fundamental bad faith only within the perspective of a fundamental choice of inferiority. Whereas in the form of reflective consciousness the will constitutes in bad faith false psychic objects as motives, on the other hand in the capacity of a non-reflective and non-thetic self-consciousness, it is consciousness (of) being in bad faith and consequently (of) the fundamental project pursued by the for-itself. Thus the divorce between the spontaneous and willed consciousness is not a purely established factual given. On the contrary this duality is projected and initially realized by our fundamental freedom; it is conceived only in and through the profound unity of our fundamental project, which is to choose ourselves as inferior. But precisely, this divorce implies that the voluntary deliberation decides in bad faith to offset or to hide our inferiority by means of works whose inner goal is actually to enable us on the contrary to measure this inferiority.

Thus, as is seen, our analysis enables us to accept the two levels on which Adler places the inferiority complex: like him we admit a fundamental recognition of this inferiority, and like him we admit a heavy and ill-balanced development of acts, works, and statements designed to offset or to hide this deep feeling. But there are these differences: (1) We do not allow ourselves to conceive of the fundamental recognition as unconscious; it is so far from being unconscious that it even constitutes the bad faith of the will. Due to this fact we do not establish between the two levels considered the difference between the unconscious and the conscious, but rather that which separates the fundamental unreflective consciousness and its tributary, the consciousness reflected-on. (2) It seems to us that the concept of bad faith—as we established in Part One—should replace those of the censor, repression, and the unconscious which Adler uses. (3) The unity of the consciousness such as it is revealed to the *cogito* is too profound for us to admit a division into two levels unless the unity is recovered by a more profound synthetic intention leading from one level to the other and unifying them. Consequently we feel that there is something of deeper significance than the inferiority complex itself; not only is the inferiority complex recognized, but this recognition is a *choice*. Not only does the will seek to hide this inferiority by means of shifting and feeble affirmations; a more profound intention traverses it and *chooses* precisely the feebleness and shiftiness of these affirmations with the intention of rendering more noticeable this inferiority which we claim to flee and which we shall experience in shame and in the feeling of failure. Thus the man who suffers from *Minderwertigkeit* has *chosen* to be his own tormenter. He has chosen shame and suffering, which does not mean, however, that he is to experience any joy when they are most forcefully realized.

But if these new possibles are chosen in bad faith by a will which is produced within the limits of our initial project, they must nevertheless be realized to a certain extent *against* the initial project. To the extent that we wish to hide our inferiority from ourselves precisely in order to *create* it, we can wish to overcome the timidity and the stuttering which on the spontaneous level manifest our initial project of inferiority. We shall then undertake a systematic and reflective effort to cause these manifestations to disappear. We make this attempt in the state of mind of patients who come to consult the psychoanalyst. That is, on the one hand we work for an achievement which on the other hand we refuse. Thus the patient decides voluntarily to come to consult the psychoanalyst in order to be cured of certain troubles which he can no longer hide from himself; and by the mere fact that he puts himself in the hands of the physician he runs the risk of being cured. But on the other hand, if he runs this risk, it is in order to persuade himself that he has in vain done everything possible in order to be cured and that therefore he is incurable. Hence he approaches the psychoanalytic treatment with bad faith and bad will. All his efforts will have as their goal causing the attempt to fail although he voluntarily continues to lend himself to the enterprise. Similarly the psychasthenics whom Janet studied *suffer* from an obsession which they intentionally enter into and *wish* to be cured of. But, to be precise, their *will* to be cured has for its goal the confirmation of these obsessions as *sufferings* and consequently the realization of them in all their strength. We know the result; the patient can not confess his obsessions; he lies sobbing on the floor, but he does not determine himself to make the requisite confession. It would be useless to speak here of a struggle between the will and the disease; these processes unfold within the ekstatic unity of bad faith in a being who is what he is not and who is not what he is. Similarly when the psychoanalyst is close to grasping the initial project of the patient, the latter abandons the treatment or begins to lie. It would be uselesss to try to explain this resistance by a revolt or an unconscious anxiety. How then could the unconscious be informed of the progress of the psychoanalytical investigation unless precisely by being a consciousness? But if the patient plays the game to the end, it is necessary that he experience a partial cure; that is, there must be produced in him the disappearance of the morbid phenomena which have brought him to seek the help of the physician. Thus he will have chosen the lesser evil: having come in order to persuade himself that he is incurable, he is forced—in order to avoid apprehending his project in full light and consequently having to nihilate it and to become freely another project—he is forced to depart pretending to be cured. Similarly the methods which I shall employ to cure myself of stuttering and of timidity may have been attempted in bad faith. Nonetheless the fact remains that I have been forced to recognize their efficacy. In this case the timidity and the stuttering will disappear; it is the lesser evil. An artificial and voluble assurance will come to replace them. But it is the same with these cures as it is with the cure of hysteria by electric shock treatment. We know that this therapy can effect the disappearance of an hysterical contraction of the leg, but as one will see, some time later the contraction will appear in the arm. This is because the hysteria can be cured only as a totality, for it is a total project of the for-itself. Partial medications only succeed in displacing the manifestations. Thus the cure of the timidity or of the stuttering is consented to and chosen in a project which extends to the appearance of other troubles—for example, to the realization of a foolish and equally unbalanced self-assurance.

Since the upsurge of a *voluntary* decision finds its motive in the fundamental free choice of my ends, it can attack these ends in appearance only. It is therefore only within the compass of my fundamental project that the will can be efficacious; and I can be "freed" from my "inferiority complex" only by a radical modification of my project which could in no way find its causes and its motives in the prior project, not even in the suffering and shame which I experience, for the latter are designed expressly to *realize* my project of inferiority. Thus so long as I am "in" the inferiority complex, I can not even conceive of the possibility of getting out of it. Even if I dream of getting out of it, the precise function of this dream is to make me experience even further the abjection of my state; it can be interpreted therefore only in and through the intention which makes me inferior. Yet at each moment I apprehend this initial choice as contingent and unjustifiable; at each moment therefore I am on the site suddenly to consider it objectively and consequently to surpass it and to make-it-past by causing the liberating *instant* to arise. Hence my anguish, the fear which I have of being suddenly exorcized (*i.e.*, of becoming radically other); but hence also the frequent upsurge of "conversions" which cause me totally to metamorphose my original project. These conversions which have not been studied by philosophers, have often inspired novelists.[11] One may recall the *instant* at which Gide's Philoctetes casts off his hate, his fundamental project, his reason for being, and his being. One may recall the *instant* when Raskolnikoff decides to give himself up. These extraordinary and marvelous instants when the prior project collapses into the past in the light of a new project which rises on its ruins and which as yet exists only in outline, in which humiliation, anguish, joy, hope are delicately blended, in

---

[11] Sartre seems not to have read or to have forgotten William James, *The Varieties of Religious Experience.* Tr.

which we let go in order to grasp and grasp in order to let go—these have often appeared to furnish the clearest and most moving image of our freedom. But they are only one among others of its many manifestations.

Thus presented, the "paradox" of the inefficacy of voluntary decisions will appear less offensive. It amounts to saying that by means of the will, we can *construct* ourselves entirely, but that the will which presides over this construction finds its meaning in the original project which it can appear to deny, that consequently this construction has a function wholly different from that which it advertises, and that finally it can reach only details of structures and will never modify the original project from which it has issued any more than the consequences of a theorem can turn back against it and change it.

At the end of this long discussion, it seems that we have succeeded in making a little more precise our ontological understanding of freedom. It will be well at present to gather together and summarize the various results obtained.

(1) A first glance at human reality informs us that for it being is reduced to doing. The psychologists of the nineteenth century who pointed out the "motor" structures of drives, of the attention, of perception, *etc.* were right. But motion itself is an act. Thus we find no *given* in human reality in the sense that temperament, character, passions, principles of reason would be acquired or innate *data* existing in the manner of things. The empirical consideration of the human being shows him as an organized unity of conduct patterns or of "behaviors." To be ambitious, cowardly, or irritable is simply to conduct oneself in this or that way in this or that circumstance. The Behaviorists were right in considering that the sole positive psychological study ought to be of conduct in strictly defined situations. Just as the work of Janet and the Gestalt School have put us in a position to discover types of emotional conduct, so we ought to speak of types of perceptive conduct since perception is never conceived outside an attitude with respect to the world. Even the disinterested attitude of the scientist, as Heidegger has shown, is the assumption of a disinterested position with regard to the object and consequently one conduct among others. Thus human reality does not exist first in order to act later; but for human reality, to be is to act, and to cease to act is to cease to be.

(2) But if human reality is action, this means evidently that its determination to action is itself action. If we reject this principle, and if we admit that human reality can be determined to action by a prior state of the world or of itself, this amounts to putting a *given* at the beginning of the series. Then these *acts* disappear as acts in order to give place to a series of *movements*. Thus the notion of conduct is itself destroyed with Janet and with the Behaviorists. The existence of the act implies its autonomy.

(3) Furthermore, if the act is not pure *motion*, it must be defined by an

*intention*. No matter how this intention is considered, it can be only a surpassing of the given toward a result to be obtained. This given, in fact, since it is
pure presence, can not get out of itself. Precisely because it is, it is fully and
solely what it is. Therefore it can not provide the reason for a phenomenon
which derives all its meaning from a result to be attained; that is, from a non-
existent. When the psychologists, for example, view the drive as a factual
state, they do not see that they are removing from it all its character as an
*appetite* (*ad-petitio*). In fact, if the sexual drive can be differentiated from the
desire to sleep, for example, this can be only by means of its end, and this end
does not exist. Psychologists ought to have asked what could be the ontological structure of a phenomenon such that it makes known to itself what it
is by means of something which does not yet exist. The intention, which is
the fundamental structure of human-reality, can in no case be explained by a
given, not even if it is presented as an emanation from a given. But if one
wishes to interpret the intention by its end, care must be taken not to confer
on this end an existence as a *given*. In fact if we could admit that the end is
given prior to the result to be attained, it would then be necessary to concede
to this end a sort of being-in-itself at the heart of its nothingness and an
attractive virtue of a truly magical type. Moreover we should not succeed any
better in understanding the connection between a given human reality and a
given end than in understanding the connection between consciousness-
substance and reality-substance in the realists' arguments. If the drive or the
act is to be interpreted by its end, this is because the intention has for its
structure *positing* its end outside itself. Thus the intention makes itself be by
choosing the end which makes it known.

(4) Since the intention is a choice of the end and since the world reveals
itself across our conduct, it is the intentional choice of the end which reveals
the world, and the world is revealed as this or that (in this or that order)
according to the end chosen. The end, illuminating the world, is a state of the
world to be obtained and not yet existing. The intention is a thetic consciousness of the end. But it can be so only by making itself a non-thetic consciousness of its own possibility. Thus my *end* can be a good meal if I am hungry.
But this meal which beyond the dusty road on which I am traveling is
projected as the *meaning* of this road (it goes *toward* a hotel where the table is
set, where the dishes are prepared, where I am expected, *etc.*) can be apprehended only correlatively with my non-thetic project toward my own possibility of eating this meal. Thus by a double but unitary upsurge the intention
illuminates the world in terms of an end not yet existing and is itself defined
by the choice of its possible. My end is a certain objective state of the world,
my possible is a certain structure of my subjectivity; the one is revealed to the
thetic consciousness, the other flows back over the non-thetic consciousness
in order to characterize it.

(5) If the given can not explain the intention, it is necessary that the intention by its very upsurge realize a rupture with the given, whatever it may be. Such must be the case, for otherwise we should have a present plenitude succeeding in continuity a present plenitude, and we could not prefigure the future. Moreover, this rupture is necessary for the *appreciation* of the given. The given, in fact, could never be a *cause* for an action if it were not appreciated. But this appreciation can be realized only by a withdrawal in relation to the given, a putting of the given into parentheses, which exactly supposes a break in continuity. In addition, the appreciation if it is not to be gratuitous, must be effected in the light of something. And this something which serves to appreciate the given can be only the end. Thus the intention by a single unitary upsurge posits the end, chooses itself, and appreciates the given in terms of the end. Under these conditions the given is appreciated in terms of something which does not yet exist; it is in the light of non-being that being-in-itself is illuminated. There results a double nihilating coloration of the given; on the one hand, it is nihilated in that the rupture makes it lose all efficacy over the intention; on the other hand, it undergoes a new nihilation due to the fact that efficacy is returned to it in terms of a nothingness that is, the appreciation. Since human reality is act, it can be conceived only as being at its core a rupture with the given. It is the being which causes *there to be* a given by breaking with it and illuminating it in the light of the not-yet-existing.

(6) The necessity on the part of the given to appear only within the compass of a nihilation which reveals it is actually the same as the *internal negation* which we described in Part Two. It would be in vain to imagine that consciousness can exist without a given; in that case it would be consciousness (of) itself as consciousness of nothing—that is, absolute nothingness. But if consciousness exists in terms of the given, this does not mean that the given conditions consciousness; consciousness is a pure and simple negation of the given, and it exists as the disengagement from a certain existing given and as an engagement toward a certain not yet existing end. But in addition this internal negation can be only the fact of a being which is in perpetual withdrawal in relation to itself. If this being were not its own negation, it would be what it is—i.e., a pure and simple given. Due to this fact it would have no connection with any other *datum* since the given is by nature only what it is. Thus any possibility of the appearance of a world would be excluded. In order not to be a given, the for-itself must perpetually constitute itself as in withdrawal in relation to itself; that is, it must leave itself behind it as a *datum* which it already no longer is. This characteristic of the for-itself implies that it is the being which finds *no help, no pillar of support* in what it *was*. But on the other hand, the for-itself is free and can cause there to be a world because the for-itself is *the being which has to be what it was in the light of what it will be.* Therefore the freedom of the for-itself appears as its *being.* But since this

freedom is neither a given nor a property, it can be only by choosing itself. The freedom of the for-itself is always *engaged*; there is no question here of a freedom which could be undetermined and which would pre-exist its choice. We shall never apprehend ourselves except as a choice in the making. But freedom is simply the fact that this choice is always unconditioned.

(7) Such a choice made without base of support and dictating its own causes to itself, can very well appear *absurd*, and in fact it is absurd. This is because freedom is a *choice* of its being but not the *foundation* of its being. We shall return to this relation between freedom and facticity in the course of this chapter. For the moment it will suffice us to say that human-reality can choose itself as it intends but is not able not to choose itself. It can not even refuse to be; suicide, in fact, is a choice and affirmation of being. By this being which is *given* to it, human reality participates in the universal contingency of being and thereby in what we may call absurdity. This choice is absurd, not because it is without reason but because there has never been any possibility of not choosing oneself. Whatever the choice may be, it is founded and reapprehended by being, for it is choice which *is*. But what must be noted here is that this choice is not absurd in the sense in which in a rational universe a phenomenon might arise which would not be bound to others by any *reasons*. It is absurd in this sense—that the choice is that by which all foundations and all reasons come into being, that by which the very notion of the absurd receives a meaning. It is absurd as being beyond all reasons. Thus freedom is not pure and simple contingency in so far as it turns back toward its being in order to illuminate its being in the light of its end. It is the perpetual escape from contingency; it is the interiorization, the nihilation, and the subjectivizing of contingency, which thus modified passes wholly into the gratuity of the choice.

(8) The free project is fundamental, for it is my being. Neither ambition nor the passion to be loved nor the inferiority complex can be considered as fundamental projects. On the contrary, they of necessity must be understood in terms of a primary project which is recognized as the project which can no longer be interpreted in terms of any other and which is total. A special phenomenological method will be necessary in order to make this initial project explicit. This is what we shall call existential psychoanalysis. We shall speak of this in the next chapter. For the present we can say that the fundamental project which I am is a project concerning not my relations with this or that particular object in the world, but my total being-in-the-world; since the world itself is revealed only in the light of an end, this project posits for its end a certain type of relation to being which the for-itself wills to adopt. This project is not instantaneous, for it can not be "in" time. Neither is it non-temporal in order to "give time to itself" afterwards. That is why we reject Kant's "choice of intelligible character." The structure of the choice

necessarily implies that it be a choice in the world. A choice which would be a choice in terms of nothing, a choice against nothing would be a choice of nothing and would be annihilated as choice. There is only phenomenal choice, provided that we understand that the phenomenon is here the absolute. But in its very upsurge, the choice is temporalized since it causes a future to come to illuminate the present and to constitute it as a present by giving the meaning of *pastness* to the in-itself "data." However we need not understand by this that the fundamental project is coextensive with the entire "life" of the for-itself. Since freedom is a being-without-support and without-a-springboard, the project in order to be must be constantly renewed. I choose myself perpetually and can never be merely by virtue of having-been-chosen; otherwise I should fall into the pure and simple existence of the in-itself. The necessity of perpetually choosing myself is one with the pursued-pursuit which I am. But precisely because here we are dealing with a *choice*, this choice as it is made indicates in general other choices as possibles. The possibility of these other choices is neither made explicit nor posited, but it is lived in the feeling of unjustifiability; and it is this which is expressed by the fact of the *absurdity* of my choice and consequently of my being. Thus my freedom eats away my freedom. Since I am free, I project my total possible, but I thereby posit that I am free and that I can always nihilate this first project and make it past.

Thus at the moment at which the for-itself thinks to apprehend itself and make known to itself by a projected nothingness what it *is*, it escapes itself; for it thereby posits that it can be other than it is. It will be enough for it to make explicit its unjustifiability in order to cause the *instant* to arise; that is, the appearance of a new project on the collapse of the former. Nevertheless this upsurge of the new project has for its express condition the nihilation of the former, and hence the for-itself can not confer on itself a new existence. As soon as it rejects the project which has lapsed into the past, it has to be this project in the form of the "was"; this means that this lapsed project belongs henceforth to the for-itself's situation. No law of being can assign an *a priori* number to the different projects which I am. The existence of the for-itself in fact conditions its essence. But it is necessary to consult each man's history in order to get from it a particular idea with regard to each individual for-itself. Our particular projects, aimed at the realization in the world of a particular end, are united in the global project which we are. But precisely because we are wholly choice and act, these partial projects are not determined by the global project. They must themselves be choices; and a certain margin of contingency, of unpredictability, and of the absurd is allowed to each of them although each project as it is projected is the specification of the global project on the occasion of particular elements in the situation and so is always understood in relation to the totality of my being-in-the-world.

With these few observations we think that we have described the freedom of the for-itself in its original existence. But it will have been observed that this freedom requires a given, not as its condition but for several reasons. First, freedom is conceived only as the nihilation of a given (5); and to the extent that it is an internal negation and a consciousness, it participates (6) in the necessity which prescribes that consciousness be consciousness of something. In addition freedom is the freedom of choosing but not the freedom of not choosing. Not to choose is, in fact, to choose not to choose. The result is that the choice is the foundation of being-chosen but not the foundation of choosing. Hence the absurdity (7) of freedom. There again we are referred to a given which is none other than the very facticity of the for-itself. Finally the global project while illuminating the world in its totality can be made specific on the occasion of this or that element of the situation and consequently of the contingency of the world. All these remarks therefore refer us to a difficult problem: that of the relation of freedom to facticity. Moreover we shall inevitably meet other concrete objections. Can I choose to be tall if I am short? To have two arms if I have only one? etc. These depend on the "limitations" which my factual situation would impose on my free choice of myself. It will be well therefore to examine the other aspect of freedom, its "reverse side:" its relation to facticity.

## II. FREEDOM AND FACTICITY: THE SITUATION

The decisive argument which is employed by common sense against freedom consists in reminding us of our powerlessness. Far from being able to modify our situation at our whim, we seem to be unable to change ourselves. I am not "free" either to escape the lot of my class, of my nation, of my family, or even to build up my own power or my fortune or to conquer my most insignificant appetites or habits. I am born a worker, a Frenchman, an hereditary syphilitic, or a tubercular. The history of a life, whatever it may be, is the history of a failure. The coefficient of adversity of things is such that years of patience are necessary to obtain the feeblest result. Again it is necessary "to obey nature in order to command it"; that is, to insert my action into the network of determinism. Much more than he appears "to make himself," man seems "to be made" by climate and the earth, race and class, language, the history of the collectivity of which he is a part, heredity, the individual circumstances of his childhood, acquired habits, the great and small events of his life.

This argument has never greatly troubled the partisans of human freedom. Descartes, first of all, recognized both that the will is infinite and that it is necessary "to try to conquer ourselves rather than fortune." Here certain distinctions ought to be made. Many of the facts set forth by the determinists do not actually deserve to enter into our considerations. In particular the coefficient of adversity in things can not be an argument against our freedom, for it is *by us*—i.e., by the preliminary positing of an end—that this coefficient of adversity arises. A particular crag, which manifests a profound resistance if I wish to displace it, will be on the contrary a valuable aid if I want to climb upon it in order to look over the countryside. In itself—if one can even imagine what the crag can be in itself—it is neutral; that is, it waits to be illuminated by an end in order to manifest itself as adverse or helpful. Again it can manifest itself in one or the other way only within an instrumental-complex which is already established. Without picks and piolets, paths already worn, and a technique of climbing, the crag would be neither easy nor difficult to climb; the question would not be posited, it would not support any relation of any kind with the technique of mountain climbing. Thus although brute things (what Heidegger calls "brute existents") can from the start limit our freedom of action, it is our freedom itself which must first constitute the framework, the technique, and the ends in relation to which they will manifest themselves as limits. Even if the crag is revealed as "too difficult to climb," and if we must give up the ascent, let us note that the crag is revealed as such only because it was originally grasped as "climbable"; it is therefore our freedom which constitutes the limits which it will subsequently encounter.

Of course, even after all these observations, there remains an unnamable and unthinkable *residuum* which belongs to the *in-itself considered* and which is responsible for the fact that in a world illuminated by our freedom, this particular crag will be more favorable for scaling and that one not. But this *residue* is far from being originally a limit for freedom; in fact, it is thanks to this residue—that is, to the brute in-itself as such—that freedom arises as freedom. Indeed common sense will agree with us that the being who is said to be *free* is the one who can *realize* his projects. But in order for the act to be able to allow a *realization*, the simple projection of a possible end must be distinguished *a priori* from the realization of this end. If conceiving is enough for realizing, then I am plunged in a world like that of a dream in which the possible is no longer in any way distinguished from the real. I am condemned henceforth to see the world modified at the whim of the changes of my consciousness; I can not practice in relation to my conception the "putting into brackets" and the suspension of judgment which will distinguish a simple fiction from a real choice. If the object appears as soon as it is simply conceived, it will no longer be chosen or merely wished for. Once the distinction between the simple *wish*, the *representation* which I could choose, and the *choice* is abolished, freedom disappears too. We are free when the final term by which we make known to ourselves what we are is an end; that is, not a real existent like that which in the supposition which we have made could fulfill our wish, but an object which does not yet exist. But consequently this *end* can be transcendent only if it is separated from us at the same time that it is accessible. Only an ensemble of real existents can separate us from this end—in the same way that this end can be conceived only as a state to-come of the real existents which separate me from it. It is nothing but the outline of an order of existents—that is, a series of dispositions to be assumed by existents on the foundation of their actual relations. By the internal negation, in fact, the for-itself illuminates the existents in their mutual relations by means of the end which it posits, and it projects this end in terms of the determinations which it apprehends in the existent. There is no circle, as we have seen, for the upsurge of the for-itself is effected at one stroke. But if this is the case, then the very order of the existents is indispensable to freedom itself. It is by means of them that freedom is separated from and reunited to the end which it pursues and which makes known to it what it is. Consequently the resistance which freedom reveals in the existent, far from being a danger to freedom, results only in enabling it to arise as freedom. There can be a free for-itself only as engaged in a resisting world. Outside of this engagement the notions of freedom, of determinism, of necessity lose all meaning.

In addition it is necessary to point out against "common sense" that the formula "to be free" does not mean "to obtain what one has wished" but rather "by oneself to determine oneself to wish" (in the broad sense of choosing). In other words success is not important to freedom. The discussion which opposes common sense to philosophers stems here from a misunderstanding: the empirical and popular concept of "freedom" which has been produced by historical, political, and moral circumstances is equivalent to "the ability to obtain the ends chosen." The technical and philosophical concept of freedom, the only one which we are considering here, means only the autonomy of choice. It is necessary, however, to note that the choice, being identical with acting, supposes a commencement of realization in order that the choice may be distinguished from the dream and the wish. Thus we shall not say that a prisoner is always free to go out of prison, which would be absurd, nor that he is always free to long for release, which would be an irrelevant truism, but that he is always free to try to escape (or get himself liberated); that is, that whatever his condition may be, he can project his escape and learn the value of his project by undertaking some action. Our description of freedom, since it does not distinguish between choosing and doing, compels us to abandon at once the distinction between the intention and the act. The intention can no more be separated from the act than thought can be separated from the language which expresses it; and as it happens that our speech informs us of our thought, so our acts will inform us of our intentions—that is, it will enable us to disengage our intentions, to schematize them, and to make objects of them instead of limiting us to living them—i.e., to assume a non-thetic consciousness of them. This essential distinction between the freedom of choice and the freedom of obtaining was certainly perceived by Descartes, following Stoicism. It puts an end to all arguments based on the distinction between "willing" and "being able," which are still put forth today by the partisans and the opponents of freedom.

It is nonetheless true that freedom encounters or seems to encounter limitations on account of the *given* which it surpasses or nihilates. To show that the coefficient of adversity of the thing and its character as an obstacle (joined to its character as an instrument) is indispensable to the existence of a freedom is to use an argument that cuts two ways; for while it enables us to establish that freedom is not invalidated by the given, it indicates, on the other hand, something like an ontological conditioning of freedom. Would it not be reasonable to say, along with certain contemporary philosophers: if no obstacle, then no freedom? And as we can not admit that freedom by itself creates its own obstacle—which would be absurd for anyone who has understood the meaning of spontaneity—there seems to be here a kind of ontological priority of the in-itself over the for-itself. Therefore we must consider the previous remarks as simple attempts to clear the ground, and we must take up again from the beginning the question of facticity.

We have established that the for-itself is free. But this does not mean that it is its own foundation. If to be free meant to be its own foundation, it would be necessary that freedom should decide the *existence* of its being. And this necessity can be understood in two ways. First, it would be necessary that freedom should decide its being-free; that is, not only that it should be a choice of an end, but that it should be a choice of itself as freedom. This would suppose therefore that the possibility of being-free and the possibility of not-being-free exist equally before the free choice of either one of them— i.e., before the free choice of freedom. But since then a previous freedom would be necessary which would choose to be free—i.e., basically, which would choose to be what it is already—we should be referred to infinity; for there would be need of another prior freedom in order to choose this and so on. In fact we are a freedom which chooses, but we do not choose to be free. We are condemned to freedom, as we said earlier, thrown into freedom or, as Heidegger says, "abandoned." And we can see that this abandonment has no other origin than the very existence of freedom. If, therefore, freedom is defined as the escape from the *given*, from fact, then there is a *fact* of escape from fact. This is the facticity of freedom.

But the fact that freedom is not its own foundation can be understood also in another way which will lead to identical conclusions. Actually if freedom decided the existence of its being, it would be necessary not only that my being not-free should be possible, but necessary as well that my absolute non-existence be possible. In other words, we have seen that in the initial project of freedom the end turns back upon causes in order to constitute them as such; but if freedom is to be its own foundation, then the end must in addition turn back on its existence and cause it to arise. We can see what would result from this: the for-itself would itself derive from nothingness in order to attain the end which it proposes to itself. This existence made legitimate by means of its end would be existence by *right* but not in *fact*. And it is true that among the thousands of ways which the for-itself has of trying to wrench itself away from its original contingency, there is one which consists in trying to make itself recognized by the Other as an existence by right. We insist on our individual rights only within the compass of a vast project which would tend to confer existence on us in terms of the function which we fulfill. This is the reason why man tries so often to identify himself with his function and seeks to see in himself only the "Presiding Judge of the Court of Appeal," the "Chief Treasurer and Paymaster" *etc.* Each of these functions has its existence justified by its end. To be identified with one of them is to take one's own existence as saved from contingency. But these efforts to escape original contingency succeed only in better establishing the existence of this contingency. Freedom can not determine its existence by the end which it posits. Of course it exists only by the choice which it makes of an end, but it is not master of the fact that *there is* a freedom which makes known to itself what it is by means of its end. A freedom which would produce its own existence would lose its very meaning as freedom. Actually freedom is not a simple undetermined power. If it were, it would be nothingness or in-itself; and it is only by an aberrant synthesis of the in-itself and nothingness that one is able to conceive of freedom as a bare power pre-existing its choices. It determines itself by its very upsurge as a "doing." But as we have seen, *to do* supposes the nihilation of a given. One does something *with* or *to* something. Thus freedom is a lack of being in relation to a given being; it is not the upsurge of a full being. And if it is this hole of being, this nothingness of being as we have just said, it supposes *all being* in order to rise up in the heart of being as a hole. Therefore it could not determine its existence from the standpoint of nothingness, for all production from the standpoint of nothingness can be only being-in-itself.

We have proved elsewhere in Part One of this work that nothingness can appear nowhere except at the heart of being. Here we add also the demands of common sense: empirically we can be free only in relation to a state of things and in spite of this state of things. I will be said to be free in relation to this state of things when it does not constrain me. Thus the empirical and practical concept of freedom is wholly negative; it issues from the consideration of a situation and establishes that this situation *leaves me free* to pursue this or that end. One might say even that this situation conditions my freedom in this sense, that the situation *is there in order not to constrain me*. Remove the prohibition to circulate in the streets after the curfew, and what meaning can there be for me to have the freedom (which, for example, has been conferred on me by a pass) to take a walk at night?

Thus freedom is a lesser being which supposes being in order to elude it. It is not free not to exist or not to be free. We are going to grasp immediately the connection of these two structures. In fact, as freedom is the escape from being, it could not produce itself laterally *alongside* being and in a project of "surveying;" one can not escape from a gaol in which one is not imprisoned. A projection of the self on the margin of being can in no way constitute itself as the nihilation of this being. Freedom is the escape from an engagement in being; it is the nihilation of a being which it *is*. This does not mean that human-reality exists first, to be free *subsequently*. "Subsequently" and "first" are terms created by freedom itself. The upsurge of freedom is effected by the double nihilation of the *being which it is* and of the being in the midst of which it is. Naturally freedom is not this being in the sense of being-in-itself. But by freedom's illuminating insufficiencies in the light of the end chosen, *there is* this being which is its own. Freedom *has to be* behind itself this being which it has not chosen; and precisely to the extent that it turns back upon it in order to illuminate it, freedom causes this being which is its own to appear in relation with the *plenum* of being—that is, to exist in the midst of the world. We said that freedom is not free not to be free and that it is not free not to exist. This is because the fact of not being able not to be free is the *facticity* of freedom, and the fact of not being able not to exist is its *contingency*. Contingency and facticity are really one; there is a being which freedom has to be in the form of *non-being* (that is, of nihilation). To exist as *the fact* of freedom or to have to be a being in the midst of the world are one and the same thing, and this means that freedom is originally *a relation to the given*.

But what is this relation to the given? Are we to understand by this that the given (the in-itself) conditions freedom? Let us look more closely. The given does not *cause* freedom (since it can produce only the given) nor is it the *reason* of freedom (since all "reason" comes into the world through freedom). Neither is it the *necessary condition* of freedom since we are on the level of pure contingency. Neither is it an *indispensable matter* on which freedom must exercise itself, for this would be to suppose that freedom exists ready-made as an Aristotelian form or as a Stoic Pneuma and that it looks for a matter to work in. The given in no way enters into the constitution of freedom since freedom is interiorized as the internal negation of the given. It is simply the pure contingency which freedom exerts by denying the given while making itself a choice; the given is the plenitude of being which freedom colors with insufficiency and with *négatité* by illuminating it with the light of an end which does not exist. The given is freedom itself in so far as freedom *exists*; and whatever it does, freedom can not escape its existence. The reader will have understood that this given is nothing other than the in-itself nihilated by the for-itself which has to be it, that the body as a point of view on the world, that the past as the *essence* which the for-itself was—that these are three designations for a single reality. By its nihilating withdrawal, freedom causes a whole system of relations to be established, from the point of view of the end, between *all* in-itselfs; that is, between the *plenum* of being which is revealed then as the *world* and the being which it has to be in the midst of this *plenum* and which is revealed as *one* being, as *one* "this" which it has to be.

Thus by its very projection toward an end, freedom constitutes as a being in the midst of the world a particular *datum* which it has to be. Freedom does not choose it, for this would be to choose its own existence; but by the choice which it makes of its end, freedom causes the *datum* to be revealed in this or that way, in this or that light in connection with the revelation of the world itself. Thus the very contingency of freedom and the world which surrounds this contingency with its own contingency will appear to freedom only in the light of the end which it has chosen; that is, not as brute existents but in the unity of the illumination of a single nihilation. And freedom would never be able to reapprehend this ensemble as a pure *datum*, for in that case it would be necessary that this freedom be outside of all choice and therefore that it should cease to be freedom. We shall use the term *situation* for the contingency of freedom in the *plenum* of being of the world inasmuch as this *datum*, which is there only in *order not to constrain* freedom, is revealed to this freedom only as *already illuminated* by the end which freedom chooses. Thus the *datum* never appears to the for-itself as a brute existent in-itself; it is discovered always *as a cause* since it is revealed only in the light of an end which illuminates it. Situation and motivation are really one. The for-itself discovers itself as engaged in being, hemmed in by being, threatened by being; it discovers the state of things which surrounds it as the cause for a reaction of defense or attack. But it can make this discovery only because it freely posits the end in relation to which the state of things is threatening or favorable.

These observations should show us that the *situation*, the common product of the contingency of the in-itself and of freedom, is an ambiguous phenomenon in which it is impossible for the for-itself to distinguish the contribution of freedom from that of the brute existent. In fact, just as freedom is the escape from a contingency which it has to be in order to escape it, so the situation is the free coordination and the free qualification of a brute given which does not allow itself to be qualified in any way at all. Here I am at the foot of this crag which appears to me as "not scalable." This means that the rock appears to me in the light of a projected scaling—a secondary project which finds its meaning in terms of an initial project which is my being-in-the-world. Thus the rock stands out on the background-world by the effect of the initial choice of my freedom. But on the other hand, what my freedom can not determine is whether the rock "to be scaled" will or will not lend itself to scaling. This is part of the brute being of the rock. Nevertheless the rock can show its resistance to the scaling only if the rock is integrated by freedom in a "situation" of which the general theme is scaling. For the simple traveler who passes over this road and whose free project is a pure aesthetic ordering of the landscape, the crag is not revealed either as scalable or as not-scalable; it is manifested only as beautiful or ugly.

Thus it is impossible to determine in each particular case what comes from freedom and what comes from the brute being of the for-itself. The given in-itself as *resistance* or as *aid* is revealed only in the light of the projecting freedom. But the projecting freedom organizes an illumination such that the in-itself is revealed by it *as it is* (i.e., resisting or favorable); but we must clearly understand that the resistance of the given is not directly admissible as an in-itself quality of the given but only as an indication—across a free illumination and a free refraction—of an inapprehensible *quid*. Therefore it is only in and through the free upsurge of a freedom that the world develops and reveals the resistance which can render the projected end unrealizable. Man encounters an obstacle only within the field of his freedom. Better yet, it is impossible to decree *a priori* what comes from the brute existent and what from freedom in the character of this or that particular existent functioning as an obstacle. What is an obstacle for me may not be so for another. There is no obstacle in an absolute sense, but the obstacle reveals its coefficient of adversity across freely invented and freely acquired techniques. The obstacle reveals this coefficient also in terms of the value of the end posited by freedom. The rock will not be an obstacle if I wish at any cost to arrive at the top of the mountain. On the other hand, it will discourage me if I have freely fixed limits to my desire of making the projected climb. Thus the world by coefficients of adversity reveals to me the way in which I stand in relation to the ends which I assign myself, so that I can never know if it is giving me information about myself or about it. Furthermore the coefficient of adversity of the given is never a simple relation to my freedom as a pure nihilating thrust. It is a relation, illuminated by freedom, between the *datum* which is the cliff and the *datum* which my freedom has to be; that is, between the contingent which it is not and its pure facticity. If the desire to scale it is equal, the rock will be easy for one athletic climber but difficult for another, a novice, who is not well trained and who has a weak body. But the body in turn is revealed as well or poorly trained only in relation to a free choice. It is because I am there and because I have made of myself what I am that the rock develops in relation to my body a coefficient of adversity. For the lawyer who has remained in the city and who is pleading a case, whose body is hidden under his lawyer's robe, the rock is neither hard nor easy to climb; it is dissolved in the totality "world" without in any way emerging from it. And in one sense it is I who choose my body as weak by making it face the difficulties which I cause to be born (mountain climbing, cycling, sport). If I have not chosen to take part in sports, if I live in the city, and if I concern myself exclusively with business or intellectual work, then from this point of view my body will have no quality whatsoever.

Thus we begin to catch a glimpse of the paradox of freedom: there is freedom only in *a situation*, and there is a situation only through freedom. Human-reality everywhere encounters resistance and obstacles which it has not created, but these resistances and obstacles have meaning only in and through the free choice which human-reality *is*. But in order better to grasp the meaning of these remarks and to derive the advantages which they allow, it will be well at present to analyze in the light of them certain specific examples. What we have called the facticity of freedom is the given which it has to *be* and which it illuminates by its project. This given is manifested in several ways although within the absolute unity of a single illumination. It is *my place, my body, my past, my position* in so far as it is already determined by the indications of Others, finally *my fundamental relation to the Other*. We are going to examine successively and with specific examples these various structures of the situation. But we must never lose sight of the fact that no one of them is given alone and that when we consider one of them in isolation, we are restricted to making it appear on the synthetic background of the others.

## A. My place

My place is defined by the spatial order and by the particular nature of the "thises" which are revealed to me on the background-world. It is naturally the spot in which I "live" (my "country" with its sun, its climate, its resources, its hydrographic and orographic configuration). It is also more simply the arrangement and the order of the objects which at present appear to me (a table, beyond the table a window, to the left of the window a cabinet, to the right a chair, and beyond the window the street and the sea), which indicate me as the reason for their order. It is not possible for me not to have a place; otherwise my relation to the world would be a state of flying over, and the world would no longer be manifested to me in any way at all—as we have seen earlier. Moreover, although this actual place can have been assigned to me by my freedom (I have "come" here), I have been able to occupy it only in connection with that which I occupied previously and by following paths marked out by the objects themselves. This previous place refers me to another, this to another, and so on to the *pure contingency of my place;* that is, to that place of mine which no longer refers to anything else which is a part of my experience: the place which is assigned to me by my birth.

It would be useless to explain this last place by the one which my mother occupied when she brought me into the world. The chain is broken, the places freely chosen by my parents would be invalid as an explanation of my places. If one considers any one of them in its connection with my original place—as when one says, for example, "I was born at Bordeaux because my father was given a position there as a civil servant," or "I was born at Tours because my grandparents had property there and my mother took refuge near them when during her pregnancy she learned of my father's death"—this merely shows more clearly how for me birth and the place which it assigns me are contingent things. Thus to be born is, among other characteristics, to take one's place, or rather according to what we have just said, to receive it. And as this original place will be that in terms of which I shall occupy new places according to determined rules, it seems that we have here a strong restriction of my freedom. Moreover as soon as one reflects on it, the question is seen to be exceedingly complicated. The partisans of free-will point out that along with any place presently occupied, an infinity of other places is offered to my choice. The opponents of freedom insist on the fact that an infinity of places is denied me by the fact that objects turn toward me a face which I have not chosen and which is exclusive of all others; they add that my place is too profoundly bound up with other conditions of my existence (my dietary habits, climate, etc.) not to contribute to making me. Between the partisans and opponents of freedom a decision seems impossible. This is because the debate has not been placed on its true level.

If we wish to posit the question as it should be, we must proceed from this antinomy: human-reality originally receives its place in the midst of things; human-reality is that by which something we can call place comes to things. Without human-reality there would have been neither space nor place, and yet this human-reality by which placing comes to things comes to receive its place among things without mastering anything. In truth there is no mystery here, but the description must proceed from the antinomy; for it is this which will give to us the exact relation between freedom and facticity.

We have seen that geometrical space—i.e., the pure reciprocity of spatial relations—is a pure nothingness. The only concrete placing which can be revealed to me is absolute extension—i.e., that which is defined by my place considered as the center for which distances are accounted for absolutely, with me as object and without reciprocity. The only absolute extension is that which unfolds starting from a location which I am absolutely. No other point could be chosen as an absolute center of reference without being immediately involved in universal relativity. If there is an extension within the limits of which I shall apprehend myself as free or as not-free, an extension which will be presented to me as helpful or as adverse (separating), this can be only because before all else I exist my place without choice, without necessity either, as the pure absolute fact of my being-there. I am there, not here but there. This is the absolute and incomprehensible fact which is at the origin of extension and consequently of my original relations with things (with these things rather than with those). A fact of pure contingency—an absurd fact.

Yet on the other hand, this place which I *am* is a relation. A univocal relation, to be sure, but a relation all the same. If I am limited to *existing* my place, I can not at the same time be elsewhere in order to establish this fundamental relation; I can not have even a dim comprehension of the object in relation to which my place is defined. I can only exist the inward determinations which the inapprehensible and unthinkable objects which surround me without my knowing it can provoke in me. By the same token the very reality of absolute extension disappears, and I am separated from everything which resembles a place. Furthermore I am neither free nor not-free; I am a pure existent without constraint, but without any way either of denying the constraint. In order that such a thing as an extension originally defined as my place may come into the world and by the same stroke strictly define me, it is not merely necessary that I exist my place—i.e., that I *have to be there*. It is necessary as well that I be able to be not wholly here so that I can be over there, near the object which I locate at ten feet from me and from the standpoint of which I make my place known to myself. The univocal relation which defines my place functions in fact as a relation between something which I am and something which I am not. This relation in order to be revealed must be established. It supposes therefore that I am in a position to effect the following operations:

(1) I must be able to *escape what I am and to nihilate it* in such a way that what I am, although it is *existed*, can still be revealed as the term of a relation. This relation is immediately given. It is not, however, given in the simple contemplation of things (if we tried to derive space from pure contemplation, one could well object, for things are given with absolute *dimensions*, not with absolute *distances*). It is given in our immediate action ("He is coming toward us," "Let's avoid him," "I am running after him," *etc.*). It implies as such a comprehension of what I am as being-there. But at the same time it is very necessary to define what I am from the standpoint of the being-there of other "thises." I am as being-there the one toward whom someone comes running, the one who has still an hour to climb before being at the top of the mountain, *etc.* Therefore when I look at the mountain top, for example, we are dealing with an escape from myself accompanied by a reflux which I effect in terms of the summit of the mountain toward my being-there in order to situate myself. Thus I must be "what I have to be" by the very fact of escaping it. In order for me to be defined by my place, it is necessary first that I escape myself in order to proceed to posit the co-ordinates in terms of which I shall define myself more narrowly as the center of the world. It should be noted that my being-there can in no way determine the surpassing which is going to fix and to locate things since my being-there is a *pure given*, incapable of projecting and since, moreover, in order to be defined strictly as this or that

*being-there,* it is already necessary that it has been determined by the surpassing followed by the reflux.

(2) I must be able *by an internal negation to escape the* "thises"—*in the midst of— the world which I am not and by which I make known to myself what I am.* To discover them and to escape them is the result, as we have seen, of a single negation. Here again the internal negation is first and spontaneous in relation to the *datum* as discovered. We can not admit that the *datum provokes* our apprehension; on the contrary, in order that there may be a "this" which announces its distances to the Being-there which I am, it is necessary for me to escape it by a *pure* negation. Nihilation, internal negation, a determining turning back upon the being-there which I am—these three operations are really one. They are only moments of an original transcendence which launches toward an end by nihilating me so that I may make known to myself what I am by means of the future. Thus it is my freedom which comes to confer on my place and to define it as such by situating me. The sole reason that I can be strictly limited to *this* being-there which I am is that my ontological structure is not to be what I am and to be what I am not.

Furthermore this determination of placing, which presupposes all transcendence, can occur only in relation to an end. It is in the light of an end that my place takes on its meaning. For I could never be *simply there.* My place is grasped as an *exile* or, on the contrary, as that natural, reassuring and favored location which Mauriac called *querencia,* comparing it to the place to which the wounded bull always returns in the arena. In relation to what I project doing, in relation to the world in totality and hence to my being-in-the-world, my place appears to me as an aid or a hindrance. To be in place is to be far from— or near to—; that is, place is provided with a meaning in relation to a certain not-yet existing being which one wants to attain. It is the accessibility or the inaccessibility of this end which defines place. It is therefore in the light of not-being and of the future that my position can be actually understood. "To be there" is to have to take just one step in order to reach the teapot, to be able to dip the pen in the ink by stretching my arm, to have to turn my back to the window if I want to read without tiring my eyes, to have to ride my bicycle and to put up with the fatigue of a hot afternoon for two hours if I wish to see my friend Pierre, to take the train and pass a sleepless night if I want to see Annie. For a Colonial, "to be there" is to be twenty days away from France; better yet, if he is a civil servant and is waiting for a trip at government expense, it is to be six months and seven days from Bordeaux or from Etaples. For a soldier, "to be there" is to be a hundred and ten, a hundred and twenty days from his discharge. The future—a projected future—intervenes everywhere; it is my future life at Bordeaux, at Etaples, the future discharge of the soldier, the future word which I shall write with a pen wet with ink—it is all this which means my place to me and which makes me exist with nervousness or impatience or nostalgia. On the other hand, if I am fleeing from a group of men or from public opinion, then my place is defined by the time which would be necessary for these people to discover me at the far end of the village where I am lodging, for them to arrive at this village, *etc.* In this case the isolation is what makes my place known to me as favorable. Here to be in place is to be sheltered.

This choice of my end slips into even purely spatial relations (high and low, right and left, *etc.*) so as to give them an existential meaning. The mountain is "overwhelming" if I live at the foot of it; on the other hand, if I am at its peak, the mountain is recovered by the very project of my pride and symbolizes the superiority which I attribute to myself over other men. The place of rivers, the distance from the sea, *etc.* come into play and are provided with symbolic meaning; constituted in the light of my end, my place reminds me symbolically of this end in all its details as in its connections. We shall return to this point when we want to define more exactly the object and the method of existential psychoanalysis. The brute relation of *distance* to objects can never be allowed to get its meaning and symbols from outside, for these are our very way of constituting it. Even more this brute relation itself has meaning only in relation to the choice of techniques which allow distances to be measured and to be traversed. A particular city situated twenty miles from my village and connected with it by a streetcar is much nearer to me than a rocky peak situated four miles away but at an altitude of two thousand eight hundred meters. Heidegger has shown how daily concerns assign to instruments a place which has nothing in common with pure geometric distance: my glasses, he says, once they are on my nose, are much farther from me than the object which I see through them.

Thus it must be said that the facticity of my place is revealed to me only in and through the free choice which I make of my end. Freedom is indispensable to the discovery of my facticity. I learn of this facticity from all the points of the future which I project; it is from the standpoint of this chosen future that facticity appears to me with its characteristics of impotence, of contingency, of weakness, of absurdity. It is in relation to my dream of seeing New York that it is absurd and painful for me to live at Mont-de-Marsan. But conversely facticity is the only reality which freedom can discover, the only one which it can nihilate by the positing of an end, the only thing in terms of which it is meaningful to posit an end. For if the end can illuminate the situation, this is because the end is constituted as a projected modification of this situation. My place appears in terms of the changes which I project. But *to change* implies something to be changed, which is precisely my place. Thus *freedom is the apprehension of my facticity.* It would be absolutely useless to seek to define or to describe the "quid" of this facticity "before" freedom turns back upon it in order to apprehend it as a determined deficiency. My place, before freedom has circumscribed my placing as a lack of a certain kind, "is" not, strictly speaking, anything at all since the very extension in terms of which all place is understood does not exist. On the other hand, the question itself is unintelligible, for it involves "before" which has no meaning; it is freedom, in fact, which temporalizes itself along the lines of a "before" and "after." Nevertheless the fact remains that this brute and unthinkable "quid" is that without which freedom could not be freedom. It is the very facticity of my freedom.

It is only in the act by which freedom has revealed facticity and apprehended it as *place* that this place thus defined is manifested as an *impediment* to my desires, an obstacle, *etc.* Otherwise how could it possibly be an obstacle? An obstacle to *what*? A compulsion *to do what*? The story is told of an emigrant who was going to leave France for Argentina after the failure of his political party: When someone remarked to him that Argentina was "very far away," he asked, "Far from what?" And it is very certain that if Argentina appears "far away" to those who live in France, it is *so* in relation to an implicit national project which valorizes their place as French. For the internationalist revolutionary, Argentina is a center of the world as is any other country. But if we have by a primary project first constituted French territory as our absolute place, and if some catastrophe forces us to go into exile, it is in relation to this initial project that Argentina will appear to us as "very far away," as a "land of exile"; it is in relation to this project that we shall feel ourselves expatriated.

Thus our freedom itself creates the obstacles from which we suffer. It is freedom itself which by positing its end and by choosing this end as inaccessible or accessible with difficulty, causes our placing to appear to our projects as an insurmountable resistance or a resistance to be surmounted with difficulty. It is freedom again which establishes the spatial connections between objects as the first type of a relation of instrumentality, which decides on techniques permitting distances to be measured and cleared, and thus constitutes its own *restriction*. But to be precise, freedom can exist only as *restricted* since freedom is choice. Every choice, as we shall see, supposes elimination and selection; every choice is a choice of finitude. Thus freedom can be truly free only by constituting facticity as its own restriction. It would therefore be to no point to say that I *am not free* to go to New York because of the fact that I am a minor government official at Mont-de-Marsan. On the contrary, it is in relation to my project of going to New York that I am going to *situate* myself at Mont-de-Marsan. My placing in the world, the relation of Mont-de-Marsan to New York and to China would be altogether different if, for example, my project were to become a wealthy farmer at Mont-de-Marsan. In the first case Mont-de-Marsan appears on the ground of a world which maintains an organized connection with New York, Melbourne, and Shanghai; in the second it emerges on the ground of an undifferentiated world. As for the *real* importance of my project of going to New York, I alone decide it. It can be just a way of choosing myself as discontented with Mont-de-Marsan; and in this case everything is centered on Mont-de-Marsan; I simply make proof of the need of perpetually nihilating my place, of living in a perpetual withdrawal in relation to the city which I inhabit. It can also be a project in which I wholly engage myself. In the first case I shall apprehend my place as an insurmountable obstacle, and I shall have simply used an indirect means to define it indirectly in the world. In the second case, on the other hand, the obstacles will no longer exist; my place will be no longer a point of attachment but a point of departure, for in order to go to New York, some point of departure is necessary. Thus I shall apprehend myself at any moment whatsoever as engaged in the world at my contingent place. But it is precisely this engagement which gives meaning to my contingent place and which is my freedom. To be sure, in being born I *take a place*, but I am responsible for the place which I take. We can see clearly here the inextricable connection of freedom and facticity in the situation. Without facticity freedom would not exist—as a power of nihilation and of choice—and without freedom facticity would not be discovered and would have no meaning.

## B. My past

We have a past. Of course we have been able to establish that this past does not determine our acts as a prior phenomenon determines a consequent phenomenon; we have shown that the past is without force to constitute the present and to sketch out the future. Nevertheless the fact remains that the freedom which escapes toward the future can not give itself any past it likes according to its fancy; there are even more compelling reasons for the fact that it can not produce itself without a past. It has to be its own past, and this past is irremediable. It even seems at first glance that freedom can not modify its past in any way; the past is that which is out of reach and which haunts us at a distance without our even being able to turn back to face it in order to consider it. If the past does not determine our actions, at least it is such that we can not take a new decision except in terms of it. If I have been trained at a naval academy, and if I have become an officer in the Navy, whenever I look back to myself, I am engaged; at the very instant when I apprehend myself, I am on watch on the bridge of the ship of which I am second in command. I can suddenly revolt against this fact, hand in my resignation, decide on suicide. These extreme measures are taken in connection with the past which is mine; if they aim at destroying it, this is because my past exists, and my most radical decisions can succeed only in taking a negative position with respect to my past. But basically this is to recognize the past's immense importance as a platform and a point of view. Every action designed to wrench me away from my past must first be conceived in terms of my particular past; that is, the action must before all recognize that it is born out of the particular past which it wishes to destroy. Our acts, says the proverb, follow after us. The past is present and melts insensibly into the present; it is the suit of clothes which I selected six months ago, the house which I have had built, the book which I began last winter, my wife, the promises which I have made to her, my children; all which I *am* I have to be in the mode of having-been. Thus the importance of the past can not be exaggerated since for me "Wesen ist was gewesen ist," essence is what has been. But we find here the paradox pointed out previously: I can not conceive of myself without a past; better yet, I can no longer think anything about myself since I think about what I *am* and since I am in the past; but on the other hand I am the being through whom the past comes to myself and to the world.

Let us examine this paradox more closely. Since freedom is choice, it is change. It is defined by the end which it projects; that is, by the future which it has to be. But precisely because the future is *the not-yet-existing-state of what is,* it can be conceived only within a close connection with what is. It is not possible that what is should illuminate what is not yet, for what is is a *lack* and consequently can be known as such only in terms of that which it lacks. The end illuminates what is. But to go looking for the end to-come in order by means of it to make known that-which-is, requires being already beyond what-is in a nihilating withdrawal which makes what-is appear clearly in the state of an isolated-system. What-is, therefore, takes on its meaning only when it is *surpassed* toward the future. Therefore what-is is the past. We see how the past as "that which is to be changed" is indispensable to the choice of the future and how consequently no free surpassing can be effected except in terms of a past, but we can see too how the very *nature* of the past comes to the past from the original choice of a future. In particular the irremediable quality of the past comes from my actual choice of the future; if the past is that in terms of which I conceive and project a new state of things in the future, then the past itself is that which *is left in place,* that which consequently is itself outside all perspective of change. Thus in order for the future to be realizable, it is necessary that the past be irremediable.

It is possible for me not to exist; but if I exist, I can not lack having a past. Such is the form which is assumed here by the "necessity of my contingency." But on the other hand, as we have seen, two existential characteristics in particular qualify the For-itself:

(1) Nothing is in consciousness which is not consciousness of being.

(2) In my being, my being is in question. This means that nothing comes to me which is *not chosen.*

We have seen, indeed, that a Past which was only Past would collapse in an honorary existence in which it would have lost all connection with the present. In order for us to "have" a past, it is necessary that we maintain it in existence by our very project towards the future; we do not receive our past, but the necessity of our contingency implies that we are not able not to choose it. This is what it means "to have to be one's own past." We see that this necessity, considered here from a purely temporal point of view, is not basically distinct from the primary structure of freedom, which must be the nihilation of the being which it is and which, by this very nihilation, brings it about that there is a being which it is.

But while freedom is the choice of an end in terms of the past, conversely the past is what it is only in relation to the end chosen. There is an unchangeable element in the past, (e.g., I had whooping cough when I was five years old) and an element which is eminently variable (the meaning of the brute fact in relation to the totality of my being). But since, on the other hand, the meaning of the past fact penetrates it through and through (I can not "recall" my childhood whooping cough outside of a precise project which defines its meaning), it is finally impossible for me to distinguish the unchangeable brute existence from the variable meaning which it includes. To say, "I had whooping cough when I was four years old"[12] supposes a thousand projects, in particular the adoption of the calendar as a system of reference for my individual existence (hence the adoption of an original position with regard to the social order) and a confident belief in the accounts which third persons give of my childhood, a belief which certainly goes along with a respect or an affection for my parents, a respect which shapes its meaning for me, etc. That brute fact itself is, but apart from the witness of others, its date, the technical name of the illness (an ensemble of meanings which depend on my projects) what can it be? Thus this brute existence, although necessarily existent and unchangeable stands as the ideal end—beyond reach—of a systematic specification of all the meanings included in a memory. There is, of course, a "pure matter" of memory in the sense in which Bergson speaks of pure memory; but when it shows itself, it is always in and through a project which includes the appearance of this matter in its purity.

Now the meaning of the past is strictly dependent on my present project. This certainly does not mean that I can make the meaning of my previous acts vary in any way I please; quite the contrary, it means that the fundamental project which I am decides absolutely the meaning which the past which I have to be can have for me and for others. I alone in fact can decide at each moment the bearing of the past. I do not decide it by debating it, by deliberating over it, and in each instance evaluating the importance of this or that prior event; but by projecting myself toward my ends, I preserve the past with

---

[12] Sartre's uncertainty as to just when he had whooping cough seems to imply even more shiftiness on the part of the past than his philosophy justifies! Tr.

me, and by action I *decide* its meaning. Who shall decide whether that mystic crisis in my fifteenth year "was" a pure accident of puberty or, on the contrary, the first sign of a future conversion? I myself, according to whether I shall decide—at twenty years of age, at thirty years—to be converted. The project of conversion by a single stroke confers on an adolescent crisis the value of a premonition which I had not taken seriously. Who shall decide whether the period which I spent in prison after a theft was fruitful or deplorable? I—according to whether I give up stealing or become hardened. Who can decide the educational value of a trip, the sincerity of a profession of love, the purity of a past intention, *etc.*? It is I, always I, according to the ends by which I illuminate these past events.

Thus all my past is there pressing, urgent, imperious, but its meanings and the orders which it gives me I choose by the very project of my end. Of course the engagements which I have undertaken weigh upon me. Of course the marriage I made earlier, the house I bought and furnished last year limit my possibilities and dictate my conduct; but precisely because my projects are such I reassume the marriage contract. In other words, precisely because I do not make of it a "marriage contract which is past, surpassed, dead" and because, on the contrary, my projects imply fidelity to the engagements undertaken or the decision to have an "honorable life" as a husband and a father, *etc.*, these projects necessarily come to illuminate the past marriage vow and to confer on it its always present value. Thus the urgency of the past comes from the future.

Suppose that in the manner of Schlumberger's hero[13] I radically modify my fundamental project, that I seek, for example, to free myself from a continued state of happiness, and my earlier engagements will lose all their urgency. They will no longer be here except as the towers and ramparts of the Middle Ages are here, structures which one can not deny but which have no other meaning than that of recalling a stage previously traversed, a civilization and a period of political and economic existence which today are surpassed and perfectly dead. It is the future which decides whether the past is living or dead. The past, in fact, is originally a project, as the actual upsurge of my being. And to the same extent that it is a project, it is an anticipation; its meaning comes to it from the future which it sketches in outline. When the past slips wholly into the past, its absolute value depends on the validation or invalidation of the anticipations which it was. But it depends on my actual freedom to confirm the meaning of these anticipations by again accepting responsibility for them—i.e., by anticipating the future which they anticipated—or to invalidate them by simply anticipating another future. In this case the past falls back as a disarmed and duped expectation; it is "without

---

[13] Schlumberger. *Un homme heureux.* N.R.F.

force." This is because the only force of the past comes to it from the future; no matter how I live or evaluate my past, I can do so only in the light of a project of myself toward the future.

Thus the order of my choices of the future is going to determine an order of my past, and this order will contain nothing of the chronological. There will be first the *always living* past which is always confirmed: my promise of love, certain business contracts, a certain picture of myself to which I am faithful. Then there is the ambiguous past which has ceased to please me and to which I still hold indirectly: for example, this suit which I am wearing, and which I bought at a certain period when I had the desire to be fashionable, displeases me extremely at present; hence the past in which I "chose" the suit is truly dead. But on the other hand, my actual project of economy is such that I must continue to wear this suit rather than get another. Hence it belongs to a past which is both dead and living like those social institutions which having been created for a determined end, have now outlived the regime which established them and have been made to serve altogether different ends, sometimes even opposed ends. A living past, a half-dead past, survivals, ambiguities, discrepancies: the ensemble of these layers of pastness is organized by the unity of my project. It is by means of this project that there is installed the complex system of references which causes any fragment of my past to enter into an hierarchical, plurivalent organization in which, as in a work of art, each partial structure indicates in different ways, various other partial structures and the total structure.

Furthermore this decision with respect to the value, the order, and the nature of our past is simply the *historical choice* in general. If human societies are historical, this does not stem simply from the fact that they have a past but from the fact that they reassume the past by making it a *memorial*. When American capitalism decides to enter the European war of 1914–1918 because it sees there the opportunity for profitable transactions, it is not *historical*; it is only utilitarian. But when in the light of its utilitarian projects, it recovers the previous relations of the United States with France and gives to them the *meaning* of the paying of a debt of honor by Americans to France, then it becomes historical. In particular it makes itself historical by the famous sentence: "La Fayette, we are here!" It goes without saying that if a different view of her real interests had led the United States to place itself on the side of Germany, she would not have lacked past elements to recover on the memorial level. One can imagine, for example, propaganda based on "blood kinship," which chiefly would have taken into account the proportion of Germans in the emigration to America in the nineteenth century. It would be in vain to try to view these references to the past as purely publicity enterprises; actually the essential fact is that they are *necessary* in order to gain the adherence of the masses and that therefore the masses demand a political project which illuminates and justifies their past. Moreover, it is evident that the past is thus *created*. *There has been* in this way the construction of a common French-American past which, on the one hand, *signified* the great economic interests of the Americans and, on the other hand, the *actual* affinities of two democratic capitalisms. Similarly about 1938 we saw how a new generation, concerned with the international events which were in preparation, now suddenly illuminated the period of 1918–1938 with a new light by calling it "the period between the wars" even before war actually had burst forth in 1939. Suddenly the period under consideration (1918–1938) was constituted in a form which was limited, surpassed, and repudiated whereas those who had lived through it by projecting themselves toward a future in continuity with their present and their immediate past had experienced it as the start of a continuous and unlimited progress. The actual project therefore decides whether a defined period of the past is in continuity with the present or whether it is a discontinuous fragment from which one is emerging and which is put at a distance.

Thus human history would have to be *finished* before a particular event, for example the taking of the Bastille, could receive a definitive *meaning*. Nobody denies, of course, that the Bastille was taken in 1789; there is the immutable fact. But are we to see in this event a revolt without consequence, a popular outburst against a half dismantled fortress, an event which the Convention, anxious to create a famous past for itself, was able to transform into a glorious deed? Or should we consider it as the first manifestation of popular strength by which the populace asserted itself, give itself confidence, and put itself in a position to effect the march on Versailles in those "Last Days of October"? He who would like to decide the question today forgets that the historian is himself *historical*; that is, that he historicizes himself by illuminating "history" in the light of his projects and of those of his society. Thus it is necessary to say that the meaning of the social past is perpetually "in suspense."

Now exactly like societies, the human person has a *memorial* past *in suspense*. It is this perpetual putting into question of the past which the sages realized very early and which the Greek tragedians expressed, for example, by that proverb which appears in all their plays: "No man can be called happy before his death." The perpetual historization of the For-itself is the perpetual affirmation of its freedom.

Once this fact is established, it is not necessary to hold that the past's character as "in suspense" appears to the For-itself in the form of a vague or incomplete aspect of its prior history. On the contrary, quite as much as the choice of the For-itself, which in its own way it expresses, the Past is apprehended by the For-itself each moment as strictly defined. Similarly the Arch of Titus or the Column of Trajan, whatever may be the historical evolution of their meaning, appear to the Roman or the tourist who considers them, as realities perfectly individualized. In the light of the project which illuminates it, the Past is revealed as perfectly compelling. The suspended character of the Past is in no way miraculous; it only serves to express—on the level of making-past and of the in-itself—the projective and expectant aspect which human reality *had* before turning to the past. It is because this human-reality was a free project eaten away by an unpredictable freedom that it becomes "in the past" a tributary of the further projects of the For-itself. Human-reality is condemned to make-itself-past and hence to wait forever for the confirmation which it expected from the future. Thus the past is indefinitely in suspense because human-reality "was" and "will be" perpetually expecting. Expectation and suspense only succeed in affirming still more plainly that freedom is their original constituent. To say that the past of the For-itself is in suspense, to say that its present is an expecting, to say that its future is a free project, or that it can be nothing without having to be it, or that it is a totality-detotalized—all these are one and the same thing. But this does not imply any indetermination in my past as it is revealed to me at present; it means simply that the right of my present revelation of my past to be definitive is put into question. But just as my present is an expectation of a confirmaion or of an invalidation which nothing allows it to foresee, so the past, which is involved in this expectation is precise to the same extent that the expectation is precise. But the meaning of the past, although strictly individualized, is totally dependent on this expectation which itself depends on an absolute nothingness; that is, on a free project which does not yet exist. My past therefore is a concrete and precise proposition which *as such* awaits ratification. This is certainly one of the meanings which Kafka's *The Trial* tries to bring to light, the characteristic in human reality of being perpetually *in court*. To be free is to *have one's freedom perpetually on trial*. The result is that the past while confined within my actual free choice is—once this choice has determined it—an integral and necessary condition of my project.

An example may make this point clearer. The past of a "half-pay" soldier under the Restoration is to have been a hero of the retreat from Russia. And what we have explained just now enables us to understand that this past itself is a free choice of the future. It is by choosing not to join in with the government of Louis XVIII and the new customs, by choosing until the end to hope for the triumphal return of the Emperor, by choosing even to con-spire to hasten this return and to prefer to be a "half-pay" rather than a full-pay soldier that the old soldier of Napoleon chooses for himself a past as a hero of Beresina. Another soldier who had formed the project of going over to the new government would certainly not have chosen the same past. But conversely, if we are considering only a "half-pay" solider, if he lives in almost indecent poverty, if he is embittered, and if he longs for the Emperor's return, this is because he was a hero of the retreat from Russia. We must be sure to understand this: the past does not act before any constituting recovery, and it does not in any way act deterministically; but once the past "soldier of the Empire" has been chosen, then the conduct of the for-itself *realizes* this past. There is even no difference between the soldier's choosing this past and his realizing it by his behavior. Thus the for-itself by endeavoring to make of its past glory an intersubjective reality, constitutes it in the eyes of others as being an objectivity-for-others (the reports of the officials, for example, on the danger represented by these old soldiers). Treated as such by others, the soldier acts henceforth in such a way as to render himself worthy of a past which he has chosen in order to compensate for his present misery and failure. He shows himself intransigent, he loses every chance of a pension; this is because he "can not" be unworthy of his past.

Thus we choose our past in the light of a certain end, but from then on it imposes itself upon us and devours us. This is not because this past has an existence *by itself* different from that which we have to be but simply because: (1) it is the presently revealed materialization of the end which we are; (2) it appears in the midst of the world for us and for others, is never alone but sinks into the universal past and thereby offers itself to the evaluation of others. Just as the geometrician is free to create a particular figure which pleases him but can not conceive of one which does not immediately enter into an infinity of relations with the infinity of other possible figures, so our free choice of ourselves by causing the upsurge of a certain evaluative order of our past, causes the appearance of an infinity of relations of this past to the world and to the Other. And this infinity of relations is presented to us as an *infinity of conducts to be adopted* since it is in the future that we evaluate our past. We are *compelled* to adopt these conducts in so far as our past appears within the compass of our essential project. To will this project, in fact, is to will this past; and to will this past is to will to realize it by a thousand secondary behaviors. Logically the requirements of the past are hypothetical imperatives: "If you wish to have such and such a past, act in such and such a way." But as the first term is a concrete and categorical choice, the imperative also is transformed into a categorical imperative.

But since the force of compulsion in my past is borrowed from my free, reflecting choice and from the very power which this choice has given itself, it is impossible to determine *a priori* the compelling power of a past. It is not only its content and the order of this content which my free choice decides; it is also the adherence of my past to my present. If within a fundamental perspective which we do not yet have to determine, one of my principal projects is to *progress*—i.e., to be always at any cost a little further advanced along a certain path than I was yesterday or an hour earlier, this progressive project involves in relation to my past a series of "uprootings." The past—which now from the height of my progress I regard with a slightly scornful pity—is that which is strictly a *passive object* for moral evaluation and judgment. "How stupid I was then!" or "How wicked I was!" It exists only because I can dissociate myself from it. I no longer enter into it, nor do I any longer wish to enter into it. This is not, of course, because it ceases to exist, but it exists only as *that self which I no longer am*—i.e., that being which I have to *be as the self which I am no longer*. Its function is to be what I have chosen of myself in order to oppose myself to it, that which enables me to measure myself. Such a for-itself chooses itself therefore without solidarity with itself, which means not that it abolishes its past but that it posits its past so as not to be associated with it, exactly so as to affirm its total freedom (that which is past is a certain kind of engagement with respect to the past and a certain kind of tradition). On the other hand, there are other for-itselfs whose project implies the rejection of time and a narrow solidarity with the past. In their desire to find a solid ground these latter have, by contrast, chosen the past as that which they *are*, everything else being only an indefinite and unworthy flight from tradition. They have chosen *at the start* the refusal of flight; that is, *the refusal to refuse*. The past consequently has the function of requiring of them a fidelity. Thus we shall see that the former persons admit scornfully and easily to a mistake which they have made whereas the very admission will be impossible for the others without their deliberately changing their fundamental project; the latter will then employ all the bad faith in the world and all the subterfuges which they can invent in order to avoid breaking that faith in "what is" which constitutes an essential structure of their project.

Thus like place, the past is integrated with the situation when the for-itself by its choice of the future confers on its past facticity a value, an hierarchical order, and an urgency in terms of which this facticity *motivates* the act and conduct of the for-itself.

## C. My environment

My "environment" must not be confused with the place which I occupy and which we have already discussed. My environment is made up of the instrumental-things which surround me, including their peculiar coefficients of adversity and utility. Of course in occupying my place, I prepare the ground for the revelation of my environment, and by changing place—an operation, which, *as* we have seen, I freely realize—I provide the basis for the appearance of a new environment. But on the other hand the environment can change or be changed by others without my having any hand in the change. To be sure, Bergson has shown in *Matter and Memory* that a single modification of my place involves the total change of my environment while it would be necessary to imagine a total and simultaneous modification of all my environment in order to be able to speak of a modification of my place.

Now this global change of the environment is inconceivable, but the fact remains that my field of action is perpetually traversed by the appearances and disappearances of objects with which I have nothing to do. In a general way the coefficient of adversity and utility of complexes does not depend solely on my place, but on the particular potentiality of the instruments. Thus as soon as I exist I am thrown into the midst of existences different from me which develop their potentialities around me, for and against me. For example, I wish to arrive on my bicycle as quickly as possible at the next town. This project involves my personal ends, the appreciation of my place and of the distance from my place to the town, and the free adaptation of means (efforts) to the end pursued. But I have a flat tire, the sun is too hot, the wind is blowing against me, *etc.*, all phenomena which I had not foreseen: these are the environment. Of course they manifest themselves in and through my principal project; it is through the project that the wind can appear as a head wind or as a "good" wind, through the project that the sun is revealed as a propitious or an inconvenient warmth. The synthetic organization of these perpetual "accidents" constitutes the unity of what the Germans call my *Umwelt*, and this *Umwelt* can be revealed only within the limits of a free project—i.e., of the choice of the ends which I am.

If our description stopped here, however, it would be much too simple. If it is true that each object in my surroundings is made known in a situation already revealed and that the sum of these objects can not by itself alone constitute a situation, if it is true that each instrument is raised on the ground of a situation in the world, still the fact remains that the abrupt transformation or the abrupt appearance of another instrument can contribute to a radical change in the situation. Let my tire be punctured, and my distance from the next town suddenly changes; now it is a distance to be counted by steps and not by the revolutions of the wheels. From this fact I can acquire the certainty that the person whom I wish to see will have already taken the train when I arrive at his house, and this certainty can involve other decisions on my part (a return to my point of departure, the sending of a telegram, *etc.*) It is even possible, for example, that sure of not being able to conclude a projected deal with this person, I may return to some one else and sign another contract. Perhaps I shall even give up the whole attempt. And shall I count my project as a total failure? In this case I shall say that I *was not able* to inform Pierre in time, to come to an understanding with him, *etc.* Is not this explicit recognition of my *powerlessness* the clearest admission of the limits of my freedom? Of course my freedom *to choose*, as we have seen, must not be confused with my freedom *to obtain*. But is it not my very choice which is here brought into play since the adversity of the environment is in many cases precisely the occasion for the changing of my project?

Before attacking the fundamental question at issue here, it will be well for us to make the question precise and to delimit it. If the changes which occur in my environment can involve modifications of my projects, they must be subject to two reservations. First, they can not by themselves effect the abandoning of my principal project which, on the contrary, serves to measure their importance. In fact, if they are grasped as the *causes* of my abandoning this or that project, it can be only in the light of a more fundamental project; otherwise they could not be causes since the cause is apprehended by the motivating-consciousness which is itself a free choice of an end. If the clouds which cover the sky can move me to give up my project of an outing, this is because they are grasped in a free projection in which the value of the outing is bound to a certain state of the sky, which step by step refers back to the value of an outing in general, to my relation to nature, and to the place which this relation occupies in the ensemble of relations which I sustain with the world. Secondly, under no circumstances can the object which has appeared or disappeared *induce* even a partial renunciation of a project. This object must of necessity be apprehended as a *lack* in the original situation; it is necessary therefore that the *given* of its appearance or of its disappearance be nihilated, that I effect a withdrawal "in relation to it," and consequently that I myself determine myself in its presence. We have already shown that even the red hot pincers of the torturer do not exempt us from being free. This does not mean that it is always *possible* to get around the difficulty, to repair the damage, but simply that the *very impossibility* of continuing in a certain direction must be freely constituted. This impossibility comes to things by means of our free renunciation; our renunciation is not induced by the impossibility of maintaining the behavior.

Once this fact has been established, we must recognize that the presence of the given here again, far from being an obstacle to our freedom, is demanded by the very existence of freedom. This freedom is a certain freedom which I am. But what am I if not a certain internal negation of the in-itself? Without this in-itself which I deny, I should vanish into nothingness. In our Introduction we pointed out that consciousness can serve as the "ontological proof" of the existence of an in-itself. In fact, if there is consciousness of something, then it is necessary at the start that this "something" have a *real* being—that is, a being *not relative to consciousness.* But we see at present that this proof has a larger bearing: if I am to be able to *do* something—anything—it is necessary that I exercise my action upon beings whose existence is in general *independent* of my existence and in particular independent of my action. My action can *reveal* this other existence to me but does not condition it. To be free is to-be-free-to-change. Freedom implies therefore the existence of an environment to be changed: obstacles to be cleared, tools to be used. Of course it is freedom which reveals them as obstacles, but by its free choice it can only interpret the *meaning* of their being. It is necessary that they be simply there, wholly brute, in order that there may be freedom. To be free is to-be-free-to-do, and it is to-be-free-in-the-world. But if this is the case, then freedom by recognizing itself as the freedom to change, recognizes and implicitly foresees in its original project the independent existence of the given on which it is exercised. The internal negation reveals the in-itself as independent, and it is this independence which constitutes in the in-itself its character as a thing. But consequently what freedom posits by the simple upsurge of its being is the fact that it is as having to do with something other than itself. To do is precisely to change what has no need of something other than itself in order to exist; it is to act on that which on principle is indifferent to the action, that which can pursue its existence or its becoming without the action. Without this indifference of exteriority on the part of the in-itself, the very notion of doing would lose its meaning (as we have shown earlier in connection with wish and decision), and consequently freedom itself would collapse. Thus the very project of a freedom in general is a choice which implies the anticipation and acceptance of some kind of resistance somewhere. Not only does freedom constitute the compass within which in-itselfs otherwise indifferent will be revealed as resistances, but freedom's very project is in general to do in a resisting world by means of a victory over the world's resistances.

Every free project in projecting itself anticipates a margin of unpredictability due to the independence of things precisely because this independence is that in terms of which a freedom is constituted. As soon as I project going to the nearby village to find Pierre, the punctures, the "headwind," a thousand foreseeable and unforeseeable accidents are given in my very project and constitute its meaning. Thus the unexpected puncture which upsets my projects comes to take its place in a world pre-outlined by my choice, for I have never ceased, if I may say so, to expect it as unexpected. And even if my path has been interrupted by something which I should never have dreamed of—like a flood or a landslide—in a certain sense this unpredictability was foreseen. Just as the Romans reserved in their temple a place for unknown gods, so in my project a certain margin of indetermination was created "for the unpredictable," and this was done not because of experience with "hard blows" or an empirical prudence but by the very nature of my project. Thus in a certain way, we can say that human reality is surprised by nothing.

These observations allow us to bring to light a new characteristic of a free choice: every project of freedom is an open project and not a closed project. Although entirely individualized, it contains within it the possibility of its further modifications. Every project implies in its structure the comprehension of the Selbständigkeit of the things in the world. This perpetual foreseeing of the unforeseeable as the margin of indetermination of the project which I am enables us to understand how it is that an accident or a catastrophe, instead of surprising me by its unknown or its extraordinary quality, always overwhelms me by a certain quality which it has of "being already seen—already foreseen," by its very obviousness and a kind of fatalistic necessity, which we express by saying, "This was bound to happen." There is nothing which astonishes in the world, nothing which surprises us without our determining ourselves to be surprised. The original theme of astonishment is not that this or that particular thing exists within the limits of the world but rather that there is a world in general; that is, that I am thrown among a totality of existents thoroughly indifferent to me. This is because in choosing an end, I choose to have relations with these existents and because these existents have relations among themselves. I choose that they should enter into combination to make known to me what I am. Thus the adversity of which things bear witness to me is pre-outlined by my freedom as one of its conditions, and it is on a freely projected meaning of adversity in general that this or that complex can manifest its individual coefficient of adversity.

But whenever there is a question of the situation it is necessary to insist on the fact that the state of things described has a reverse side. Here also if freedom pre-outlines adversity in general, then this is one way of sanctioning the exteriority and indifference of the in-itself. Of course adversity comes to things through freedom, but this is in so far as freedom illuminates its facticity as "being-in-the-midst-of-an-in-itself-of-indifference." Freedom gives itself things as adverse (i.e., it confers on them a meaning which makes them things), but it is by assuming the very given which will be meaningful; that is, freedom assumes its exile in the midst of an indifferent in-itself in order to surpass this exile. Conversely, furthermore, the contingent given which is assumed can support even this primary meaning which is the support of all others, this "exile in the midst of indifference" only in and through a free assumption of the for-itself.

Such, in fact, is the primitive structure of the situation; it appears here in all its clarity. It is by its very surpassing of the given toward its ends that freedom causes the given to exist as *this* given *here* (previously there was neither *this* nor *that* nor *here*) and the given thus *designated* is not formed in any way whatsoever; it is a brute existent, assumed in order to be surpassed. But at the same time that freedom is a surpassing of *this given*, it chooses itself as *this* surpassing of the given. Freedom is not just any kind of surpassing of any kind of given. By assuming the brute given and by conferring meaning on it, freedom has suddenly chosen itself; its end is exactly *to change this given*, just as the given appears as this given in the light of the end chosen. Thus the upsurge of freedom is the crystallization of an end *across a given* and the revelation of a given *in the light of* an end; these two structures are simultaneous and inseparable. We shall see later in fact that the universal values of the chosen ends are disengaged only by analysis; every choice is the choice of a concrete change to be bestowed on a concrete given. Every situation is concrete.

Thus the adversity of things and their potentialities in general are illuminated by the end chosen. But there is an end only for a for-itself which assumes itself as abandoned in the midst of indifference. By this assumption it brings *nothing* new into this contingent, brute abandonment except for a *meaning*. It is responsible for the fact that henceforth *there is* an abandonment, that this abandonment is revealed as a situation.

We have seen in Part II, chapter IV, that the for-itself by its upsurge causes the in-itself to come into the world; still more generally, it is by means of nothingness that "there is" the in-itself—that is, things. We have seen also that the reality-in-itself is there at hand, with its *qualities*, without any distortion or adjunction. We are simply separated from it by the various types of nihilation which we instate by our very upsurge: world, space and time, potentialities. We have seen in particular that although we are surrounded by *presences* (this glass, this inkwell, this table, *etc.*), these presences are inapprehensible as such, for they release whatever it may be of them only after a gesture or an act projected by us—that is, in the future. At present we are able to understand the meaning of this state of things: We are separated from things by nothing *except by our freedom*; it is our freedom which is responsible for the fact that *there are* things with all their indifference, their unpredictability, and their adversity, and for the fact that we are inevitably separated from them; for it is on the ground of nihilation that they appear and that they are revealed as bound one to another. Thus the project of my freedom adds *nothing* to things: it causes *there to be* things; that is, precisely, realities provided with a coefficient of adversity and utilizable instrumentality. Freedom makes these things reveal themselves in *experience*—that is, raise themselves successively on the ground of the world in the course of a process of temporalization. Finally our freedom causes these things to manifest themselves as out of reach, independent, separated from me by the very nothingness which I secrete and which I am. It is because freedom is condemned to be free—i.e., can not choose itself as freedom—that there are things; that is, a plenitude of contingency at the heart of which it is itself contingency. It is by the assumption of this contingency and by its surpassing that there can be at once a *choice* and an organization of things in *situation*; and it is the contingency of freedom and the contingency of the in-itself which are expressed in *situation* by the unpredictability and the adversity of the environment. Thus I am absolutely free and absolutely responsible for my situation. But I am never free except in *situation*.

## D. My neighbor

To live in a world haunted by my neighbor is not only to be able to encounter the Other at every turn of the road; it is also to find myself engaged in a world in which instrumental-complexes can have a meaning which my free project has not first given to them. It means also that in the midst of this world *already* provided with meaning I meet with a meaning which is *mine* and which I have not given to myself, which I discover that I "possess already." Thus when we ask what the original and contingent fact of existing in a world in which "there are" also Others can mean for our situation, the problem thus formulated demands that we study successively three layers of reality which come into play so as to constitute my concrete situation: instruments which are *already* meaningful (a station, a railroad sign, a work of art, a mobilization notice), the meaning which I discover as *already mine* (my nationality, my race, my physical appearance), and finally the Other as a center of reference to which these meanings refer.

Everything would be very simple if I belonged to a world whose meanings were revealed simply in the light of my own ends. In this case I would dispose of things as instruments or as instrumental complexes within the limits of my own choice of myself; it is this choice which would make of the mountain an obstacle difficult to overcome or a spot from which to get a good view of the landscape, *etc*; the problem would not be posed of knowing what meaning this mountain could have *in itself* since I would be the one by whom meanings come to reality in itself. The problem would again be very much simplified if I were a monad without doors or windows and if I merely knew in some way or other that other monads existed or were possible, each of them conferring new meanings on the things which I see. In this case, which is the one to which philosophers have too often limited themselves in their inquiry, it would be sufficient for me to hold other meanings as *possible*, and finally the plurality of meanings corresponding to the plurality of consciousnesses would coincide very simply for me with the possibility always open to me of making *another choice* of myself. But we have seen that this monadic conception conceals a hidden solipsism precisely because it is going to confuse the plurality of meanings which I can attach to the real and the plurality of meaningful systems each one of which refers to a consciousness which I am not. Moreover on the level of concrete experience this monadic description is revealed as inadequate. There exists, in fact, something in "my" world other than a plurality of possible meanings; there exist objective meanings which are given to me as not having been brought to light by me. I, by whom meanings come to things, I find myself engaged in an *already meaningful* world which reflects to me meanings which I have not put into it.

One may recall, for example, the innumerable host of meanings which are independent of my choice and which I discover if I live in a city: streets, houses, shops, streetcars and buses, directing signs, warning sounds, music on the radio, etc. In solitude, of course, I should discover the brute and unpredictable existence—this rock, for example—and I should limit myself, in short, to making there be a rock; that is, that there should be this existent here and outside of it nothing. Nevertheless I should confer on it its meaning as "to be climbed," "to be avoided," "to be contemplated," etc. When there where the street curves, I discover a building, it is not only a brute existent which I reveal in the world; I do not only cause there to be a "this" qualified in this or that way; but the meaning of the object which is revealed then resists me and remains independent of me. I discover that the property is an apartment house, or a group of offices belonging to the Gas Company, or a prison, etc. The meaning here is contingent, independent of my choice; it is presented with the same indifference as the reality of the in-itself; it is made a thing and is not distinguished from the quality of the in-itself. Similarly the coefficient of adversity in things is revealed to me before being experienced by me. Hosts of notices put me on my guard: "Reduce Speed. Dangerous curve," "Slow. School," "Danger," "Narrow Bridge 100 feet ahead," etc. But these meanings while deeply imprinted on things and sharing in their indifferent exterior-ity—at least in appearance—are nonetheless indications for a conduct to be adopted, and they directly concern me. I shall cross the street in the lanes indicated. I shall go into this particular shop to buy this particular instru-ment, and a page with directions for using it is given to buyers. Later I shall use this instrument, a pen, for example, to fill out this or that printed form under determined conditions.

Am I not going to find in all this strict limits to my freedom? If I do not follow point by point the directions furnished by others, I shall lose my bearings, I shall take the wrong street, I shall miss my train, etc. Moreover these notices are most often imperatives: "Enter here," "Go out here." Such is the meaning of the words "Entrance" and "Exit" painted over doorways. I obey. They come to add to the coefficient of adversity which I cause to be born in things, a strictly human coefficient of adversity. Furthermore if I submit to this organization, I depend on it. The benefits which it provides me can cease; come civil disturbance, a war, and it is always the items of prime necessity which become scarce without my having any hand in it. I am dispossessed, arrested in my projects, deprived of what is necessary in order for me to accomplish my ends. In particular we have observed that directions, instructions, orders, prohibitions, billboards are addressed to me in so far as I am just anybody; to the extent that I obey them, that I fall into line, I submit to the goals of a human reality which is just anybody and I realize them by just any techniques. I am therefore modified in my own being since I am the ends which I have chosen and the techniques which realize them—to any ends whatsoever, to *any* techniques whatsoever, any human reality whatsoever. At the same time since the world never appears except through the techniques which I use, the world—it also—is modified. This world, seen through the use which I make of the bicycle, the automobile, the train in order that I may traverse the world, reveals to me a countenance strictly correlative with the means which I employ; therefore it is *the countenance which the world offers to everybody*. Evidently it must follow, someone will say, that my freedom escapes me on every side; there is no longer a *situation* as the organization of a meaningful world around the free choice of my spontaneity; there is a *state* which is imposed upon me. It is this problem which we must now examine.

There is no doubt that my belonging to an inhabited world has the value of a *fact*. It refers to the original fact of the Other's presence in the world, a fact which, as we have seen, can not be deduced from the ontological structure of the for-itself. And although this fact only makes our facticity more deep-rooted, it does not evolve from our facticity in so far as the latter expresses the necessity of the contingency of the for-itself. Rather we must say: the for-itself *exists in fact*; that is, its existence can not be identical with a reality engendered in conformity to a law, nor can it be identical with a free choice. And among the factual characteristics of this "facticity"—i.e., among those which can neither be deduced nor proven but which simply "let themselves be seen"—there is one of these which we call the existence-in-the-world-in-the-presence-of-others. Whether this factual characteristic does or does not need to be recovered by my freedom in order to be efficacious in any manner whatsoever is what we shall discuss a little later. Yet the fact remains that on the level of techniques of appropriating the world, the very *fact* of the Other's existence results in the fact of the collective ownership of techniques. Therefore facticity is expressed on this level by the fact of my appearance in a world which is revealed to me only by collective and already constituted techniques which aim at making me apprehend the world in a form whose meaning has been defined outside of me. These techniques are going to determine my belonging to collectivities: to the *human species*, to the national collectivity, to the professional and to the family group.

It is even necessary to underscore this fact further: outside of my being-for-others—of which we shall speak later—the only positive way which I have *to exist my factual belonging* to these collectivities is the use which I constantly make of the techniques which arise from them. Belonging to the *human species* is defined by the use of very elementary and very general techniques: to know how to walk, to know how to take hold, to know how to pass judgment on the surface and the relative size of perceived objects, to know how to speak, to know how in general to distinguish the true from the false, *etc.* But we do not possess these techniques in this abstract and universal form: to know how to speak is not to know how to pronounce and understand words in general; it is to know how to speak a certain language and by it to manifest one's belonging to humanity on the level of the national collectivity. Moreover to know how to speak a language is not to have an abstract and pure knowledge of the language as it is defined by academic dictionaries and grammars; it is to make the language one's own across the peculiar changes and emphasis brought in by one's province, profession, and family. Thus it can be said that the *reality* of our belonging to the human is our *nationality* and that the reality of our nationality is our belonging to the family, to the region, to the profession, *etc.* in the sense that the *reality* of speech is language and that the reality of language is dialect, slang, jargon, *etc.* And conversely the *truth* of the dialect is the language, the *truth* of the language is speech. This means that the concrete techniques by which we manifest our belonging to the family and to the locality refer us to more abstract and more general structures which constitute its meaning and essence; these refer to others still more general until we arrive at the universal and perfectly simple essence of any technique whatsoever by which any being whatsoever appropriates the world.

Thus to be French, for example, is only the truth of being a Savoyard. But to be a Savoyard is not simply to inhabit the high valleys of Savoy; it is, among a thousand other things, to ski in the winters, to use the ski as a mode of transportation. And precisely, it is to ski according to the French method, not that of Arlberg or of Norway.[14] But since the mountain and the snowy slopes are apprehended only through a technique, this is precisely to discover the *French* meaning of ski slopes. In fact according to whether one will employ the Norwegian method, which is better for gentle slopes, or the French method which is better for steep slopes, the same slope will appear as steeper or more gentle exactly as an upgrade will appear as more or less steep to the bicyclist according to whether he will "put himself into neutral or low gear." Thus the French skier employs a French "gear" to descend the ski fields, and this "gear" reveals to him a particular type of slope wherever he may be. This is to say that the Swiss or Bavarian Alps, the Telemark, or the Jura will always offer to him a meaning, difficulties, an instrumental complex, or a complex of adversity which are purely French. Similarly it would be easy to show that the majority of attempts to define the working class amount to taking as a criterion production, consumption or a certain type of *Weltanschauung* springing out of an inferiority complex (Marx-Halbwachs-de Man); that is, in all cases certain techniques for the elaboration or the appropriation of the world across which there is offered what we shall be able to call the "proletarian

---

[14] This is a simplification: There are influences and interferences in the matter of technique; the Arlberg method has been prevalent with us for a long time. The reader will easily be able to re-establish the facts in their complexity.

BEING AND DOING: FREEDOM **535**

countenance" with its violent oppositions, its great uniform and desert masses, its zones of shadow and its shores of light, the simple and urgent ends which illuminate it.

Now it is evident that although my belonging to a particular class or nation does not derive from my facticity as an ontological structure of my for-itself, my factual existence—i.e., my birth and my place—involves my apprehension of the world and of myself through certain techniques. Now these techniques which I have not chosen confer on the world its meanings. It appears that it is no longer I who decide in terms of my ends whether the world appears to me with the simple, well-marked oppositions of the "proletarian" universe or with the innumerable interwoven nuances of the "bourgeois" world. I am not only thrown face to face with the brute existent. I am thrown into a worker's world, a French world, a world of Lorraine or the South, which offers me its meanings without my having done anything to disclose them.

Let us look more closely. We showed earlier that my nationality is only the truth of my belonging to a province, to a family, to a professional group. But must we stop there? If the language is only the truth of the dialect, is the dialect absolutely concrete reality? Is the professional jargon as "they" speak it, or the Alsatian dialect as a linguistic and statistical study enables us to determine its laws—is this the primary phenomenon, the one which finds its foundation in pure fact, in original contingency? Linguistic research can be mistaken here; statistics bring to light constants, phonetic or semantic changes of a given type; they allow us to reconstruct the evolution of a phoneme or a morpheme in a given period so that it appears that the *word* or the *syntactical* rule is an individual reality with its meaning and its history. And in fact individuals seem to have little influence over the evolution of language. Social facts such as invasions, great thoroughfares, commercial relations seem to be the essential causes of linguistic changes. But this is because the question is not placed on the true level of the concrete. Also we find only what we are looking for.

For a long time psychologists have observed that the *word* is not the concrete element of speech—not even the word of the dialect or the word of the family with its particular variation; the elementary structure of speech is the *sentence*. It is within the sentence, in fact, that the word can receive a real function of designation; outside of the sentence the word is just a propositional function—when it is not a pure and simple rubric designed to group absolutely disparate meanings. Only when it appears in discourse, does it assume a "holophrastic" character, as has often been pointed out. This does not mean that the word can be limited by itself to a precise meaning but that it is integrated in a context as a secondary form in a primary form. The word therefore has only a purely *virtual* existence outside of complex and active organizations which integrate it. It can not exist "in" a consciousness or an unconscious *before* the use which is made of it: the sentence is not *made out of words*. But we need not be content with this. Paulhan has shown in *Fleurs de Tarbes* that entire sentences, "commonplaces," do not, any more than words, pre-exist the use which is made of them. They are mere commonplaces if they are looked at from the outside by a reader who recomposes the paragraph by passing from one sentence to the next, but they lose their banal and conventional character if they are placed within the point of view of the author who saw *the thing to be expressed* and who attended to the most pressing things first by producing an act of designation or re-creation without slowing down to consider the very elements of this act. If this is true, then neither the words nor the syntax, nor the "readymade sentences" pre-exist the use which made of them. Since the verbal unity is the meaningful sentence, the latter is a constructive act which is conceived only by a transcendence which surpasses and nihilates the given toward an end. To understand the word in the light of the sentence is *very exactly* to understand any given whatsoever in terms of the situation and to understand the situation in the light of the original ends.

To understand a sentence spoken by my companion is, in fact, to understand what he is trying to say—that is, to espouse his movement of transcendence, to throw myself with him toward possibles, toward ends, and to return again to the ensemble of organized means so as to understand them by their function and their end. The spoken language, moreover, is always interpreted in terms of the situation. References to the weather, to time, to place, to the environment, to the situation of the city, of the province, of the country are given before the talking. It is enough for me to have read the papers and to have *seen* Pierre's healthy appearance and anxious expression in order for me to understand the "Things aren't so good" with which he greets me this morning. It is not his health which "is not so good" since he has a rosy complexion, nor is it his business nor his household; it is the situation of our city or of our country. I *knew it already*. In asking him, "How goes it?", I was already outlining an interpretation of his reply; I transported myself already to the four corners of the horizon, ready to *return* from there to Pierre in order to understand him. To listen to speech is to "speak with," not simply because we imitate in order to interpret, but because we originally project ourselves toward the possibles and because we must understand *in terms of the world*.

But if the sentence pre-exists the word, then we are referred to the *speaker* as the concrete foundation of speech. A word can indeed seem to have a "life" of its own if one comes upon it in sentences of various epochs. This borrowed life resembles that of an object in a film fantasy; for example, a knife which by itself starts slicing a pear. It is effected by the juxtaposition of instantaneities; it is cinematographic and is constituted in universal time. But if words appear to live when one projects a semantic or morphological film, they are not going to constitute whole sentences; they are only the tracks of the passage of sentences as highways are only the tracks of the passage of pilgrims or caravans. The sentence is a project which can be interpreted only in terms of the nihilation of a given (the very one which one wishes to *designate*) in terms of a posited end (its *designation* which itself supposes other ends in relation to which it is only a means). If the given can not determine the sentence any more than the word can, if on the contrary the sentence is necessary to illuminate the given and to make the word understandable, then the sentence is a moment of the free choice of myself, and it is as such that it is understood by my companion. If a language is the reality of speech, if a dialect or jargon is the reality of a language, then the reality of the dialect is the *free act* of designation by which I choose myself as *designating*. And this free act can not be an *assembling* of words. To be sure, if it were a pure assembling or words in conformity with technical prescriptions (grammatical laws), we could speak of factual limits imposed on the freedom of the speaker; these limits would be marked by the material and phonetic nature of the words, the vocabulary of the language employed, the personal vocabulary of the speaker (the n words which he has at his command), the "spirit of the language," etc., *etc.* But we have just shown that such is not the case. It has been maintained recently that there is a sort of living order of words, of the dynamic laws of speech, an impersonal life of the logos—in short that speech is a Nature and that to some extent man must obey it in order to make use of it as he does with Nature.[15] But this is because people in considering speech frequently will take speech that is *dead* (i.e., already spoken) and infuse into it an impersonal life and force, affinities and repulsions all of which in fact have been borrowed from the personal freedom of the for-itself which spoke. People have made of speech a *language which speaks all by itself.* This is an error which should not be made with regard to speech or any other technique. If we are to make man arise in the midst of techniques which are applied all by themselves, of a language which speaks itself, of a science which constructs itself, of a city which builds itself according to its own laws, if meanings are fixed in in-itself while we preserve a human transcendence, then the role of man will be reduced to that of a pilot employing the determined forces of winds, waves, and tides in order to direct a ship. But gradually each technique in order to be directed toward human ends will require another technique; for example, to direct a boat, it is necessary to speak. Thus we shall perhaps arrive at the technique of techniques—which in turn will be applied by

[15] Brice Parain: *Essai sur le logos platonicien.*

itself—but we shall have lost forever the possibility of meeting the technician.

If on the other hand, it is by speaking that we cause words to exist, we do not thereby suppress the *necessary technical* connections or the connections in *fact* which are articulated inside the sentence. Better yet, we *found* this necessity. But in order for it to appear, in order for words to enter into relations with one another, in order for them to latch on to one another or repulse one another, it is necessary that they be united in a synthesis which does not come from them. Suppress this synthetic unity and the block which is called "speech" disintegrates; each word returns to its solitude and at the same time loses its unity, being parcelled out among various incommunicable meanings. Thus it is within the free project of the sentence that the laws of speech are organized; it is by speaking that I make grammar. Freedom is the only possible foundation of the laws of language.

Furthermore, *for whom* do the laws of language exist? Paulhan has given the essential answer: they are not for the one who speaks, they are for the one who listens. The person who speaks is only the choice of a *meaning* and apprehends the order of the words only in so far as he *makes* it.[16] The only relations which he will grasp within this organized complex are specifically those which he has established. Consequently if we discover that two (or several) words hold between them not one but several defined relations and that there results from this a multiplicity of meanings which are arranged in an hierarchy or opposed to each other—all for one and the same sentence—if, in short, we discover the "Devil's share," this can be only under the two following conditions: (1) The words must have been assembled and presented by a meaningful rapprochement; (2) this synthesis must be seen *from outside*—i.e., by *The Other* and in the course of a hypothetical deciphering of the possible meanings of this rapprochement. In this case, in fact, each word grasped first as a cross-roads of meanings is bound to another word similarly apprehended. And the rapprochement will be multivocal. The apprehension of the *true* meaning (i.e., the one expressly willed by the speaker) will be able to put other meanings in the shade or subordinate them, but it will not suppress them. Thus speech, which is a free project *for me*, has specific laws for *others*. And these laws themselves can come into play only within an original synthesis.

Thus we can grasp the clear distinction between the event "sentence" and a natural event. The natural fact is produced in conformity to a law which it

---

[16] I am simplifying: one can also learn one's own thought from one's sentence. But this is because it is possible to a certain extent to adopt with respect to the sentence the point of view of the Other—exactly as in the case of one's own body.

manifests but which is a purely external rule of production of which the considered fact is only one example. The "sentence" as an event contains within itself the law of its organization, and it is inside the free project of *designating* that legal (i.e., grammatical) relations can arise between the words. In fact, there can be no laws of speaking before one speaks. And each utterance is a free project of designation issuing from the choice of a personal for-itself and destined to be interpreted in terms of the global situation of this for-itself. What is primary is the situation in terms of which I understand the *meaning* of the sentence; this meaning is not in itself to be considered as a given but rather as an end chosen in a free surpassing of means. Such is the only *reality* which the working linguist can encounter. From the standpoint of this reality a regressive analytical work will be able to bring to light certain more general and more simple structures which are like legal schemata. But these schemata which would function as laws of dialect, for example, are in themselves abstract. Far from presiding over the constitution of the sentence and being the mould into which it flows, they exist only in and through this sentence. In this sense the sentence appears as a free invention of its own laws. We find here simply the original characteristic of every situation; it is by its very surpassing of the given as such (the linguistic apparatus) that the free project of the sentence causes the given to appear *as this* given (these laws of word order and dialectal pronunciation). But the free project of the sentence is precisely a scheme to assume *this given*; it is not just any assumption but is aimed at a not yet existing end across existing means on which it confers their exact meaning as a means.

Thus the sentence is the order of words which become *these words* only by means of their very order. This is indeed what linguists and psychologists have perceived, and their embarrassment can be of use to us here as a counter-proof; they believed that they discovered a circle in the formulation of speaking, for in order to speak it is necessary to know one's thought. But how can we know this thought as a reality made explicit and fixed in concepts except precisely by speaking it? Thus speech refers to thought and thought to speech. But we understand now that there is no circle or rather that this circle—from which linguists and psychologists believed they could escape by the invention of pure psychological idols such as the verbal image or an imageless, wordless thought—is not unique with speech; it is the characteristic of the situation in general. It means nothing else but the ekstatic connection of the present, the future, and the past—that is, the free determination of the existent by the not-yet-existing and the determination of the non-yet-existing by the existent. Once we have established this fact, it will be permissible to uncover abstract operational schemata which will stand as the legal truth of the sentence: the dialectal schema—the schema of the national language—the linguistic schema in general. But these schemata far from pre-existing the concrete sentence are in themselves affected with Unselb-ständigkeit and exist always only incarnated and sustained in their very incarnation by a freedom.

It must be understood, of course, that speech is here only the example of one social and universal technique. The same would be true for any other technique. It is the blow of the axe which reveals the axe, it is the hammering which reveals the hammer. It will be permissible in a particular run to reveal the French method of skiing and in this method the general skill of skiing as a human possibility. But this human skill is never anything by itself alone; it does not exist *potentially*; it is incarnated and manifested in the *actual* and concrete skill of the skier. This enables us to outline tentatively a solution for the relations of the individual to the species. Without the human species, there is no truth; that is certain. There would remain only an irrational and contingent swarming of individual choices to which no law could be assigned. If some sort of truth exists capable of unifying the individual choices, it is the human species which can furnish this truth for us. But if the species is the truth of the individual, it can not be a *given* in the individual without profound contradiction. As the laws of speech are sustained by and incarnated in the concrete free project of the sentence, so the human species (as an ensemble of peculiar techniques to define the activity of men) far from pre-existing an individual who would manifest it in the way that this particular fall exemplifies the law of falling bodies, is the ensemble of abstract relations sustained by the free individual choice. The for-itself in order to choose itself *as a person* effects the existence of an internal organization which the for-itself surpasses toward itself, and this internal technical organization is in it the national or the human.

Very well, someone will say. But you have dodged the question. For these linguistic organizations or techniques have not been created by the for-itself so that it may find itself; it has got them from others. The rule for the agreement of participles does not exist, I admit, outside of the free rapprochement of concrete participles in view of an end with a particular designation. But when I employ this rule, I have learned it from others; it is because others in their personal projects cause it to be that I make use of it myself. My speech is then subordinated to the speech of others and ultimately to the national speech.

We should not think of denying this fact. For that matter our problem is not to show that the for-itself is the free foundation of its being; the for-itself is free but in *condition*, and it is the relation of this condition to freedom that we are trying to define by making clear the meaning of the situation. What we have just established, in fact, is only a part of reality. We have shown that the existence of meanings which do not emanate from the for-itself can not constitute an external limit of its freedom. As a for-itself one is not man first in order to be oneself subsequently and one does not constitute oneself as oneself in terms of a human essence given *a priori*. Quite the contrary, it is in its effort to choose itself as a personal self that the for-itself sustains in existence certain social and abstract characteristics which make of it a man (or a woman); and the necessary connections which accompany the essential elements of man appear only on the foundation of a free choice; in this sense each for-itself is responsible in its being for the existence of a human race. But it is necessary for us again to stress the undeniable fact that the for-itself can choose itself only beyond certain meanings of which it is not the origin. Each for-itself, in fact, is a for-itself only by choosing itself beyond nationality and race just as it speaks only by choosing the designation beyond the syntax and morphemes. This "beyond" is enough to assure its total independence in relation to the structures which it surpasses; but the fact remains that it constitutes itself as *beyond* in relation to *these* particular structures. What does this mean? It means that the for-itself arises in a world which is a world for other for-itselfs. Such is the *given*. And thereby, as we have seen, the meaning of the world is *alien* to the for-itself. This means simply that each man finds himself in the presence of *meanings* which do not come into the world through him. He arises in a world which is given to him as *already looked-at*, furrowed, explored, worked over in all its meanings, and whose very contexture is already defined by these investigations. In the very act by which he unfolds his time, he temporalizes himself in a world whose temporal meaning is already defined by other temporalizations: this is the fact of simultaneity. We are not dealing here with a limit of freedom; rather it is in *this world* that the for-itself must be free; that is, it must choose itself by taking into account these circumstances and not *ad libitum*. But on the other hand, the for-itself— i.e., man—in rising up *does not merely suffer* the Other's existence; he is compelled to make the Other's existence manifest to himself in the form of a choice. For it is by a choice that he will apprehend the Other as The-Other-as-subject or as The-Other-as-object.[17] Inasmuch as the Other is for him the Other-as-a-look, there can be no question of *techniques* or of foreign meanings; the for-itself experiences itself as an object in the Universe beneath the Other's look. But as soon as the for-itself by surpassing the Other toward its ends makes of him a transcendence-transcended, that which was a free surpassing of the given toward ends appears to it as meaningful, given conduct in the world (fixed in in-itself). The Other-as-object becomes an *indicator of ends* and by its own free project, the For-itself throws itself into a world in which conducts-as-objects designate ends. Thus the Other's presence as a transcended transcendence reveals *given* complexes of means to ends. And as

---

[17] We shall see later that the problem is more complex. But these remarks are sufficient for the present.

the end decides the means and the means the end by its upsurge in the face of the Other-as-object, the For-itself causes ends in the world to be indicated to itself; it comes into a world peopled by ends. But if consequently the techniques and their ends arise in the look of the For-itself, we must necessarily recognize that it is by means of the free assumption of a position by the For-itself confronting the Other that they become *techniques*. The Other by himself alone can not cause these projects to be revealed to the For-itself as techniques; and due to this fact there *exists for the Other* in so far as he transcends himself toward his possibles, *no technique* but a concrete *doing* which is defined in terms of his individual end. The shoe-repairer who puts a new sole on a shoe does not experience himself as "in the process of applying a technique;" he apprehends the situation as demanding this or that action, that particular piece of leather, as requiring a hammer, *etc.* The For-itself as soon as it assumes a position with respect to the Other, causes techniques to arise in the world as the conduct of the Other *as a transcendence-transcended*. It is at this moment and at this moment only that there appear in the world—bourgeois and workers, French and Germans, in short, men.

Thus the For-itself is responsible for the fact that the Other's conduct is revealed in the world as techniques. The for-itself can not cause the world in which it arises to be furrowed by this or that particular technique (it can not make itself appear in a world which is "capitalistic" or "governed by a natural economy" or in a "parasitic civilization"), but it causes that which is lived by the Other as a free project to exist *outside* as technique; the for-itself achieves this precisely by making itself the one by whom an outside comes to the Other. Thus it is by choosing itself and by historicizing itself in the world that the For-itself historicizes the world itself and causes it to be *dated* by its techniques. Henceforth, precisely because the techniques appear as objects, the For-itself can choose to appropriate them. By arising in a world in which Pierre and Paul speak in a certain way, stick to the right when driving a bicycle or a car, *etc.*, and by constituting these free patterns of conduct into meaningful objects, the For-itself is responsible for the fact that there is a world in which they stick to the right, in which they speak French, etc. It causes the internal laws of the Other's act, which were originally founded and sustained by a freedom engaged in a project, to become now objective rules of the conduct-as-object; and these rules become universally valid for all analogous conduct, while the supporter of the conduct or the agent-as-object becomes simply *anybody*. This historization, which is the effect of the for-itself's free choice, in no way restricts its freedom; quite the contrary, it is in this world and no other that its freedom comes into play; it is in connection with its existence in this world that it puts itself into question. For to be free is not to choose the historic world in which one arises—which would have no meaning—but to choose oneself in the world whatever this may be.

In this sense it would be absurd to suppose that a certain *state* of techniques is restrictive to human possibilities. Of course a contemporary of Duns Scotus is ignorant of the use of the automobile or the airplane; but he appears as ignorant *to us* and only from our point of view because we privately apprehend him in terms of a world where the automobile and the airplane exist. For him, who has no relation of any kind with these objects and the techniques which refer to them, there exists a kind of absolute, unthinkable, and undecipherable nothingness. Such a nothingness *can in no way limit* the For-itself which is choosing itself; it can not be apprehended as a lack, no matter how we consider it. The For-itself which historicizes itself in the time of Duns Scotus therefore nihilates itself in the heart of a fullness of being—that is, of a world which like ours is *everything which it can be*. It would be absurd to declare that the Albigenses lacked heavy artillery to use in resisting Simon de Montfort; for the Seigneur de Trencavel or the Comte de Toulouse chose themselves such as they were in a world in which artillery had no place: they conceived politics in that world; they made plans for military resistance in that world; they chose themselves as sympathizers with the Cathari *in that world*; and as they were only what they chose to be, they were *absolutely* in a world as absolutely full as that of the Panzer-divisionen or of the R.A.F.

What is true for material techniques applies as well to more subtle techniques. The fact of existing as a petty noble in Languedoc at the time of Raymond VI is not *determining* if it is placed in the feudal world in which this lord exists and in which he chooses himself. It appears as privative only if we commit the error of considering this divison of *Francia* and of the Midi from the actual point of view of French unity. The feudal world offered to the vassal lord of Raymond VI infinite possibilities of choice; we do not possess more. A question just as absurd is often posited in a kind of utopian dream: what would Descartes have been if he had known of contemporary physics? This is to suppose that Descartes possesses an *a priori* nature more or less limited and altered by the state of science in his time and that we could transport this brute nature to the contemporary period in which it would react to more extensive and more exact knowledge. But this is to forget that Descartes is what he has chosen to be, that he is an absolute choice of himself from the standpoint of a world of various kinds of knowledge and of techniques which this choice both assumes and illuminates. Descartes is an absolute upsurge at an absolute date and is perfectly unthinkable at another date, for he has made his date by making himself. It is he and not another who has determined the exact state of the mathematical knowledge immediately before him, not by an empty inventory which would be made from no point of view and would be related to no axis of coordination, but by establishing the principles of analytical geometry—that is, by inventing precisely the axis of coordinates which would permit us to define the state of this knowledge.

Here again it is free invention and the future which enable us to illuminate the present; it is the perfecting of the technique in view of an end which enables us to evaluate the state of the technique.

Thus when the For-itself affirms itself in the face of the Other-as-object, by the same stroke it reveals *techniques*. Consequently it can appropriate them—that is, *interiorize* them. But suddenly there are the following consequences: (1) By employing a technique, the For-itself surpasses the technique toward its own end; it is always beyond the technique which it employs. (2) The technique which was originally a pure, meaningful conduct fixed in some Other-as-object, now, because it is interiorized, loses its character as a technique and is integrated purely and simply in the free surpassing of the given toward ends; it is recovered and sustained by the freedom which founds it exactly as dialect or speech is sustained by the free project of the sentence. Feudalism as a technical relation between man and man does not exist; it is only a pure abstract, sustained and surpassed by the thousands of individual projects of a particular man who is a liege in relation to his lord. By this we by no means intend to arrive at a sort of historical nominalism. We do not mean that feudalism is the sum of the relations of vassals and suzerains. On the contrary, we hold that it is the abstract structure of these relations; every project of a man of this time must be realized as a surpassing toward the concrete of this abstract moment. It is therefore not necessary to generalize in terms of numerous detailed experiences in order to establish the principles of the feudal technique; this technique exists necessarily and completely in each individual conduct, and it can be brought to light in each case. But it is there only to be surpassed. In the same way the For-itself can not be a person—i.e., choose the ends which it is—without being a man or woman, a member of a national collectivity, of a class, of family, *etc*. But these are abstract structures which the For-itself sustains and surpasses by its project. It makes itself French, a man of a southern province, a workman to order to be *itself* at the horizon of these determinations. Similarly the world which is revealed to the For-itself appears as provided with certain meanings correlative with the techniques adopted. It appears as a world-for-the-Frenchman, a world-for-the-worker, *etc*., with all the characteristics which would be expected. But these characteristics do not possess *Selbständigkeit*. The world which allows itself to be revealed as French, proletarian, *etc*., is before all else a world which is illuminated by the For-itself's own ends, its own world.

Nevertheless the Other's existence brings a factual limit to my freedom. This is because of the fact that by means of the upsurge of the Other there appear certain determinations which I *am* without having chosen them. Here I am—Jew, or Aryan, handsome or ugly, one-armed, etc. All this I am *for the Other* with no hope of apprehending this meaning which I have *outside* and, still more important, with no hope of changing it. Speech alone will inform me of what I am; again this will never be except as the object of an empty intention; any intuition of it is forever denied me. If my race or my physical appearance were only an image in the Other or the Other's opinion of me, we should soon have done with it; but we have seen that we are dealing with objective characteristics which define me in my being-for-others. As soon as a freedom other than mine arises confronting me, I begin to exist in a new dimension of being; and this time it is not a question of my conferring a meaning on brute existents or of accepting responsibility on my own account for the meaning which Others have conferred on certain objects. It is I myself who see a meaning conferred upon me, and I do not have the recourse of accepting the responsibility for this meaning which I have since it can not be given to me except in the form of an empty indication. Thus something of myself—according to this new dimension—exists in the manner of the *given*; at least *for me*, since this being which I am *is suffered*, it *is* without *being existed*. I learn of it and suffer it in and through the relations which I enter into with others, in and through their conduct with regard to me. I encounter this being at the origin of a thousand prohibitions and a thousand resistances which I bump up against at each instant: Because I am a *minor* I shall not have this or that privilege. Because I *am a Jew* I shall be deprived—in certain societies—of certain possibilities, *etc.* Yet I am unable in *any way* to feel myself as a Jew or as a minor or as a Pariah. It is at this point that I can react against these interdictions by declaring that race, for example, is purely and simply a collective fiction, that only individuals exist. Thus here I suddenly encounter the total alienation of my person: I am something which I have not chosen to be. What is going to be the result of this for the situation?

We must recognize that we have just encountered a real limit to our freedom—that is, a way of being which is imposed on us without our freedom being its foundation. Still it is necessary to understand this: the limit imposed does not come from the *action* of others. In a preceding chapter we observed that even torture does not dispossess us of our freedom; when we give in, we do so *freely*. In a more general way the encounter with a prohibition in my path ("No Jews allowed here," or "Jewish restaurant. No Aryans allowed," etc.) refers us to the case considered earlier (collective techniques), and this prohibition can have meaning only on and through the foundation of my free choice. In fact according to the free possibilities which I choose, I can disobey the prohibition, pay no attention to it, or, on the contrary, confer upon it a coercive value which it can hold only because of the weight which I attach to it. Of course the prohibition fully retains its character as an "emanation from an alien will;" of course it has for its specific structure the fact of *taking me for an object* and thereby manifesting a transcendence which transcends me. Still the fact remains that it is not incarnated in my universe, and it loses its peculiar force of compulsion only within the limits of my own choice and according to whether under any circumstances I prefer life to death or whether, on the contrary, I judge that in certain particular cases death is preferable to certain kinds of life, etc. The true limit of my freedom lies purely and simply in the very fact that an Other apprehends me as the Other-as-object and in that second corollary fact that my situation ceases for the Other to be a situation and becomes an objective form in which I exist as an objective structure. It is this alienating process of making an object of my situation which is the constant and specific limit of my situation, just as the making an object of my being-for-itself in being-for-others is the limit of my being. And it is precisely these two characteristic limits which represent the boundaries of my freedom.

In short, by the fact of the Other's existence, I exist in a situation which *has an outside* and which due to this very fact has a dimension of alienation which I can in no way remove from the situation any more than I can act directly upon it. This limit to my freedom is, as we see, posited by the Other's pure and simple existence—that is, by the *fact* that my transcendence exists for a transcendence. Thus we grasp a truth of great importance: we saw earlier, keeping ourselves within the compass of existence-for-itself, that only my freedom can limit my freedom; we see now, when we include the Other's existence in our considerations, that my freedom on this new level finds its limits also in the existence of the Other's freedom. Thus on whatever level we place ourselves, the only limits which a freedom can encounter are found in freedom. Just as thought according to Spinoza can be limited only by thought, so freedom can be limited only by freedom. Its limitation as internal finitude stems from the *fact* that it can not not-be freedom—that is, it is condemned to be free; its limitation as external finitude stems from the *fact* that being freedom, it *is* for other freedoms, freedoms which freely apprehend it in the light of their own ends.

Once this is posited, we must observe first that this alienation of the situation does not represent an inner flaw nor the introduction of the given as a brute resistance in the situation such as I live it. Quite the contrary, the alienation is neither an inner modification nor a partial change of the situation; it does not appear in the course of the temporalization; I never encounter it in the situation, and it is consequently never released to my intuition. But on principle it escapes me; it is the very exteriority of the situation—that is, its being-outside-for-others. Therefore we have to do with an essential characteristic of all situation in general; this characteristic can not act upon its content, but it is accepted and recovered by the same being who *puts himself into a situation*. Thus the very meaning of our free choice is to cause a situation to arise which expresses this choice, a situation the essential characteristic of which is to be *alienated; that is,* to exist as a form in itself for the Other. We can not escape this alienation since it would be absurd even to think of existing otherwise than in situation. This characteristic is not manifested by an internal resistance; on the contrary, one makes proof of it in and through its very inapprehensibility. It is therefore ultimately not an head-on obstacle which freedom encounters but a sort of centrifugal force in the very nature of freedom, a weakness in the basic "stuff" of freedom which causes everything which it undertakes to have always one face which freedom will not have chosen, which escapes it and which for the Other will be pure existence. A freedom which would will itself freedom could by the same token will only this character. Yet this character does not belong to the *nature* of freedom; for there is here no nature; moreover if there were one, this characteristic could not be deduced from it since Others' existence is an entirely contingent fact. To come into the world as a freedom confronting Others is to come into the world as alienable. If to will oneself free is to choose to be in this world confronting Others, then the one who wills himself such must will also the *passion* of his freedom.

Besides, I do not objectively disclose and establish the alienated situation and my own being-alienated. In the first place, indeed, we have just seen that on principle everything which is alienated exists only for *the Other*. But in addition a pure establishment, even if it were possible, would be insufficient. In fact I can not *make proof* of this alienation without by the same stroke *recognizing* the Other as a transcendence. And this recognition, as we have seen, would have no meaning if it were not a *free* recognition of the Other's freedom. By this free recognition of the Other across the proof which I make of my alienation, I *assume* my being-for-others, whatever it may be, and I assume it precisely because it is my link with the Other. Thus I can apprehend the Other as a freedom only within the free project of apprehending him as such (in fact it always remains possible for me to apprehend the Other freely as an object); and the free project of the *recognition* of the Other is not distinct from the free assumption of my being-for-others.

Now then we can see how my freedom in a way recovers its own limits, for I can grasp myself as limited by the Other only in so far as the Other exists for me, and I can make the Other exist for me only as a subjectivity recognized by my assuming my being-for-others. There is no circle here. By the free assumption of this being-alienated which I experience, I suddenly make the Other's transcendence exist for me as such. It is only by my recognizing the *freedom* of anti-Semites (whatever use they may make of it) and by my assuming this *being-a-Jew* that I am a Jew for them; it is only thus that being-a-Jew will appear as the external objective limit of the situation. If, on the contrary, it pleases me to consider the anti-Semites as pure *objects*, then my being-a-Jew disappears immediately to give place to the simple consciousness (of) being a free, unqualifiable transcendence. To recognize others and, if I am a Jew, to assume my being-a-Jew are one and the same. Thus the Other's freedom confers limits on my situation, but I can *experience* these limits only if I recover this being-for-others which I am and if I give to it a meaning in the light of the ends which I have chosen. Of course, this very assumption is *alienated*; it has its outside, but it is through this assumption that I can experience my being-outside as outside.

How then shall I experience the objective limits of my being: Jew, Aryan, ugly, handsome, king, a civil servant, an untouchable, *etc.*—when will language have informed me as to which of these are my limits? It can not be in the way in which I intuitively *apprehend* the Other's beauty, ugliness, race, nor in the way if which I have a non-thetic consciousness (of) projecting myself toward this or that possibility. It is not that these objective characteristics must necessarily be *abstract*; some are abstract, others not. My beauty or my ugliness or the insignificance of my features are apprehended by the Other in their full concreteness, and it is this concreteness which the Other's speech will indicate to me; it is toward this that I shall emptily direct myself. Therefore we are not dealing with an abstraction but with an ensemble of structures, of which certain are abstract but whose totality is an absolute concrete, an ensemble which simply is indicated to me as on principle escaping me. This ensemble is in fact what I *am*. Now we observed at the beginning of Part Two that the for-itself can not *be* anything. For-myself I am not a professor or a waiter in a café, nor am I handsome or ugly, Jew or Aryan, witty, vulgar, or distinguished. We shall call these characteristics *unrealizables*. We must be careful not to confuse them with the *imaginaries*. We have to do with perfectly real existences; but those for which these characteristics are really *given are not* these characteristics, and I who *am* them can not realize them. If I am told that I am *vulgar*, for example, I have often grasped by intuition as regards others the nature of vulgarity; thus I can apply the word "vulgar" to my person. But I can not join the meaning of this word to my person. There is here exactly the indication of a connection to be effected but one which could be made only by an interiorization and a subjectivizing of the vulgarity or by the objectivizing of the *person*—two operations which involve the immediate collapse of the reality in question.

Thus we are surrounded by an infinity of *unrealizables*. Certain among these unrealizables we feel vividly as irritating absences. Who has not felt a profound disappointment at not being able after his return from a long exile to *realize* that he "*is in Paris.*" The objects are there and offer themselves familiarly, but I am only an absence, only the pure nothingness which is necessary in order that there may be a Paris. My friends, my relatives offer the image of a promised land when they say to me: "At last you are here! You have returned! You are in Paris!" But access to this promised land is wholly denied me. And if the majority of people deserve the reproach of "applying a double standard" according to whether they are considering others or themselves, if when

they perceive that they are guilty of a fault which they had blamed in someone else the day before, they have a tendency to say, "That's not the same
thing," this is because in fact "it is not the same thing." The one action is a
given object of moral evaluation; the other is a pure transcendence which
carries its justification in its very existence since its being is a choice. We shall
be able to convince its agent by a comparison of the *results* that the two acts
have a strictly identical "outside", but the best will in the world will not allow
him to *realize* this identity. Here is the source of a good part of the troubles of
the moral consciousness, in particular despair at not being able truly to con-
temn oneself, at not being able to realize oneself as guilty, at feeling perpetually a gap between the expressed meaning of the words: "I *am* guilty, I have
sinned," *etc.*, and the real apprehension of the situation. In short this is the
origin of all the anguish of a "bad conscience,"[18] that is, the consciousness of
bad faith which has for its ideal a self-judgment—i.e., taking toward oneself
the point of view of the Other.

But if some particular kinds of *unrealizables* have impressed us more than
others, if they have become the object of psychological descriptions, they
must not blind us to the fact that unrealizables are infinite in number since
they represent the reverse side of the situation.

These unrealizables, however, are not only appresented to us as unrealizables; in fact in order that they may have the character of unrealizables, they
must be revealed in the light of some project aiming at realizing them. This is
indeed what we noted earlier when we were showing how the for-itself
*assumes* its being-for-others in and by the very act which *recognizes* the existence
of others. Correlatively therefore with this assuming project, the unrealizables
are revealed as *to be realized*. At first, indeed, the assumption is made in the
perspective of my fundamental project. I do not limit myself to receiving
passively the meaning "ugliness," "infirmity," "race," *etc.*, but, on the contrary, I can grasp these characteristics—in the simple capacity of a meaning—only in the light of my own ends. This is what is expressed—but by
completely reversing the terms—when it is said that the fact of being of a
certain race can *determine* a reaction of pride or an inferiority complex. In
actual fact the race, the infirmity, the ugliness can *appear* only within the limits
of my own choice of inferiority or of pride;[19] in other words, they can appear
only with a meaning which my freedom confers on them. This means once
again that they *are* for the Other but that they can be for me only if I *choose*
them. The law of my freedom which makes me unable to be without choosing

---

[18] There is no distinction in French between "conscience" and "consciousness," both of which
are expressed by the word *conscience*. This is, I believe, the only passage in *Being and Nothingness* in
which Sartre intends to emphasize the idea of a "conscience" (English sense), which, of course,
has no place in his philosophy. Tr.

[19] Or of any other choice of my ends.

myself applies here too: I do not choose to be for the Other what I am, but I can try to be for myself what I am for the Other, by choosing myself such as I appear to the Other—i.e., by an elective assumption. A Jew is not a Jew first in order to be *subsequently* ashamed or proud; it is his pride of being a Jew, his shame, or his indifference which will reveal to him his being-a-Jew; and this being-a-Jew is nothing outside the free manner of adopting it. Although I have at my disposal an infinity of ways of assuming my being-for-others, *I am not able not to assume it.* We find here again that condemnation to freedom which we defined above as *facticity.* I can neither abstain totally in relation to what I am (for the Other)—for to refuse is not to abstain but still to assume—nor can I submit to it passively (which in a sense amounts to the same thing). Whether in fury, hate, pride, shame, disheartened refusal or joyous demand, it is necessary for me to choose to be what I am.

Thus the unrealizables are revealed to the for-itself as "unrealizables-to-be-realized." They do not thereby lose their character as limits; quite the contrary, it is as objective and external limits that they are presented to the for-itself as *to be interiorized.* They have therefore a character which is distinctly *obligatory.* In fact we are not dealing with an instrument revealing itself as "to be employed" in the movement of the free project which I am. Here the unrealizable appears as an *a priori* limit given to my situation (since I am such for the Other) and hence as an existent which does not wait for me to give it existence; but also it appears as able to exist only in and through the free project by which I shall assume it—the assumption evidently being identical with the synthetic organization of all the conduct aimed at *realizing* the unrealizable *for me.* At the same time since it is given in the capacity of an unrealizable, it is manifested as beyond all the attempts which I can make to realize it. The unrealizable is an *a priori* which requires my engagement in order to be, while depending only on this engagement and while placing itself at the start beyond any attempt to realize it. What then is this if not precisely an *imperative?* It is indeed *to be interiorized* (that is, it comes from the outside as does *every fact*) but the *order*, whatever it may be, is defined always as an exteriority recovered in interiority. If an order is to be order—and not a *flatus vocis* or a pure factual given which one merely seeks to change—it is necessary that I reassume it with my freedom, that I make of it a structure of my free projects. But if the order is to be *order* and not a free movement toward my own ends, it must necessarily preserve at the very heart of my free choice its character as *exteriority.* It is the exteriority which remains exteriority even in and through the attempt on the part of the For-itself to interiorize it. This is precisely the definition of the *unrealizable to be realized*; that is why it is given as an imperative.

But we can go further in the description of this unrealizable; it is in fact my limit. But precisely because it is my limit it can not exist as the limit of a given being but only as the limit of my freedom. This means that my freedom by freely choosing itself chooses its limits; or, if you prefer, the free choice of my ends (i.e., of what I am for myself) includes the assumption of the limits of this choice, whatever they may be. Here again the choice is a choice of finitude as we indicated earlier, but whereas the chosen finitude is an inner finitude—i.e., the determination of freedom by itself—the finitude assumed by the recovery of unrealizables is an external finitude. I choose to have a being at a distance, which limits all my choices and constitutes their reverse side; that is, I choose that my choice be limited by something other than itself. If I should grow angry over it and attempt in every way to recover these limits, as we saw in the preceding section of this work, even the most energetic of these attempts at recovery must of necessity have its foundation in the free recovery *as limits* of the limits which one wishes to interiorize. Thus freedom is fully responsible and makes the unrealizable limits enter into the situation by choosing to be a freedom limited by the Other's freedom. Consequently the external limits of the situation become a *situation-limit* —that is, they are incorporated in the interior of the situation with the characteristic "unrealizable" as "unrealizables to be realized." As a chosen and fugitive reverse side of my choice, they become a meaning of my desperate effort to *be* although they are situated *a priori* beyond this effort exactly as death—another type of unrealizable which we do not have to consider for the moment— becomes a situation-limit on condition that it be taken as an *event of life* even though it points toward a world where my presence and my life are no longer realized—i.e., toward what is beyond life.

The fact that *there is* a beyond for life, a beyond which derives its meaning only through and in my life and which yet remains for me an unrealizable, and the fact that there is a freedom beyond my freedom, a situation beyond my situation and one for which what I live as a situation is given as an objective form in the midst of the world: here are two types of situation-limit which have the paradoxical character of limiting my freedom on every side and yet not having any other meaning than that which my freedom confers on them. For class, for race, for the body, for the Other, for function, *etc.*, there is a "being-free-for ———." By it the For-itself projects itself towards one of its possibles which is always its *ultimate possible*, for the envisaged possibility is a possibility of *seeing itself*; that is, of being another than itself in order to see itself from outside. In one case as in the other there is a projection of self towards an "ultimate" which thereby interiorized becomes a thematic out-of-reach meaning of hierarchized possibles. One can "be-in-order-to-be-French," "be-in-order-to-be-a-worker," the son of a king can "be-in-order-to-reign." We are dealing here with limits and negating *states* of our being which we have to assume in the sense in which, for example, the Zionist Jew resolutely assumes himself within his race—that is, assumes concretely and once and for all the permanent *alienation* of his being; in the same way the revolutionary worker by his very revolutionary project assumes a "being-in-order-to-be-a-worker." And we shall note as Heidegger did (although the expressions "authentic" and "unauthentic" which he employs are dubious and insincere because of their implicit moral content) that the attitude of refusal and of flight which remains always possible is despite itself the free assumption of what it is fleeing. Thus the bourgeois makes himself a bourgeois by denying that there are any classes, just as the worker makes himself a worker by asserting that classes exist and by realizing through his revolutionary activity his "being-in-a-class." But these external limits of freedom, precisely because they are external and are interiorized only as unrealizables, will never be either a *real* obstacle for freedom or a limit suffered. Freedom is total and infinite, which does not mean that it has no limits but that it *never encounters them*. The only limits which freedom bumps up against at each moment are those which it imposes on itself and of which we have spoken in connection with the past, with the environment, and with techniques.

## E. My death

After death had appeared to us as pre-eminently non-human since it was what there was on the other side of the "wall," some people decided suddenly to consider it from a wholly different point of view—that is, as an event of human life. This change is easily explained: death is a *boundary*, and every boundary (whether it be final or initial) is a *Janus bifrons*. Whether it is thought of as adhering to the nothingness of being which limits the process considered or whether on the contrary it is revealed as agglutinated to the series which it terminates, in either case it is a being which belongs to an existent process and which in a certain way constitutes the meaning of the process. Thus the final chord of a melody always looks on the one side toward silence—that is, toward the nothingness of sound which will follow the melody; in one sense it is made with the silence since the silence which will follow is already present in the resolved chord as its meaning. But on the other side it adheres to this *plenum* of being which is the melody intended; without the chord this melody would remain in the air, and this final indecision would flow back from note to note to confer on each of them the quality of being unfinished.

Death has always been—rightly or wrongly is what we can not yet determine—considered as the final boundary of human life. As such it was natural that a philosophy which was primarily concerned to make precise the human position in relation to the non-human which surrounded it, would first consider death as a door opening upon the nothingness of human-reality, and that this nothingness would be the absolute cessation of being or else existence in a non-human form. Thus we may say that there has been—in correlation with the great realist theories—a realistic conception of death such that death appeared as an immediate contact with the non-human. Thus death escaped man at the same time that it rounded him off with the non-human absolute. It was not possible, of course, for an idealist and humanistic conception of the real to tolerate the idea that man would encounter the non-human even as his limit. It would then have sufficed in fact, to adopt the point of view of this limit in order to illuminate man with a non-human light.[20] The idealist attempt to *recover* death was not originally the fact of philosophers but that of poets like Rilke or novelists like Malraux. It was sufficient to consider death as the final term *belonging to the series*. If the series thus recovers its *terminus ad quem*, then precisely because of this *ad* which indicates its interiority, death as the end of life is interiorized and humanized. Man can no longer encounter anything but the human; there is no longer any *other side* of life, and death is a human phenomenon; it is the final phenomenon of life and is still life. As such it influences the entire life by a reverse flow. Life is limited by life; it becomes like the world of Einstein, "finite but unlimited." Death becomes the meaning of life as the resolved chord is the meaning of the melody. There is nothing miraculous in this; it is one term in the series under consideration, and, as one knows, each term of a series is always present in all the terms of the series.

But death thus recovered does not remain simply human; it becomes *mine*. By being interiorized it is individualized. Death is no longer the great unknowable which limits the human; it is the phenomenon of my personal life which makes of this life a unique life—that is, a life which does not begin again, a life in which one never recovers his stroke. Hence I become responsible for my death as for my life. Not for the empirical and contingent phenomenon of my decease but for this character of finitude which causes my life like my death to be my life. It is in this sense that Rilke attempts to show that the end of each man resembles his life because all his individual life has been a preparation for this end. In this sense Malraux in *Les Conquérants* shows that European culture by giving to certain Asiatics the meaning of their death suddenly penetrates them with this despairing and intoxicating truth that "life is unique." It was left to Heidegger to give a philosophical form to this humanization of death. In fact if the *Dasein* actually *suffers nothing* precisely because it is a project and an anticipation, then it must be an anticipation and a project of its own death as the possibility of no longer realizing presence in the world. Thus death has become the peculiar possibility of the *Dasein*, the being of human-reality is defined as *Sein zum Tode*. Inasmuch as the *Dasein*

---

[20] See, for example, the realistic Platonism of Morgan in *Sparkenbroke*.

determines its project toward death, it realizes freedom-to-die and constitutes itself as a totality by its free choice of finitude.

It appears at first that we can not but be attracted to such a theory: by interiorizing death, it serves our own ends; this apparent limit of our freedom by being interiorized is recovered by freedom. Yet neither the advantage of these views nor the undeniable portion of truth which they include should mislead us. It is necessary to take the question up again from the beginning.

It is certain that human-reality, by whom the quality of being a world comes to the real, can not encounter the non-human; the very concept of the non-human is man's concept. Therefore even if in-itself death were a passage to an absolute non-human, we should still have to abandon any hope of considering it as a window giving out upon that absolute. Death reveals to us only ourselves and that from a human point of view. Does this mean that death belongs a priori to human reality?

What must be noted first is the absurd character of death. In this sense every attempt to consider it as a resolved chord at the end of a melody must be sternly rejected. It has often been said that we are in the situation of a condemned man among other condemned men who is ignorant of the day of his execution but who sees each day that his fellow prisoners are being executed. This is not wholly exact. We ought rather to compare ourselves to a man condemned to death who is bravely preparing himself for the ultimate penalty, who is doing everything possible to make a good showing on the scaffold, and who meanwhile is carried off by a flu epidemic. This is what Christian wisdom understands when it recommends preparing oneself for death as if it could come at any hour. Thus one hopes to recover it by metamorphosing it into an expected death. If the meaning of our life becomes the expectation of death, then when death occurs, it can only put its seal upon life. This is basically the most positive content of Heidegger's "resolute decision" (Entschlossenheit).

Unfortunately this advice is easier to give than to follow, not because of a natural weakness in human-reality or because of an original project of unauthenticity, but because of death itself. One can, in fact, expect a particular death but not death. The sleight of hand introduced by Heidegger is easy enough to detect. He begins by individualizing the death of each one of us, by pointing out to us that it is the death of a person, of an individual, the "only thing which nobody can do for me." Then this incomparable individuality which he has conferred upon death in terms of the Dasein, he uses to individualize the Dasein itself; it is by projecting itself freely towards its final possibility that the Dasein will attain authentic existence and wrench itself away from everyday banality in order to attain the irreplaceable uniqueness of the person. But there is a circle here. How indeed can one prove that death has this individuality and the power of conferring it? Of course, if death is described as my death, I can await it; it is a possibility which is characterized and distinct. But is the death which will overtake me *my* death? In the first place it is perfectly gratuitous to say that "to die is the only thing which nobody can do for me." Or rather there is here an evident bad faith in the reasoning; if one considers death as the ultimate subjective possibility, the event which concerns only the for-itself, then it is evident that nobody can die for me. But then it follows that none of my possibilities taken from this point of view—which is that of the *cogito*—whether taken in authentic existence or unauthentic—can be projected by anyone other than me. Nobody can love for me—if we mean by that to make vows which are my vows, to experience the emotions (however commonplace they may be) which are my emotions. And the *my* here has nothing to do with a personality won by overcoming everyday banality (which would allow Heidegger to retort that it is very necessary that I be "free to die," in order that a love which I experience should be *my* love and not the love in me of the "they"); it refers simply to that selfness which Heidegger expressly recognizes in every *Dasein*—whether it exists in the authentic or unauthentic mode—when he declares that "Dasein ist je meines." Thus from this point of view the most commonplace love is, like death, irreplaceable and unique; nobody can love for me.

On the other hand, if my acts in the world are considered from the point of view of their function, their efficacy, and their result, it is certain that the Other can always do what I do. If it is a quesion of making this woman happy, of safeguarding her life or her freedom, of giving her the means of finding her salvation, or simply of realizing a home with her, of "giving her" children, if *that* is what we call loving, then another will be able to love in my place, he will even be able to love for me. This is the actual meaning of those sacrifices recounted thousands of times in sentimental novels which show us the amorous hero longing for the happiness of the woman whom he loves and effacing himself before his rival because the latter "will be able to love better than he." Here the rival is specifically charged to *love for*, for to love is defined simply as "to make happy by the love which is borne to her." And so it will be with all my conduct. In this case, however, my death *also* will fall into this category. If to die is to die in order to inspire, to bear witness, for the country, *etc.*, then anybody at all can die in my place—as in the song in which lots are drawn to see who is to be eaten. In short there is no personalizing virtue which is peculiar to my death. Quite the contrary, it becomes my death only if I place myself already in the perspective of subjectivity; it is my subjectivity defined by the pre-reflective *cogito* which makes of my death a subjective irreplaceable, and not death which would give an irreplaceable selfness to my for-itself. In this case death can not be characterized; for *it is death as my* death, and consequently its essential structure as death is not sufficient to make of it that personalized and qualified event which one can wait for.

Furthermore death can not be awaited unless it is very precisely designated as my condemnation to death (the execution which will take place in eight days, the issue of my illness, which I know to be immanent and ruthless, etc.), for it is nothing but the revelation of the absurdity of every expectation even though it be the expectation of death itself. To begin with, we must carefully distinguish between two meanings of the verb "expect" which are continually confused: to *expect* death is not to *wait* for death.[21] We can "wait for" only a determined event which equally determined processes are in the act of realizing. I can wait for the arrival of the train from Chartres because I know that it has left the station at Chartres and that each turn of the wheels brings it closer to the station at Paris. Of course the train can be late; an accident even can happen. But the fact remains that the process itself by which the entrance into the station will be realized is "underway;" and the phenomena which can delay or prevent this entrance into the station mean here simply that the process is only a relatively closed, relatively isolated system and that it is in fact immersed in a universe with a "fibrous structure," as Meyerson put it. Thus I can say that I am waiting for Pierre and that "I expect that his train is late." But in the same way the possibility of my death means only that I am biologically only a relatively closed, relatively isolated system; it indicates only the fact that my body belongs to the totality of existents. It is of the same type as the probable delay of trains, not of the type of Pierre's arrival. It stands with the unforeseen, *unexpected* impediment which we must always take into account even while it preserves its specific character as unexpected, the impediment which one can not *wait* for because it is itself lost in the undetermined. Indeed even if we admit that the factors are strictly conditioned, which is not even proved and which requires therefore a metaphysical option, still their number is infinite and their implications infinitely infinite; their ensemble does not constitute a system. At least from the point of view considered, the envisioned result— my death—can not be foreseen for any date, and consequently it can not be waited for. Perhaps while I am peacefully writing in this room, the state of the universe is such that my death has approached considerably closer; but perhaps, on the contrary, it has just been considerably removed. For example, if I am waiting for a a mobilization order, I can consider that my death is imminent—i.e., that the chances of an imminent death are considerably increased; but it can happen that at the same moment an international

---

[21] Sartre here is distinguishing between the reflexive and non-reflexive form of the verb *attendre*. I am translating *s'attendre* as "to expect" and *attendre* as "to wait for." As Sartre indicates, the distinction ordinarily is not sharply maintained. Tr.

conference is being held in secret and that it has discovered a way of prolonging the peace.

Thus I can not say that the minute which is passing is bringing death closer to me. It is true that death is coming to me if I consider very broadly that my life is limited. But within these very elastic limits (I can die at the age of a hundred or at thirty-seven, tomorrow) I can not know whether this end is coming closer to me or being removed farther from me. This is because there is a considerable difference in quality between death at the limit of old age and sudden death which annihilates us at the prime of life or in youth. To wait for the former is to accept the fact that life is a limited enterprise; it is one way among others of choosing finitude and electing our ends on the foundation of finitude. To wait for the second would be to wait with the idea that my life is an enterprise which is lacking. If only deaths from old age existed (or deaths by explicit condemnation), then I could wait for my death. But the unique quality of death is the fact that it can always before the end surprise those who wait for it at such and such a date. And while death from old age can be confused with the finitude of our choice and consequently can be lived as the resolved chord of our life (we are given a task and we are given time to accomplish it), sudden death, on the contrary, is such that it can in no way be waited for. Sudden death is undetermined and by definition can not be waited for at any date; it always, in fact, includes the possibility that we shall die in surprise before the awaited date and consequently that our waiting may be, qua waiting, a deception or that we shall survive beyond this date; in the latter case since we were only this waiting, we shall outlive ourselves.

Moreover as the sudden death is qualitatively different from the other only to the extent that we live one or the other biologically (that is, from the point of view of the universe they differ in no way as to their causes and the factors which determine them) the indetermination of the one actually is reflected in the other. This means that one can wait for a death from old age only blindly or in bad faith. We have, in fact, every chance of dying before we have accomplished our task, or, on the other hand, of outliving it. There is therefore a very slim chance that our death will be presented to us as that of Sophocles was, for example, in the manner of a resolved chord. And if it is only chance which decides the character of our death and therefore of our life, then even the death which most resembles the end of a melody can not be waited for as such; luck by determining it for me removes from it any character as an harmonious end. An end of a melody in order to confer its meaning on the melody must emanate from the melody itself. A death like that of Sophocles will therefore resemble a resolved chord but will not be one, just as the group of letters formed by the falling of alphabet blocks will perhaps resemble a word but will not be one. Thus this perpetual appearance of chance at the heart of my projects can not be apprehended as my possibility but, on the contrary, as the nihilation of all my possibilities, a nihilation which *itself is no longer a part of my possibilities.* Thus death is not my possibility of no longer realizing a presence in the world but rather *an always possible nihilation of my possibles which is outside my possibilities.*

This can be expressed in a slightly different way if we approach the problem from the consideration of meanings. Human reality is meaningful, as we know. This means that human reality makes known to itself what it is by means of that which is not, or if you prefer, that it is *to come* to itself. If therefore it is perpetually engaged in its own future, this compels us to say that it waits for the confirmation of this future. As future, in fact, that which is to come is pre-outlined by a present which *will be*; one puts oneself in the hands of this present which alone, by virtue of being present, is to be able to confirm or invalidate the pre-outlined meaning which I am. As this present will be itself a free recovery of the past in the light of a new future, we shall not be able to *determine* it but only to project it and wait for it. The meaning of my actual conduct is the reprimand which I wish to be administered to a particular person who has seriously offended me. But how do I know whether this reprimand will not be transformed into irritated and timid stammerings and whether the meaning of my present conduct will not be transformed *in the past*? Freedom limits freedom; the past derives its meaning from the present. This, as we have shown, explains the paradox that our actual conduct is both totally translucent (the pre-reflective *cogito*) and at the same time totally hidden by a free determination which we must wait for. The adolescent is perfectly conscious of the mystic sense of his conduct, and at the same time he must entrust himself to all his future in order to determine whether he is in the process of "passing through a crisis of puberty" or of engaging himself in earnest in the way of devotion.

Thus our further freedom, inasmuch as it is not our actual possibility but the foundation of possibilities which we are not yet, constitutes as a sort of opacity in full translucency something like what Barrès called "the mystery in broad daylight." Hence this necessity for us *to wait for ourselves.* Our life is only a long waiting: first a waiting for the realization of our ends (to be engaged in an undertaking is to wait for its outcome) and especially a waiting for ourselves (even if this undertaking is realized, even if I am able to make myself loved, to obtain this distinction, this favor, it remains for me to determine the place, the meaning, and the value of this very enterprise in my life). This does not stem from a contingent lack in human "nature," from a nervousness which would prevent us from limiting ourselves to the present and which could be *corrected* by practice, but rather from the very nature of the for-itself which "is" to the extent that it temporalizes itself. Thus it is necessary to consider our life as being made up not only of waitings but of waitings which themselves wait for waitings. There we have the very structure of selfness: to be oneself is to come to oneself. These waitings evidently all include a reference to a final term which would be *waited for* without waiting for anything more. A repose which would be *being* and no longer a waiting for being. The whole series is suspended from this final term which on principle is never *given* and which is the value of our being—that is, evidently, a plenitude of the type "in-itself-for-itself." By means of this final term the recovery of our past would be made once and for all. We should know for always whether a particular youthful experience had been fruitful or ill-starred, whether a particular crisis of puberty was a caprice or a real pre-formation of my later engagements; the curve of our life would be fixed forever. In short, the account would be closed. Christians have tried to take death as this final term. The Reverend Father Boisselot in a private conversation with me gave me to understand that the "Last Judgment" was precisely this closing of the account which renders one unable any longer to recover his stroke and which makes one finally *be* what one *has been*—irremediably.

But there is an error here analogous to that which we pointed out earlier in connection with Leibniz although it is put at the other end of existence. For Leibniz we are free since our acts derive from our essence. Yet the single fact that our essence has not been chosen by us shows that all this freedom in particulars actually covers over a total slavery. God chose Adam's essence. Conversely if it is the closing of the account which gives our life its meaning and its value, then it is of little importance that all the acts of which the web of our life is made have been free; the very meaning of them escapes us if we do not ourselves choose the moment at which the account will be closed. This has been clearly perceived by the free-thinking author of an anecdote echoed in the work of Diderot. Two brothers appeared at the divine tribunal on the Day of Judgment. The first said to God, "Why did you make me die so young?" And God said, "In order to save you. If you had lived longer, you would have committed a crime as your brother did." Then the brother in turn asked, "Why did you make me die so old?" If death is not the free determination of our being, it can not *complete* our life. If one minute more or less may perhaps change everything and if this minute is added to or removed from my account, then even admitting that I am free to use my life, the meaning of my life escapes me. Now the Christian death comes from God. He chooses our hour, and in a general way I know clearly that even if it is I who by temporalizing myself cause there to be minutes and hours in general, still the minute of my death is not fixed by me; the sequences of the universe determine it.

If this is the case, we can no longer even say that death confers a meaning on life from the outside; a meaning can come only from subjectivity. Since death does not appear on the foundation of our freedom, it can only *remove all meaning from life*. If I am a waiting for waitings for waiting and if suddenly the object of my final waiting and the one who awaits it are suppressed, the waiting takes on retrospectively the character of *absurdity*. For example, this young man has lived for thirty years in the expectation of becoming a great writer, but this waiting itself is not enough; it becomes a vain and senseless obstinacy or a profound comprehension of his value according to the books which he writes. His first book has appeared, but by itself what does it mean? It is the book of a beginner. Let us admit that it is good; still it gets its meaning through the future. If it is unique, it is at once inauguration and testament. He had only one book to write; he is limited and cut off by his work; he will not be "a great writer." If the novel is one in a mediocre series, it is an "accident." If it is followed by other better books, it can classify its author in the first rank. But exactly at this point death strikes the author—at the very moment when he was anxiously testing himself to find out "whether he had the stuff" to write another work, at the moment when he was still *expecting* to become a great writer. This is enough to cause everything to fall into the undetermined: I can not say that the dead writer is the author of a *single* book (in the sense that he would have had only one book to write) nor that he would have written several (since in fact only one has appeared). I can say nothing. Suppose that Balzac had died before *Les Chouans*; he would remain the author of some execrable novels of intrigue. But suddenly the very expectation which this young man *was*, this expectation of being a great man, loses any kind of meaning; it is neither an obstinate and egotistical blindness nor the true sense of his own value since nothing shall ever decide it. It would be useless indeed to try to decide it by considering the sacrifices which he made to his art, the obscure and hard life which he was willing to lead; just as many mediocre figures have had the strength to make comparable sacrifices. On the contrary, the final value of this conduct remains forever in suspense; or if you prefer, the ensemble (particular kinds of conduct, expectations, values) falls suddenly into the absurd. Thus death is never that which gives life its meanings; it is, on the contrary, that which on principle removes all meaning from life. If we must die, then our life has no meaning because its problems receive no solution and because the very meaning of the problems remains undetermined.

It would be in vain for us to resort to suicide in order to escape this necessity. Suicide can not be considered as an end of life for which I should be the unique foundation. Since it is an act of my life, indeed, it itself requires a meaning which only the future can give to it; but as it is the *last* act of my life, it is denied this future. Thus it remains totally undetermined. If I escape death, or if I "misfire," shall I not judge later that my suicide was cowardice? Will the outcome not show me that other solutions were possible? But since these solutions can be only my own projects, they can appear only if I live. Suicide is an absurdity which causes my life to be submerged in the absurd.

These remarks, it will be noted, are not derived from the consideration of death but, on the contrary from the consideration of life; this is because the for-itself is the being in whose being being is in question; since the for-itself is the being which always lays claim to an "after," there is no place for death in the being which is for-itself. What then could be the meaning of a waiting for death if it is not the waiting for an undetermined event which would reduce all waiting to the absurd, even including that of death itself. A waiting for death would be self-destructive, for it would be the negation of all waiting. My project toward a particular death is comprehensible (suicide, martyrdom, heroism) but not the project toward my death as the undetermined possibility of no longer realizing a presence in the world, for this project would be the destruction of all projects. Thus death can not be my peculiar possibility; it can not even be one of my possibilities.

Furthermore, death, in so far as it can be revealed to me, is not only the always possible nihilation of my possibles, a nihilation outside my possiblities. It is not only the project which destroys all projects and which destroys itself, the impossible destruction of my expectations. It is also the triumph of the point of view of the Other over the point of view which I am toward myself. This is doubtless what Malraux means when in l'Espoir he says of death that it "transforms life into destiny." Death, in fact, is only on its negative side the nihilation of my possibilities; since indeed I am my possibilities only through the nihilation of being-in-itself which I have to be, death as the nihilation of a nihilation is a positing of my being as in-itself in the sense in which for Hegel the negation of a negation is an affirmation. So long as the for-itself is "in life" it surpasses its past toward its future, and the past is that which the for-itself has to be. When the for-itself "ceases to live," this past is not thereby abolished. The disappearance of the nihilating being does not touch that part of its being which is of the type of the in-itself; it is engulfed in the in-itself. My whole life is. This means not that it is an harmonious totality but that it has ceased to be its own suspense and that it can no longer change itself by the simple consciousness which it has of itself. Quite the contrary, the meaning of any phenomenon whatsoever in that life is henceforth fixed not by itself but by this open totality which is the arrested life. This meaning in the primary and fundamental sense is an *absence of meaning*, as we have seen. But in a secondary and derived sense thousands of shimmering, iridescent relative meanings can come into play upon this fundamental absurdity of a "dead" life.

For example, whatever may have been its ultimate vanity, the fact remains that Sophocles' life was happy, that Balzac's life was prodigiously industrious, etc. Naturally these general qualifications can be made tighter; we can risk a description, an analysis, along with a narration of this life. We shall obtain more distinct characteristics; for example, we shall be able to speak of a particular dead woman in the same way as Mauriac speaks of one of his heroines when he says that she lived in "prudent desperation." We shall be able to grasp the meaning of Pascal's "soul" (i.e., of his inward "life") as "magnificent and bitter" as Nietzsche described it. We can go on to qualify a particular episode as "cowardly" or "tactless" without, however, ever losing sight of the fact that only the contingent arrest of this "being-in-perpetual-suspense" which is the living for-itself allows us on the foundation of a radical absurdity to confer a relative meaning on the episode considered, and that this meaning is an *essentially provisory* meaning, the provisory quality of which has *accidentally passed* into the definitive. But these various explanations of the meaning of Pierre's life—when it was Pierre himself who effected them in his own life—resulted in changing the meaning and the orientation; for every description of one's own life when it is attempted by the for-itself is a project of the self beyond this life. And as the altering project is by the same token bound to life which it alters, it is Pierre's own life which metamorphoses its meaning by continually temporalizing itself. Now that his life is dead, only the *memory of the Other* can prevent Pierre's life from shriveling up in its plenitude in-itself by cutting all its moorings with the present.

The unique characteristic of a dead life is that it is a life of which the Other makes himself the guardian. This does not mean simply that the Other preserves the life of the "deceased" by effecting an explicit, cognitive reconstruction of it. Quite the contrary, such a reconstruction is only one of the possible attitudes of the Other in relation to the dead life; consequently the character of a "reconstructed life" (in the midst of the family through the memories of relatives, in the historic environment) is a particular destiny which is going to mark some lives to the exclusion of others. The necessary result is that the opposite quality "a life fallen into oblivion"—also represents a specific destiny capable of description, one which comes to certain lives again in terms of the Other. To be forgotten is to be made the object of an attitude of another, and of an implicit decision on the part of the Other. To be forgotten is, in fact, to be resolutely apprehended forever as one element dissolved into a mass (the "great feudal lords of the thirteenth century," the "bourgeois Whigs" of the eighteenth century, the Soviet officials," etc.); it is in no way to be *annihilated*, but it is to lose one's personal existence in order to be constituted with others in a collective existence.

This shows us clearly what we hoped to prove: it is that the Other can not be first without any contact with the dead so as to decide *subsequently* (or so that circumstances may decide) that he will have this or that relation with certain particular dead (those whom he has known while they were alive, the "famous dead," *etc.*). In reality the relation with the dead—with *all* the dead—is an essential structure of the fundamental relation which we have called "being-for-others." In its upsurge into being, the for-itself must assume a position in relation to the dead; his initial project organizes them in large anonymous masses or as distinct individualities. And for these collective masses as for these individualities he determines their removal or their absolute proximity; he unfolds temporal distances between them and himself by temporalizing himself just as he unfolds spatial distances in terms of his surroundings. While making himself known to himself through his end he decides the peculiar importance of the extinct collectivities or individualities. A particular group which will be strictly anonymous and amorphous for Pierre will be specific and structured for me; another, purely uniform for me, will for Jean effect the appearance of its component individuals. Byzantium, Rome, Athens, the second Crusade, the Convention, as many immense necropoleis as I can see from near or far, from casual observation or careful scrutiny according to the position which I take, which I "am." It is not impossible (provided one understands this properly) to define a "person" by his dead—i.e., by the areas of individualization or of collectivization which he has determined in the necropolis, by the roads and pathways which he has traced, by the information which he has decided to get for himself, by the "roots" which he has put down there.

Of course the dead choose us, but it is necessary first that we have chosen them. We find here again the original relation which binds facticity to freedom: we choose our own attitude toward the dead, but it is not possible for us not to choose an attitude. Indifference with respect to the dead is a perfectly possible attitude (examples of it will be found among the heimatlos, among certain revolutionaries, or among individualists). But this indifference—which consists of making the dead "die again"—is one conduct among others with respect to them. Thus by its very facticity, the for-itself is thrown into full "responsibility" with respect to the dead; it is obliged to decide freely the fate of the dead. In particular, when it is a question of the dead who surround us, it is not possible for us not to decide—explicitly or implictly—the fate of their enterprises; this is obvious when it is a question of the son who continues his father's business or the disciple who continues the school and the teachings of his master. But although the bond is less clearly visible in a good number of circumstances, it is there also in every case in which the dead and the living belong to the same historical and concrete collectivity. It is I, it is the men of my generation who decide the meaning of the efforts and the enterprises of the preceding generation whether we resume and continue their social and political attempts, or whether we realize a decisive rupture and throw the dead back into inefficacy. As we have seen, it is the America of 1917 which decides the value and the meaning of the deeds of La Fayette.

Thus from this point of view we can see clearly the difference between life and death: life decides its own meaning because it is always in suspense; it possesses essentially a power of self-criticism and self-metamorphosis which causes it to define itself as a "not-yet" or, if you like, makes it be as the changing of what it is. The dead life does not thereby cease to change, and yet it is *all done*. This means that for it the chips are down and that it will henceforth undergo its changes without being in any way responsible for them. For this life it is not a question only of an arbitrary and definitive totalization. In addition there is a radical transformation: nothing more can *happen* to it from the inside; it is entirely closed; nothing more can be made to enter there; but its meaning does not cease to be modified from the outside. Until the death of this apostle of peace the meaning of his enterprises (as folly or as a profound sense of the truth of things, as successful or a failure) was in his own hands. "So long as I am here, there will not be any war." But to the extent that this meaning surpasses the limits of a simple individuality, to the extent that the person makes himself known to himself through an objective situation to be realized (the peace in Europe), death represents a total *dispossession*; it is the Other who *dispossesses* the Apostle of peace of the very meaning of his efforts and therefore of his being, for the Other despite himself and by his very upsurge undertakes to transform into failure or success, into folly or an intuition of genius the very enterprise by which the person made himself known to himself and which he was in his being.

Thus the very existence of *death* alienates us wholly in our own life to the advantage of the Other. To be dead is to be a prey for the living. This means therefore that the one who tries to grasp the meaning of his future death must discover himself as the future prey of others. We have here therefore a case of alienation which we did not consider in the section of this work which we devoted to the For-others. The alienations which we studied there, in fact, were those which we could nihilate by transforming the Other into a transcendence-transcended, just as we could nihilate our *outside* by the absolute and subjective positing of our freedom. So long as I live I can escape what I *am* for the Other by revealing to myself by my freely posited ends that I *am* nothing and that I make myself be what I am; so long as I live, I can give the lie to what others discover in me, by projecting myself already toward other ends and in every instance by revealing that my dimension of being-for-myself is incommensurable with my dimension of being-for-others. Thus ceaselessly I escape my outside and ceaselessly I am reapprehended by the Other; and in this "dubious battle" the definitive victory belongs to neither the one nor the other of these modes of being. But the *fact of death* without being precisely allied to either of the adversaries in this same combat gives the final victory to the point of view of the Other by transferring the combat and the prize to another level—that is, by suddenly suppressing one of the combatants. In this sense to die is to be condemned no matter what ephemeral victory one has won over the Other; even if one has made use of the

Other to "sculpture one's own statue," to die is to exist only through the Other, and to owe to him one's meaning and the very meaning of one's victory.

If we share the realist views which we presented in Part Three, we must recognize that my *existence after death* is not the simple spectral survival "in the Other's consciousness" of simple representations (images, memories, *etc.*) concerning me. My being-for-others is a real being. If it remains in the hands of the Other like a coat which I leave to him after my disappearance, this is by virtue of a real dimension of my being—a dimension which has become my unique dimension—and not in the form of an unsubstantial specter. Richelieu, Louis XV, my grandfather are by no means the simple sum of my memories, nor even the sum of the memories or the pieces of knowledge of all those who have heard of them; they are objective and opaque beings which are reduced to the single dimension of exteriority. In this capacity they will pursue their history in the human world, but they will never be more than transcendences-transcended in the midst of the world. Thus not only does death disarm my waiting by definitively removing the *waiting* and by abandoning in indetermination the realization of the ends which make known to me what I am—but again it confers a meaning from the outside on everything which I live in subjectivity. Death reapprehends all this subjective which while it "lived" defended itself against exteriorization, and death deprives it of all subjective meaning in order to hand it over to any *objective* meaning which the Other is pleased to give to it. Nevertheless it should be noted that this "destiny" thus conferred on *my life* remains also in suspense, in reprieve. The reply to the question, "What will be the definitive historical destiny of Robespierre?" depends on the reply to this preliminary question: "Does history have a meaning?" That is, "Is history completed or *only terminated?*" This question is not resolved. Perhaps it is insolvable since all answers which can be made to it (including the answer of idealism: "The history of Egypt is the history of Egyptology") are themselves historical.

Thus by admitting that my death can be revealed in my life, we see that it can not be a pure arresting of my subjectivity; for such an arresting, since it is an inner event of this subjectivity, could finally be concerned only with the subjectivity. If it is true that dogmatic realism was wrong in viewing death as *the state of death*—i.e., as a transcendent to life—the fact remains that death such that I can discover it as *mine* necessarily engages something other than myself. In fact in so far as it is the always possible nihilation of my possibles, it is outside my possibilities and therefore I can not wait for it; that is, I can not thrust myself toward it as towards one of my possibilities. Death can not therefore belong to the ontological structure of the for-itself. In so far as it is the triumph of the Other over me, it refers to a fact, fundamental to be sure, but totally contingent as we have seen, a fact which is the Other's existence.

We should not know this death if the Other did not exist; it could not be revealed to us, nor could it be constituted as the metamorphosis of our being into a destiny; it would be in fact the simultaneous disappearance of the for-itself and of the world, of the subjective, and of the objective, of the meaning-ful and of all meanings. If death can to a certain extent be revealed to us as the metamorphosis of these particular meanings which are my meanings, it is owing to the fact of the existence of a meaningful Other which guarantees the location of meanings and of signs. It is because of the Other that my death is the fact that as a subjectivity I fall out of the world and it is not the annihilation of both consciousness and the world. There is then an undeni-able and fundamental character of fact—i.e., a radical contingency—in death as in the Other's existence. This contingency at once puts death out of reach of all ontological conjectures. And to contemplate my life by considering it in terms of death would be to contemplate my subjectivity by adopting with regard to it the Other's point of view. We have seen that this is not possible.

Thus we must conclude in opposition to Heidegger that death, far from being my peculiar possibility, is a *contingent fact* which as such on principle escapes me and originally belongs to my facticity. I can neither discover my death nor wait for it nor adopt an attitude toward it, for it is that which is revealed as undiscoverable, that which disarms all waiting, that which slips into all attitudes (and particularly into those which are assumed with respect to death) so as to transform them into externalized and fixed conducts whose meaning is forever entrusted to others and not to ourselves, Death is a pure fact as is birth; it comes to us from outside and it transforms us into the outside. At bottom it is in no way distinguished from birth, and it is the identity of birth and death that we call facticity.

Does this mean that death marks the limits of our freedom? In renouncing Heidegger's being-unto-death, have we abandoned forever the possibility of freely giving to our being a meaning for which we are responsible?

Quite the contrary. As it seems to us, death by being revealed to us as it really is frees us wholly from its so-called constraint. This will be clearer if we but reflect on the matter.

First, however, it will be well to separate radically the two usually com-bined ideas of death and finitude. Ordinarily the belief seems to be that it is death which constitutes our finitude and which reveals it to us. From this combination it results that death takes on the shape of an ontological neces-sity and that finitude, on the other hand, borrows from death its contingent character. Heidegger in particular seems to have based his whole theory of *Sein-zum-Tode* on the strict identification of death and finitude. In the same way Malraux when he tells us that death reveals to us the uniqueness of life, seems to hold that it is just because we die that we are powerless to recover our stroke and are therefore finite. But if we consider the matter a little more closely, we detect their error: death is a contingent fact which belongs to facticity; finitude is an ontological structure of the for-itself which determines freedom and exists only in and through the free project of the end which makes my being known to me. In other words human reality would remain finite even if it were immortal, because it *makes* itself finite by choosing itself as human. To be finite, in fact, is to choose oneself—that is, to make known to oneself what one is by projecting oneself toward one possible to the exclusion of others. The very act of freedom is therefore the assumption and creation of finitude. If I make myself, I make myself finite and hence my life is unique. Consequently even if I were immortal, it would be forbidden me to "recover my stroke;" it is the irreversibility of temporality which forbids me, and this irreversibility is nothing but the peculiar character of a freedom which temporalizes itself. Of course if I am immortal and have had to reject the possible B in order to realize the possible A, the opportunity may be offered me later to realize the refused possible. But by the very fact that this opportunity will be presented *after* the refused opportunity, it will not be the same, and consequently I shall for all eternity have *made myself finite* by irremediably rejecting the first opportunity. From this point of view, the immortal man like the mortal is born several and makes himself one. Even if one is temporally indefinite—i.e., without limits—one's "life" will be nevertheless finite in its very being because it makes itself unique. Death has nothing to do with this. Death occurs "within time," and human-reality by revealing to itself its unique finitude does not thereby discover its mortality.

Thus death is in no way an ontological structure of my being, at least not in so far as my being is *for itself*; it is the Other who is mortal in his being. There is no place for death in being-for-itself; it can neither wait for death nor realize it nor project itself toward it; death is in no way the foundation of the finitude of the for-itself. In a general way death can neither be founded from within like the project of original freedom, nor can it be received from the outside as a quality by the for-itself. What then is death? Nothing but a certain aspect of facticity and of being-for-others—i.e., nothing other than the *given*. It is absurd that we are born; it is absurd that we die. On the other hand, this absurdity is presented as the permanent alienation of my being-possibility which is no longer my possibility but that of the Other. It is therefore an external and factual limit of my subjectivity.

But do we not recognize at this point the description which we attempted in the preceding section? This factual limit which on the one hand we must affirm since nothing penetrates us from outside and since in one sense it is very necessary that we *experience* death if we are to be able even to name it, this factual limit which, on the other hand, is never *encountered* by the for-itself since it does not enter into the for-itself save as the indefinite permanence of its being-for-others—what is this limit if not precisely one of the *unrealizables*?

What is it if not a synthetic aspect of our *reverse side?* Mortal represents the present being which I am for the Other; *dead* represents the future meaning of my actual for-itself for the Other. We are dealing therefore with a permanent limit of my projects; and as such this limit is to be assumed. It is therefore an exteriority which remains exteriority even in and through the attempt of the for-itself to realize it. It is what we defined above as the *unrealizable to be realized.* There is basically no difference between the choice by which freedom assumes its death as the inapprehensible and inconceivable limit of its subjectivity and that by which it chooses to be a freedom limited by the fact of the Other's freedom. Thus death is not my possibility in the sense previously defined; it is a situation-limit as the chosen and fugitive reverse side of my choice. It is not my possible in the sense that it would be my own end which would make known to me my being. But due to the fact that it is an unavoidable necessity of existing elsewhere as an outside and an in-itself, it is interiorized as "ultimate;" that is, as a thematic meaning of the hierarchical possibles, a meaning out of reach.

Thus death haunts me at the very heart of each of my projects as their inevitable reverse side. But precisely because this "reverse" is to be assumed not as my possibility but as the possibility that there are for me no longer any possibilities, it does not penetrate me. The freedom which is my freedom remains total and infinite. Death is not an obstacle to my projects; it is only a destiny of these projects elsewhere. And this is not because death does not limit my freedom but because freedom never encounters this limit. I am not "free to die," but I am a free mortal. Since death escapes my projects because it is unrealizable, I myself escape death in my very project. Since death is always beyond my subjectivity, there is no place for it in my subjectivity. This subjectivity does not affirm itself *against* death but independently of it although this affirmation is immediately alienated. Therefore we can neither think of death nor wait for it nor arm ourselves against it; but also our projects as projects are independent of death—not because of our blindness, as the Christian says, but on principle. And although there are innumerable possible attitudes with which we may confront this unrealizable which "into the bargain" is to be realized, there is no place for classifying these attitudes as authentic or unauthentic since we always die *into the bargain.*

These various descriptions relating to my place, my past, my environment, my death, and my fellowman do not claim to be exhaustive or even detailed. Their aim is simply to grant us a clearer conception of the "situation." Thanks to these descriptions, it is going to be possible for us to define more precisely this "being-in-situation" which characterizes the For-itself in so far as it is responsible for its manner of being without being the foundation of its being.

(1) I am an existent *in the midst of* other existents. But I can not "realize"

this existence in the midst of others; I can not apprehend as *objects* the existents which surround me nor apprehend myself as a *surrounded* existence nor even give a meaning to this notion of "in the midst of" except by choosing myself—not in my being but in my manner of being. The choice of this end is the choice of what is *not-yet-existing*. My position in the midst of the world is defined by the relation between the instrumental utility or adversity in the realities which surround me and my own facticity; that is, the discovery of the dangers which I risk in the world, of the obstacles which I can encounter there, the aid which can be offered me, all in the light of a radical nihilation of myself and of a radical, internal negation of the in-itself and all effected from the point of view of a freely posited end. This is what we mean by the *situation*.

(2) The situation exists only in correlation with the surpassing of the given toward an end. It is the way in which the given which I am and the given which I am not are revealed to the For-itself which I am in the mode of not-being it. When we speak of *situation* therefore we are speaking of a "position apprehended by the For-itself which is in situation." It is impossible to consider a situation from the outside; it is fixed in a form *in itself*. Consequently the situation can not be called either objective nor subjective although the partial structures of this situation (the cup which I use, the table on which I lean, *etc.*) can and must be strictly objective.

The situation can not be *subjective*, for it is neither the sum nor the unity of the *impressions* which things make on us. It is *the things themselves* and myself among things; for my upsurge into the world as the pure nihilation of being has no other result but to cause there to be things, and it adds *nothing*. In this aspect the situation betrays my *facticity*; that is, the fact that things simply are there as they are without the necessity or the possibility of being otherwise and that I *am* there among them.

But neither can the situation be *objective* in the sense that it would be a pure given which the subject would establish without being in any way engaged in the system thus constituted. In fact the situation by the very meaning of the given (a meaning without which there *would not even be* any given) reflects to the for-itself its freedom. If the situation is neither subjective nor objective, this is because it does not constitute a *knowledge* nor even an affective comprehension of the state of the world by a subject. The situation is a *relation of being* between a for-itself and the in-itself which the for-itself nihilates. The situation is the whole subject (he is *nothing* but his situation) and it is also the whole "thing" (*there is* never anything more than things). The situation is the subject illuminating things by his very surpassing, if you like; it is things referring to the subject his own image. It is the total facticity, the absolute contingency of the world, of my birth, of my place, of my past, of my environment, of the fact of my fellowman—and it is my freedom without limits as that which causes there to be for me a facticity. It is this dusty, ascending road, this burning thirst which I have, the refusal of these people to give me anything to drink because I do not have any money or because I am not of their country or of their race; it is my abandonment in the midst of these hostile populations along with this fatigue in my body which will perhaps prevent me from reaching the goal which I had set for myself. But also it is precisely this *goal*, not in so far as I clearly and explicitly formulate it but in so far as it is there everywhere around me as that which unifies and explains all these facts, that which organizes them in a totality capable of description instead of making of them a disordered nightmare.

(3) If the for-itself is nothing other than its situation, then it follows that being-in-situation defines human reality by accounting both for its *being-there* and for its *being-beyond*. Human reality is indeed the *being which is always beyond its being-there*. And the situation is the organized totality of the being-there, interpreted and lived in and through being-beyond. Therefore there is no priviledged situation. We mean by this that there is no situation in which the *given* would crush beneath its weight the freedom which constitutes it as such— and that conversely there is no situation in which the for-itself would be *more free* than in others. This must not be understood in the sense of that "inward freedom" of Bergson's which Politzer ridiculed in *La fin d'une parade philosophique* (*The End of a Philosophical Parade*) and which simply amounted to recognizing in the slave the independence of the inner life and of the heart in chains. When we declare that the slave in chains is as free as his master, we do not mean to speak of a freedom which would remain undetermined. The slave in chains is free to *break them*; this means that the very meaning of his chains will appear to him in the light of the end which he will have chosen: to remain a slave or to risk the worst in order to get rid of his slavery. Of course the slave will not be able to obtain the wealth and the standard of living of his master; but these are not the objects of his *projects*; he can only dream of the possession of these treasures. The slave's *facticity* is such that the world appears to him with another countenance and that he has to posit and to resolve different problems; in particular it is necessary fundamentally to choose himself on the ground of *slavery* and thereby to give a meaning to this obscure constraint. For example, if he chooses revolt, then slavery, far from being *at the start* an obstacle to this revolt, takes on its meaning and its coefficient of adversity only through the revolt. To be exact, just because the life of the slave who revolts and dies in the course of this revolt is a free life, just because the situation illuminated by a free project is full and concrete, just because the urgent and principal problem of this life is "Shall I attain my goal?"—just because of all this, the situation of the slave *can not be compared* with that of the master. Each of them in fact takes on its meaning only for the for-itself in situation and in terms of the free choice of its ends. A comparison could be

made only by a third person and consequently it could take place only between two objective forms in the midst of the world; moreover it could be established only in the light of a project freely chosen by this third person. There is no absolute point of view which one can adopt so as to compare different situations; each person realizes only one situation—his own.

(4) Since the situation is illumined by ends which are themselves projected only in terms of the being-there, which they illuminate, it is presented as eminently concrete. Of course it contains and sustains abstract and universal structures, but it must be understood as the single countenance which the world turns toward us as our unique and personal chance. We may recall here a fable of Kafka's: A merchant comes to plead his case at the castle where a forbidding guard bars the entrance. The merchant does not dare to go further; he waits and dies still waiting. At the hour of death he asks the guardian, "How does it happen that I was the only one waiting?" And the guardian replies, "This gate was made only for you." Such is precisely the case with the for-itself if we may add in addition that each man makes for himself his own gate. The concreteness of the situation is expressed particularly by the fact that the for-itself never aims at ends which are fundamentally abstract and universal. Of course we shall see in the next chapter that the profound meaning of the choice is universal and that consequently the for-itself causes a human-reality to exist as a species. Again it is necessary to disengage the meaning which is implicit, and it is for this that we shall use existential psychoanalysis. Once disengaged the terminal and initial meaning of the for-itself will appear as an Unselbständig which in order to manifest itself needs a particular kind of concretion.[22] But the end of the for-itself as it is lived and pursued in the project by which the for-itself surpasses and founds the real is revealed in its concreteness to the for-itself as a particular change in the situation which it lives (e.g., to break its chains, to be King of the Franks, to liberate Poland, to fight for the proletariat). At first the for-itself will not project fighting for the proletariat in general but will aim at the proletariat across a particular concrete group of workers to which the person belongs. This is due to the fact that the end illuminates the given only because the end is chosen as the surpassing of this given. The for-itself does not arise with a wholly given end. But by "making" the situation, the for-itself "makes itself"—and conversely.

(5) Just as the situation is neither objective or subjective, so it can be considered neither as the free result of a freedom nor as the ensemble of the constraints to which I am subject; it stems from the illumination of the constraint by freedom which gives to it its meaning as constraint. Among brute existents there can be no connection; it is freedom which founds the connections by grouping the existents into instrumental-complexes; and it is

---

[22] Cf. the following chapter.

freedom which projects the *reason* for the connections—that is, its end. But precisely because I project myself toward an end through a world of *connections*, I now meet with sequences, with linked series, with complexes, and I must determine to act according to laws. These laws and the way I make use of them decide the failure or the success of my attempts. But it is through freedom that legal relations come into the world. Thus freedom enchains itself in the world as a free project toward ends.

(6) The For-itself *is* temporalization. This means that it *is* not but that it "makes itself." It is the *situation* which must account for that *substantial perman-ence* which we readily recognize in people ("He has not changed." "He is always the same.") and which the person experiences empirically in most cases as being his own. The free perseverance in a single project does not imply any permanence; quite the contrary, it is a perpetual renewal of my engagement—as we have seen. On the other hand, the realities enveloped and illuminated by a project which develops and confirms itself present the per-manence of the in-itself; and to the extent that they refer our image to us, they support us with their everlastingness; in fact it frequently happens that we take their permanence for our own. In particular the permanence of place and environment, of the judgments passed on us by our neighbors, of our past—all that *represents* a degraded image of our *perseverance*. While I am tem-poralizing myself, I am *always* French, a civil servant or a proletarian *for others*. This unrealizable has the character of an invariable limit for my situation.

Similarly what we call a person's temperament or character but which is nothing but his free project in so far as it is-for-the-Other, appears also for the For-itself as an invariable unrealizable. Alain has perceived correctly that character is a *vow*. When a man says, "I am not easy to please," he is entering into a free engagement with his ill-temper, and by the same token his words are a free interpretation of certain ambiguous details in his past. In this sense there is no character; there is only a project of oneself. But we must not, however, misunderstand the *given* aspect of the character. It is true that for the Other who apprehends me as the Other-as-object, I *am* ill-tempered, hypo-critical or frank, cowardly or courageous. This aspect is referred to me by the Other's look; by the experience of the look, this character, which was a free project lived and self-conscious, becomes an unrealizable *ne varietur* to be assumed. It depends then not only on the Other but on the position which I have taken with respect to the Other and on my perseverance in maintaining this position. So long as I let myself be fascinated by the Other's look, my character will figure in my own eyes as an unrealizable *ne varietur*, the substan-tial permanence of my being—the kind of thing expressed in such ordinary everyday remarks as "I am forty-five years old, and I'm not going to start changing myself today." The Character often is what the For-itself tries to recover in order to become the In-itself-for-itself which it projects being.

Nevertheless it should be noted that this permanence of the past, of the environment, and of character are not given qualities; they are revealed on things only in correlation with the continuity of my project. For example, after a war, after a long exile, one finds a particular mountain landscape unchanged; however it would be vain to try to found a hope for a renascence of the past on the inertia and apparent permanence of its stones. This land-scape reveals its permanence only through a persevering project. These mountains have a *meaning* inside my situation; in one way or another they shape my belonging to a nation at peace, independent, one who holds a certain rank in the international hierarchy. Let me find them again after a defeat and during the occupation of a part of the national territory, and they can not offer me the same countenance. This is because I myself have other projects, because I am engaged differently in the world.

Finally we have seen that internal upheavals of the situation because of autonomous changes in the environment are always to be anticipated. These changes can never *provoke* a change of my project, but on the foundation of my freedom they can effect a simplification or a complication of the situation. Consequently my initial project will be revealed to me with more or less simplicity. For a person is never either simple or complex; it is his situation which can be one or the other. In fact I am nothing but the project of myself beyond a determined situation, and this project *pre-outlines* me in terms of the concrete situation as in addition it illumines the situation in terms of my choice. If therefore the situation in its ensemble is simplified, even if land-slides, cave-ins, erosions have imprinted upon it a well-marked aspect of heavier features with violent contrasts, I shall myself be simple, for my choice—the choice which I am—is an apprehension of *this situation here* and can only be simple. The birth of new complications will have the result of presenting me with a complicated situation beyond which I shall find myself complicated. This is something which everyone could establish if he had observed to what almost animal simplicity prisoners of war regress, as a result of the extreme simplification of their situation. This simplification can not modify the meaning of their project; but on the very foundation of my freedom it causes my environment to become condensed and uniform and to be constituted in and through a clearer, more brutal, and more condensed apprehension of the fundamental ends of the captive person. In short we are dealing with an internal metabolism, not with a global metamorphosis which would affect as well the form of the situation. These are, nevertheless, changes which I discover *as* changes "in my life"—that is, changes within the unitary compass of a single project.

## III. FREEDOM AND RESPONSIBILITY

Although the considerations which are about to follow are of interest primarily to the moralist, it may nevertheless be worthwhile after these descriptions and arguments to return to the freedom of the for-itself and to try to understand what the fact of this freedom represents for human destiny.

The essential consequence of our earlier remarks is that man being condemned to be free carries the weight of the whole world on his shoulders; he is responsible for the world and for himself as a way of being. We are taking the word "responsibility" in its ordinary sense as "consciousness (of) being the incontestable author of an event or of an object." In this sense the responsibility of the for-itself is overwhelming since he[23] is the one by whom it happens that there is a world; since he is also the one who makes himself be, then whatever may be the situation in which he finds himself, the for-itself must wholly assume this situation with its peculiar coefficient of adversity, even though it be insupportable. He must assume the situation with the proud consciousness of being the author of it, for the very worst disadvantages or the worst threats which can endanger my person have meaning only in and through my project; and it is on the ground of the engagement which I am that they appear. It is therefore senseless to think of complaining since nothing foreign has decided what we feel, what we live, or what we are.

Furthermore this absolute responsibility is not resignation; it is simply the logical requirement of the consequences of our freedom. What happens to me happens through me, and I can neither affect myself with it nor revolt against it nor resign myself to it. Moreover everything which happens to me is mine. By this we must understand first of all that I am always equal to what happens to me qua man, for what happens to a man through other men and through himself can be only human. The most terrible situations of war, the worst tortures do not create a non-human state of things; there is no non-human situation. It is only through fear, flight, and recourse to magical types of conduct that I shall decide on the non-human, but this decision is human, and I shall carry the entire responsibility for it. But in addition the situation is mine because it is the image of my free choice of myself, and everything which it presents to me is mine in that this represents me and symbolizes me. Is it not I who decide the coefficient of adversity in things and even their unpredictability by deciding myself?

Thus there are no accidents in a life; a community event which suddenly bursts forth and involves me in it does not come from the outside. If I am mobilized in a war, this war is my war; it is in my image and I deserve it. I

---

[23] I am shifting to the personal pronoun here since Sartre is describing the for-itself in concrete personal terms rather than as a metaphysical entity. Strictly speaking, of course, this is his position throughout, and the French "il" is indifferently "he" or "it." Tr.

deserve it first because I could always get out of it by suicide or by desertion; these ultimate possibles are those which must always be present for us when there is a question of envisaging a situation. For lack of getting out of it, I have *chosen* it. This can be due to inertia, to cowardice in the face of public opinion, or because I prefer certain other values to the value of the refusal to join in the war (the good opinion of my relatives, the honor of my family, *etc.*). Anyway you look at it, it is a matter of a choice. This choice will be repeated later on again and again without a break until the end of the war. Therefore we must agree with the statement by J. Romains, "In war there are no innocent victims."[24] If therefore I have preferred war to death or to dishonor, everything takes place as if I bore the entire responsibility for this war. Of course others have declared it, and one might be tempted perhaps to consider me *as a* simple accomplice. But this notion of complicity has only a juridical sense, and it does not hold here. For it depended on me that for me and by me this war should not exist, and I have decided that it does exist. There was no compulsion here, for the compulsion could have got no hold on a freedom. I did not have any excuse; for as we have said repeatedly in this book, the peculiar character of human-reality is that it is without excuse. Therefore it remains for me only to lay claim to this war.

But in addition the war is *mine* because by the sole fact that it arises in a situation which I cause to be and that I can discover it there only by engaging myself for or against it, I can no longer distinguish at present the choice which I make of myself from the choice which I make of the war. To live this war is to choose myself through it and to choose it through my choice of myself. There can be no question of considering it as "four years of vacation" or as a "reprieve," as a "recess," the essential part of my responsibilities being elsewhere in my married, family, or professional life. In this war which I have chosen I choose myself from day to day, and I make it mine by making myself. If it is going to be four empty years, then it is I who bear the responsibility for this.

Finally, as we pointed out earlier, each person is an absolute choice of self from the standpoint of a world of knowledges and of techniques which this choice both assumes and illumines; each person is an absolute upsurge at an absolute date and is perfectly unthinkable at another date. It is therefore a waste of time to ask what I should have been if this war had not broken out, for I have chosen myself as one of the possible meanings of the epoch which imperceptibly led to war. I am not distinct from this same epoch; I could not be transported to another epoch without contradiction. Thus I *am* this war which restricts and limits and makes comprehensible the period which preceded it. In this sense we may define more precisely the responsibility of the

---

[24] J. Romains: *Les hommes de bonne volonté*; "Prélude à Verdun."

for-itself if to the earlier quoted statement, "There are no innocent victims," we add the words, "We have the war we deserve." Thus, totally free, undistinguishable from the period for which I have chosen to be the meaning, as profoundly responsible for the war as if I had myself declared it, unable to live without integrating it in my situation, engaging myself in it wholly and stamping it with my seal, I must be without remorse or regrets *as* I am without excuse; for from the instant of my upsurge into being, I carry the weight of the world by myself alone without anything or any person being able to lighten it.

Yet this responsibility is of a very particular type. Someone will say, "I did not ask to be born." This is a naive way of throwing greater emphasis on our facticity. I am responsible for everything, in fact, except for my very responsibility, for I am not the foundation of my being. Therefore everything takes place as if I were compelled to be responsible. I am *abandoned* in the world, not in the sense that I might remain abandoned and passive in a hostile universe like a board floating on the water, but rather in the sense that I find myself suddenly alone and without help, engaged in a world for which I bear the whole responsibility without being able, whatever I do, to tear myself away from this responsibility for an instant. For I am responsible for my very desire of fleeing responsibilities. To make myself passive in the world, to refuse to act upon things and upon Others is still to choose myself, and suicide is one mode among others of being-in-the-world. Yet I find an absolute responsibility for the fact that my facticity (here the fact of my birth) is directly inapprehensible and even inconceivable, for this fact of my birth never appears as a brute fact but always across a projective reconstruction of my for-itself. I am ashamed of being born or I am astonished at it or I rejoice over it, or in attempting to get rid of my life I affirm that I live and I assume this life as bad. Thus in a certain sense I *choose* being born. This choice itself is integrally affected with facticity since I am not able not to choose, but this facticity in turn will appear only in so far as I surpass it toward my ends. Thus facticity is everywhere but inapprehensible; I never encounter anything except my responsibility. That is why I can not ask, "*Why* was I born?" or curse the day of my birth or declare that I did not ask to be born, for these various attitudes toward my birth—i.e., toward the *fact* that I realize a presence in the world—are absolutely nothing else but ways of assuming this birth in full responsibility and of making it *mine*. Here again I encounter only myself and my projects so that finally my abandonment—i.e., my facticity—consists simply in the *fact* that I am condemned to be wholly responsible for myself. I am the being which *is* in such a way that in its being its being is in question. And this "*is*" of my being *is as* present and inapprehensible.

Under these conditions since every event in the world can be revealed to me only as an *opportunity* (an opportunity made use of, lacked, neglected, *etc.*), or better yet since everything which happens to us can be considered *as a chance* (i.e., can appear to us only as a way of realizing this being which is in question in our being) and since others as transcendences-transcended are themselves only *opportunities* and *chances*, the responsibility of the for-itself extends to the entire world as a peopled-world. It is precisely thus that the for-itself apprehends itself in anguish; that is, as a being which is neither the foundation of its own being nor of the Other's being nor of the in-itselfs which form the world, but a being which is compelled to decide the meaning of being—within it and everywhere outside of it. The one who realizes in anguish his condition as *being* thrown into a responsibility which extends to his very abandonment has no longer either remorse or regret or excuse; he is no longer anything but a freedom which perfectly reveals itself and whose being resides in this very revelation. But as we pointed out at the beginning of this work, most of the time we flee anguish in bad faith.

# 2

## DOING AND HAVING

### I. EXISTENTIAL PSYCHOANALYSIS

If it is true that human reality—as we have attempted to establish—identifies and defines itself by the ends which it pursues, then a study and classification of these ends becomes indispensable. In the preceding chapter we have considered the For-itself only from the point of view of its free project, which is the impulse by which it thrusts itself toward its end. We should now question this end itself, for it forms *a part* of absolute subjectivity and is, in fact, its transcendent, objective limit. This is what empirical psychology has hinted at by admitting that a particular man is defined by his desires. Here, however, we must be on our guard against two errors. First, the empirical psychologist, while defining man by his desires, remains the victim of the illusion of substance. He views desire as being *in* man by virtue of being "contained" by his consciousness, and he believes that the meaning of the desire is inherent in the desire itself. Thus he avoids everything which could evoke the idea of transcendence. But if I desire a house or a glass of water or a woman's body, how could this body, this glass, this piece of property reside in my desire, and how can my desire be anything but the consciousness of these objects *as* desirable? Let us beware then of considering these desires as little psychic entities dwelling in consciousness; they are consciousness itself in its original projective, transcendent structure, for consciousness is on principle consciousness of something.

The other error, which fundamentally is closely connected with the first, consists in considering psychological research as terminated as soon as the investigator has reached the concrete ensemble of empirical desires. Thus a man would be defined by the bundle of drives or tendencies which empirical observation could establish. Naturally the psychologist will not always limit himself to making up the sum of these tendencies; he will want to bring to light their relationships, their agreements and harmonies; he will try to present the ensemble of desires as a synthetic organization in which each desire acts on the others and influences them. A critic, for example, wishing to explain the "psychology" of Flaubert, will write that he "appeared in his early youth to know as his normal state, a continual exaltation resulting from the two-fold feeling of his grandiose ambition and his invincible power. . . . The effervescence of his young blood was then turned into literary passion as happens about the eighteenth year in precocious souls who find in the energy of style or the intensities of fiction some way of escaping from the need of violent action or of intense feeling, which torments them."[1]

In this passage there is an effort to reduce the complex personality of an adolescent to a few basic desires, as the chemist reduces compound bodies to merely a combination of simple bodies. The primitive givens will be grandiose ambition, the need of violent action and of intense feeling; these elements when they enter into combination, produce a permanent exaltation. Then—as Bourget remarks in a few words which we have not quoted—this exaltation nourished by numerous well chosen readings, is going to seek to delude itself by self-expression in fictions which will appease it symbolically and channel it. There in outline is the genesis of a literary "temperament."

Now in the first place such a psychological *analysis* proceeds from the postulate that an individual fact is produced by the intersection of abstract, universal laws. The fact to be explained—which is here the literary disposition of the young Flaubert—is resolved into a combination of *typical*, abstract desires such as we meet in "the average adolescent." What is concrete here is only their combination; in themselves they are only possible patterns. The abstract then is by hypothesis prior to the concrete, and the concrete is only an organization of abstract qualities; the individual is only the intersection of universal schemata. But—aside from the logical absurdity of such a postulate—we see clearly in the example chosen, that it simply fails to explain what makes the individuality of the project under consideration. The fact that "the need to feel intensely," a universal pattern, is disguised and channeled into becoming the need to write—this is not the *explanation* of the "calling" of Flaubert; on the contrary, it is what must be explained. Doubtless one could invoke a thousand circumstances, known to us and unknown, which have shaped this need to feel into the need to act. But this is to give up at the start all attempt to explain and refers the question to the undiscoverable.[2] In addition this method rejects the pure individual who has been

---

[1] Paul Bourget: *Essai de Psychologie contemporaine: G. Flaubert.*

[2] Since Flaubert's adolescence, so far as we can know it, offers us nothing specific in this connection, we must suppose the action of imponderable facts which on principle escape the critic.

banished from the pure subjectivity of Flaubert into the external circumstances of his life. Finally, Flaubert's correspondence proves that long before the "crisis of adolescence," from his earliest childhood, he was tormented by the need to write.

At each stage in the description just quoted, we meed with an hiatus. Why did ambition and the feeling of his power produce in Flaubert *exaltation* rather than tranquil waiting or gloomy impatience? Why did this exaltation express itself specifically in the need to act violently and feel intensely? Or rather why does this need make a sudden appearance by spontaneous generation at the end of the paragraph? And why does this need instead of seeking to appease itself in acts of violence, by amorous adventures, or in debauch, choose precisely to satisfy itself symbolically? And why does Flaubert turn to writing rather than to painting or music for this symbolic satisfaction; he could just as well not resort to the artistic field at all (there is also mysticism, for example). "I could have been a great actor," wrote Flaubert somewhere. Why did he not try to be one? In a word, we have understood nothing; we have seen a succession of accidental happenings, of desire springing forth fully armed, one from the other, with no possibility for us to grasp their genesis. The *transitions*, the becomings, the transformations, have been carefully veiled from us, and we have been limited to putting order into the succession by invoking empirically established but literally unintelligible sequences (the need to act preceding in the adolescent the need to write).

Yet this is called psychology! Open any biography at random, and this is the kind of description which you will find more or less interspersed with accounts of external events and allusions to the great explanatory idols of our epoch—heredity, education, environment, physiological constitution. Occasionally, in the better works the connection established between antecedent and consequent or between two concornitant desires and their reciprocal action is not conceived merely as a type of regular sequence; sometimes it is "comprehensible" in the sense which Jaspers understands in his general treatise on psychopathology. But this comprehension remains a grasp of general connections. For example we will realize the link between chastity and mysticism, between fainting and hypocrisy. But we are ignorant always of the concrete relation between this chastity (this abstinence in relation to a particular woman, this struggle against a definite temptation) and the individual content of the mysticism; in the same way psychiatry is too quickly satisfied when it throws light on the general structures of delusions and does not seek to comprehend the individual, concrete content of the psychoses (why this man believes himself to be that particular historical personality rather than some other; why his compensatory delusion is satisfied with specifically these ideas of grandeur instead of others, *etc.*).

But most important of all, these "psychological" explanations refer us ultimately to inexplicable original givens. These are the simple bodies of psychology. We are told, for example, that Flaubert had a "grandiose ambition" and all of the previously quoted description depends on this original ambition. So far so good. But this ambition is an irreducible fact which by no means satisfies the mind. The irreducibility here has no justification other than refusal to push the analysis further. There where the psychologist stops, the fact confronted is given as primary. This is why we experience a troubled feeling of mingled resignation and dissatisfaction when we read these psychological treatises. "See," we say to ourselves, "Flaubert was ambitious. He was that kind of man." It would be as futile to ask why he was such as to seek to know why he was tall and blond. Of course we have to stop somewhere; it is the very contingency of all real existence. This rock is covered with moss, the rock next to it is not. Gustave Flaubert had literary ambition, and his brother Achille lacked it. That's the way it is. In the same way we want to know the properties of phosphorus, and we attempt to reduce them to the structure of the chemical molecules which compose it. But why are there molecules of this type? That's the way it is, that's all. The explanation of Flaubert's psychology will consist, if it is possible, in referring the complexity of his behavior patterns, his feelings, and his tastes back to certain properties, comparable to those of chemical bodies, beyond which it would be foolish to attempt to proceed. Yet we feel obscurely that Flaubert had not "received" his ambition. It is meaningful; therefore it is free. Neither heredity, nor bourgeois background nor education can account for it, still less those physiological considerations regarding the "nervous temperament," which have been the vogue for some time now. The nerve is not meaningful; it is a colloidal substance which can be described in itself and which does not have the quality of transcendence; that is, it does not transcend itself in order to make known to itself by means of other realities what it is. Under no circumstances could the nerve furnish the basis for meaning. In one sense Flaubert's ambition is a fact with all a fact's contingency—and it is true that it is impossible to advance beyond that fact—but in another sense it makes itself, and our satisfaction is a guarantee to us that we may be able to grasp beyond this ambition something more, something like a radical decision which, without ceasing to be contingent, would be the veritable psychic irreducible.

What we are demanding then—and what nobody ever attempts to give us—is a veritable irreducible; that is, an irreducible of which the irreducibility would be self-evident, which would not be presented as the postulate of the psychologist and the result of his refusal or his incapacity to go further, but which when established would produce in us an accompanying feeling of satisfaction. This demand on our part does not come from that ceaseless pursuit of a cause, that infinite regress which has often been described as constitutive of rational research and which consequently—far from being exclusively associated with psychological investigation—may be found in all disciplines and in all problems. This is not the childish quest of a "because," which allows no further "why?" It is on the contrary a demand based on a pre-ontological comprehension of human reality and on the related refusal to consider man as capable of being analyzed and reduced to original givens, to determined desires (or "drives"), supported by the subject as properties by an object. Even if we were to consider him as such, it would be necessary to choose: either Flaubert, the man, whom we can love or detest, blame or praise, who represents for us the Other, who directly attacks our being by the very fact that he has existed, would be originally a substratum unqualified by these desires; that is, a sort of indeterminate clay which would have to receive them passively or he would be reduced to the simple bundle of these irreducible drives or tendencies. In either case the man disappears; we can no longer find "the one" to whom this or that experience has happened; either in looking for the person, we encounter a useless, contradictory metaphysical substance—or else the being whom we seek vanishes in a dust of phenomena bound together by external connections. But what each one of us requires in his very effort to comprehend another is that he should never have to resort to this idea of substance which is inhuman because it is well this side of the human. Finally the fact is that the being considered does not crumble into dust, and one can discover in him that unity—for which substance was only a caricature— which must be a unity of responsibility, a unity agreeable or hateful, blamable and praiseworthy, in short personal. This unity, which is the being of the man under consideration, is a free unification, and this unification can not come after a diversity which it unifies.

But to be, for Flaubert, as for every subject of "biography," means to be unified in the world. The irreducible unification which we ought to find, which is Flaubert, and which we require biographers to reveal to us—this is the unification of an original project, a unification which should reveal itself to us as a non-substantial absolute. Therefore we should forego these so-called irreducible details and, taking the very evidence of them for a criterion, not stop in our investigation before it is evident that we neither can nor ought to go any further. In particular we must avoid trying to reconstruct a person by means of his inclinations, just as Spinoza warns us not to attempt to reconstruct a substance or its attributes by the summation of its modes. Every desire if presented as an irreducible is an absurd contingency and involves in absurdity human reality taken as a whole. For example, if I declare of one of my friends that he "likes to go rowing," I deliberately intend to stop my investigation there. But on the other hand, I thus establish a contingent fact, which nothing can explain and which, though it has the gratuity of free decision, by no means has its autonomy. I can not in fact consider this fondness for rowing as the fundamental project of Pierre; it contains something secondary and derived. Those who portray a character in this way by successive strokes come close to holding that each of these strokes—each one of the desires confronted—is bound to the others by connections which are purely contingent and simply external. Those who, on the other hand, try to explain this liking will fall into the view of what Comte called *materialism*; that is, of explaining the higher by the lower. Someone will say, for example, that the subject considered is a sportsman who likes violent exercise and is in addition a man of the outdoors who especially likes open air sports. By more general and less differentiated tendencies he will try to explain this desire, which stands in exactly the same relation to them as the zoological species does to the genus. Thus the psychological explanation when it does not suddenly decide to stop, is sometimes the mere putting into relief relations of pure concomitance or of constant succession, and it is at other times a simple classification. To explain Pierre's fondness for rowing is to make it a member of the family of fondness for open air sports and to attach this family to that of fondness for sport in general. Moreover we will be able to find still more general and barren rubrics if we classify the taste for sports as one aspect of the love of risk, which will itself be given as a specific instance of the fundamental fondness for play. It is obvious that this so-called explanatory classification has no more value or interest than the classifications in ancient botany; like the latter it amounts to assuming the priority of the abstract over the concrete—as if the fondness for play existed first in general to be sub-sequently made specific by the action of these circumstances in the love of sport, the latter in the fondness for rowing, and finally the rowing in the desire to row on a particular stream, under certain circumstances in a particu-lar season—and like the ancient classifications it fails to explain the concrete enrichment which at each stage is undergone by the abstract inclination considered.

Furthermore how are we to believe that a desire to row is only a desire to row? Can we truthfully admit that it can be reduced so simply to what it is? The most discerning moralists have shown how a desire reaches beyond itself. Pascal believed that he could discover in hunting, for example, or tennis, or in a hundred other occupations, the need of being diverted. He revealed that in an activity which would be absurd if reduced to itself, there was a meaning which transcended it; that is, an indication which referred to the reality of man in general and to his condition. Similarly Stendhal in spite of his attach-ment to ideologists, and Proust in spite of his intellectualistic and analytical tendencies, have shown that love and jealousy can not be reduced to the strict desire of possessing a *particular* woman, but that these emotions aim at laying hold of the world in its entirety through the woman. This is the meaning of Stendhal's crystallization, and it is precisely for this reason that love as Stendhal describes it appears as a mode of being in the world. Love is a fundamental relation of the for-itself to the world and to itself (selfness) through a particular woman; the woman represents only a conducting body which is placed in the circuit. These analyses may be inexact or only partially true; nevertheless they make us suspect a method other than pure analytical description. In the same way Catholic novelists immediately see in carnal love its surpassing toward God—in Don Juan, "the eternally unsatisfied," in sin, "the place empty of God." There is no question here of finding again an abstract behind the concrete; the impulse toward God is no *less concrete* than the impulse toward a particular woman. On the contrary, it is a matter of rediscovering under the partial and incomplete aspects of the subject the veritable concreteness which can be only the totality of his impulse toward being, his original relation to himself, to the world, and to the Other, in the unity of internal relations and of a fundamental project. This impulse can be only purely individual and unique. Far from estranging us from the person, as Bourget's analysis, for example, does in constituting the individual by means of a summation of general maxims, this impulse will not lead us to find in the need of writing—and of writing particular books—the need of activity in general. On the contrary, rejecting equally the theory of malleable clay and that of the bundle of drives, we will discover the individual person in the initial project which constitutes him. It is for this reason that the irreducibility of the result attained will be revealed as self-evident, not because it is the poorest and the most abstract but because it is the richest. The intuition here will be accompanied by an individual fullness.

The problem must be posed in approximately these terms: If we admit that the person is a totality, we can not hope to reconstruct him by an addition or by an organization of the diverse tendencies which we have empirically discovered in him. On the contrary, in each inclination, in each tendency the person expresses himself completely, although from a different angle, a little as Spinoza's substance expresses itself completely in each of its attributes. But if this is so, we should discover in each tendency, in each attitude of the subject, a meaning which transcends it. A jealousy of a particular date in which a subject historicizes himself in relation to a certain woman, signifies for the one who knows how to interpret it, the total relation to the world by which the subject constitutes himself as a self. In other words this *empirical* attitude is by itself the expression of the "choice of an intelligible character." There is no mystery about this. We no longer have to do with an intelligible pattern which can be present in our thought only, while we apprehend and conceptualize the unique pattern of the subject's empirical existence. If the empirical attitude signifies the choice of the intelligible character, it is because it is itself this choice. Indeed the distinguishing characteristic of the intelligible choice, as we shall see later, is that it can exist only as the transcendent meaning of each concrete, empirical choice. It is by no means first effected in some unconscious or on the noumenal level to be *subsequently* expressed in a particular observable attitude; there is not even an *ontological* pre-eminence over the empirical choice, but it is on principle that which must always detach itself from the empirical choice as its *beyond* and the infinity of its transcendence. Thus if I am rowing on the river, I am nothing— either here or in any other world—save this concrete project of rowing. But this project itself inasmuch as it is the totality of my being, expresses my original choice in particular circumstances; it is nothing other than the choice of myself as a totality in these circumstances. That is why a special method must aim at detaching the fundamental meaning which the project admits and which can be only the individual secret of the subject's being-in-the-world. It is then rather by a *comparison* of the various empirical drives of a subject that we try to discover and disengage the fundamental project which is common to them all—and not by a simple summation or reconstruction of these tendencies; each drive or tendency is the entire person.

There is naturally an infinity of possible projects as there is an infinity of possible human beings. Nevertheless, if we are to recognize certain common characteristics among them and if we are going to attempt to classify them in larger categories, it is best first to undertake individual investigations in the cases which we can study more easily. In our research, we will be guided by this principle: to stop only in the presence of evident irreducibility; that is, never to believe that we have reached the initial project until the projected end appears as *the very being* of the subject under consideration. This is why we can not stop at those classifications of "authentic project" and "unauthentic project of the self" which Heidegger wishes to establish. In addition to the fact that such a classification, in spite of its author's intent, is tainted with an ethical concern shown by its very terminology, it is based on the attitude of the subject toward his own death. Now if death causes anguish, and if consequently we can either flee the anguish or throw ourselves resolutely into it, it is a truism to say that this is because we wish to hold on to life. Consequently anguish before death and resolute decision or flight into unauthenticity can not be considered as fundamental projects of our being. On the contrary, they can be understood only on the foundation of an original project of living; that is, on an original choice of our being. It is right then in each case to pass beyond the results of Heidegger's interpretation toward a still more fundamental project.

This fundamental project must not of course refer to any other and should be conceived by itself. It can be concerned neither with death nor life nor any particular characteristic of the human condition; the original project of a for-itself *can aim only at its being.* The project of being or desire of being or drive toward being does not originate in a physiological differentiation or in an empirical contingency; in fact it is not distinguished from the being of the for-itself. The for-itself is a being such that in its being, its being is in question in the form of a project of being. To the for-itself *being* means to make known to oneself what one is by means of a possibility appearing as a value. Possibility and value belong to the being of the for-itself. The for-itself is defined ontologically as a *lack of being*, and possibility belongs to the for-itself as that which it lacks, in the same way that value haunts the for-itself as the totality of being which is lacking. What we have expressed in Part Two in terms of lack can be just as well expressed in terms of *freedom*. The for-itself chooses because it is lack; freedom is really synonymous with lack. Freedom is the concrete mode of being of the lack of being. Ontologically then it amounts to the same thing to say that value and possibility exist as internal limits of a lack of being which can exist only as a lack of being—or that the upsurge of freedom determines its possibility and thereby circumscribes its value.

Thus we can advance no further but have encountered the self-evident irreducible when we have reached the *project of being*; for obviously it is impossible to advance further than *being*, and there is no difference between the project of being, possibility, value, on the one hand, and *being*, on the other. Fundamentally man is *the desire to be*, and the existence of this desire is not to be established by an empirical induction; it is the result of an *a priori* description of the being of the for-itself, since desire is a lack and since the for-itself is the being which is to itself its own lack of being. The original project which is expressed in each of our empirically observable tendencies is then the *project of being*; or, if you prefer, each empirical tendency exists with the original project of being, in a relation of expression and symbolic satisfaction just as conscious drives, with Freud, exist in relation to the complex and to the original libido. Moreover the desire to be by no means exists *first* in order to cause itself to be expressed subsequently by desires *a posteriori*. There is nothing outside of the symbolic expression which it finds in concrete desires. There is not first a single desire of being, then a thousand particular feelings, but the desire to be exists and manifests itself only in and through jealousy, greed, love of art, cowardice, courage, and a thousand contingent, empirical expressions which always cause human reality to appear to us only as *manifested by a particular man*, by a specific person.

As for the being which is the object of this desire, we know *a priori* what this is. The for-itself is the being which is to itself its own lack of being. The being which the for-itself lacks is the in-itself. The for-itself arises as the nihilation of the in-itself and this nihilation is defined as the project toward the in-itself. Between the nihilated in-itself and the projected in-itself the for-itself is nothingness. Thus the end and the goal of the nihilation which I am is the in-itself. Thus human reality is the desire of being-in-itself. But the in-itself which it desires can not be pure contingent, absurd in-itself, comparable at every point to that which it encounters and which it nihilates. The nihilation, as we have seen, is in fact like a revolt of the in-itself, which nihilates itself against its contingency. To say that the for-itself lives its facticity, as we have seen in the chapter concerning the body, amounts to saying that the nihilation is the vain effort of a being to found its own being and that it is the withdrawal to found being which provokes the minute displacement by which nothingness enters into being. The being which forms the object of the desire of the for-itself is then an in-itself which would be to itself its own foundation; that is, which would be to its facticity in the same relation as the for-itself is to its motivations. In addition the for-itself, being the negation of the in-itself, could not desire the pure and simple return to the in-itself. Here as with Hegel, the negation of the negation can not bring us back to our point of departure. Quite the contrary, what the for-itself demands of the in-itself is precisely the totality detotalized—"In-itself nihilated in for-itself." In other words the for-itself projects *being as for-itself*, a being which is what it is. It is as being which is what it is not, and which is not what it is, that the for-itself projects being what it is. It is as consciousness that it wishes to have the impermeability and infinite density of the in-itself. It is as the nihilation of the in-itself and a perpetual evasion of contingency and of facticity that it wishes to be its own foundation. This is why the possible is projected in general as what the for-itself lacks in order to become in-itself-for-itself. The fundamental value which presides over this project is exactly the in-itself-for-itself; that is, the ideal of a consciousness which would be the foundation of its own being-in-itself by the pure consciousness which it would have of itself. It is this ideal which can be called God. Thus the best way to conceive of the fundamental project of human reality is to say that man is the being whose project is to be God. Whatever may be the myths and rites of the religion considered, God is first "sensible to the heart" of man as the one who identifies and defines him in his ultimate and fundamental project. If man possesses a pre-ontological comprehension of the being of God, it is not the great wonders of nature nor the power of society which have conferred it upon him. God, value and supreme end of transcendence, represents the permanent limit in terms of which man makes known to himself what he is. To be man means to reach toward being God. Or if you prefer, man fundamentally is the desire to be God.

It may be asked, if man on coming into the world is tending toward God as toward his limit, if he can choose only to be God, what becomes of freedom? For freedom is nothing other than a choice which creates for itself its own possibilities, but it appears here that the initial project of being God, which "defines" man, comes close to being the same as a human "nature" or an "essence." The answer is that while the *meaning* of the desire is ultimately the project of being God, the desire is never *constituted* by this meaning; on the contrary, it always represents a particular discovery of its ends. These ends in fact are pursued in terms of a particular empirical situation, and it is this very pursuit which constitutes the surroundings *as a situation*. The desire of being is always realized as the desire of a mode of being. And this desire of a mode of being expresses itself in turn as the meaning of the myriads of concrete desires which constitute the web of our conscious life. Thus we find ourselves before very complex symbolic structures which have *at least* three stories. In empirical desire I can discern a symbolization of a fundamental concrete desire which is the person himself and which represents the mode in which he has decided that being would be in question in his being. This fundamental desire in turn expresses concretely in the world within the particular situation enveloping the individual, an abstract meaningful structure which is the desire of being in general; it must be considered as human reality in the person, and it brings about his community with others, thus making it possible to state that there is a truth concerning man and not only concerning individuals who cannot be compared. Absolute concreteness, completion, existence as a totality belong then to the free and fundamental desire which is the unique person. Empirical desire is only a symbolization of this; it refers to this and derives its meaning from it while remaining partial and reducible, for the empirical desire can not be conceived in isolation. On the other hand, the desire of being in its abstract purity is the *truth* of the concrete fundamental desire, but it does not exist by virtue of reality. Thus the fundamental project, the person, the free realization of human truth is everywhere in all desires (save for those exceptions treated in the preceding chapter, concerning, for example, "indifferents"). It is never apprehended except through desires—as we can apprehend space only through bodies which shape it for us, though space is a specific reality and not a concept. Or, if you like, it is like the *object* of Husserl, which reveals itself only by *Abschattungen*, and which nevertheless does not allow itself to be absorbed by any one *Abschattung*. We can understand after these remarks that the abstract, ontological "desire to be" is unable to represent the fundamental, *human* structure of the individual; it cannot be an obstacle to his freedom. Freedom in fact, as we have shown in the preceding chapter, is strictly identified with nihilation. The only being which can be called free is the being which nihilates its being. Moreover we know that nihilation is *lack of being* and can not be otherwise. Freedom is precisely the being which makes itself a lack of being. But since desire, as we have established, is identical with lack of being, freedom can arise only as being which makes itself a desire of being; that is, as the project-for-itself of being in-itself-for-itself. Here we have arrived at an abstract structure which can by no means be considered as the nature or essence of freedom. Freedom is existence, and in it existence precedes essence. The upsurge of freedom is immediate and concrete and is not to be distinguished from its choice; that is, from the person himself. But the structure under consideration can be called the truth of freedom; that is, it is the human meaning of freedom.

It should be possible to establish the human truth of the person, as we have attempted to do by an ontological phenomenology. The catalogue of empirical desires ought to be made the object of appropriate psychological investigations, observation and induction and, as needed, experience can serve to draw up this list. They will indicate to the philosopher the comprehensible relations which can unite to each other various desires and various patterns of behaviors, and will bring to light certain concrete connections between the subject of experience and "situations" experientially defined (which at bottom originate only from limitations applied in the name of positivity to the fundamental situation of the subject in the world). But in establishing and classifying fundamental desires of *individual persons* neither of these methods is appropriate. Actually there can be no question of determining *a priori* and ontologically what appears in all the unpredictability of a free act. This is why we shall limit ourselves here to indicating very summarily the possibilities of such a quest and its perspectives. The very fact that we can subject any man whatsoever to such an investigation—that is what belongs to human reality in general. Or, if you prefer, this is what can be established by an ontology. But the inquiry itself and its results are on principle wholly outside the possibilities of an ontology.

On the other hand, pure, simple empirical description can only give us catalogues and put us in the presence of pseudo-irreducibles (the desire to write, to swim, a taste for adventure, jealousy, etc.). It is not enough in fact to draw up a list of behavior patterns, of drives and inclinations, it is necessary also to *decipher* them; that is, it is necessary to know how to *question* them. This research can be conducted only according to the rules of a specific method. It is this method which we call existential psychoanalysis.

The *principle* of this psychoanalysis is that man is a totality and not a collection. Consequently he expresses himself as a whole in even his most insignificant and his most superficial behavior. In other words there is not a taste, a mannerism, or an human act which is not *revealing*.

The *goal* of psychoanalysis is to *decipher* the empirical behavior patterns of man; that is to bring out in the open the revelations which each one of them contains and to fix them conceptually.

Its *point of departure is experience*; its pillar of support is the fundamental, pre-ontological comprehension which man has of the human person. Although the majority of people can well ignore the indications contained in a gesture, a word, a sign and can look with scorn on the revelation which they carry, each human individual nevertheless possesses *a priori* the *meaning* of the revelatory value of these manifestations and is capable of deciphering them, at least if he is aided and guided by a helping hand. Here as elsewhere, truth is not encountered by chance; it does not belong to a domain where one must seek it without ever having any presentiment of its location, as one can go to look for the source of the Nile or of the Niger. It belongs *a priori* to human comprehension and the essential task is an hermeneutic; that is, a deciphering, a determination, and a conceptualization.

Its *method* is comparative. Since each example of human conduct symbolizes in its own manner the fundamental choice which must be brought to light, and since at the same time each one disguises this choice under its occasional character and its historical opportunity, only the comparison of these acts of conduct can effect the emergence of the unique revelation which they all express in a different way. The first outline of this method has been furnished for us by the psychoanalysis of Freud and his disciples. For this reason it will be profitable here to indicate more specifically the points where existential psychoanalysis will be inspired by psychoanalysis proper and those where it will radically differ from it.

Both kinds of psychoanalysis consider all objectively discernible manifestations of "psychic life" as symbols maintaining symbolic relations to the fundamental, total structures which constitute the individual person. Both consider that there are no primary givens such as hereditary dispositions, character, *etc.* Existential psychoanalysis recognizes nothing *before* the original upsurge of human freedom; empirical psychoanalysis holds that the original affectivity of the individual is virgin wax *before* its history. The libido is nothing besides its concrete fixations, save for a permanent possibility of fixing anything whatsoever upon anything whatsoever. Both consider the human being as a perpetual, searching, historization. Rather than uncovering static, constant givens they discover the meaning, orientation, and adventures of this history. Due to this fact both consider man in the world and do not imagine that one can question the being of a man without taking into account all his *situation*. Psychological investigations aim at reconstituting the life of the subject from birth to the moment of the cure; they utilize all the objective documentation which they can find; letters, witnesses, intimate diaries, "social" information of every kind. What they aim at restoring is less a pure psychic event than a twofold structure: the crucial event of infancy and the psychic crystallization around this event. Here again we have to do with a *situation*. Each "historical" fact from this point of view will be considered at once as *a factor* of the psychic evolution and as a *symbol* of that evolution. For it is nothing in itself. It operates only according to the way in which it is taken and this very manner of taking it expresses symbolically the internal disposition of the individual.

Empirical psychoanalysis and existential psychoanalysis both search within an existing situation for a fundamental attitude which can not be expressed by simple, logical definitions because it is prior to all logic, and which requires reconstruction according to the laws of specific syntheses. Empirical psychoanalysis seeks to determine the *complex*, the very name of which indicates the polyvalence of all the meanings which are referred back to it. Existential psychoanalysis seeks to determine the *original choice*. This original choice operating in front of the world and being a choice of position in the world is total like the complex; it is prior to logic like the complex. It is this which decides the attitude of the person when confronted with logic and principles; therefore there can be no possibility of questioning it in conformance to logic. It brings together in a prelogical synthesis the totality of the existent, and as such it is the center of reference for an infinity of polyvalent meanings.

Both our psychoanalyses refuse to admit that the subject is in a privileged position to proceed in these inquiries concerning himself. They equally insist on a strictly objective method, using as documentary evidence the data of reflection as well as the testimony of others. Of course the subject *can* undertake a psychoanalytic investigation of himself. But in this case he must renounce at the outset all benefit stemming from his peculiar position and must question himself exactly as if he were someone else. Empirical psychoanalysis in fact is based on the hypothesis of the existence of an unconscious psyche, which on principle escapes the intuition of the subject. Existential psychoanalysis rejects the hypothesis of the unconscious; it makes the psychic act coextensive with consciousness. But if the fundamental project is fully experienced by the subject and hence wholly conscious, that certainly does not mean that it must by the same token be *known* by him; quite the contrary. The reader will perhaps recall the care we took in the Introduction to distinguish between consciousness and knowledge. To be sure, as we have seen earlier, reflection can be considered as a quasi-knowledge. But what it graps at each moment is not the pure project of the for-itself as it is symbolically expressed—often in several ways at once—by the concrete behavior which it apprehends. It grasps the concrete behavior itself; that is, the specific dated desire in all its characteristic network. It grasps at once symbol and symbolization. This apprehension, to be sure, is entirely constituted by a preontological comprehension of the fundamental project; better yet, in so far as reflection is almost a non-thetic consciousness of itself as reflection, it is this same project, as well as the non-reflective consciousness. But it does not follow that it commands the instruments and techniques necessary to isolate the choice symbolized, to fix it by concepts, and to bring it forth into the full light of day. It is penetrated by a great light without being able to express what this light is illuminating. We are not dealing with an unsolved riddle as the Freudians believe; all is there, luminous; reflection is in full possession of it, apprehends all. But this "mystery in broad daylight" is due to the fact that this possession is deprived of the means which would ordinarily permit *analysis* and *conceptualization*. It grasps everything, all at once, without shading, without relief, without any scale of sizes—not that these shades, these values, these reliefs exist somewhere and are hidden from it, but rather because they must be established by another human attitude and because they can exist only *by means of* and *for* knowledge. Reflection, unable to serve as the basis for existential psychoanalysis, will then simply furnish us with the brute materials toward which the psychoanalyst must take an objective attitude. Thus only will he be able to *know* what he *already understands*. The result is that complexes uprooted from the depths of the unconscious, like projects revealed by existential psychoanalysis, will be apprehended from *the point of view of the Other*. Consequently the *object* thus brought into the light will be articulated according to the structures of the transcended-transcendence; that is, its being will be the being-for-others even if the psychoanalyst and the subject of the psychoanalysis are actually the same person. Thus the project which is brought to light by either kind of psychoanalysis can be only the totality of the individual human being, the irreducible element of the transcendence with the structure of *being-for-others*. What always escapes these methods of investigation is the project as it is for itself, the complex in its own being. This project-for-itself can be enjoyed; there is an incompatibility between existence for-itself and objective existence. But the object of the two psychoanalyses has nonetheless the *reality of a being*; the subject's knowledge of it can in addition contribute to *clarify* reflection, and that reflection can then become a possession which will be a quasi-knowing.

At this point the similarity between the two kinds of psychoanalysis ceases. They differ fundamentally in that empirical psychoanalysis has decided upon its own irreducible instead of allowing this to make itself known in a self-evident intuition. The libido or the will to power in fact constitutes a psycho-biological residue which is not clear in itself and which does not appear to us as having to be the irreducible limit of the investigation. Finally it is experience which establishes that the foundation of complexes is this libido or this will to power; and these results of empirical inquiry are perfectly contingent, they are not convincing. Nothing prevents our conceiving *a priori* of a "human reality" which would not be expressed by the will to power, for which the libido would not constitute the original, undifferentiated project.

On the contrary, the choice to which existential psychoanalysis will lead us, precisely because it is a choice, accounts for its original contingency, for the contingency of the choice is the reverse side of its freedom. Furthermore, inasmuch as it is established on the *lack of being*, conceived as a fundamental characteristic of being, it receives its legitimacy *as a choice*, and we know that we do not have to push further. Each result then will be at once fully contingent and legitimately irreducible. Moreover it will always remain *particular*;

that is, we will not achieve as the ultimate goal of our investigation and the foundation of all behavior an abstract, general term, libido for example, which would be differentiated and made concrete first in complexes and then in detailed acts of conduct, due to the action of external facts and the history of the subject. On the contrary, it will be a choice which remains unique and which is from the start absolute concreteness. Details of behavior can express or *particularize* this choice, but they can not make it more concrete than it already is. That is because the choice is nothing other than the being of each human reality, and because it amounts to the same thing to say that a particular partial behavior *is* or that it expresses the original choice of this human reality since for human reality there is no difference between existing and choosing for itself. From this fact we understand that existential psychoanalysis does not have to proceed from the fundamental "complex," which is exactly the choice of being, to an abstraction like the libido which would explain it. The complex is the ultimate choice, it is the choice of being and *makes itself such*. Bringing it into the light will reveal it each time as evidently irreducible. It follows necessarily that the libido and the will to power will appear to existential psychoanalysis neither as general characteristics common to all mankind nor as irreducibles. At most it will be possible after the investigation to establish that they express by virtue of particular ensembles in certain subjects a fundamental choice which can not be reduced to either one of them. We have seen in fact that desire and sexuality in general express an original effort of the for-itself to recover its being which has become alienated through contact with the Other. The will to power also originally supposes being-for-others, the comprehension of the Other, and the choice of winning its own salvation by means of the Other. The foundation of this attitude must be an original choice which would make us understand the radical identification of being-in-itself-for-itself with being-for-others.

The fact that the ultimate term of this existential inquiry must be a *choice*, distinguishes even better the psychoanalysis for which we have outlined the method and principal features. It thereby abandons the supposition that the environment acts mechanically on the subject under consideration. The environment can act on the subject only to the exact extent that he understands it; that is, transforms it into a situation. Hence no objective description of this environment could be of any use to us, From the start the environment conceived as a situation refers to the for-itself which is choosing, just as the for-itself refers to the environment by the very fact that the for-itself is in the world. By renouncing all mechanical causation, we renounce at the same time all *general* interpretation of the symbolization confronted. Our goal could not be to establish empirical laws of succession, nor could we constitute a universal symbolism. Rather the psychoanalyst will have to rediscover at each step a symbol functioning in the particular case which he is considering. If each being is a totality, it is not conceivable that there can exist elementary symbolic relationships (*e.g.*; the faeces = gold, or a pincushion = the breast) which preserve a constant meaning in all cases; that is, which remain unaltered when they pass from one meaningful ensemble to another ensemble. Furthermore the psychoanalyst will never lose sight of the fact that the choice is living and consequently can be *revoked* by the subject who is being studied. We have shown in the preceding chapter the importance of the *instant*, which represents abrupt changes in orientation and the assuming of a new position in the face of an unalterable past. From this moment on, we must always be ready to consider that symbols change meaning and to abandon the symbol used hitherto. Thus existential psychoanalysis will have to be completely flexible and adapt itself to the slightest observable changes in the subject. Our concern here is to understand what is *individual* and often even instantaneous. The method which has served for one subject will not necessarily be suitable to use for another subject or for the same subject at a later period.

Precisely because the goal of the inquiry must be to discover a *choice* and not a *state*, the investigator must recall on every occasion that his object is not a datum buried in the darkness of the unconscious but a free, conscious determination—which is not even resident in consciousness, but which is one with this consciousness itself. Empirical psychoanalysis, to the extent that its method is better than its principles, is often in sight of an existential discovery, but it always stops part way. When it thus approaches the fundamental choice, the resistance of the subject collapses suddenly and he *recognizes* the image of himself which is presented to him as if he were seeing himself in a mirror. This involuntary testimony of the subject is precious for the psychoanalyst; he sees there the sign that he has reached his goal; he can pass on from the investigation proper to the cure. But nothing in his principles or in his initial postulates permits him to understand or to utilize this testimony. Where could he get any such right? If the complex is really unconscious— that is, if there is a barrier separating the sign from the thing signified—how could the subject *recognize* it? Does the unconscious complex recognize itself? But haven't we been told that it lacks *understanding*? And if of necessity we granted to it the faculty of understanding the signs, would this not be to make of it by the same token a conscious unconscious? What is understanding if not to be conscious that we have understood? Shall we say on the other hand that it is the subject as conscious who recognizes the image presented? But how could he compare it with his true state since that is out of reach and since he has never had any knowledge of it? At most he will be able to judge that the psychoanalytic explanation of his case is a *probable* hypothesis, which derives its probability from the number of behavior patterns which it explains. His relation to this interpretation is that of a third party, that of the psychoanalyst himself; he has no privileged position. And if he *believes* in the probability of the psychoanalytic hypothesis, is this simple belief, which lives in the limits of his consciousness, able to effect the breakdown of the barriers which dam up the unconscious tendencies? The psychoanalyst doubtless has some obscure picture of an abrupt coincidence of conscious and unconscious. But he has removed all methods of conceiving of this coincidence in any positive sense.

Still, the enlightenment of the subject is a fact. There is an intuition here which is accompanied by evidence. The subject guided by the psychoanalyst does more and better than to give his agreement to an hypothesis; he touches it, he sees what it is. This is truly understandable only if the subject has never ceased being conscious of his deep tendencies; better yet, only if these drives are not distinguished from his conscious self. In this case as we have seen, the traditional psychoanalytic interpretation does not cause him to attain *consciousness* of what he is; it causes him to attain *knowledge* of what he is. It is existential psychoanalysis then which claims the final intuition of the subject as decisive.

This comparison allows us to understand better what an existential psychoanalysis must be if it is entitled to exist. It is a method destined to bring to light, in a strictly objective form, the subjective choice by which each living person makes himself a person; that is, makes known to himself what he is. Since what the method seeks is a *choice of being* at the same time as a *being*, it must reduce particular behavior patterns to fundamental relations—not of sexuality or of the will to power, but *of being*—which are expressed in this behavior. It is then guided from the start toward a comprehension of being and must not assign itself any other goal than to discover being and the mode of being of the being confronting this being. It is forbidden to stop before attaining this goal. It will utilize the comprehension of being which characterizes the investigator inasmuch as he is himself a human reality; and as it seeks to detach being from its symbolic expressions, it will have to rediscover each time on the basis of a comparative study of acts and attitudes, a symbol destined to decipher them. Its criterion of success will be the number of facts which its hypothesis permits it to explain and to unify as well as the self-evident intuition of the irreducibility of the end attained. To this criterion will be added in all cases where it is possible, the decisive testimony of the subject. The results thus achieved—that is, the ultimate ends of the individual—can then become the object of a classification, and it is by the comparison of these results that we will be able to establish general considerations about human reality as an empirical choice of its own ends. The behavior studied by this psychoanalysis will include not only dreams, failures, obsessions, and neuroses, but also and especially the thoughts of waking life, successfully adjusted acts, style, *etc*. This psychoanalysis has not yet found its Freud. At most we can find the foreshadowing of it in certain particularly successful biographies. We hope to be able to attempt elsewhere two examples in relation to Flaubert and Dostoevsky. But it matters little to us whether it now exists; the important thing is that it is possible.

## II. "DOING" AND "HAVING": POSSESSION

The information which ontology can furnish concerning behavior patterns and desire must serve as the basic principles of existential psychoanalysis. This does not mean that there is an over-all pattern of abstract desires common to all men; it means that concrete desires have structures which emerge during the study of ontology because each desire—the desire of eating or of sleeping as well as the desire of creating a work of art—expresses all human reality. As I have shown elsewhere,[3] the knowledge of man must be a totality; empirical, partial pieces of knowledge on this level lack all significance. We shall succeed in our task if we utilize the pieces of knowledge achieved up to this point, for laying down the bases of existential psychoanalysis. Indeed this is the point where ontology must stop; its final discoveries are the first principles of psychoanalysis. Henceforth we must have another method since the object is different. What then does ontology teach us about desire, since desire is the being of human reality?

Desire is a lack of being. As such it is directly oriented toward the being of which it is a lack. This being, as we have said, is the in-itself-for-itself, consciousness become substance, substance become the cause of itself, the Man-God. Thus the being of human reality is originally not a substance but a lived relation. The limiting terms of this relation are first the original In-itself, fixed in its contingency and its facticity, its essential characteristic being that it is, that it exists; and second the In-itself-for-itself or value, which exists as the Ideal of the contingent In-itself and which is characterized as beyond all contingency and all existence. Man is neither the one nor the other of these beings, for strictly speaking, we should never say of him that he *is* at all. He is what he is not and he is not what he is; he is the nihilation of the contingent In-itself in so far as the self of this nihilation is its flight ahead toward the In-itself as self-cause. Human reality is the pure effort to become God without there being any given substratum for that effort, without there being *anything* which so endeavours. Desire expresses this endeavour.

Nevertheless desire is not defined solely in relation to the In-itself-as-self-cause. It is also relative to a brute, concrete existent which we commonly call the object of the desire. This object may be now a slice of bread, now an

---

[3] *Esquisse d'une théorie phénoménologique des émotions.* Hermann, 1939.

automobile, now a woman, now an object not yet realized and yet defined—as when the artist desires to create a work of art. Thus by its very structure desire expresses a man's relation to one or several objects in the world; it is one of the aspects of Being-in-the-world. From this point of view we see first that this relation is not of a unique type. It is only by a sort of abbreviation that we speak of "the desire of something." Actually a thousand empirical examples show that we desire to *possess* this object or to *do* that thing or to *be* someone. If I desire this picture, it means that I desire to buy it, to appropriate it for myself. If I desire to write a book, to go for a walk, it means that I desire to "do" this book, to "do" this walk. If I dress up, it is because I desire to be well-groomed. I train myself in order to *be* a scientist, *etc.* Thus from the outset, the three big categories of concrete human existence appear to us in their original relation: *to do, to have, to be.*[4]

It is easy to see, however, that the desire to do is not irreducible. One does (= makes) an object in order to enter into a certain relation with it. This new relation can be immediately reducible to *having.* For example, I cut a cane from a branch of a tree (I *do* a cane out of a branch) in order to *have* this cane. The "doing" is reduced to a mode of having. This is the most common example. But it can also happen that my activity does not appear on the surface as reducible. It can appear gratuitous as in the case of scientific research, or sport, or aesthetic creation. Yet in these various examples doing is still not irreducible. If I create a picture, a drama, a melody, it is in order that I may be at the origin of a concrete existence. This existence interests me only to the degree that the bond of creation which I establish between it and me gives to me a particular right of ownership over it. It is not enough that a certain picture which I have in mind should exist; it is necessary as well that it exist *through me.* Evidently in one sense the ideal would be that I should sustain the picture in being by a sort of continuous creation and that consequently it should be *mine* as though by a perpetually renewed emanation. But in another sense it must be radically distinct from myself—in order that it may be *mine* but not *me.* Here as in the Cartesian theory of substances, there is danger that the being of the created object may be reabsorbed in my being because of lack of independence and objectivity; hence it must of necessity exist also *in itself,* must perpetually renew its existence *by itself.* Consequently my work appears to me as a continuous creation but fixed in the in-itself; it carries indefinitely my "mark"; that is, it is for an indefinite period "my" thought. Every work of art is a thought, an "idea"; its characteristics are plainly ideal to the extent that it is nothing but a meaning. But on the other hand, this meaning, this thought which is in one sense perpetually active as if I were

[4] The reader will recall that as stated earlier the French word *faire* means both "do" and "make." Tr.

perpetually forming it, as if a mind were conceiving it without respite—a mind which would be my mind—this thought sustains itself alone in being; it by no means ceases to be active when I am not actually thinking it. I stand to it then in the double relation of the consciousness which conceives it and the consciousness which encounters it. It is precisely this double relation which I express by saying that it is mine. We shall see the meaning of it when we have defined precisely the significance of the category "to have." It is in order to enter into this double relation in the synthesis of appropriation that I create my work. In fact it is this synthesis of self and not-self (the intimacy and translucency of thought on the one hand and the opacity and indifference of the in-itself on the other) that I am aiming at and which will establish my ownership of the work. In this sense it is not only strictly artistic works which I appropriate in this manner. This cane which I have cut from the branch is also destined to belong to me in this double relation: first as an object for everyday use, which is at my disposition and which I possess as I possess my clothes or my books, and second as my own work. Thus people who like to surround themselves with everyday objects which they themselves have made, are enjoying subtleties of appropriation. They unite in a single object and in one syncretism the appropriation by enjoyment and the appropriation by creation. We find this same uniting into a single project everywhere from artistic creation to the cigarette which "is better when I roll it myself." Later we shall meet this project in connection with a special type of ownership which stands as the degradation of it—luxury—for we shall see that luxury is distinguished not as a quality of the object possessed but as a quality of possession.

Knowing also—as we showed in the introduction to Part Four—is a form of appropriation. That is why scientific research is nothing other than an effort to appropriate. The truth discovered, like the work of art, is my knowledge; it is the noema of a thought which is discovered only when I form the thought and which consequently appears in a certain way as maintained in existence by me. It is through me that a facet of the world is revealed; it is to me that it reveals itself. In this sense I am creator and possessor, not that I consider the aspect of being which I discover, as a pure representation, but on the contrary, because this aspect although it is revealed only by me, exists profoundly and really. I can say only that I manifest it in the sense that Gide tells us that "we always ought to manifest." But I find again an independence analogous to that of the work of art in the character of the truth of my thought; that is, in its objectivity. This thought which I form and which derives its existence from me pursues at the same time its own independent existence to the extent that it is thought by everybody. It is doubly "I": it is the world revealing itself to me and it is "I" in relation to others, I forming my thought with the mind of others. At the same time it is doubly closed against me: it is the being which I am not (inasmuch as it reveals itself to me), and since it is thought by all from the moment of its appearance, it is a thought devoted to anonymity. This synthesis of self and not-self can be expressed here by the term "mine."

In addition the idea of discovery, of revelation, includes an idea of appropriative enjoyment. What is seen is possessed; to see is to *deflower*. If we examine the comparisons ordinarily used to express the relation between the knower and the known, we see that many of them are represented as being a kind of *violation by sight*. The unknown object is given as immaculate, as virgin, comparable to a *whiteness*. It has not yet "delivered up" its secret; man has not yet "snatched" its secret away from it. All these images insist that the object is ignorant of the investigations and the instruments aimed at it; it is unconscious of being known; it goes about its business without noticing the glance which spies on it, like a woman whom a passerby catches unaware at her bath. Figures of speech, sometimes vague and sometimes more precise, like that of the "unviolated depths" of nature suggest the idea of sexual intercourse more plainly. We speak of snatching away her veils from nature, of unveiling her (cf. Schiller's *Veiled Image of Saïs*). Every investigation implies the idea of a nudity which one brings out into the open by clearing away the obstacles which cover it, just as Actaeon clears away the branches so that he can have a better view of Diana at her bath. More than this, knowledge is a hunt. Bacon called it the hunt of Pan. The scientist is the hunter who surprises a white nudity and who violates by looking at it. Thus the totality of these images reveals something which we shall call the *Actaeon complex*.

By taking this idea of the hunt as a guiding thread, we shall discover another symbol of appropriation, perhaps still more primitive: a person hunts for the sake of eating. Curiosity in an animal is always either sexual or alimentary. To know is to devour with the eyes.[5] In fact we can note here, so far as knowledge through the senses is concerned, a process the reverse of that which was discovered in connection with the work of art. We remarked that the work of art is like a fixed emanation of the mind. The mind is continually creating it and yet it stands alone and indifferent in relation to that creation. This same relation exists in the act of knowing, but its opposite is not excluded. In knowing, consciousness attracts the object to itself and incorporates it in itself. Knowledge is assimilation. The writings of French epistemology swarm with alimentary metaphors (absorption, digestion, assimilation). There is a movement of dissolution which passes from the object to the knowing subject. The known is transformed into *me*; it becomes my thought and thereby consents to receive its existence from me alone. But this movement of dissolution is fixed by the fact that the known remains in

[5] For the child, knowing involves actually eating. He wants to taste what he sees. (We might, I suppose, compare Ben Jonson's "Drink to Me Only with Thine Eyes"! Tr.)

the same place, indefinitely absorbed, devoured, and yet indefinitely intact, wholly digested and yet wholly outside, as indigestible as a stone. For naive imaginations the symbol of the "digested indigestible" is very important; for example, the stone in the stomach of the ostrich or Jonah in the stomach of the whale. The symbol represents the dream of a non-destructive assimilation. It is an unhappy fact—as Hegel noted—that desire destroys its object. In this sense, he said, desire is the desire of devouring. In reaction against this dialectical necessity, the For-itself dreams of an object which may be entirely assimilated by me, which would be me, without dissolving into me but still keeping the structure of the in-itself; for what I desire exactly is this object; and if I eat it, I do not have it any more, I find nothing remaining except myself.

This impossible synthesis of assimilation and an assimilated which maintains its integrity, has deep-rooted connections with basic sexual drives. The idea of "carnal possession" offers us the irritating but seductive figure of a body perpetually possessed and perpetually new, on which possession leaves no trace. This is deeply symbolized in the quality of "smooth" or "polished." What is smooth can be taken and felt but remains no less impenetrable, does not give way in the least beneath the appropriative caress—it is like water. This is the reason why erotic descriptions insist on the smooth whiteness of a woman's body. Smooth— it is what re-forms itself under the caress, as water re-forms itself in its passage over the stone which has pierced it. At the same time, as we have seen earlier, the lover's dream is to identify the beloved object with himself and still preserve for it its own individuality; let the Other become me without ceasing to be the Other. It is at this point that we encounter the similarity to scientific research: the known object, like the stone in the stomach of the ostrich, is entirely within me, assimilated, transformed into myself, and it is entirely me; but at the same time it is impenetrable, untransformable, entirely smooth, with the indifferent nudity of a body which is beloved and caressed in vain. It remains outside; to know it is to devour it yet without consuming it. We see here how the sexual and alimentary currents mingle and interpenetrate in order to constitute the Actaeon complex and the Jonah complex; we can see the digestive and sensual roots which are reunited to give birth to the desire of knowing. Knowledge is at one and the same time a *penetration* and a *superficial* caress, a digestion and the contemplation from afar of an object which will never lose its form, the production of a thought by a continuous creation and the establishment of the total objective independence of that thought. The known object is *my thought as a thing*. This is precisely what I profoundly desire when I undertake my research —to apprehend my thought as a thing and the thing as my thought. The syncretic relation which provides the basis for the ensemble of such diverse tendencies can be only a relation of *appropriation*. That is why the desire to know, no matter how disinterested it may appear, is a relation of appropriation. To *know* is one of the forms which can be assumed by to *have*.

There remains one type of activity which is willingly presented as entirely gratuitous; the activity of *play* and the "drives" which relate back to it. Can we discover an appropriative drive in sport? To be sure, it must be noted first that play as contrasted with the spirit of seriousness appears to be the least possessive attitude; it strips the real of its reality. The serious attitude involves starting from the world and attributing more reality to the world than to oneself; at the very least the serious man confers reality on himself to the degree to which he belongs to the world. It is not by chance that materialism is serious; it is not by chance that it is found at all times and places as the favorite doctrine of the revolutionary. This is because revolutionaries are serious. They come to know themselves first in terms of the world which oppresses them, and they wish to change this world. In this one respect they are in agreement with their ancient adversaries, the possessors, who also come to know themselves and appreciate themselves in terms of their position in the world. Thus all serious thought is thickened by the world; it coagulates; it is a dismissal of human reality in favor of the world. The serious man is "of the world" and has no resource in himself. He does not even imagine any longer the possibility of *getting out* of the world, for he has given to himself the type of existence of the rock, the consistency, the inertia, the opacity of being-in-the-midst-of-the-world. It is obvious that the serious man at bottom is hiding from himself the consciousness of his freedom; he is in *bad faith* and his bad faith aims at presenting himself to his own eyes as a consequence; everything is a consequence for him, and there is never any beginning. That is why he is so concerned with the consequences of his acts. Marx proposed the original dogma of the serious when he asserted the priority of object over subject. Man is serious when he takes himself for an object.

Play, like Kierkegaard's irony, releases subjectivity. What is play indeed if not an activity of which man is the first origin, for which man himself sets the rules, and which has no consequences except according to the rules posited? As soon as a man apprehends himself as free and wishes to use his freedom, a freedom, by the way, which could just as well be his anguish, then his activity is play. The first principle of play is man himself; through it he escapes his natural nature; he himself sets the value and rules for his acts and consents to play only according to the rules which he himself has established and defined. As a result, there is in a sense "little reality" in the world. It might appear then that when a man is playing, bent on discovering himself as free in his very action, he certainly could not be concerned with *possessing* a being in the world. His goal, which he aims at through sports or pantomime or games, is to attain himself as a certain being, precisely the being which is in question in his being.

The point of these remarks, however, is not to show us that in play the desire to *do* is irreducible. On the contrary we must conclude that the desire to do is here reduced to a certain desire to be. The act is not its own goal for itself; neither does its explicit end represent its goal and its profound meaning; but the function of the act is to make manifest and to present to *itself* the absolute freedom which is the very being of the person. This particular type of project, which has freedom for its foundation and its goal, deserves a special study. It is radically different from all others in that it aims at a radically different type of being. It would be necessary to explain in full detail its relations with the project of being-God, which has appeared to us as the deep-seated structure of human reality. But such a study can not be made here; it belongs rather to an *Ethics* and it supposes that there has been a preliminary definition of nature and the role of purifying reflection (our descriptions have hitherto aimed only at *accessory* reflection); it supposes in addition taking a position which can be *moral* only in the face of values which haunt the For itself. Nevertheless the fact remains that the desire to play is fundamentally the desire to be.

Thus the three categories "to be," "to do," and "to have" are reduced here as everywhere to two; "to do" is purely transitional. Ultimately a desire can be only the desire *to be* or the desire *to have*. On the other hand, it is seldom that play is pure of all appropriative tendency. I am passing over the desire of achieving a good performance or of beating a record which can act as a stimulant for the sportsman; I am not even speaking of the desire "to have" a handsome body and harmonious muscles, which springs from the desire of appropriating objectively to myself my own being-for-others. These desires do not always enter in and besides they are not fundamental. But there is always in sport an appropriative component. In reality sport is a free transformation of the worldly environment into the supporting element of the action. This fact makes it creative like art. The environment may be a field of snow, an Alpine slope. To see it is already to possess it. In itself it is already apprehended by sight as a symbol of being.[6] It represents pure exteriority, radical spatiality; its undifferentiation, its monotony, and its whiteness manifest the absolute nudity of substance; it is the in-itself which is only in-itself, the being of the phenomenon, which being is manifested suddenly outside all phenomena. At the same time its *solid* immobility expresses the permanence and the objective resistance of the In-itself, its opacity and its impenetrability. Yet this first intuitive enjoyment can not suffice me. That pure in-itself, comparable to the absolute, intelligible plenum of Cartesian

[6] See section III.

extension, fascinates me as the pure appearance of the not-me; What I wish precisely is that this in-itself might be a sort of emanation of myself while still remaining in itself. This is the meaning even of the snowmen and snowballs which children make; the goal is to "do something out of snow"; that is, to impose on it a form which adheres so deeply to the matter that the matter appears to exist for the sake of the form. But if I approach, if I want to establish an appropriative contact with the field of snow, everything is changed. Its scale of being is modified; it exists bit by bit instead of existing in vast spaces; stains, brush, and crevices come to individualize each square inch. At the same time its solidity melts into water. I sink into the snow up to my knees; if I pick some up with my hands, it turns to liquid in my fingers; it runs off; there is nothing left of it. The in-itself is transformed into nothingness. My dream of appropriating the snow vanishes at the same moment. Moreover I *do not know what to do* with this snow which I have just come to see close at hand. I can not get hold of the field; I can not even reconstitute it as that substantial total which offered itself to my eyes and which has abruptly, doubly collapsed.

To ski means not only to enable me to make rapid movements and to acquire a technical skill, nor is it merely to *play* by increasing according to my whim the speed or difficulties of the course; it is also to enable me to *possess* this field of snow. At present I *am doing something to it*. That means that by my very activity as a skier, I am changing the matter and meaning of the snow. From the fact that now in my course it appears to me as a slope to go down, it finds again a continuity and a unity which it had lost. It is at the moment connective tissue. It is included between two limiting terms; it unites the point of departure with the point of arrival. Since in the descent I do not consider it in itself, bit by bit, but am always fixing on a point to be reached beyond the position which I now occupy, it does not collapse into an infinity of individual details but is *traversed toward* the point which I assign myself. This traversal is not only an activity of movement; it is also and especially a synthetic activity of organization and connection; I spread the skiing field before me in the same way that the geometrician, according to Kant, can apprehend a straight line only by drawing one. Furthermore this organization is marginal and not focal; it is not for itself and in itself that the field of snow is unified; the goal, posited and clearly perceived, the object of my attention is the spot at the edge of the field where I shall arrive. The snowy space is massed underneath implicitly; its cohesion is that of the blank space understood in the interior of a circumference, for example, when I look at the black line of the circle without paying explicit attention to its surface. And precisely because I maintain it marginal, implicit, and understood, it adapts itself to me, I have it well in hand; I pass beyond it toward its end just as a man hanging a tapestry passes beyond the hammer which he uses, toward its end, which is to nail an arras on the wall.

No appropriation can be more complete than this instrumental appropriation; the synthetic activity of appropriation is here a technical activity of utilization. The upsurge of the snow is the matter of my act in the same way that the upswing of the hammer is the pure fulfillment of the hammering. At the same time I have chosen a certain point of view in order to apprehend this snowy slope: this point of view is a determined *speed*, which emanates from me, which I can increase or diminish as I like; through it the field traversed is constituted as a definite object, entirely distinct from what it would be at another speed. The speed organizes the ensembles at will; a specific object does or does not form a part of a particular group according to whether I have or have not taken a particular speed. (Think, for example, of Provence seen "on foot," "by car," "by train," "by bicycle." It offers as many different aspects according to whether or not Béziers is one hour, a morning's trip, or two days distant from Narbonne: that is, according to whether Narbonne is isolated and posited for itself with its environs or whether it constitutes a coherent group with Béziers and Sète, for example. In this last case Narbonne's *relation to the sea* is directly accessible to intuition; in the other it is denied; it can form the object only of a pure concept.) It is I myself then who give form to the field of snow by the free speed which I give myself. But at the same time I am acting upon *my matter*. The speed is not limited to imposing a form on a matter given from the outside; it *creates* its matter. The snow, which sank under my weight when I walked, which melted into water when I tried to pick it up, solidifies suddenly under the action of my speed; it supports me. It is not that I have lost sight of its lightness, its nonsubstantiality, its perpetual evanescence. Quite the contrary. It is precisely that lightness, that evanescence, that secret liquidity which hold me up; that is, which condense and melt in order to support me. This is because I hold a special relation of appropriation with the snow: *sliding*. This relation we will study later in detail. But at the moment we can grasp its essential meaning. We think of sliding as remaining on the surface. This is inexact; to be sure, I only skim the surface, and this skimming in itself is worth a whole study. Nevertheless I realize a synthesis which has depth. I realize that the bed of snow organizes itself in its lowest depths in order to hold me up; the sliding is action *at a distance*; it assures my mastery over the material without my needing to plunge into that material and engulf myself in it in order to overcome it. To slide is the opposite of taking root. The root is already half assimilated into the earth which nourishes it; it is a living concretion of the earth; it can utilize the earth only by making itself earth; that is, by submitting itself, in a sense, to the matter which it wishes to utilize. Sliding, on the contrary, realizes a material unity in depth without penetrating farther than the surface; it is like the dreaded master who does not need to insist nor to raise his voice in order to be obeyed. An admirable picture of power. From this comes that famous advice: "Slide, mortals, don't bear down!" This does not mean "Stay on the surface, don't go deeply into things," but on the contrary, "Realize syntheses in depth without compromising yourself."

Sliding is appropriation precisely because the synthesis of support realized by the speed is valid only for the slider and during the actual time when he is sliding. The solidity of the snow is effective only for me, is sensible only to me; it is a secret which the snow releases to me alone and which is already no longer true *behind my back.* Sliding realizes a strictly individual relation with matter, an historical relation; the matter reassembles itself and solidifies in order to hold me up, and it falls back exhausted and scattered behind me. Thus by my passage I have realized that which is unique *for me.* The ideal for sliding then is a sliding which does not leave any trace. It is sliding on water with a rowboat or motor boat or especially with water skis which, though recently invented, represent from this point of view the ideal limit of aquatic sports. Sliding on snow is already less perfect; there is a trace behind me by which I am compromised, however light it may be. Sliding on ice, which scratches the ice and finds a matter already organized, is very inferior, and if people continue to do it despite all this, it is for other reasons. Hence that slight disappointment which always seizes us when we see behind us the imprints which our skis have left on the snow. How much better it would be if the snow re-formed itself as we passed over it! Besides when we let ourselves slide down the slope, we are accustomed to the illusion of not making any mark; we ask the snow to behave like that water which secretly it is. Thus the sliding appears as identical with a continuous creation. The speed is comparable to consciousness and here symbolizes consciousness.[7] While it exists, it effects in the material the birth of a deep quality which lives only so long as the speed exists, a sort of reassembling which overcomes its indifferent exteriority and which falls back like a sheaf behind the moving slider. The informing unification and synthetic condensation of the field of snow, which masses itself into an instrumental organization, which is *utilized,* like the hammer or the anvil, and which docilely adapts itself to an action which understands it and fulfills it; a continued and creative action on the very matter of the snow; the solidification of the *snowy mass* by the sliding; the similarity of the snow to the water which gives support, docile and without memory, or to the naked body of the woman, which the caress leaves intact and troubled in its inmost depths—such is the action of the skier on the real. But at the same time the snow remains impenetrable and out of reach; in one sense the action of the skier only develops its *potentialities. The skier makes it produce*

---

[7] We have seen in Part Three the relation of motion to the for-itself.

what it can produce; the homogeneous, solid matter releases for him a solidity and homogeneity only through the act of the sportsman, but this solidity and this homogeneity dwell as properties enclosed in the matter. This synthesis of self and not-self which the sportsman's action here realizes is expressed, as in the case of speculative knowledge and the work of art, by the affirmation of the right of the skier over the snow. It is my field of snow; I have traversed it a hundred times, a hundred times I have through my speed effected the birth of this force of condensation and support; it is mine.

To this aspect of appropriation through sport, there must be added another—a difficulty overcome. It is more generally understood, and we shall scarcely insist on it here. Before descending this snowy slope, I must climb up it. And this ascent has offered to me another aspect of the snow—resistance. I have realized this resistance through my fatigue, and I have been able to measure at each instant the progress of my victory. Here the snow is identical with the Other, and the common expressions "to overcome," "to conquer," "to master," etc. indicate sufficiently that it is a matter of establishing between me and the snow the relation of master to slave. This aspect of appropriation which we find in the ascent, exists also in swimming, in an obstacle course, etc. The peak on which a flag is planted is a peak which has been appropriated. Thus a principal aspect of sport—and in particular of open air sports—is the conquest of these enormous masses of water, of earth, and of air, which seem a priori indomitable and unutilizable; and in each case it is a question of possessing not the element for itself, but the type of existence in-itself which is expressed by means of this element; it is the homogeneity of substance which we wish to possess in the form of snow; it is the impenetrability of the in-itself and its non-temporal permanence which we wish to appropriate in the form of the earth or of the rock, etc. Art, science, play are activities of appropriation, either wholly or in part, and what they want to appropriate beyond the concrete object of their quest is being itself, the absolute being of the in-itself.

Thus ontology teaches us that desire is originally a desire of being and that it is characterized as the free lack of being. But it teaches us also that desire is a relation with a concrete existent in the midst of the world and that this existent is conceived as a type of in-itself; it teaches us that the relation of the for-itself to this desired in-itself is appropriation. We are, then, in the presence of a double determination of desire: on the one hand, desire is determined as a desire to be a certain being, which is the in-itself-for-itself and whose existence is ideal; on the other hand, desire is determined in the vast majority of cases as a relation with a contingent and concrete in-itself which it has the project of appropriating.[8] Does one of these determinations dominate the

---

[8] Except when it is simply a desire to be—the desire to be happy, to be strong, etc.

other? Are the two characteristics compatible? Existential psychoanalysis can be assured of its principles only if ontology has given a preliminary defin- ition of the relation of these two beings—the concrete and contingent in- itself or object of the desire, and the in-itself-for-itself or ideal of the desire— and if it has made explicit the relation which unites appropriation as a type of relation to the in-itself, to being, as a type of relation to the in-itself-for-itself. This is what we must attempt at present.

What is meant by "to appropriate"? Or if you prefer, what do we under- stand by possessing an object? We have seen the reducibility of the category "to do," which allows us to see in it at one time "to be" and at another "to have." Is it the same with the category "to have"?

It is evident that in a great number of cases, to possess an object is to be able to *use* it. However, I am not satisfied with this definition. In this café I use this plate and this glass, yet they are not mine. I can not "use" that picture which hangs on my wall, and yet it *belongs to me*. The right which I have in certain cases to *destroy* what I possess is no more decisive. It would be purely abstract to define ownership by this right, and furthermore in a society with a "planned economy" an owner can possess his factory with- out having the right to close it; in imperial Rome the master possessed his slave but did not have the right to put him to death. Besides what is meant here by the *right* to destroy, the right to use? I can see that this right refers me to the social sphere and that ownership seems to be defined within the compass of life in society. But I see also that the right is purely negative and is limited to preventing another from destroying or using what belongs to me. Of course we could try to define ownership *as a* social function. But first of all, although society confers in fact the *right* to possess according to certain rules, it does not follow that it creates the relation of appropriation. At the very most it makes it legal. If ownership is to be elevated to the rank of the *sacred*, it must first of all exist as a relation spontaneously established between the for-itself and the concrete in-itself. If we can imagine the future existence of a more just collective organization, where individual possession will cease to be protected and sanctified at least within certain limits—this does not mean that the appropriative tie will cease to exist; it can remain indeed by virtue of a *private* relation of men to things. Thus in primitive societies where the matrimonial bond is not yet a legal one and where hereditary descent is still matrilineal, the sexual tie exists at the very least as a kind of concubinage. It is necessary then to distinguish between possession and the right to possess. For the same reason I must reject any definition of the type which Proudhon gives—such as "ownership is theft"—for it begs the question. It is possible of course for private property to be the *product* of theft and for the holding of this property to have for its *result* the robbing of another. But whatever may be its origin and its results, ownership can be nevertheless described and defined in itself. The thief considers himself the owner of the money which he has stolen. Our problem then includes describing the precise relation of the thief to the stolen goods as well as the relation of the lawful owner to property "honestly acquired."

If I consider the object which I possess, I see that the quality of *being possessed* does not indicate a purely external denomination marking the object's external relation to me; on the contrary, this quality affects its very depths; it appears to me and it appears to others as making a part of the object's being. This is why primitive societies say of certain individuals that they are "possessed"; the "possessed" are thought of as *belonging to* . . . This is also the significance of primitive funeral ceremonies where the dead are buried with the objects which belong to them. The rational explanation, "so that they can use the objects," is evidently after the event. It is more probable that at the period when this kind of custom appeared spontaneously, no explanation seemed to be required. The objects had the specific quality *belonging to the deceased.* They formed a whole with him; there was no more question of burying the dead man without his usual objects than of burying him without one of his legs. The corpse, the cup from which the dead man drank, the knife which he used *make a single dead person.* The custom of burning widows in Malabar can very well be included under this principle; the woman has been possessed; the dead man takes her along with him in his death. In the eyes of the community, by rights she is dead; the burning is only to help her pass from this death by right to death in fact. Objects which can not be put in the grave are haunted. A ghost is only the concrete materialization of the idea that the house and furnishings "are possessed." To say that a house is haunted means that neither money nor effort will efface the metaphysical, absolute fact of *its possession* by a former occupant. It is true that the ghosts which haunt ancestral castles are degraded Lares. But what are these Lares if not layers of possession which have been deposited one by one on the walls and furnishings of the house? The very expression which designates the relation of the object to its owner indicates sufficiently the deep penetration of the appropriation; to be possessed means *to be for someone* (être à . . .). This means that the possessed object is touched *in its being.* We have seen moreover that the destruction of the possessor involves the destruction of the right of the possessed and inversely the survival of the possessed involves the survival of the right of the possessor. The bond of possession is an internal bond of *being.* I meet the possessor in and through the object which he possesses. This is evidently the explanation of the importance of *relics*; and we mean by this not only religious relics, but also and especially the totality of the property of a famous man in which we try to rediscover him, the souvenirs of the beloved dead which seem to "perpetuate" his memory. (Consider, for example, the

Victor Hugo Museum, or the "objects which belonged" to Balzac, to Flaubert.)

This internal, ontological bond between the possessed and the possessor (which customs like branding have often attempted to materialize) can not be explained by a "realistic" theory of appropriation. If we are right in defining realism as a doctrine which makes subject and object two independent substances possessing existence for themselves and by themselves, then a realistic theory can no more account for appropriation than it can for knowledge, which is one of the forms of appropriation; both remain external relations uniting temporarily subject and object. But we have seen that a substantial existence must be attributed to the object known. It is the same with ownership in general: the possessed object exists in itself, is defined by permanence, non-temporality, a sufficiency of being, in a word by substantiality. Therefore we must put *Unselbständigkeit* on the side of the possessing subject. A substance cannot appropriate another substance, and if we apprehend in things a certain quality of "being possessed," it is because originally the internal relation of the for-itself to the in-itself, which is ownership, derives its origin from the insufficiency of being in the for-itself. It is obvious that the object possessed is not *really* affected by the act of appropriation, any more than the object known is affected by knowledge. It remains untouched (except in cases where the possessed is a human being, like a slave or a prostitute). But this quality on the part of the possessed does not affect its meaning *ideally* in the least; in a word, its meaning is to reflect this possession to the for-itself.

If the possessor and the possessed are united by an internal relation based on the insufficiency of being in the for-itself, we must try to determine the nature and the meaning of the *dyad* which they form. In fact the internal relation is synthetic and effects the unification of the possessor and the possessed. This means that the possessor and the possessed constitute ideally a unique reality. To possess is to be united with the object possessed in the form of appropriation; to wish to possess is to wish to be united to an object in this relation. Thus the desire of a particular object is not the simple desire of this object; it is the desire to be united with the object in an internal relation, in the mode of constituting with it the unity "possessor-possessed." The desire *to have* is at bottom reducible to the desire to be related to a certain object in a certain *relation of being.*

In determining this relation, observations made earlier on the behavior of the scientist, the artist, and the sportsman will be very useful to us. We discovered in the behavior of each one a certain appropriative attitude, and the appropriation in each case was marked by the fact that the object appeared simultaneously to be a kind of subjective emanation of ourselves and yet to remain in an indifferently external relation with us. The "mine" appeared to us then as a relation of being intermediate between the absolute interiority of the *me* and the absolute exteriority of the *not-me*. There is within the same syncretism a self becoming not-self and a not-self becoming self. But we must describe this relation more carefully. In the project of possession we meet a for-itself which is "*Unselbständig*," separated by a nothingness from the possibility which it is. This possibility is the possibility of appropriating the *object*. We meet in addition a *value* which haunts the for-itself and which stands as the ideal indication of the total being which would be realized by the union in identity of the possible and the for-itself which is its possible; I mean here the being which would be realized if I were in the indissoluble unity of identity—myself and my property. Thus appropriation would be a relation of being between a for-itself and a concrete in-itself, and this relation would be haunted by the ideal indication of an identification between this for-itself and the in-itself which is possessed.

To possess means *to have for myself*; that is, to be the unique end of the existence of the object. If possession is entirely and concretely given, the possessor is the *raison d'être* of the possessed object. I possess this pen; that means this pen exists *for me*, has been made *for me*. Moreover originally it is I who make for myself the object which I want to possess. My bow and arrows—that means the objects which I have made for myself. Division of labor can dim this original relation but cannot make it disappear. Luxury is a degradation of it; in the primitive form of luxury I possess an object which I *have had made (done)* for myself by people belonging to me (slaves, servants born in the house). Luxury therefore is the form of ownership closest to primitive ownership; it is this which next to ownership itself throws the most light on the relation of *creation* which originally constitutes appropriation. This relation in a society where the division of labor is pushed to the limit, is hidden but not suppressed. The object which I possess is one which I *have bought*. Money represents my strength; it is less a possession in itself than an instrument for possessing. That is why except in most unusual cases of avarice, money is effaced before its possibility for purchase; it is evanescent, it is made to unveil the object, the concrete thing; money has only a transitive being. But to *me* it appears as a creative force: to buy an object is a symbolic act which amounts to creating the object. That is why money is synonymous with power; not only because it is in fact capable of procuring for us what we desire, but especially because it represents the effectiveness of my desire as such. Precisely because it is transcended toward the thing, surpassed, and simply *implied*, it represents my magical bond with the object. Money suppresses the *technical* connection of subject and object and renders the desire immediately operative, like the magic wishes of fairy tales. Stop before a show case with money in your pocket; the objects displayed are already more than half yours. Thus money establishes a bond of appropriation between the for-itself and the total collection of objects in the world. By means of money desire as such is already informer and creator.

Thus through a continuous degradation, the bond of creation is maintained between subject and object. To have is first to create. And the bond of ownership which is established then is a bond of continuous creation; the object possessed is inserted by me into the total form of my environment; its existence is determined by my situation and by its integration in that same situation. My lamp is not only that electric bulb, that shade, that wrought iron stand; it is a certain power of lighting this desk, these books, this table; it is a certain luminous nuance of my work at night in connection with my habits of reading or writing late; it is animated, colored, defined by the use which I make of it; it is that use and exists only through it. If isolated from my desk, from my work, and placed in a lot of objects on the floor of a salesroom, my lamp is radically extinguished; it is no longer my lamp; instead, merely a member of the class of lamps, it has returned to its original matter. Thus I am responsible for the existence of my possessions in the human order. Through ownership I raise them up to a certain type of functional being; and my simple life appears to me as creative exactly because by its continuity it perpetuates the quality of being possessed in each of the objects in my possession. I draw the collection of my surroundings into being along with myself. If they are taken from me, they die as my arm would die if it were severed from me.

But the original, radical relation of creation is a relation of emanation, and the difficulties encountered by the Cartesian theory of substance are there to help us discover this relation. What I create is still me—if by creating we mean to bring matter and form to existence. The tragedy of the absolute Creator, if he existed, would be the impossibility of getting out of himself, for whatever he created could be only himself. Where could my creation derive any objectivity and independence since its form and its matter are from me? Only a sort of inertia could close it off from my presence, but in order for this same inertia to function, I must sustain it in existence by a continuous creation. Thus to the extent that I appear to myself as creating objects by the sole relation of appropriation, these objects are myself. The pen and the pipe, the clothing, the desk, the house—are myself. The totality of my possessions reflects the totality of my being. I am what I have. It is I myself which I touch in this cup, in this trinket. This mountain which I climb is myself to the extent that I conquer it; and when I am at its summit, which I have "achieved" at the cost of this same effort, when I attain this magnificent view of the valley and the surrounding peaks, then I am the view; the panorama is myself dilated to the horizon, for it exists only through me, only for me.

But creation is an evanescent concept which can exist only through its movement. If we stop it, it disappears. At the extreme limits of its acceptance, it is annihilated; either I find only my pure subjectivity or else I encounter a naked, indifferent materiality which no longer has any relation to me. *Creation* can be conceived and maintained only as a continued transition from one term to the other. As the object rises up in my world, it must simultaneously be wholly me and wholly independent of me. This is what we believe that we are realizing in possession. The possessed object as possessed is a continuous creation; but still it remains there, it exists by itself; it is in-itself. If I turn away from it, it does not thereby cease to exist; if I go away, it *represents* me in my desk, in my room, in this place in the world. From the start it is impenetrable. This pen is entirely myself, at the very point at which I no longer even distinguish it from the act of writing, which is my act. And yet, on the other hand, it is intact; my ownership does not change it; there is only an ideal relation between it and me. In a sense I enjoy my ownership if I surpass it toward use, but if I wish to contemplate it, the bond of possession is effaced, I no longer understand what it means to possess. The pipe there on the table is independent, indifferent. I pick it up, I feel it, I contemplate it so as to realize this appropriation; but just because these gestures are meant to give me the *enjoyment* of this appropriation, they miss their mark. I have merely an inert, wooden stem between my fingers. It is only when I pass beyond my objects toward a goal, when I utilize them, that I can enjoy their possession.

Thus the relation of continuous creation incloses within it as its implicit contradiction the absolute, in-itself independence of the objects created. Possession is a magical relation; I *am* these objects which I possess, but outside, so to speak, facing myself; I create them as independent of me; what I possess is mine outside of me, outside all subjectivity, as an in-itself which escapes me at each instant and whose creation at each instant I perpetuate. But precisely because I am always somewhere outside of myself, as an incompleteness which makes its being known to itself by what it is not, now when I possess, I transfer myself to the object possessed. In the relation of possession the dominant term is the object possessed; without it I am nothing save a nothingness which possesses, nothing other than pure and simple possession, an incompleteness, an insufficiency, whose sufficiency and completion are there in that object. In possession, I am my own foundation in so far as I exist in an in-itself. In so far as possession is a continuous creation, I apprehend the possessed object as founded by me in its being. On the other hand, in so far as creation is emanation, this object is reabsorbed in me, it is only myself. Finally, in so far as it is originally in itself, it is not-me, it is myself facing myself, objective, in itself, permanent, impenetrable, existing in relation to me in the relation of exteriority, of indifference. Thus I am the foundation for myself in so far as I exist as an indifferent in-itself in relation to myself. But this is precisely the project of the in-itself-for-itself. For this ideal being is defined as an in-itself which, for-itself, would be its own foundation, or as a for-itself whose original project would not be a mode of being, but a being precisely the being-in-itself which it is. We see that appropriation is nothing save the *symbol* of the ideal of the for-itself or value. The dyad, for-itself possessing and in-itself possessed, is the same as that being which is in order to possess itself and whose possession is in its own creation—God. Thus the possessor aims at enjoying his being-in-itself, his being-outside. Through possession I recover an object-being identical with my being-for-others. Consequently the Other can not surprise me; the being which he wishes to bring into the world, which is myself-for-the-Other— this being I already enjoy possessing. Thus possession is in addition a *defense against others*. What is mine is myself in a non-subjective form inasmuch as I am its free foundation.

We can not insist too strongly on the fact that this relation is *symbolic* and *ideal*. My original desire of being my own foundation for myself is never satisfied through appropriation any more than Freud's patient satisfies his Oedipus complex when he dreams that a soldier kills the Czar (*i.e.*, his father). This is why ownership appears to the owner simultaneously as some-thing given at one stroke in the eternal and as requiring an infinite time to be realized. No particular act of utilization really realizes the enjoyment of full possession; but it refers to other appropriative acts, each one of which has the value of an incantation. To possess a bicycle is to be able first to look at it, then to touch it. But touching is revealed as being insufficient; what is necessary is to be able to get on the bicycle and take a ride. But this *gratuitous* ride is likewise insufficient; it would be necessary to use the bicycle to go on some errands. And this refers us to longer uses and more complete, to long trips across France. But these trips themselves disintegrate into a thousand appropriative behavior patterns, each one of which refers to others. Finally as one could foresee, handing over a bank-note is enough to make the bicycle belong to me, but my entire life is needed to realize this possession. In acquiring the object, I perceive that possession is an enterprise which death always renders still unachieved. Now we can understand why; it is because it is impossible to realize the relation symbolized by appropriation. In itself appropriation contains nothing concrete. It is not a real activity (such as eating, drinking, sleeping) which could serve in addition as a symbol for a particular desire. It exists, on the contrary, only as a symbol; it is its symbol-ism which gives it its meaning, its coherence, its existence. There can be found in it no positive enjoyment outside its symbolic value; it is only the indication of a supreme enjoyment of possession (that of the being which would *be its own foundation*), which is always beyond all the appropriative conduct meant to realize it.

This is precisely why the recognition that it is impossible to *possess* an object involves for the for-itself a violent urge to *destroy* it. To destroy is to reabsorb into myself; it is to enter along with the being-in-itself of the destroyed object into a relation as profound as that of creation. The flames which burn the farm which I myself have set on fire, gradually effect the fusion of the farm with myself. In annihilating it I am changing it into *myself*. Suddenly I rediscover the relation of being found in creation, but in reverse; I *am* the foundation of the barn which is burning; I *am* this barn since I am destroying its being. Destruction realizes appropriation perhaps more keenly than creation does, for the object destroyed is no longer there to show itself impenetrable. It has the impenetrability and the sufficiency of being of the in-itself which it *has been*, but at the same time it has the invisibility and translucency of the nothingness which I am, since it *no longer exists*. This glass which I have broken and which "was" on this table, is there still, but as an absolute transparency. I see all beings through it. This is what movie producers have attempted to render by overprinting the film. The destroyed object resembles a consciousness although it has the irreparability of the in-itself. At the same time it is positively mine because the mere fact that I have to be what I was keeps the destroyed object from being annihilated. I recreate it by recreating myself; thus to destroy is to recreate by assuming oneself as solely responsible for the being of what existed *for all*.

Destruction then is to be given a place among appropriative behaviors. Moreover many kinds of appropriative conduct have a destructive structure along with other structures. To utilize is to use. In *making use* of my bicycle, I *use* it up—wear it out; that is, continuous appropriative creation is marked by a partial destruction. This wear can cause distress for strictly practical reasons, but in the majority of cases it brings a secret joy, almost like the joy of possession; this is because it is coming from us—we are consuming. It should be noted that the word "consume" holds the double meaning of an appropriative destruction and an alimentary enjoyment. To consume is to annihilate and it is to eat; it is to destroy by incorporating into oneself. If I ride on my bicycle, I can be annoyed at wearing out its tires because it is difficult to find others to replace them; but the image of enjoyment which my body invokes is that of a destructive appropriation, of a "creation-destruction." The bicycle gliding alone, carrying me, by its very movement is created and made mine; but this creation is deeply imprinted on the object by the light, continued wear which is impressed on it and which is like the brand on the slave. The object is mine because it is I who have used it up; the using up of what is *mine* is the reverse side of my life.[9]

These remarks will enable us to understand better the meaning of certain

---

[9] Brummell carried his elegance to the extent of wearing only clothes which had been worn a little. He had a horror of anything new; what is new is "dressed up" because it does not belong to anybody.

feelings or behavior ordinarily considered as irreducible; for example, *generosity*. Actually the *gift* is a primitive form of destruction. We know for example that the potlatch involves the destruction of enormous quantities of merchandise. These destructions are challenges to the Other; the gifts enchain him. On this level it is indifferent whether the object is destroyed or given to another; in any case the potlatch is destruction and enchaining of the Other. I destroy the object by giving it away as well as by annihilating it; I suppress in it the quality of being *mine*, which constituted it to the depths of its being; I remove it from my sight; I constitute it—in relation to my table, to my room—as *absent*; I alone shall preserve for it the ghostly, transparent being of *past* objects, because I am the one through whom beings pursue an honorary existence after their annihilation. Thus generosity is above all a destructive function. The craze for giving which sometimes seizes certain people is first and foremost a craze to destroy; it is equivalent to an attitude of madness, a "love" which accompanies the shattering objects. But the craze to destroy which is at the bottom of generosity is nothing else than a craze to possess. All which I abandon, all which I give, I enjoy in a higher manner through the fact that I give it away; giving is a keen, brief enjoyment, almost sexual. To give is to enjoy possessively the object which one gives; it is a destructive-appropriative contact. But at the same time the gift casts a spell over the recipient; it obliges him to recreate, to maintain in being by a continuous creation this bit of myself which I no longer want, which I have just possessed up to its annihilation, and which finally remains only as an image. To give is to enslave. That aspect of the gift does not interest us here, for it concerns primarily our relations with others. What we wish to emphasize is that generosity is not irreducible; to give is to appropriate by destruction while utilizing this destruction to enslave another. Generosity then is a feeling structured by the existence of the Other and indicates a preference for *appropriation by destruction*. In this way it leads us toward *nothingness* still more than toward the in-itself (we have here a nothingness of in-itself which is evidently itself in-itself but which as nothingness can symbolize with the being which is its own nothingness). If then existential psychoanalysis encounters evidence of *generosity* in a subject, it must search further for his original project and ask why the subject has chosen to appropriate by destruction rather than by creation. The answer to this question will reveal that original relation to being which constitutes the *person* who is being studied.

These observations aim only at bringing to light the *ideal* character of the appropriative tie and the symbolic function of all appropriative conduct. It is necessary to add that the symbol is not deciphered by the subject himself. It has not been prepared by a symbolic process in an unconscious but comes from the very structure of being-in-the-world. We have seen in the chapter devoted to transcendence that the order of instruments in the world is the result of my projecting into the in-itself the image of my possibilities—that is, of what I am—but that I could never decipher this worldly image since it would require nothing less than reflective scissiparity to enable me to consider myself in the pattern of an object. Thus since the circuit of selfness is non-thetic and consequently the identification of what I am remains non-thematic, this "being-in-itself" of myself which the world refers to as me is necessarily hidden from my *knowledge*. I can only adapt myself to it in and through the approximative action which gives it birth. Consequently to possess does not mean to know that one holds with the object possessed a relation identified as creation-destruction; rather to possess means to *be in this relation* or better yet to be this *relation*. The possessed object has for us an immediately apprehensible quality which transforms it entirely—the quality of being *mine*—but this quality is in itself strictly undecipherable; it reveals itself in and through action. It makes clear that it has a particular meaning, but from the moment that we want to withdraw a little in relation to the object and to contemplate it, the quality vanishes without revealing its deeper structure and its meaning. This withdrawal indeed is itself destructive of the appropriative connection. An instant earlier I was engaged in an ideal totality, and precisely because I was engaged in my being, I could not know it; an instant later the totality has been broken and I can not discover the meaning of it in the disconnected fragments which formerly composed it. This can be observed in that contemplative experience called depersonalization which certain patients have in spite of efforts to resist it. We are forced then to have recourse to existential psychoanalysis to reveal in each particular case the meaning of the appropriative synthesis for which we have just determined the general, abstract meaning by ontology.

It remains to determine in general the meaning of the object possessed. This investigation should complete our knowledge of the appropriative project. What then is it which we seek to appropriate?

In the first place it is easy to see abstractly that we originally aim at possessing not so much the mode of being of an object as the actual being of this particular object. In fact it is as a concrete representative of being-in-itself that I desire to appropriate it; that is, to apprehend that ideally I am the foundation of its being in so far as it is a part of myself and on the other hand to apprehend that empirically the appropriated object is never valid in itself alone nor for its individual use. No particular appropriation has any meaning outside its indefinite extensions: the pen which I possess is the same as *all* other pens; it is the class of pens which I possess in it. But in addition I possess in it the possibility of writing, of tracing with certain characteritic forms and color (for I combine the instrument itself and the ink which I use in it). These characteristic forms and color with their meaning are condensed in the pen as well as the paper, its special resistance, its odor, *etc.* With *all* possession there is made the crystallizing synthesis which Stendhal has described for the one case of love. Each possessed object which raises itself on the foundation of the world, manifests the entire world, just as a beloved woman manifests the sky, the shore, the sea which surrounded her when she appeared. To appropriate this object is then to appropriate the world symbolically. Each one can recognize it by referring to his own experience: for myself, I shall cite a personal example, not to prove the point but to guide the reader in his inquiry.

Some years ago I brought myself to the decision not to smoke any more. The struggle was hard, and in truth, I did not care so much for the *taste* of the tobacco which I was going to lose, as for the *meaning* of the act of smoking. A complete crystallization had been formed. I used to smoke at the movies, in the morning while working, in the evening after dinner, and it seemed to me that in giving up smoking I was going to strip the film of its interest, the evening meal of its savor, the morning work of its fresh animation. Whatever unexpected happening was going to meet my eye, it seemed to me that it was fundamentally impoverished from the moment that I could not welcome it while smoking. To-be-capable-of-being-met-by-me-smoking: such was the concrete quality which had been spread over everything. It seemed to me that I was going to snatch it away from everything and that in the midst of this universal impoverishment, life was not so worth living. But to smoke is an appropriative, destructive action. Tobacco is a symbol of "appropriated" being, since it is destroyed in the rhythm of my breathing, in a mode of "continuous destruction," since it passes into me and its change in myself is manifested symbolically by the transformation of the consumed solid into smoke. The connection between the landscape seen while I was smoking and this little crematory sacrifice was such that as we have just seen, the tobacco symbolized the landscape. This means then that the act of destructively appropriating the tobacco was the symbolic equivalent of destructively appropriating the entire world. Across the tobacco which I was smoking was the world which was burning, which was going up in smoke, which was being reabsorbed into vapor so as to reenter into me. In order to maintain my decision not to smoke, I had to realize a sort of decrystallization; that is, without exactly accounting to myself for what I was doing, I reduced the tobacco to being nothing but itself—an herb which burns. I cut its symbolic ties with the world; I persuaded myself that I was not taking anything away from the film at the cinema, from the landscape, from the book which I was reading, if I considered them without my pipe; that is, I rebuilt my possession of these objects in modes other than that sacrificial ceremony. As soon as I was persuaded of this, my regret was reduced to a very small matter; I deplored the thought of not perceiving the odor of the smoke, the warmth of the bowl between my fingers and so forth. But suddenly my regret was disarmed and quite bearable.

Thus what fundamentally we desire to appropriate in an object is its being and it is the world. These two ends of appropriation are in reality only one. I search behind the phenomenon to possess the being of the phenomenon. But this being, as we have seen, is very different from the phenomenon of being; it is being-in-itself, and not only the being of a particular thing. It is not because there is here a passage to the universal but rather the being considered in its concrete nudity becomes suddenly the being of the totality. Thus the relation of possession appears to us clearly: to possess is to wish to possess the the world across a particular object. And as possession is defined as the effort to apprehend ourselves as the foundation of a being in so far as it is ourselves ideally, every possessive projcct aims at constituting the For-itself as the foundation of the world or a concrete totality of the in-itself, and this totality is, as totality, the for-itself itself existing in the mode of the in-itself. To-be-in-the-world is to form the project of possessing the world; that is, to apprehend the total world as that which is lacking to the for-itself in order that it may become in-itself-for-itself. It is to be engaged in a totality which is precisely the ideal or value or totalized totality and which would be ideally constituted by the fusion of the for-itself as a detotalized totality which has to be what it is, with the world, as the totality of the in-itself which is what it is.

It must be understood of course that the project of the for-itself is not to establish a conceptual being, that is a being which the for-itself would first conceive—form and matter—and then endow with existence. Such a being actually would be a pure abstraction, a universal; its conception could not be prior to being-in-the-world; on the contrary its conception would presuppose being-in-the-world as it supposes the pre-ontological comprehension of a being which is eminently concrete and present at the start, which is the "there" of the first being-there of the for-itself; that is the being of the world. The for-itself does not exist so as first to think a universal and then determine itself in terms of concepts. It is its choice and its choice can not be abstract without making the very being of the for-itself abstract. The being of the for-itself is an individual venture, and the choice must be an individual choice of a concrete being. This applies, as we have seen, to the *situation* in general. The choice of the for-itself is always a choice of a concrete situation in its incomparable uniqueness. But it is true as well for the ontological meaning of this choice. When we say that the for-itself is a project of *being*, we do not mean that the being-in-itself which it forms the project of being, is conceived by the for-itself as a structure common to all existents of a certain type; its project is in no way a conception, as we have seen. That which it forms the project of being appears to it as an eminently concrete totality; it is *this* particular being. Of course we can foresee in this project the possibilities of a universalizing development; but it is in the same way as we say of a lover that he loves all women or all womankind in one woman. The for-itself has the project of being the foundation of this concrete being, which as we have just seen, can not be *conceived*—for the very reason that it is concrete; neither can it be imagined, for the imaginary is nothingness and this being is eminently being. It must *exist*; that is, it must be encountered, but this encounter is identical with the choice which the for-itself makes. The for-itself is an encountered-choice; that is, it is defined as a choice of founding the being which it encounters. This means that the for-itself as an individual enterprise is a choice of *this world*, as an individual totality of being; it does not surpass it towards a logical universality but towards a new concrete "state" of the same world, in which being would be an in-itself founded by the for-itself; that is, it surpasses it towards a concrete-being-beyond-the-concrete-existing-being. Thus being-in-the-world is a project of possessing this world, and the value which haunts the for-itself is the concrete indication of an individual being constituted by the synthetic function of *this* for-itself and *this* world. Being, in fact, whatever it may be, wherever it may come from and in whatever mode we may consider it, whether it is in-itself or for-itself or the impossible ideal of in-itself-for-itself, is in its original contingency an individual venture.

Now we can define the relations which unite the two categories, *to be* and *to have*. We have seen that desire can be originally either the desire to be or the desire to have. But the desire to have is not irreducible. While the desire *to be* bears directly on the for-itself and has the project of conferring on it without intermediary the dignity of in-itself-for-itself, the desire *to have* aims at the for-itself on, in and through the world. It is by the appropriation of the world that the project *to have* aims at realizing the same value as the desire *to be*. That is why these desires, which can be distinguished by analysis, are in reality inseparable. It is impossible to find a desire to be which is not accompanied by a desire to have, and conversely. Fundamentally we have to do with two ways of looking toward a single goal, or if you prefer, with two interpretations of the same fundamental situation, the one tending to confer being on the For-itself without detour, the other establishing the circuit of selfness; that is, inserting the world between the for-itself and its being. As for the original situation, it is the lack of being which I am; that is, which I make myself be. But the being of which I make myself a lack is strictly individual and concrete; it is the being which *exists already* and in the midst of which I arise as being *its* lack. Thus the very nothingness which I am is individual and concrete, as being *this* nihilation and not any other.

Every for-itself is a free choice; each of its acts—the most insignificant as well as the most weighty—expresses this choice and emanates from it. This is what we have called our freedom. We have now grasped the *meaning* of this choice; it is a choice of being, either directly or by the appropriation of the world, or rather by both at once. Thus my freedom is a choice of being God and all my acts, all my projects translate this choice and reflect it in a thousand and one ways, for there is an infinity of ways of being and of ways of having. The goal of existential psychoanalysis is to rediscover through these empirical, concrete projects the original way in which each man has chosen his being. It remains to explain, someone will say, why I choose to possess the world through this particular object rather than another. We shall reply that here we see the peculiar character of freedom.

Yet the object itself is not irreducible. In it we aim at its *being* through its mode of being or quality. Quality—particularly a material quality like the fluidity of water or the density of a stone—is a mode of being and so can only present being in one certain way. What we choose is a certain way in which being reveals itself and lets itself be possessed. The yellow and red, the taste of a tomato, or that of split peas, roughness and softness, are by no means irreducible givens. They translate symbolically to our perception a certain way which being has of giving itself, and we react by disgust or desire, according to how we see being spring forth in one way or another from their surface. Existential psychoanalysis must bring out the *ontological meaning* of qualities. It is only thus—and not by considerations of sexuality— that we can explain, for example, certain constants in poetic "imaginations" (Rimbaud's "geological," Poe's fluidity of water) or simply the *tastes* of each one, those famous tastes about which people say "there is no accounting for them", without understanding that they symbolize in their own way a whole *Weltanschauung*, a whole choice of being and that hence comes their *self-evidence* to the eyes of the man who has made them his. Our next procedure then is to sketch in outline this particular attempt of existential psychoanalysis, for the sake of making suggestions for further research. For it is not on the level of a taste for sweetness or for bitterness and the like that the free choice is irreducible, but on the level of the choice of the aspect of being which is revealed *through and by means* of sweetness, bitterness, and the rest.

## III. QUALITY AS A REVELATION OF BEING

What we must do is to attempt a psychoanalysis of *things*. M. Bachelard has tried this and shown much talent in his last book, *Water and Dreams*. There is great promise in this work; in particular the author has made a real discovery in his "material imagination." Yet in truth this term *imagination* does not suit us and neither does that attempt to look behind things and their gelatinous, solid, or fluid matter, for the "images" which we project there. Perception, as I have shown elsewhere,[10] has nothing in common with imagination; on the

---

[10] *L'Imaginaire*. N.R.F., 1940.

contrary each strictly excludes the other. To perceive does not mean to assemble images by means of sensations; this thesis, originating with the association theory in psychology, must be banished entirely. Consequently psychoanalysis will not look for images but rather will seek to explain the *meaning* which really belongs to things. Of course the "human" meaning of *sticky*, of *slimy*, *etc.* does not belong to the in-itself. But potentialities do not belong to it either, as we have seen, and yet it is these which constitute the world. *Material* meanings, the human sense of icicles, of grained, of crowded, of greasy, *etc.*, are as real as the world, neither more nor less, and to come into the world means to rise up in the midst of these meanings. But no doubt we have to do here with a simple difference in terminology. M. Bachelard appears bolder and seems to reveal the basis of his thought when he speaks in his studies of psychoanalyzing plants or when he entitles one of his works *The Psychoanalysis of Fire*. Actually he is applying not *to the subject* but to things a method of objective interpretation which does not suppose any previous reference to the subject. When for instance I wish to determine the objective meaning of snow, I see, for example, that it melts at certain temperatures and that this melting of the snow is its death. Here we merely have to do with objective confirmation. When I wish to determine the meaning of this melting, I must compare it to other objects located in other regions of existence but equally objective, equally transcendent—ideas, friendship, persons—concerning which I can also say that they melt. Money *melts* in my hands. I am perspiring and I *melt* into water. Certain ideas—in the sense of socially objective meanings—"snowball" and others *melt* away.[11] We say, "How thin he has become! How he has melted away!" (*Comme il a fondu!*) Doubtless I shall thus obtain a certain relation binding certain forms of being to certain others.

It is instructive to compare the melting snow to certain other more mysterious examples of melting. Take for example the content of certain old myths. The tailor in Grimm's fairy tales takes a piece of cheese in his hands, pretends it is a stone, squeezes it so hard that the whey oozes out of it; the onlookers believe that he has made a stone drip, that he is extracting the liquid from it. Such a comparison informs us of a secret liquid quality in solids, in the sense in which Audiberti by a happy inspiration spoke of the secret blackness of milk. This liquidity which ought to be compared to the juice of fruits and to human blood—which is to man something like his own secret and vital liquidity—this liquidity refers us to a certain permanent possibility which the "granular compact" (designating a certain quality of the being of the *pure in-itself*) possesses of changing itself into *homogenous, undifferentiated fluidity* (another quality of the being of the pure in-itself). We apprehend here in its

[11] We may recall also the "melting money" of Daladier.

origin and with all its ontological significance the polarity of the continuous and discontinuous, the feminine and masculine poles of the world, for which we shall subsequently see the dialectical development all the way to the quantum theory and wave mechanics. Thus we shall succeed in deciphering the secret meaning of the snow, which is an ontological meaning.

But in all this where is the relation to the subjective? To imagination? All we have done is to compare strictly objective structures and to formulate the hypothesis which can unify and group these structures. That is why psycho-analysis depends here on the things themselves, not upon men. That is also why I should have less confidence than M. Bachelard in resorting at this level to the material imaginations of poets, whether Lautréamont, Rimbaud, or Poe. To be sure, it is fascinating to look for the "Bestiary of Lautréamont." But actually if in this research we have returned to the subjective, we shall attain results truly significant only if we consider Lautréamont as an original and pure preference for animality and if we have first determined the objective meaning of animality.[12] In fact if Lautréamont *is what he prefers*, it is necessary first to understand the nature of what he prefers. To be sure, we know well that he is going "to put" into the animal world, something different and more than I put into it. But the subjective enrichments which inform us about Lautréamont are polarized by the objective structure of animality. This is why the existential psychoanalysis of Lautréamont supposes first an inter-pretation of the objective meaning of *animal*. Similarly I have thought for a long time of establishing a *lapidary* for Rimbaud. But what meaning would it have unless we had previously established the significance of the geological in general?

It will be objected that a meaning presupposes man. We do not deny this. But man, being transcendence, establishes the meaningful by his very coming into the world, and the meaningful because of the very structure of tran-scendence is a reference to other transcendents which can be interpreted without recourse to the subjectivity which has established it. The potential energy of a body is an objective quality of that body which can be objectively calculated taking into account only objective circumstances. And yet this energy can come to dwell in a body only in a world whose appearance is a correlate of that of a for-itself. Similarly a rigorously objective psycho-analysis will discover that deeply engaged in the matter of things there are other potentialities which remain entirely transcendent even though they correspond to a still more fundamental choice of human reality, a choice of *being*.

That brings us to the second point in which we differ with M. Bachelard. Certainly any psychoanalysis must have its principles *a priori*. In particular it

---

[12] One aspect of this animality is exactly what Scheler calls *vital values*.

must know *what it is looking for*, or how will it be able to find it? But since the goal of its research can not itself be established by the psychoanalysis, without falling into a vicious circle, such an end must be the object of a postulate; either we seek it in experience, or we establish it by means of some other discipline. The Freudian libido is obviously a simple postulate; Adler's will to power seems to be an unmethodical generalization from empirical data—and in fact it is this very lack of method which allows him to lay down the basic principles of a psychoanalytic method. M. Bachelard seems to rely upon these predecessors; the postulate of sexuality seems to dominate his research; at other times we are referred to *Death*, to the trauma of birth, to the will to power. In short his psychoanalysis seems more sure of its method than of its principles and doubtless will count on its results to enlighten it concerning the precise goal of its research. But this is to put the cart before the horse; consequences will never allow us to establish the principle, any more than the summation of finite modes will permit us to grasp substance. It appears to us therefore that we must here abandon these empirical principles or these postulates which would make man *a priori* a sexuality or a will to power, and that we should establish the goal of psychoanalysis strictly from the standpoint of ontology. This is what we have just attempted. We have seen that human reality, long before we can describe it as *libido* or will to power, is a *choice of being*, either directly or through appropriation of the world. And we have seen—when the choice is expressed through appropriation—that each *thing* is chosen in the last analysis, not for its sexual potential but depending on the mode in which it *renders* being, depending on the manner in which being springs forth from its surface. A psychoanalysis of *things* and of their *matter* ought above all to be concerned with establishing the way in which each thing is the *objective* symbol of being and of the relation of human reality to this being. We do not deny that we should discover afterwards a whole sexual symbolism in nature, but it is a secondary and reducible stratum, which supposes first a psychoanalysis of pre-sexual structures. Thus M. Bachelard's study of water, which abounds in ingenious and profound insights, will be for us a set of suggestions, a precious collection of materials which should now be utilized by a psychoanalysis which is aware of its own principles.

What ontology can teach psychoanalysis is first of all the *true* origin of the meanings of things and their *true* relation to human reality. Ontology alone in fact can take its place on the plane of transcendence and from a single viewpoint apprehend being-in-the-world with its two terms, because ontology alone has its place originally in the perspective of the *cogito*. Once again the ideas of facticity and situation will enable us to understand the existential symbolism of things. We have seen that it is in theory possible but in practice impossible to distinguish facticity from the project which constitutes it into situation. This observation can be of use to us here; we have seen that there is no necessity to hold that the "this" has any meaning whatever when considered in the indifferent exteriority of its being and independently from the upsurge of the for-itself. Actually its quality, as we have seen, is nothing other than its being. The yellow of the lemon, we said, is not a subjective mode of apprehending the lemon; it is the lemon. We have shown also that the whole lemon extends throughout its qualities and that each one of the qualities is spread over the others; that is what we have correctly called "this."[13] Every quality of being is all of being; it is the presence of its absolute contingency; it is its indifferent irreducibility. Yet in Part Two we insisted on the inseparability of project and facticity in the single quality. "For in order for there to be quality, there must be being for a nothingness which by nature is not being . . . Quality is the whole of being unveiling itself within the limitations of the there is." Thus from the beginning we could not attribute the meaning of a quality to being-in-itself, since the "there is" is already necessary; that is, the nihilating mediation of the for-itself must be there in order for qualities to be there. But it is easy to understand in view of these remarks that the meaning of quality in turn indicates something as a re-enforcement of "there is," since we take it as our support in order to surpass the "there is" toward being as it is absolutely and in-itself.

In each apprehension of quality, there is in this sense a metaphysical effort to escape from our condition so as to pierce through the shell of nothingness about the "there is" and to penetrate to the pure in-itself. But obviously we can apprehend quality only as a symbol of a being which totally escapes us, even though it is totally there before us; in short, we can only make revealed being function as a symbol of being-in-itself. This means that a new structure of the "there is" is constituted which is the meaningful level although this level is revealed in the absolute unity of one and the same fundamental project. This structure we shall call the metaphysical purport of all intuitive revelation of being; and this is precisely what we ought to achieve and disclose by psychoanalysis. What is the metaphysical purport of yellow, of red, of polished, of wrinkled? And after these elementary questions, what is the metaphysical coefficient of lemon, of water, of oil, etc.? Psychoanalysis must resolve all these problems if it wants to understand someday why Pierre likes oranges and has a horror of water, why he gladly eats tomatoes and refuses to eat beans, why he vomits if he is forced to swallow oysters or raw eggs.

We have shown also, however, the error which we would make by believing that we "project" our affective dispositions on the thing, to illuminate it or color it. First, as was seen early in the discussion, a feeling is not an inner disposition but an objective, transcending relation which has as its object to

---

[13] Part Two, ch. III, section iii.

learn what it is. But this is not all. The explanation by projection, which is found in such trite sayings as "A landscape is a spiritual state," always begs the question. Take for example that particular quality which we call "slimy."[14] Certainly for the European adult it signifies a host of human and moral characteristics which can easily be reduced to relations of being. A handshake, a smile, a thought, a feeling can be slimy. The common opinion is that first I have experienced certain behavior and certain moral attitudes which displease me and which I condemn, and that in addition I have a sensory intuition of "slimy." Afterwards, says the theory, I should establish a connection between these feelings and sliminess and the slimy would function as a symbol of a whole class of human feelings and attitudes. I would then have enriched the slimy by projecting upon it my knowledge with respect to that human category of behavior.

But how are we to accept this explanation by projection? If we suppose that we have first grasped the feelings as pure psychic qualities, how will we be able to grasp their relation to the slimy? A feeling apprehended in its qualitative purity will be able to reveal itself only as a certain purely unextended disposition, culpable because of its relation to certain values and certain consequences; in any case it will not "form an image" unless the image has been given first. On the other hand if "slimy" is not originally charged with an affective meaning, if it is given only as a certain material quality, one does not see how it could ever be chosen as a symbolic representation of certain psychic unities. In a word, if we are to establish consciously and clearly a symbolic relation between sliminess and the sticky baseness of certain individuals, we must apprehend baseness already in sliminess and sliminess in certain baseness. Consequently the explanation by projection explains nothing since it takes for granted what it ought to explain. Furthermore even if it escaped this objection on principle, it would have to face another, drawn from experience and no less serious; the explanation by projection implies actually that the projecting subject has arrived by experience and analysis at a certain knowledge of the structure and effects of the attitudes which he calls slimy. According to this concept the recourse to sliminess does not as knowledge enrich our experience of human baseness. At the very most it serves as a thematic unity, as a picturesque rubric for bits of knowledge already acquired. On the other hand, sliminess proper, considered in its isolated state, will appear to us harmful in practice (because slimy substances stick to the hands, and clothes, and because they stain), but sliminess then is not repugnant. In fact the disgust which it inspires can be explained only by the combination

---

[14] French visqueux. This at times comes closer to the English "sticky", but I have consistently used the word "slimy" in translating because the figurative meaning of "slimy" appears to be identical in both languages. Tr.

of this physical quality with certain moral qualities. There would have to be a kind of apprenticeship for learning the symbolic value of "slimy." But observation teaches us that even very young children show evidence of repulsion in the presence of something slimy, as if it were already combined with the psychic. We know also that from the time they know how to talk, they *understand* the value of the words "soft," "low," *etc.*, when applied to the description of feelings. All this comes to pass as if we come to life in a universe where feelings and acts are all charged with something material, have a substantial stuff, are *really* soft, dull, slimy, low, elevated, *etc.* and in which material substances have originally a psychic meaning which renders them repugnant, horrifying, alluring, etc. No explanation by projection or by analogy is acceptable here. To sum up, it is impossible to derive the value of the psychic symbolism of "slimy" from the brute quality of the this and equally impossible to project the meaning of the this in terms of a *knowledge* of psychic attitudes. How then are we to conceive of this immense and universal symbolism which is translated by our repulsion, our hates, our sympathies, our attractions toward objects whose materiality must on principle remain non-meaningful? To progress in this study it is necessary to abandon a certain number of postulates. In particular we must no longer postulate *a priori* that the attribution of sliminess to a particular feeling is only an image and not knowledge. We must also refuse to admit—until getting fuller information— that the psychic allows us to view the physical matter symbolically or that our experience with human baseness has any priority over the apprehension of the "slimy" as meaningful.

Let us return to the original project. It is a project of appropriation. It compels the slimy to reveal its being; since the upsurge of the for-itself into being is appropriative, the slimy when perceived is "a slimy to be possessed"; that is, the original bond between the slimy and myself is that I form the project of being the foundation of its being, inasmuch as it is myself ideally. From the start then it appears as a possible "myself" to be established; from the start it has a psychic quality. This definitely does not mean that I endow it with a soul in the manner of primitive animism, nor with metaphysical virtues, but simply that even its materiality is revealed to me as having a psychic meaning—this psychic meaning, furthermore, is identical with the symbolic value which the slimy has in relation to being-in-itself. This appropriative way of forcing the slimy to produce all its meanings can be considered as a formal *a priori*, although it is a free project and although it is identified with the being of the for-itself. In fact the appropriative mode does not depend originally on the mode of being of the slimy but only on its brute being there, on its pure encountered existence; it is like any other encounter since it is a simple project of appropriation, since it is not distinguished in any way from the pure "there is" and since it is, according to whether we consider it from one point of view or the other, either pure freedom or pure nothingness. But it is precisely within the limits of this appropriative project that the slimy reveals itself and develops its sliminess. From the first appearance of the slimy, this sliminess is already a response to a demand, already a *bestowal of self*; the slimy appears as already the outline of a fusion of the world with myself. What it teaches me about the world, that it is like a *leech sucking me*, is already a reply to a concrete question; it responds with its very being, with its mode of being, with all its matter. The response which it gives is at the same time fully appropriate to the question and yet opaque and indecipherable, for it is rich with all its inexpressible materiality. It is clear inasmuch as the reply is exactly appropriate; the slimy lets itself be apprehended as that which I lack; it lets itself be examined by an appropriative inquiry; it allows its sliminess to be revealed to this outline of appropriation. Yet it is opaque because if the meaningful form is evoked in the slimy by the for-itself, all its sliminess comes to succour and replenish it. We are referred then to a meaning which is full and dense, and this meaning releases for us first being-in-itself in so far as the slimy is at the moment that which is manifesting the world, and second an *outline of ourselves*, in so far as the appropriation outlines something like a founding act on the part of the slimy.

What comes back to us then as an objective quality is a new *nature* which is neither material (and physical) nor psychic, but which transcends the opposition of the psychic and the physical, by revealing itself to us as the ontological expression of the entire world; that is, which offers itself as a rubric for classifying all the "thises" in the world, so that we have to deal with material organizations or transcended transcendences. This means that the apprehension of the slimy as such has, by the same stroke, created for the in-itself of the world a particular mode of giving itself. In its own way it symbolizes being; that is, so long as the contact with the slimy endures, everything takes place for us as if sliminess were the meaning of the entire world or the unique mode of being of being-in-itself—in the same way as for the primitive clan of lizards all objects *are* lizards.

What mode of being is symbolized by the slimy? I see first that it is the homogeneity and the imitation of liquidity. A slimy substance like pitch is an aberrant fluid. At first, with the appearance of a fluid it manifests to us a being which is everywhere fleeing and yet everywhere similar to itself, which on all sides escapes yet on which one can float, a being without danger and without memory, which eternally is changed into itself, on which one leaves no mark and which could not leave a mark on us, a being which slides and on which one can slide, which can be possessed by something sliding (by a rowboat, a motor boat, or water ski), and which never possesses because it rolls over us, a being which is eternity and infinite temporality because it is a perpetual change without anything which changes, a being which best symbolizes in this synthesis of eternity and temporality, a possible fusion of the for-itself as pure temporality and the in-itself as pure eternity. But immediately the slimy reveals itself as essentially ambiguous because its fluidity exists in slow motion; there is a sticky thickness in its liquidity; it represents in itself a dawning triumph of the solid over the liquid—that is, a tendency of the indifferent in-itself, which is represented by the pure solid, to fix the liquidity, to absorb the for-itself which ought to dissolve it.

Sliminess is the death of water. It presents itself as a phenomenon in constant transformation, it does not have the permanence within change that water has but on the contrary represents an accomplished break in a change of state. This fixed instability in the slimy discourages possession. Water is more fleeting, but it can be possessed in its very flight as something fleeing. The slimy flees with a heavy flight which has the same relation to water as the unwieldy earthbound flight of the chicken has to that of the hawk. Even this flight can not be possessed because it denies itself as flight. It is already almost a solid permanence. Nothing testifies more clearly to its ambiguous character as a "substance in between two states" than the slowness with which the slimy melts into itself. A drop of water touching the surface of a large body of water is instantly transformed into the body of water; we do not see the operation as buccal absorption, so to speak, of the drop of water by the body of water but rather as a spiritualizing and breaking down of the individuality of a single being which is dissolved in the great whole from which it had issued. The symbol of the body of water seems to play a very important role in the construction of pantheistic systems; it reveals a particular type of relation of being to being. But if we consider the slimy,[15] we note that it presents a constant hysteresis in the phenomenon of being transmuted into itself. The honey which slides off my spoon on to the honey contained in the jar first sculptures the surface by fastening itself on it in relief, and its fusion with the whole is presented as a gradual sinking, a collapse which appears at once as a deflation (think for example of children's pleasure in "blowing" a balloon-doll which groans mournfully when deflating) and as display—like the flattening out of the full breasts of a woman who is lying on her back.

In the slimy substance which dissolves into itself there is a visible resistance, like the refusal of an individual who does not want to be annihilated in the whole of being, and at the same time a softness pushed to its ultimate limit. For the soft is only an annihilation which is stopped half way; the soft is

---

[15] Although slime has mysteriously preserved all fluidity in slow motion; it must not be confused with purées where fluidity roughly outlined, undergoes abrupt breaks and stoppages and where the substance after a preliminary show of pouring, rolls abruptly head over heels.

what furnishes us with the best image of our own destructive power and its limitations. The slowness of the disappearance of the slimy drop in the bosom of the whole is grasped first in *softness*, which is like a retarded annihilation and seems to be playing for time, but this softness lasts up to the end; the drop is sucked into the body of the slimy substance. This phenomenon gives rise to several characteristics of the slimy. First it is *soft* to touch. Throw water on the ground; it *runs*. Throw a slimy substance; it draws itself out, it displays itself, it flattens itself out, it is *flaccid*; touch the slimy; it does not flee, it yields. There is in the very fact that we cannot grasp water a pitiless hardness which gives to it a secret sense of being *metal*; finally it is incompressible like steel. The slimy is compressible. It gives us at first the impression that it is a being which can be *possessed*. Doubly so: its sliminess, its adherence to itself prevent it from escaping; I can take it in my hands, separate a certain quantity of honey or of pitch from the rest in the jar, and thereby *create* an individual object by a continuous creation; but at the same time the softness of this substance which is squashed in my hands gives me the impression that I am perpetually *destroying* it.

Actually we have here the image of destruction-creation. The slimy is *docile*. Only at the very moment when I believe that I possess it, behold by a curious reversal, it possesses me. Here appears its essential character: its softness is leech-like. If an object which I hold in my hands is solid, I can let go when I please; its inertia symbolizes for me my total power; I give it its foundation, but it does not furnish any foundation for me; the For-itself collects the In-itself in the object and raises the object to the dignity of the In-itself without compromising itself (*i.e.*, the self of the For-itself) but always remaining an assimilating and creative power. It is the For-itself which absorbs the In-itself. In other words, possession asserts the primacy of the For-itself in the synthetic being "In-itself-For-itself." Yet here is the slimy reversing the terms; the For-itself is suddenly *compromised*. I open my hands, I want to let go of the slimy and it sticks to me, it draws me, it sucks at me. Its mode of being is neither the reassuring inertia of the solid nor a dynamism like that in water which is exhausted in fleeing from me. It is a soft, yielding action, a moist and feminine sucking, it lives obscurely under my fingers, and I sense it like a dizziness; it draws me to it as the bottom of a precipice might draw me. There is something like a tactile fascination in the slimy. I am no longer the master in *arresting* the process of appropriation. It continues. In one sense it is like the supreme docility of the possessed, the fidelity of a dog who *gives himself* even when one does not want him any longer, and in another sense there is underneath this docility a surreptitious appropriation of the possessor by the possessed.

Here we can see the symbol which abruptly discloses itself: some possessions are venomous; there is a possibility that the In-itself might absorb the

For-itself; that is, that a being might be constituted in a manner just the reverse of the "In-itself-For-itself," and that in this new being the In-itself would draw the For-itself into its contingency, into its indifferent exteriority, into its foundationless existence. At this instant I suddenly understand the snare of the slimy: it is a fluidity which holds me and which compromises me; I can not *slide* on this slime, all its suction cups hold me back; it can not slide over me, it clings to me like a leech. The sliding however is not simply denied as in the case of the solid; it is *degraded*. The slimy seems to lend itself to me, it invites me; for a body of slime at rest is not noticeably distinct from a body of very dense liquid. But it is a trap. The sliding is *sucked* in by the sliding substance, and it leaves its traces upon me. The slime is like a liquid seen in a nightmare, where all its properties are animated by a sort of life and turn back against me. Slime is the revenge of the In-itself. A sickly-sweet, feminine revenge which will be symbolized on another level by the quality "sugary." This is why the sugar-like sweetness to the taste—an indelible sweetness, which remains indefinitely in the mouth even after swallowing—perfectly completes the essence of the slimy. A sugary sliminess is the ideal of the slimy; it symbolizes the sugary death of the For-itself (like that of the wasp which sinks into the jam and drowns in it).

But at the same time the slimy is *myself*, by the very fact that I have outlined an appropriation of the slimy substance. That sucking of the slimy which I feel on my hands outlines a kind of *continuity* of the slimy substance in myself. These long, soft strings of substance which fall from me to the slimy surface (when, for example, I plunge my hand into it and then pull it out again) symbolize a flowing of myself toward the slime. And the hysteresis which I establish in the fusion of the ends of these strings with the larger body, symbolizes the resistance of my being to absorption into the In-itself. If I sink into the water, if I plunge into it, if I let myself sink in it, I experience no discomfort, for I do not have any fear whatsoever that I may dissolve in it; I remain a solid in its liquidity. If I sink in the slimy, I feel that I am going to be lost in it; that is, that I may dissolve in the slime precisely because the slimy is in process of solidification. The *pasty* would present the same aspect as the slimy from this point of view, but it does not fascinate, it does not compromise because it is inert. In the very apprehension of the slimy, a gluey substance, compromising and without stability, there is the haunting memory of a *metamorphosis*.

To touch the slimy is to risk being dissolved in sliminess. Now this dissolution by itself is frightening enough, because it is the absorption of the For-itself by the In-itself as ink is absorbed by a blotter. But it is still more frightening in that the metamorphosis is not just into a thing (bad as that would be) but into slime. Even if I could conceive of a liquefaction of myself (that is, a transformation of my being into water) I would not be inordinately affected because water is the symbol of consciousness—its movement, its fluidity, its deceptive appearance of being solid, its perpetual flight—everything in it recalls the For-itself; to such a degree that psychologists who first noted the characteristics of *duration* of consciousness (James, Bergson) have very often compared it to a river. A river best evokes the image of the constant interpenetration of the parts by a whole and their perpetual dissociation and free movement.

But the slimy offers a horrible image; it is horrible in itself for a consciousness to *become slimy*. This is because the being of the slimy is a soft clinging, there is a sly solidarity and complicity of all its leechlike parts, a vague, soft effort made by each to individualize itself, followed by a falling back and flattening out that is emptied of the individual, sucked in on all sides by the substance. A consciousness which became slimy would be transformed by the thick stickiness of its ideas. From the time of our upsurge into the world, we are haunted by the image of a consciousness which would like to launch forth into the future, toward a projection of self, and which at the very moment when it was conscious of arriving there would be slyly held back by the invisible suction of the past and which would have to assist at its own slow dissolution in this past which it was fleeing, would have to attend the invasion of its project by a thousand parasites until finally it completely lost itself. The "stealing of thoughts" found in the psychosis of influence gives us the best image of this horrible condition. But what is it then which is expressed by this fear on the ontological level if not exactly the flight of the For-itself before the In-itself of facticity; that is, exactly temporalization.

The horror of the slimy is the horrible fear that time might become slimy, that facticity might progress continually and insensibly and absorb the For-itself which *exists* it. It is the fear not of death, not of the pure In-itself, not of nothingness, but of a particular type of being, which does not actually exist any more than the In-itself-For-itself and which is only *represented* by the slimy. It is an ideal being which I reject with all my strength and which haunts me *as value* haunts my being, an ideal being in which the foundationless In-itself has priority over the For-itself. We shall call it an *Antivalue*.

Thus in the project of appropriating the slimy, the sliminess is revealed suddenly as a symbol of an antivalue: it is a type of being not realized but threatening which will perpetually haunt consciousness as the constant danger which it is fleeing, and hence will suddenly transform the project of appropriation into a project of flight. Something has appeared which is not the result of any prior experience but only of the pre-ontological comprehension of the In-itself and the For-itself, and this is the peculiar meaning of the slimy. In one sense it is an experience since sliminess is an intuitive discovery; in another sense it is like the discovery of an adventure of being. Henceforth for the For-itself there appears a new danger, a threatening mode of being which must be avoided, a concrete category which it will discover every-where. The slimy does not symbolize any psychic attitude *a priori*; it manifests a certain relation of being with itself and this relation has originally a psychic quality because I have discovered it in a plan of appropriation and because the sliminess has returned my image to me. Thus I am enriched from my first contact with the slimy, by a valid ontological pattern beyond the distinction between psychic and non-psychic, which will interpret the meaning of being and of all the existents of a certain category, this category arising, moreover, like an empty skeletal framework *before* the experience with different kinds of sliminess. I have projected it into the world by my original project when faced with the slimy; it is an objective structure of the world and at the same time an antivalue; that is, it determines an area where slimy objects will arrange themselves. Henceforth each time that an object will manifest to me this relation of being, whether it is a matter of a handshake, of a smile, or of a thought, it will be apprehended by by definition as slimy: that is, beyond its phenomenal context, it will appear to me as constituting along with pitch, glue, honey, *etc.* the great ontological region of sliminess.

Conversely, to the extent that the this which I wish to appropriate, repre-sents the entire world, the slimy, from my first intuitive contact, appears to me rich with a host of obscure meanings and references which surpass it. The slimy is revealed in itself as "much more than the slimy." From the moment of its appearance it transcends all distinctions between psychic and physical, between the brute existent and the meanings of the world; it is a possible meaning of being. The first experience which the infant can have with the slimy enriches him psychologically and morally; he will not need to reach adulthood to discover the kind of sticky baseness which we figuratively name "slimy"; it is there near him in the very sliminess of honey or of glue. What we say concerning the slimy is valid for all the objects which surround the child. The simple revelation of their matter extends his horizon to the extreme limits of being and bestows upon him at the same stroke a collection of clues for deciphering the being of all human facts. This certainly does not mean that he *knows* from the start the "ugliness," the "characteristics," or the "beauties" of existence. He is merely in possession of all the *meanings of being* of which ugliness and beauty, attitudes, psychic traits, sexual relations, *etc.* will never be more than particular exemplifications. The gluey, the sticky, the hazy, *etc.*, holes in the sand and in the earth, caves, the light, the night, *etc.*— all reveal to him modes of pre-psychic and pre-sexual being which he will spend the rest of his life explaining. There is no such thing as an "innocent" child. We will gladly recognize along with the Freudians the innumerable relations existing between sexuality and certain matter and forms in the child's environment. But we do not understand by this that a sexual instinct already constituted has charged them with a sexual significance. On the contrary it seems to us that this matter and these forms are apprehended in themselves, and they reveal to the child the For-itself's modes of being and relations to being which will illuminate and shape his sexuality.

To cite only one example—many psychoanalysts have been struck by the attraction which all kinds of holes exert on the child (whether holes in the sand or in the ground, crypts, caves, hollows, or whatever), and they have explained this attraction either by the anal character of infant sexuality, or by prenatal shock, or by a presentiment of the adult sexual act. But we can not accept any of these explanations. The idea of "birth trauma" is highly fantastic. The comparison of the hole to the feminine sexual organ supposes in the child an experience which he can not possibly have had or a presentiment which we can not justify. As for the child's anal sexuality, we would not think of denying it; but if it is going to illuminate the holes which he encounters in the perceptual field and charge them with symbolism, then it is necessary that the child apprehend his anus as a hole. To put it more clearly, the child would have to apprehend the essence of the hole, of the orifice, as corresponding to the sensation which he receives from his anus. But we have demonstrated sufficiently the subjective character of "my relation with my body" so that we can understand the impossibility of saying that the child apprehends a particular part of his body as an objective structure of the universe. It is only to another person that the anus appears as an orifice. The child himself can never have experienced it as such; even the intimate care which the mother gives the child could not reveal the anus in this aspect, since the anus as an erogenous zone, or a zone of pain is not provided with tactile nerve endings. On the contrary it is only through another—through the words which the mother uses to designate the child's body—that he learns that his anus is a hole. It is therefore the objective nature of the hole perceived in the world which is going to illuminate for him the objective structure and the meaning of the anal zone and which will give a transcendent meaning to the erogenous sensations which hitherto he was limited to merely "existing." In itself then the hole is the symbol of a mode of being which existential psychoanalysis must elucidate.

We can not make such a detailed study here. One can see at once, however, that the hole is originally presented as a nothingness "to be filled" with my own flesh; the child can not restrain himself from putting his finger or his whole arm into the hole. It presents itself to me as the empty image of myself. I have only to crawl into it in order to make myself exist in the world which awaits me. The ideal of the hole is then an excavation which can be carefully moulded about my flesh in such a manner that by squeezing myself into it and fitting myself tightly inside it, I shall contribute to making a fullness of being exist in the world. Thus to plug up a hole means originally to make a sacrifice of my body in order that the plenitude of being may exist; that is, to subject the passion of the For-itself so as to shape, to perfect, and to preserve the totality of the In-itself.[16]

Here at its origin we grasp one of the most fundamental tendencies of human reality—the tendency to fill. We shall meet with this tendency again in the adolescent and in the adult. A good part of our life is passed in plugging up holes, in filling empty places, in realizing and symbolically establishing a plenitude. The child recognizes as the results of his first experiences that he himself has holes. When he puts his fingers in his mouth, he tries to wall up the holes in his face; he expects that his finger will merge with his lips and the roof of his mouth and block up the buccal orifice as one fills the crack in a wall with cement; he seeks again the density, the uniform and spherical plenitude of Parmenidean being; if he sucks his thumb, it is precisely in order to dissolve it, to transform it into a sticky paste which will seal the hole of his mouth. This tendency is certainly one of the most fundamental among those which serve as the basis for the act of eating; nourishment is the "putty" which will seal the mouth; to eat is among other things to be filled up.

It is only from this standpoint that we can pass on to sexuality. The obscenity of the feminine sex is that of everything which "gapes open." It is *an appeal to being* as all holes are. In herself woman appeals to a strange flesh which is to transform her into a fullness of being by penetration and dissolution. Conversely woman feels her condition as an appeal precisely because she is "in the form of a hole." This is the true origin of Adler's complex. Beyond any doubt her sex is a mouth and a voracious mouth which devours the penis—a fact which can easily lead to the idea of castration. The amorous act is the castration of the man; but this is above all because sex is a hole. We have to do here with a *pre-sexual* contribution which will become one of the components of sexuality as an empirical, complex, human attitude but which far from deriving its origin from the sexed being has nothing in common with basic sexuality, the nature of which we have explained in Part III. Nevertheless the experience with the hole, when the infant sees the reality, includes the ontological presentiment of sexual experience in general; it is with his flesh that the child stops up the hole and the hole, before all sexual specification, is an obscene expectation, an appeal to the flesh.

We can see the importance which the elucidation of these immediate and concrete existential categories will assume for existential psychoanalysis. In this way we can apprehend the very general projects of human reality. But what chiefly interests the psychoanalyst is to determine the free project of the unique person in terms of the individual relation which unites him to these

---

[16] We should note as well the importance of the opposite tendency, to dig holes, which in itself demands an existential analysis.

various symbols of being. I can love slimy contacts, have a horror of holes, *etc*. That does not mean that for me the slimy, the greasy, a hole, *etc*. have lost their general ontological meaning, but on the contrary that *because* of this meaning, I determine myself in this or that manner in relation to them. If the slimy is indeed the symbol of a being in which the for-itself is swallowed up by the in-itself, what kind of a person am I if, unlike the others, I love the slimy? To what fundamental project of myself am I referred if I want to explain this love of an ambiguous, sucking in-itself? In this way *tastes* do not remain irreducible givens; if one knows how to question them, they reveal to us the fundamental projects of the person. Down to even our alimentary preferences they all have a meaning. We can account for this fact if we will reflect that each taste is presented, not as an absurd *datum* which we must excuse but as an evident value. If I like the taste of garlic, it seems irrational to me that other people can not like it.

To eat is to appropriate by destruction; it is at the same time to be filled up with a certain being. And this being is given as a synthesis of temperature, density, and flavor proper. In a word this synthesis signifies *a certain being*; and when we eat, we do not limit ourselves to *knowing* certain qualities of this being through taste; by tasting them we appropriate them. Taste is assimilation; by the very act of biting the tooth reveals the density of a body which it is transforming into gastric contents. Thus the synthetic intuition of food is in itself an assimilative destruction. It reveals to me the being which I am going to make my flesh. Henceforth, what I accept or what I reject with disgust is the very being of that existent, or if you prefer, the totality of the food proposes to me a certain mode of being of the being which I accept or refuse. This totality is organized as a form in which less intense qualities of density and of temperature are effaced behind the flavor proper which expresses them. The *sugary*, for example, *expresses* the slimy when we eat a spoonful of honey or molasses, just as an analytical function expresses a · geometric curve. This means that all qualities which are not strictly speaking flavor but which are massed, melted, buried in the flavor, represent the *matter* of the flavor. (The chocolate biscuit which at first offers a resistance to my tooth, soon abruptly gives way and crumbles; its resistance first, then its crumbling is chocolate.) In addition they are united to certain temporal characteristics of flavor; that is, to its mode of temporalization. Certain tastes give themselves all at once, some are like delayed-action fuses, some release themselves by degrees, certain ones dwindle slowly until they disappear, and still others vanish at the very moment one thinks to possess them. These qualities are organized along with density and temperature; in addition on another level they express the visual aspect of the food. If I eat a pink cake, the taste of it is pink; the light sugary perfume, the oiliness of the butter cream *are* the pink. Thus I eat the pink as I see the sugary. We understand that flavor, due to this fact, has a complex architecture and differentiated matter; it is this structured matter—which offers us a particular type of being—that we can assimilate or reject with nausea, according to our original project. It is not a matter of indifference whether we like oysters or clams, snails or shrimp, if only we know how to unravel the existential significance of these foods.

Generally speaking there is no irreducible taste or inclination. They all represent a certain appropriative choice of being. It is up to existential psychoanalysis to compare and classify them. Ontology abandons us here; it has merely enabled us to determine the ultimate ends of human reality, its fundamental possibilities, and the value which haunts it. Each human reality is at the same time a direct project to metamorphose its own For-itself into an In-itself-For-itself and a project of the appropriation of the world as a totality of being-in-itself, in the form of a fundamental quality. Every human reality is a passion in that it projects losing itself so as to found being and by the same stroke to constitute the In-itself which escapes contingency by being its own foundation, the *Enscausa sui*, which religions call God. Thus the passion of man is the reverse of that of Christ, for man loses himself as man in order that God may be born. But the idea of God is contradictory and we lose ourselves in vain. Man is a useless passion.

# CONCLUSION

## I. IN-ITSELF AND FOR-ITSELF: METAPHYSICAL OUTLOOKS

We are finally in a position to form conclusions. Already in the Introduction we discovered consciousness as an appeal to being, and we showed that the *cogito* refers immediately to a being-in-itself which is the *object* of consciousness. But after our description of the In-itself and the For-itself, it appeared to us difficult to establish a bond between them, and we feared that we might fall into an insurmountable dualism. This dualism threatened us again in another way. In fact to the extent that it can be said of the For-itself that it is, we found ourselves confronting two radically distinct modes of being: that of the For-itself which has to be what it is—i.e., which is what it is not and which is not what it is—and that of the In-itself which is what it is. We asked then if the discovery of these two types of being had resulted in establishing an hiatus which would divide Being (as a general category belonging to all existents) into two incommunicable regions, in each one of which the notion of Being must be taken in an original and unique sense.

Our research has enabled us to answer the first of these questions: the For-itself and the In-itself are reunited by a synthetic connection which is nothing other than the For-itself itself. The For-itself, in fact, is nothing but the pure nihilation of the In-itself; it is like a hole of being at the heart of Being. One may be reminded here of that convenient fiction by which certain popularizers are accustomed to illustrate the principle of the conservation of energy. If, they say, a single one of the atoms which constitute the universe were annihilated, there would result a catastrophe which would extend to the entire universe, and this would be, in particular, the end of the Earth and of the solar system. This metaphor can be of use to us here. The For-itself is like a tiny nihilation which has its origin at the heart of Being; and this nihilation is sufficient to cause a total upheaval to *happen* to the In-itself. This upheaval is the world. The for-itself has no reality save that of being the nihilation of being. Its sole qualification comes to it from the fact that it is the nihilation of an individual and particular In-itself and not of a being in general. The For-itself is not nothingness in general but a particular privation; it constitutes itself as the privation of *this being*. Therefore we have no business asking about the way in which the for-itself can be united with the in-itself since the for-itself is in no way an autonomous substance. As a nihilation it *is made-to-be* by the in-itself; as an internal negation it must by means of the in-itself make known to itself what it is not and consequently what it has to be. If the *cogito* necessarily leads outside the self, if consciousness is a slippery slope on which one cannot take one's stand without immediately finding oneself tipped outside onto being-in-itself, this is because consciousness does not have by itself any sufficiency of being as an absolute subjectivity; from the start it refers to the thing.

For consciousness there is no being except for this precise obligation to be a revealing intuition of something. What does this mean except that consciousness is the Platonic Other? We may recall the fine description which the Stranger in the *Sophist* gives of this "other,"[1] which can be apprehended only "as in a dream," which has no being except its being-other (i.e., which enjoys only a borrowed being), which if considered by itself disappears and which takes on a marginal existence only if one fixes his look on being, this other which is exhausted in being other than itself and other than being. It even seems that Plato perceived the dynamic character which the otherness of the other presented in relation to itself, for in certain passages he sees in this the origin of motion. But he could have gone still further; he would have seen then that the other, or relative non-being, could have a semblance of existence only by virtue of consciousness. To be other than being is to be self-consciousness in the unity of the temporalizing ekstases. Indeed what can the otherness be if not that game of musical chairs played by the reflected and the reflecting which we described as at the heart of the for-itself? For the only way in which the other can exist as other is to be consciousness (of) being other. Otherness is, in fact, an internal negation, and only a consciousness can be constituted as an internal negation. Every other conception of otherness will amount to positing it as an in-itself—that is, establishing between it and being an external relation which would necessitate the presence of a witness so as to establish that the other is other than the in-itself. However the other can not be other without emanating from being; in this respect it is relative to the in-itself. But neither can it be other without *making itself other*; otherwise its otherness would become a given and therefore a *being* capable of being considered in-itself. In so far as it is relative to the in-itself, the other is affected with facticity; in so far as it makes itself, it is an absolute. This is what we

---

[1] "The other" in this passage must of course not be confused with "The Other" discussed in connection with the problem of human relationships. Tr.

pointed out when we said that the for-itself is not the foundation of its being-as-nothingness-of-being but that it perpetually founds its nothingness-of-being. Thus the for-itself is an absolute *Unselbständig*, what we have called a non-substantial absolute. Its reality is purely *interrogative*. If it can posit questions this is because it is itself always in *question*; its being is never *given* but *interrogated* since it is always separated from itself by the nothingness of otherness. The for-itself is always in suspense because its being is a perpetual reprieve. If it could ever join with its being, then the otherness would by the same stroke disappear and along with it possibles, knowledge, the world. Thus the *ontological* problem of knowledge is resolved by the affirmation of the ontological primacy of the in-itself over the for-itself.

But this immediately gives rise to a *metaphysical* interrogation. The upsurge of the for-itself starting from the in-itself is in no way comparable to the *dialectical* genesis of the Platonic Other starting from being. "Being" and "other" are, for Plato, *genera*. But we, on the contrary, have seen that being is an individual venture. Similarly the appearance of the for-itself is the absolute event which comes to being. There is therefore room here for a *metaphysical problem which could be formulated* thus: Why does the for-itself arise from being? We, indeed, apply the term "metaphysics" to the study of individual processes which have given birth to *this* world as a concrete and particular totality. In this sense metaphysics is to ontology as history is to sociology. We have seen that it would be absurd to ask why being is other, that the question can have meaning only within the limits of a for-itself and that it even supposes the ontological priority of nothingness over being. It can be posited only if combined with another question which is externally analogous and yet very different: Why is it that *there is* being? But we know now that we must carefully distinguish between these two questions. The first is devoid of meaning: all the "Whys" in fact are subsequent to being and presuppose it. Being is, without reason, without cause, and without necessity; the very definition of being reveals to us its original contingency. To the second question we have already replied, for it is not posited on the metaphysical level but on that of ontology: "There is" being because the for-itself is such that there is being. The character of a *phenomenon* comes to being through the for-itself.

But while questions on the origin of being or on the origin of the world are either devoid of meaning or receive a reply within the actual province of ontology, the case is not the same for the origin of the for-itself. The for-itself is such that it has the right to turn back on itself toward its own origin. The being by which the "Why" comes into being has the right to posit its own "Why" since it is itself an interrogation, a "Why." To this question ontology can not reply, for the problem here is to explain an event, not to describe the structures of a being. At most it can point out that the nothingness which is *made-to-be* by the in-itself is not a simple emptiness devoid of meaning. The meaning of the nothingness of the nihilation is to-be-made-to-be in order to found being. Ontology furnishes us two pieces of information which serve as the basis for metaphysics: first, that every process of a foundation of the self is a rupture in the identity-of-being of the in-itself, a withdrawal by being in relation to itself and the appearance of presence to self or consciousness. It is only by making itself for-itself that being can aspire to be the cause of itself. Consciousness as the nihilation of being appears therefore as one stage in a progression toward the immanence of causality—i.e., toward being a self-cause. The progression, however, stops there as the result of the insufficiency of being in the for-itself. The temporalization of consciousness is not an ascending progress toward the dignity of the *causa sui*; it is a surface run-off whose origin is, on the contrary, the impossibility of being a self-cause. Also the *ens causa sui* remains as the *lacked*, the indication of an impossible vertical surpassing which by its very non-existence conditions the flat movement of consciousness; in the same way the vertical attraction which the moon exercises on the ocean has for its result the horizontal displacement which is the tide. The second piece of information which metaphysics can draw from ontology is that the for-itself is *effectively* a perpetual project of founding itself qua being and a perpetual failure of this project. Presence to itself with the various directions of its nihilation (the ekstatic nihilation of the three temporal dimensions, the twin nihilation of the dyad reflected-reflecting) represents the primary upsurge of this project; reflection represents the splitting of the project which turns back on itself in order to found itself at least as a project, and the aggravation of the nihilating hiatus by the failure of this project itself. "Doing" and "having," the cardinal categories of human reality, are immediately or mediately reduced to the project of being. Finally the plurality of both *can* be interpreted as human reality's final attempt to found itself, resulting in the radical separation of being and the consciousness of being.

Thus ontology teaches us two things: (1) If the in-itself were to found itself, it could attempt to do so only by making itself consciousness; that is, the concept of *causa sui* includes within it that of presence to self—i.e., the nihilating decompression of being; (2) Consciousness is in *fact* a project of founding itself; that is, of attaining to the dignity of the in-itself-for-itself or in-itself-as-self-cause. But we can not derive anything further from this. Nothing allows us to affirm on the ontological level that the nihilation of the in-itself in for-itself has for its meaning—from the start and at the very heart of the in-itself—the project of being its own self-cause. Quite the contrary. Ontology here comes up against a profound contradiction since it is through the for-itself that the possibility of a foundation comes to the world. In order to be a project of founding itself, the in-itself would of necessity have to be originally a presence to itself—i.e., it would have to be already consciousness.

Ontology will therefore limit itself to declaring that *everything takes place as* if the in-itself in a project to found itself gave itself the modification of the for-itself. It is up to metaphysics to form the *hypotheses* which will allow us to conceive of this process as the absolute event which comes to crown the individual venture which is the existence of being. It is evident that these hypotheses will remain hypotheses since we can not expect either further validation or invalidation. What will make their *validity* is only the possibility which they will offer us of unifying the *givens* of ontology. This unification naturally must not be constituted in the perspective of an historical becoming since temporality comes into being through the for-itself. There would be therefore no sense in asking what being was *before* the appearance of the for-itself. But metaphysics must nevertheless attempt to determine the nature and the meaning of this prehistoric process, the source of all history, which is the articulation of the individual venture (or existence of the in-itself) with the absolute event (or upsurge of the for-itself). In particular the task belongs to the metaphysician of deciding whether the movement is or is not a first "attempt" on the part of the in-itself to found itself and to determine what are the relations of motion as a "malady of being" with the for-itself as a more profound malady pushed to nihilation.

It remains for us to consider the second problem which we formulated in our Introduction: If the in-itself and the for-itself are two modalities of *being*, is there not an hiatus at the very core of the idea of being? And is its comprehension not severed into two incommunicable parts by the very fact that its extension is constituted by two radically heterogenous classes? What is there in common between the being which is what it is, and the being which is what it is not and which is not what it is? What can help us here, however, is the conclusion of our preceding inquiry. We have just shown in fact that the in-itself and the for-itself are not juxtaposed. Quite the contrary, the for-itself without the in-itself is a kind of abstraction; it could not exist any more than a color could exist without form or a sound without pitch and without timbre. A consciousness which would be consciousness of nothing would be an absolute nothing. But if consciousness is bound to the in-itself by an *internal* relation, doesn't this mean that it is articulated with the in-itself so as to constitute a totality, and is it not this totality which would be given the name *being* or reality? Doubtless the for-itself is a nihilation, but as a nihilation it *is*; and it is in *a priori* unity with the in-itself. Thus the Greeks were accustomed to distinguish cosmic reality, which they called Tò πᾶν, from the totality constituted by this and by the infinite void which surrounded it—a totality which they called Tò ὅλον. To be sure, we have been able to call the for-itself a nothing and to declare that there is "outside of the in-itself" *nothing* except a reflection of this nothing which is itself polarized and defined by the in-itself—inasmuch as the for-itself is precisely the nothingness of *this in-itself*.

But here as in Greek philosophy a question is raised: which shall we call *real*? To which shall we attribute *being*? To the cosmos or to what we called Tὸ ὅλον? To the pure in-itself or to the in-itself surrounded by that shell of nothingness which we have designated by the name of the for-itself?

But if we are to consider total being as constituted by the synthetic organization of the in-itself and of the for-itself, are we not going to encounter again the difficulty which we wished to avoid? And as for that hiatus which we revealed in the concept of being, are we not going to meet it at present in the existent itself? What definition indeed are we to give to an existent which as in-itself would be what it is and as for-itself would be what it is not?

If we wish to resolve these difficulties, we must take into account what is required of an existent if it is to be considered as a totality: it is necessary that the diversity of its structures be held within a unitary synthesis in such a way that each of them considered apart is only an abstraction. And certainly consciousness considered apart is only an abstraction; but the in-itself has no need of the for-itself in order to be; the "passion" of the for-itself only causes there to be in-itself. The *phenomenon* of in-itself is an abstraction without consciousness but its *being* is not an abstraction.

If we wish to conceive of a synthetic organization such that the for-itself is inseparable from the in-itself and conversely such that the in-itself is indissolubly bound to the for-itself, we must conceive of this synthesis in such a way that the in-itself would receive its existence from the nihilation which caused there to be consciousness of it. What does this mean if not that the indissoluble totality of in-itself and for-itself is conceivable only in the form of a being which is its own "self-cause"? It is this being and no other which could be valid absolutely as that ὅλον of which we spoke earlier. And if we can raise the question of the being of the for-itself articulated in the in-itself, it is because we define ourselves *a priori* by means of a pre-ontological comprehension of the *ens causa sui*. Of course this *ens causa sui* is *impossible*, and the concept of it, as we have seen, includes a contradiction. Nevertheless the fact remains that since we raise the question of the being of the ὅλον by adopting the point of view of the *ens causa sui*, it is from this point of view that we must set about examining the credentials of this ὅλον. Has it not appeared due to the mere fact of the upsurge of the for-itself, and is not the for-itself originally a project of being its own self-cause? Thus we begin to grasp the nature of total reality. Total being, the concept of which would not be cleft by an hiatus and which would nevertheless not exclude the nihilating-nihilated being of the for-itself, that being whose existence would be a unitary synthesis of the in-itself and of consciousness—this ideal being would be the in-itself founded by the for-itself and identical with the for-itself which founds it—i.e., the *ens causa sui*. But precisely because we adopt the point of view of this ideal being in order to judge the *real* being which we call ὅλον, we must notice that the real is an abortive effort to attain to the dignity of the self-cause. Everything happens as if the world, man, and man-in-the-world succeeded in realizing only a missing God. Everything happens therefore as if the in-itself and the for-itself were presented in a state of disintegration in relation to an ideal synthesis. Not that the integration has ever *taken place* but on the contrary precisely because it is always indicated and always impossible.

It is this perpetual failure which explains both the indissolubility of the in-itself and of the for-itself and at the same time their relative independence. Similarly when the unity of the cerebral functions is shattered, phenomena are produced which simultaneously present a relative autonomy and which at the same time can be manifested only on the ground of the disintegration of a totality. It is this failure which explains the hiatus which we encounter both in the concept of being and in the existent. If it is impossible to pass from the notion of being-in-itself to that of being-for-itself and to reunite them in a common genus, this is because the *passage in fact* from the one to the other and their reuniting can not be effected. We know that for Spinoza and for Hegel, for example, if a synthesis is arrested before its completion and the terms fixed in a relative dependence and at the same time in a relative independence, the synthesis is constituted at once as an error. For example, it is in the notion of a sphere that for Spinoza the rotation of a semicircle around its diameter finds its justification and its meaning. But if we imagine that the notion of a sphere is on principle out of reach, then the phenomenon of the rotation of the semicircle becomes *false*. It has been decapitated; the idea of rotation and the idea of a circle are held together without being able to be united in a synthesis which surpasses them and justifies them; the one remains irreducible to the other. This is precisely what happens here. We shall say therefore that the ὅλον we are considering is like a decapitated notion in perpetual disintegration. And it is in the form of a disintegrated ensemble that it presents itself to us in its ambiguity—that is, so that one can *ad libitum* insist on the dependence of the beings under consideration or on their independence. There is here a passage which is not completed, a short circuit.

On this level we find again that notion of a detotalized totality which we have already met in connection with the for-itself itself and in connection with the consciousnesses of others. But this is a third type of detotalization. In the simply detotalized totality of reflection the reflective *had to be* reflected-on, and the reflected-on had to be the reflected. The double negation remained evanescent. In the case of the for-others the (reflection-reflecting) reflected was distinguished from the (reflection-reflecting) reflecting in that each one *had to not-be* the other. Thus the for-itself and the-other-for-itself constitute a being in which each one confers the being-other on the other by making himself other. As for the totality of the for-itself and the in-itself, this has for its characteristic the fact that the for-itself makes itself *other* in relation to the in-itself but that the in-itself is in no way other than the for-itself in its being; the in-itself purely and simply is. If the relation of the in-itself to the for-itself were the reciprocal of the relation of the for-itself to the in-itself, we should fall into the case of being-for-others. But this is definitely not the case, and it is this absence of reciprocity which characterizes the ὅλον of which we spoke earlier. To this extent it is not absurd to raise the question of the totality. In fact when we studied the for-others, we established that it was necessary that there be a being which was an "other-me" and which had to be the reflective scissiparity of the for-others. But at the same time this being which is an other-me appeared to us as being able to exist only if it included an inapprehensible non-being of exteriority. We asked then if the paradoxical character of the totality was in itself an irreducible and if we could posit the mind as the being which is and which is not. But we decided that the question of the synthetic unity of consciousnesses had no meaning, for it presupposed that it was possible for us to assume a point of view on the totality; actually we exist on the foundation of this totality and as engaged in it.

But if we can not "adopt a point of view on the totality," this is because the Other on principle denies that he is I as I deny that I am he. It is the reciprocity of the relation which prevents me from ever grasping it in its integrity. In the case of the internal negation for-itself-in-itself, on the contrary, the relation is not reciprocal, and I am both one of the terms of the relation and the relation itself. I apprehend being, I *am* the apprehension of being, I am *only* an apprehension of being. And the being which I apprehend is not posited *against* me so as to apprehend me in turn; it is what is apprehended. Its *being* simply does not coincide in any way with its being-apprehended. In one sense therefore I can pose the question of the totality. To be sure, I exist here as *engaged* in this totality, but I can be an *exhaustive consciousness* of it since I am at once consciousness of the being and self-consciousness. This question of the totality, however, does not belong to the province of ontology. For ontology the only regions of being which can be elucidated are those of the in-itself, of the for-itself, and the ideal region of the "self-cause." For ontology it makes no difference whether we consider the for-itself articulated in the in-itself as a well marked *duality* or as a disintegrated being. It is up to metaphysics to decide which will be more profitable for knowledge (in particular for phenomenological psychology, for anthropology, *etc.*): will it deal with a being which we shall call the *phenomenon* and which will be provided with two dimensions of being, the dimension in-itself and the dimension for-itself (from this point of view there would be *only one* phenomenon: the world), just as in the physics of Einstein it has been found advantageous to speak of an event conceived as having spatial dimensions and a temporal dimension and as determining its place in a space-time; or, on the other hand will it remain preferable despite all to preserve the ancient duality "consciousness-being." The only observation which ontology can hazard here is that in case it appears useful to employ the new notion of a phenomenon as a disintegrated totality, it will be necessary to speak of it *both* in terms of immanence and in terms of transcendence. The danger, in fact, would be of falling into either a doctrine of pure immanence (Husserlian idealism) or into one of pure transcendence which would look on the *phenomenon* as a new kind of *object*. But immanence will be always limited by the phenomenon's dimension in-itself, and transcendence will be limited by its dimension for-itself.

After having decided the question of the origin of the for-itself and of the nature of the phenomenon of the world, the metaphysician will be able to attack various problems of primary importance, in particular that of action. Action, in fact, is to be considered simultaneously on the plane of the for-itself and on that of the in-itself, for it involves a project which has an immanent origin and which determines a modification in the being of the transcendent. It would be of no use to declare that the action modifies only the phenomenal appearance of the thing. If the phenomenal appearance of a cup can be modified up to the annihilation of the cup qua cup, and if the being of the cup is nothing but its *quality*, then the action envisaged must be capable of modifying the very being of the cup. The problem of action therefore supposes the elucidation of the transcendent efficacy of consciousness, and it puts us on the path of its veritable relation of being with being. It reveals to us also, owing to the repercussions of an act in the world, a relation of being with being which, although apprehended in exteriority by the physicist, is neither pure exteriority nor immanence but which refers us to the notion of the Gestalt form. It is therefore in these terms that one might attempt a metaphysics of nature.

## II. ETHICAL PERSPECTIVES

Ontology itself can not formulate ethical precepts. It is concerned solely with what is, and we can not possibly derive imperatives from ontology's indicatives. It does, however, allow us to catch a glimpse of what sort of ethics will assume its responsibilities when confronted with a *human reality in situation*. Ontology has revealed to us, in fact, the origin and the nature of value; we have seen that value is the *lack* in relation to which the for-itself determines its being as *a lack*. By the very fact that the for-itself *exists*, as we have seen, value arises to haunt its being-for-itself. It follows that the various tasks of the for-itself can be made the object of an existential psychoanalysis, for they all aim at producing the missing synthesis of consciousness and being in the form of value or self-cause. Thus existential psychoanalysis is *moral description*, for it releases to us the ethical meaning of various human projects. It indicates to us the necessity of abandoning the psychology of interest along with any utilitarian interpretation of human conduct—by revealing to us the *ideal* meaning of all human attitudes. These meanings are beyond egoism and altruism, beyond also any behavior which is called *disinterested*. Man makes himself man in order to be God, and selfness considered from this point of view can appear to be an egoism; but precisely because there is no common measure between human reality and the self-cause which it wants to be, one could just as well say that man loses himself in order that the self-cause may exist. We will consider then that all human existence is a passion, the famous *self-interest* being only one way freely chosen among others to realize this passion.

But the principal result of existential psychoanalysis must be to make us repudiate the *spirit of seriousness*. The spirit of seriousness has two characteristics: it considers values as transcendent givens independent of human subjectivity, and it transfers the quality of "desirable" from the ontological structure of things to their simple material constitution. For the spirit of seriousness, for example, *bread* is desirable because it is *necessary* to live (a value written in an intelligible heaven) and because bread is nourishing. The result of the serious attitude, which as we know rules the world, is to cause the symbolic values of things to be drunk in by their empirical idiosyncrasy as ink by a blotter; it puts forward the opacity of the desired object and posits it in itself as a desirable irreducible. Thus we are already on the moral plane but concurrently on that of bad faith, for it is an ethics which is ashamed of itself and does not dare speak its name. It has obscured all its goals in order to free itself from anguish. Man pursues being blindly by hiding from himself the free project which is this pursuit. He makes himself such that he is *waited* for by all the tasks placed along his way. Objects are mute demands, and he is nothing in himself but the passive obedience to these demands.

Existential psychoanalysis is going to reveal to man the real goal of his pursuit, which is being as a synthetic fusion of the in-itself with the for-itself; existential psychoanalysis is going to acquaint man with his passion. In truth there are many men who have practiced this psychoanalysis on themselves and who have not waited to learn its principles in order to make use of them as a means of deliverance and salvation. Many men, in fact, know that the goal of their pursuit is being; and to the extent that they possess this knowledge, they refrain from appropriating things for their own sake and try to realize the symbolic appropriation of their being-in-itself. But to the extent that this attempt still shares in the spirit of seriousness and that these men can still believe that their mission of effecting the existence of the in-itself-for-itself is written in things, they are condemned to despair; for they discover at the same time that all human activities are equivalent (for they all tend to sacrifice man in order that the self-cause may arise) and that all are on principle doomed to failure. Thus it amounts to the same thing whether one gets drunk alone or is a leader of nations. If one of these activities takes precedence over the other, this will not be because of its real goal but because of the degree of consciousness which it possesses of its ideal goal; and in this case it will be the quietism of the solitary drunkard which will take precedence over the vain agitation of the leader of nations.

But ontology and existential psychoanalysis (or the spontaneous and empirical application which men have always made of these disciplines) must reveal to the moral agent that he *is the being by whom values exist*. It is then that his freedom will become conscious of itself and will reveal itself in anguish as the unique source of value and the nothingness by which the *world* exists. As soon as freedom discovers the quest for being and the appropriation of the in-itself as *its own possibles*, it will apprehend by and in anguish that they are possibles only on the ground of the possibility of other possibles. But hitherto although possibles could be chosen and rejected *ad libitum*, the theme which made the unity of all choices of possibles was the value or the ideal presence of the *ens causa sui*. What will become of freedom if it turns its back upon this value? Will freedom carry this value along with it whatever it does and even in its very turning back upon the in-itself-for-itself? Will freedom be reapprehended from behind by the value which it wishes to contemplate? Or will freedom by the very fact that it apprehends itself as a freedom in relation to itself, be able to put an end to the reign of this value? In particular is it possible for freedom to take itself for a value as the source of all value, or must it necessarily be defined in relation to a transcendent value which haunts it? And in case it could will itself as its own possible and its determining value, what would this mean? A freedom which wills itself freedom is in fact a being-which-is-not-what-it-is and which-is-what-it-is-not, and which chooses as the ideal of being, being-what-it-is-not and not-being-what-it-is.

This freedom chooses then not to *recover* itself but to flee itself, not to coincide with itself but to be always at a distance *from* itself. What are we to understand by this being which wills to hold itself in awe, to be at a distance from itself? Is it a question of bad faith or of another fundamental attitude? And can one *live* this new aspect of being? In particular will freedom by taking itself for an end escape all *situation*? Or on the contrary, will it remain situated? Or will it situate itself so much the more precisely and the more individually as it projects itself further in anguish as a freedom within conditions and assumes more fully its responsibility as an existent by whom the world comes into being? All these questions, which refer us to a pure and not an accessory (or impure) reflection, can find their reply only on the ethical plane. We shall devote to them a future work.

THE END

# KEY TO SPECIAL TERMINOLOGY[1]

Abolition (*disparition*). The fact of ceasing to exist on the part of an object. This is, of course, from the point of view of the For-itself, not of the In-itself since Being does not increase or diminish.

*Abschattungen*. Used by Sartre in the usual phenomenological sense to refer to the successive appearances of the object "in profile."

Absurd. That which is meaningless. Thus man's existence is absurd because his contingency finds no external justification. His projects are absurd because they are directed toward an unattainable goal (the "desire to become God" or to be simultaneously the free For-itself and the absolute In-itself.)

Actaeon Complex. Totality of images which suggest that "knowing" is a form of appropriative violation with sexual overtones.

Anguish. The reflective apprehension of the Self as freedom, the realization that a nothingness slips in between my Self and my past and future so that nothing relieves me from the necessity of continually choosing myself and nothing guarantees the validity of the values which I choose. Fear is of something in the world, anguish is anguish before myself (as in Kierkegaard).

Apparition (*apparition*). The coming into existence of an object. This is only from the point of view of the For-itself since Being itself neither "comes" nor "goes."

Appearance (*apparition*). See "Phenomenon" and "*Abschattungen*."

Bad Faith. A lie to oneself within the unity of a single consciousness. Through

---

[1] This far from exhaustive list of terms will perhaps be confusing to the person who has read none of BEING AND NOTHINGNESS and will certainly appear inadequate to anyone who has completed the volume. I am nevertheless including it in the hope that these approximate definitions may serve as a guide for readers so that they may thus more easily attain for themselves a full comprehension of Sartre's philosophy. I am including here both technical terms coined by Sartre and familiar words to which he gives special meanings. All direct quotations are from *Being and Nothingness*. Tr.

bad faith a person seeks to escape the responsible freedom of Being-for-itself. Bad faith rests on a vacillation between transcendence and facticity which refuses to recognize either one for what it really is or to synthesize them.

Being (être). "Being is. Being is in-itself. Being is what it is." Being includes both Being-in-itself and Being-for-itself, but the latter is the nihilation of the former. As contrasted with Existence, Being is all-embracing and objective rather than individual and subjective.

Being-for-itself (être-pour-soi). The nihilation of Being-in-itself; consciousness conceived as a lack of Being, a desire for Being, a relation to Being. By bringing Nothingness into the world the For-itself can stand out from Being and judge other beings by knowing what it is not. Each For-itself is the nihilation of a particular being.

Being-in-itself (être-en-soi). Non-conscious Being. It is the Being of the phenomenon and overflows the knowledge which we have of it. It is a plenitude, and strictly speaking we can say of it only that it is.

Being-for-others (être-pour-autrui). The third ekstasis (q.v.) of the For-itself. There arises here a new dimension of being in which my Self exists outside as an object for others. The For-others involves a perpetual conflict as each For-itself seeks to recover its own Being by directly or indirectly making an object out of the other.

Cause. Occasionally used in the ordinary sense of physical cause and effect. In the human sphere cause (motif) is empty of all deterministic quality and stands for an objective apprehension of a situation which in the light of a certain end may serve as a means for attaining that end.

Coefficient of adversity. A term borrowed from Gaston Bachelard. It refers to the amount of resistance offered by external objects to the projects of the For-itself.

Cogito. Sartre claims that the pre-reflective cogito (see "consciousness") is the pre-cognitive basis for the Cartesian cogito.

There is also, he says, a sort of cogito concerning the existence of Others. While we can not abstractly prove the Other's existence, this cogito will disclose to me his "concrete, indubitable presence," just as my own "contingent but necessary existence" has been revealed to me.

Consciousness. The transcending For-itself. "Consciousness is a being such that in its being, its being is in question in so far as this being implies a being other than itself." Like Husserl Sartre insists that consciousness is always consciousness of something. He sometimes distinguishes types of consciousness according to psychic objects; e.g. pain-consciousness, shame-consciousness. Two more basic distinctions are made:

(1) Unreflective consciousness (also called non-thetic consciousness or non-positional self-consciousness). This is the pre-reflective cogito. Here

there is no knowledge but an implicit consciousness of being conscious-ness of an object.

(2) Reflective consciousness (also called thetic consciousness or pos-itional self-consciousness). For this see "reflection."

Contingency. In the For-itself this equals facticity, the brute fact of being this For-itself in the world. The contingency of freedom is the fact that freedom is not able not to exist.

Dasein. Heidegger's term for the human being as a conscious existent. Basic meaning is "Being-there."

Dissociation (dédoublement). The never completed split in consciousness attempted by consciousness in reflection. The two parts (if they were separated) would be the reflective consciousness and the consciousness reflected-on.

Distraction. An act by which consciousness in order to flee anguish forces itself to look on certain of its own future possibilities as if they were actually possibilities of someone else. Distraction as regards the Past tries to view the Self as a fully constituted personality and to hold that acts are free when in conformity with this Essence, thus avoiding a free, new choice of Being. More generally distraction is any act by which consciousness deter-mines itself not to see certain of its own reactions.

Eidetic Reduction. (Husserl). The process of considering any object or isol-ated example of subjectivity as merely an example of what it is apart from any affirmation of its actual existence. Sartre refers to it as meaning simply that "one can always pass beyond the concrete phenomenon toward its essence."

Ekstasis. Used in the original Greek sense of "standing out from." The For-itself is separated from its Self in three successive ekstases:

(1) Temporality. The For-itself nihilates the In-itself (to which in one sense it still belongs) in the three dimensions of past, present, and future (the three temporal ekstases).

(2) Reflection. The For-itself tries to adopt an external point of view on itself.

(3) Being-for-others. The For-itself discovers that it has a Self for-the-Other, a Self which it is without ever being able to know or get hold of it.

Engage (engager). Includes both the idea of involvement and the idea of delib-erate commitment. Thus the human being is inescapably engaged in the world, and freedom is meaningful only as engaged by its free choice of ends.

Epoché. Husserl's "putting into parentheses" all ideas about the existence of the world so as to examine consciousness independently of the question of any worldly existence. Sartre, of course, can not follow this procedure since his task is to examine consciousness in-the-world.

Essence. For Sartre as for Hegel, essence is what has been. Sartre calls it man's past. Since there is no pre-established pattern for human nature, each man makes his essence as he lives.

Existence. Concrete, individual being here and now. Sartre says that for all existentialists existence precedes essence. Existence has for them also always a subjective quality when applied to human reality.

External negation. "An external bond established between two beings by a witness."

Facticity (facticité). The For-itself's necessary connection with the In-itself, hence with the world and its own past. It is what allows us to say that the For-itself is or exists. The facticity of freedom is the fact that freedom is not able not to be free.

Finitude. To be carefully distinguished from "mortality." Finitude refers not to the fact that man dies but to the fact that as a free choice of his own project of being, he makes himself finite by excluding other possibilities each time that he chooses the one which he prefers. Man would thus because of his facticity be finite even if immortal.

Freedom. The very being of the For-itself which is "condemned to be free" and must forever choose itself—i.e., make itself. " 'To be free' does not mean 'to obtain what one has wished' but rather 'by oneself to determine oneself to wish' (in the broad sense of choosing). In other words success is not important to freedom."

Future. The "possibles" of the For-itself. The future is what the For-itself has to be. It is "the determining being which the For-itself has to be beyond being."

Historicize (state or quality, "historicity"; active process, "historization"). To become involved as a concrete existent in an actual world so as to have an "history."

Human-reality. Sartre's term for the human being or For-itself. Used both generally (like "mankind") and for the individual man.

Instant. Sartre denies that time is a succession of instants. The instant is psychologically important, however, as indicating the everpresent possibility that the For-itself may at any point suddenly effect a rupture in its existence by choosing a new project of being. The instant thus becomes simultaneously the final and the initial terms for the respective projects.

Internal negation. Found only in connection with the action of the For-itself. A negation which influences the inner structure of a being who or which is denied something. "Such a relation between two beings that the one which is denied to the other qualifies the other at the heart of its essence—by absence."

Jonah complex. Irrational desire to assimilate and to identify with oneself either the object of knowledge or a beloved person—without in any way impairing that object's character as an external object.

Made-to-be. An unsatisfactory translation of *est été*, literally "is been." Sartre's use of the verb "to be" as transitive is, so far as I know, unique.

Metaphysics. "The study of individual processes which have given birth to this world as a concrete and particular totality." Metaphysics is thus concerned with the problem of why concrete existents are as they are. Sartre says that metaphysics is to ontology as history is to sociology.

Mine. "A synthesis of self and not-self."

Motive (*mobile*). "The ensemble of the desires, emotions, and passions which urge me to accomplish a certain act." Sartre holds that these are freely constituted as a motive, not psychologically determined.

Nausea. The "taste" of the facticity and contingency of existence. "A dull and inescapable nausea perpetually reveals my body to my consciousness." On the ground of this fundamental nausea are produced all concrete, empirical nauseas (caused by spoiled meat, excrement, *etc.*).

Négatité. Sartre's word for types of human activity which while not obviously involving a negative judgment nevertheless contain negativity as an integral part of their structure; *e.g.*, experiences involving absence, change, interrogation, destruction.

Nihilate. (*néantir*). A word coined by Sartre. Consciousness exists as consciousness by making a nothingness (q.v.) arise between it and the object of which it is consciousness. Thus nihilation is that by which consciousness exists. To nihilate is to encase with a shell of non-being. The English word "nihilate" was first used by Helmut Kuhn in his *Encounter with Nothingness*.

Noema (Husserl). The objective "pole" of conscious experience viewed after the epoché (q.v.); the object intended by consciousness—as it is in itself plus all its phenomenal essential features.

Noesis. Husserl's term for the intentional direction by consciousness toward an object external to it. The intending act as such with all its essential features.

Nothingness (*Néant*). Nothingness does not itself have Being, yet it is supported by Being. It comes into the world by the For-itself and is the recoil from fullness of self-contained Being which allows consciousness to exist as such.

Objectness. (*Objectité*). Not quite objectivity but rather the quality or state of being an object. Sometimes *objectité* is here translated as "object-state." "Objectivation" and "objectivize" are related words and refer to making an object out of something or someone.

Ontology. The study "of the structures of being of the existent taken as a totality." Ontology describes Being itself, the conditions by which "there is" a world, human reality, *etc.* Cf. "metaphysics."

Past. What the For-itself has been. The Past thus becomes Being-in-itself and is the For-itself's essence and substance as well as part of its facticity. This is the only sense in which the For-itself has either essence or substance since in its living present it "is what it is not and is not what it is."

Phenomenon. *Being* as it appears or is revealed. Sartre uses the word in its usual phenomenological sense though he differs in his view of the transphenomenality of Being. He, of course, denies any distinction between phenomena and noumena.

Phenomenology. In general in speaking of the theory of phenomenology Sartre refers to the work of Husserl. It should be noted, however, that in spite of many points of disagreement with Husserl, Sartre considers his own work a phenomenological study. When he says that an idea merits phenomenological investigation, he means, of course, a study conducted according to his own method.

Possibilize (*possibilise*). Refers to the free act by which consciousness constitutes an action as capable of being performed or an attitude as capable of being assumed.

Possible (*possible*). A noun almost equal to "possibility." Sartre generally prefers "possible" which signifies a concrete action to be performed in a concrete world rather than an abstract idea of possibility in general. The For-itself makes itself by choosing its possibles and projecting itself toward those preferred.

Presence. Concerns the relation of the For-itself to the rest of Being and involves an internal negation. "Presence to —— is an internal relation between the being which is present and the being to which it is present." "The For-itself is presence to all of Being-in-itself" by making Being-in-itself "exist as a totality."

Present. The Present *is not*. The For-itself is presence to Being-in-itself by means of an internal negation. But this very presence is a flight toward the Future as a further project of the For-itself.

Presentation. That which is present to the mind as an object of consciousness. Sometimes distinguished from *representation*. When this distinction is observed, *presentation* refers to actual objects of which the mind is conscious, *representation* to imaginary ones.

Probability. A potentiality which refers back to the object though it is not made by the object nor does it have to be. It belongs to the In-itself whereas possibility lies in the province of the For-itself.

Project. Both verb and noun. It refers to the For-itself's choice of its way of being and is expressed by action in the light of a future end.

Reflection (*reflet*). In the dyad "the-reflection-reflecting," the form in which the For-itself founds its own nothingness. "The For-itself can be only in the mode of a reflection causing itself to be reflected as not being a certain being." In other words consciousness exists as a translucent consciousness of being other than the objects of which it is consciousness.

Reflection (*réflexion*). The attempt on the part of consciousness to become its own object. "Reflection is a type of being in which the For-itself is in order to be to itself what it is." There are two types.

(1) Pure reflection. The presence of the reflective consciousness to the consciousness reflected-on. This requires a Katharsis effected by consciousness on itself.

(2) Impure (accessory) reflection. The constitution of "psychic temporality," the For-itself's contemplation of its psychic states.

Representation. See "Presentation."

Responsibility. "Consciousness (of) being the incontestable author of an event or an object."

Serious. The "Spirit of seriousness" (*l'esprit de sérieux*) views man as an object and subordinates him to the world. It thinks of values as having an absolute existence independent of human-reality.

Situation. The For-itself's engagement in the world. It is the product of both facticity and the For-itself's way of accepting and acting upon its facticity.

Space. "The nothingness of relation apprehended as a relation by the being which is its own relation." Space is primarily subjective because it is the result of the For-itself's act of organizing relations between external objects—always in the light of the For-itself's own ends.

Survey, project of surveying (*survoler, survol*). Process of thought or perception such that objects are grasped in a global act and can not be separated into points or instants.

Temporality. Subjective process whereby the For-itself continuously lives its project of nihilating the In-itself. Through temporality the For-itself sets up its own measure for the duration and self-identity of things. Time is not in things but flows over them. The For-itself as what it has been (Past) is a flight (Present) toward what it projects to be (Future).

"There is" (*il y a*). Used by Sartre to indicate that the world and objects exist *as a world* and *as objects* rather than as meaningless, undifferentiated Being-in-itself. The "there is" results, of couse from the upsurge into Being on the part of the For-itself.

Transcendence. Often refers simply to the process whereby the For-itself goes beyond the given in a further project of itself. Sometimes the For-itself is itself called a transcendence. If I make an object out of the Other, then he is for me a transcendence-transcended. On the other hand, the Being-in-itself which overflows all its appearances and all attempts of mine to grasp it is called a transcendent Being. The word "transcendence" is sometimes purely a substantive, sometimes refers to a process.

Transphenomenality. Refers to the fact that Being although coextensive with its appearance is not limited to it, that Being "surpasses the knowledge which we have of it and provides the basis for such knowledge."

Unrealizable. An ideal which although by nature unattainable dominates human conduct as man strives to realize this goal. Sartre uses this for ideals common to all human reality, not for concrete, individual goals which might be realized by some people and not by others.

Value. In general value arises as the For-itself constitutes objects as desirable. More specifically value is the "beyond of all surpassings as the For-itself seeks to be united with its Self. It is what the For-itself lacks in order to be itself.

World. The whole of non-conscious Being as it appears to the For-itself and is organized by the For-itself in "instrumental complexes." Because of its facticity the For-itself is inescapably engaged in the world. Yet strictly speaking, without the For-itself, there would be not a world but only an undifferentiated plenitude of Being.

# NAME INDEX

# Routledge Classics
## Get inside a great mind

### What is Literature?
Jean-Paul Sartre

'This is a book that can neither be assimilated nor bypassed. There is probably no better way to encounter it than in this translation, with these notes and this introduction.'
*Notes and Queries*

Jean-Paul Sartre was one of the most important philosophical and political thinkers of the twentieth century. His writings had a potency that was irresistible to the intellectual scene that swept post-war Europe, and have left a vital inheritance to contemporary thought. In *What is Literature?* Sartre the novelist and Sartre the philosopher combine to address the phenomenon of literature, exploring why we read, and why we write.

Hb: 0–415–25557–0     Pb: 0–415–25404–3

### A Short History of Modern Philosophy
#### From Descartes to Wittgenstein
Roger Scruton

'Anyone seeking a short and intelligible introduction to the ideas and intentions of Spinoza, Hume, Kant, Hegel and Marx, among others, need look no further.'
*Good Book Guide*

In this guide, Scruton takes us on a fascinating tour of modern philosophy, from founding father René Descartes to Ludwig Wittgenstein. He clearly summarizes the thought of each major figure and outlines the major preoccupations of Western philosophy. This book paints a vivid, animated and engaging picture of modern philosophy and is already established as the classic introduction. Read it and find out why.

Hb: 0–415–26762–5     Pb: 0–415–26763–3

For these and other classic titles from Routledge, visit
**www.routledgeclassics.com**

Some titles not available in North America

# Routledge Classics
## Get inside a great mind

### A Short History of Ethics
#### A history of moral philosophy from the Homeric Age to the twentieth century
### Alasdair MacIntyre

'Very powerful . . . this book is an impressive contribution to our endless argument about the meaning of ethical concepts.'
*The Observer*

What is right? What is wrong? How do we decide? To a remarkable extent, our decision-making is determined by the origins of the ethical ideas that we employ and the history of their development. This classic work is widely acknowledged as the perfect introduction to the subject, presenting in concise form an insightful yet exceptionally complete history of moral philosophy in the West from the Greeks to contemporary times. In clear and readable prose, Alasdair MacIntyre, one of the finest living philosophers, leads the reader towards a greater understanding of what lies behind our ethical decisions.

Hb: 0–415–28748–0      Pb: 0–415–28749–9

### Sketch for a Theory of the Emotions
### Jean-Paul Sartre

'The best source for Sartre's theoretical views on the nature of psychology.'
*Mary Warnock*

Anticipating his great work, *Being and Nothingness*, this book is considered to be one of Jean-Paul Sartre's most important pieces of writing. By arguing that we choose how to utilize our emotions, and identifying their evanescent nature, Sartre places *us* firmly in control. A witty and dazzling journey into one of the most intriguing theories of our time.

Hb: 0–415–26751–X      Pb: 0–415–26752–8

For these and other classic titles from Routledge, visit
### www.routledgeclassics.com

# Routledge Classics
## Get inside a great mind

### The Birth of the Clinic
#### An archaeology of medical perception
#### Michel Foucault

'Foucault's importance is that he has boldly attempted to create a new method of historical analysis and a new framework for the study of the human sciences as a whole. . . . The homage that is paid to Foucault as commentator on medical history is fully justified.'
*Theodore Zeldin, New Statesman*

In this remarkable book, Michel Foucault calls on us to look critically at specific historical events in order to uncover new layers of significance, and analyses the methods of observation that underpin the origins of modern medical techniques. The scope of such an undertaking is vast, but it is Foucault's skill that, by means of his uniquely engaging narrative style, his penetrating gaze is able to confront our own.

0–415–30772–4

### The Order of Things
#### Michel Foucault

'Michel Foucault is a very brilliant writer . . . he has a remarkable angle of vision, a highly disciplined and coherent one, that informs his work to such a degree as to make the work *sui generis* original.'
*Edward W. Said*

In this virtuoso history of thought, Foucault takes us far beyond the limits of our usual categories into a realm of what he calls 'exotic charm', taking in literature, art, economics and even biology along the way. This work, which offers an insight into the early development of postmodernism, established Foucault as an intellectual giant and remains one of the most significant works of the twentieth century. A must.

Hb: 0–415–26736–6    Pb: 0–415–26737–4

For these and other classic titles from Routledge, visit
**www.routledgeclassics.com**